e Richardson Dimensions of Communication

Qv

DIMENSIONS
OF
COMMUNICATION

DIMENSIONS OF COMMUNICATION

Edited by
Lee Richardson
Louisiana State University

APPLETON-CENTURY-CROFTS
EDUCATIONAL DIVISION
MEREDITH CORPORATION

New York

669-1

Library of Congress Card Number: 69-11705

PRINTED IN THE UNITED STATES OF AMERICA

390-73890-5

To Lee-Ellen,
A pertinacious communicator

Contents

Preface

      Dimensions of Communication is designed for use in principles courses in communications, journalism, marketing communications, advertising, and communications-oriented courses such as political science, social psychology, sociology, psychology, speech, management, and English. It brings together many developments in communications research, consumer behavior, advertising research, and areas of the behavioral sciences, in order to focus upon the problems of communication and persuasion. Through these clearly written introductory readings, the student becomes familiar with the fundamental developments in varied fields that assist his understanding of contemporary problems of communications.

      Part I introduces the reader to the fundamentals of communications. With the basic concepts and terms of communications in firm grasp, the student is prepared to apply the findings in later readings.

      Part II introduces communications at the level of the individual. The implications of research in persuasion and the psychology of communications are evident for problems in a number of fields. Many principles of individual behavior are developed, and the student should be prepared to relate the findings and presentations of the readings to realistic applied situations. By application of the findings to familiar situations, the student begins to see the fallacies of many communications strategies currently used and their failure to employ accepted principles.

      A mere look at the relationship of the individual to communications patterns does not reveal a number of the special problems of mass communications as developed in Part III. While mass communications can be understood partially as the involvement of many individuals in the communication process, the problems of operating on a large scale introduce such concepts as audience, propaganda, and public opinion, as well as technological terms relating to media operations.

      The communications story is hopelessly incomplete unless informal communications are considered. Communications problems are not only concerned with the direct communication between the paid sponsor and the immediate audience. Within the audience there is much intracommunication.

xii   PREFACE

Part IV explores problems of innovation, adoption, influence, and the relative strengths of informal and formal communications.

Part V presents specific applications of communications science to advertising. Of course, much of the material in other parts has clear implications for advertising, whose problems can be looked at in terms of the message to be delivered and the medium by which to deliver that message. Communications researchers, however, show us that word-of-mouth advertising, a form of informal communication which is explored here in depth, is of critical importance.

Personal selling and salesmanship, discussed in Part VI, are often overlooked by communications scholars. Yet personal selling is a form of marketing communications, delivered by a medium different from the advertising media. In the present state of our understanding, it is important just to realize that personal selling can benefit from communications science. The student will be surprised to find, however, both that research has gone far beyond the point of simply recognizing the relationship between personal selling and communications, and that definite principles have been established and additional work is under way to bring science further into the area known as personal selling.

Communicators, involved in their day-to-day problems, often overlook the immense social implications of communications. Many outsiders criticize the methods that are employed and the social complications that result unwittingly from advertising campaigns. Part VII contains criticism of advertising; its articles are definitely at conflict with the nature of our advertising today. The student cannot ignore the clever and sometimes sarcastic assertions of these writers if he is to become a responsible professional communicator.

Many aspects of communications cannot be covered in depth, simply because of the limitations of time and space. Part VIII presents some of the new aspects and new directions found in communications. The area of communications cannot be considered as merely a rather well-defined tool in the hands of the promotional expert. Instead, it must be seen from many points of view. If communications research is to become more valuable than it is currently, research methods—many of which are already being developed in other disciplines—must be developed in a manner that can be adopted by practitioners in many communications fields.

Numerous authors and publishers in diverse fields cooperated by giving permission to include their articles in this book. Researchers in communications at Louisiana State University offered many of the insights necessary in preparing this material. No small thanks should go to the undergraduate students who "student tested" these readings. Full responsibility in selecting the articles rests, of course, with the editor.

L.R.

Introduction

Communications is still basically an art. Yet, we endeavor to introduce science into this field in order to advance it. Managers of organizations, for instance, have come to recognize the importance of mathematics and statistics in the behavioral sciences for varied purposes in the development and execution of their programs. Applications of behavioral sciences are manifold in promotion; but, in this important subarea of business strategy, art still dominates practitioners' decisions. We cannot be displeased by this fact because science simply has not developed complete theories and working models that the practitioner can readily employ. Communicators of all descriptions are still seeking better answers to their questions concerning multimillion-dollar communications programs.

Business promotion is a communication process. Whether we wish to discuss promotion as basically a persuasion process or as an informational process, the pieces that we work with and fit together to describe this process are elements of communication. The term "selling" conjures up the image of a party trying to cause another party to act. Since the communicator cannot use force, he must use words, or in some other way communicate ideas to effect the desired action on the part of the audience.

If we ask just what we do know for certain about applied communications, we begin to see the void that exists. Below are some fundamental questions about different areas of applied communications. If answers to these questions are available to you, then there is no need to read this book. On the other hand, if you feel that these questions are posed because the exact answers are available somewhere in these readings, you are drawing an equally invalid conclusion. Consider that if the question is significant, the efforts to obtain the answers deserve time, energy, and money.

1. What kinds of persons are most likely to respond favorably to a given type of printed message?
2. Under what conditions is a persuasive printed message likely to be most effective?
3. What types of persuasive printed messages are best for certain situations and for certain types of audiences?

4. What types of advertisements sell what types of products under what conditions and to what types of consumers?

5. When should persuasive communication be written, voiced, or expressed nonverbally?

6. Does everyone get the information he needs about products from advertisements, or from neighbors, friends, or relatives, or doctors, or lawyers, or dentists, or professors, or baseball players, or simply by the example of strangers?

7. How do you persuade a person to repeat an action as opposed to acting on a message the first time?

8. If a person has the wrong idea about our product, service, or institution, how can we change his mind?

9. Does advertising brainwash us, or just offer information, or affect us in some other way?

10. How do people resolve conflicting statements from different communicators?

11. What is the difference between promoting a type of product such as automobiles as opposed to a particular brand of a product type?

12. Why are some personal communicators so persuasive?

13. How can a person's personality affect his ability to convince others?

14. What kinds of salesmen are able to sell what kinds of products best in what kinds of situations to what kinds of consumers with what kinds of messages, information, or persuasion?

15. What does the salesman have to do in order to make the sale as opposed to simply getting a chance to make a pitch?

16. How can you teach a personal communicator to handle many kinds of people and their varied reactions to his communications?

Communications research has to measure its progress against the chasm of problems it faces. Likewise, scientific developments in applied communications have to be measured against problems such as those illustrated above which challenge and plague the practitioner. Each seemingly small step toward solutions of problems can result in more efficiency and success. To these ends, the practitioner dedicates his study of communications.

The subject of communications has been studied in many fields for different purposes. Findings in particular fields are often not of apparent use to others. Yet the scope of communications problems in most fields is so broad that communications research of nearly all varieties can be shown to have at least an indirect bearing. Communications research has been done in journalism, sociology, psychology, social psychology, and anthropology; by advertisers who may not have called it communications research; and by a new breed of researcher who is simply a communications researcher. A practitioner in a particular field must switch gears and understand the background from which each of these researchers writes. Various social sciences, for instance, have special languages; and even different schools of communications researchers use different terms and are concerned with different problems.

We are strictly at the outset in applied communications, as evidenced by many different points of view. As a case in point, only a few colleges of business administration, such as the one at Louisiana State University, offer courses in marketing communications at either the graduate or the undergraduate level. Today, however, communication specialists recognize the need to have some glimpse of the tremendous problems in their particular fields and have begun to see what others have found out about communication. Organized research efforts directed at specialized problems will increase and bear better results if the findings of communications and behavioral sciences are used as building blocks.

DIMENSIONS
OF
COMMUNICATION

I

FUNDAMENTALS OF COMMUNICATION

ONE OF THE OUTSTANDING CHARACTERISTICS OF A HIGHLY developed society such as the United States is its huge volume of communication activity. Combined with the extensive person-to-person communication found in most societies, the communications of a specialized technical society are of a bewildering assortment. Fundamentals of communication underlie this apparently different activity at its many levels and intensities. These fundamentals are explored in this section.

While specialists seek answers to different problems of their discipline or practice, there is a common ground. Sociologists seek answers to problems of group behavior, and psychologists focus on individual behavior. Social psychologists may want to apply the findings to small group interaction, and marketing specialists to problems of product promotion. Public relations, management, and other business disciplines will have particular current problems to solve. Political scientists, journalists, speech scientists all bring individual sets of circumstances to which general principles will apply. These articles introduce the general field of communication science, which is the beginning point for all.

Wilbur Schramm's article presents a complete treatment, and is perhaps the classic general explanation of the nature of communication. In the article by Maloney, some of the things that we now know and do not know about communications are reviewed. It becomes clear that the study of communication is not easy to delineate because of the all-persuasive nature of the subject. Scarcely any dynamics occur in an organization or group without communications being involved.

1

1

How Communication Works

WILBUR SCHRAMM

The Process

It will be easier to see how mass communication works if we first look at the communication process in general.

Communication comes from the Latin *communis*, common. When we communicate we are trying to establish a "commonness" with someone. That is, we are trying to share information, an idea, or an attitude. At this moment I am trying to communicate to you the idea that the essence of communication is getting the receiver and the sender "tuned" together for a particular message. At this same moment, someone somewhere is excitedly phoning the fire department that the house is on fire. Somewhere else a young man in a parked automobile is trying to convey the understanding that he is moon-eyed because he loves the young lady. Somewhere else a newspaper is trying to persuade its readers to believe as it does about the Republican Party. All these are forms of communication, and the process in each case is essentially the same.

Communication always requires at least three elements—the source, the message, and the destination. A *source* may be an individual (speaking, writing, drawing, gesturing) or a communication organization (like a newspaper, publishing house, television station or motion picture studio). The *message* may be in the form of ink on paper, sound waves in the air, impulses in an electric current, a wave of the hand, a flag in the air, or any other signal capable of being interpreted meaningfully. The *destination* may be an *individual* listening, watching, or reading; or a member of a *group*, such as a discussion group, a lecture audience, a football crowd, or a mob; or an individual member of the particular group we call the *mass audience*, such as the reader of a newspaper or a viewer of television.

This paper, first published in the Shimbun Kenkyu of Tokyo and later in the 53rd Yearbook of the Society for the Study of Education, is a general introduction to the communication process. Reprinted from *The Process and Effects of Mass Communication*, Wilbur Schramm, ed., Urbana, Illinois: University of Illinois Press, 1955, pp. 3-26.

Now what happens when the source tries to build up this "commonness" with his intended receiver? First, the source encodes his message. That is, he takes the information or feeling he wants to share and puts it into a form that can be transmitted. The "pictures in our heads" can't be transmitted until they are coded. When they are coded into spoken words, they can be transmitted easily and effectively, but they can't travel very far unless radio carries them. If they are coded into written words, they go more slowly than spoken words, but they go farther and last longer. Indeed, some messages long outlive their senders—the *Iliad*, for instance; the Gettysburg address; Chartres cathedral. Once coded and sent, a message is quite free of its sender, and what it does is beyond the power of the sender to change. Every writer feels a sense of help-lessness when he finally commits his story or his poem to print; you doubtless feel the same way when you mail an important letter. Will it reach the right person? Will he understand it as you intend him to? Will he respond as you want him to? For in order to complete the act of communication the message must be decoded. And there is good reason, as we shall see, for the sender to wonder whether his receiver will really be in tune with him, whether the mes-sage will be interpreted without distortion, whether the "picture in the head" of the receiver will bear any resemblance to that in the head of the sender.

We are talking about something very like a radio or telephone circuit. In fact, it is perfectly possible to draw a picture of the human communication system that way:

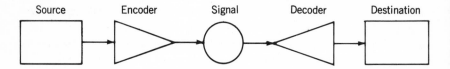

Figure 1-1.

Substitute "microphone" for encoder, and "earphone" for decoder and you are talking about electronic communication. Consider that the "source" and "en-coder" are one person, "decoder" and "destination" are another, and the sig-nal is language, and you are talking about human communication.

Now it is perfectly possible by looking at those diagrams to predict how such a system will work. For one thing, such a system can be no stronger than its weakest link. In engineering terms, there may be filtering or distortion at any stage. In human terms, if the source does not have adequate or clear in-formation; if the message is not encoded fully, accurately, effectively in trans-mittible signs; if these are not transmitted fast enough and accurately enough, despite interference and competition, to the desired receiver; if the message is not decoded in a pattern that corresponds to the encoding; and finally, if the destination is unable to handle the decoded message so as to produce the desired response—then, obviously, the system is working at less than top efficiency. When we realize that *all* these steps must be accomplished with relatively high efficiency if any communication is to be successful, the everyday act of explaining something to a stranger, or writing a letter, seems a minor miracle.

A system like this will have a maximum capacity for handling information and this will depend on the separate capacities of each unit on the chain—for example, the capacity of the channel (how fast can one talk?) or the capacity of the encoder (can your student understand something explained quickly?). If the coding is good (for example, no unnecessary words) the capacity of the channel can be approached, but it can never be exceeded. You can readily see that one of the great skills of communication will lie in knowing how near capacity to operate a channel.

This is partly determined for us by the nature of the language. English, like every other language, has its sequences of words and sounds governed by certain probabilities. If it were organized so that no set of probabilities governed the likelihood that certain words would follow certain other words (for example, that a noun would follow an adjective, or that "States" or "Nations" would follow "United") then we would have nonsense. As a matter of fact, we can calculate the relative amount of freedom open to us in writing any language. For English, the freedom is about 50 per cent. (Incidentally, this is about the required amount of freedom to enable us to construct interesting crossword puzzles. Shannon has estimated that if we had about 70 per cent freedom, we could construct three-dimensional crossword puzzles. If we had only 20 per cent, crossword puzzle making would not be worth while.)

So much for language *redundancy*, as communication theorists call it, meaning the percentage of the message which is not open to free choice. But there is also the communicator's redundancy, and this is an important aspect of constructing a message. For if we think our audience may have a hard time understanding the message, we can deliberately introduce more redundancy; we can repeat (just as the radio operator on a ship may send "SOS" over and over again to make sure it is heard and decoded), or we can give examples and analogies. In other words, we always have to choose between transmitting more information in a given time, or transmitting less and repeating more in the hope of being better understood. And as you know, it is often a delicate choice, because too slow a rate will bore an audience, whereas too fast a rate may confuse them.

Perhaps the most important thing about such a system is one we have been talking about all too glibly—the fact that receiver and sender must be in tune. This is clear enough in the case of a radio transmitter and receiver, but somewhat more complicated when it means that a human receiver must be able to understand a human sender.

Let us redraw our diagram in very simple form, like this:

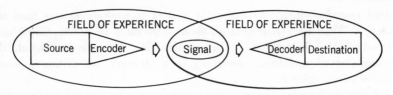

Figure 1-2.

Think of those circles as the accumulated experience of the two individuals trying to communicate. The source can encode, and the destination can decode, only in terms of the experience each has had. If we have never learned any Russian, we can neither code nor decode in that language. If an African tribesman has never seen or heard of an airplane, he can only decode the sight of a plane in terms of whatever experience he has had. The plane may seem to him to be a bird, and the aviator a god borne on wings. If the circles have a large area in common, then communication is easy. If the circles do not meet—if there has been no common experience—then communication is impossible. If the circles have only a small area in common—that is, if the experiences of source and destination have been strikingly unlike—then it is going to be very difficult to get an intended meaning across from one to the other. This is the difficulty we face when a non-science-trained person tries to read Einstein, or when we try to communicate with another culture much different from ours.

The source, then, tries to encode in such a way as to make it easy for the destination to tune in the message—to relate it to parts of his experience which are much like those of the source. What does he have to work with?

Messages are made up of signs. A sign is a signal that stands for something in experience. The word "dog" is a sign that stands for our generalized experience with dogs. The word would be meaningless to a person who came from a dog-less island and had never read of or heard of a dog. But most of us have learned that word by association, just as we learn most signs. Someone called our attention to an animal, and said "dog." When we learned the word, it produced in us much the same response as the object it stood for. That is, when we heard "dog" we could recall the appearance of dogs, their sound, their feel, perhaps their smell. But there is an important difference between the sign and the object: the sign always represents the object at a reduced level of cues. By this we mean simply that the sign will not call forth all the responses that the object itself will call forth. The sign "dog," for example, will probably not call forth in us the same wariness or attention a strange dog might attract if it wandered into our presence. This is the price we pay for portability in language. We have a sign system that we can use in place of the less portable originals (for example, Margaret Mitchell could re-create the burning of Atlanta in a novel, and a photograph could transport world-wide the appearance of a bursting atomic bomb), but our sign system is merely a kind of shorthand. The coder has to be able to write the shorthand, the decoder to read it. And no two persons have learned exactly the same system. For example, a person who has known only Arctic huskies will not have learned exactly the same meaning for the shorthand sign "dog" as will a person who comes from a city where he has known only pekes and poms.

We have come now to a point where we need to tinker a little more with our diagram of the communication process. It is obvious that each person in the communication process is both an encoder and a decoder. He receives and transmits. He must be able to write readable shorthand, and to read other people's shorthand. Therefore, it is possible to describe either sender or receiver in a human communication system thus:

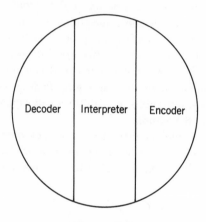

Figure 1-3.

What happens when a signal comes to you? Remember that it comes in the form of a sign. If you have learned the sign, you have learned certain responses with it. We can call these mediatory responses, because they mediate what happens to the message in your nervous system. These responses are the *meaning* the sign has for you. They are learned from experience, as we said, but they are affected by the state of your organism at the moment. For example, if you are hungry, a picture of a steak may not arouse exactly the same response in you as when you are overfed.

But subject to these effects, the mediatory responses will then determine what you do about the sign. For you have learned other sets of reactions connected to the mediatory responses. A sign that means a certain thing to you will start certain other processes in your nerves and muscles. A sign that means "fire," for example, will certainly trigger off some activity in you. A sign that means you are in danger may start the process in your nerves and muscles that makes you say "help!" In other words, the meaning that results from your decoding of a sign will start you *encoding*. Exactly *what* you encode will depend on your choice of the responses available in the situation and connected with the meaning.

Whether this encoding actually results in some overt communication or action depends partly on the barriers in the way. You may think it better to keep silent. And if an action does occur, the nature of the action will also depend on the avenues for action available to you and the barriers in your way. The code of your group may not sanction the action you want to take. The meaning of a sign may make you want to hit the person who has said it, but he may be too big, or you may be in the wrong social situation. You may merely ignore him, or "look murder at him," or say something nasty about him to someone else.

But whatever the exact result, this is the process in which you are constantly engaged. You are constantly decoding signs from your environment, interpreting these signs, and encoding something as a result. In fact, it is misleading to think of the communication process as starting somewhere and ending somewhere. It is really endless. We are little switchboard centers handling and rerouting the great endless current of communication. We can accurately think of communication as passing through us—changed, to be sure, by our interpretations, our habits, our abilities and capabilities, but the input still being reflected in the output.

We need now to add another element to our description of the communication process. Consider what happens in a conversation between two people. One is constantly communicating back to the other, thus:

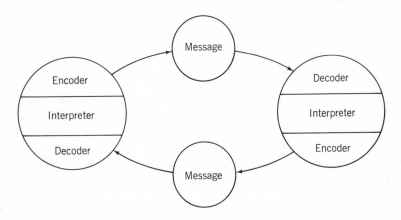

Figure 1-4.

The return process is called *feedback*, and plays a very important part in communication because it tells us how our messages are being interpreted. Does the hearer say, "Yes, yes, that's right," as we try to persuade him? Does he nod his head in agreement? Does a puzzled frown appear on his forehead? Does he look away as though he were losing interest? All these are feedback. So is a letter to the editor of a newspaper, protesting an editorial. So is an answer to a letter. So is the applause of a lecture audience. An experienced communi-cator is attentive to feedback, and constantly modifies his messages in light of what he observes in or hears from his audience.

At least one other example of feedback, also, is familiar to all of us. We get feedback from our own messages. That is, we hear our own voices and can correct mispronunciations. We see the words we have written on paper, and can correct misspellings or change the style. When we do that, here is what is happening:

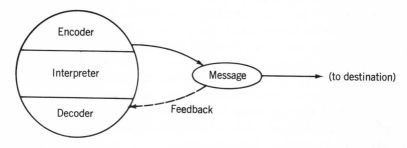

Figure 1-5.

It is clear that in any kind of communication we rarely send out mes-sages in a single channel, and this is the final element we must add to our account of the communication process. When you speak to me, the sound waves from your voice are the primary message. But there are others: the expression on your face, your gestures, the relation of a given message to past messages. Even the primary message conveys information on several levels. It gives me words to decode. It emphasizes certain words above others. It presents the words in a pattern of intonation and timing which contribute to the total meaning. The quality of your voice (deep, high, shrill, rasping, rich, thin, loud, soft) itself carries information about you and what you are saying.

This multiple channel situation exists even in printed mass communica-tion, where the channels are perhaps most restricted. Meaning is conveyed, not only by the words in a news item, but also by the size of the headline, the position on the page and the page in the paper, the association with pictures, the use of boldface and other typographical devices. All these tell us something about the item. Thus we can visualize the typical channel of communication, not as a simple telegraph circuit, in which current does or does not flow, but rather as a sort of coaxial cable in which many signals flow in parallel from source toward the destination.

These parallel relationships are complex, but you can see their general pattern. A communicator can emphasize a point by adding as many parallel messages as he feels are deserved. If he is communicating by speaking, he can stress a word, pause just before it, say it with a rising inflection, gesture while he says it, look earnestly at his audience. Or he can keep all the signals parallel—except *one*. He can speak solemnly, but wink, as Lowell Thomas sometimes does. He can stress a word in a way that makes it mean something else—for example, "That's a *fine* job you did!" And by so doing he conveys secondary meanings of sarcasm or humor or doubt.

The same thing can be done with printed prose, with broadcast, with television or films. The secondary channels of the sight-sound media are especially rich. I am reminded of a skillful but deadly job done entirely with secondary channels on a certain political candidate. A sidewalk interview program was filmed to run in local theaters. Ostensibly it was a completely impartial program. An equal number of followers of each candidate were interviewed—first, one who favored Candidate A, then one who favored Candidate B, and so on. They were asked exactly the same questions, and said about the same things, although on opposite sides of the political fence, of course. But there was one interesting difference. Whereas the supporters of Candidate A were ordinary folks, not outstandingly attractive or impressive, the followers of Candidate B who were chosen to be interviewed invariably had something slightly wrong with them. They looked wild-eyed, or they stuttered, or they wore unpressed suits. The extra meaning was communicated. Need I say which candidate won?

But this is the process by which communication works, whether it is mass communication, or communication in a group, or communication between individuals.

Communication in Terms of Learning Theory

So far we have avoided talking about this complicated process in what may seem to you to be the obvious way to talk about it—in the terminology and symbols of learning theory.[1] We have done so for the sake of simplicity. Now in order to fill in the picture it seems desirable to sketch the diagram of how communication looks to a psychologist of learning. If psychological diagrams bother you, you can skip to section 3.

Let's start with the diagram, then explain it.

The diagram isn't as complicated as it looks. Remember that time in the diagram moves from left to right, and then follow the numbers and you won't get far off the road.

Begin with (1). This is the input. At the message level we have a collection of objectivity measurable signs $\boxed{S}$. These come to your sense or-

---

[1]For the model in the following pages the author is indebted to his colleague, Dr. Charles E. Osgood. Dr. Osgood has since published the model in a more advanced form.

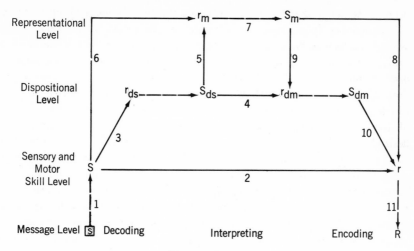

Figure 1-6.

gans, where they constitute a stimulus for action. This stimulus we call s. When the process gets as far as s, you are paying attention. The message has been accepted. It may not have been accepted as intended; s may not equal [s]; the sensory mechanism may have seen or heard it incompletely. But everything else that happens as a result of the message in that particular destination will now necessarily be the result of the stimulus accepted by your sense organs.

Now look at number (2). The message may not have to go to any other level in order to bring about a response. If a man waves his fist near your nose, you may dodge. If he squeezes your hand, you may say "ouch!" These are learned, almost automatic, responses on the sensory and motor skill level.

But the stimulus may also bring about other kinds of activity within your nervous system. Look at number (3). The stimulus s may be translated into a grammatical response on your dispositional level—by which we mean the level of learned integrations (attitudes, values, sets, etc.) which make it so easy for you to dispose of the variety of stimuli that come to you in the course of a day. These are what we call the intervening variables. Suppose the stimulus stirs up activity in this area of intervening variables. Two things may happen. Look at number (4). The response may be so well learned that it doesn't even have to go to the level of thinking. You hear a line of a poem, and almost automatically say the second line. In that case the activity is through numbers (4) and (10).

More often, however, the activity goes through number (5). Here the original stimulus has been decoded into grammar, fed through the intervening variables, and sent up to the representational level of the central nervous system, where meanings are assigned and ideas considered. Occasionally a stimulus comes to that level without going through the intervening variables —as is number (6). These stimuli create activity in the central nervous system (r_m) which is the terminus of the decoding part of the process. This is equivalent to the meaning or the significance of the signs s . What happens in number (7), then, is what we have been referring to as interpretation. The response r_m which we call meaning becomes in turn a stimulus which sets the encoding process in action, so that (7) is both the terminus of decoding and the start of encoding. We learn to associate meanings with desired responses. And so the encoding process moves through (8) or (9). That is, we give certain orders which either pass directly to the neuro-muscular system (through 8) or are passed through the intervening variables (through 9 and 10). In any case, all this activity of the nervous system finally results in a response on the motor skill level (r), which results in output (number 11). If the output is an overt response (R), then we have another message, which may offer itself as a collection of signs s and be accepted by still another person as a stimulus (s).

This is what we believe happens when someone says to you, "cigarette?" and you answer "yes, please," or "no, thanks." If you are interested in doing so, you can translate all that is said about the communication process in this paper into the psychological symbols we have just been using. But to make the account simpler, we are going to shift gears at this point and talk about communication effects and mass communication in the terms we used in section 1.

How Communication Has an Effect

The chief reason we study this process is to learn something about how it achieves effects. We want to know what a given kind of communication does to people. Given a certain message content, we should like to be able to predict what effect that content will have on its receivers.

Every time we insert an advertisement in a newspaper, put up a sign, explain something to a class, scold a child, write a letter, or put our political candidate on radio or television, we are making a prediction about the effect communication will have. I am predicting now that what I am writing will help you understand the common everyday miracle of communication. Perhaps I am wrong. Certainly many political parties have been proved wrong in their predictions about the effects of their candidates' radio speeches. Some ads sell goods; others don't. Some class teaching "goes over"; some does not. For it is apparent to you, from what you have read so far, that there is no such thing as a simple and easily predictable relationship between message content and effect.

Nevertheless, it is possible to describe simply what might be called the conditions of success in communication—by which we mean the conditions that must be fulfilled if the message is to arouse its intended response. Let us set them down here briefly, and then talk about them:

1. The message must be so designed and delivered as to gain the attention of the intended destination.

2. The message must employ signs which refer to experience common to source and destination, so as to "get the meaning across."

3. The message must arouse personality needs in the destination and suggest some ways to meet those needs.

4. The message must suggest a way to meet those needs which is appropriate to the group situation in which the destination finds himself at the time when he is moved to make the desired response.

You can see, by looking at these requirements, why the expert communicator usually begins by finding out as much as he can about his intended destination, and why "know your audience" is the first rule of practical mass communication. For it is important to know the right timing for a message, the kind of language one must use to be understood, the attitudes and values one must appeal to in order to be effective, and the group standards in which the desired action will have to take place. This is relatively easy in face-to-face communication, more difficult in mass communication. In either case, it is necessary.

Let us talk about these four requirements.

1. *The message must be so designed and delivered as to gain the attention of the intended destination.* This is not so easy as it sounds. For one thing, the message must be made available. There will be no communication if we don't talk loud enough to be heard, or if our letter is not delivered, or if we smile at the right person when she isn't looking. And even if the message is available, it may not be selected. Each of us has available far more communication than we can possibly accept or decode. We therefore scan our environment in much the same way as we scan newspaper headlines or read a table of contents. We choose messages according to our impression of their general characteristics—whether they fit our needs and interests. We choose usually on the basis of an impression we get from one cue in the message, which may be a headline, a name in a radio news story, a picture, a patch of color, or a sound. If that cue does not appeal to us, we may never open our senses to the message. In different situations, of course, we choose differently among these cues. For example, if you are speaking to me at a time when I am relaxed and unbusy, or when I am waiting for the kind of message you have (for instance, that my friends have come to take me fishing), then you are more likely to get good attention than if you address me when noise blots out what you say, or when all my attention is given to some competing message, or when I am too sleepy to pay attention, or when I am thinking about something else and have simply "tuned out." (How many times have you finished speaking and realized that your intended

receiver had simply not heard a word you said?) The designing of a message for attention, then, involves timing, and placing, and equipping it with cues which will appeal to the receiver's interests.

2. *The message must employ signs which refer to experience common to both source and destination, in order to "get the meaning across."* We have already talked about this problem of getting the receiver in tune with the sender. Let us add now that as our experience with environment grows, we tend to classify and catalog experience in terms of how it relates to other experience and to our needs and interests. As we grow older that catalog system grows harder and firmer. It tends to reject messages that do not fit its structure, or distort them so that they do fit. It will reject Einstein, perhaps, because it feels it can't understand him. If an airplane is a completely new experience, but a bird is not, it may, as we have said, interpret the plane as a large, noisy bird. If it is Republican it will tend to reject Democratic radio speeches or to recall only the parts that can be made into pro-Republican arguments; this is one of the things we have found out about voting behavior. Therefore, in designing a message we have to be sure not only that we speak the "same language" as the receiver, and that we don't "write over his head," but also that we don't conflict too directly with the way he sees and catalogs the world. There are some circumstances, true, in which it works well to conflict directly, but for the most part these are the circumstances in which our understandings and attitudes are not yet firm or fixed, and they are relatively few and far between. In communicating, as in flying an airplane, the rule is that when a stiff wind is blowing, one doesn't land cross-wind unless he has to.

3. *The message must arouse personality needs in the destination and suggest some way to meet those needs.* We take action because of need and toward goals. In certain simple situations, the action response is quite automatic. When our nerves signal "pain-heat-finger" we jerk our fingers back from the hot pan. When our optic nerve signals "red traffic light" we stop the car. In more complicated situations we usually have more freedom of choice, and we choose the action which, in the given situation, will come closest to meeting our needs or goals. The first requisite of an effective message, therefore (as every advertising man knows), is that it relate itself to one of our personality needs—the needs for security, status, belongingness, understanding, freedom from constraint, love, freedom from anxiety, and so forth. It must arouse a drive. It must make the individual feel a need or a tension which he can satisfy by action. Then the message can try to control the resulting action by suggesting what action to take. Thus an advertisement usually tells you to buy, what, and where. Propaganda to enemy troops usually suggests a specific action, such as surrender, subversion, or malingering. The suggested action, of course, is not always the one taken. If an easier, cheaper, or otherwise more acceptable action leading to the same goal is seen, that will probably be selected instead. For instance, it may be

that the receiver is not the kind of person to take vigorous action, even though that seems called for. The person's values may inhibit him from doing what is suggested. Or his group role and membership may control what action he takes, and it is this control we must talk about now.

4. *The message must suggest a way to meet those needs which is appropriate to the group situation in which the destination finds himself at the time when he is moved to make the desired response.* We live in groups. We get our first education in the primary group of our family. We learn most of our standards and values from groups. We learn roles in groups, because those roles give us the most orderly and satisfying routine of life. We make most of our communication responses in groups. And if communication is going to bring about change in our behavior, the first place we look for approval of this new behavior is to the group. We are scarcely aware of the great importance our group involvements have for us, or of the loyalties we develop toward our several groups and institutions, until our place in the group or the group itself is threatened. But yet if our groups do not sanction the response we are inclined to make to communication, then we are very unlikely to make it. On the other hand, if our group strongly approves of a certain kind of action, that is the one we are likely to select out of several otherwise even choices.

You can see how this works in practical situations. The Jewish culture does not approve the eating of pork; the Indian culture does not approve the slaughter of cows, and the eating of beef. Therefore, it is highly unlikely that even the most eloquent advertisement will persuade an orthodox Jewish family to go contrary to their group sanctions, and buy pork; or an orthodox Hindu family, to buy beef. Or take the very simple communication situation of a young man and a young woman in a parked automobile. The young man communicates the idea that he wants a kiss. There isn't much likelihood of his not gaining attention for that communication or of its not being understood. But how the young woman responds will depend on a number of factors, partly individual, partly group. Does she want to be kissed at that moment? Does she want to be kissed by that young man? Is the situation at the moment—a moon, soft music from the radio, a convertible?—conducive to the response the young man wants? But then, how about the group customs under which the girl lives? If this is a first date, is it "done" to kiss a boy on a first date? Is petting condoned in the case of a girl her age? What has she learned from her parents and her friends about these things? Of course, she won't knowingly have a little debate with herself such as we have suggested here, but all these elements and more will enter into the decision as to whether she tilts up her chin or says, "No, Jerry. Let's go home."

There are two things we can say with confidence about predicting communication effects. One is that a message is much more likely to succeed if it fits the patterns of understandings, attitudes, values and goals that a receiver has; or at least if it starts with this pattern and tries to reshape it slightly. Communication research men call this latter process "canalizing," meaning that the sender provides a channel to direct the already existing motives in the receiver. Advertising men and propagandists say it more bluntly; they say that a communicator must "start where the audience is." You can see why this is. Our personalities—our patterns of habits, attitudes, drives, values, and so forth—grow very slowly but firmly. I have elsewhere compared the process to the slow, sure, ponderous growth of a stalagmite on a cave floor. The stalagmite builds up from the calcareous residue of the water dripping on it from the cave roof. Each drop leaves only a tiny residue, and it is very seldom that we can detect the residue of any single drop, or that any single drop will make a fundamental change in the shape or appearance of the stalagmite. Yet together all these drops do build the stalagmite, and over the years it changes considerably in size and somewhat in shape. This is the way our environment drips into us, drop by drop, each drop leaving a little residue, each tending to follow the existing pattern. This personality pattern we are talking about is, of course, an active thing—not passive, like the stalagmite—but still the similarity is there. When we introduce one drop of communication into a person where millions of drops have already fallen and left their residue, we can hardly expect to reshape the personality fundamentally by that one drop. If we are communicating to a child, it is easier, because the situation is not so firmly fixed. If we are communicating in an area where ideas and values are not yet determined—if our drop of communication falls where not many have fallen before—then we may be able to see a change as a result of our communication.

But in general we must admit that the best thing we can do is to build on what already exists. If we take advantage of the existing pattern of understanding, drives, and attitudes to gain acceptance for our message, then we may hope to divert the pattern slightly in the direction we want to move it. Let's gó back to elections again for an example. It is very hard to change the minds of convinced Republicans or Democrats through communication, or even to get them to listen to the arguments of the opposing party. On the other hand, it is possible to start with a Republican or Democratic viewpoint and slightly modify the existing party viewpoints in one way or other. If this process goes on for long enough, it may even be possible to get confirmed party-men to reverse their voting pattern. This is what the Republicans were trying to do in the 1952 election by stressing "the mess in Washington," "time for a change," "the mistakes in Korea," and "the threat of Communism," and apparently they were successful in getting some ordinarily Democratic votes. But in 1952, as in every campaign, the real objectives of the campaigning were the new voters and the undecided voters.

The second thing we can say with confidence about communication effects is that they are resultants of a number of forces, of which the communicator can really control only one. The sender, that is, can shape his message and can decide when and where to introduce it. But the message is only one of at least four important elements that determine what response occurs. The other three are the situation in which the communication is received and in which the response, if any, must occur; the personality state of the receiver; and his group relationships and standards. This is why it is so dangerous to try to predict exactly what will be the effect of any message except the simplest one in the simplest situation.

Let us take an example. In Korea, in the first year of the war there, I was interviewing a North Korean prisoner of war who had recently surrendered with one of our surrender leaflets on his person. It looked like an open and shut case: the man had picked up the leaflet, thought it over, and decided to surrender. But I was interviewing him anyway, trying to see just how the leaflet had its effect. This is what he told me.

He said that when he picked up the leaflet, it actually made him fight harder. It rather irritated him, and he didn't like the idea of having to surrender. He wasn't exactly a warlike man; he had been a clerk, and was quiet and rather slow; but the message actually aroused a lot of aggression in him. Then the situation deteriorated. His division was hit hard and thrown back, and he lost contact with the command post. He had no food, except what he could find in the fields, and little ammunition. What was left of his company was isolated by itself in a rocky valley. Even then, he said, the morale was good, and there was no talk of surrendering. As a matter of fact, he said, the others would have shot him if he had tried to surrender. But then a couple of our planes spotted them, shot up their hideout, and dropped some napalm. When it was over, he found himself alone, a half mile from where he had been, with half his jacket burned off, and no sign of any of his company. A couple of hours later some of our tanks came along. And only then did the leaflet have an effect. He remembered it had told him to surrender with his hands up, and he did so.

In other words, the communication had no effect (even had an opposite effect from the one intended) so long as the situation, the personality, and the group norms were not favorable. When the situation deteriorated, the group influence was removed, and the personality aggression was burned up, then finally the message had an effect. I tell you this story hoping it will teach you what it taught me: that it is dangerous to assume any simple and direct relationship between a message and its effect without knowing all the other elements in the process.

The Nature of Mass Communication

Now let us look at mass communication in the light of what we have already said about communication in general.

The process is exactly what we have described, but the elements in the process are not the same.

The chief source, in mass communication, is a communication organization or an institutionalized person. By a communication organization we mean a newspaper, a broadcasting network or station, a film studio, a book or magazine publishing house. By an institutionalized person we mean such a person as the editor of a newspaper, who speaks in his editorial columns through the facilities of the institution and with more voice and prestige than he would have if he were speaking without the institution.

The organization works exactly as the individual communicator does. It operates as decoder, interpreter, and encoder. On a newspaper, for example, the input to be decoded flows in through the news wires and the reporters. It is evaluated, checked, amplified where necessary, written into a story, assigned headline and position, printed, distributed. This is the same process as goes on within an individual communicator, but it is carried out by a group of persons rather than by one individual. The quality of organization required to get a group of reporters, editors, and printers working together as a smooth communication unit, decoding, interpreting, and encoding so that the whole operation and product has an individual quality, is a quite remarkable thing. We have become so used to this performance that we have forgotten how remarkable it is.

Another difference between the communication organization and the individual communicator is that the organization has a very high ratio of output to input. Individuals vary, of course, in their output-input ratios. Persons who are in the business of communicating (preachers or teachers, for example) ordinarily have higher ratios than others, and so do naturally talkative persons who are not professional communicators. Very quiet persons have relatively higher input. But the communication institution is so designed as to be able to encode thousands—sometimes millions—of identical messages at the same time. To carry these, intricate and efficient channels must be provided. There have to be provisions for printing and delivering thousands of newspapers, magazines, or books, for making prints of a film and showing them in hundreds or thousands of theaters, for translating sound waves into electricity and distributing it through wires and through the air to millions of receiving sets.

The *destinations* of mass communication are individuals at the ends of these channels—individuals reading the evening paper, looking through the new magazine, reading the new book, sitting in the motion picture theater, turning the dial on the radio set. This receiving situation is much different from that which pertains in face-to-face communication, for one thing, because there is very little direct *feedback* from the receivers to the sender. The destination who, in a face-to-face situation, will nod his head and smile or frown while the sender is speaking, and then encode a reply himself, will very seldom talk back to the radio network or write a letter to the editor. Indeed, the kind of feedback that comes to a mass communication organization is a kind of inferential expression —receivers stop buying the publication, or no longer listen to the program, or cease to buy the product advertised. Only in rare instances do these organizations have an opportunity to see, more directly than that, how their messages are going over. That is one reason why mass communication conducts so much audience research, to find out what programs are being listened to, what stories are being read, what ads attended to. It is one of their few substitutes for the feedback which makes interpersonal communication so relatively easy to plan and control.

The following chapters will have something to say about the audiences of the different media, and we need not discuss them in any detail here. These audiences cluster, not only around a newspaper, magazine, or television station, but also around certain stories in the paper, certain parts of the magazine, certain television or radio programs. For example, Station A will not have the same audience at 8:00 as it had at 7:00, because some of these listeners will have moved to Stations B or C, and some of the listeners from B and C will have moved to A. Newspaper D will not have the same audience on its sports pages as on its society pages, although there will be some overlap. What determines which offering of mass communication will be selected by any given individual? Perhaps the easiest way to put it is to say that choice is determined by the Fraction of Selection—

$$\frac{\text{Expectation of reward}}{\text{Effort required}}$$

You can increase the value of that fraction either by increasing the numerator or decreasing the denominator, which is to say that an individual is more likely to select a certain communication if it promises him more reward or requires less effort than comparable communications. You can see how this works in your own experience. You are much more likely to read the newspaper or magazine at hand than to walk six blocks to the news stand to buy a bigger newspaper or magazine. You are more likely to listen to a station which has a loud clear signal than to one which is faint and fading and requires constant effort from you to hear at all. But if the big game of the week is on that faint station, or if your favorite author is in the magazine at the news stand, then there is more likelihood that you will make the additional effort. If you were a member of the underground in occupied France during World War II, you probably risked your life to hear news from the forbidden Allied radio. You aren't likely to stay up until 2 a.m. simply to hear a radio program, but if by staying up that long you can find out how the Normandy invasion is coming or who has won the Presidential election—then you will probably make the extra effort just as most of the rest of us did. It is hardly necessary to point out that no two receivers may have exactly the same fraction of selection. One of them may expect more reward from Milton Berle than will the other. One of them may consider it less effort to walk six blocks to the news stand than does the other. But according to how this fraction looks to individuals in any given situation, the audience of mass communication is determined.

Unlike lecture audiences and small groups, mass communication audiences (with the exception of the people in a motion picture theater at the same time) have very little contact with each other. People in one house listening to Jack

Benny don't know whether anybody in the next house is listening to him or not. A person reading an editorial in the New York *Times* has little group feeling for the other people in this country who read editorials in the New York *Times*. These audiences are individuals, rather than groups. But each individual is connected with a group or groups—his family, his close friends, his occupational or school group—and this is a very important thing to remember about mass communication. The more we study it, the more we are coming to think that the great effects of mass communication are gained by feeding ideas and information into small groups through individual receivers. In some groups, as you well know, it is a sign of status to be familiar with some part of mass communication (for example, in the teen-age group to hear the currently screamable crooner, or in some business groups to read the *Wall Street Journal*). In many a group, it is a news story from the radio, or an editorial from the *Tribune*, or an article from the *Times*, or an article from one of the big magazines, that furnishes the subject of conversation on a given day. The story, or article, or editorial, is then re-interpreted by the group, and the result is encoded in group opinion and perhaps in group action. Thus it may well be that the chief influence of mass communication on individuals is really a kind of secondary influence, reflected to the group and back again.

We are ready now to draw a diagram of mass communication, and to talk about the kinds of messages this sort of system requires and what we know about predicting their effects. This is the way mass communication seems to work:

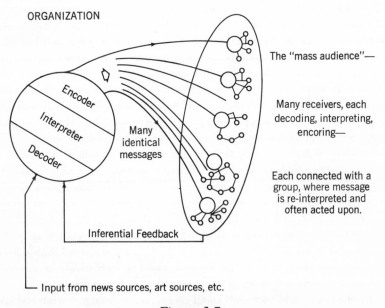

ORGANIZATION

Encoder

Interpreter

Decoder

Many
identical
messages

The "mass audience"—

Many receivers, each
decoding, interpreting,
encoring—

Each connected with a
group, where message
is re-interpreted and
often acted upon.

Inferential Feedback

Input from news sources, art sources, etc.

Figure 1-7.

Now it is easy to see that there will be certain restrictions on the kinds of program which can be carried over these identical circuits to these little-known and changing audiences. The communication organization knows it is dealing with individuals, yet does not know them as individuals. Its audience research classifies, rather than individualizes, the audience. Audience research, that is, says that so many people are listening at a given time, or that so many men and so many women are likely to read a given kind of article, or that the readers of a given magazine are in the upper economic bracket and have had on the average 12 years of schooling. Whereas the individual communicator is dealing with individuals and able to watch the way his message is received and modify it if necessary, the organization is dealing only with averages and classes. It must pitch its reading level somewhere below the estimated average of its audience, in order not to cut off too many of the lower half of the audience. It must choose its content according to the best estimate it can make of what the broadest classes of receivers want and need. Whereas the individual communicator is free to experiment because he can instantly correct any mistake, the organization is loathe to experiment. When it finds an apparently successful formula, it keeps on that way. Or it changes the details but not the essentials. If one organization makes a great success with a given kind of message, others tend to copy it—not because of any lack of originality, but because this is one of the few kinds of feedback available from the mass audience. That is why we have so much sameness on the radio, why one successful comic strip tends to be followed by others of the same kind, one successful news or digest magazine by others, one kind of comedy program by others of the same kind, and so forth.

What can we say about the effects of these mass communication messages? For one thing, mass communication has pervasive effect because in many respects it has taken over the function of *society communicating*. Our society, like any other communication unit, functions as decoder, interpreter, and encoder. It decodes our environment for us, watches the horizon for danger and promise and entertainment. It then operates to interpret what it has decoded, arrives at a consensus so that it can put policy into effect, keep the ordinary interactions of communal life going, and helps its members

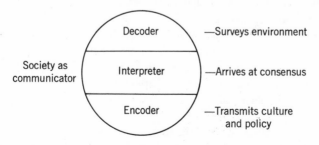

Figure 1-8.

enjoy life. It also encodes—messages to maintain our relations with other societies in the world, and messages to transmit our culture to its new members. Mass communication, which has the power to extend our eyes and ears almost indefinite distances, and to multiply our voices and written words as far as we can find listeners or readers, has taken over a large share of the responsibility for this social communication. Newspapers, radio, television watch the horizon for us. By telling us what our leaders and experts think, by conducting a discussion of public issues, these media, and magazines and films as well, help us to interpret what is seen on the horizon and decide what to do about it. The textbook and educational films have led all the other media in encoding our culture so that the young persons coming into our society may learn as quickly and easily as possible the history, standards, roles, and skills they must know in order to be good members of society. This is not to say that all the media do not contribute in some degree to all these functions. For example, a book like *1984* may be as much a report of the horizon as the most current news story. And on the other hand, it is certainly true that a great deal of our culture is transmitted currently through television, radio, newspapers, and magazines. But the faster media are better equipped to be watchmen, and are more often so used. The slower, longer lasting media are better equipped to be teaching aids and are so used. The important thing is that *all* the mass media have important uses in providing the network of understandings without which the modern large community could not exist.

So much for the basic effect, which we see every day in the kind of customs around us, the people and problems talked about, and the language we speak. This is the slow, imperceptible effect. This is like building the stalagmite. But how about the specific effect of a given message transmitted by mass communication? How can we predict what the effect will be on the mass audience?

We can't predict the effect on the mass audience. We can only predict the effect on individuals. Communication organizations have developed group encoding, but there is only individual decoding. Therefore, we can predict the effect of mass communication only in the way we try to predict the effect of other communication—that is, in terms of the interaction of message, situation, personality, and group.

The first thing which becomes obvious, therefore, is that inasmuch as there are many different combinations of personality, situation, and group in any mass audience, there are likely to be many different kinds of effects. It is equally obvious that since mass communication doesn't know much about the individuals in its audience, predicting effects is going to be extremely difficult.

Nevertheless, there are certain things to be said. The problem of attention constantly faces mass communication. The average American (whoever he is) probably gives four or five hours a day to mass communication. If he lives in a big city, he gets a paper that would itself take half that time to read. (He doesn't read all of it.) He is offered the equivalent of two weeks of radio and television every day from which he can choose. He is offered a bewildering array of magazines and books and films. From these also he must choose. Other attractive ways to spend leisure compete with communication. He sometimes combines them—listening to music while he reads, playing cards or eating while he hears a newscast, playing with the baby while he watches television. Therefore, we can predict at least that any individual will have a fairly small chance of selecting any given item in mass communication, and that if he does select it, his level of attention may be rather low. This is responsible for many cases of "mis-hearing" radio. We know also that readership of the average newspaper story falls off sharply after the first few paragraphs, so that a member of the mass audience is likely not to see at all the latter part of a long newspaper story.

There are of course many cases in which markedly high attention is aroused by mass communication, and plentiful instances of listeners identifying closely with radio characters and adopting the mannerisms and language of movie heroes. It has been said that the mass media have brought Hollywood, Broadway, and Washington nearer than the next town, and there is a great deal of truth in this. There are also some cases in which very spectacular overt results have been accomplished by mass communication.

Let us recall one of them. Can you remember when CBS broadcast Orson Welles' performance of H. G. Wells' "War of the Worlds"? The script featured the invasion of the United States by armies from outer space. Perhaps you were one of the people who ran screaming for the hills, or armed yourself to wait for the invaders, or tried to call your loved ones long distance for a farewell talk. Or perhaps you were not. Perhaps you were one of those who heard the CBS announcers explain carefully that it was a play made from a book of fiction. Those who didn't hear those announcements were engaged in proving what we have just said about the low level of attention to some parts of mass communication.

But that doesn't entirely explain why people became hysterical and did things they were rather ashamed of the next day. And in truth, this is one of the really spectacular examples of mass communication effect. This happened without any specific reference to groups; it happened spontaneously in thousands of homes near the supposed scene of invasion. Why did it happen? Research men have studied the incident, and think they have put together the puzzle. For one thing, it was a tense time. People were full of anxiety, which could have been triggered off in many ways. In the second place, people trusted—still trust—radio news; the play was in the form of newscasts and commentaries. Therefore, the communication as it was interpreted really represented a spectacular change in the situation: the Martians were invading! Apparently the group element played no large part in this event, but the other three did. The message was accepted (minus the important identification as fiction). The listeners had a good deal of anxiety ready to be used. The message convinced them that the situation had indeed changed for the worse. Each according to his own personality and situation then took action.

As we have said, that was, fortunately, one of the few really spectacular examples of mass behavior. Another one was the Gold Rush that resulted in the 1890's when the newspapers brought word of gold in Alaska. Some people might say that what the Communists have been able to accomplish is a spectacular advertisement for the power of mass communication, and that subject is worth looking at because it shows us not only some of the differences between the ways we use the mass media and the way dictators use them, but also some of the principles of communication effect.

It is true that one of the first acts of the Communists, when they take over a country, is to seize the mass communication system. (That was also one of Hitler's first acts.) They also seize the police power and the control of productive resources, and they organize an intricate system of Party groups and meetings. I don't know of any case in which the Communists have put the whole burden of convincing people and gaining members on mass communications alone. They always provide a group structure where a convert can get reinforcement, and meetings to which a potential convert can be drawn. They use mass communication almost as an adjunct to these groups. In Korea and China, the mass media actually become texts for the groups. And the Communists do one thing more. If at all possible, they secure a monopoly on the mass communication reaching the people whom they are taking over. When they took Seoul, Korea, in 1950, they confiscated radio receivers wherever they found receivers despite the fact that they had captured Radio Seoul, intact, the most powerful transmitter in that part of Asia. They were willing to give up the use of Radio Seoul, if by so doing they could keep their subjects from foreign radio.

Now obviously, a state monopoly on communication, as well as control of resources and organization of a police state, is a long way from our system. And as long as our mass media are permitted free criticism and reporting, and as long as they represent more than one political point of view, we have little to worry about in a political way from them. But even though we may look with revulsion at the Communist way of using mass communication, still we can study it. And let us refer back to the four elements which we said were instrumental in bringing about communication effects—message, situation, personality, and group. The Communists control the messages. By their police power, control of resources (and hence of food and pay), they can structure the situation as they see fit. Their group organization is most careful, and offers a place—in fact compels a place—for every person. Thus they control three of the four elements, and can use those three to work on the fourth— the personalities of their receivers.

The Communists, who have now had 35 years practice in the intensive use of mass communication for accomplishing specified effects, are apparently unwilling to predict the results of their communication unless they can control three of the four chief elements which enter into the effect.

Let us take one final example. There is a great deal of violence in mass communication content today. Violence is interesting to children. Yet only a few children actually engage in acts of criminal violence. Most children do no such things. They sample the violent material, and decide they would rather play football. Or they attend faithfully to the violent material, use it to clear out vicariously some of the aggressions they have been building up, and emerge none the worse for the experience. Or they adopt some of the patterns in a mild and inoffensive way when they play cops and robbers. Only a few children learn, from the mass media, techniques of crime and violence which they and their pals actually try out. Now what is it that determines which of those children will be affected harmfully by those messages of violence, and which will not?

We can attempt to answer this question from cases we have studied. And the answer is simply that the other three elements—personality, situation, and group influence—will probably determine the use made of the message. If the child is busy with athletics, Scouts, church, or other wholesome activities, he is not likely to feel the need of violent and antisocial actions. On the other hand, if he is bored and frustrated, he may experiment with dangerous excitement. If he has a healthy personality, if he has learned a desirable set of values from his family group, he is less likely to give in to motivation toward violence. On the other hand, if his value standards are less certain, if he has lost some of his sense of belonging and being loved (possibly because of a broken home), he may entertain more hospitably the invitation to violence. If the group he admires has a wholesome set of standards, he is not likely to try an undesirable response, because the group will not reinforce it. On the other hand, if he belongs to a "gang" there is every reason to expect that he will try some of the violence, because in so doing he will win admiration and status in the group. Therefore, what he does will depend on the delicate balancing of these influences at a given time. Certainly no one could predict—except possibly on an actuarial basis—from merely seeing such a message exactly what the response to it would be. And it is entirely probable in the case we have mentioned that the community, the home, and the school—because they influence so greatly the other three elements—would have much more to do with the young person's response than would the message itself.

The all-pervasive effect of mass communication, the ground swell of learning that derives from mass communication acting as *society communicating*— this we can be sure of, and over a long period we can identify its results in our lives and beliefs. The more specific effects, however, we must predict only with caution, and never from the message alone without knowing a great deal about the situation, the personality, and the group relationship where the message is to be acted upon.

2

Advertising Research and an Emerging Science of Mass Persuasion

JOHN C. MALONEY

In an age of specialization we are often frustrated in our natural search for the "oneness of things." But the intellectual pursuits of many converge today in the study of public opinion. Public opinion holds a fascination for theologian and politician, propagandist and editor, social scientist and advertiser.

Goethe spoke of public opinion in terms of the *Zeitgeist*, the "spirit of the times." Modern anthropologists express a similar notion when they speak of the "cultural metaphysics" that is reflected in the communications patterns which shape the thinking of those within the culture.

Psychologist-historian E. G. Boring recently spoke of public opinion in terms of the "current of credence, the stream of change in what the culture carries as truth at any particular time."[1]

But it is doubtful that anyone has put the matter as clearly as did the priest-paleontologist Pierre Teilhard de Chardin when he described what he called the *noosphere*.[2]

The *noosphere*, says Teilhard, is the layer of information which surrounds us all. It is as pervasive as the atmosphere which provides the air we breathe. It is, in fact, so pervasive that few men are aware of this layer of information or of its effects.

We are all constantly awash with information from pulpit and classroom, from television, radio, books, magazines, billboards, car cards, match covers

This article was adapted from an address at the 1964 convention of the Association for Education in Journalism at University of Texas. At the time he wrote the article, Dr. Maloney was employed by the Leo Burnett Company. Reprinted from *Journalism Quarterly* (Autumn, 1964), pp. 517-525, by permission of the author and publisher.
[1]Edwin G. Boring, "Cognitive Dissonance: Its Use in Science," *Science*, 145: 680-85 (Aug. 14, 1964).
[2]Pierre Teilhard de Chardin, *The Phenomenon of Man* (New York: Harper & Row, First Harper Torchbook Edition, 1961), pp. 180-83, 220 ff.

and personal conversations. Like fish in the ocean, we can never get up out of the noosphere long enough to notice that it is there. But this continuous flow of information bearing stimulation *is* there. The noosphere is every bit as real as the atmosphere even though it is the product of men themselves communicating with men.

Just as we breathe out and breathe in we write and we read. We speak and we listen. We show and we learn. We continuously put something of ourselves *into* the noosphere and we withdraw our thoughts, our biases and our plans *from* the noosphere. Walt Whitman was no doubt thinking about this noosphere when he wrote years ago about the child that went forth each day and became what he saw.

Mass Communication, Persuasion and Control of the Noosphere

The average man takes more out of this stream of thought than he puts into it. But there is a large privileged class which communicates to many. Within this privileged class we find the novelist, journalist, minister, professor, politician and advertiser. Each decides what he wants others to know, think, or feel and each communicates to his respective audience accordingly.

No one, of course, can manipulate more than a portion of the noosphere. Some of the swirls and eddies in this stream of information come from the pen of a Dewey or a James or a Faulkner. Some emanate from the White House and some from Republican party headquarters. Some come from the National Council of Churches, Baptist headquarters or the Vatican.

Some come from *True Story* and some from the *Saturday Review*. And some of this communication flows from the public relations department of the Ford Motor Company, the product planning divisions of General Motors and the package design section of the American Tobacco Company. With their $13 billion per year efforts, advertisers also contribute a little something to this unceasing stream of information.

These are a few of the groups which have been called the "mind makers." They all have their effects on the noosphere. The contributions of all bear upon our conscious thoughts, our hidden assumptions and biases, our plans and our actions.

An Emerging Science of Mass Persuasion

From the times of Aristotle and the early Roman Empire we have inherited how-to manuals for winning arguments and elections, converting heathens, indoctrinating the young, obtaining gifts and making sales. History teaches us that religious missionaries and emperors' public relations experts were very astute propagandists two thousand years ago. But certain developments of the 20th century have brought us toward a true science of mass persuasion.

A new psychophysics has provided us with laws of attention which govern people's probabilities of watching certain sights or hearing certain sounds. We have recently noticed that these same laws of attention control attention to competing communication stimuli in the noosphere.

A new psychology has provided us with some fairly clearcut principles of perception and cognition. We are beginning to see how these explain the ways in which people make sense of or "understand" the communication symbols to which they attend.

New learning and attitude formation theories teach us a good deal about the so-called acceptance or belief of information once it is noted and minimally understood. Information-flow theories of sociology and social psychology teach us how mass media information interacts with word-of-mouth information in the formation of public opinion. And the modern computer, with its prodigious capacities for mixing and matching all sorts of information promises to explain the translation of public opinion to mass action in the marketplace, at the polls, or in other areas of social action.

Attention - Comprehension - Conviction - Action; Awareness - Interest - Desire - Action — These were clichés of the mass persuader just a few years ago. Today these terms suggest a new kind of behavioral science. A science of mass persuasion is well on its way.

Evolution of the Communication Research Movement

It is the purpose of this paper to describe the role of advertising research as a catalyst for the development of this mass persuasion science, and indeed many of the earliest detailed studies of persuasive communication were in the area of advertising research. A Minnesota psychologist, Harlow Gale, published a book on the psychology of advertising in 1900 and a surprising number of advertising psychology books were published in the first quarter of the century. (Outstanding among these were the works of Starch, Poffenberger and Walter Dill Scott, who later became president of Northwestern University.)

However, the particular role of present day advertising research can not be appreciated without an understanding of the relationship between such research and the broader context of a general communication research movement.

The impetus for this movement came largely through the federal government's support of persuasive mass communication studies during World War II. These included studies of indoctrination and training procedures for servicemen; studies of the effects of psychological warfare and propaganda; studies of special efforts to sell war bonds and to gain civilian support for government rationing and other war effort programs.

While the government's mobilization of the social sciences to study mass persuasion during World War II launched the first large scale communications research movement, the trend continued at the close of the war. The Department of Agriculture underwrote the special studies of rural sociologists who set out to determine the patterns of new idea and new product adoption in farm communities. Marketing and advertising research groups were set up within this same department and government-sponsored studies of psychological warfare, propaganda and other forms of mass persuasion have continued (though on a rather modest scale, through such agencies as the United States Information Agency) to the present day.

Meanwhile, academicians whose efforts had contributed to these wartime studies were turning their attention to studies of political persuasion during presidential campaigns, studies of rumor, studies of the effects of different forms of rhetoric, and general studies of information flow within groups. Much of this early work came from the Bureau of Applied Social Research at Columbia University and through special Institutes of Communication Research set up at Yale, Stanford and Illinois. Similar communication research groups appeared in rapid succession at other major universities. A rather amazing growth rate for such facilities continues to the present time.

As a result of this rapidly accelerating trend in recent years, communications research has attracted the interests of a broad range of behavioral science specialists (anthropologists, sociologists, psychologists, semanticists and a host of others). It has also attracted the attention of physical scientists whose work involved communication problems—communication engineers, information theorists, and finally the cyberneticists whose fruitful human brain-electronic brain analogies have had a marked impact upon the field.

Early paradigms of "who says what to whom with what effect" gave way to more sophisticated terminologies of source and destination, sender and receiver, encode, transmit, decode and feedback.

With a jargon of its own, burgeoning literature of its own, and an impressive variety of professional organizations of its own "communications research" had, during the decade of the 1950s, taken on the earmarks of a unique scientific discipline.

Until very recently, however, the main effect of the communication research movement has been to direct the attentions of separate behavioral science disciplines toward the communication aspects of their own areas of specialty. Psychologists have been more inclined to study the communication implications of psychology; sociologists have been more inclined to explore the communication facets of sociology and so on. Each behavioral science, though much influenced within its own ranks, has been reluctant to subordinate its own theories and traditions to a general discipline of "communications research."[3]

The separate bits and pieces of knowledge of human behavior have clearly begun to fall in place, and it is clear that this knowledge is of great practical value to the "mind makers," the "noosphere manipulators" or those privileged groups who control the mass media of communication and persuasion.

But one must look to the sociologists or social psychologists (or, in some cases the Operations Research specialists) to find this new knowledge as it applies to *communication campaigns*. They are the ones who can tell us how to identify those segments of the population most likely to respond to a given campaign of persuasion and those who are most likely to make the big difference in the marketplace or at the polling booth. They are the experts in the "two-step flow of communication" from the mass media to especially interested opinion leaders and from opinion leaders to less interested groups. They know the most about the mass media—word-of-mouth interactions in the flow of information.

Those who seek new knowledge of communication *message effects* might turn, instead, to the learning theorists and those who specialize in attitude formation. They could offer the best guidance for selecting message texts, issues, editorial stances or "selling ideas" that might move groups with certain predeveloped attitudes toward specific mass behaviors (e.g., voting behaviors, buying behaviors or other mass action behaviors). They know the most about the use of fear appeals and promises of reward; the use of one-sided and two-sided arguments and sales messages; and the selection of message spokesmen who will be believable to particular audience segments.

If one's interests run to communication *symbol effects* he would turn to another group of specialists—to the semanticists, for example, or to certain other learning and cognition theorists. Within their own specialties they have learned most about the effects of novelty, familiarity and repetition with variation. They might know most about finding the words or pictures, sights or sounds which would be most easily understood or most in tune with a given audience's own experiences. They have learned a good deal about the proper relationships of pictures, headlines and copy in printed messages and the integration of audio and video symbols in broadcast messages. They could well advise the "mind maker" regarding the optimum redundancy in headline and

---

[3]Thus, key figures in the communication research field have retained their basic identification with original disciplines. Sociologists Paul Lazarsfeld and Elihu Katz have retained positions as professors of sociology, the former at Columbia and the latter at the University of Chicago. Harold Lasswell, long regarded by many as the father of communication research, continued his career as professor of law at Yale. The late Dr. Carl Hovland and Dr. Charles Osgood, dominant figures in the field through their work as directors of Institutes of Communications Research at Yale and the University of Illinois, respectively, retained primary identities as psychologists. Dr. Hovland served as president of the American Psychological Association in 1958; Dr. Osgood was accorded the same honor by his fellow psychologists in 1964.

body copy and the kind of dominance a new message element must have if it is not to get lost in the background clutter of other elements.

Still other specialists could offer good advice regarding communication *stimulus or signal effects,* whether the concern is with page size, picture size, type face or the use of color.

Thus, the communication research movement has had a profound effect upon the behavioral sciences. And as each of the sciences has gone about its specialized study of sensation, perception, cognition, learning or public opinion formation each has contributed much to a general knowledge of communication processes. But this general research trend (since the time of the problem-oriented wartime studies) has lacked a unifying force or sense of urgency for finding workable answers to actual communication problems. The science of mass persuasion will trace its origins to the general communication research movement, but its main form is more likely to take shape in the advertising agency than in the university.

Behavioral Science in Advertising Research

At first glance the advertising business environment seems like a most unlikely spawning ground for a new behavioral science, and a good deal of advertising research practice remains today what it has been in the past—a pseudoscientific rationalization for advertising expenditures. But all of this has been changing in the past five or ten years and the change is rapid.

The successes of modern cost accounting, production planning, inventory controlling procedures and other "management science" methods have created a new climate in American business. Businessmen feel a new need for rational understanding of the business processes for which they make major expenditures. The profit squeeze is on and business leaders are growing impatient with the fact that their vast advertising budgets are spent largely on the basis of trial and error experimentation. With a very real sense of urgency surrounding the issue of advertising accountability increasing sums are spent each year on advertising research.

Behavioral scientists, many with advanced training in their respective fields at the Ph.D. level, are coming into the field in unprecedented numbers. When they come they find research funds, computer facilities, interviewing staffs, laboratory equipment and better mass behavior criterion data (in the form of product sales records) than they could ever find outside of the business community. The best of these people can, in a word, find an environment that is most conducive to accomplishment.

Emboldened by the fact that multimillion dollar mass persuasion decisions must be made with them or without them, these people are encouraged to wade into the complexities, to stretch their powers of reason.

The traditional barriers which would separate sociologists from experimental psychologist or behavioral scientist from mathematician or economist in another setting are starting to fall. Theories are not espoused out of loyalty to a discipline or the provincial doctrines of a research professor. Facts are marshalled to produce actionable conclusions. Theories are milked for their practical value and revised rather unceremoniously when they fail to stand on their own.

The figure-ground contrast theories of one discipline are seen as the equivalents of the signal-to-noise ratio notions of another. Stimulus or input; response or output; cognitive dissonance or doubt; feedback, curiosity or mental set—the polyglot jargon of behavioral science and communication theory is being distilled to produce a pragmatic language for decision makers.

But, for all of this pragmatism, the new professionals in advertising research make few compromises with sound research practice. There are already enough true professionals in the field today to provide checks and balances on each other's work. These checks and balances and strivings for achievement are all the more effective since these people are sprinkled throughout many competing business firms and since it is now becoming commonplace for them to move back and forth between positions in business and positions on the university campus.

The scientist who is sensitive to criticism for research shoddiness or theoretical naivete on the university campus is no less sensitive to such criticism applied to studies undertaken in the business community.[4]

Research facilities in the author's own firm may serve as an example of this trend. We have 60 to 70 people employed full time in the research phases of planning and evaluating advertising. Eight of these are trained at the Ph.D. level; many more hold masters' degrees. The Ph.D.'s represent advanced training in business administration, economics, communications, experimental psychology, applied psychology and the psychology of human development.

We operate a fully equipped psycho-physical laboratory to measure people's immediate short term responses to advertising layouts and commercial storyboards. Twelve thousand people served as "subjects" for this facility last year. For field studies our researchers may draw upon a highly competent interviewing staff and high speed electronic computer facilities are readily available. (The latter include an I.B.M. 1401 computer located in the office itself.)

Many months of literature review and experimental research have gone into development of a standardized on-the-air testing procedure for evaluating

[4]While these remarks are made primarily with advertising agency personnel in mind they apply equally to a growing number of behavioral scientists in marketing and advertising consulting firms, those on the staffs of major manufacturing firms, and those employed by newspapers and magazine publishers and broadcasters.

the attention value, clarity and "believability" of commercial messages and a project for the development of an objective campaign evaluation procedure is now entering its second year.

Pilot tests for the campaign evaluation project are underway and we have a good deal of encouraging evidence concerning the way in which our *campaign effect* measures may be expected to vary with lower order *message effects* (e.g., from commercial tests measures) and predict higher order *mass behavior effects* (e.g., product sales and brand share changes as measured at retail level).

Our overall experience with these studies of symbols, finished commercial messages and overall campaigns has taught us something that few of the highly specialized communication research centers outside of the business world are likely to notice. It is the relationship *between* these various levels of effectiveness that matters a good deal more than separate studies of the effectiveness of symbols, messages or campaigns themselves. (The most persuasive of all messages, for example, will be of little value to the mass persuader unless its frequency and timing of exposure to the proper audience is aptly controlled at the campaign level.) Hovland's presidential address to the American Psychological Association in 1958 is one of very few noncommercial communication research treatments of such relationships between different communications effectiveness measures.

A Universal View of Audience Response to Communication

It is important to recognize the correspondence between advertising research (i.e., commercial mass persuasion research) and other forms of communication research. Effective marketing today calls for close coordination of advertising, salesmanship, publicity, package design and all other forms of communication to the consumer public. Other modern mass persuaders have likewise learned that they must shape audience thought patterns through the manipulation and timing of *all* of the relevant audience information that they can control.

The study of mass persuasion teaches us, as we take audience members' mental machinery apart from top to bottom, that the processes of selling soup or soap are basically the same as those involved in "selling" seat belts, polio vaccinations, or support for cancer research, the United Nations or the church or college of your choice. Except for the subordinate details, the same "Attention-Comprehensive-Conviction-Action" processes (or the same "Awareness-Interest-Desire-Decision" processes) come into play when the "action" or "decision" payoff involves buying, voting or further study of a particular subject matter.

The Crucial Issues: Stimulus and Response

The public is accustomed to viewing advertising, public education, political and religious campaigns in different lights. But there are no objective bases for distinction between these various forms of mass persuasion. Within each broad class of persuasion the relative impact of the mass persuader's influence will vary; the use of various communications media will vary; the complexity of relevant public opinions and audience behaviors will vary. Advertising, political and religious appeals all vary a good deal in terms of "truth" or importance for individual audience members, and one may easily find examples of both overt and "hidden" or subtle forms of persuasion within each of these areas.

But there are two basic facts about *all* forms of mass persuasion or "public information." All such mass communications:

1) reach the audience in the form of physical *stimuli;* and

2) are aimed at influencing the behavior or a mental *response* of the audience.

It is obvious that audience attention to advertising involves stimulus input through the same eyes and ears as are used in attending to any other communication or information source. (This stimulus input function is suggested by the funnel symbol in Figure 2-1.)

Response may take many different forms—a selection of brand X, a vote for Senator Y, a purchase of another copy of the "Daily Blatt" or an answer that a professor is looking for on an examination. But all such responses in-

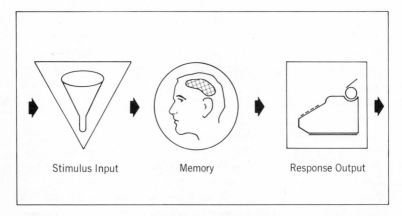

Figure 2-1. A universal view of audience response to communications

volve audience behaviors—more or less observable behaviors which do or do not conform to the intentions of the communicator. In such very general terms response is represented by the crude symbolism of the printout device in Figure 2-1.

Thus, the universal paradigm of our new mass persuasion science is the same as that which has always applied to the study of human behavior: STIM-ULUS—RESPONSE. The main challenge of this new science is to understand how the stimulus inputs function to produce altered probabilities of various response outputs.

In general terms at least all of the behavioral scientists involved might agree that the key to this process lies in the integration of the stimulus inputs with audience memory.

The integration or *memory* functions in Figure 2-1 suggest the cybernetic human brain—electronic brain analogy. In this sense we might speak of "information storage." In the jargon of other relevant sciences we are speaking of "neutral trace patterns," "engram patterns," "cognitive structures," "attitude structures" or "public opinions." For present purposes let us keep things simple: we will call this *memory*.

The Decoding Function of Memory

The point is that people can only decode communication symbols by relating them to past experiences; people can only understand things in the light of prior learning. This is true whether we are dealing with the words of idioms of a particular language (such as "extremism," "Christian love," "lip smackin' good") or whether we are dealing with nonverbal stimuli such as the cartoon figure of the G.O.P. elephant, a picture of the Christian cross, the sound of the national anthem or a demonstration of rich chocolate cake batter pouring into a pan.

Audience memory, then, provides the signal decoding equipment that is needed to make sense of communication inputs. Without it these inputs would have no meaning for the audience. And if the communicator and his audience hold different meanings in their memories for the symbols which the communicator uses, the communication is almost sure to be misunderstood.

The Accumulation and Storage Functions of Memory

But memory is important for another reason. It is in the audience memory that the effects of communications must be accumulated or stored between the time that messages are received and the time that decisions or responses are made.

The STIMULUS-RESPONSE pattern we are dealing with here is not like that studied with rats in a learning box. A considerable time period often intervenes between the time a commercial is viewed and the time a purchase decision is made—between the time the political speech is heard and the time the ballot is marked—or between the time a college catalogue is read and the time the student registers for classes. In the meantime, any positive effects of the communication must be stored in audience members' memories.

Please note that we are not talking about the literal recall of the commercial, speech or catalogue. The fact that there may be some such recall is almost irrelevant. We are talking here about the storage of communication-altered probabilities of response. These probabilities of response are what many refer to as attitudes or opinions. While the definition is somewhat inexact we might, therefore, think of the audience memory as an attitude or opinion storage compartment.

The "Noise" Factor

To complete this basic paradigm of audience response to communication, we should add two additional features. We should allow for the com-

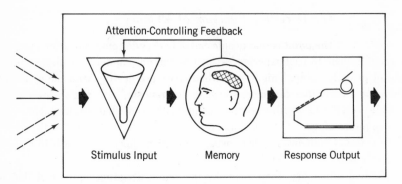

Attention-Controlling Feedback

Stimulus Input   Memory   Response Output

Figure 2-2.   Audience response diagram—modified to show input noises and attention-controlling feedback

peting "background noises," the extraneous inputs or cross currents of information which compete for audience attention, often in the form of conflicting or contradictory communications. These are suggested by the dashed input arrows in Figure 2-2. (In this way we symbolize what communications engineers refer to as "noise," what psychologists refer to in their descriptions of "figure-ground contrast," or what has otherwise been described as a "nexus of mediating factors.") [5]

[5]This "nexus of mediating factors" is discussed in the light of dozens of communication research studies by Joseph Klapper in *The Effects of Mass Communications* (Glencoe, Ill.: The Free Press, 1960), p. 8 and p. 18, ff.

Curiosity: Attention-controlling Feedback

The second additional feature in our Figure 2-2 diagram, the reverse arrow, represents an attention-controlling feedback process. This arrow thus represents a rather common agreement that different people are receptive to or "interested in" different sorts of information inputs at different times. Beyond this, there is now rather broad agreement that such curiosity, interest or feedback results from "surprisal," "tension," "negative entropy," "dissonance" or "anastasis" (that is, an imbalance or an unfinished business of one sort or another) within the memory structure.

Common examples of such feedback are the following: recent car buyers or those in the market for a new car are most likely to notice automobile advertisements, particularly for the make of car they have just bought or the make they tentatively plan to buy. Republicans are particularly likely to take note of Republican campaign materials, particularly those which promise a liberal or a conservative view, according to their own tentative commitments to liberal or conservative opinions.

On the other hand, those without prior interests in a given communication's subject matter tend to screen out the material from their fields of attention and often express resentment at its intrusion into their lives.[6]

There is nothing new in any of this, is there? So far we have merely described the basic elements that are common to almost all communication and behavioral science theory. We have simply said that . . .

> 1) We are always dealing with STIMULUS, INTEGRATION and RESPONSE.
>
> 2) The audience takes in or attends to those stimuli which stand out most against background noises or competing stimuli, favoring those most compatible with preexisting memories, interests or curiosities.
>
> 3) These stimuli are integrated with memories from prior learning or experience and the effects of such integration are stored in the memory structure. They remain there until they are themselves buried (that is, "forgotten") or altered by later inputs, or until they are reactivated to form a decision, a response or a pattern of response.

[6]It is worth noting that this concept of attention-controlling feedback has had more attention in studies of persuasive communication than it had ever before been accorded. While each of the parent disciplines for our mass persuasion science acknowledged this phenomenon it has usually been treated as a "contaminant" of other studies. Attention to the concept in persuasive communication studies has now resolved many separate points of confusion. Learning theorists suddenly learned, for example, that there is no contradiction in their frequent findings that learning seems to be both the cause and the effect of curiosity; just as there is no contradiction in the fact that brand awareness can be both cause and effect of attention to advertising. See, for example, O. Hobart Mowrer, *Learning Theory and Behavior* (New York; John Wiley and Sons, 1960), p. 174. The author's own research and discussion of such feedback may be found in John C. Maloney, "Curiosity versus Disbelief in Advertising," *Journal of Advertising Research*, 2:2-8 (June 1962).

4) Meanwhile the imbalance, or unfinished business within the audience's memory structure, provides the interests or feedbacks which partially control attention to subsequent inputs.

So much for the similarities between many separate "parent discipline" theories of audience response to communication. The embryo science of mass persuasion can not be content to simply find such points of agreement; its most significant contributions (and advertising researchers' most significant findings) will come from the resolution of *differences* between these similar but separate theories.

The Communication Response Hierarchy

Various theories of human response to information differ primarily in their inclusiveness. Each theory, in other words, tends to occupy a different place in a hierarchy of part-whole relationships. This hierarchy is implicit in the different theories and research methods used to evaluate different levels of persuasive communication.

At one communication level messages interact with messages and with message noises within the audience memory—so long as our "memory" is viewed as public opinion or the aggregate of certain group attitudes. Under these circumstances the message interactions take place over weeks, months or even years. In the case of advertising the resulting campaign effects are typically measured with repeated consumer surveys of product awareness, attitude, trial and use.

Message *symbols*, on the other hand, also interact with other symbols, and with symbol noises, within the audience memory. But at this level "memory" is conceived to be the individual audience member's attitude structure and the combined or accumulated effects of these symbols are the message effects which advertising researchers measure with shorter term advertisement or commercial tests.[7]

The interactions of signals or physical stimuli to produce symbol effects take place on a still shorter term basis; "memory" is then viewed in a smaller scale, physiological sense and the proper effectiveness measures at this level are likely to employ special laboratory equipment, and so on. (The reader who is familiar with current events in the study of molecular biology may even see the way in which the DNA-RNA "memory molecule" theories fit the pattern.)

Thus we see, in Figure 2-3, a pragmatic view of the relationship between

---

[7]A general discussion of advertising stimulus-audience memory interactions at this level is offered in John C. Maloney, "Is Advertising Believability Really Important?," *Journal of Marketing*, 27:1-8 (October 1963).

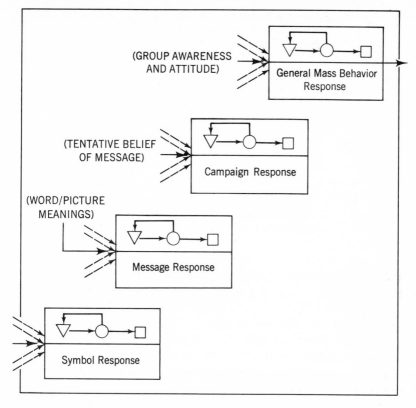

Figure 2-3. The communication response hierarchy

various levels of human response to sight and sound stimuli in the noospheric environment—a schematic view of relationships between sight and sound stimulus effects on up to and through mass behavioral effects in the marketplace, in the polling place, or in other spheres of social behavior.

In response to businessmen's demands for "advertising accountability" this embryo discipline promises to resolve the big-picture vs. little-picture views of human behavior that have plagued the behavioral sciences for years.

In a letter to a friend a year or so ago, I resorted to a bit of doggerel verse to describe this hierarchy. Part of that verse went something like this . . .

> We start with stimulus signals;
>   Then on to symbols of communication.
> From symbols we get messages.
>   (Starting to see the whole relation?)
>
> From messages we move on up
>   To effects of the whole campaign.
> We have to track the whole thing through
>   Or the task is all in vain.

So, from sensation to perception.
From perception to cognition.
From cognition up to attitude
And right on through to public mood.

There is a plot; there is a plan.
It stems from cybernetics.
It can give us all the wondrous key
To this challenge in synthetics.

All inputs are with memories mixed.
Things move along this vein.
It is stimulus, memory, and response . . .
All three on every plane.

From RNA or DNA within the nervous system
To social norms.
They're all just forms of memories.
How could we have missed 'em?

As serious scholars of mass persuasion, in advertising research or else-where, recognize the system-subsystem or part-whole relationhips which make up consumer memory, and as they learn to take proper account of the time spans and "noises" relevant to each type of memory, they will improve the reliability and sensitivity of their effectiveness measures at each communication level.

As they share knowledge about human behavior at each level (knowledge about attention factors, learning phenomena, attitude change processes, mass media and personal influence interactions and other such knowledge which has already been found relevant to mass persuasion efforts on piece-meal bases) they will improve their abilities to *predict* communication effects from one level to the next.

As they continue to "track the whole thing through" this energetic new breed of behavioral scientists may very well unravel the whole skein of events that comprise the "Attention-Comprehension-Conviction-Action" response to mass persuasion.

Most of the necessary basic research has already been done by the separate behavioral science disciplines. Those who will bother to look may note that in recent years the pieces of information have begun to fall rapidly into place.[8]

[8]The reader will recognize that the communication response hierarchy notion is presented here in a very superficial form. The many detailed research and planning implications of the notion are well beyond the scope of the present paper. It should be noted, however, that the general concept of such a hierarchy has lain dormant in the behavioral sciences for many years waiting for quantitative measures of multilevel effects. The Stoics spoke of such a hierarchy over two thousand years ago and the notion revealed itself in the writings of John Locke in the 17th century. Charles Pierce's 19th century syntactic, semantic, and pragmatic notions of "semiotics" reflect the same general concept and the author's review of current behavioral science theory reveals that the notion is implicit or explicit in almost all new developments in the field. An excellent treatment of the concept's relevance to current psychological theory is offered by Charles Solley and Gardner Murphy, *Development of the Perceptual World* (New York: Basic Books, Inc., 1960), pp. 310-14. Relevance of this hierarchy to the current status of advertising research is discussed in John C. Maloney, "Copy Testing—What Course Is It Taking?," 9th Annual Conference of the Advertising Research Foundation, Inc., *Proceedings, 1963*, pp. 89-94.

An Increasingly Urgent Issue of Moral Judgment

All professional mind makers have been criticized at one time or another for the indiscreet use of their meager powers to manipulate the noosphere.

Science professors are criticized for instilling a narrow, mechanistic simple-mindedness in their students while humanities instructors are blamed for encouraging an impractical muddle-headedness. Television and movie producers are accused of encouraging an emotional immaturity in the public mind and the press is lambasted for its vested interest in catastrophe and its supposed tendency to raise the "hostility potential" of the public.

Politicians, priests and ministers are regularly attacked by all but their own converts and advertisers are criticized for their "hidden persuasion" and inclinations to make people want things for all the wrong reasons.

Whether these criticisms are just or unjust in any given instance each group has had two consistent lines of defense. First of all, each group acknowledges a potential danger of mass persuasion by other groups but claims a singular immunity from such guilt on its own part. As a second line of defense each group points to the rugged independence of its audience membership and cites its own record of incompetence.

But the scientific study of mass persuasion puts a new face on both the criticisms and the defenses. There is surely nothing ethical or unethical about the basic process of mass persuasion itself. Any of us might agree that we would prefer to be the persuader, rather than the persuaded, but no one can deny that modern society would stop functioning effectively without some means of ordering public opinions and mass behaviors in many different spheres.

Neither is there anything sinister or laudable in the mere fact that man is learning more about the mass persuasion processes. No advertiser, politician, minister nor any other "mind maker" can remain ethical merely by remaining incompetent.

There can be no doubt, however, that the ethics of mass persuasion take on a greater importance as sophistication in the field increases. Mass persuaders are being deprived of the generalized defense of incompetence.

In a recent address, Kingman Brewster Jr., president of Yale University, offered some advice that might well be heeded by mass persuasion scientists and practitioners alike: "Experimentation and quantification of human and social behavior will mark the intellectual revolution of your time. Do not fight it. But having welcomed it, do not expect the newly scientific study of man and society to relieve you of the moral overload of judgment."

II

COMMUNICATIONS, PERSUASION, AND THE INDIVIDUAL

THE FUNDAMENTAL CONSIDERATION IN ANY COMMUNICATION from source to receiver is the impact that the message will have upon that receiver. Regardless of how we define the communication process, the goal is to affect the behavior of the potential receiver. Thus, in all stages of decisions in communications, the source must be aware of the principles of communications as they relate to individuals. Individual behavior is therefore a critical element in effective communications. The elements of behavior that indeed are many and varied do not fit along a neat spectrum or into a precise model. Terms such as drives, emotions, attention, motivation, beliefs, learning, and desires are related to the impact of communications on the individual. Before making prescriptions for his situations, the practitioner must understand human behavior in order to make the best fit of communications. Making the communications fit or be effective will require much research into particular situations, individual behavior patterns, and other factors before the effectiveness of communication can be maximized in a particular situation. Because science has made so little progress toward understanding individual behavior, we begin to see why communication strategy is still basically an art. Communicators must use incomplete and partial information in making the decisions that must be reached if they are to affect the audience.

The articles in this part present only a glimpse of what is known about the interrelationships between the individual and communications, and only an infinitesimal portion of what needs to be known. The findings presented here are, however, clearly steps forward. We can say, at least, that responsible attempts are being made to increase our knowledge of and our ability to predict the effects of messages on individuals.

43

3

Relating the Selling Effort
to Patterns of Purchase Behavior
ROBERT C. BROOKS, JR.

What is the relative effectiveness of advertising as opposed to that of personal selling? Are there variations in the extent to which each should be used at various stages of a marketing program? For which selling tasks is advertising best suited, and, alternatively, which tasks should be assigned to personal selling? Does testimonial advertising afford a way of combining the advantages of both personal selling and advertising?

Considerable light on these important questions has been provided by sociological research on the nature of the communications process. The entire marketing activity of a firm could well be summarized as that of the maintenance of useful communication between the firm and its market. Marketing research deals with communication which flows from the consumer to the producer, while advertising and personal selling deal with communication from the producer to the consumer. Only the latter type will be considered here.

Advertising and personal selling are means of *direct* communication to present and potential customers, but these are not the only sources from which consumers receive communications regarding new products. Networks of interpersonal relations within the consumer market also serve this purpose. While beyond the direct control of the firm, these networks are of great significance, and knowledge of the way they operate can be of great value in making the selling effort more effective.[1]

Reprinted from *Business Topics* (Winter, 1963), pp. 73-79, by permission of the publisher, Graduate School of Business Administration, Michigan State University.
[1]For a more extended discussion of these networks and a consideration of some of their implications in relation to the selling effort of the firm, see my article, " 'Word-of-mouth' Advertising in Selling New Products," *Journal of Marketing*, XXII (October 1957), 154-61.

A Sequence of Influences

From the standpoint of a consumer, three separate processes are involved in the initial purchase of a product:

(1) the consumer must be informed of the existence and characteristics of the product, (2) the consumer must make a decision to buy the product, and (3) the decision to buy must be translated into an actual purchase.

Some interesting analyses have been made of the time sequence of purchase influences concerning new type products. Ryan and Gross, in their study of the diffusion of hybrid seed corn in Iowa, found that commercial channels, especially salesmen, were most important as original sources of knowledge, while neighbors were most important as influences leading to actual adoption of the improved type of seed.[2] There appeared to be a time lag of approximately five years between first knowledge of the product and the decision for adoption. In another study, one of the adoption of a new drug by the medical profession, the Bureau of Applied Social Research found that the primary sources of original knowledge of the drug were commercial, particularly the "detail men" (representatives of the drug house who call on doctors), while the "sanctioning" forces which led to decisions for adoption of the drug were the influences of colleagues and medical journal articles.[3] Thus, both in the case of a new type of seed and in the case of a new type of drug, we see a similar tendency toward specialization of sources of communications by types of purchase influences.

In the studies cited, the commercial sources have generally performed the first, or notification, process, while neighbors and colleagues were most important in the second, or decision-making process. In the introduction of a product, the inter-personal network, which is subsequently so important in influencing decisions to buy, is inoperative until at least some of the members of that network are brought to adopt the product.

Information and Decision

In the initial stage, the selling and advertising effort should result not only in notification that the product exists, but also in the bringing about of a number of decisions to buy the product, at least on a trial basis.

[2]Bryce Ryan and Neal Gross, "The Diffusion of Hybrid Seed Corn in Two Iowa Communities," *Rural Sociology*, VIII (March 1943), 15-24.

[3]Bureau of Applied Social Research, Columbia University, "On the Flow of Scientific Information in the Medical Profession" (2 vols.), unpublished research reports, 1955. Also see Elihu Katz, "The Two-step Flow of Communication: An Up-to-date Report on an Hypothesis," *Public Opinion Quarterly*, XXI (Spring 1957), 61-78.

The firm must do this necessary spadework in the introductory period, in order to set the stage for a "snowballing" of adoptions through the subsequent influence of the interpersonal network.[4] To illustrate this point, although Ryan and Gross found that neighbors were *in general* the most important influence leading to adoption of the improved seed corn, at the *earlier* stages of diffusion the commercial salesmen themselves accounted for most of the adoptions. Whyte, in reporting on his study of air conditioner ownership, also stresses that group pressure to consider an appliance as a "necessity" does not develop until a significant proportion of the group has purchased one.[5] While early purchasers are victims of the "raised eyebrow," once the proportion of ownership has grown sufficiently, the group begins to act as a force for further purchases and to "punish" those who lag behind. This emphasizes the need for the application of aggressive selling effort at the *initial* stage, since it is at this time that it is most effective, both in its direct effect on sales, and as a prerequisite for valuable assistance from the "web of word of mouth" later on.

Purchase

In regard to the third phase of the buying process, the actual purchase, Wilkening, in a summarization of a number of studies in rural sociology, has shown that, after a farmer has decided to adopt a new technique, he seeks out a source of instruction as to how and when to put the changes into effect.[6] The principal sources of this information are the county agents and the commercial sources of supply. The commercial sources are primarily consulted in this connection in regard to the handling of items purchased from these sources, such as seed, fertilizer, and spray.[7] In other words, as part of their functions as suppliers of farm materials, these commercial sources are also expected to give instruction in the use of the materials they supply. This illustrates a point made by Wiebe, who states that, in order for a motivation—such as a motivation to buy—to be translated into action, there must exist an adequate and accessible mechanism appropriate to the direction of the motivation.[8] If a farmer decides to buy a new type of seed, he expects the source of supply not only to furnish the material, but also to be able to give adequate advice concerning its handling, and—furthermore—the source must be both physically and psychologically "accessible," both for the material itself and for the necessary instruction.

Although marketing institutions are held up as a model for the provision

[4]Brooks, op. cit., pp. 154-55.
[5]William H. Whyte, Jr., "The Web of Word of Mouth," *Fortune*, L (November 1954), 140 ff.
[6]E. A. Wilkening, "Communicating Agents and Technological Change among Farmers," paper read at annual meeting of the Rural Sociology Society, September 1954.
[7]E. A. Wilkening, "Sources of Information for Improved Farm Practices," *Rural Sociology*, XV (March 1950), 19-30.
[8]G. D. Wiebe, "Merchandising Commodities and Citizenship on Television," *Public Opinion Quarterly*, XV (Winter 1951), 679-91.

of the "mechanism compatible with the direction of the motivation," there are many cases where potential sales have been lost because the distribution of the product was inadequate for the demand, or where the distribution outlets were physically or psychologically inaccessible—or were not willing or able to provide the information or service expected in connection with the utilization of the product. For example, a survey of Chicago housewives showed that, while the three most preferred brands of all-purpose flour enjoyed approximately the same degree of preference, one of the brands was actually being purchased by less than half the number of housewives purchasing each of the other two brands. While 31 percent of the housewives gave Brand C top-rating, only 19 percent were actually using Brand C. The author of the study suggested that the discrepancy was due to a lack of availability of the brand in many of the outlets where flour was purchased.[9] To give another illustration, it is reported that during the heyday of the "$64,000 Question," the particular item advertised on a given date would be out of stock in many outlets two days later. An example of psychological inaccessibility is provided by bookstores, which 93 percent of the population have never entered, according to a study sponsored by the Book Manufacturers' Institute. Similarly, it has been found that many patrons of small-loan companies are highly reluctant to enter the premises of banks, unless the bank gives its small-loan department a separate store-front of the type to which small-loan customers are accustomed.

It is clear from the preceding discussion that far more is involved in the bringing of a consumer to purchase a new type product than is usually encompassed in the concepts of advertising and personal selling. In fact, it is obviously unrealistic to judge the effectiveness of these activities in terms of sales, unless an evaluation is also made of the activities of friends, neighbors, and colleagues as well as of the adequacy and accessibility of the distribution system.

Influence of Advertising and Personal Selling

The importance of advertising and personal selling in the diffusion of acceptance of new products has been shown in the preceding section. They are the principal elements in the process of notification, and, in the introductory period, are crucial factors in leading to decisions on the part of early adopters. The firm should not only utilize advertising and personal selling, but through its organization of distribution, also provide for an adequate and accessible source of instructions and service regarding the use of a new product, as well as of the product itself.

[9]George H. Brown, "Measuring Consumer Attitudes Toward Products," *Journal of Marketing*, XIV (April 1950), 691, 694-95.

This section will indicate some the functions of advertising and personal selling for the marketing of established—as well as of new—products. Many of these functions have to do with the canalization of the satisfaction of an existing want through purchase of a specific item and brand which the firm is attempting to sell. It has been pointed out by Lazarsfeld and Merton that it is in this area that mass communications are most effective, and that the explanation of the relative success of commercial campaigns is in large part the fact that they usually attempt to canalize rather than to make basic changes in opinions, attitudes, or wants.[10]

In the studies cited earlier the interpersonal networks were concerned with general types of products almost to the exclusion of brands. Only one of three types of networks found among doctors discussed brands, and a lack of homogeneity of brands was noted within clusters of air conditioners. In view of such findings, it is clear that, even in selling a new type product, a firm faced by competition from other brands would be dependent on the canalization power of the mass media in order to direct favorably the purchase decisions generated by interpersonal networks.

Advertising by the Firm

In their study of opinion changes in the 1940 election, Lazarsfeld, Berelson, and Gaudet found that, although the mass media were of little consequence in *changing* opinion, they played a major role in the reinforcement and activation of opinions already held.[11] The significance for advertising is clearly that one should not limit an analysis of advertising effectiveness simply to the amount of *increased* sales which can be ascribed to the advertising. One must also consider the contribution of the advertising to the maintenance and reinforcement of favorable opinions already in the minds of customers, and must also consider its activation of these opinions into purchases on the part of these *present* customers, exclusive of any additional purchases that result from its effect on new customers. In other words, not only the additional sales the advertising is bringing in must be considered, but also the number of sales the firm would be losing were the advertising not in effect.

Another aspect of mass media which is almost impossible to measure in the case of advertising, but which was demonstrated by means of controlled experiment by Hovland, Lumsdaine, and Sheffield,[12] is the "sleeper" effect. Although their experiments on the effects of a series of Army I&E films failed

---

[10]Paul F. Lazarsfeld and Robert K. Merton, "Mass Communication, Popular Taste, and Organized Social Action," in Swanson, Newcomb, and Hartley, eds., *Readings in Social Psychology* (New York: Holt, 1952).

[11]Paul F. Lazarsfeld, Bernard Berelson, and Hazel Gaudet, *The People's Choice* (New York: Columbia University Press, 1948).

[12]Carl I. Hovland, Arthur A. Lumsdaine, and Fred D. Sheffield, *Experiments in Mass Communication* (Princeton, N.J.: Princeton University Press, 1949).

to show any significant change in opinion as an immediate effect, there was evidence that the desired change in opinion took place rather slowly over a substantial period of time following the viewing of the series. It is apparent that such sleeper effects from advertising are not measured by any of the commonly used tests of advertising effectiveness.

A concept of great importance to the selling effort of a firm is that of the "supplementation" role of advertising, as developed by Lazarsfeld and Merton.[13] This is based upon the fact that being represented in the mass media confers prestige upon an organization. The increased status reinforces the position of a face-to-face representative of the organization, and, combined with the advantages of the personal contact, has an extremely effective result.

Personal Selling by the Firm

Personal selling appears to be superior to advertising in its ability to cause *changes* in behavior, although still not as effective as those interpersonal influences which are beyond the direct control of the firm. In a study of changes in fashions and of changes in brand of small household purchases, Katz and Lazarsfeld report data which indicate the effectiveness of retail salespersons to be intermediate between those of the mass media and the interpersonal consumer network.[14] In discussing the greater effectiveness of personal influence among consumers, Katz and Lazarsfeld explain that, while formal media influence only by means of indirect attraction or by what they tell, people exert influence both in this way and also by control. It might be added, in this connection, that, while the salesperson may have less effective control than the friend or neighbor, the elements of control are present to some extent in almost any type of personal contact.

In their study of the 1940 election, Lazarsfeld, Berelson, and Gaudet found that person-to-person influences were much more effective in causing changes in vote intention than were any of the mass media.[15] Their analysis of the reasons for this greater effectiveness is to some extent applicable to the methods of personal selling. Among their explanations for the success of the personal contact in causing *changes* in intention are:

- less opportunity for self-selection of messages by the person being influenced.

- flexibility of timing and message to individual conditions.

- immediate and personal award for compliance—through the approval and friendship of the influencer.

- trust by the contact in an intimate and respected source to pick out the factors relevant to the contact's specific case.

[13]*Op. cit.*
[14]Elihu Katz and Paul F. Lazarsfeld, *Personal Influence* (Glencoe, Illinois: Free Press, 1955), pp. 175-82.
[15]*Op. cit.*

- decision on the basis of positive personal factors, when there is no other element leading to a specific choice.

While all of these advantages of personal—as opposed to mass media—influence are particularly applicable to the influence of other people in voting, it seems reasonable to assume that these are the same factors, operating to a somewhat lesser extent, which account for the relative effectiveness of personal selling.[16]

Testimonial Advertising

On the surface, one might be led to consider testimonial advertising as partaking heavily of the advantages of personal selling. However, when the list of advantages given in the preceding section is considered, it is apparent that only the last reason has any validity in the case of "celebrity" testimonials, and that only the fourth reason can be effective in those cases where the testimonial is given by a consumer "like one's self."

In the case of celebrity testimonials, Smith found that the believability of such testimonials is low,[17] but Starch made a study of five consumer magazines which shows that readership of celebrity testimonials is considerably higher than that of non-testimonial advertisements or of non-celebrity testimonials.[18] The reason for the higher readership apparently lies in the greater *attention*-getting power of the celebrity, rather than any believability, as Rudolph reports a study of 2,500 *Saturday Evening Post* advertisements which shows the testimonial to be the second highest ranking of all categories analyzed in terms of attention value.[19] Thus it appears that celebrity testimonials have the advantage of getting more people to notice and read the content, and a liking for the celebrity may cause the reader to buy the product recommended when, as is frequently the case, there is no other important basis for the decision. It must also be recognized that some radio celebrities, such as Kate Smith in her war bond drives, have been shown to have exhibited great sincerity and believability in the eyes of their audience, and it is believed by many that Arthur Godfrey's effectiveness was largely due to his gift for believability. Although the audience may be aware that such personalities are paid for their commercials, there is no reason why they should be any less believable than a known and respected salesperson, who is also paid.

In the case of non-celebrity testimonials, as mentioned before, there is no evidence of any superior attention-getting value. However, since the non-

---

[16]Some very interesting research on antecedents and consequences of various specific types of influence is reported by Herbert C. Kelman, "Processes of Opinion Change," *Public Opinion Quarterly*, XXV (Spring 1961), 66-77.

[17]George H. Smith, *Motivation Research in Advertising and Marketing* (New York: McGraw-Hill, 1954).

[18]Daniel Starch, "Testimonial Ads Get Nod," *Printers' Ink* (February 19, 1954), p. 21.

[19]Harold J. Rudolph, *Attention and Interest Factors in Advertising* (New York: Funk & Wagnalls, 1947).

celebrity may frequently be considered as a consumer like us, there is some reason for believing such a source to have acted on the basis of factors relevant to our own specific case, and thus believe the given product to be the best one for our purposes. Studies involving over 5,000 women exposed to non-celebrity testimonials by the Schwerin Research Corporation showed that, for the testimonial to have the essential characteristic of believability, it was of the greatest importance that the testimonial giver be established as bona fide and as like the audience in general. The most believable testimonial studied was delivered by a mother who went into detail about everyday problems of caring for her house and five children, while the least believable testimonial was delivered by a professional model, identified as such. In other words, there must be a realistic basis for transfer for the testimonial giver's experience to the specific case of the listener.[20]

Direction and Coordination

In all types of communications activities under the direct control of the firm, it is possible to some extent to select the audience to whom the message is directed. Since the mass media are most effective in giving information and in reinforcing and activating already held opinions, it is indicated that the audience to which the firm should direct the mass media message is that to which it wishes to give information not previously possessed concerning the product, and that which already holds a position favorable to the product. Because personal selling has certain advantages in its ability to *change* opinion and behavior, it would appear desirable to direct the personal selling effort to those people who are not now using the product but whom the firm may be able to influence. This would be particularly true in the introductory phase of a new product, as there would be no possibility of any other personal influence working until at least some of the members of the consumer network were induced to adopt the product.

[20]I am grateful to William Kalan, Manager of Consumer Research for the Toni Company, for valuable comments on testimonial commercials.

4

Seven Principles
in Image Formation

BARDIN H. NELSON

The creation of markets for products is as necessary as the creation of products for the market. And modern management, through costly experience, has become aware of the significance of consumer attitudes or expectancies. Most executives now realize that the decision makers in industry are so remote from their customers that they do not know what customers really want. This awareness has created a desire for sounder evidence about consumer patterns of response or resistance to products, to help guide management decision making.

The needs of people with respect to physiological necessities in the United States have by and large been fulfilled, and are taken for granted by most people. Discriminative buying of items from the viewpoint of satisfying other motives has allowed consumers to play a more significant role in marketing decisions and product development.

A psychological break occurred after World War II. Buying sentiments were no longer characterized by the pessimism of depression years. The increasing psychological acceptance of credit buying enabled consumers to make greater annual expenditures than their current incomes and cash reserves formerly warranted.

Management, realizing that it must have predictive information to adjust to the consumer's optimism or pessimism, began to turn to the behavioral sciences for further help. After reviewing research concerning consumer attitudes and the group actions of consumers, some heads of businesses became enamored with the possibility of attitude measurement as an indicator for necessary future adjustments by business. Although the instruments used were imperfect in many respects, they provided the kinds of information which enabled business to have greater ability to anticipate changing market situations and to make necessary adjustments.

Reprinted from *Journal of Marketing* (January, 1962), pp. 67-71, by permission of the publisher, the American Marketing Association.

53

Individuals in a mass society have difficulty in maintaining a strong sense of personal identity because of competing reference groups, conflicting social norms, and various other cultural influences. Increasingly, businessmen became aware that an important factor in group influence is the impact of uniform stimuli reaching people in similar situations with similar attitudes, needs, and aspirations. This awareness opened the eyes of management to the feasibility of giving direction to such stimuli in order to maintain optimum sales volume of their products.

Thus, psychological and sociological principles to some extent have become important business principles. In their attempts to forecast business trends, research economists at Michigan State University, Texas A. & M., and other institutions now study "consumer sentiments" as well as levels of income, prices, liquid assets, and debts.

Although they represent oversimplifications, the following ideas have emerged:

1. An attitude is preparation for behavior. A composite of the attitudes which a group of people hold toward a product constitutes an image. Influence their images, and you influence their behavior.

2. People have hidden urges or desires which have been repressed or buried in the subconscious areas of the mind. Build an image around a product that satisfies these needs, and people will buy the product. Satisfy the hidden motives.

As early as 1918, Thomas and Znaniecki demonstrated that the effect of a phenomenon upon an individual depended not only on the objective content, but more specifically on the subjective standpoint taken by an individual toward the phenomenon.[1] What the individual's mind defines as reality is real in its consequences for that individual. Thomas and Znaniecki revealed that a product was not just a *physical* object, but that it was what people *thought* it was.

Physical attributes of a product act only as stimuli capable of developing certain associations in the minds of individuals. Such associations may be pleasant or unpleasant. The image makers strive to translate these stimuli into images favorable to their product.

Although there are numerous complex psychological processes relevant to image formation, only a limited number of steps involved in creating an image will be dealt with here.

Reference Points

Human beings in a complex society are constantly making choices or judgments. Perhaps it is a judgment concerning financial affairs,

[1]W. I. Thomas and F. Znaniecki, *The Polish Peasant in Europe and America* (Boston: Richard G. Badger, 1918-1920), 5 vols.

or the proper degree of control to exercise over children. In making such judgments they utilize standards derived from many sources. To judge anything, they must have something as a basis for comparison.

If no objects or experiences are available as reference points, it becomes virtually impossible for individuals to orient to their surroundings or circumstances. Captain Charles Yeager tells of his experiences when he flew the first plane to reach and maintain supersonic speed: "I had a hard time judging my speed. The little Mach needle and other instruments kept telling me that no one had ever gone faster, but I was so high and so remote, and the airplane was so very quiet that I might almost have been motionless. You sense speed in terms of something stationary, something outside yourself."[2]

In social life, individuals frequently make immediate on-the-spot judgments of persons or of performance and achievement of other people. The anchorages or reference points involved in making such judgments stem from past experience, from a positive or negative stand on an issue, or from positive or negative relationships with the persons in question. What is distinct or significant in experience depends upon our "anchorages" which may be external, internal, or both.

External factors include social influences such as instruction, suggestion, group pressures, or group participation. Intensity, size, novelty, repetition, contrast, and movement are also external factors that may determine what stands out in experience.

Internal factors include: personal interest; state of the organism, such as emotional state or physical state; motives, such as hunger or thirst; and attitudes, prejudices, or other feelings concerning individuals or groups.

Principles Involved in Image Formation

Following are seven principles:

Principle No. 1: People are not "exclusively" rational creatures. Their behavior is usually determined, not entirely by knowledge and reason, but also by feelings and unconscious drives. At best, behavior or thought of the average individual represents a combination of emotional and rational elements. We must always recognize the obvious impossibility of any individual's capability of recognizing and tracing back all the influences upon his behavior, some of which may have originated in early childhood.

A group of Swazi tribesmen from South Africa visited London. After they returned home, it was noted that the thing which remained most vividly fixed in the tribesmen's minds was their image of the English policeman reg-

[2]M. Sherif and C. Sherif, *An Outline of Social Psychology*, revised edition (New York: Harper and Bros., 1956), p. 47.

ulating traffic with uplifted hand. The Swazi greets his fellowman or visitor with uplifted hand. Here was the familiar gesture, warm with friendliness, in a foreign country. It was one of the few things they saw that fitted immediately into their own well-established social framework and thus produced an enduring effect.[3] From a rational standpoint, one might point to thousands of objects in London that possess more significance than the raised hand of a policeman.

Housewives seemingly influenced by the color factor in certain selections readily admitted that color did not affect the utility of particular products. They had difficulty in explaining the bases for their particular color preferences. The following excerpts from an interview show this response pattern:

Mrs. B: "The three major grocery stores where I buy my groceries carry three brands which I've used. There's really not enough difference to tell between _____, _____, and _____. I think _____ is real nice because of its rich yellow color. I like the yellow wrapper on _____. It's a pretty yellow. I'm like a child. If you fix things up pretty, I'll buy them. I didn't see any way it was put in the can or any way it was different from the others."

Interviewer X: "Do you have any ideas about what causes frying failures?"

Mrs. B: "As I told you, any one of the three good shortenings I've used is all right for frying or baking. They probably weren't watching what they were doing."

Principle No. 2: People respond to situations in ways which appear to them to protect their self-images.

Human beings have emotional foundations which undergird their behavior and which are as much a part of them as their arms or legs. For one to attack or threaten an individual's psychological being is almost as bad as hacking at his hands or legs with a knife. Whenever an individual faces activity or events which produce disequilibrium, the mind seeks ways and means for restoring the equilibrium. Such attempts explain why individuals will give socially acceptable answers or even completely erroneous answers concerning their behavior.

For example, respondents were asked the direct question: "Why don't you serve chicken and dumplings more often?" Only 20 per cent answered either "hard to make" or "can't make good ones." Respondents were shown a picture frustration question in which a little boy was saying to his mother, "Tommy's having chicken and dumplings for supper. Why don't we ever have them?" When asked to give their ideas as to what the mother's answer was, 54 per cent said, "She told him she didn't know how to make good dumplings."[4]

Principle No. 3: We need to determine the various images and reference

---

[3]*Ibid.* p. 82.
[4]Henry V. Courtenay, *An Analysis of Response Variation Encountered With Selected Interviewing Techniques in Consumer Marketing Research,* unpublished Master's Thesis, College Station, Texas, May, 1960, pp. 13-14.

points or anchorages which already exist in the minds of a particular group or society. Seldom are there revolutionary changes in people's images.

"The weight of evidence indicates that actually very little change occurs during college in the essential standards by which students govern their lives. The values with which they arrive and which are integral elements of their personality, are still there when most students leave."[5]

Messages received may clarify the image—make something which was less certain, more certain. However, messages or stimuli may have the reverse effect. They may introduce doubt or uncertainty concerning the image. In either case, the significance of the stimuli usually depends on the reinforcement received from other like stimuli or messages. To tear down a conflicting image or to build upon one that is compatible, the image maker must first know the images that already exist in the minds of people. The necessity for such knowledge has given social-psychological research new status, particularly in the eyes of management. Projective tests are being more widely used. "Depth interview" has become a frequently used phrase among corporate heads.

The image that people held of a certain chain store operation could best be described as "high priced." Considerable probing revealed, however, that the interviewees felt that numerous items in specific departments were priced well in line or even cheaper than at other chains in the same locality. A word-association test revealed that interviewees associated good food with the advertised products of a certain company. Comparison shopping revealed that these products were priced higher at the chain operation being studied than at other chain stores.

A revision of prices of a nationally advertised brand of canned goods, plus the promotion of brand-name specials, gradually produced a significant change in the image which people held of these stores. There are key factors which appear on the surface to be incidental, but which exert tremendous influence in the formation of images. Shop-worn vegetables in the vegetable bins of a food store may establish a negative image concerning cleanliness in a store which is otherwise spotless.

Principle No. 4: If an image appears stable and if reference groups surrounding the individual continue to support the image, both internal and external forces opposing the image will be resisted.

At the A. & M. College of Texas a very stable image exists concerning the role of a freshman. Organizational structures strongly support the image. A freshman's father told him, "Explain to your Commanding Officer that you didn't clean up your room because you weren't feeling well."

The father did not fully understand when he was told, "Sir, there is only one response I can make to my C.O. and that is 'No excuse, Sir.' " The freshman's image of his role was important to him.

[5]Philip E. Jacob, *Changing Values in College* (New York: Harper and Bros., 1957), p. 53.

Excerpts taken from an interview are typical of responses obtained in a survey conducted in a large residential area surrounding an industrial section.

Interviewer X: "_____ has a supermarket in _____ Shopping Center. Do you ordinarily buy some of your groceries at that unit?"

Mr. S: "My wife and I buy most of our groceries on Friday afternoon. That's my afternoon off from the plant. I guess we bought the bulk of our groceries from _____ until last year. They have good stuff and it's real convenient—close and the parking and all. But we quit them last year. They had always been a real friendly place, but last year they ordered me over to a little window to get my check cashed. They'd built this little room off the office. I let them belittle me, standing there in that line. I talked to several of my buddies at the plant. They felt just like I did. We decided somebody new must have come in. Some of them still go there, but me and most of my buddies don't like this new management."

The initial purpose of the survey was to determine why particular units of the chain operation had suffered a loss in volume of business the preceding year.

Principle No. 5: If an image is marked by doubt, uncertainty, or insecurity, utilize additional means for creating further doubts. Present the new image in a form whereby it will dispel anxiety or doubts.

The Chinese Communists were aware of considerable resistance among U.S. citizens to our entry into the Korean War. Newspapers carried headlines, "Is This War Necessary?" Some disgruntlement also existed because of a mild economic recession prior to our involvement in Korea. Furthermore, the Chinese Communists knew that the image which the average American soldier held of them was a type of Dr. Fu Manchu who had all kinds of exquisite Oriental tortures, including that of burning bamboo splinters under one's fingernails. They also knew that many soldiers thought of themselves as peacetime boys who could hardly wait to get back to their families, wives, sweethearts, and the comforts of home.

Based upon this and other knowledge of the image held by U.S. soldiers, the Communists developed an approach to creating new images. This procedure began when a soldier was captured. It began first of all with a speech of welcome and introduction. A young English-speaking Chinese officer appeared, often a graduate of an American university, in civilian clothes and affecting a friendly and conciliatory attitude:

> We welcome you to the ranks of the people. We are happy and privileged to have liberated you from the imperialist Wall Street warmongers who started this war. We have nothing against you personally. We are not going to abuse you. We are going instead to offer you a fair shake. Let us present to you our side of the picture, and in return we promise you there'll be no slave camps, no work groups, no road crews. We ask only that you hear us out, which is only American fair play, and make up your minds about what is true.

How much better this plan sounded as compared to one involving burning bamboo splinters; it was a reprieve from almost certain death. This procedure was the first step in a plan which followed well-known psychological principles.

The president and founder of an old, reliable, well-established business in the downtown area of a major city experienced feelings of doubt and anxiety when lower management suggested that three new units be established in shopping centers. The president was so fearful that the reputation of the business would be endangered that he suggested there be no further discussion of the matter.

Lower management began to emphasize in subtle fashion various problems and negative forces confronting the business. The research department included as a part of their field studies an investigation which revealed: (1) that the average customer of the business came to the downtown area of the city only twice a year; (2) that generally interviewees thought that a business which did not have some units in the new shopping centers was either extremely limited in scope of operation, was failing, or would be failing shortly; and (3) that interviewees thought that the effect of additional units upon the prestige of an old established downtown business would depend largely on design, styling, type of operation, and particular location of the new units.

The president's increasing uncertainty concerning the future was replaced with a degree of certainty, based upon his confidence in the research department. He gave leadership to the development of two new units in shopping centers. The information which influenced his actions was used as promotional material for the general public to remove their doubts about the company's plans for the future. The campaign utilized the selection of particular centers, the styling of the units, and various other special features to create a new and stronger image of a business that could adjust to social, economic, and technological change and still maintain an exclusive personality.

Principle No. 6: Place the desired image in the most favorable setting. If at all possible, clothe the new image in the already accepted values of the people.

In the 1960 political campaign, President Kennedy made widespread use of the names Woodrow Wilson and Franklin Delano Roosevelt—identified as men of action who moved America out of the doldrums.

Restaurant managers are aware that most people prefer the traditional items offered on the menu. Consumer research indicates, however, that preference for new or "exotic" dishes varies according to educational levels. Customers with a college education may choose "exotic" dishes twice as frequently as customers with junior high-school education. Significant differences are also observed between selections of customers with junior high-school education and customers with high-school education.

Thus, a restaurant operator should consider carefully the educational level of his potential clientele as he seeks to determine the most appropriate image for his business.

Principle No. 7: To stimulate development of a new image, one must attract the attention of large numbers of potential consumers.

Based on consumer research conducted in Texas, the housewife's image of chicken with respect to method of preparation focuses on one method—frying. Since use of chicken tends to be confined to frying, it is used mostly for variety among other meats rather than being used as a dish frequently served but varied by preparation in several different ways. Little effort has been expended by the poultry industry to establish a broader image by promotional campaigns emphasizing the ease of preparation and the tastes of other chicken dishes, such as Chicken Tetrazzini or Coq au Vin. In areas where favorable images already exist concerning the economy and flavor of chicken dishes, the probabilities of projecting a broader and increasingly favorable image of chicken seem excellent; but such a change in image would require the transfer of new ideas and information to broad cultural groups.

The more striking the attraction used to gain attention, the better. Reinforce an image by clear-cut, simple imagery such as catch phrases or slogans. Fairly continuous repetition of slogans or catch words is necessary for a long period of time.

Enable individuals through the imagery to escape the known and to conquer the unknown. Allow them to experience the magnificent, and thus escape the small perimeters of their daily lives. Ernest Dichter tells his clients: "Sell emotional security or go under."[6]

However, where images are stable, any techniques designed to replace them will be resisted. It is true that a change which might take a generation to accomplish in a slow-moving, nonliterate society may be accomplished in months or even days in a society with mass communications. Nevertheless, the message is not always as important as the kind of image that it produces.

The success of any method of influencing people depends upon a favorable climate or environment for its use. The question then arises as to what is the most favorable environment. It is one where the people experience (1) painful uneasiness or anxiety; (2) a feeling of separation from the group or isolation from group standards; and (3) a feeling of pointlessness or that no certain goals exist.[7]

Can we defend the use of the social sciences in influencing people? As Dichter says: "People have tried to influence each other since the origins of intelligent behavior in mankind. The real issue is one of determination of goals. A butcher knife can be used to murder or to cut meat."[8]

Perhaps a more appropriate illustration might be, "It's a good fire that warms you and a bad fire that burns you."

[6]Ernest Dichter, *The Strategy of Desire* (Garden City: Doubleday and Co., 1960), pp. 112, 169.
[7]Sebastian De Grazia, *The Political Community* (Chicago: The University of Chicago Press, 1948), pp. 105-106.
[8]Dichter, same reference as footnote 6.

5

The Psychology of Communication

JON EISENSON,
J. JEFFERY AUER,
and JOHN V. IRWIN

It is important to distinguish between the act and art of oral communication, for we are here primarily concerned with the latter. The act of speech is simple vocal utterance; it may be performed by the untutored, crudely and ineffectively, as well as by those schooled in the art, effectively, intelligently, and responsibly. But since man first communicated with man, the act has engendered the art. Jebb (1876, II, 370), for example, affirms that "It was of the essence of Greek oratory . . . that its practice should be connected with a theory. Art is the application of rules . . . and the Greek conception of speaking as an art implied a Rhetoric." The unschooled act of verbal communication may reflect only a knack; the best communication is based upon a compend of theory.

As we have previously noted, it was Aristotle, *c.* 336 B.C., who set down the earliest extant complete and systematic theory of rhetoric, or scientific rationale for oral discourse. Essentially the peripatetic Greek conceived of rhetoric, or communication, as an instrumental discipline, a powerful social force by means of which man could interpret, control, modify, or adapt to his environment. Aristotle did not deal with transmitting information as a specific end of speech, but limited its purpose to persuasion: "So let Rhetoric be defined as the faculty [power] of discovering in the particular case what are the available means of persuasion." Aristotle and later classical writers structured the discipline of persuasive discourse around five canons: *invention,* the source and substance of ideas in a speech; *disposition,* the structure and sequence of the discourse; *style,* the specific language used in communicating; *memory,* the recall and retention resources of the speaker; and *delivery*, the vocal and physical attributes of speaking.

While eighteenth- and nineteenth-century writers maintained these canons in structuring their treatments of rhetoric, they restated the classical doctrines for a new society, and adapted to newer understandings of the behavior of man. This was notable in George Campbell's *Philosophy of Rhetoric*, 1776, strong psychological orientation in establishing the ends of speech as (a) to enlighten the understanding, (b) to please the imagination, (c) to move the passions, and (d) to influence the will. This division of purposes was influenced by the prevailing faculty psychology of his day, especially as it attempted to distinguish between belief and action, a dichotomy no longer in psychological fashion. Greater insight into human behavior was reflected in Campbell's definition of persuasion as argument or logic based upon desire: "To say that it is possible to persuade without speaking to the passions, is but, at best, a kind of specious nonsense."

Early twentieth-century rhetoricians, such as James A. Winans, adopted the psychological concept of attention as a determinant of action, and later writers, notably William Norwood Brigance, incorporated more of the findings of contemporary psychologists to expand the concept of desire, or motivation, as the heart of the persuasive process.

From this point on, students of the art of communication drew with increasing frequency from the researches in the behavioral sciences. As Wallace (1954, p. 125) wrote, the field of speech "cannot deal fully with either the act or the art of communication unless it knows all it can about the behavior of the speaking and listening individual, the behavior of individuals in group situations, the psychology of motives, emotions, and attitudes, the psychology of the speech-handicapped person, and the methods of tests and measurements." Beyond this draft on the funds of psychological research, students of communication must also, on occasion, become acquainted with related studies in linguistic behavior, logic, ethics, and semantics, as well as those in physiology, anatomy, and neurology, in literary history and criticism, and in general culture. As a consequence, the standard research bibliographies in speech have been drawn about equally from the humanities, the natural sciences, and the social sciences. The references and additional readings cited in chapters of this book attest to the almost universal resources employed for the study of speech, as well as to its singularity among the academic disciplines.

Both the act and art of communication, then, are concerned with the behavior of man communicating with man for reasons practical, cultural, or aesthetic. The chief sources for our understanding of man's communicative behavior are the traditional concepts of rhetorical theory as modified by the contemporary contributions of the behavioral sciences. As we shall try to exemplify, these disciplines provide the conceptual framework, the analytical and critical methods, and the evaluative techniques for any comprehensive study of oral communication.

Speaker-Listener Relationships

We commonly identify only two elements in the communicative process, speaker and listener, but it is really more complex. The traditional rhetorical analysis has always recognized four distinct elements: the speaker, the speech, the individual listener or the audience, and the occasion for speaking. Harold Lasswell (1946, p. 121) identified similar elements commonly phrased in a formula question: *"Who says what to whom, how,* and with *what effect?"* Considering communication as an electronic system, Shannon and Weaver (1949) isolated source, transmitter, channel, receiver, and destination.

When these several approaches to the communicative process are articulated we may describe it something like this: Any oral communication act (whether in face-to-face groups, co-acting groups, or via the mass media) begins with an idea, concept, or proposition in the mind of the communicator. He then encodes the idea into a communication consisting of a set of audible (and sometimes visible) symbols and transmits it, with light and sound waves as his channel. The receiver is an individual listener (sometimes a member of an audience group) who decodes the symbols into terms meaningful to him, and the communication, or at least a facsimile of it, reaches his mind and elicits some kind of response. This response may be covert only. It may also be overt, in clearly distinguishable physical movement or vocal response, apparent to the communicator and acting as a "feedback" from the impact of his initial communication. Thus his further communication may be affected by his own reaction to his hearer's response.

This simple tracing of the communicative process . . . shows how much more complicated it is than the commonly conceived speaker-listener interplay. We now explain in some greater detail three of the elements in that relationship.

1. *Individuals may play either specialized or alternating roles in the communicative process.* In face-to-face groups, such as committees, each member may play alternating roles, sometimes acting as communicator, sometimes as listener. Especially in informal discussions, the transitions from one role to another may come irregularly and rapidly. In co-acting groups, on the other hand, individuals commonly have specialized roles: one stands on a stage or behind a lectern, consistently communicating in a "solo performance," while the others are auditors, normally all attending and responding to the single stimulus of the speaker. Except for overt responses, such as applause, shouts of "hear, hear!" and the like, the communicative behavior of the listeners is limited both by custom and by the degree of their polarization (psychological and physiological orientation toward the speaker). In communicating via the

mass media the speaker normally plays a specialized role, but his listeners, gathered in small groups in living rooms, taverns, or automobiles, play alternating roles, sometimes attending to him, sometimes distracted by other stimuli and ignoring him.

2. *Response from the listener is the ultimate goal of all communication.* Earlier in this book we dealt with the nature of psychological response, commonly manifested in muscular or glandular activity when one or more sense organs are stimulated. Response is what the individual does when he reacts to a stimulus. Thus we use the term response as the goal of all communication. The speaker wants the listener to respond, preferably in a way that will implement the speaker's specific purpose. But . . . if we understand response to be physiological reaction to a speaker's words, then there is no real psychological difference between such terms as belief and action or conviction and persuasion. Each one is merely a special way of describing response, but all are response. It is true, of course, that some levels of response are easier to achieve than others; for example, "I *understand* what you are saying," "I *believe* what you are saying," and "I will *act* upon what you are saying," may often represent a sequence of increasingly difficult response-goals for the communicator.

3. *Individuals respond most readily when they are highly involved in the purpose of the communication.* At some point in any communication situation the basic purpose becomes clear to everyone. In a face-to-face situation, such as a committee meeting, that purpose is the "group task," normally understood in advance, but often recalled by the chairman's opening remarks: "Our assignment is to prepare a slate of officers. . . ." or in an informal group: "I believe that we all agreed to discuss this evening the kind of foreign policy which . . ." The more intensively group members are committed to and involved in the group task, the more likely it is that they will participate freely and work toward the group's goals. To achieve this positive orientation toward the purpose of the communicative situation may require, as we shall see later, a careful selection of group members, a collective approach to agenda planning, and specific encouragement for members to assume active group roles. In the co-acting group situation, such as for a persuasive speech, the speaker's specific purpose may not always be understood in advance, and he may even want to conceal it during part of his speech. In any event, the speaker's message should seem as important to his hearers as it does to him; unless the hearers have a sense of personal involvement or at least interest in his subject, they are unlikely to respond to his purpose-proposition.

The Impact of Communications Upon Behavior

We have already observed that response is the aim of all purposeful communication. As Hovland, Janis, and Kelley (1953, p. 12) state this premise for their psychological studies of opinion change, communication is "the process by which an individual (the communicator) transmits stimuli (usually verbal) to modify the behavior of other individuals (the audience)." But how are these modifications in behavior manifested, and how can they be measured and evaluated? Psychologists generally agree that *attitudes* and *beliefs* are key indexes to behavior and that both are measurable in such ways as to reflect the influence of communication upon behavior.

Attitudes

One of the most useful definitions of attitude is Allport's (1935, p. 906): "a mental and neural state of readiness, organized through experience, exerting a directive or dynamic influence upon the individual's responses to all objects with which it is connected." An attitude toward any person, object, or situation, is thus a tendency to respond, either favorably or unfavorably. Attitudes may be as general as a favorable response to "physical fitness" or as specific as an unfavorable response to a particular person.

Some writers classify pairs of attitudes, such as personal and social, or general and specific. Especially significant for communication is the distinction between *dominant* and *latent* attitudes. Dominant attitudes are those that are active at the moment; they tend to give the individual a psychological "set" or readiness to react in a patterned way when confronted with a general problem or a specific stimulus situation. It is the dominant attitude that the communicator hopes to touch off when persuading an audience; more difficult is the task of securing a response by connecting a proposition with the latent attitudes of his hearers.

Attitudes are not a part of the individual's native psychological equipment; they are acquired or developed throughout his life. Like other mental or emotional patterns of behavior, they are learned, modified, or discarded as the individual reacts to his environment and his experiences. A child may develop a dislike for certain foods, but later come to like them as his taste matures. The same child may also acquire from his environment an unfavorable attitude toward other racial or religious groups, but subsequent pleasant experiences with individuals in those groups may modify or destroy that attitude.

Beliefs

In contrast to the generalized nature of an attitude, a belief is the acceptance of a specific proposition. An individual may have a general attitude of religious tolerance, but be quite categorical about the question "Do you believe in God?" Although beliefs may be covertly held, we commonly identify them by an individual's verbal utterances. Skinner (1957, p. 88) implies a progression in a listener's behavior from attitude to belief, describing the latter as "the probability that he will take effective action with respect to a particular verbal stimulus."

Men are born without beliefs. We commonly say that beliefs are socially determined; while they may be based partly upon personal experiences, they depend more largely upon the advice, testimony, and influence of others. Even traditional beliefs in a family or a sect are social in character since they have been transmitted from one generation to the next.

It is important to note that all men tend to formulate beliefs about most situations they encounter; both problems and people are perceived with meaning and interpretation, even though with limited evidence. As Krech and Crutchfield (1948, p. 86) observe: "Man is an organizing animal. . . . As soon as we experience any facts, they will be perceived as organized into some sort of meaningful whole. This is a universal characteristic of the cognitive process and not a weakness of the impatient or prejudiced individual . . ." It follows that the establishment of a belief involves some thinking on the part of an individual; this is not necessarily true about an attitude. The difference is that individuals verbalize their beliefs and prefer to be able to state supporting reasons. There is something unsatisfactory even to the believer in confessing that "I don't know why, I just believe this is true." Thus the individual tends to rationalize, or to organize reasons for, his beliefs, a procedure he seldom follows in justifying his attitudes.

Generalizations About Attitudes and Beliefs

In concluding our discussion of attitudes and beliefs as they relate to communication a number of general observations are pertinent:

1. Attitudes and beliefs are in large part products of an individual's general culture, including his family, religious, and educational backgrounds. So long as an individual remains in the context of this culture these same influences tend to preserve existent attitudes and beliefs, by exerting social pressure for conformity.

2. Attitudes and beliefs are also products of what the individual thinks are pertinent "facts." These alleged facts, however, are often selectively perceived: new information uncongenial to dominant attitudes and beliefs may be rejected, and only information reinforcing prior attitudes and beliefs may be accepted. Moreover, individuals may not always be equipped to apply appropriate validity tests to these "facts," nor competency tests to "authorities" who purvey them.

3. Attitudes and beliefs vary in strength. These studies indicate some significant variables:

(a) Marple (1933) concludes that "there appears to be a decline of suggestibility with increasing age," that as we grow older and preserve our beliefs they tend to become stronger, and we are less likely to relinquish them.

(b) Marple's study also indicates a positive correlation between group opinion and personal belief: "Group opinion . . . is more powerful in affecting individual agreement than is expert opinion." Burtt and Falkenberg (1941) and Wheeler and Jordan (1929) support this judgment, although Kulp (1934) and Lorge (1936) found evidence to support the stronger prestige of the expert. We must conclude that group opinion is probably strongest in influencing individual attitudes and beliefs, but that the subject under discussion and the prestige of a particular expert may make for exceptions.

(c) Asch (1956) found that in situations where group members each announced publicly his conclusion on a question of judgment, only about one third of those in an extreme minority position (8 or 9 to 1) tended to distort their conclusions to conform with the majority. When the minority persons knew the judgments of others, but did not have to announce their own position, even fewer of them shifted toward the majority view. In a different type of situation, however, Sawyer (1955) found that audience members who were persuaded by a speaker's arguments judged that the majority of their fellow listeners were equally persuaded. Together these studies indicate that individuals have some concern for the congruity of their beliefs with what they feel to be the view of the majority, but that other resistant factors are also operative.

(d) Simpson (1938, p. 87) reported that in discussion situations, those who are the most influential with others are least likely to be influenced by others, indicating that belief-strength may be greater for those possessing attributes effective in influencing the beliefs of others.

(e) Schanck and Goodman (1939) found that existing beliefs and prejudices were intensified when listeners heard both sides of a fairly academic controversy, but that there was more open-mindedness, or a lessening of the intensity of belief, when the listeners felt the issue was closer to reality.

(f) Lund (1925) discovered a correlation of over $+.80$ in ranking between the order for "belief strength" and "desirability" of the belief.

Opinions

Any discussion of attitudes and beliefs inevitably leads to a consideration of opinions. While attitudes and beliefs tend to interact, sometimes making them difficult to distinguish from each other, opinions are clearly responses derived from a combination of attitudes and beliefs. In practice an opinion is an overtly verbalized attitude or belief, sometimes both. Like a belief, it is a statement of a proposition; like an attitude, it is favorable or unfavorable. Operationally, say Hovland, Janis, and Kelley (1953, p. 6), "opinions are viewed as verbal 'answers' that an individual gives in response to stimulus situations in which some general 'question' is raised." The communicator normally thinks about "influencing opinions" rather than attitudes or beliefs, since he assumes that opinions are indexes of probable action by his hearers. This is not always a safe assumption: sometimes various pressures may induce an individual to state an opinion that he feels will be socially acceptable, rather than one truly reflecting his attitudes or beliefs.

Measuring Attitudes and Opinions

Any communicator is naturally concerned with measuring his message's impact upon his listeners. We will briefly describe five measurement methods, each useful in determining the impact of communication on attitudes, beliefs, or opinions, but not the amount of information that may be conveyed to the respondent. The measurement of impact, of course, necessitates using the instruments both before and after the communicative act.

1. The simplest device for measuring attitudes is the *linear* scale, a line theoretically representing the possible range of attitude on a specific issue from complete endorsement to complete rejection. The respondent is asked to check a point representing his present attitude on, for example, "What is my attitude toward federal aid to education?" from "10-extremely favorable" to "0-extremely unfavorable."

2. A more sophisticated device, and more time-consuming both in preparation and application, is the *attitude test*. The standard procedure is to formulate a final test by (a) collecting as many relevant, simple, and unambiguous statements as possible about a specific issue, (b) having these statements sorted by a panel of experts into eleven categories, ranging from "extremely favorable" to "extremely unfavorable," in order to establish scale values, and (c) selecting for the final test perhaps twenty or thirty statements, spread across the whole range of eleven scale values. In administering the test the respondent is instructed to check "agree" or "disagree" for each statement. A simple mathematical calculation of responses indicates the position of the respondent on the "extremely favorable" to "extremely unfavorable" continuum.

3. The *public opinion poll* is the most familiar measuring instrument, consisting of a series of "Do you favor . . . ?" or "What do you think about . . . ?" questions, designed to be asked in personal interviews. When the questions are properly phrased, presented in the right context, and to a representative sample of respondents, this is a satisfactory method.

4. The *shift-of-opinion ballot* has also frequently been used in measuring impact, especially where an effort has been made to present both sides of an issue, as in a public discussion or a debate. On the pre-test the respondent is presented with three choices: "I am in favor . . ." "I am undecided . . ." "I am opposed . . ." The post-test ballot carries the same three and two additional options, one at each extreme: "I am more strongly in favor . . ." and "I am more strongly opposed . . ." Thus the post-test form permits the respondent to reflect an intensification of his original opinion, a shift in varying degrees to the opposite opinion, or no change at all.

5. The most recently developed measuring instrument is the *semantic differential*, posited on the assumption that human judgments as reflected

in verbal behavior may be reduced to a limited number of primary dimensions such as evaluation, activity, and potency. While studies in the field of speech are just developing applications of this method of analysis (Smith, 1959) they show great promise. The instrument itself usually consists of a set of ten to a dozen seven-step, bi-polar adjectival scales (such as "optimistic . . . pessimistic," "true . . . false," and "calm . . . excitable") designed to tap previously determined dimensions of meaning. The subject rates a concept (such as "emotional appeals" or "reasoning") by checking the appropriate cell of a linear scale. While the test is easy to administer, researchers are still working on a simple method of analyzing and interpreting its data.

Functional Factors

An understanding of the relation of psychology to communication requires familiarity with pertinent functional psychological factors. In the rest of this chapter we shall describe a number of these in general terms, saving until later chapters the specific applications of these factors to various patterns of communicative behavior.

Attention and Perception

Attention has always been a central concept in psychology, and it is also a key functional factor in communication. No matter how significant the communicator's message, and no matter how strongly he feels about it, it will be lost unless his hearers attend to it . . . the psychology of listening is predicated upon the concepts of attention and perception. When we listen we attend: we organize a maximum concentration of our sensory receptors upon the communicative stimulus consisting of audible (spoken words) and visible (bodily action) symbols. Only after we attend can we perceive: we are aware of the stimulus symbols and of the objects, conditions, or relationships which they represent. When we both attend and perceive we respond: we manifest this response by some overt or covert muscular movement or glandular activity.

It is no mistake if this description of the attention-perception-response sequence suggests an inseparability of the elements. Attention is a preparatory process, leading into perception, and culminating with response, sequentially but almost simultaneously. In the following discussion of attention, therefore, we are inevitably also referring to perception.

Before examining the concept of attention in detail we should underscore its significance in the communicative situation: it is one of the two major psychological contributions to rhetorical theory. The psychologist William James (1892, pp. 448-449) stated the basic principle: "What holds attention determines action. . . . What checks our impulses is the mere thinking of reasons to the contrary—it is their bare presence to the mind which gives the veto." Psychologist James R. Angell (1908, p. 402) expanded the principle: "No idea can dominate our movements which does not catch and hold attention. When we keep our attention firmly fixed upon a line of conduct, to the exclusion of all competitors, our decision is already made." And rhetorician James A. Winans (1915, p. 194) incorporated the principle into his then-revolutionary definition: "Persuasion is the process of inducing others to give fair, favorable, or undivided attention to propositions."

1. *The duration and span of attention.* A listener cannot give continuous attention; even when he tries very hard to attend, he does not hear everything. Attention comes in spurts, like an irregular succession of waves breaking on a beach. While early experimenters estimated that the length of an attention unit is from five to eight seconds, psychologists now conclude simply that the duration of attention is brief, and that it is impossible to specify an absolute time value since that depends upon the intensity of the stimulus. Even assuming that an individual's capacity for sustained stimulus selection is thirty seconds, however, it is obvious that when listening to a speech delivered at the rate of 150 words per minute, the listener would hear only about 75 words in one unit of attention. The duration of attention varies with individuals, and their powers of concentration are affected by such factors as interest in the communication, fatigue, and so on.

The span of an individual's attention also varies. Psychologists commonly refer to a *focus,* where perception is sharp, and a *margin,* where awareness is slight. As Chapman and Brown (1935) found, clarity of perception is greatest when the stimuli are clustered in focus. While individual differences and the type of stimuli involved will affect the span of attention, laboratory experiments suggest that four or five visual stimuli and five to eight auditory ones, represent practical limits.

2. *Types of attention.* Thus far we have spoken of attention as though it always takes the same form. In fact, psychologists commonly recognize three varieties of attention: involuntary, voluntary, habitual.

(a) *Involuntary attention* is sometimes called passive, since it requires no effort on the part of the individual; instead, he attends because some stimulus is compellingly attractive compared with other stimuli. Operationally this may be illustrated by the "figure-ground" concept, in which unusual stimulus symbols stand out from the background of the familiar. Thus a printed word is a "figure" against the "ground" of a white page, a speaker's striking gesture is a "figure" against the "ground" of normal delivery. Everyday life is filled with fire sirens, neon signs, dramatic slogans, and even certain social forces, that compel our involuntary attention.

(b) *Voluntary attention* results from deliberate action on our part, sometimes requiring great effort. Studying for a final examination, performing an unpleasant task in the office, or listening to an uninspiring speaker, exemplifies attention of this sort. These examples also explain why voluntary attention is often referred to as active, demanding conscious, although perhaps reluctant, focus on the stimulus.

(c) *Habitual attention* is sometimes referred to as nonvoluntary, suggesting its roots in both of the other types. If it is caused by aroused interests, or opportunities to satisfy needs (such as a listless lecturer but one who presents vital pre-examination information), it will have some qualities of voluntary attention. If it comes from a psychological "set" for a repeated experience (it *is* customary to listen to classroom lecturers), it will have some characteristics of involuntary attention.

In many situations the listener may shift or be shifted, from one type of attention to another. For example, a communicator who lacks prestige, or whose message will not command voluntary attention, may begin with a device that compels involuntary attention, then try to develop sustained habitual attention.

3. *Unlearned attention* values. The communicator who wants the attention of audience members must recognize that his stimulus must not only be strong enough to energize their sensory organs, but compelling enough to compete successfully with other stimuli. Thus he must find what Murphy (1951, p. 140) calls "factors of advantage," stimulus attributes commanding priority. Psychologists are in general agreement on the nature of these attributes and in considering some of them to be unlearned, others learned. Here are five natural or unlearned values:

(a) *Change* is the most basic and significant attention value. When the attention-perception-response cycle has been completed for any one stimulus it tends to lose its potency, and a new stimulus is necessary to attract further attention. A changing stimulus is one that moves in some direction, from high to low, weak to strong, background to foreground, and so on. Thus the television director tries to maintain attention by alternating "long" and "close-up" camera shots. If the diversification of stimuli becomes too rhythmical, however, as in the "sing-song" recitation of a poem, then the movement becomes predictable and the value of change is lost. In using vocal and physical energy as attention devices, therefore, the stimuli need not only change, but must also incorporate a variety of change.

(b) *Intensity* as an attention value may be described this way: whenever there are competing stimuli the most intense one (strongest, loudest, brightest, largest, etc.) will command our attention. This principle operates with both visible and audible symbols, such as the full-page color advertisement against the quarter-page black and white one, or the strong and vibrant voice against the weak and flat one. As with the principle of change, however, variety is also an important concomitant of intensity. Actors, for example, learn to vary the vocal intensity of their playing in order to extract maximum value from its use in "building" a scene.

(c) *Striking quality*, sometimes simply in the form of novelty of stimulus, has obvious attention value. Some of its virtue may be drawn from the incorporation of the values of change or intensity. If we suddenly shout in a high pitch we probably use greater intensity, but even without increasing the intensity the high pitch alone would attract attention. Even a physically stronger stimulus may yield to a lesser one of striking quality, such as a smooth pressure on a large area to a light pinch in a localized area, pastels to saturated colors, or an open trumpet to a muted one.

(d) *Repetition,* within limits, has high attention value. Its advantages lie in the added strength given to the stimulus by repeating it and in the consequent increase in our sensitivity to the stimulus. This increased sensitivity develops from what is often described as a "summation of stimuli" and a consequent "neurological summation" of response. Plutarch reported that when Demosthenes was asked what were the three parts of oratory he replied, "Action, *action,* ACTION!" With this repetition we cannot fail to get the point. The possibility of monotony may be avoided and even greater potency often achieved if the repeated stimulus is varied slightly in form while retaining the central theme. This application of repetition is a hallmark of good design and composition, whether in music, architecture, stage scenery, or public relations campaigns.

(e) *Definiteness of form* has great natural attention value because perception is easier when stimulus objects are sharply outlined, or when multiple stimuli can be viewed as a patterned group. Thus we attend to the grouping of stars into the Big Dipper, the arrangement of musical notes into a melody, or the organization of arguments into a cumulative sequence. Our ability to perceive stimuli in patterns is so strong that we often fill in gaps, in effect "seeing" a whole even though some parts may be missing. We expect to find eleven men in a football lineup and so may not notice when the ball is snapped with one player still on the sideline. Our tendency to attend to, and to perceive, definiteness of form is strengthened when the stimulus objects are similar to each other, close enough together to be seen as a whole, arranged in an orderly or a symmetrical pattern, or forming some sort of continuity.

4. *Individualized attention values.* In addition to the natural and universal values influencing the direction of attention there is a complex of subjective or individualized "factors of advantage." Psychologists also agree generally on three types of learned values.

(a) *The organic condition* of the individual may determine the stimulus to which he is most apt to respond at any given moment. If we are fatigued, stimuli related to rest will have special potency; hunger renders us unusually receptive to stimuli related to food; and if we are perplexed about a problem we respond to stimuli offering resolution. Thus the individual selectively attends to whatever stimulus is most closely related to his paramount biological needs.

(b) *Social suggestion* is often a determinant of attention and perception. What is pointed out to us by others—or what we see others doing—often influences our own behavior. Especially is this true if the suggested action will gain social approval or special prestige. Opera halls and art galleries alike are populated not only by true connoisseurs, but also by those seeking status rather than culture. Even "sidewalk superintendents" may be attracted not so much by the construction project as by the fact that others have apparently been attracted.

(c) *Predispositions* of an individual also operate as selective factors in determining what he attends to. His interests, wants, experiences, or habits predispose him to attend to associated stimuli. A fire siren may not disturb a sleeping mother, but she will awaken with a start at the slightest outcry from her baby. An audience may be unaware of an actor's miscue, but a person familiar with the script will discern the mistake at once. Or, to put the matter another way, several individuals may attend to the same stimulus but be guided by their predispositions into "seeing" it quite differently. A mathematician may see a simple circle as a symbol for zero, a garage mechanic interpret it as a piston ring, and an artist view it as a design element.

Interest

In considering functional psychological factors in communicative behavior it is logical to move from attention to interest for they are not only associated but nearly inseparable. As William James (1892, p. 448) put it: "What-we-attend-to and what-interests-us are synonymous terms." The distinction between them, a thin one, is that attention is concerned with the initial organization of our sensory receptors toward a given stimulus and that interest is what maintains subsequent orientation. We have already noted that the only thing constant about attention is that it ebbs and flows; the effect of factors having inherent interest is to stabilize it as much as that is possible. We describe here the most common natural factors of interest.

1. *Animation* as an interest factor is analogous to the attention values of change and intensity. When the attention-perception-response cycle set off by one stimulus is completed, a change in the stimulus requires a readjustment and tends to evoke new interest. The stationary painted barber pole, the revolving pole, and the new one with neon lights, illustrate our point. So do the animated television commercials where few products are static but shaving cream lathers and beer foams, and the digestive tract is in a constant state of upset.

2. *Vitalness* in a stimulus almost guarantees interest, especially when its vital quality is related to self. Even the individual who prides himself on objectivity and intellectuality is seldom able to suppress interest in anything affecting his basic physiological needs. Those who sell medical nostrums rely on this fact, and so do those who promote safety on the highways. What affects our vital interests concerns us because they are *our* interests.

3. *Familiarity* in a situation sustains interest because it gives us a sense of security; we "feel at home" with what we already know. This is why politicians often apply accepted labels to new proposals: "The undistributed profits tax is merely an extension of the individual income tax." Even what is not itself familiar, but similar to something previously experienced, may also hold interest; we have some confidence in likenesses and do much of our learning by association.

4. *Novelty* contrasts sharply with familiarity, but may be no less potent as an interest factor. If situations are too familiar, repeated exposure to them may become monotonous. Instead of feeling secure, we may become apathetic. "This is where I came in" is a common phrase indicating a loss of interest. A novel stimulus tends to counter this reaction; because it is new it excites curiosity and revives interest. Perhaps the most effective presentation combines familiarity and novelty: "Old wine in new bottles." In terms of communication this might mean familiar ideas and sentiments applied to new situations and in novel language.

5. *Conflict* interests almost everyone. Most of us regularly engage in some form of it, playing in team sports, working to earn promotions, trying to write better books, or just "keeping up with the Joneses." It is natural, therefore, that we also become interested observers of the presentation of conflict and may identify with and respond especially to one of the combatants. The modern mass audiences for professional sports illustrate the point, and so does the theatre-goer whose interest in a play is at least partially due to its resolving a conflict situation. Burke (1945) even views persuasive speaking from a dramatistic approach and sees its modes of action in the form of conflict.

6. *Suspense* is inextricably tied to conflict in the maintenance of interest; if we become involved in a conflict situation, even as observers, we want to know how it comes out. Psychologically, an unresolved conflict is an incomplete configuration; we are annoyed because part of the picture is missing, and we sustain our interest until the picture is filled in and we can react to the complete situation.

7. *Concreteness* commonly holds interest while abstractness loses it. The psychological principle is the simple one that any stimulus is a symbol which must be interpreted in terms of our experiences, and that our experiences seldom survive as abstractions but rather as memories of concrete things we have seen, sounds we have heard, and so on. Thus concrete stimuli are most effective in calling up concrete images. It is true, however, that the more intelligent and sophisticated individual usually finds it easier to translate abstractions, and may even enjoy doing it.

8. *Humor* is an ambivalent factor of interest unless it is clearly relevant to the total situation. A humorous anecdote, built on incongruity, becomes itself incongruous when unrelated to the central experience: "It's funny, but what's the point?" Both variety and relaxation of tension may be introduced

into a situation, however, by an occasional and pertinent turn of phrase, an unexpected comparison, or a play on sound or sense.

Motivation

In an earlier chapter, we introduced the concept of emotion in our discussion of affective behavior and speech. Here we restate briefly some of what was said, as a prelude to our comments on motivation. We give this subject emphasis by repetition because it is so commonly believed that man is a completely rational being, that we always "make up our minds" by applying reason to problem situations and in choosing among alternative reactions. Our study of psychology compels us to disagree with this view. Man's fulfillment of his maximum potentialities does depend upon the controlling force of reason, but he seldom achieves this goal. "Reason," says Overstreet (1949, pp. 104-105), "is a *capacity* in man, not necessarily an achievement. In most men it lies largely dormant while something else, which is far from reason, takes over."

A major factor in that "something else" which takes over from pure reason is emotion. Psychologists do not always agree upon how to classify emotions; indeed, they prefer not to consider emotions as discrete entities, but to think of affective behavior as a single, basic, and confused pattern of response. This behavior they measure by such indicators of satisfaction, relaxation, irritation, or frustration as galvanic skin response, blood pressure and volume, muscular tensions, heart rate, and respiration. In general it would be agreed that both bodily states and expressive actions reveal characteristics of affective behavior commonly elicited by three basic situations:

1. Those situations that are completely new or strange, that develop suddenly and unexpectedly, threatening an individual's physical or social security and creating anxiety, tend to arouse a *fear* response.

2. Those situations which restrain the individual in any way, frustrating his desires or preventing him from behaving in ways that will satisfy him, tend to arouse an *anger* response.

3. Those situations which remove threats to the individual's feeling of security, relieve his anxieties, or eliminate frustration, and thus permit the satisfaction of his desires and needs, tend to arouse a *pleasure* response.

From this application of what we have said earlier about affective behavior, we conclude that any physiological or environmental circumstance which annoys or satisfies the individual does so not solely because it brings him pleasure or pain, contentment or irritation, joy or depression, but primarily because it either satisfies or thwarts particular desires and wants. These desires and wants give an emotional impulse toward behavior which helps the individual adjust to the circumstance confronting him. In short, his behavior is motivated.

In 1938, one of the authors of this book introduced a discussion of motivation by declaring that: "The amount of organized human behavior that is not determined by an individual's wants, interests, and purposes is so small as to merit attention only because of its rarity." Despite the enormous amount of psychological research in the subsequent quarter of a century, there is no reason to modify this statement. The more we study human behavior the more sure we are that it is dynamic, characterized by great energy stemming from basic inner drives—wants, interests, and purposes.

These motives are so closely articulated with our behavior that we seldom identify them in isolation. Indeed, we may never recognize them unless we are caught in the vise of conflicting motives operating upon us simultaneously. After momentary frustration we normally resolve the conflict and shape our behavior to satisfy one drive or the other. In abnormal behavior, of course, the individual fails to make a choice and meets the conflict by various stratagems of avoidance or dissembling, such as rationalization, projection, repression, or sublimation.

Since we cannot observe motivational drives directly, we are obliged to identify them by observing the characteristics of motivated behavior. Stagner and Karwoski (1952, pp. 35-36) list three primary ones: energy, persistence, and variability. Motivation operates, they say, in proportion to the energy expended in a given situation, and thus they assume that if one student works more energetically than another, he is more strongly motivated. They also point out that a highly motivated person does not give up easily; if his initial behavior does not lead directly to his goal, he persists by trying other behaviors. The third characteristic of variability is thus a product of the second; the highly motivated person varies his techniques as he continues to seek satisfaction.

These observations suggest that motivation operates in a sequence of three steps. First, the individual feels a need, stemming from his wants, interests, or purposes. Second, this feeling of need leads him into some form of instrumental or problem-solving behavior. Third, if this behavior is efficient, it achieves a specific end that satisfies the original need. The omnibus term describing this complete sequence is motivated behavior.

Before we attempt a classification of basic drives that result in motivated behavior, note should be taken of the significance of motivation in the communicative situation. In discussing the concept of attention we observed that it was one of two major psychological contributions to rhetorical theory; the second is the concept of motivation. Winans (1915, p. xiii), building upon the concept set forth by James, was explicit: "The key word [in public speaking] is Attention." Concurrently he held that persuasion was a mental process. Brigance (1935) took cognizance of later psychological research on motivation: "the generally accepted view today, however, is that persuasion takes place, not on an intellectual, but rather on a motor level," and "the lines of modern research, to say nothing of common sense, converge to show that desires are the basic determinant of persuasion." Thus Brigance accepted the James-Winans notion that attention was the *channel* for the flow of persuasive communication, but argued that its *headspring* was desire. This view of the dominant function of motivation is standard today.

We now conclude this discussion of motivation by describing the fundamental drives affecting normal human behavior. While modern psychologists agree upon the existence and the significance of these wants, purposes, and interests, each tends to draw up his own list of exactly what they are. We shall follow that precedent and present our own list. These are the basic, unlearned drives, universally present in all human beings:

1. *Human beings direct their activities toward the satisfaction of physical wants and general well-being.* They avoid, whenever possible, situations that may bring about physical deprivation, including pain, hunger, thwarting of sex impulses, and a need for sleep. Much contemporary advertising promises these satisfactions, whether from headache remedies, fancy foods, or form-fitting mattresses. An individual can suffer any of these deprivations temporarily, however, and he may knowingly enter into situations which will deprive him for a time if he believes that there will be ultimate satisfaction. The willingness of astronauts to undergo periods of intense training is at least partially explainable in terms of the ultimate respite they know will come at the end of their missions.

2. *Human beings normally behave in ways that will lead them toward success, mastery, and achievement.* They try to avoid situations that may thwart, frustrate or disappoint them. Again, however, individuals may often knowingly accept temporary disappointment when there is promise of future success or achievement. Some students, for example, may withdraw from athletic competition if they fear that the cannot "make the team"; but others willingly engage in rigorous drills if they believe that "practice pays off." It is normal to want to "be the best of whatever you are."

3. *Human beings tend to behave in ways that will help them to gain recognition, admiration, respect, and approval.* They avoid action that may result in being ignored, looked down upon, or merely tolerated. Even temporary disdain may be accepted by an individual if he feels there is a possibility of gaining lasting respect; tomorrow's cheers will compensate for today's jeers. Those who study social influence on behavior often refer to "status needs," the drives to achieve favorable prominence in one's own social hierarchy. Some groups accord high status to great intellect or creative talent; in others these virtues count for little, but material possessions—costly cars, lavish wardrobes, or unlimited expense accounts—are status symbols. So common is this drive for recognition that "status seeker" is now a widely used label.

4. *Human beings generally act in ways that will lead toward their being loved, and the realization of a feeling of being wanted.* They tend to avoid behavior that keeps them from "belonging," and to indulge in activities that are not intrinsically satisfying—such as going to concerts or attending cocktail parties—if participation will strengthen group ties. Human beings usually

prefer the company of others rather than being alone, and prefer to be with familiar persons rather than strange ones. There are notable exceptions, however; explorers may visit isolated areas or strange people, and recluses may shun all human contacts. But such persons may well be motivated in their behavior by other drives which are for them, at least at the moment, more fundamental.

5. *Human beings usually act in ways that will bring about peace of mind, security, and a feeling of release from worry and anxiety.* They try to avoid involvement in situations that create fear, anxiety, or insecurity. Students lacking confidence in their mathematical abilities may avoid science courses; others, feeling deficient in social qualities, may refuse opportunities for group memberships. In some circumstances, of course, individuals may be oppressed by more than one of these concerns, and be forced to accept a lesser, and perhaps temporary, worry in order to put off a more serious one. Thus "robbing Peter to pay Paul" or "choosing the lesser of two evils" are common behavioral guides.

6. *Finally, human beings indicate by their behavior that they seek some adventure, new experiences, and zestful living.* They tend to avoid boredom and monotony. How much adventure or how many new experiences a person seeks is a highly individual matter. The man who is responsible only to and for himself may often enter into situations that are not only new but dangerous, in his search for zestful living. But the less mobile man, such as the head of a family, tends to suppress his drive for new experiences in favor of mundane security. Generally, however, individuals seek a condition of life with enough novelty to prevent monotony, but not so much novelty that living will be difficult because of the necessity of making continuous adjustments to too rapid change. The appeal of eating in exotic restaurants or of watching adventure programs on television may thus be compensation for otherwise humdrum living.

Learning and Remembering

The primary aim of the communicator, we have said, is so to transmit his message to his hearers that it will change their behavior. Another way to say this is that the communicator wants his hearers to "learn" his propositions and to "remember" them as bases for immediate or future action. In short, as Berlo (1960, pp. 99-100) has compared the two, a "model of the communication process encompasses the model of learning. . . . The two models represent only a difference in point of view. A learning model usually starts with the decoding function, a communication model usually starts with a discussion of purpose. That is the primary distinction between the two, and it is not important theoretically." What is important is that the concepts of learning and remembering are important functional factors in the psychology of communication.

For our purposes we need review here only that type of learning called perceptual. Learning results from our discriminating understanding of concepts. Concepts are generalizations that remain constant as our guides to the meaning of objects, persons, qualities, or relationships. We learn literally thousands of concepts, usually in terms of word symbols but occasionally in terms of visual or other sensory images, such as "purple," "Easterner," "vitality," or "love." (By the process of abstraction our concepts may be extended, broadened, reduced in complexity.) Working from a base of acquired concepts we perceive a wide range of stimuli. This perception becomes discriminative learning as a consequence of what is called differential reinforcement. The reinforcement consists of providing an incentive for responding (perceiving) in a particular way to a specific stimulus. To be effective this incentive must be related to the satisfaction of a physiological need or one of the basic drives we have previously discussed. We refer to the reinforcement as differential because it rewards the response to one stimulus but not to another. Thus we identify perceptual learning as that involving the perception of new concepts (or the modification of old ones) about objects, persons, qualities, or relationships, and resulting from the presentation of reinforced stimuli.

With this limited review we now consider learning and remembering in a variety of communication situations. Specifically, communicators should appreciate the influence of the listener's selectivity upon what he will attend to, the utility of categorization and of suggestion in stimulating both learning and remembering, and specific techniques of impressiveness in assuring retention.

1. *Selectivity in attending and perceiving.* An understanding of psychological barriers to communication, and an appreciation of the elements creating resistance to change, are both important in a complete assessment of learning in communicative situations. For our purposes, it is sufficient to generalize about the influence upon learning of selective perception. It is apparent that not all persons attend and perceive in the same way, to the same degree, or for the same reasons. In addition to such variations explainable by differences in personality, it should be recognized that individuals may be deliberately selective in exposing themselves to learning opportunities. This fact is underscored in the following conclusions about the relationships between opportunity for learning and actual learning. They were derived from a careful examination by Hyman and Sheatsley (1947) of surveys made by the National Opinion Research Center:

(a) There exists a hard core of chronic "know-nothings." "There is something about the uninformed which makes them harder to reach, no matter what the level or nature of the information."

(b) Interested people acquire the most information. "The widest possible dissemination of material may be ineffective if it is not geared to the public's interest."

(c) People seek information congenial to prior attitudes, and tend to ignore uncongenial information. "Merely 'increasing the flow' is not enough, if the information continues to 'flow' in the direction of those already on your side."

(d) People interpret the same information differently. It is "false to assume that exposure, once achieved, results in uniform interpretation and retention of the material." Memory and perception are distorted by wishes, motives, and attitudes.

(e) Information does not necessarily change attitudes. Informed people react differently from uninformed, "but it is naïve to suppose that information always affects attitudes, or that it affects all attitudes equally. . . . There is evidence . . . that individuals, once they are exposed to information, change their views *differentially*, each in the light of his own *prior* attitude."

2. *Learning and remembering by categorizing.* Outstanding in recent psychological research has been that in the Harvard University Cognition Project. Of particular interest here is its focus upon a process called categorizing, the way a person establishes equivalences or distinctive similarities among concepts, as he "sorts out and responds to the world around him." This process is related to learning and remembering in communicative situations, as we can see by summarizing from Bruner, Goodnow, and Austin (1956, pp. 11-15) the utility for the individual of categorizing discriminably different objects, persons, qualities, relationships, or events:

(a) By categorizing, the individual reduces the complexity of his environment, abstracting and defining in terms of previously perceived groupings.

(b) Categorizing provides an individual the means for identifying the objects of the world about him and assigning each one to its established class.

(c) Because categorizing does reduce the complexity of the environment by establishing identification patterns, it also reduces the necessity for constant learning by the individual. He can capitalize upon his recollections of previous experiences.

(d) Categorizing provides the individual with direction for instrumental or problem-solving activity; it gives him a set of relatively reliable a priori judgments about how to behave with respect to recognized concepts.

(e) The individual is enabled by his categorizing to order and relate different classes of objects, events, and so on. Organized and related systems of categorized classes permit him to relate classes of objects and events rather than individual ones.

Closely related to the process of learning and remembering by categorization is the process of generalization in critical thinking, or developing universal conclusions from inductive analyses of particular instances. Categorizing and generalizing are both ways of learning about events, relationships, and other concepts.

3. *Suggestion in learning and remembering.* We observed that individuals exercise some selectivity about what they choose to learn, but we must turn the coin over and note that individuals may also be quite unselective in this respect *if the force of positive suggestion is strong enough* (Coffin, 1941). "I

would like to suggest," says the professor, "that my lecture today will cover materials that are significant for the final examination." This unsubtle suggestion is a stimulus sure to evoke attention, interest, and learning from all but the most indolent student.

Any positive suggestion is a social stimulus designed to elicit an uncritical and more or less automatic response. That it can do so results from the fact that humans tend to prefer being in a passive rather than an active state. Acceptance of a suggestion is a normal response, requiring little or no discriminative activity. To doubt, on the other hand, is more difficult; it demands active and critical analysis. If the suggestion comes from a person with prestige or authority, it is even more likely to be accepted. In our illustration of the preceding paragraph, the psychological odds are all in favor of the professor.

We conclude these observations on the role of suggestion in learning with a series of generalizations about the nature of suggestion and its demonstrated effects upon behavior:

(a) Suggestion operates most effectively when it is directed toward an existent response-pattern.

(b) Suggestion operates most effectively when it encounters a receptive attitude; there must be no other suggestions that set off stronger or better established response patterns.

(c) Suggestion is increased when there is a lack of adequate knowledge concerning the subject at hand.

(d) Suggestion is increased when it is related to desire—a fundamental want, drive, or belief.

(e) Suggestion is increased by the prestige of the person making it.

(f) Suggestion is increased by excitement which is usually accompanied by a relaxation of reason.

(g) Suggestion is usually increased by group situations.

4. *Impressiveness in learning and remembering.* A final significant influence upon the learning and remembering process is the impressiveness of the stimulus employed to bring about the desired response. A general principle is that the stronger or the more potent the stimulus, the greater impress it will make upon the responding person. The best omnibus word to describe this principle in operation is *emphasis*, the special stress or weight given to particular stimuli. In the communicative situation this means the emphasis given to particular stimulus units (whole arguments, propositional sentences, important phrases, key words) by presenting them with special potency. To give emphasis of this sort implies, realistically, that in any total learning some parts are more critical to understanding than others. We apply this fact whenever we reduce a fifty-word message to a ten-word telegram, retaining only the essential information.

Some of the earliest investigations into the relative potency of stimuli in oral communication situations were reported by Jersild (1928) and Ehrensberger (1945), and many subsequent studies have been done by researchers in the field of speech. From these experimental inquiries into the impressiveness of stimuli we draw the following generalizations:

(a) The intensity of a stimulus increases its potency: loud sounds more than soft ones, vivid hues more than moderate ones, and so on.

(b) The potency of a stimulus is related to its duration. The prolonged wail of the fire siren has more impact than a short blast, and an argument fully explained makes more impress than one merely alluded to.

(c) Even though a stimulus may be intense and prolonged, its potency may further be increased by the specific reinforcement of an accompanying stimulus such as a vigorous gesture, or an orienting one such as an anticipatory pause.

(d) Stimuli repeated as many as three or four times tend to be more impressive than those presented only once. Beyond four, however, further repetitions do not appear to affect responses proportionately.

(e) Repetitions of stimuli appear to be most potent when they are spaced out in intervals of time. This may well be because distributed repetitions have a better chance of striking the listener during one or more of his spurts of attention than do successive ones.

(f) In any series of stimuli a specific one may be given greater potency by being placed first or last. While there seems to be greater experimental support for an anticlimax order of stimuli, whether primacy or recency is most effective is a matter still in doubt.

(g) Finally, the potency of a stimulus may also be increased when it is reinforced by the phenomenon of social facilitation. An individual who is aware of favorable responses to a specific stimulus by other viewers or listeners, tends to be more impressed by that same stimulus. The mere sight or sound of others responding makes it more comfortable and desirable for him to respond in the same way.

References

ALLPORT, G. W. in Murchison, C., ed., *Handbook of Social Psychology.* Worcester, Mass., Clark University Press, 1937.

ANGELL, J. R. *Psychology.* New York, Holt, Rinehart, and Winston, 1908.

ASCH, S. E. "Studies of Independence and Conformity: I. A Minority of One Against a Unanimous Majority." *Psychol. Monogr.,* 1956, 70, 416, 70 pp.

BERLO, D. K. *The Process of Communication.* New York, Holt, Rinehart, and Winston, 1960.

BRIGANCE, W. N. "Can We Redefine the James-Winans Theory of Persuasion?" *Quart. J. Spch,* 1935, 21, 19-26.

BRUNER, J. S., GOODNOW, J. J., & AUSTIN, G. A. *A Study of Thinking.* New York, Wiley, 1956.

BURKE, K. *A Grammar of Motives.* Englewood Cliffs, N. J., Prentice-Hall, 1945.

BURTT, H. E., & FALKENBERG, D. R. "The Influence of Majority and Expert Opinion on Religious Attitudes." *J. Soc. Psychol.,* 1941, 14, 269-278.

CHAPMAN, D. W., & BROWN, H. E. "The Reciprocity Between Clearness and Range of Attention." *J. Gen. Psychol.,* 1935, 13, 357-366.

COFFIN, T. E. "Some Conditions of Suggestibility: A Study of Certain Attitudinal and Situational Factors Influencing the Process of Suggestion." *Psychol. Monogr.,* 1941, 53, 241, 125 pp.

EHRENSBERGER, R. "The Relative Effectiveness of Certain Forms of Emphasis in Public Speaking." *Spch. Monogr.,* 1945, 12, 94-111.

HOVLAND, C. I., JANIS, I. L., & KELLEY, H. H. *Communication and Persuasion.* New Haven, Yale University Press, 1953.

HYMAN, H. H., & SHEATSLEY, P. B. "Some Reasons Why Information Campaigns Fail." *Publ. Opin. Quart.,* 1947, 11, 412-423.

JAMES, W. *Psychology, Briefer Course.* New York, Holt, Rinehart, and Winston, 1892.

JEBB, R. C. *The Attic Orators.* New York, Macmillan, 1876. 2 vols.

JERSILD, A. T. "Modes of Emphasis in Public Speaking." *J. Appl. Psychol.,* 1928, 12, 611-620.

KRECH, D., & CRUTCHFIELD, R. S. *Theory and Problems of Social Psychology.* New York, McGraw-Hill, 1948.

KULP, D. H. "Prestige, as Measured by Single-experience Changes and Their Permanency." *J. Educ. Res.,* 1934, 27, 663-672.

LASSWELL, H. D. in Smith, B. L., Lasswell, H. D., & Casey, R. D. eds., *Propaganda, Communication and Public Opinion.* Princeton, Princeton University Press, 1946.

LORGE, I. "Prestige, Suggestion and Attitudes." *J. Soc. Psychol.,* 1936, 7, 386-402.

LUND, F. H. "The Psychology of Belief." *J. Abnorm. Soc. Psychol.,* 1925, 20, 63-112, 174-224.

MARPLE, C. H. "The Comparative Susceptibility of Three Age Levels to the Suggestion of Group Versus Expert Opinion." *J. Soc. Psychol.,* 1933, 4, 176-186.

MURPHY, G. *An Introduction to Psychology.* New York, Harper & Row, 1951.

OVERSTREET, H. A. *The Mature Mind.* New York, W. W. Norton, 1949.

SAWYER, T. M., JR., "Shift of Attitude Following Persuasion as Related to Estimate of Majority Attitude." *Spch. Monogr.,* 1955, 22, 68-78.

SCHANCK, R. L. & GOODMAN, C. "Reactions to Propaganda on Both Sides of a Controversial Issue." *Publ. Opin. Quart.,* 1939, 3, 107-112.

SCOTT, W. D. *The Psychology of Public Speaking.* Philadelphia, Pearson Brothers, 1906.

SHANNON, C., & WEAVER, W. *The Mathematical Theory of Communication.* Urbana, Ill., University of Illinois Press, 1949.

SIMPSON, R. H. *A Study of Those Who Influence and of Those Who Are Influenced in Discussion.* New York, Teachers College, Columbia University, 1938.

SKINNER, B. F. *Verbal Behavior.* New York, Appleton-Century-Crofts, 1957.

SMITH, R. G. "Development of a Semantic Differential for Use with Speech Related Concepts." *Spch Monogr.,* 1959, 26, 263-272.

STAGNER, R., & KARWOSKI, T. F. *Psychology.* New York, McGraw-Hill, 1952.

WALLACE, K. R. "The Field of Speech, 1953: An Overview." *Quart. J. Spch,* 1954, 40, 117-129.

WHEELER, D., & JORDAN, H. "Change of Individual Opinion to Accord with Group Opinion." *J. Abnorm. Soc. Psychol.,* 1929, 24, 203-206.

WINANS, J. A. *Public Speaking.* New York, Appleton-Century-Crofts, 1915.

6

Reconciling Conflicting Results Derived from Experimental and Survey Studies of Attitude Change

CARL I. HOVLAND

Two quite different types of research design are characteristically used to study the modification of attitudes through communication. In the first type, the *experiment,* individuals are given a controlled exposure to a communication and the effects evaluated in terms of the amount of change in attitude or opinion produced. A base line is provided by means of a control group not exposed to the communication. The study of Gosnell (1927) on the influence of leaflets designed to get voters to the polls is a classic example of the controlled experiment.

In the alternative research design, the *sample survey,* information is secured through interviews or questionnaires both concerning the respondent's exposure to various communications and his attitudes and opinions on various issues. Generalizations are then derived from the correlations obtained between reports of exposure and measurements of attitude. In a variant of this method, measurements of attitude and of exposure to communication are obtained during repeated interviews with the same individual over a period of weeks or months. This is the "panel method" extensively utilized in studying the impact of various mass media on political attitudes and on voting behavior (cf., e.g., Kendall & Lazarsfeld, 1950).

Generalizations derived from experimental and from correlational studies of communication effects are usually both reported in chapters on the effects of mass media and in other summaries of research on attitude, typically without much stress on the type of study from which the conclusion was derived. Close scrutiny of the results obtained from the two methods, however, suggests a marked difference in the picture of communication effects obtained from each. The object of my paper is to consider the conclusions derived from these two types of design, to suggest some of the factors responsible for the frequent

Reprinted from *American Psychologist* (1959), pp. 8-17.

divergence in results, and then to formulate principles aimed at reconciling some of the apparent conflicts.

Divergence

The picture of mass communication effects which emerges from correlational studies is one in which few individuals are seen as being affected by communications. One of the most thorough correlational studies of the effects of mass media on attitudes is that of Lazarsfeld, Berelson, and Gaudet published in *The Peoples' Choice* (1944). In this report there is an extensive chapter devoted to the effects of various media, particularly radio, newspapers, and magazines. The authors conclude that few changes in attitudes were produced. They estimate that the political positions of only about 5% of their respondents were changed by the election campaign, and they are inclined to attribute even this small amount of change more to personal influence than to the mass media. A similar evaluation of mass media is made in the recent chapter in the *Handbook of Social Psychology* by Lipset and his collaborators (1954).

Research using experimental procedures, on the other hand, indicates the possibility of considerable modifiability of attitudes through exposure to communication. In both Klapper's survey (1949) and in my chapter in the *Handbook of Social Psychology* (Hovland, 1954) a number of experimental studies are discussed in which the opinions of a third to a half or more of the audience are changed.

The discrepancy between the results derived from these two methodologies raises some fascinating problems for analysis. This divergence in outcome appears to me to be largely attributable to two kinds of factors: one, the difference in research design itself; and, two, the historical and traditional differences in general approach to evaluation characteristic of researchers using the experimental as contrasted with the correlational or survey method. I would like to discuss, first, the influence these factors have on the estimation of overall effects of communications and, then, turn to other divergences in outcome characteristically found by the use of the experimental and survey methodology.

Undoubtedly the most critical and interesting variation in the research *design* involved in the two procedures is that resulting from differences in definition of exposure. In an experiment the audience on whom the effects are being evaluated is one which is fully exposed to the communication. On the other hand, naturalistic situations with which surveys are typically concerned, the outstanding phenomenon is the limitation of the audience to those who *expose themselves* to the communication. Some of the individuals in a captive audience experiment would, of course, expose themselves in the course of natural events to a communication of the type studied; but many others would not. The group which does expose itself is usually a highly biased one, since most individuals "expose themselves most of the time to the kind of material with which they agree to begin with" (Lipset et al., 1954, p. 1158). Thus one reason for the difference in results between experiments and correlational studies is that experiments describe the effects of exposure on the whole range of individuals studied, some of whom are initially in favor of the position being advocated and some who are opposed, whereas surveys primarily describe the effects produced on those already in favor of the point of view advocated in the communication. The amount of change is thus, of course, much smaller in surveys. Lipset and his collaborators make this same evaluation, stating that: "As long as we test a program in the laboratory we always find that it has great effect on the attitudes and interests of the experimental subjects. But when we put the program on as a regular broadcast, we then note that the people who are most influenced in the laboratory tests are those who, in a realistic situation, do not listen to the program. The controlled experiment always greatly overrates effects, as compared with those that really occur, because of the self-selection of audiences (Lipset et al., 1954, p. 1158)."

Differences in the second category are not inherent in the design of the two alternatives, but are characteristic of the way researchers using the two methods typically proceed.

The first difference within this class is in the size of the communication unit typically studied. In the majority of survey studies the unit evaluated is an entire program of communication. For example, in studies of political behavior an attempt is made to assess the effects of all newspaper reading and television viewing on attitudes toward the major parties. In the typical experiment, on the other hand, the interest is usually in some particular variation in the content of the communications, and experimental evaluations much more frequently involve single communications. On this point results are thus not directly comparable.

Another characteristic difference between the two methods is in the time interval used in evaluation. In the typical experiment the time at which the effect is observed is usually rather soon after exposure to the communication. In the survey study, on the other hand, the time perspective is such that much more remote effects are usually evaluated. When effects decline with the passage of time, the net outcome will, of course, be that of accentuating the effect obtained in experimental studies as compared with those obtained in survey researches. Again it must be stressed that the difference is not inherent in the designs as such. Several experiments, including our own on the effects of motion pictures (Hovland, Lumsdaine, & Sheffield, 1949) and later studies on the "sleeper effect" (Hovland & Weiss, 1951; Kelman & Hovland, 1953), have studied retention over considerable periods of time.

Some of the difference in outcome may be attributable to the types of communicators characteristically used and to the motive-incentive conditions operative in the two situations. In experimental studies communications are frequently presented in a classroom situation. This may involve quite different types of factors from those operative in the more naturalistic communication situation with which the survey researchers are concerned. In the classroom there may be some implicit sponsorship of the communication by the teacher and the school administration. In the survey studies the communicators may often be remote individuals either unfamiliar to the recipients, or outgroupers clearly known to espouse a point of view opposed to that held by many members of the audience. Thus there may be real differences in communicator credibility in laboratory and survey researches. The net effect of the differences will typically be in the direction of increasing the likelihood of change in the experimental as compared with the survey study.

There is sometimes an additional situational difference. Communications of the type studied by survey researchers usually involve reaching the individual in his natural habitat, with consequent supplementary effects produced by discussion with friends and family. In the laboratory studies a classroom situation with low postcommunication interaction is more typically involved. Several studies, including one by Harold Kelley reported in our volume on *Communication and Persuasion* (Hovland, Janis, & Kelley, 1953), indicate that, when a communication is presented in a situation which makes group membership salient, the individual is typically more resistant to counternorm influence than when the communication is presented under conditions of low salience of group membership (cf. also, Katz & Lazarsfeld, 1955, pp. 48-133).

A difference which is almost wholly adventitious is in the types of populations utilized. In the survey design there is, typically, considerable emphasis on a random sample of the entire population. In the typical experiment, on the other hand, there is a consistent overrepresentation of high school students and college sophomores, primarily on the basis of their greater accessibility. But as Tolman has said: "college sophomores may not be people." Whether differences in the type of audience studied contribute to the differences in effect obtained with the two methods is not known.

Finally, there is an extremely important difference in the studies of the experimental and correlational variety with respect to the type of issue discussed in the communications. In the typical experiment we are interested in studying a set of factors or conditions which are expected on the basis of theory to influence the extent of effect of the communication. We usually deliberately try to find types of issues involving attitudes which are susceptible to modification through communication. Otherwise, we run the risk of no measurable effects, particularly with small-scale experiments. In the survey procedures, on the other hand, socially significant attitudes which are deeply rooted in prior experience and involve much personal commitment are typically involved. This is especially true in voting studies which have provided us with so many of our present results on social influence. I shall have considerably more to say about this problem a little later.

The differences so far discussed have primarily concerned the extent of overall effectiveness indicated by the two methods: why survey results typically

show little modification of attitudes by communication while experiments indicate marked changes. Let me now turn to some of the other differences in
generalizations derived from the two alternative designs. Let me take as the
second main area of disparate results the research on the effect of varying distances between the position taken by the communicator and that held by the
recipient of the communication. Here it is a matter of comparing changes for
persons who at the outset closely agree with the communicator with those for
others who are mildy or strongly in disagreement with him. In the naturalistic
situation studied in surveys the typical procedure is to determine changes in
opinion following reported exposure to communication for individuals differing from the communicator by varying amounts. This gives rise to two possible
artifacts. When the communication is at one end of a continuum, there is little
room for improvement for those who differ from the communication by small
amounts, but a great deal of room for movement among those with large discrepancies. This gives rise to a spurious degree of positive relationship between the degree of discrepancy and the amount of change. Regression effects
will also operate in the direction of increasing the correlation. What is needed
is a situation in which the distance factor can be manipulated independently
of the subject's initial position. An attempt to set up these conditions experimentally was made in a study by Pritzker and the writer (1957). The method
involved preparing individual communications presented in booklet form
so that the position of the communicator could be set at any desired distance
from the subject's initial position. Communicators highly acceptable to the
subjects were used. A number of different topics were employed, including the

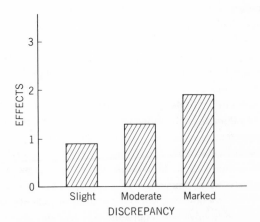

Figure 6-1. Mean opinion change score with
three degrees of discrepancy (deviation between subject's position and position advocated
in communication). [From Hovland & Pritzker, 1957]

likelihood of a cure for cancer within five years, the desirability of compulsory voting, and the adequacy of five hours of sleep per night.

The amount of change for each degree of advocated change is shown in Fig. 6-1. It will be seen that there is a fairly clear progression, such that the greater the amount of change advocated the greater the average amount of opinion change produced. Similar results have been reported by Goldberg (1954) and by French (1956).

But these results are not in line with our hunches as to what would happen in a naturalistic situation with important social issues. We felt that here other types of response than change in attitude would occur. So Muzafer Sherif, O. J. Harvey, and the writer (1957) set up a situation to simulate as closely as possible the conditions typically involved when individuals are exposed to major social issue communications at differing distances from their own position. The issue used was the desirability of prohibition. The study was done in two states (Oklahoma and Texas) where there is prohibition or local option, so that the wet-dry issue is hotly debated. We concentrated on three aspects of the problem: How favorably will the communicator be received when his position is at varying distances from that of the recipient? How will what the communicator says be perceived and interpreted by individuals at varying distances from his position? What will be the amount of opinion change produced when small and large deviations in position of communication and recipient are involved?

Three communications, one strongly wet, one strongly dry, and one moderately wet, were employed. The results bearing on the first problem, of *recep-*

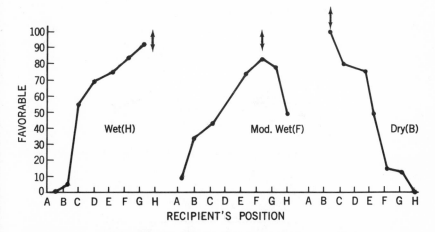

Figure 6-2. Percentage of favorable evaluation ("fair," "unbiased," etc.) of wet (H), moderately wet (F), and dry (B) communications for subjects holding various positions on prohibition. Recipients' positions range from A (very dry) to H (very wet). Position of communications indicated by arrow. [From Hovland, Harvey, & Sherif, 1957]

tion, are presented in Fig. 6-2. The positions of the subjects are indicated on the abscissa in letters from A (extreme dry) to H (strongly wet). The positions of the communication are also indicated in the same letters, *B* indicating a strongly dry communication, *H* a strongly wet, and *F* a moderately wet. Along the ordinate there is plotted the percentage of subjects with each position on the issue who described the communication as "fair" and "unbiased." It will be seen that the degree of distance between the recipient and the communicator greatly influences the evaluation of the fairness of the communication. When a communication is directed at the pro-dry position, nearly all of the dry subjects consider it fair and impartial, but only a few per cent of the wet subjects consider the identical communication fair. The reverse is true at the other end of the scale. When an intermediate position is adopted, the percentages fall off sharply on each side. Thus under the present conditions with a relatively ambiguous communicator one of the ways of dealing with strongly discrepant positions is to *discredit* the communicator, considering him unfair and biased.

A second way in which an individual can deal with discrepancy is by distortion of what is said by the communicator. Thus is a phenomenon extensively studied by Cooper and Jahoda (1947). In the present study, subjects were asked to state what position they thought was taken by the communicator on the prohibition question. Their evaluation of his position could then be analyzed in relation to their own position. These results are shown in Fig. 6-3 for the moderately wet communication. It will be observed that there is a tendency for

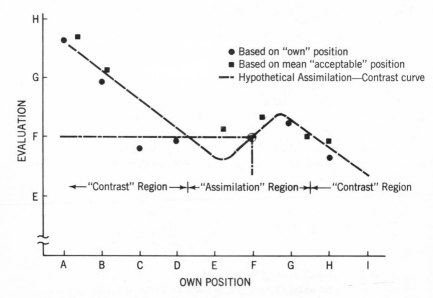

Figure 6-3. Average placement of position of moderately wet communication (F) by subjects holding various positions on the issue, plotted against hypothetical assimilation-contrast curve. [From Hovland, Harvey, & Sherif. 1957]

individuals whose position is close to that of the communicator to report on the communicator's position quite accurately, for individuals a little bit removed to report his position to be substantially more like their own (which we call an "assimilation effect"), and for those with more discrepant positions to report the communicator's position as more extreme than it really was. This we refer to as a "contrast effect."

Now to our primary results on opinion change. It was found that individuals whose position was only slightly discrepant from the communicator's were influenced to a greater extent than those whose positions deviated to a larger extent. When a wet position was espoused, 28% of the middle-of-the-road subjects were changed in the direction of the communicator, as compared with only 4% of the drys. With the dry communication 14% of the middle-of-the-roaders were changed, while only 4% of the wets were changed. Thus, more of the subjects with small discrepancies were changed than were those with large discrepancies.

These results appear to indicate that, under conditions when there is some ambiguity about the credibility of the communicator and when the subject is deeply involved with the issue, the greater the attempt at change the higher the resistance. On the other hand, with highly respected communicators, as in the previous study with Pritzker using issues of lower involvement, the greater the discrepancy the greater the effect. A study related to ours has just been completed by Zimbardo (1959) which indicates that, when an influence attempt is made by a strongly positive communicator (i.e., a close personal friend), the greater the discrepancy the greater the opinion change, even when the experimenter made a point of stressing the great importance of the subject's opinion.

The implication of these results for our primary problem of conflicting results is clear. The types of issues with which most experiments deal are relatively uninvolving and are often of the variety where expert opinion is highly relevant, as for example, on topics of health, science, and the like. Here we should expect that opinion would be considerably affected by communications and furthermore that advocacy of positions quite discrepant from the individual's own position would have a marked effect. On the other hand, the types of issues most often utilized in survey studies are ones which are very basic and involve deep commitment. As a consequence small changes in opinion due to communication would be expected. Here communication may have little effect on those who disagree at the outset and function merely to strengthen the position already held, in line with survey findings.

A third area of research in which somewhat discrepant results are obtained by the experimental and survey methods is in the role of order of presentation. From naturalistic studies the generalization has been widely adopted that primacy is an extremely important factor in persuasion. Numerous writers have reported that what we experience first has a critical role in what we believe. This is particularly stressed in studies of propaganda effects in various countries when the nation getting across its message first is alleged to have a great advantage and in commercial advertising where "getting a beat on the field" is stressed. The importance of primacy in political propaganda is indicated in the following quotation from Doob:

> The propagandist scores an initial advantage whenever his propaganda reaches people before that of his rivals. Readers or listeners are then biased to comprehend, forever after, the event as it has been initially portrayed to them. If they are told in a headline or a flash that the battle has been won, the criminal has been caught, or the bill is certain to pass the legislature, they will usually expect subsequent information to substantiate this first impression. When later facts prove otherwise, they may be loath to abandon what they believe to be true until perhaps the evidence becomes overwhelming (Doob, 1948, pp. 421-422).

A recent study by Katz and Lazarsfeld (1955) utilizing the survey method compares the extent to which respondents attribute major impact on their decisions about fashions and movie attendance to the presentations to which they were first exposed. Strong primacy effects are shown in their analyses of the data.

We have ourselves recently completed a series of experiments oriented toward this problem. These are reported in our new monograph on *Order of Presentation in Persuasion* (Hovland, Mandell, Campbell, Brock, Luchins, Cohen, McGuire, Janis, Feierabend, & Anderson, 1957). We find that primacy is often *not* a very significant factor when the relative effectiveness of the first side of an issue is compared experimentally with that of the second. The research suggests that differences in design may account for much of the discrepancy. A key variable is whether there is exposure to both sides or whether only one side is actually received. In naturalistic studies the advantage of the first side is often not only that it is first but that it is often then the only side of the issue to which the individual is exposed. Having once been influenced, many individuals make up their mind and are no longer interested in other communications on the issue. In most experiments on order of presentation, on the other hand, the audience is systematically exposed to both sides. Thus under survey conditions, self-exposure tends to increase the impact of primacy.

Two other factors to which I have already alluded appear significant in determining the amount of primacy effect. One is the nature of the communicator, the other the setting in which the communication is received. In our volume Luchins presents results indicating that, when the same communicator presents contradictory material, the point of view read first has more influence. On the other hand, Mandell and I show that, when two different communicators present opposing views successively, little primacy effect is obtained. The communications setting factor operates similarly. When the issue and the conditions of presentation make clear that the points of view are controversial, little primacy is obtained.

Thus in many of the situations with which there had been great concern as to undesirable effects of primacy, such as in legal trials, election campaigns, and political debate, the role of primacy appears to have been exaggerated, since the conditions there are those least conducive to primacy effects: the issue is clearly defined as controversial, the partisanship of the communicator is usually established, and different communicators present the opposing sides.

Time does not permit me to discuss other divergences in results obtained in survey and experimental studies, such as those concerned with the effects of repetition of presentation, the relationship between level of intelligence and susceptibility to attitude change, or the relative impact of mass media and personal influence. Again, however, I am sure that detailed analysis will reveal differential factors at work which can account for the apparent disparity in the generalizations derived.

Integration

On the basis of the foregoing survey of results I reach the conclusion that no contradiction has been established between the data provided by experimental and correlational studies. Instead it appears that the seeming divergence can be satisfactorily accounted for on the basis of a different definition of the communication situation (including the phenomenon of self-selection) and differences in the type of communicator, audience, and kind of issue utilized.

But there remains the task of better integrating the findings associated with the two methodologies. This is a problem closely akin to that considered by the members of the recent Social Science Research Council summer seminar on *Narrowing the Gap Between Field Studies and Laboratory Studies in Social Psychology* (Riecken, 1954). Many of their recommendations are pertinent to our present problem.

What seems to me quite apparent is that a genuine understanding of the effects of communications on attitudes requires both the survey and the experimental methodologies. At the same time there appear to be certain inherent limitations of each method which must be understood by the researcher if he is not to be blinded by his preoccupation with one or the other type of design. Integration of the two methodologies will require on the part of the experimentalist an awareness of the narrowness of the laboratory in interpreting the larger and more comprehensive effects of communication. It will require on the part of the survey researcher a greater awareness of the limitations of the correlational method as a basis for establishing causal relationships.

The framework within which survey research operates is most adequately and explicitly dealt with by Berelson, Lazarsfeld, and McPhee in their book on *Voting* (1954). The model which they use, taken over by them from the economist Tinbergen, is reproduced in the top half of Fig. 6-4. For comparison, the model used by experimentalists is presented in the lower half of the figure. It will be seen that the model used by the survey researcher, particularly when he employs the "panel" method, stresses the large number of simultaneous and interacting influences affecting attitudes and opinions. Even more significant is its provision for a variety of "feedback" phenomena in which

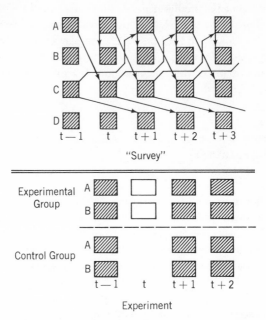

Figure 6-4. Top Half: "Process analysis" schema used in panel research. (Successive time intervals are indicated along abscissa. Letters indicate the variables under observation. Arrows represent relations between the variables.) From Berelson, Lazarsfeld, & McPhee, 1954. Bottom Half: Design of experimental research. (Letters on vertical axis again indicate variables being measured. Unshaded box indicates experimentally manipulated treatment and blanks indicate the absence of such treatment. Time periods indicated as in top half of chart.)

consequences wrought by previous influences affect processes normally considered as occurring earlier in the sequence. The various types of interaction are indicated by the placement of arrows showing direction of effect. In contrast the experimentalist frequently tends to view the communication process as one in which some single manipulative variable is the primary determinant of the subsequent attitude change. He is, of course, aware in a general way of the importance of context, and he frequently studies interaction effects as well as main effects; but he still is less attentive than he might be to the complexity of the influence situation and the numerous possibilities for feedback loops. Undoubtedly the real life communication situation is better described in terms of the survey type of model. We are all familiar, for example, with the interactions in which attitudes predispose one to acquire certain types of information, that this often leads to changes in attitude which may result in further acquisition of knowledge, which in turn produces more attitude change, and so on. Certainly the narrow question sometimes posed by experiments as to the effect of knowledge on attitudes greatly underestimates these interactive effects.

But while the conceptualization of the survey researcher is often very valuable, his correlational research design leaves much to be desired. Advocates of correlational analysis often cite the example of a science built on observation exclusively without experiment: astronomy. But here a very limited number of space-time concepts are involved and the number of competing theoretical formulations is relatively small so that it is possible to limit alternative theories rather drastically through correlational evidence. But in the area of communication effects and social psychology generally the variables are so numerous and so intertwined that the correlational methodology is primarily useful to suggest hypotheses and not to establish causal relationships (Hovland et al., 1949, pp. 329-340; Maccoby, 1956). Even with the much simpler relationships involved in biological systems there are grave difficulties of which we are all aware these days when we realize how difficult it is to establish through correlation whether eating of fats is or is not a cause of heart disease or whether or not smoking is a cause of lung cancer. In communications research the complexity of the problem makes it inherently difficult to derive causal relationships from correlational analysis where experimental control of exposure is not possible. And I do not agree with my friends the Lazarsfelds (Kendall & Lazarsfeld, 1950) concerning the effectiveness of the panel method in circumventing this problem since parallel difficulties are raised when the relationships occur over a time span.

These difficulties constitute a challenge to the experimentalist in this area of research to utilize the broad framework for studying communication effects suggested by the survey researcher, but to employ well controlled experimental design to work on those aspects of the field which are amenable to experimental manipulation and control. It is, of course, apparent that there are important communication problems which cannot be attacked directly by experimental methods. It is not, for example, feasible to modify voting behavior by manipulation of the issues discussed by the opposed parties during a particular campaign. It is not feasible to assess the effects of communications over a very long span of time. For example, one cannot visualize experimental procedures for answering the question of what has been the impact of the reading of *Das Kapital* or *Uncle Tom's Cabin*. These are questions which can be illuminated by historical and sociological study but cannot be evaluated in any rigorous experimental fashion.

But the scope of problems which do lend themselves to experimental attack is very broad. Even complex interactions can be fruitfully attacked by experiment. The possibilities are clearly shown in studies like that of Sherif and Sherif (1953) on factors influencing cooperative and competitive behavior in a camp for adolescent boys. They were able to bring under manipulative control many of the types of interpersonal relationships ordinarily considered impossible to modify experimentally, and to develop motivations of an intensity characteristic of real-life situations. It should be possible to do similar studies in the communication area with a number of the variables heretofore only investigated in uncontrolled naturalistic settings by survey procedures.

In any case it appears eminently practical to minimize many of the differences which were discussed above as being not inherent in design but more or less adventitiously linked with one or the other method. Thus there is no reason why more complex and deeply-involving social issues cannot be employed in experiments rather than the more superficial ones more commonly used. The resistance to change of socially important issues may be a handicap in studying certain types of attitude change; but, on the other hand, it is important to understand the lack of modifiability of opinion with highly-involving issues. Greater representation of the diverse types of communicators found in naturalistic situations can also be achieved. In addition, it should be possible to do experiments with a wider range of populations to reduce the possibility that many of our present generalizations from experiments are unduly affected by their heavy weighting of college student characteristics, including high literacy, alertness, and rationality.

A more difficult task is that of experimentally evaluating communications under conditions of self-selection of exposure. But this is not at all impossible in theory. It should be possible to assess what demographic and personality factors predispose one to expose oneself to particular communications and then to utilize experimental and control groups having these characteristics. Under some circumstances the evaluation could be made on only those who select themselves, with both experimental and control groups coming from the self-selected audience.

Undoubtedly many of the types of experiments which could be set up involving or simulating naturalistic conditions will be too ambitious and costly to be feasible even if possible in principle. This suggests the continued use of small-scale experiments which seek to isolate some of the key variables operative in complex situations. From synthesis of component factors, prediction of complex outcomes may be practicable. It is to this analytic procedure for narrowing the gap between laboratory and field research that we have devoted major attention in our research program. I will merely indicate briefly here some of the ties between our past work and the present problem.

We have attempted to assess the influence of the communicator by varying his expertness and attractiveness, as in the studies by Kelman, Weiss, and the writer (Hovland & Weiss, 1951; Kelman & Hovland, 1953). Further data on this topic were presented earlier in this paper.

We have also been concerned with evaluating social interaction effects. Some of the experiments on group affiliation as a factor affecting resistance to counternorm communication and the role of salience of group membership by Hal Kelley and others are reported in *Communication and Persuasion* (Hovland et al., 1953).

Starting with the studies carried out during the war on orientation films by Art Lumsdaine, Fred Sheffield, and the writer (1949), we have had a strong interest in the duration of communication effects. Investigation of effects at various time intervals has helped to bridge the gap between assessment of immediate changes with those of longer duration like those involved in survey studies. More recent extensions of this work have indicated the close relationship between the credibility of the communicator and the extent of postcommunication increments, or "sleeper effects" (Hovland & Weiss, 1951; Kelman & Hovland, 1953).

The nature of individual differences in susceptibility to persuasion via communication has been the subject of a number of our recent studies. The generality of persuasibility has been investigated by Janis and collaborators and the development of persuasibility in children has been studied by Abelson and Lesser. A volume concerned with these audience factors to which Janis, Abelson, Lesser, Field, Rife, King, Cohen, Linton, Graham, and the writer have contributed will appear under the title *Personality and Persuasibility* (1959).

Lastly, there remains the question on how the nature of the issues used in the communication affects the extent of change in attitude. We have only made a small beginning on these problems. In the research reported in *Experiments on Mass Communication*, we showed that the magnitude of effects was directly related to the type of attitude involved: film communications had a significant effect on opinions related to straightforward interpretations of policies and events, but had little or no effect on more deeply intrenched attitudes and motivations. Further work on the nature of issues is represented in the study by Sherif, Harvey, and the writer (1957) which was discussed above. There we found a marked contrast between susceptibility to influence and the amount of ego-involvement in the issue. But the whole concept of ego-involvement is a fuzzy one, and here is an excellent area for further work seeking to determine the theoretical factors involved in different types of issues.

With this brief survey of possible ways to bridge the gap between experiment and survey I must close. I should like to stress in summary the mutual importance of the two approaches to the problem of communication effectiveness. Neither is a royal road to wisdom, but each represents an important emphasis. The challenge of future work is one of fruitfully combining their virtues so that we may develop a social psychology of communication with the conceptual breadth provided by correlational study of process and with the rigorous but more delimited methodology of the experiment.

References

BERELSON, B. R., LAZARSFELD, P. F., & McPHEE, W. N. *Voting: A Study of Opinion Formation in a Presidential Campaign.* Chicago, Univer. Chicago Press, 1954.

COOPER, EUNICE, & JAHODA, MARIE. "The Evasion of Propaganda: How Prejudiced People Respond to Antiprejudice Propaganda." *J. Psychol.,* 1947, 23, 15-25.

DOOB, L. W. *Public Opinion and Propaganda.* New York, Holt, 1948.

FRENCH, J. R. P., JR. "A Formal Theory of Social Power." *Psychol. Rev.,* 1956, 63, 181-194.

GOLDBERG, S. C. "Three Situational Determinants of Conformity to Social Norms." *J. Abnorm. Soc. Psychol.,* 1954, 49, 325-329.

GOSNELL, H. F. *Getting Out the Vote: An Experiment in the Stimulation of Voting.* Chicago, Univer. Chicago Press, 1927.

HOVLAND, C. I. "Effects of the Mass Media of Communication." In G. LINDZEY (Ed.), *Handbook of Social Psychology.* Vol. II. *Special Fields and Applications.* Cambridge, Mass.: Addison-Wesley, 1954. Pp. 1062-1103.

HOVLAND, C. I., HARVEY, O. J., & SHERIF, M. "Assimilation and Contrast Effects in Reactions to Communication and Attitude Change." *J. Abnorm. Soc. Psychol.,* 1957, 55, 244-252.

HOVLAND, C. I., JANIS, I. L., & KELLEY, H. H. *Communication and Persuasion.* New Haven, Yale Univer. Press, 1953.

HOVLAND, C. I., LUMSDAINE, A. A., & SHEFFIELD, F. D. *Experiments on Mass Communication.* Princeton, Princeton Univer. Press, 1949.

HOVLAND, C. I., MANDELL, W., CAMPBELL, ENID H., BROCK, T., LUCHINS, A. S. COHEN, A. R., McGUIRE, W. J., JANIS, I. L., FEIERABEND, ROSALIND L., & ANDERSON, N. H. *The Order of Presentation in Persuasion.* New Haven, Yale Univer. Press, 1957.

HOVLAND, C. I., & PRITZKER, H. A. "Extent of Opinion Change as a Function of Amount of Change Advocated." *J. Abnorm. Soc. Psychol.,* 1957, 54, 257-261.

HOVLAND, C. I., & WEISS, W. "The Influence of Source Credibility on Communication Effectiveness." *Publ. Opin. Quart.,* 1951, 15, 635-650.

JANIS, I. L., HOVLAND, C. I., FIELD, P. B., LINTON, HARRIETT, GRAHAM, ELAINE, COHEN, A. R., RIFE, D., ABELSON, R. P., LESSER, G. S., & KING, B. T. *Personality and Persuasibility.* New Haven, Yale Univer. Press, 1959.

KATZ, E., & LAZARSFELD, P. F. *Personal Influence.* Glencoe, Ill., Free Press, 1955.

KELMAN, H. C., & HOVLAND, C. I. " 'Reinstatement' of the Communicator in Delayed Measurement of Opinion Change." *J. Abnorm. Soc. Psychol.,* 1953, 48, 327-335.

KENDALL, PATRICIA L., & LAZARSFELD, P. F. "Problems of Survey Analysis." In R. K. MERTON & P. F. LAZARSFELD (Eds.), *Continuities in Social Research: Studies in the Scope and Method of "The American Soldier."* Glencoe, Ill., Free Press, 1950. Pp. 133-196.

KLAPPER, J. T. *The Effects of Mass Media.* New York, Columbia Univer. Bureau of Applied Social Research, 1949. (Mimeo.)

LAZARSFELD, P. F., BERELSON, B., & GAUDET, HAZEL. *The People's Choice.* New York, Duell, Sloan, & Pearce, 1944.

LIPSET, S. M., LAZARSFELD, P. F., BARTON, A. H., & LINZ, J. "The Psychology of Voting: An Analysis of Political Behavior." In G. LINDZEY (Ed.), *Handbook of Social Psychology*. Vol. II. *Special Fields and Applications*. Cambridge, Mass., Addison-Wesley, 1954. Pp. 1124-1175.

MACCOBY, ELEANOR E. "Pitfalls in the Analysis of Panel Data: A Research Note on Some Technical Aspects of Voting." *Amer. J. Sociol.*, 1956, 59, 359-362.

RIECKEN, H. W. (Chairman). "Narrowing the Gap Between Field Studies and Laboratory Experiments in Social Psychology: A Statement by the Summer Seminar." *Items Soc. Sci. Res. Council*, 1954, 8, 37-42.

SHERIF, M., & SHERIF, CAROLYN W. *Groups in Harmony and Tension: An Integration of Studies on Intergroup Relations*. New York, Harper, 1953.

ZIMBARDO, P. G. "Involvement and Communication Discrepancy as Determinants of Opinion Change." Unpublished doctoral dissertation, Yale University, 1959.

7

Message Exaggeration
by the Receiver

MAX WALES,
GALEN RARICK,
and HAL DAVIS

Much discussion—and some research—has been devoted to the problem of message distortion by the communicator, whether he be newspaper reporter, advertising copywriter or broadcaster. Interest has often centered on distortion in the direction of exaggeration or sensationalism, and discussion usually revolves around the biases, predispositions and motives of the communicator.

As early as 1870, a critic wrote that "If we could only have newspapers which simply professed to give the news, we might begin to get some glimmering of truth from them. . . . Distortion of perspective is what some of the gentlemen who conduct the daily press seem to consider their charter of success."[1]

As recently as the spring of 1962, Greenberg and Tannenbaum reported that communicator accuracy is related to cognitive stress. That is, when journalism students had to write stories about a faculty committee report, they made more errors when the report was contrary to their biases and predispositions than they did when the report supported them. Furthermore, substantively the message distortion was in the direction of supporting the communicators.[2]

These are but two of the many articles in which communicator errors have been examined or decried. On the other hand, relatively few observers have concerned themselves with the possibility that the message may tend to suffer the same sort of distortion from the receiver as it does from the sender,

Reprinted from *Journalism Quarterly* (Summer, 1963), pp. 339-342, by permission of the authors and publisher.

[1]A. G. Sedgewick, Editorial in the *Nation*, 10:34 (Jan. 27, 1870).

[2]Bradley S. Greenberg and Persy H. Tannenbaum, "Communicator Performance under Cognitive Stress," JOURNALISM QUARTERLY, 39:169-78 (Spring 1962).

i.e., the extent and direction of distortion are dependent upon the needs and predispositions of the communicator *and* the audience.

In other words, most of the literature on the mass media dealing with message exaggeration has examined *what encoders do to messages;* it is suggested here that it should also be helpful to examine *what decoders do to messages.*

Hastorf and Cantril,[3] Cooper and Jahoda,[4] and Hyman and Sheatsley[5] have provided data on perceptual processes which support this line of reasoning. Hastorf and Cantril found that college students err in their perception of a football game film in keeping with their biases. Cooper and Jahoda found that prejudiced people tend to react to antiprejudice propaganda by evading the message or by distorting it to make it consistent with, or at least not contrary to, their prejudices. Hyman and Sheatsley present evidence in support of their theory that a person's perception and memory of messages are often dependent upon his wishes, motives and attitudes.

It follows then that in developing a hypothesis concerning message distortion by the receiver, one should take into account the needs and predispositions of audiences.

Studies of media consumption have frequently shown that a majority of people spend a great deal of time attending to fantasy or escapist fare. Klapper devoted an entire chapter to the research literature concerning audience consumption of and addiction to what he called "escapism."[6]

The evidence presented by Klapper seems to indicate that one reason people attend to such fare is that they need drama and excitement in their lives. That is, they are predisposed to "escape" from dull, frustrating circumstances. Consequently, it is postulated in this study that one way a person can fulfill the need for drama and excitement is to invest the messages he receives with these qualities by exaggerating their contents.

An experiment was designed to test the following hypothesis: *More people will exaggerate messages they receive than will minimize them.*

If this hypothesis is correct, it means that when people recall the content of a communication, they will not make random errors. Instead, more of them will commit errors in the direction of exaggeration than in the direction of minimization. It should be noted that this hypothesis does not predict the frequency or proportion of error but rather stipulates the predominant direction of error when it occurs.

[3]A. H. Hastorf and H. Cantril, "They Saw a Game: A Case Study," *Journal of Abnormal and Social Psychology,* 49:129-34 (1954).

[4]E. Cooper and M. Jahoda, "The Evasion of Propaganda," *Journal of Psychology,* 23:15-25 (1947).

[5]H. Hyman and P. Sheatsley, "Some Reasons Why Information Campaigns Fail," *Public Opinion Quarterly,* 11:412-23 (1947).

[6]J. T. Klapper, *The Effects of Mass Communication* (Glencoe, Ill.: Free Press, 1960), Chapter VII, "The Effects of Escapist Media Material."

The Study Design

The subjects for this experiment were 39 sophomores and juniors attending a college course in advertising. An "after-only" design was utilized.

At the beginning of the experiment, the subjects were told merely that it was desired that they read "some copy." The regular instructor was absent, and the students had been informed that they were to have a guest lecturer. Each student was given three pieces of copy to read, with the order of presentation being systematically rotated. One piece of copy was a fictitious news release from the university concerning recommendations that the academic requirements of the university be made more rigorous. The other two were advertisements: one for a certain type of kitchen sink and the other for an Oriental air line.

Immediately after the subjects had read the copy, they were given a multiple-choice recall test. There were five questions about the news release, two about the kitchen sink advertisement, and one about the air line copy. The ordering of these questions was systematically rotated.

Three possible answers were provided for each question, and the subject was asked to check the correct ones. Only one answer for each question was correct, i.e., repeated a statement of fact from the copy. Another answer exaggerated that statement, and the third minimized it. The order of these three possible answers was also systematically rotated throughout the test. Following are the findings and analysis of the study.

Findings and Analysis

On the recall test, 254 (81.7%) of the 311 responses were correct. (One of the 39 subjects failed to respond to one of the eight items.) Since this test was given immediately after the copy was read, it is not surprising that so many of the answers were correct. However, the question remains: When errors were made, did more subjects exaggerate the message than minimize it?

A net score was computed for each subject by assigning a value of 0 to a correct answer, -1 to a minimization, and $+1$ to an exaggeration. This meant that the possible range of net scores was from -8 to $+8$. However, the obtained range, as shown in Table 7-1, was from -2 to $+4$.

Table 7-1. Distribution of net scores on recall test for all 39 subjects.

Net score	−2	−1	0	+1	+2	+3	+4
Frequency	2	4	13	11	6	2	1

Out of a total of 57 error responses, 41 were exaggerations and only 16 were minimizations. Nine of the subjects made no errors, and four others made "balanced" errors, i.e., there was a minimization for each exaggeration. Consequently, 26 subjects committed net error in one direction or the other. Of these, 20 had net positive (exaggeration) scores, while only six had net negative (minimization) scores.

If people are as likely to minimize as they are to exaggerate messages received, one would predict that out of the 26 scores which were not zero, 13 would be positive and 13 would be negative. Consequently, a Chi Square test was employed to see if the obtained distribution differed significantly from these figures. Obviously, the difference is in the hypothesized direction. The Chi Square value of 7.54 with one degree of freedom is significant at well beyond the .005 level by one-tailed test. So, in this experiment, when the receivers of messages made recall errors, there was a highly significant tendency to exaggerate rather than minimize.

There is the possibility, of course, that the bias was in the measuring instrument rather than in the subjects. That is, it may be that the multiple-choice items were such that it was "psychologically easier" to make an exaggerated error than it was to make a minimized one. However, the experimenters attempted to make the two error alternatives to each item equally plausible, and it is suggested that a more definite answer to this question could be provided by added research.

Such studies might also attempt to answer such questions as: What are the educational, sociological, and psychological characteristics of people who tend to exaggerate messages received as contrasted to those of people who tend to minimize them and to those of people who tend to do neither? Are people more likely to exaggerate messages which are threatening or potentially punishing to them than they are to exaggerate messages which are comforting or potentially rewarding? Can certain techniques of writing be employed to reduce greatly the exaggeration of a message by a receiver?

Summary and Discussion

Many observers have concerned themselves with the problem of exaggeration by the communicator. Relatively few, however, have considered the matter of exaggeration of a message by the receiver. There is much research evidence that many people are addicted to escapist or fantasy fare in the mass media. Consequently, it was inferred that there is a need for drama or excitement, and that this predisposition will tend to lead to exaggeration when errors are made in the recall of a message.

In this experiment, students read some copy and were immediately given a multiple-choice recall test. It was found that significantly more students committed error in the direction of exaggeration than committed error in the direction of minimization even though most of the responses were correct.

It can be inferred from the results of this experiment that in the communication process, the tendency toward exaggeration may be as much a part of decoding as it is a part of encoding. It is suggested that research might make it possible to specify the type of personality most likely to exaggerate and the conditions under which exaggeration is most likely to occur.

For the journalist, there are implications that in addition to trying to avoid making exaggerated statements, he should attempt to find ways of writing that will reduce exaggeration by his audience. Perhaps the skillful use of intentional redundancy would be one of them.

8

Behavioral Support
for Opinion Change

LEON FESTINGER

The last three decades have seen a steady and impressive growth in our knowledge concerning attitudes and opinions—how they are formed, how they are changed, and their relations to one another. For example, we now know a good deal about the effects on opinion change of varying the structure of a persuasive communication—whether it is one-sided or two-sided, whether it is fear-arousing or not, whether pro arguments precede or follow con arguments, and whether it is attributed to trustworthy or untrustworthy sources. Phenomena such as sleeper effects, immunization to counterpropaganda, assimilation and contrast effects, are beginning to be understood. We have also learned a great deal about attitude and opinion change in small face-to-face groups, about the relationship between personality variables and opinion change, about factors affecting resistance to persuasive communications, and so on. I do not intend to review seriously all this work. Anyone who wants to has only to start looking for the names of Hovland, Janis, Kelley, McGuire, Newcomb, Katz, Peak, Kelman—there are many others but these would do for a start.

There is, however, one important gap in our knowledge about attitude and opinion change—a gap that is doubly peculiar when seen in relation to the strong behavioral emphasis in psychology in the United States. I first realized the existence of this gap on reading a manuscript by Arthur R. Cohen. Let me read to you the paragraph that startled me. Cohen's manuscript focuses on the ". . . ways in which persuasive communicators and members of one's social group come to influence the attitudes of the individual." In his concluding remarks he says:

> Probably the most important and long-range research problem in the sphere of attitude theory has to do with the implications of attitude change for subsequent behavior. In general, most of the researchers whose work we have examined make the widespread psychological as-

Reprinted from *Public Opinion Quarterly* (Fall, 1964), pp. 404-417.

sumption that since attitudes are evaluative predispositions, they have consequences for the way people act toward others, for the programs they actually carry out and the manner in which they perform these programs. Thus attitudes are always seen to be a precursor to behavior, a determinant of what behaviors the individual will actually go about doing in his daily affairs. However, though most psychologists assume such a state of affairs, very little work on attitude change has explicitly dealt with the behavior that may follow upon a change in attitudes. Most researchers in this field are content to demonstrate that there are factors which affect attitude change and that these factors are open to orderly exploration, without actually carrying through to the point where they examine the links between changed attitudes and changes in learning, performance, perception and interaction. Until a good deal more experimental investigation demonstrates that attitude change has implications for subsequent behavior, we cannot be certain that our change procedures do anything more than cause cognitive realignments, or even, perhaps, that the attitude concept has any critical significance whatever for psychology.[1]

I was, at first reading, slightly skeptical about the assertion that there is a dearth of studies relating attitude or opinion change to behavior. Although I could not think of any offhand, it seemed reasonable that many of them would be scattered through the journals. Consequently, I started looking for such studies and asked others if they knew of any. After prolonged search, with the help of many others, I succeeded in locating only three relevant studies, one of which is of dubious relevance and one of which required re-analysis of data. The absence of research, and of theoretical thinking, about the effect of attitude change on subsequent behavior is indeed astonishing.

Before telling you about these three studies I would like to make sure that the problem is clear. I am not raising the question of whether or not attitudes are found to relate to relevant behavior. Let us accept the conclusion that they are related, at least to some extent, although even here relatively few studies in the literature address themselves to this question. A fairly recent study by De Fleur and Westie provides a good example of the kind of relationship between existing attitudes and relevant overt behavior that may be found under controlled conditions with good measurement.[2]

The investigators obtained measures of attitudes toward Negroes from 250 college students. The particular attitude measure employed was apparently reliable, test-retest measures over a five-week interval yielding a correlation of +.96. They selected, from these 250 students, 23 who had scored in the upper quartile and 23 who had scored in the lower quartile, matching the two groups on a number of other variables. These two extreme groups were then compared on a rather clever measure of overt behavior with respect to Negroes. A situation was constructed in which it was believable to ask each of them to sign an

---

[1]Arthur R. Cohen, *Attitude Change and Social Influence*, New York, Basic Books [1964].

[2]M. L. De Fleur and F. R. Westie, "Verbal Attitudes and Overt Act: An Experiment on the Salience of Attitudes," *American Sociological Review*, Vol. 23, 1958, pp. 667-673.

authorization permitting use of a photograph of himself sitting with a Negro. The subject was free not to permit the photograph to be taken at all, or, if he signed the authorization, to permit any of a number of possible uses of the photograph ranging from very limited use in laboratory experiments to, at the other extreme, use in a nationwide publicity campaign. The signing of the authorization was real, and may be regarded as an instance of overt commitment. As the authors say: "In American society, the affixing of one's signature to a document is a particularly significant act. The signing of checks, contracts, agreements, and the like is clearly understood to indicate a binding obligation on the part of the signer to abide by the provisions of the document."

What, then, is the relationship found between the measure of general attitudes toward Negroes and the behavioral measure? Table 8-1 presents a summary of the data. Clearly, there is a relationship between the attitude and the behavior. Those who are prejudiced are less willing to have the photograph taken and widely used. True, it is a relatively small relationship, although highly significant statistically. The smallness of the relationship is emphasized when we recall that we are comparing extreme groups. But nevertheless, it is comforting to know that a relation does exist. One can understand the smallness of the relationship by realizing that overt behavior is affected by many other variables in addition to one's own private attitude.

Table 8-1. Relationship between race attitudes and level of signed agreement to be photographed with Negro.

Signed Level of Agreement	Prejudiced Group	Unprejudiced Group
Below mean	18	9
Above mean	5	14

But data such as these do not answer the question we wish to raise here. The fact that existing attitudes relate to overt behavior does not tell us whether or not an attitude *change* brought about by exposure to a persuasive communication will be reflected in a *change* in subsequent behavior. To answer this question we need studies in which, after people have been exposed to a persuasive communication, a measure of attitude or opinion is obtained on the basis of which attitude change can be assessed. Such studies must also, some time later, provide an indication of behavior change relevant to the opinion or attitude, so that one can see whether the cognitive change had any effect on subsequent behavior. We may even be content with studies in which overt behavior is not actually observed. If the subjects are asked questions about what they actually did, this may suffice.

As I mentioned before, we were able to locate only three studies reasonably close to meeting these requirements. One of these, the data from which I reanalyzed, was part of a larger series of studies conducted by Maccoby et al.[3] These investigators selected a sample of mothers whose only child was between three and twelve months old. Each of these mothers was interviewed and was asked, among other questions, at what age she believed toilet training of the child should begin. Three weeks later, each of these women was again interviewed. This time, however, two different procedures were followed. Half the mothers, selected at random, were designated as a control group and were simply re-interviewed. In this second interview they were again asked the age at which they thought toilet training of the child should begin. The other half of the sample, the experimental group, were first exposed to a persuasive communication and then re-interviewed with the same interview used in the control group. The persuasive communication was a specially prepared, illustrated pamphlet entitled "When to Toilet Train Your Child." Each mother in the experimental group was handed this pamphlet and asked to read it, then and there, while the interviewer waited. The pamphlet argued strongly for starting toilet training at the age of twenty-four months. The re-interview occurred immediately after the mother had read the pamphlet. Thus, a comparison of the results of the two groups on the first and second interviews indicated how successful the pamphlet was in changing their opinion concerning when toilet training should start.

In order to assess the persistence of the change in opinion brought about by the pamphlet, both groups of mothers were again interviewed about six months later and were again asked at what age they thought toilet training should begin. Finally, and most importantly for our present concern, about a year after the initial interviews, on the assumption that most of the mothers would have started toilet training already, they were interviewed again and asked at *what age they had actually started.* This last may certainly be regarded as a simple, and probably truthful, report of their actual behavior. Consequently, one can look at the relationship between attitude change and behavior.

In any study in which people are interviewed and re-interviewed over a period of a year, there is an inevitable attrition. Some mothers left the area, others simply could not be reached for one or another interview, and the like. Actually, in this study the drop-out rate was remarkably small. About 80 per cent of the initial sample was actually interviewed all four times, 45 mothers in the experimental group and 47 mothers in the control group. At the time of the fourth interview 34 mothers in each of the two groups had begun toilet training their child and, consequently, it is only for these 68 mothers that we have a measure of actual behavior. The other 24 mothers (11 in the experimental group and 13 in the control group) who had not yet started toilet training by the time of the last interview were asked when they intended to start. Although for these we cannot say that we have a measure of actual behavior, we will present the results for them also.

[3]N. Maccoby, A. K. Romney, J. S. Adams, and Eleanor E. Maccoby, *"Critical Periods" in Seeking and Accepting Information,* Paris-Stanford Studies in Communication, Stanford, Calif., Institute for Communication Research, 1962.

First, however, let us look at the data presented in Table 8-2 for those who had started toilet training. The data are rather startling to contemplate—although perhaps not too startling. It is clear that the persuasive communication was quite effective in immediately changing the opinions of the mothers in the experimental group. The change, on the average, was to advocate toilet training 2.3 months later than on the initial interview. The control group did not change materially—actually moving slightly in the direction of advocating earlier toilet training.

Table 8-2. Attitude change and behavior of mothers who had started with respect to toilet training (data in months)

	Control (N = 34)	Experimental (N = 34)
Immediate opinion change (Interview 2—Interview 1)	−0.2	+2.3
Delayed opinion change (Interview 3—Interview 1)	+0.8	+1.6
Effect of opinion change on behavior (Interview 4—Interview 1)	+2.0	+1.2

Six months later the change was still maintained, although somewhat reduced in magnitude. The experimental group still advocated that toilet training begin 1.6 months later than they had on the initial interview. The control group, however, also now advocated somewhat later toilet training. Nevertheless, there was still a clear difference between the two groups.

When we examine when these mothers actually started to toilet train their child, however, we are met with a surprise. There is, if anything, a reverse relationship between attitude change and behavior. The mothers in the experimental group actually started toilet training 1.2 months later on the average then they had initially advocated. But the mothers in the control group, who had never been subjected to any experimental persuasive communication to change their opinion, started toilet training 2.0 months later than their initial opinion would have indicated. Apparently, in the usual American home, as the child gets older, events conspire to delay toilet training somewhat beyond what the mothers think is probably desirable. But the opinion change in the experimental group clearly did not carry over to affect behavior.

We can also see evidence of the same thing in the data for those mothers who had not as yet started to toilet train their children at the time of the fourth interview. These are presented in Table 8-3. Here again it is clear that the persuasive communication had a strong immediate effect on the opinions of the mothers in the experimental group and that, six months later, this effect had been maintained. The difference between the control and the experimental groups was almost as large after six months as it was immediately after the persuasive communication. It is also clear that events conspired to make these mothers delay the actual onset of toilet training and conspired equally for both groups. The changed opinion had no effect on the actual behavior of these mothers. The difference between their initial opinion and their intention at the time of the fourth interview was high because these data are for a selected group who had not yet started to toilet train their children. The important thing, however, is that there was no difference between the experimental and control groups.

Table 8-3. Attitude change and intentions of mothers who had not started with respect to toilet training (data in months)

	Control (N = 13)	Experimental (N = 11)
Immediate opinion change (Interview 2—Interview 1)	−1.2	+2.2
Delayed opinion change (Interview 3—Interview 1)	+0.3	+3.0
Effect of opinion change on intention (Interview 4—Interview 1)	+5.1	+5.2

Another way to look at the data is as follows. Both Table 8-2 and Table 8-3 show that the persuasive communication was effective for the experimental group and that the impact of the persuasive communication was still present six months later. If this opinion change had had any effect on behavior, we would expect that, by the time of the fourth interview, a larger percentage of the mothers in the control group would have already started to toilet train their children. More of the mothers in the experimental group, having become convinced that toilet training should start later, would *not* yet have started. Actually, the difference was negligible and slightly in the reverse direction. Thirty-four out of 45 mothers in the experimental group and 34 out of 47 mothers in the control group had already started toilet training by the time of the fourth interview. All in all, we can detect no effect on behavior of a clear and persistent change in opinion brought about by a persuasive communication.

Let us proceed to examine another relevant study. This study, reported by Fleishman, Harris, and Burtt, attempted to measure the effects of a two-week training course for foremen in industry.[4] This training course stressed principles of human relations in dealing with subordinates. Clearly, we are not faced here with the impact of one short persuasive communication but rather with a series of such communications extending over a two-week period. These per-

[4]E. Fleishman, E. Harris, and H. Burtt, *Leadership and Supervision in Industry: An Evaluation of a Supervisory Training Program*, Columbus, Ohio State University, Bureau of Educational Research, 1955.

suasive communications took the form of lectures and group discussions, assisted by visual aids and role playing. For our purposes here, we may, perhaps, safely regard this two-week training session as a concerted attempt to persuade the foremen that mutual trust, warmth, and consideration for the other person are important aspects of effective leadership. (Before anyone misinterprets what I have said, let me hasten to add that undoubtedly other things went on during the two weeks. I have simply abstracted the aspect of the training session that resembles a persuasive communication.)

Given such a prolonged exposure to such a heavy dose of persuasion, we can well imagine that the opinions of the trainees would change from before to after the two-week session. The investigators attempted to measure any such opinion change in the following way. Before the training session and on its last day, the foremen were given a questionnaire measuring their opinions concerning leadership on the part of foremen. The major dimension on the questionnaire of interest to us here is one the authors label "consideration," made up of questions on such things as friendship, mutual trust, and warmth between the leader and his group. As one would expect, the investigators found a clear, appreciable, and significant change on this dimension from before to after the training session. The two weeks of persuasion were effective and the foremen now thought that the dimension of "consideration" was more important than they had previously believed.

This study is relevant for our present purposes because the investigators proceeded to obtain a subsequent on-the-job behavioral measure relevant to the dimension of "consideration." They compared the behavior of those foremen who had attended the training session with a comparable group of foremen who had not. The results are rather surprising. In general, there were no very consistent differences in behavior between the group of foremen who had, and the group who had not, been exposed to the two-week training session. This, in itself, is worrisome. Significant opinion change brought about as a result of a two-week exposure to a series of persuasive communications shows no relationship to behavior. But the results are actually even more surprising than this. The investigators divided their group of "trained" foremen into subgroups according to how recently they had completed the training course. After all, it might be reasoned that the effect of the training disappears with time. If so, one should at least be able to observe an effect on behavior among those who had most recently completed their two-week training course. The results show that the "most recently trained sub-group" was actually *lower* in consideration *behavior* than the group that had never been exposed to any training—had never been exposed to the impact of the persuasive communications. Once more we see the hint of a slightly inverse relationship between attitude change and behavior.

We will now proceed to examine the only other study we were able to find bearing on the question of the relation between opinion change and behavior. This is the well known study by Janis and Feshbach on the effects of fear-arousing communications.[5] Because the authors of this study did not interpret their data as bearing on this question, we will have to put a different interpretation on their experiment in order to make it relevant. Perhaps this different interpretation is not justifiable. But since so few published studies could be found that bear on our problem at all, I will proceed with the re-interpretation.

Of four groups of high school students used in the experiment, one, the control group, was not exposed to the relevant persuasive communication. The other three groups each heard an illustrated lecture about proper care of teeth and gums that attempted to persuade them that it was important to care for the teeth properly in order to avoid unpleasant consequences. The lectures each of the three groups heard differed in their emphasis on the painful consequences of improper oral hygiene. In the words of the authors:

> One of the main characteristics of the *Strong* appeal was the use of personalized threat-references explicitly directed to the audience, i.e., statements to the effect that "this can happen to you." The *Moderate* appeal, on the other hand, described the dangerous consequences of improper oral hygiene in a more factual way using impersonal language. In the *Minimal* appeal, the limited discussion of unfavorable consequences also used a purely factual style.

One might expect that the more emphasis put upon the importance of proper oral hygiene, and the more personal the importance is made, the more effective the communication would be in making the listener feel that proper oral hygiene is something to be concerned about. Thus, we might expect that the Strong appeal would be most effective, and the Minimal appeal least effective, in persuading people to be concerned about proper oral hygiene. One week before hearing the lecture, and immediately after hearing the lecture, all the subjects were asked two questions about how concerned or worried they were about the possibility of developing diseased gums and decayed teeth. The authors interpret these questions as indicating the degree of emotionality aroused by the persuasive communication, but, for the sake of our re-interpretation, let us look at the answers as reflecting opinion change. After all, the communications attempted to concern the listeners about these things. Let us see how well they succeeded. The data are shown in Table 8-4.

Table 8-4. Percentage who felt "somewhat" or "very" worried about decayed teeth and diseased gums

	Before	After
Strong appeal (N = 50)	34	76
Moderate appeal (N = 50)	24	50
Minimal appeal (N = 50)	22	46
Control group (N = 50)	30	38

[5] I. Janis and S. Feshbach, "Effects of Fear-arousing Communications," *Journal of Abnormal and Social Psychology*, Vol. 48, 1953, pp. 78-92.

As one might expect, the persuasive communications were all effective to some extent—they all succeeded in creating more change in concern about oral hygiene than appeared in the control group. Within the experimental conditions we find that the Strong appeal was, plausibly, most effective. The Moderate and Minimal appeals seem to have been about equally effective.

The three persuasive communications, in addition to attempting to persuade the listeners of the importance of oral hygiene, also attempted to persuade them about the proper way to brush one's teeth and the characteristics of a "proper" type of toothbrush. Here, however, the three communications were equal. Before and after measures were obtained concerning the beliefs in the desirability of the recommended characteristics of a toothbrush. On these issues, where the communications did not differ, the authors state, ". . . all three experimental groups, as compared with the Control group, showed a significant change in the direction of accepting the conclusions presented in the communication. Among the three experimental groups, there were no significant differences with respect to net changes."

In other words, the three experimental groups were equally persuaded about the proper procedures to use in caring for the gums and teeth, but the Strong appeal group was made to feel these procedures were more important. If there were a simple, straightforward relationship between opinion or attitude change and behavior, one would expect the control group to change their behavior least (or not at all) and the Strong appeal group to change their behavior most.

On the initial questionnaire, given one week before the students heard the persuasive communications, five questions asked them to describe the way they were currently brushing their teeth—in other words, asked them to report their behavior. A week after having been exposed to the persuasive communications they were again asked these same five questions, covering aspects of tooth brushing that were stressed in the persuasive communications as the proper way to brush one's teeth. The answers were scored in terms of whether the student did or did not use the recommended practice. Since these questions asked the students about what they actually did when they brushed their teeth, perhaps it is legitimate to regard their answers as truthful reports concerning their actual behavior. This may or may not be a valid interpretation of their responses, but, assuming that it is, let us see what the relationship is between attitude change and their reported behavior. Table 8-5 presents the data on the percentage of subjects in each group who changed in the direction of increased use of the practices recommended in the persuasive communication.

It is clear from even a cursory glance at the data that the results do not represent a simple relation between attitude change and behavior. It is true that those who heard any of the persuasive communications reported more change in their behavior than the control group. This, however, may simply reflect the fact that subjects in the experimental conditions learned the proper terminology and what is approved. The interesting comparison is among the

Table 8-5. Percentage who changed toward increased use of recommended dental practices

	Per Cent Who Changed
Strong appeal	28
Moderate appeal	44
Minimal appeal	50
Control group	22

experimental groups. Within the experimental conditions, the relation between behavior and the degree to which students were made to feel concerned about oral hygiene was actually in the reverse direction from what one would expect from any simple relationship between attitude change and behavior.

The authors offer as an explanation for the inverse relationship the hypothesis that the Strong appeal created strong fear and, hence, subjects exposed to this communication were motivated to avoid thinking about it. Perhaps this is the correct explanation, although little evidence is presented in the study to support the assertion that strong fear was aroused in the Strong appeal condition. And it is certainly not clear why people who are more concerned about something are not more likely to take action. If we think of the results of this study together with the results of the previous studies I described (and let me stress again that these are the only three studies I have been able to find that are at all relevant to the issue at hand), it seems clear that we cannot glibly assume a relationship between attitude change and behavior. Indeed, it seems that the absence of research in this area is a glaring omission and that the whole problem needs thinking through.

Let us, for the sake of the present discussion, put aside the possibility that responses to a questionnaire after having been exposed to a persuasive communication may reflect nothing more than "lip service;" that is, the person's real opinions and attitudes may not have changed at all but his responses may simply reflect a desire not to appear unreasonable in the eyes of the experimenter. This kind of thing may affect responses to questionnaires to some extent, but it seems unreasonable to imagine that it is a dominant effect or that it could count for differences among experimental conditions. Undoubtedly, to a major extent, a person's answers to a questionnaire reflect how he really feels about the issue at that moment. Then why should one not observe a clear relationship with behavior?

I would like to suggest one possible reason for a complex relationship between attitude or opinion change and behavior. I have no data to support this suggestion, but perhaps it may offer some conceptual basis for future research that will clarify the problem. I want to suggest that when opinions or attitudes are changed through the momentary impact of a persuasive communication, this change, all by itself, is inherently unstable and will disappear or remain isolated unless an environmental or behavioral change can be brought about to support and maintain it.

To illustrate and amplify this suggestion, let us imagine a person who held the unlikely opinion that giving speeches was a productive and worthwhile thing to do. Undoubtedly, such an opinion would have been developed over many years on the basis of his own experience, what other people say about it, and also his own needs and motives. For example, he has observed that many people engage in the practice of giving speeches and from this it seems clear that it must have some desirable aspects. He has even read that at A.P.A. conventions papers are held to short periods of time because so many people (more than can be accommodated) want to make speeches. Surely, giving a speech must be a good thing to do. What is more, he has observed that many people actually go to listen to such speeches—a fact that certainly supports his opinion.

There is even more to the "reality" basis he has for this opinion. Once when he gave a speech, two people came up to him afterward and told him how wonderful they thought it was. What better evidence could he have that it was indeed worthwhile to engage in this activity? Furthermore, no one ever came up to him to tell him it was a waste of time. In addition, he found that he got quite a bit of personal satisfaction out of having all those people listening to what he said. All in all, the opinion became rather well established. There was considerable evidence to support it, none to contradict it, and it was a pleasant opinion to hold.

Needless to say, such a well-established opinion would affect the person's behavior. This does not mean that at every possible opportunity he would give a speech, but rather that he would be more likely to do so than someone who did not hold the opinion that such speeches were very worthwhile. It would not be a perfect relationship, since many other factors would affect his behavior, for example, the availability of time and whether or not he really had anything to say. But, by and large, one would observe a positive relationship.

Let us now imagine that the following unhappy incident occurs in the life of this contented speechmaker. One day, shortly before he is to leave town to go to some distant place to deliver a speech, he happens to engage in conversation with a few of his friends. One of them, on learning about the imminent trip, raises the question as to why it is necessary or valuable to do this kind of thing. After all, the monetary cost and the time spent are rather large. What does an audience get out of a personally delivered speech that they couldn't get just as well out of reading it?

Let is imagine the highly unlikely event that, in the ensuing discussion, no one is able to come up with a good answer to this question and so a real impact is made on the speechmaker's opinion. If one were to give this person a questionnaire at this moment, one would discover that a change in his opinion had been brought about. He would feel less certain that it was a good thing to do. But what are the implications for the future of this change in his opinion? After this friendly but unsettling discussion, our speechmaker returns to the same environment that produced his opinion initially, and, we can consequently assume, there will be pressures to return to his former opinion. Pressures, indeed, that he has not felt in a long time. Furthermore, he is about to leave to make a speech and he goes ahead with what he is already committed to doing. This obviously further helps to restore his former opinion. The world he encounters remains the same, his experiences remain the same, and so his opinion will tend to revert. His behavior will remain the same or perhaps even intensify in an effort to restore his former opinion. The exact content of his opinion may indeed have changed somewhat and became more differentiated. He may buttress his original opinion by the notion that many people will listen to a speech who would not read it and that it is important to communicate to many people; he may persuade himself that the personal contact is in some unspecified way very important; he may even tell himself that a practice so widespread must be good even if he, at the moment, cannot see its good aspects clearly.

It is my present contention that, in order to produce a stable behavior change following opinion change, an environmental change must also be produced which, representing reality, will support the new opinion and the new behavior. Otherwise, the same factors that produced the initial opinion and the behavior will continue to operate to nullify the effect of the opinion change.

Thus far we have speculated mainly about some possible reasons for the *absence* of a relationship between opinion change following a persuasive communication and resulting behavior. We have not grappled with the perplexing question raised by the persistent hint of a slightly inverse relationship (if three times may be called persistent). I must confess that I have no very good or interesting speculations to offer here. Let me also emphasize that the data certainly do not warrant assuming that such an inverse relationship really does exist: they do not more than raise a possible suspicion. If this inverse relation is found not to exist, there is, of course, nothing to explain. If, however, it does exist, we must find some explanation for it.

What I want to stress is that we have been quietly and placidly ignoring a very vital problem. We have essentially persuaded ourselves that we can simply assume that there is, of course, a relationship between attitude change and subsequent behavior and, since this relationship is obvious, why should we labor to overcome the considerable technical difficulties of investigating it? But the few relevant studies certainly show that this "obvious" relationship probably does not exist and that, indeed some nonobvious relationships may exist. The problem needs concerted investigation.

9

The Learning of Tastes

HERBERT E. KRUGMAN
and EUGENE L. HARTLEY

The subject of consumer taste has proved an elusive one for social scientists and businessmen alike. But while the latter energetically pursue the public on a day-to-day basis with ever new baubles and gadgets, the social sciences have for the most part confined their interest to a broad and distant view and only rarely descended to research on the specific processes of taste formation. For students of public opinion the particular process of familiarization has special relevance in view of their concern with the *new*, if not in products then certainly in ideas. Too often in the past, furthermore, explanations for public acceptance or rejection of the new have wandered without restraint between such commonplaces as "Repetition equals reputation," and "Familiarity breeds contempt," *or* "It's the novelty that attracts people," and "It's too new for the public."

All the social sciences have made at least some broad-gauged attempts to come to grips with the problem. Anthropologists like Kroeber and sociologists like Sorokin have made long-term historical analyses of changing styles in dress fashion and art, respectively.[1] Psychologists like Hurlock have studied personality factors in dress.[2] Social historians like Wector have traced the course of a broad variety of taste and style changes in upper-class American society.[3] A great deal of interest has been focused by sociologists on what is called "mass culture," or "popular culture," and here Rosenberg and White have brought together a wealth of material on the changing contents and func-

Reprinted from *Public Opinion Quarterly* (Winter, 1960), pp. 621-631.

[1]A. L. Kroeber, and J. Richardson, *Three Centuries of Women's Dress Fashions: A Quantitative Analysis*, Berkeley, Calif., University of California Press, 1940, and P. Sorokin, *Social and Cultural Dynamics*, Vol. I, *Fluctuations in Forms of Art*, New York, American Book, 1941.

[2]E. B. Hurlock, *The Psychology of Dress: An Analysis of Fashion and Its Motive*, New York, Ronald, 1929.

[3]D. Wector, *The Saga of American Society*, New York, Scribner, 1937.

tions of this culture.[4] Russell Lynes has written entertainingly about the differences between high-brow, middle-brow, and low-brow culture in America,[5] and Vance Packard has attempted to create a social issue out of the malevolent and omnipotent business forces which he sees as controlling the taste and buying habits of the general public.[6] What has not been dealt with, however, is the close study of the rise and/or fall of specific tastes. In a way, the sudden rise and often equally sudden fall of "fads" and fancies in the marketplace are treated as temporary aberrations not worthy of serious attention—perhaps in part because of the plainly trivial nature of some of the objects involved, for example, beanie caps, hula-hoops, and beards. When perchance a fad or newly popular item becomes generalized into a broad acceptance for some new theme, i.e. when a new "style" or "fashion" is born, then it is true there is talk of norms and mores and the social scientists may be interested. The question of how a fad turns into a style or fashion is necessarily unanswered, however, since the antecedent fad and the whole subject of fads have been left unexplored and ununderstood. This applies equally to the new style or fashion which achieves a quiet and unobtrusive acceptance without benefit of an antecedent and much-commented-upon fad.

The subject is important for several reasons. To the small businessman it represents a particularly tragic area of decision making. How often a manufacturer finds a sudden "hit" on his hands and borrows capital to expand plant and equipment, only to find in the midst of trebled production that the will-o'-the-wisp public has lost interest. At the other extreme, we have the manufacturer who is rightly convinced of the worth and potential of his new product, who miscalculates the time it will take for his product to catch on, and who closes his doors financially, unable to wait even in the face of mounting public interest.

For the social sciences, and especially for psychology, the subject is important because it concerns the question of how we *learn to like* objects or ideas. While there is a great deal of research and tested knowledge concerning our ability to learn new skills or solve new problems, we do not confidently know if the principles uncovered in those areas apply to the learning of likes or dislikes or, if not, what principles do apply.

To the market or consumer researcher, the subject is also unclear. Most tests of consumer likes and dislikes involve one-time exposure procedures, for example, "Madam, how do you feel about this new product X (Like ..... dislike ..... or no opinion .....) ?" No single-exposure procedure can allow for so many of the problems inherent in the learning process. Learning often implies time and repeated trials or exposures. What we like today may seem dull tomorrow. What seems uninteresting on first view may prove somewhat intriguing with a

---

[4]B. Rosenberg, and D. M. White, *Mass Culture: The Popular Arts in America*, Glencoe, Ill., Free Press, 1957.

[5]R. Lynes, *The Tastemakers*, New York, Harper, 1954.

[6]V. O. Packard, *The Hidden Persuaders*, New York, McKay, 1957.

second look, etc. Indeed the market researchers' pre-testing of television and other programs on a single-exposure basis may in part be responsible for the low levels of taste in much of what is presented to the public. If repeated- rather than single-exposure tests were made, it might be demonstrated that the audience could "develop a taste" for something new and different, and the sponsor might thereby be encouraged to forego the luxury of immediate popularity for his show.

When time *is* taken into account, and when it is determined how well an object or idea might wear ("Will it prove popular in the long run? Will it hold up?") we encounter another equally significant part of the subject of consumer taste, the problem of familiarity. At the other extreme from faddism, yet theoretically its blood brother, we find innumerable examples of manufacturers offering beautiful and superior new styles, fabrics, devices or packages to a strange market that seems perversely to prefer going along with the older but more familiar items. The psychologist's interest may be engaged here as he identifies a familiar problem, "resistance to social change." While it is a familiar problem in those terms, however, it may not be so familiar when linked with fads and fancies as one and the same problem. That problem concerns the beginning and the end points of *learning* to like. It is the problem of some new things becoming popular quickly and others slowly, of some dying out quickly and others slowly, of some fads broadening into fashions and some fashions persisting indefinitely. It concerns the question of when novelty is delightful and when familiarity outweighs all other considerations. Put simply and perhaps best, however, it is the question of how we learn to like, and what is the influence of the extent of familiarity on the degree of liking. We would like to know more, therefore, about familiarity and liking, about fads becoming fashions, and about the qualities that enable some individuals to "make" fashions or sense new ones in the making while others dismiss them as "only fads." The subject, it may be noted, involves not only the suddenly successful novelties known as fads but the liking or disliking, popularity or unpopularity, of any and all tastes and styles evoking different kinds and degrees of public comment and reaction.

Background

The study of learning, especially in its relation to the phenomenon of memory, is perhaps the oldest of the classic interests of academic psychology. Indeed, it goes well back into the nineteenth century. Since that time the world of education has created enormous pressures and opportunities for psychologists to contribute to better understanding of the learning process in the classroom situation. Out of the vast body of research and literature produced to meet this challenge there developed several major and competing theories of learning, differing in important theoretical respects but similar in the factors or variables considered important to study, and similar also in many of the principles which later emerged as practical guides in the classroom.

The most widely accepted principles can be summarized thus: In learning new skills, repetition or practice is effective; active practice, or recitation, is more effective than passive practice; the learning of the task as a whole is more effective than learning it piece by piece; short practice sessions spread over a longer period of time are more effective than longer practice sessions crammed into a shorter period of time; when practice is continued beyond what is required for successful accomplishment of the task at hand, there is little forgetting of what has been learned even after long periods without practice.

Now the businessman may become interested and ask what implications there are here for how complete his advertisements should be in describing his product, how often and over how long a period his advertisements should be spaced, etc. To some extent practical implications do exist, but as far as we know only in terms of product awareness. We do not know but are now asking what implications there are in terms of product liking and disliking. One difficulty lies in the difference between classroom and marketplace. In the former we have motivated individuals actively coping with difficult problems, whereas in the latter we are much more involved with capturing the attention of a passive audience and creating likes for objects, forms, and ideas which, despite the manufacturers' pride, may be quite trivial in importance or consumer concern. These qualifications do not prevent us, however, from singling out the major factor in learning, i.e. repetition, and putting it in terms of exposure and familiarity, to see where and how it can be linked to the development of likes and dislikes.

Two aspects of repetition and familiarity may be defined. One concerns what is called cognitive, or perceptual, learning, for example, how often do we have to look at an object or hear a theme before we recognize it as "familiar"? The second concerns what is called affective learning, for example, how often do we have to look or hear before we "like"? Both aspects will concern us, and the interrelationship of the two will be our particular focus.

Three Experiments

Familiarity may affect our attitudes toward a wide variety of items from everyday life. A pioneer attempt to study such variety in an experimental setting was made by Maslow.[7] He recruited fifteen students for a ten-day, two-hours-a-day experiment. During each session the students met in the same room and took the same seats. The room had large, bright pictures on the wall and a metronome ticking in the background. The sessions were devoted to looking at a series of paintings by fifteen well-known artists, trying to write down and spell correctly the names of Russian women read to them by the experimenter, copying out of a book those sentences that contained key words provided on a separate list, and marking true-false tests. Throughout the experiment the students wore smocks, used grey rubber bands, large paper clips, yellow blotters, unlined 3 × 5 cards, used copies of books, yellow paper, and pens. Cookies were available for refreshment. These conditions prevailed generally throughout the sessions until the last few, when periodically the students were offered something different, without warning, or asked to make a judgment of personal preference.

The students were offered a chance to change seats, to have the pictures on the wall removed, to have the metronome stopped; they were shown a matched series of paintings by the same fifteen artists and asked which in each matched pair was more beautiful; they were read a similar series of Russian women's names and asked which in each matched pair sounded nicer; they were offered the choice of copying significant parts rather than whole sentences, and of writing original sentences rather than copying; they were offered an easier test-marking system; in addition, they were offered a chance to remove their smocks and to use red rubber bands, small paper clips, orange blotters, lined 3 × 5 cards, new books, blue writing pads, pencils, and a new kind of cookie.

The results showed a general tendency to choose the "familiar," although some students were more likely to do this than others. More important, there was a great difference in what kinds of choice were affected by familiarity and what kinds were not.

Students did not care to change their seats and were no longer aware enough of the bright pictures on the wall or the metronome ticking in the background to care about these matters one way or another. These items were apparently peripheral to the tasks at hand and, while distracting at first, eventually disappeared into the background. Thus familiarity *neutralized* them to the point where no liking or disliking was involved, but only indifference.

Judgments of paintings and names were clearly affected by familiarity, that is, the more familiar were preferred as more beautiful. In addition, half or more of the students preferred the familiar ways of copying sentences or marking tests even though the new methods offered were easier. It is in these two areas that familiarity seemed to have its most positive effect. These repre-

[7]A. H. Maslow, "The Influence of Familiarization on Preference," *Journal of Experimental Psychology*, Vol. 21, 1937, pp. 162-180.

sented, of course, the focus of the students' attention. In the case of paintings and names, however, it was more surely demonstrated that familiarity was responsible for preference of the original series by showing that another group of students, not previously exposed to the original series, split their preferences more evenly between the two.

Students did not, at first, care about removing their smocks, but half of them did so with further encouragement. No preference was shown for rubber bands or blotters of one or another color, or for large or small paper clips. There were some tendencies to prefer the familiar unlined 3×5 cards, old books, pens, and original cookies. In one case, that of blue writing pads versus yellow paper, the new item was preferred. However, results might have been different if single sheets of blue paper had been compared with the single sheets of yellow paper.

In all, this study is a challenging demonstration of the potent and yet varied influence of familiarity. Some items were affected greatly, others less, and still others not at all. We would understand more, perhaps, if we knew how repeated exposures affected the responses of those who initially liked a picture or name as opposed to those who initially disliked a picture or name. We would also like to know which kinds of familiarized preference stood up over a long period of time and which disappeared with time.

Most important, we would want to bring more directly into play the concept of the learning process. In Maslow's study he deals with items that are familiar and not familiar, on a cognitive level, rather than with items of a measured degree of more or less familiarity. Thus it would be instructive to know if the influence of repeated exposures upon preference for a picture or name was greater among those students who had learned to remember the pictures more vividly or to spell the names of Russian women more correctly.

A later study of Krugman attempts to control initial familiarity with the items used in the experiment, and also raises the question of generalization, that is, what happens to liking for the general category within which one may have learned for the first time to like a single item.[8] In his study he used "swing" and "classical" music as the categories and individual musical selections as the items. He first measured students' attitudes toward swing and classical music, then selected nine students, three each who were pro-swing, pro-classical, and indifferent to both. The three at each extreme were clearly prejudiced in their attitude and rarely listened to music of the other category.

A second step was to play classical music to the swing fans and to the indifferent students, and to play swing music to the classical fans. For each student the items to be played were selected by playing a number of records until three were found which he neither liked nor disliked. From then on the same selections were played once a week for eight weeks. Degree of liking was rated by the student after every playing.

Results showed a general increase in liking from week to week, typically for at least two of the three selections per student, at least until the sixth week, when some flattening of the general upward trend appeared. At the end of the experiment all the students agreed that they could get to like some selections representing a category of music to which they had previously felt a marked prejudice. Furthermore, when the initial measure of attitudes toward categories of music was repeated, it was found that some had shifted in their attitudes toward the category as well as toward the individual items.

The questions posed by the Maslow study apply to this one as well. What would the results be if one started with items that were initially liked or disliked by the students? Which likes persist and which fade away? Do eight sessions or exposures constitute the same degree of learned familiarity and recognition for one student as they do for another? In addition, what is the difference between those students who learned to like the individual items but maintained their attitude toward the category and those who shifted in their attitude toward the category?

Perhaps the main contribution of this experiment was to suggest that the development of "new" likes for specific items is closely correlated with number of exposures, that the learning involves a gradual but regular process. A secondary contribution was to show that some students generalize from their experience with the new while others do not.

A third and more recent experiment by Hartley takes a closer look at the relationship between familiarity and liking for items and categories, and he does this for different types of categories, in an attempt to discover for what categories generalization from item to category is most and least likely.[9] In his study he used "Oriental," "modern," "portrait," "floral," and "landscape" as his categories, and individual paintings as his items.

Hartley had twenty-three students rate each of ten paintings on a five-point scale of familiarity, and then again on a five-point scale of liking. The ten paintings involved two each representing Oriental, modern, portrait, floral, and landscape subjects or styles. These he called the test paintings. A week later and five times during the three weeks thereafter the students were shown five other paintings, one for each of the categories above, and asked to study them carefully for twenty seconds. They then were asked to imagine the paintings and rate them for various aspects of clarity. These were called the familiarization paintings. After the five exposures were over and these exercises in imagery completed, the original test paintings were re-rated for familiarity and liking.

Comparison of the before and after ratings of the test paintings showed a general increase in familiarity for the ten items, but with different degrees of increase by category. Thus increases were greatest for Oriental, floral, modern, and landscape in that (decreasing) order, while portraits showed a decrease in familiarity, that is, exposure to portraits made them seem less

[9] E. L. Hartley, unpublished manuscript, February 1960.

familiar. Comparison also showed that there was no general change in liking for the categories but that moderns, especially, and portraits, slightly, were more liked, while florals were less liked.

In order to discover what these differential shifts implied for the relationship between items and categories, the question was raised as to the extent to which the two Orientals, moderns, portraits, florals, and landscapes were seen or treated as members of the same category. This was done by correlating the initial ratings of familiarity and of liking for each of the two paintings in the test series: did the two Orientals get similar or dissimilar ratings on familiarity and on liking?

Keeping the very rough (N=2) definition of category in mind, it may be reported nevertheless that all correlations on familiarity were significant and positive, and that this was especially true of portraits and florals; on a cognitive level these were all true categories or fell into accepted categories. As for liking, however, the correlations were both negative and positive, and only landscapes and moderns showed significant and positive correlations. In short, there were no prejudices or tendencies to like or dislike the items as a category except for landscapes and moderns. Furthermore, when familiarity and liking were correlated with each other by category, it was found that portraits and florals showed consistent and high negative correlations for the four items involved—the more familiar the more disliked. Orientals showed a consistent positive correlation for the two items involved—the more familiar the more liked.

What, then, are the implications of these initial reactions? First let us summarize the results as follows (with F=familiarity, L=liking, and D=disliking):

Table 9-1.

Category	Initial Test of F as a Category	Initial Test of L or D as a Category	Initial Relation of L and D as Items	Re-test Increase in F of the Category	Re-test Shifts in L of the Category
Oriental	Yes	No	Increased F = L	Most	None
Floral	Especially	No	Increased F = D	Second	Decrease
Modern	Yes	Yes	None	Third	Increase
Landscape	Yes	Yes	None	Fourth	None
Portraits	Especially	No	Increased F = D	Decrease	Increase (slight)

The Oriental paintings were seen as a category but were (predominantly) liked more on an item-by-item than on a category basis. Familiarity with the category increased more than any other, perhaps because the category is strange to Americans, but no increase in liking for the category took place.

Floral paintings were especially seen as a category but were (predominantly) disliked more on an item-by-item than a category basis. Familiarity with the category increased significantly and apparently produced dislike for the category as such.

Modern paintings were seen and liked or disliked as a category without much item-by-item sensitivity. Familiarity with the category increased moderately, while liking for the category increased significantly.

Landscape paintings were also seen and liked or disliked as a category without item-by-item sensitivity. Familiarity with the category increased, but liking for the category did not.

Portraits were especially seen as a category, but were (predominantly) disliked more on an item-by-item than a category basis. Familiarity with the category decreased, i.e. began to be seen as different, and even produced some increase in liking for the category.

One might characterize the Oriental situation as "open"; individual items can be liked, but familiarity with the category still provides room for increase without any shift in liking for the category. Florals, on the other hand, could be characterized as a dead category, where further exposure and familiarity will only broaden the dislike for individual items into a dislike for the category as a whole. Moderns and landscapes are perhaps the most popular categories of those studied here, and further familiarity with the more popular moderns increases their popularity, while further familiarity with landscapes has no further effect on their popularity. Portraits, on the other hand, represent a dead category that apparently can be resurrected or re-appreciated.

In general, then, Hartley has shown that familiarity with and study of items (in this case, the exercises in imagery) for the most part increase familiarity with the category. What then happens to liking for the category may depend on what room for further familiarity still exists (as with Orientals), on the relationship between familiarity and liking for individual items (as with florals), on the popularity of the category (as with moderns), or possibly on other factors not involved in the categories used in this study. The case of the portraits suggests that the students learned to see the category differently. It would have been useful therefore to have had a direct measure of how successful or revealing the imagery exercises were. It would seem that something was learned there about portraits which would have been measurably larger than what was learned about other categories.

To sum up the three experiments discussed, it may be said that Maslow demonstrated that familiarity with items created liking for some items but not for others; Krugman demonstrated that when familiarity with items created liking for the items then some combination of familiarity and liking could create liking for the category. Hartley showed that familiarity with items created familiarity with the category, but that this might or might not create liking for the category depending upon a number of different factors.

Taken as a group these three experiments suggest what elements ought to be included in a more ideal experiment or series of experiments:

1. Measures of initial familiarity with, and liking for, items representing categories that are old and new, popular and unpopular, familiar and unfamiliar.

2. Measures of initial familiarity with, and liking for, each category, using more than two items as a basis for measurement, or using a more direct measure.

3. Measures of the individual's ability to learn, and to generalize from learning.

4. Repeated measures of liking for items.

5. Repeated measures of "true" familiarity (i.e. cognitive learning) apart from judgments of "apparent" familiarity.

6. Comparison of results with different degrees of exposure or number of trials (i.e. "assumed" familiarity).

7. Repeated but less frequent measures of familiarity with, and liking for, the category.

8. Comparisons between items that showed more and less change.

9. Comparisons between categories that showed more and less change.

10. Comparison between people who showed more and less change.

The elements above may be used to conduct research on products, brands, tastes, styles, or ideas. It matters less what is actually studied than the fact that a real gap in our knowledge is represented here, a gap that should be a matter of concern to both the social scientist and the businessman.

10

A Behavioristic Approach to Communication: A Selective Review of Learning Theory and a Derivation of Postulates

FRANK R. HARTMAN

A body of theory and research which may be loosely united under the term behaviorism has been sifted and principles applicable to communications derived and discussed. The available empirical evidence primarily consists of conditioning experiments on lower animals and verbal learning experiments on human subjects. Thus the extrapolation to applied communications is a long one, and we should do well to ponder whether or not such extrapolation is justified. There are several arguments in justification of extrapolating: (a) Learning problems translate easily into communication problems. (b) Learning research has been very extensive, resulting in a large body of empirical findings and in procedural refinements and sophistication in the kind of question posed; it would be both time consuming and expensive for communication research to replow the same ground. (c) Many issues which can be explored through learning research cannot be duplicated in communication research because there are no techniques sufficient for controlling the relevant variables at the more complex level. (d) Many of the principles derived from behavioristic learning research find confirmation in the rules of thumb of applied communications.

While it is possible to justify the extrapolation, one can still wish for a program of research to confirm or reject the extrapolated principles as valid for applied communications. There are numerous instances where the learning research data were sufficiently shaky to make the extrapolation based upon them highly speculative in nature. Communications research which confines

Reprinted from *Audio-Visual Communications Review* (September-October, 1963), pp. 182-186, with permission from the Department of Audiovisual Instruction, National Education Association, Washington, D. C.

itself to testing the validity of the extrapolations is both feasible and mandatory. However, the tests should first be made under the controlled conditions of the laboratory rather than in the field.

The following principles are enumerated with what is only proper hesitancy. They are derived from what appeared to the writer to be the best currently available information. But the best available information often leaves much to be desired, and the importance of the label "tentative" in the heading of the list cannot be exaggerated.

Tentative Findings for Communication

The following findings have been extrapolated from behavioristic learning research:

1. Communication is the arrangement of environmental stimuli to produce certain desired behavior on the part of the organism.

2. A communication can achieve some changes in behavior through its own reinforcing power. A communication can acquire reinforcing power through association with other stimuli which are reinforcing.

3. Since the aim of communication is to bring about a desired modification of behavior, the natural discriminative stimuli for the desired responses should be isloated and, if possible, incorporated into the communication.

4. Since no communication is effective unless it is attended to, attending behavior must be reinforced.

5. The same unit of a message may have both discriminative and reinforcing functions.

6. To increase the strength of a communication, increase the attendance on the communication for the discriminative stimuli governing behavior.

7. The estimated success of a communication in achieving a desired response is a function of the number of possibilities for interference both during the message and during the interval of time elapsing between the message and the desired response.

8. There are three principal factors contributing to interference: frustration, fatigue, and low motivation. The reduction of these factors is a matter of being careful to fulfill the recipient's expectations, of exceeding neither his comprehension nor his attention span, and of reinforcing him frequently for attending.

9. A fourth factor producing interference is resistance. Resistance to a communication is learned. The discriminative stimuli for this behavior have not been clearly identified, and it would appear profitable to further their identification. Resistance behavior takes several forms, such as avoiding the communication, competing with it, and attacking it. The two latter modes

seem preferable since the behavior remains to some extent under the control of the communicator even though the response is negative.

10. When the ultimate response to a communication cannot be immediately performed but must be delayed in time, the communication should pertain not to specific behaviors but to generalized predispositions for behavior or attitudes. Attitudes are less susceptible to forgetting and to countercommunications and generalize to a wide range of situations. They are established by pairing certain identifying stimuli or labels with emotional reactions.

11. Communication efficiency is increased when delivered by a "live" communicator, provided the desired response is carried out in the presence of this communicator.

12. The provision of useful or interesting information in a communication is an efficient reinforcer of attention to this and similar communications.

13. A relatively meaningless communication unit can be made meaningful by related metaphorical or illustrative stimuli. The meaning of the metaphors is extended through association to the neutral unit. The recipient, if he is properly cued, will often provide his own metaphorical extensions through the normal processes of association. However, recipient-produced metaphorical extensions require time adequate for completion. Since a communicator who controls the rate of presentation of the message units also controls the rate of the recipient's response to those units, the communicator must manipulate the rate of presentation to allow the recipient time for response if he wishes to take advantage of recipient-produced metaphor.

14. There exists considerable potential behavior for which the discriminative stimuli are not present either in the form of external stimuli or in the form of internal motivation of sufficient strength. However, the motivation is often sufficiently strong that a communicator can translate this behavior from potential to actual by supplying the proper external discriminative stimuli.

15. The most exact test of the comprehension of a communication is to discover whether the communication elicits the same responses from the recipient as it elicits from the communicator himself.

16. Regardless of relative meaningfulness, the units of long and complex messages tend to generalize and interfere with one another. Successful reduction of this tendency can be achieved through active practice by the recipient in reproducing the units of the message.

17. Communication effectiveness is a function of the meaningfulness of the message units. This effect is more pronounced if the recipient is required to reproduce some or all of the message units.

18. The meaningfulness of message units may be increased by increasing the frequency of the recipient's exposure to them. This increase is much more pronounced if the recipient responds actively to the message.

19. Frequency of exposure to message units increases their positive evaluation by the recipient and, therefore, the likelihood of his accepting them. If a choice exists between two positive qualifiers equivalent in meaning but

differing in frequency of usage, the more frequently used qualifier should be chosen.

20. Repetition (particularly massed repetition) of communications reduces the number and variety of the meaningful responses which they produce in their recipients. For some purposes this results in the end of the usefulness of the communication; for others, the corresponding increase in the speed of recognition and assimilation of the communication is an advantage.

21. The connotative reactions which underlie values and attitudes can be shifted from one message unit to another by repeatedly pairing the two units in the same message. This effect should take place independent of overt practice on the part of the recipient.

22. The connotative or affective shift of meaning from one message unit to another is heightened by the expectation on the part of the recipient that a noun and its modifier will have the same connotative value.

23. Connotative reactions are easily attached to any communication unit, regardless of whether the unit is verbalizable by the recipient.

24. The connotative meaning of a communication unit persists long after the denotative meaning of the unit ceases to be demonstrable.

25. Connotative reactions increase and decrease slowly. Rapid shifts in connotative meaning during a communication thus will be unsuccessful.

26. The generalized nature of connotative meanings makes them less subject to interference.

27. Two aspects of meaning may be successfully measured: (a) *Meaningfulness*, which affects the ease with which a communications unit may be learned, is measured by the frequency of occurrence in either print or free association. (b) *Quality*, definition by means of synonyms, is measured by listing the strong associates of the communications unit. These measures reflect *denotative meaning*. *Connotative meaning* remains tentative as a concept. The *intensity or meaningfulness* of *connotative meaning* may be assessed by any of the usual measures of emotional intensity such as the Psycho-Galvanic Response. The *quality* of *connotative meaning* may be reflected in the bipolar adjectives which anchor the scales of the Semantic Differential. However, Semantic Differential ratings are probably contaminated by *denotative* factors.

28. Of the existing instruments for measuring the various aspects of meaning, only the Semantic Differential appears useful to the practical communicator. Any communication unit may be rated and evaluated with comparative ease. The meaning of the unit is given with respect to the bipolar scales or to the *evaluative, potency*, and *activity* factors as estimated from the communalities of the bipolar scales with these factors. The meaning measured is probably both connotative and denotative, and Osgood believes that intensity or *meaningfulness* may also be evaluated. Osgood has found the factor structure to be remarkably stable, but the user of the Semantic Differential would be well advised to perform his own factor analysis on data from the population in which he is interested.

If communications research should show some of these principles to be valid, what use can the practical communicator make of them? With such a set of validated principles, one could aspire to an engineering of human communications. With sufficient pains and ingenuity in application, messages then might be constructed with some precision. Precisely engineered communications will require considerable time and resources. Such expenditure may be justifiable only for communications in the mass media. Here the possibility of extensive reproduction and wide dissemination of communications compensates for expense in their original design and construction. But for any communicator a set of valid communication principles will provide a standard against which a communication may be checked and weaknesses discovered and corrected. In view of our current intuitive procedures, this would be a considerable step forward.

III

MASS COMMUNICATIONS

MASS COMMUNICATIONS IS A POPULAR TERM TODAY BECAUSE THE impact of mass communications is pervasive, affecting the very structure of our society. The practitioner is mostly concerned, however, with the ability of mass communications media to deliver the results that will enable his organization to prosper.

Mass communications, as opposed to small-scale or personal communications, does offer certain advantages and disadvantages to the communicator, at least in theory. The communicator has great control over mass communications, because the messages and the method of delivery are, for the most part, uniform and predictable. Personal communication, on the other hand, will vary considerably in quality and nature from person to person and situation to situation. Mass communications also offers a chance to lower the cost per communication. Advertisers, for instance, may find their cost per thousand messages delivered by certain mass media lower than one dollar.

Terminology in some of the following articles will duplicate that of the previous part because mass communications to some extent is simply communication between individuals on a large scale. On the other hand, new problems are introduced and new solutions are required for mass communications. The readings here contain new insights for mass communicators as well as findings useful in all types of communications. Again, the progress made in mass communications has been slight because the field, as an area of scholarly study, is a new one relative to many other sciences. The field is basically interdisciplinary, in that researchers of many different backgrounds are working on problems of mass communications. Their considerable attempts, including some failures as well as controversial findings, are reviewed.

11

What We Know About the Effects of Mass Communication: The Brink of Hope

JOSEPH T. KLAPPER

Twenty years ago writers who undertook to discuss mass communication typically felt obliged to define that unfamiliar term. In the intervening years conjecture and research upon the topic, particularly in reference to the effects of mass communication, have burgeoned. The literature has reached that stage of profusion and disarray, characteristic of all burgeoning disciplines, at which researchers and research administrators speak wistfully of establishing centers where the cascading data might be sifted and stored. The field has grown to the point at which its practitioners are periodically asked by other researchers to attempt to assess the cascade, to determine whither we are tumbling, to attempt to assess, in short, "what we know about the effects of mass communication." The present paper is one attempt to partially answer that question.

The author is well aware that the possibility of bringing any order to this field is regarded in some quarters with increasing pessimism. The paper will acknowledge and document this pessimism, but it will neither condone nor share it. It will rather propose that we have come at last to the brink of hope.

The Bases of Pessimism

The pessimism is, of course, widespread and it exists both among the interested lay public and within the research fraternity.

Some degree of pessimism, or even cynicism, is surely to be expected

Reprinted from *Public Opinion Quarterly* (Winter, 1958), pp. 453-466. This paper may be identified as publication A-242 of the Bureau of Applied Social Research, Columbia University. It was originally presented as an address at the National Education Association's Centennial Seminar on Communications, at Dedham, Mass., May 21-22, 1957.

from the lay public, whose questions we have failed to answer. Teachers, preachers, parents, and legislators have asked us a thousand times over these past fifteen years whether violence in the media produces delinquency, whether the media raise or lower public taste, and just what the media can do to the political persuasions of their audiences. To these questions we have not only failed to provide definitive answers, but we have done something worse: we have provided evidence in partial support of every hue of every view. We have on the one hand demonstrated that people's existing tastes govern the way they use media,[1] and on the other hand reported instances in which changed media usage was associated with apparently altered tastes.[2] We have hedged on the crime and violence question, typically saying, "Well, probably there is no causative relationship, but there just might be a triggering effect."[3] In reference to persuasion, we have maintained that the media are after all not so terribly powerful,[4] and yet we have reported their impressive successes in such varied causes as promoting religious intolerance,[5] the sale of war bonds,[6] belief in the American Way,[7] and disenchantment with boy scout activities.[8] It is surely no wonder that a bewildered public should regard with cynicism a research tradition which supplies, instead of definitive answers, a plethora of relevant but inconclusive, and at times seemingly contradictory, findings.

Considerable pessimism, of a different hue, is also to be expected within the research fraternity itself. Such anomalous findings as have been cited above seemed to us at first to betoken merely the need of more penetrating and rigid research. We shaped insights into hypotheses and eagerly set up research designs in quest of the additional variables which we were sure would bring order out of chaos, and enable us to describe the process of effect with sufficient precision to diagnose and predict. But the variables emerged in such a cataract that we almost drowned. The relatively placid waters of *"who* says *what* to *whom"* were early seen to be muddied by audience predispositions, "self-selection," and selective perception. More recent studies, both in the laboratory and the social world, have documented the influence

---

[1]E.g., Lazarsfeld (1940), pp. 21-47; Wiebe (1952), pp. 185 ff. (*For complete bibliographical details, refer to Bibliography.*)

[2]E.g., Lazarsfeld (1940), pp. 126 ff.; Suchman (1941). Both Lazarsfeld and Suchman point out that although media may seem to be causative agents, further research reveals that their influence was energized by other factors. The point is discussed at length below.

[3]This is the typical, if perhaps, inevitable conclusion, of surveys of pertinent literature and comment. See, for example, Bogart (1956), pp. 258-274.

[4]E.g., Lazarsfeld and Merton (1949); Klapper (1948). The point is elaborately demonstrated in regard to political conversion in Lazarsfeld, Berelson, and Gaudet (1948), and in Berelson, Lazarsfeld, and McPhee (1954).

[5]Klapper (1949), pp. II-25, IV-47, IV-52.

[6]Merton (1946).

[7]The efficacy, as well as the limitations, of media in this regard, are perhaps most exhaustively documented in the various unclassified evaluation reports of the United States Information Agency.

[8]Kelley and Volkhart (1952).

of a host of other variables, including various aspects of contextual organization;[9] the audiences' image of the source; [10] the simple passage of time;[11] the group orientation of the audience member and the degree to which he values group membership;[12] the activity of opinion leaders;[13] the social aspects of the situation during and after exposure to the media,[14] and the degree to which the audience member is forced to play a role;[15] the personality pattern of the audience member,[16] his social class, and the level of his frustration;[17] the nature of the media in a free enterprise system,[18] and the availability of "social mechanism[s] for implementing action drives."[19] The list, if not endless, is at least overwhelming, and it continues to grow. Almost every aspect of the life of the audience member and the culture in which the communication occurs seems susceptible of relation to the process of communicational effect. As early as 1948, Berelson, cogitating on what was then known, came to the accurate if perhaps moody conclusion that "some kinds of *communication* on some kinds of *issues,* brought to the attention of some kinds of *people* under some kinds of *conditions* have some kinds of *effects.*"[20] It is surely no wonder that today, after eight more years at the inexhaustible fount of variables, some researchers should feel that the formulation of any systematic description of what effects are how effected, and the predictive application of such principles, is a goal which becomes the more distant as it is the more vigorously pursued.

This paper, however, takes no such pessimistic view. It rather proposes that we already know a good deal more about communications than we thought we did, and that we are on the verge of being able to proceed toward even more abundant and more fruitful knowledge.

[9]The effect of such variables as the number of topics mentioned, the order of topics, camera angles, detail of explanation, explicitness vs. implicitness, one side vs. both sides, and a host of other contextual variables has been exhaustively studied in virtually thousands of experiments conducted under the auspices of the U. S. Navy, the U. S. Army, and Pennsylvania State University, as well as by individual investigators. Summaries of several such studies will be found, *passim,* in Hovland, Lumsdaine, and Sheffield (1949) and Hovland, Janis, and Kelley (1953).

[10]E.g., Merton (1946), pp. 61 ff.; Freeman, Weeks and Wertheimer (1955) ; Hovland, Janis, and Kelley (1953), ch. 2, which summarizes a series of studies by Hovland, Weiss, and Kelman.

[11]Hovland, Lumsdaine, and Sheffield (1949), in re "sleeper effects" and "temporal effects."

[12]E.g., Kelley and Volkhart (1952) ; Riley and Riley (1951) ; Ford (1954) ; Katz and Lazarsfeld (1955) review a vast literature on the subject (pp. 15-133).

[13]Katz (1957) provides an exhaustive review of the topic.

[14]E.g., Friedson (1953). For an early insight, see Cooper and Jahoda (1947).

[51]Janis and King (1954), King and Janis (1953), and Kelman (1953), all of which are summarized and evaluated in Hovland, Janis, and Kelley (1953) ; also Michael and Maccoby (1953).

[16]E.g., Janis (1954) ; also Hovland, Janis, and Kelley (1953), ch. 6.

[17]E.g., Maccoby (1954).

[18]E.g., Klapper (1948) ; Klapper (1949), pp. IV-20-27; Wiebe (1952).

[19]Wiebe (1951-2).

[20]Berelson (1948), p. 172.

The Bases of Hope

This optimism is based on two phenomena. The first of these is a new orientation toward the study of communication effects which has recently become conspicuous in the literature. And the second phenomenon is the emergence, from this new approach, of a few generalizations. It is proposed that these generalizations can be tied together, and tentatively developed a little further, and that when this is done the resulting set of generalizations can be extremely helpful. More specifically, they seem capable of organizing and relating a good deal of existing knowledge about the processes of communication effect, the factors involved in the process, and the direction which effects typically take. They thus provide some hope that the vast and ill-ordered array of communications research findings may be eventually molded, by these or other generalizations, into a body of organized knowledge.

This paper undertakes to cite the new orientation, to state what seem to be the emerging generalizations, and to at least suggest the extent of findings which they seem capable of ordering. In all of this, the author submits rather than asserts. He hopes to be extremely suggestive, but he cannot yet be conclusive. And if the paper bespeaks optimism, it also bespeaks the tentativeness of exploratory rather than exhaustive thought. Explicit note will in fact be taken of wide areas to which the generalizations do not seem to apply, and warnings will be sounded against the pitfalls of regarding them as all-inclusive or axiomatic.

The Phenomenistic Approach

The new orientation, which has of course been hitherto and variously formulated, can perhaps be described, in a confessedly oversimplified way, as a shift away from the concept of "hypodermic effect"[21] toward an approach which might be called "situational," "phenomenistic," or "functional." It is a shift away from the tendency to regard mass communication as a necessary and sufficient cause of audience effects, toward a view of the media as influences, working amid other influences, in a total situation. The old quest of specific effects stemming directly from the communication has given way to the observation of existing conditions or changes—followed by an inquiry into the factors, including mass communication, which produced those conditions and changes, and the roles which these factors played relative to each other. In short, attempts to assess a stimulus which was presumed to

[21]Berelson, Lazarsfeld, and McPhee (1954), p. 234.

work alone have given way to an assessment of the role of that stimulus in a total observed phenomenon.

Examples of the new approach are fairly numerous, although they still represent only a small proportion of current research. The so-called Elmira[22] and Decatur[23] studies, for example, set out to determine the critical factors in various types of observed decisions, rather than focussing exclusively on whether media did or did not have effects. McPhee, in theoretical vein, proposes that we stop seeking direct media effects on taste and inquire instead into what produces taste and how media affect that.[24] The Rileys and Maccoby focus on the varying functions which media serve for different sorts of children, rather than inquiring whether media do or do not affect them.[25] Some of the more laboratory-oriented researchers, in particular the Hovland school, have been conducting ingeniously designed controlled experiments in which the communicational stimulus is a constant, and various extra-communicational factors are the variables.[26]

This new approach, which views mass media as one among a series of factors, working in patterned ways their wonders to perform, seems to the author to have made possible a series of generalizations which will now be advanced. They are submitted very gingerly. They seem to the author at once extremely generic and quite immature; they seem on the one hand to involve little that has not been said, and on the other hand to be frightfully daring. They do seem, however, to be capable of relating a good deal of data about the processes, factors, and directions of communication effects, and of doing this in such a way that findings hitherto thought anomalous or contradictory begin to look like orderly variations on a few basic themes.

Emerging Generalizations

The entire set of generalizations will first be presented in their bare bones, and without intervening comment. The remainder of this paper will be devoted to justifying their existence and indicating the range of data which they seem able to organize. Without further ado, then, it is proposed that we are as of now justified in making the following tentative generalizations:

1. Mass communication ordinarily does not serve as a necessary and sufficient cause of audience effects, but rather functions among and through a nexus of mediating factors and influences.

2. These mediating factors are such that they typically render mass communication a contributory agent, but not the sole cause, in a process of reinforcing the existing conditions. (Regardless of the condition in question—be it the level of public taste, the tendency of audience mem-

22*Ibid.*
23Katz and Lazarsfeld (1955).
24McPhee (1953).
25Riley and Riley (1951), and Maccoby (1954).
26E.g., the experimental program described in Hovland, Janis, and Kelley (1953).

bers toward or away from delinquent behavior, or their vote intention—
and regardless of whether the effect in question be social or individual,
the media are more likely to reinforce than to change.)

3. On such occasions as mass communication does function in the
service of change, one of two conditions is likely to obtain. Either: a) the
mediating factors will be found to be inoperative, and the effect of the
media direct; or b) the mediating factors, which normally favor reinforcement, will be found to be themselves impelling toward change.

4. There are certain residual situations in which mass communication seems to wreak direct effects, or to directly and of itself serve certain
psychophysical functions.

5. The efficacy of mass communication, either as contributory
agents or as agents of direct effect, is affected by various aspects of the
media themselves or of the communication situation (including, for
example, aspects of contextual organization, the availability of channels
for overt action, etc.).

Therewith the generalizations, and herewith the application. The schemata
will be applied first to the field of persuasive communication, and then, much
more briefly, to the data dealing with the effects of mass communication on
the levels of audience taste. The hope, in each case, is to show that the data
support the generalizations, and that the generalizations in turn organize the
data and suggest new avenues of logically relevant research.

The Generalizations Applied: Persuasion

Persuasive communication here refers to those communications
which are intended to evoke what Katz and Lazarsfeld have called "campaign"
effects,[27] i.e., to produce such short term opinion and attitude effects as are
typically the goals of campaigns—political, civic, or institutional. Long-range
phenomena, such as the building of religious values, are not here a focus of
attention, nor are the marketing goals of most advertising.

Reinforcement

It is by now axiomatic that persuasive communication of the
sort we are discussing is far more often associated with attitude reinforcement
than with conversion. The now classic *People's Choice* found reinforcement,
or constancy of opinion, approximately ten times as common as conversion
among Erie County respondents exposed to the presidential campaign of 1940,[28]
and a nine to one ratio was found in the more elaborate study of Elmira voters
in 1948.[29] Various other studies have attested that, in general, when the media

[27]Katz and Lazarsfeld (1955), pp. 17 ff.
[28]Lazarsfeld, Berelson, and Gaudet (1948).
[29]Berelson, Lazarsfeld, and McPhee (1954).

offer fare in support of both sides of given issues, the dominant effect is stasis, or reinforcement, and the least common effect is conversion.

But we are not here proposing merely that the media are more likely to reinforce than to convert. We are also proposing, as some others have proposed before us, [30] and as we have stated in generalization number 1, that the media typically do not wreak direct effects upon their audiences, but rather function among and through other factors or forces. And we are going slightly farther by proposing, in generalization number 2, that it is these very intervening variables themselves which tend to make mass communication a contributing agent of reinforcement as opposed to change. We shall here note only a few such variables, deliberately selecting both from among the long familiar and the newly identified, in order to suggest the extent of findings for which this generalization seems able to account, and which, seen in this light, become logically related manifestations of the same general phenomenon.

Audience predispositions, for example, have been recognized since the very beginnings of communications research as a controlling influence upon the effect of persuasive mass communication. A plethora of studies, some conducted in the laboratory and some in the social world, have demonstrated that such predispositions and their progeny—selective exposure, [31] selective retention, and selective perception—intervene between the supply of available mass communication stimuli and the minds of the audience members. [32] They wrap the audience member in a kind of protective net, which so sifts or deflects or remolds the stimuli as to make reinforcement a far more likely effect than conversion.

Let us turn from these very old friends to newer acquaintances. Communications research has recently "rediscovered" *the group.* Katz and Lazarsfeld, drawing on the literature of small group research, have proposed, with considerable supporting evidence, that primary-type groups to which the audience member belongs may themselves function as reinforcing agents and may influence mass communication to do likewise.[33] People tend, for example, to belong to groups whose characteristic opinions are congenial with their own; the opinions themselves seem to be intensified, or at least made more manifest,

---

[30]For explicit statements, see McPhee (1953) and Meyersohn (1957). Similar orientations are implicit in Katz (1957), in all studies cited in footnotes 22-26 above, and in various other works.

[31]"Selective exposure" seems to the author a somewhat more realistic term than the classic "self-selection." It is in a sense true that a given program "selects its audience before it affects it" (Lazarsfeld, 1940, p. 134), i.e., that it acts like a sieve in screening its particular audience from among the vast potential audience of all media offerings. But the sieve works, after all, only because the people, rather than the program, are consciously or unconsciously, selective.

[32]No attempt can be made to cite here the hundreds of studies which demonstrate one or more of these processes. Summaries of a considerable number which appeared during or before the late 1940's will be found in Klapper (1949), pp. Intro 11-12, I-15-26, and IV-27-33. For a particularly intriguing demonstration of selective exposure, see Geiger (1959), and for an extraordinarily elaborate demonstration of selective perception, see Wilner (1951).

[33]Katz and Lazarsfeld (1955), pp. 15-133.

by intra-group interaction; and the benefits, both psychological and social, of continued membership in good standing act as a deterrent against opinion change. Group-anchored norms thus serve, on a conscious or unconscious level, to mediate the effects of communications. The proposition has been empirically demonstrated by Kelley and Volkhart,[34] who found that, in general, persuasive communications were more likely to be rejected if they were not in accord with the norms of groups to which the audience member belonged; there were indications, furthermore, that the tendency was intensified in regard to issues more salient to the group, and among persons who particularly valued their membership. Groups are further likely to supplement the reinforcing effect by providing areas for oral dissemination. Various studies have shown that communications spread most widely among persons of homogeneous opinion, and especially among those who agree with the communication to begin with.[35] The "rediscovered group," in short, intervenes between the media stimuli and the people who are affected, and it does so, other conditions being equal, in favor of reinforcement.

Consider another phenomenon which is now in the limelight of communication research: *opinion leadership,* or, as it is sometimes called, "the two-step flow of communication."[36] The operation of such leadership is by definition interventive. And opinion leaders, it turns out, are usually supernormative members of the same groups to which their followers belong—i.e., persons especially familiar with and loyal to group standards and values.[37] Their influence therefore appears more likely to be exercised in the service of continuity than of change, and it seems therefore a reasonable conjecture—although it has not, to the author's knowledge, been specifically documented—that their role in the process of communication effect is more likely to encourage reinforcement than conversion.

All the intervening phenomena which have thus far been cited pertain, in one way or another, to the audience members—to the element of *whom* in the old Lasswell formula. But the range of mediating influences is not so restricted. *The nature of mass communication* in a free enterprise society, for example, falls under this same rubric. It is surely not necessary to here rehearse in detail the old adage of how the need for holding a massive audience leads the media, particularly in their entertainment fare, to hew to the accepted, and thus to tend to resanctify the sancified.[38] But it should here be noted that this is to say that the demands of the socio-economic system mediate the possible effects of mass communication in the direction of social reinforcement.

[34]Kelley and Volkhart (1952), and Kelley (1955), both of which are summarized in Hovland, Janis, and Kelley (1953), Ch. 5.

[35]E.g., Katz and Lazarsfeld (1955), pp. 82-115; also Katz (1957).

[36]Katz and Lazarsfeld (1955), pp. 309-320, and Katz (1957).

[37]Katz and Lazarsfeld (1955), pp. 82-115, and 219-334 *passim,* especially pp. 321 ff.; also Katz (1957).

[38]E.g., Klapper (1948) ; Klapper (1949), pp. IV-20-27; Wiebe (1952).

Such phenomena as these lend some credence to the proposition that the media typically work among and through other forces, and that these intervening forces tend to make the media contributing agents of reinforcement. And the generalization, to which these factors lend credence, in turn serves to organize and relate the factors. Diverse though they may be, they are seen to play essentially similar roles. One is tempted to wonder if they do not constitute a definable class of forces—whether, if the process of communicational effect were reduced to symbolic formulation, they might not be severally represented as, say Q_1, Q_2, and so forth to Q_n. The author does not propose anything so drastic. He merely notes that the generalization suggests it. It suggests, simultaneously, relevant topics for further research. *Do* opinion leaders actually function, as the generalization suggests, to render mass communication a more likely agent of reinforcement than of change? And what of all those Q's between Q_3 or Q_8 and Q_n? What other phenomena function in a similar manner and toward the same end?

We may note also that this generalization, simple though it is, not only accounts for such factors as provide its life blood. It provides as well a sort of covering shed for various bits and pieces of knowledge which have hitherto stood in discrete isolation.

Consider, for example, the phenomenon of *"monopoly propaganda"*—i.e., propaganda which is vigorously and widely pursued and nowhere opposed. Monopoly propaganda has been long recognized as widely effective, and monopoly position has been cited as a condition which virtually guarantees persuasive success.[39] But monopoly propaganda can exist only in favor of views which already enjoy such wide sanction that no opposition of any significance exists. Viewed in the light of the generalization, monopoly position is seen not as an isolated condition of propaganda success, but as a specific combination of known factors. It is a name for the situation in which both the media and virtually all the factors which interevene between the media and the audience, or which operate co-existently with the media, approach a homogeneity of directional influence. Monopoly position is, as it were, a particular setting of the machine, and its outcome is logically predictable.

Change, with Mediators Inoperative

Generalization number 3 recognizes that although the media typically function as contributory agents of reinforcement, they also function as agents of attitude change. In reference to this simple point, there is surely no need for lengthy documentation: the same studies that find reinforcement the predominant effect of campaigns typically reveal as well some small inci-

[39]E.g., Lazarsfeld and Merton (1949) ; Klapper (1948) and Klapper (1949), pp. IV-20-27.

dence of conversion, and a plethora of controlled experiments attest that media, or laboratory approximations of media, can and often do shift attitudes in the direction intended by the communicator. But the generalization further proposes—and in this it is more daring than its predecessors—that such attitude changes occur when either of two conditions obtain: when the forces which normally make for stasis or reinforcement are inoperative, or when these very same forces themselves make for change.

Let us consider first the proposition that change is likely to occur if the forces for stasis are inoperative. A set of experiments which has already been mentioned above is extremely indicative in reference to this proposition. Kelley and Volkhart, it will be recalled, found that, in general, communications opposed to group norms were likely to be rejected if the issue was particularly salient to the group, and that they were more likely to be rejected by persons who particularly valued their group membership. But there is another side to the Kelley-Volkhart coin, viz., the findings that the communication opposed to group norms was more likely to be *accepted when the issue was not particularly salient* to the group, and that it was more likely to be accepted *by persons who did not particularly value their membership* in the group.[40] Put another way, *changes were more likely to occur in those situations in which the mediating effect of the group was reduced.*

A whole slew of other findings and bits of knowledge, both old and new, and previously existing as more or less discrete axioms, seem susceptible of being viewed as essentially similar manifestations of this same set of conditions. It has long been known, for example, that although the media are relatively ineffectual in conversion, they are quite effective in forming opinions and attitudes in regard to *new issues,* particularly as these issues are the more unrelated to "existing attitude clusters."[41] But it is precisely in reference to such issues that predispositions, selective exposure, and selective perception are least likely to exist, that group norms are least likely to pertain, that opinion leaders are least ready to lead—that the mediating forces of stasis, in short, are least likely to mediate. The intervening forces, in short, are likely to be inoperative, and the media are more likely to directly influence their audience.

Much the same explanation can be offered for the observed ability of the media to influence their audience on peripheral issues[42] while simultaneously failing in the major mission of the moment, and the same situation probably obtains in regard to media's ability to *communicate facts or even change opinions on objective matters without producing the attitude changes that*

[40]Kelley and Volkhart (1952), and Kelley (1955), both of which are summarized in Hovland, Janis, and Kelley (1953), Ch. 5. As noted above, the findings are highly indicative, but not absolutely clear cut.

[41]Berelson (1948), p. 176.

[42]E.g., McPhee (1953), pp. 12-13; also Hovland (1954).

such facts and opinions are intended to engender.[43] It may well be that the facts and opinions are not related to the desired attitude change sufficiently strongly to call the protective mediating forces into play: the communication content is probably not recognized as necessarily relevant to the attitude, as not salient, and mediation does not occur. This interpretation, by the way, could very easily be tested.[44]

The inverse correlation between the capability of the media to wreak attitude change and the degree to which the attitude in question is ego-involved may well be another case in point.[45] But this paper cannot analyze and rehearse, nor has the author wholly explored, the entire range of phenomena which might be explained on the basis of the forces for stasis being inoperative. If the generalization is at all valid, it will gather such phenomena unto itself. Let it be the role of this paper to present it, to germinate as it will.

Changes Through Mediators

Let us turn now to the second part of the proposition about the conditions under which media may serve as agents of opinion change. It has been suggested that such an effect is likely when either of two conditions obtain: when the forces for stasis are inoperative—as in the cases which have just been discussed—and, secondly, when the intervening forces themselves favor change.

Let us look again, for example, at the influence of group membership and of group norms. These typically mediate the influences of mass communication in favor of reinforcement, but under certain conditions they may abet communicational influences for change.

In an ingeniously designed experiment by McKeachie,[46] for example, communications regarding attitudes toward Negroes, and the discussion which

[43]Hovland, Lumsdaine, and Sheffield (1949), pp. 42 ff. and elsewhere, *passim;* summarized in Klapper (1949), pp. IV-9-17.

[44]A rather simple controlled experiment might be set up, for example, in which two groups were exposed to communications, one of which merely presented the objective facts, and the other of which explicitly pointed out the implications for attitude change of accepting the objective facts. In line with the interpretation presented above, we would hypothesize that in the latter communication the *objective facts themselves* would be more likely to be rejected. Such an experiment would differ from the numerous studies of the relative efficacy of "implicit" vs. "explicit" conclusions, which have to date been primarily concerned with whether the *conclusions*, rather than the facts themselves, were more or less likely to be accepted.

[45]For what, after all, is an "ego-involved attitude," other than an attitude which is particularly salient to the person who holds it, and thus particularly well protected by predispositions, selective perception and the like? For an amusing statement of a similar view, see "John Crosby's Law," as quoted in Bogart (1956), p. 215. Suggestively relevant studies are numerous and include, e.g., Cooper and Jahoda (1947) ; Cooper and Dinerman (1951) ; Wilner (1951) ; Cannel and MacDonald (1956) ; and various others.

[46]McKeachie (1954).

these communications engendered, made some group members aware that they had misperceived the pertinent group norms. The great majority of such individuals showed opinion changes in the direction of the norm, which was also the direction intended by the communication. The *newly perceived norms* impelled the audience toward the communicationally recommended change.

A *switch in group loyalties or in reference groups* may likewise predispose an individual toward consonant opinion changes suggested by mass communication.[47] Studies of satellite defectors, for example, suggest that persons who have lived for years as respected members of Communist society, and then fall from grace, develop a new susceptibility to Western propaganda. As their lot deteriorates, they turn their eyes and minds to the west, and their radio dials to VOA and RFE. By the time they defect they have developed a set of extremely anti-Communist and pro-Western attitudes, quite out of keeping with their previous lives, but in accord with what they regard as normative to their new refugee primary group.[48]

Group norms, or predispositions otherwise engendered, may furthermore become dysfunctional; in learning theory terminology, the response they dictate may cease to be rewarding, or may even lead to punishment. In such situations the individual is impelled to find a new response which does provide reward, and communications recommending such a changed response are more likely to be accepted. Some such phenomenon seems to have occurred, for example, in the case of Nazi and North Korean soldiers who remained immune to American propaganda appeals while their military primary group survived, but became susceptible when the group disintegrated and adherence to its normative attitudes and conduct ceased to have survival value.[49] The accustomed group norms in such instances had not merely become inoperative; they had become positively dysfunctional and had sensitized and predisposed their adherents to changes suggested by the media.

Personality pattern appears to be another variable which may mediate the influence of communications, and particular syndromes seem to abet change. Janis, for example, found in a laboratory study that those of his subjects "who manifested social inadequacy, inhibition of aggression, and depressive tendencies, showed the greatest opinion change" in response to persuasive communication. They appeared, as Hovland puts it, to be "predisposed to be highly influenced."[50]

In sum, it appears that the generalization is supported by empirical data —that intervening variables which mediate the influence of mass communication, and which typically promote reinforcement, may also work for change. And again, the generalization, in turn, accounts for and orders the data on

---

[47]E.g., Katz and Lazarsfeld (1955), pp. 66-81.

[48]The phenomenon has not been explicitly detailed, but is implicit in various studies performed for the United States Information Agency, and in Kracauer and Berkman (1956).

[49]E.g., Shils and Janowitz (1948) ; also Schramm (1954), pp. 17-18.

[50]Janis (1954), which is summarized in Hovland, Janis, and Kelley (1953), pp. 276 ff. (Quotes are from p. 277.)

which it is based. Group membership, dysfunctional norms, and particular personality patterns can be viewed as filling similar roles in the process of communicationally stimulated opinion change. Other similarly operative variables will doubtless be identified by a continued phenomenistic approach, i.e., by the analysis of accomplished opinion changes.

The generalization furthermore serves, as did the others, to relate and explain various discrete findings and isolated bits of knowledge. It would appear to cover, for example, such hitherto unrelated phenomena as the susceptibility to persuasive appeals of persons whose primary group memberships place them under cross-pressures, and the effects of what Hovland has called "role playing."[51]

The first case—*the susceptibility to persuasive communications of persons whose primary group membership places them under cross-pressure*[52]—is fairly obvious. In terms of the generalization, such people can be said to be at the mercy of mediating factors which admit and assist communicational stimuli favoring both sides of the same issue. We may also observe that any attitude shift which such a person may make toward one side of the issue does not necessarily entail any reduction of the forceful mediation toward the other direction. On the basis of the generalization, we would therefore predict not only change, but inconstancy, which has in fact been found to be the case.[52a]

The effects of role playing seem another, if less obvious, example of opinion change occurring as a result of a mediating, or, in this case, a superimposed factor which in turn rendered a communication effective. Hovland reported that if persons opposed to a communication are forced to defend it, i.e., to act in a public situation as though they had accepted the recommended opinion, they become more likely actually to adopt it.[53] The crucial element of role playing is, of course, artificially superimposed. But in any case, the entire phenomenon might be viewed as something very akin to what occurs when an old norm, or an old predisposition, ceases to lead to reward. Successful role playing in fact invests the opposing response with reward. The communication is thus given an assist by the imposition of new factors which favor change. The potentialities of this technique, incidentally, are of course appalling. The Communists have already developed and refined it and we have christened the process "brain-washing."

Various other bits of knowledge about communication effect can be viewed as related manifestations of this same general phenomenon, i.e., the phenomenon of communications inducing attitude change through the assistance of mediating factors which themselves favor change. But it is the goal of this paper to be only suggestive, rather than exhaustive or exhausting, and thus generalization number three may be here left, to suggest whatever it will.

[51]Hovland, Janis, and Kelley (1953), Ch. 7.
[52]E.g., Berelson, Lazarsfeld, and McPhee (1954) ; also Kriesberg (1954).
[52a]Lazarsfeld, Berelson, and Gaudet (1948), p. 70.
[53]Hovland, Janis, and Kelley (1953), Ch. 7.

So much, then, for the first three generalizations, which attempt to relate the processes, the factors, and the directions of effect. It is hardly germane, at this juncture, to belabor generalizations four and five. They serve only to recognize residual categories. Thus number four merely points out that some persuasive or quasi-persuasive effects do appear, at least to our present state of knowledge, to be direct. The apparently unmotivated learning of sufficiently repeated facts or slogans is a case in point. And generalization number five merely points out that the persuasive efficacy of the media is known to be affected by numerous variables pertaining to the content, the medium itself, or the communication situation—by such matters, for example, as the number and order of topics, the degree of repetition, the likelihood of distraction, the objective possibilities of action, and the like. The proposed schemata suggests that these variables are of a different and residual order as compared with the kind of *mediating* variables which we have just been discussing.

We have thus far been laboring to make and document three points, viz., (1) the set of generalizations is supported by our knowledge of the effects of persuasive communications; (2) the generalizations organize, or bring into logical relation, or, if you will, "predict" in an *a posteriori* sense, a large portion of that knowledge; and (3) in so ordering the data they simultaneously suggest new and logically related avenues for further research.

It is proposed that the same set of generalizations is similarly applicable to other types of communication effect. To spell this out in detail is beyond the scope of a single paper.[54] It may be well for the sake of the argument, however, to at least suggest the applicability of the generalizations to one other area, the effects of mass communication upon levels of public taste.

The Generalizations Applied: Effects on Taste

Reinforcement

It has been long known that the media do not seem to determine tastes, but rather to be used in accordance with tastes otherwise determined. The typical audience member selects from the media's varied fare those commodities which are in accord with his existing likes, and typically eschews exposure to other kinds of material. His existing likes, in turn, seem largely to derive from his primary, secondary, and reference groups, although they are not uncommonly affected by his special personality needs.[55] Whatever

[54]A forthcoming book by the present author, tentatively scheduled for publication in 1958, will attempt to indicate the degree to which the schemata is applicable to a much wider array of effects. [Editor's note: Mr. Klapper's book, *The Effects of Mass Communication*, was published by the Free Press, Glencoe, Ill., in 1960.]

[55]E.g., Lazarsfeld (1940), pp. 21-47; Wiebe (1952), pp. 185 ff.; Maccoby (1954); Johnstone and Katz (1957).

their origin, they intervene between the audience member and the vast array of media fare, and between the specific content and his interpretation of it.[56] The media stimuli are thoroughly sifted and molded, and they serve, typically, as grist for the existing mill. Put in a now familiar way, the effects of mass communication are mediated, and the media serve as contributing agents of reinforcement.

Changes

But the media are also associated with changes in taste. Oddly enough, little attention has been paid to the one change which occurs continually—the changing tastes of growing children. Wolf and Fiske seem to be the only researchers who explicitly noted that the pattern of development in children's comic book preferences precisely parallels the changing needs of their developing personalities,[57] as expressed, for example, in games. And no one, to the author's knowledge, has ever pointed out that the pattern of development in comic book and TV preferences also parallels the previously characteristic patterns of development in regular reading preferences. In short, the development and its integral changes in taste are culturally wholly catholic. In terms of our present set of generalizations, this is to say that such mediating variables as personality, cultural norms, and peer group interests impel the media to function as contributory agents of taste change.

The media have also been observed, although rarely, to play a role in elevating the tastes of adults. Suchman, for example, investigated the previous habits of some 700 persons who regularly listened to classical music broadcasts, and found that in the case of 53 per cent the radio had either "initiated" their interest in music or had "nursed" a mild but previously little exercised interest. But—and here is the essential point—the radio had functioned in almost all of these cases not as a necessary and sufficient cause, but as an "energizing agent" or implementer of tendencies otherwise engendered. The so-called initiates had been urged to listen by friends, or in some cases fiancés, whose tastes they respected and whose good opinion they sought, or by their own belief that a taste for classical music would increase their social prestige.[58] The mediating factors, in short, were at it again.

The literature on taste effects is relatively sparse, and seems to offer no illustration of changes which could be ascribed to the forces of stasis being inoperative. It might be conjectured that such effects occur among extreme isolates, but the possibility seems never to have been investigated.

In any case, our two generalizations which regard both reinforcement and change as essentially products of mediating factors account for virtually

---

[56]For a curious demonstration of primary-type groups affecting *interpretation* of content, see Bogart (1955).

[57]Wolf and Fiske (1949).

[58]Suchman (1941).

all of the hard data on the effect of mass communication on public taste. The generalizations furthermore suggest that the data are neither contradictory nor anomalous, but logically related. Stasis, reinforcement, developmental patterns, and individual change appear as different but understandable and predictable products of the same machines.

Residual Matters

There remains a certain residuum of related data and respectable conjecture for which the generalizations do not account. They do not explain why tastes in the development of which media has played a large role tend to have a sort of pseudo-character—why music lovers whose passions have been largely radio-nurtured, for example, appear to be peculiarly interested in the lives of composers and performers, and to lack real depth of musical understanding.[59] Nor do the generalizations cover the phenomenon of media *created* pseudo-interests, about which much speculation exists. McPhee has noted, for example, that the tremendous availability of newscasts seem to have created in some people an addiction, an ardent hunger which is sated by the five-minute newscast, despite its lack of detail and regardless of its irrelevance to the addict's life and interests. McPhee notes a similar passion for big-league baseball results, even among people who have never been in a ball park nor even seen a game on TV.[60] Meyersohn regards this sort of thing as an indication that media create their own common denominators of national taste.[61]

We know little about this phenomenon. Perhaps it is a direct effect, or perhaps it involves mediators as yet unspotted. In any case, deeper understanding seems likely to come from what we have called the phenomenistic approach—from an inquiry into the functions which such addiction serves for the addict, and into the role of the media in creating or serving the addiction.

Application to Other Fields

We have now considered the extent to which the proposed generalizations are applicable to existing data regarding the effects of mass communication on opinions and attitudes, and upon levels of taste. It is pro-

---

[59]E.g., Suchman (1941), pp. 178 f.; Lazarsfeld (1940), p. 255; Bogart (1949). The generalizations are *relevant* to this phenomenon, in that such extra-media forces as the urging of friends are necessary causes of the changed tastes. But there is nothing in the generalization to *account* for the stoppage. There is no reason to assume that extra-media forces which impel the media toward wreaking particular effects also limit the extent of the effect, and in reference to the Suchman data there is not even any reason to presume that people who urge others to listen to good music are themselves possessed of "pseudo-tastes."

[60]McPhee (1953). The comment in footnote 59 is equally applicable here.

[61]Meyersohn (1957), pp. 352-4.

posed that they are equally applicable to questions about the effect of specific types of media fare, such as fantasy or depictions of crime and violence, on the psychological orientations and behavior of the audience. In the interests of brevity, these other areas of effect will not be discussed, except to note that the classic studies, both old and new, seem particularly suggestive. The old studies of soap opera listeners by Warner and Henry[62] and Herzog,[63] for example, and the more recent and differently focused work of the Rileys and of Maccoby,[64] all relate such variables as group orientation and personality needs to media use and media effects. They speak, implicitly and explicitly, of the *functions* served by media, and the role of the media in effects of which they are not the sole cause.

Summation and Conclusions

It is time now to look quickly back over the ground we have covered, and to evaluate the set of generalizations which have been proposed— to inquire into what they have enabled us to do, and to note their weaknesses.

On the positive side, they appear to serve three major functions:

First, as this paper has been at some pains to demonstrate, the generalizations have permitted us in some measure to organize, or to account for, a considerable number of communications research findings which have previously seemed discrete, at times anomalous, and occasionally contradictory. The author submits, tentatively and with due humility, that the schemata has in fact made possible organization of several different orders:

. . . it has enabled us to relate the *processes* of effect and the *direction* of effect, and to account for the relative incidence of reinforcement and of change.

. . . it has provided a concept of the process of effect in which both reinforcement and change are seen as related and understandable outcomes of the same general dynamic.

. . . it has enabled us to view such diverse phenomena as audience predispositions, group membership and group norms, opinion leadership, personality patterns, and the nature of the media in this society, as serving similar functions in the process of effect—as being, if you will, all of a certain order, and distinct from such other factors as the characteristics of media content.

. . . it has enabled us to view such other unrelated phenomena as monopoly propaganda, new issues, and role-playing as manifestations of the same general process—as specific combinations of known variables, the outcomes of which were predictable.

So much for the organizational capabilities of the media. But note that

[62]Warner and Henry (1948).
[63]Herzog (1944).
[64]Riley and Riley (1951) and Maccoby (1954).

this organization of existing data, even within so sketchy a framework as these generalizations provide, permitted us to see gaps—to discover, for example, that certain presumed outcomes have to date been neither documented nor shown not to occur. And thus the second contribution: the generalizations seem capable of indicating avenues of needed research, which are logically related to existing knowledge. Put another way, even this simple schemata seems capable of contributing to the cumulatibility of future research findings. This is in no way to gainsay that future thought and research must inevitably change the generalizations themselves. As presently formulated, they constitute only a single tentative step forward, and their refinement or emendation seems more likely to enlarge than to reduce the area of their applicability.

Finally, it is in the extent of this applicability, coupled with the foetal nature of the generalizations, that the author finds particular bases for hope. Sketchy and imperfect as they are, these propositions regarding the process and direction of effect seem applicable to the effects of persuasive communications, to the effects of mass communication on public taste, and, though it has not here been demonstrated, to the effects of specific media fare upon the psychological orientations and overt behavior patterns of the audience. Furthermore, the mediating variables to which they point—variables such as predisposition, group membership, personality patterns and the like—seem to play essentially similar roles in all these various kinds of effect. Even if these generalizations turn out to be wholly in error—and certainly they are imperfect—they seem nevertheless sufficiently useful and sufficiently applicable to justify the faith that some generalizations can in due time be made.

These particular generalizations, however, do not usher in the millennium. They are imperfect, and underdeveloped; they are inadequate in scope, and in some senses they are dangerous.

They do not, for example, cover the residuum of direct effects except to note that such effects exist. They are less easy to apply, and perhaps inapplicable, to certain other broad areas of effect, such as the effect of the existence of the media on patterns of daily life, on each other, and on cultural values as a whole. We have here spoken of cultural values as a mediating factor, which in part determines media content, but certainly some sort of circular relationship must exist, and media content must in turn affect cultural values.

Such concepts suggest what is perhaps the greatest danger inherent both in these generalizations and in the approach to communications research from which they derive. And that is the tendency to go overboard in blindly minimizing the effects and potentialities of mass communication. In reaping the fruits of the discovery that mass media function amid a nexus of other influences, we must not forget that the influences nevertheless differ. Mass media of communication possess various characteristics and capabilities distinct from those of peer groups or opinion leaders. They are, after all, media of *mass* communication, which daily address tremendous cross-sections of the population with a single voice. It is neither sociologically unimportant nor insignificant that the media have rendered it possible, as Wiebe has put it, for Americans from all social strata to laugh at the same joke,[65] nor is it insignificant that total strangers, upon first meeting, may share valid social expectations that small talk about Betty Furness or Elvis Presley will be mutually comprehensible. We must not lose sight of the peculiar characteristics of the media, nor of the likelihood that of this peculiar character there may be engendered peculiar effects.

In any case, the most fruitful path for the future seems clear enough. It is not the path of abstract theorizing, nor is it the path, which so many of us have deserted, of seeking simple and direct effects of which media are the sole and sufficient cause. It appears rather to be the path of the phenomenistic approach, which seeks to account for the known occurrence and to assess the roles of the several influences which produced it, and which attempts to see the respondents not as randomly selected individuals each exchangeable for the other, but rather as persons functioning within particular social contexts. It is likewise the path of the cumulating controlled experiments in which the multifarious extra-media factors being investigated are built into the research design. These are the paths which have brought us to what seems the verge of generalization and empirically documented theory. They are the paths which have brought us to the brink of hope.

Bibliography

Note: Groups of works by the same author(s) are arranged *in order of their publication dates, not alphabetically by title.*

1. BERNARD BERELSON (1948), "Communications and Public Opinion," in Schramm (1948).
2. BERNARD R. BERELSON, PAUL F. LAZARSFELD, and WILLIAM N. McPHEE (1954), *Voting: A Study of Opinion Formation During A Presidential Campaign,* Chicago, University of Chicago Press, 1954.
3. LEO BOGART (1949), "Fan Mail for the Philharmonic," *Public Opinion Quarterly,* 13, 3 (Fall, 1949), pp. 423-434.
4. LEO BOGART (1955), "Adult Talk About Newspaper Comics," *American Journal of Sociology,* 61, 1 (July, 1955), pp. 26-30.
5. LEO BOGART (1956), *The Age of Television,* New York: Frederick Ungar Publishing Co., 1956.
6. CHARLES F. CANNEL and JAMES MacDONALD (1956), "The Impact of Health News on Attitudes and Behavior," *Journalism Quarterly,* 1956 (Summer), pp. 315-23.
7. EUNICE COOPER and MARIE JAHODA (1947), "The Evasion of Propaganda," *Journal of Psychology,* 23 (1947), pp. 15-25.
8. EUNICE COOPER and HELEN DINERMAN (1951), "Analysis of the Film 'Don't Be A Sucker': A Study in Communication," *Public Opinion Quarterly,* 15, 2 (Summer, 1951).

[65]Wiebe (1952).

9. JOSEPH B. FORD (1954), "The Primary Group in Mass Communication," *Sociology and Social Research*, 38, 3 (Jan.-Feb., 1954), pp. 152-8.
10. HOWARD E. FREEMAN, H. ASHLEY WEEKS, and WALTER I. WERTHEIMER (1955), "News Commentator Effect: A Study in Knowledge and Opinion Change," *Public Opinion Quarterly*, 19, 2 (Summer, 1955), pp. 209-215.
11. ELIOT FRIEDSON (1953), "The Relation of the Social Situation of Contact to the Media of Mass Communication," *Public Opinion Quarterly*, 17, 2 (Summer, 1953), pp. 230-238.
12. THEODORE GEIGER (1950), "A Radio Test of Musical Taste," *Public Opinion Quarterly*, 14, 3 (Fall, 1950), pp. 453-60.
13. HERTA HERZOG (1944), "What Do We Really Know About Daytime Serial Listeners," in Lazarsfeld and Stanton (1944).
14. CARL I. HOVLAND (1954), "Effects of the Mass Media of Communication," in LINDZEY, GARDINER, *Handbook of Social Psychology*, Cambridge Mass.: Addison-Wesley Publishing Co., 1954, Vol. II.
15. CARL I. HOVLAND, IRVING L. JANIS, and HAROLD H. KELLEY (1953), *Communication and Persuasion*, New Haven: Yale University Press, 1953.
16. CARL I. HOVLAND, ARTHUR A. LUMSDAINE, and FRED D. SHEFFIELD (1949), *Experiments in Mass Communications* (Studies in Social Psychology in World War II, Vol. III), Princeton, N. J.: Princeton University Press, 1949.
17. I. L. JANIS (1954), "Personality Correlates of Susceptibility to Persuasion," *Journal of Personality*, 22 (1954), pp. 504-518.
18. I. L. JANIS and B. T. KING (1954), "The Influence of Role Playing on Opinion Change," *Journal of Abnormal and Social Psychology*, 49 (1954), pp. 211-218.
19. JOHN JOHNSTONE and ELIHU KATZ (1957), "Youth and Popular Music," *American Journal of Sociology*, 62, 6 (May, 1957).
20. ELIHU KATZ and PAUL F. LAZARSFELD (1955), *Personal Influence: The Part Played by People in the Flow of Mass Communications*, Glencoe, Ill.: The Free Press, 1955.
21. ELIHU KATZ (1957), "The Two-step Flow of Communication: An Up-to-date Report on an Hypothesis," *Public Opinion Quarterly*, 21, 1 (Spring, 1957), pp. 61-78.
22. HERBERT C. KELMAN (1953), "Attitude Change as a Function of Response Restriction," *Human Relations*, 6, 3 (1953), pp. 185-214.
23. H. H. KELLEY (1958), "Salience of Membership and Resistance to Change of Group Anchored Attitudes," *Human Relations*, 8 (1958), pp. 275-289.
24. H. H. KELLEY and E. H. VOLKHART (1952), "The Resistance to Change of Group-Anchored Attitudes," *American Sociological Review*, 17 (1952), pp. 453-465.
25. B. T. KING and I. L. JANIS (1953), as reported in Hovland, Janis and Kelley (1953), pp. 222-228.
26. JOSEPH T. KLAPPER (1948), "Mass Media and the Engineering of Consent," *The American Scholar*, 17, 4 (Autumn, 1948), pp. 419-429.
27. JOSEPH T. KLAPPER (1949), *The Effects of Mass Media*, New York: Bureau of Applied Social Research, Columbia University, 1949.
28. SIEGFRIED KRACAUER and PAUL L. BERKMAN (1956), *Satellite Mentality*, New York: Frederick A. Praeger, Inc., 1956.
29. MARTIN KRIESBERG (1949), "Cross-pressures and Attitudes: A Study of the Influence of Conflicting Propaganda on Opinions Regarding American Soviet Relations," *Public Opinion Quarterly*, 13, 1 (Spring, 1949) pp. 5-16.
30. PAUL F. LAZARSFELD (1940), *Radio and the Printed Page*, New York: Duell, Sloan and Pearce, 1940.

31. PAUL F. LAZARSFELD, BERNARD BERELSON, and HAZEL GAUDET (1948), *The People's Choice*, New York: Columbia University Press, 1948.
32. PAUL F. LAZARSFELD and ROBERT K. MERTON (1949), "Mass Communication, Popular Taste and Organized Social Action," in Schramm (1949), Q.V.
33. PAUL F. LAZARSFELD and FRANK N. STANTON (1941), *Radio Research, 1941*, New York: Duell, Sloan and Pearce, 1941.
34. PAUL F. LAZARSFELD and FRANK N. STANTON (1944), *Radio Research, 1942-3*, New York: Duell, Sloan and Pearce, 1944.
35. PAUL F. LAZARSFELD and FRANK N. STANTON (1949), *Communications Research, 1948-1949*, New York: Harper & Brothers, 1949.
36. ELEANOR E. MACCOBY (1954), "Why Do Children Watch Television?" *Public Opinion Quarterly*, 18, 3 (Fall, 1954), pp. 239-244.
37. WILBERT J. McKEACHIE (1954), "Individual Conformity to Attitudes of Classroom Groups," *Journal of Abnormal and Social Psychology*, 49 (1954), pp. 282-9.
38. WILLIAM N. McPHEE (1953), *New Strategies for Research in the Mass Media*, New York: Bureau of Applied Social Research, Columbia University, 1953.
39. ROBERT K. MERTON (1946), *Mass Persuasion*, New York: Harper and Brothers, 1946.
40. ROLF B. MEYERSOHN (1957), "Social Research in Television," in Rosenberg and White (1957).
41. DONALD M. MICHAEL and NATHAN MACCOBY (1953), "Factors Influencing Verbal Learning under Varying Conditions of Audience Participation," *Journal of Experimental Psychology*, 46 (1953), pp. 411-418.
42. MATILDA W. RILEY and JOHN W. RILEY, JR. (1951), "A Sociological Approach to Communications Research," *Public Opinion Quarterly*, 15, 3 (Fall, 1951), pp. 444-460.
43. BERNARD ROSENBERG and DAVID MANNING WHITE (1957), *Mass Culture: The Popular Arts in America*, Glencoe, Ill.: The Free Press, 1957.
44. WILBUR SCHRAMM (1948), *Communications in Modern Society*, Urbana, Ill.: U. of Illinois Press, 1948.
45. WILBUR SCHRAMM (1949), *Mass Communications*, Urbana, Ill.: U. of Illinois Press, 1949.
46. WILBUR SCHRAMM (1954), "How Communication Works," in his *The Process and Effects of Mass Communication*, Urbana, Ill.: U. of Illinois Press, 1954.
47. EDWARD SUCHMAN (1941), "Invitation to Music," in Lazarsfeld and Stanton (1941).
48. EDWARD A. SHILS and MORRIS JANOWITZ (1948), "Cohesion and Disintegration in the Wehrmacht in World War II," *Public Opinion Quarterly*, 12, 2 (Summer, 1948), pp. 280-315.
49. W. LLOYD WARNER and WILLIAM E. HENRY (1948), *The Radio Day Time Serial: A Symbolic Analysis*, Genetic Psychology Monographs, 37 (1948).
50. GERHART D. WIEBE (1951-2), "Merchandizing Commodities and Citizenship on Television," *Public Opinion Quarterly*, 15, 4 (Winter, 1951-2), pp. 679-691.
51. GERHART D. WIEBE (1952), "Mass Communications," in Hartley, Eugene L. and Ruth E. Hartley, *Fundamentals of Social Psychology*, New York: Alfred E. Knopf, 1952.
52. DANIEL M. WILNER (1951), *Attitude as a Determinant of Perception in the Mass Media of Communication: Reactions to the Motion Picture "Home of the Brave,"* Unpublished doctoral dissertation, U. of California, Los Angeles, 1951.
53. KATHERINE WOLF and MARJORIE FISK (1949), "The Children Talk About Comics," in Lazarsfeld and Stanton (1949).

12

Some Principles of Mass Persuasion

DORWIN CARTWRIGHT

Among the many technological advances of the past century that have produced changes in social organization, the development of the mass media of communication promises to be the most far-reaching. Techniques making possible the instantaneous transmission of visual and auditory messages around the world have greatly heightened the interdependence among ever larger numbers of people. It has now become possible from one source to influence the thinking and behavior of hundreds of millions of people. One person can now address at one time a major portion of the world's population to educate, entertain, incite, or allay fears. Only psychological and social factors make it impossible at the present time to assemble into a single audience virtually the entire population of the world.

This heightened interdependence of people means that the possibilities of mobilizing mass social action have been greatly increased. It is conceivable that one persuasive person could, through the use of mass media, bend the world's population to his will. Writers have described such a state of affairs, and demagogues have tried to create one, but nothing so drastic has yet even been approached.

Perhaps because of fears aroused by such a possibility, there has been a tendency to exaggerate both the possible evils of mass persuasion and its powers to influence behavior. An examination of the actual effectiveness of campaigns of mass persuasion may contribute to objective thinking.

In the course of a year in the United States alone, literally scores of organizations make use of a significant part of the mass media in order to carry on some campaign. Only the financial cost of using the media seems to limit their use for these purposes. One need mention but a few examples to suggest an almost endless list. The financing of social welfare agencies throughout the United States, for instance, is accomplished largely through annual campaigns

Reprinted from *Human Relations*, London, Plenum Publishing Co., Ltd., 1949, pp. 253-267, by permission of the author and publisher.

designed to enlist contributions from the general public. Political campaigns are an essential part of any democratic political system. During the war the various governments relied upon campaigns to organize public behavior behind their national war efforts. And campaigns are currently under way to induce people to drive in such a way as to reduce traffic accidents, to eat the kinds of food that will create better standards of health, to take steps necessary to cure cancer, to contribute to the endowment of educational institutions, to participate in food production programs of the government, to support or oppose specific legislation, etc., etc. Most of the activities of businesses intended to promote the sale of goods by means of advertising should be included in this list.

Despite the great reliance placed upon campaigns by organizations of all types, it is none the less evident that campaigns do not necessarily succeed in inducing desired behavior among any substantial proportion of the population. As research techniques have become available to evaluate the actual effects of campaigns, it has become a rather common experience for organizations and agencies to spend substantial sums of money on such activities only to find from objective appraisals that little perceptible effect was accomplished. It is not yet possible on the basis of research to state exactly how large a campaign of what kind is required to produce a given amount of influence on mass behavior, but evidence is accumulating to indicate that significant changes in behavior as a result of campaigns are rather the exception than the rule.

During the recent war there arose an opportunity to collect some data relevant to this problem. The United States Government undertook, as a part of its inflation control program, to sell Savings Bonds to the population by means of campaigns. Regular research projects, undertaken to make these efforts as effective and efficient as possible, provide some data concerning the effects produced by campaigns of various kinds and magnitudes. Since the major part of the effort going into these campaigns was contributed voluntarily, it was not possible to get a precise measure of their magnitude even in terms of the money value of their costs, but fairly good estimates were possible. Some illustrative findings may be cited. During the Second War Loan it was estimated that slightly more than $12,000,000 worth of measurable advertising was displayed through the various mass media. In addition to this there were countless rallies, meetings, editorials, feature articles, and the like. In other words, during a period of approximately two months there was developed an unusually concentrated campaign of social pressure to induce people to buy War Bonds. What were the measurable effects? A national survey conducted after the campaign found that 62 per cent of the adult population could recognize the name of the drive and that 20 per cent of those receiving income had bought bonds for the drive. Comparable figures for the Seventh War Loan provide an indication of the effects of an even larger effort. During this campaign over $42,000,000 worth of measurable advertising was displayed; now 94 per cent of the adult population could recognize the name of the drive and 40 per cent of the income receivers bought bonds for the drive.

There are of course many other effects of such campaigns in addition to those listed here, and comparable data are needed from campaigns of a different sort before safe generalizations can be made, but it is reasonable to conclude from these data that even the most efficiently conducted campaigns do not produce major effects upon mass behavior cheaply nor without considerable effort.

We may ask why it is that campaigns seem to require so much effort. One obvious variable influencing the outcome of campaigns is the relation between the behavior encouraged by the campaign and the behavior which the population desires. It is easier to get people to do something they want to do than something they oppose. But this seems to be only part of the story. Another reason that campaigns may fail to be fully influential is that the techniques for using the media are not always the most effective. Research on readership, listening behavior, and the like shows that some techniques, *qua* techniques, are better than others in attracting attention, creating favorable attitudes toward the media, etc. But again the evidence available indicates that the amount of improvement in the effectiveness of a medium that can be obtained by refinement of techniques is limited.

A more fruitful approach to this problem would seem to lie in an analysis of the psychological processes involved in the induction of behavior by an outside agent. What happens psychologically when someone attempts to influence the behavior of another person? The answer, in broad outline, may be described as follows: To influence behavior, a chain of processes must be initiated within the person. These processes are complex and interrelated, but in broad terms they may be characterized as (i) creating a particular cognitive structure, (ii) creating a particular motivational structure, and (iii) creating a particular behavioral (action) structure. In other words, behavior is determined by the beliefs, opinions, and 'facts' a person possesses; by the needs, goals, and values he has; and by the momentary control held over his behavior by given features of his cognitive and motivational structure. To influence behavior 'from the outside' requires the ability to influence these determinants in a particular way.

It seems to be a characteristic of most campaigns that they start strongly with the first process, do considerably less with the second, and only lightly touch upon the third. To the extent that the campaign is intended to influence behavior and not simply to 'educate,' the third process is essential.

Let us now elaborate these principles in more detail, calling upon the data concerning the sale of War Bonds to provide illustrations and documentation.

Creating a Particular Cognitive Structure

It is considered a truism by virtually all psychologists that a person's behavior is guided by his perception of the world in which he lives.

Action is taken on the basis of a person's view of the 'facts' of the situation. Alternatives are chosen according to beliefs about "what leads to what." The content and relationships among parts of a person's psychological world may be called his cognitive structure, and it may be stated that a person's behavior is a function of the nature of his cognitive structure. It follows from this formulation that one way to change a person's behavior is to modify his cognitive structure. Certain kinds of changes of behavior, moreover, seem to be possible only if certain changes of cognitive structure take place. This principle applies to all efforts to influence behavior, whether in a face-to-face situation or by communication through a distance.

The modification of cognitive structure in individuals by means of the mass media has several prerequisites. These may be stated in the form of principles.

1. The 'message' (i.e., information, facts, etc.) must reach the sense organs of the persons who are to be influenced.

Stated in such a bald fashion this principle seems obvious enough. Yet it has practical consequences which are not so commonly recognized. Research upon readership and listenership has made it clear that putting a message on a national radio network or in a national periodical by no means assures that it will actually reach the sense organs of a significant proportion of the population. Only a fraction of the population listens to the radio at any given time, and quite small proportions see a given issue of a periodical. For the most part, people choose the media and thus the 'messages' which are to reach them at any given time. They decide whether they will listen to the radio, read a magazine, go to the movies, or attend a political rally. There is no guarantee, therefore, that providing the opportunity for mass stimulation of the entire population will result in the actual stimulation of any large segment of it.

1a. Total stimulus situations are selected or rejected on the basis of an impression of their general characteristics.

Although the factors determining the way people select stimulus situations are only partially known, there appear to be broad categories which people employ in characterizing stimulus situations, such as entertainment, news, politics, advertising, and the like. Whether or not a person will choose one or another stimulus situation seems to depend upon his reaction to the general category. An illustration of this process is provided by research on the War Bond program. Early in the war the Treasury Department distributed through the mail a pamphlet about bonds to every household in most parts of the country. As a test of its effectiveness a sample survey was conducted in Baltimore, Maryland, to determine how many people had read the pamphlet. Although this pamphlet had been placed in the mailbox of nearly every family in the city, it was found that 83 per cent of those interviewed did not remember having seen it, even after being shown a copy of the publication and being allowed to examine its contents. Of the 17 per cent who recalled having received a copy, about one-third reported that they had not looked through it at all and were able to recognize only the front cover. This means, then, that only about 11 per cent of the adult population had read any part of the pamphlet. In attempting to learn why so many people failed to read the pamphlet after receiving it, it was found that many people had confused the pamphlet with other publications of similar format, such as Sunday newspaper supplements or other advertising matter. A number of people asserted that they had thrown it away because they had thought it was a commercial advertising leaflet. Another group of people took it to be a children's publication and gave it to their children without reading it themselves. What happened, then, was that upon the basis of a first general impression people categorized the pamphlet as something they did not care to read and disposed of it without further scrutiny.

1b. The categories employed by a person in characterizing stimulus situations tend to protect him from unwanted changes in his cognitive structure.

Apparently one common consequence of this categorization of stimulus situations is the protection of the person from stimuli which might produce unwanted changes in his cognitive structure. Illustrative of this principle are the tendencies of people to read newspapers whose editorial policy tends to agree with their own and to listen predominantly to political candidates who belong to their own party. Further evidence may be derived from the wartime research program for the Treasury. In the spring of 1944 Treasury Department officials were exploring the possibilities of using documentary movies in order to heighten citizen identification with the war effort. As an experiment to determine the effects of one particular movie, a week's showing was organized in a public auditorium in Bridgeport, Connecticut. Tickets were distributed widely throughout the population by labor unions, employers, civilian defense organizations, nationality groups, civic organizations, city employees, and many others. During the week approximately five per cent of the adult population of Bridgeport came to the movie. As a part of the evaluation of the effects of the movie on people's interest in participating in voluntary civilian war activities, interviews were conducted with a random sample of those attending and with a control sample of people who did not attend the movie. One of the most striking findings of this study revealed that the people who attended the movie were the ones whose behavior was already closest to that encouraged by the movie. For example, approximately 40 per cent of those attending the movie had offered blood to the Red Cross while only 20 per cent of those not attending had done so. Other measures of activity in community affairs revealed similar differences, and there was evidence that those attending the movie came disproportionately from the upper income levels of the population. In other words, the way in which the appeal to attend the movie was categorized by the public made it less attractive to those very people whom the movie was designed to influence. Had the movie been shown in commercial theaters simply as 'entertainment' it might not have selected such a special group of people.

2. Having reached the sense organs, the 'message' must be accepted as a part of the person's cognitive structure.

Even after a 'message' reaches the sense organs of an individual there are many reasons that it may not be incorporated into his cognitive structure. Everyone knows that there is often a considerable difference between telling a person something and having him pay attention to it, remember it, or accept it as true. In general the same factors operate to facilitate or inhibit the acceptance of a given 'message' that influence the selection of stimulation from the media. We may therefore note the following principles.

2a. Once a given 'message' is received it will tend to be accepted or rejected on the basis of more general categories to which it appears to belong.

2b. The categories employed by a person in characterizing 'messages' tend to protect him from unwanted changes in his cognitive structure.

Anyone desiring to influence the behavior of others must keep constantly in mind a very simple and obvious fact, namely, that everyone, after the earliest stages of infancy, possesses a remarkably stable cognitive structure upon which he depends for a satisfactory adjustment to his environment. Any effort to change behavior through a modification of this cognitive structure must overcome the forces tending to maintain the present structure. Only when a given cognitive structure seems to the person to be unsatisfactory for his adjustment is he likely readily to receive influences designed to change that structure. It is instructive to examine what happens when an item is presented which is at variance with the cognitive structure. When such a situation occurs a disequilibrium is established which must be restored in some fashion. Characteristically one or more of three things seem to happen.

2c. When a 'message' is inconsistent with a person's prevailing cognitive structure it will either (a) be rejected, (b) be distorted so as to fit, or (c) produce changes in the cognitive structure.

Which of these outcomes will actually occur depends upon the relative strength of the forces maintaining the cognitive structure and of those carried by the new 'message.' It will not be possible to explore here the factors determining the magnitude of these forces, but it may be indicated that the forces maintaining a cognitive structure are ordinarily of a very great magnitude. Evidence from the War Bond research may be cited to illustrate two points of relevance here. First, it will be seen that, despite continued efforts throughout the war to get people to understand some of the major purposes the Government had for its War Bond program, there was little actual change in people's beliefs. This is evidence of the stability of cognitive structure and its resistance to change. Second, it will be evident that this stability was maintained by people selecting from the great variety of promotional material developed for the campaigns those features which conformed to their existing cognitive structure and rejecting those which deviated.

After each of the War Loans a sample of the population was asked: "Why do you think the Government is anxious to get people to buy bonds?" The specific answers given by respondents to this question have been grouped under a few major headings in *Table 12-1.* It will be seen how little the answers changed over a period of thirty months of War Bond publicity.

Table 12-1.   Reasons attributed to Government for wanting to sell bonds

Reasons	Second Loan April 1943	Third Loan Sept. 1943	Fourth Loan Jan. 1944	Fifth Loan June 1944	Sixth Loan Nov. 1944	Seventh Loan June 1945
	%	%	%	%	%	%
To finance the war, to win the war, to help soldiers	65	75	65	65	67	68
To prevent inflation	14	11	14	15	15	14
To get people to save	4	4	7	8	7	10
To provide postwar security	4	2	2	3	2	3
Other reasons	13	8	12	9	9	5
	100	100	100	100	100	100
Number of interviews	1,358	1,583	1,441	1,925	2,148	2,263

The stability of the percentages in the table is most remarkable. With minor exceptions the variability does not exceed that expected simply from repeated samplings of a population with constant characteristics. Since the same individuals were not interviewed in the various studies it is not possible to determine with certainty that individuals were not shifting from one category to another from one time to the next, but the most likely hypothesis would seem to be that there was remarkably little change throughout the war in people's views as to why the Government was wanting to sell bonds. This stability was maintained in the face of a tremendous barrage of promotion through all the media of communication. Examination of the content of this promotion makes it clear that no single explanation of the Government's reasons was universally pushed, and it is reasonable to suppose that there was a rough correspondence between the percentage of the publicity devoted to any given reason and the number of people already holding that reason. But the remarkable fact remains that, with the great array of reasons being publicized, people seemed to keep the ones they arrived at in the very beginning of the war.

In the course of the research program considerable attention was given to the nature of popular thinking about the functioning of the economy and the role of War Bonds in the prevention of inflation. From this analysis it became clear, for example, why the promotion designed to explain the Government's interest in bond sales as a means of inflation control did not succeed in changing popular thinking. It became apparent that for many people war finance was seen simply as the collection of dollars by Uncle Sam which were then paid by him to manufacturers of war goods. If Uncle Sam sold the bonds, he could buy equipment; if he did not sell them, he could not get the supplies. Asked directly whether failure to sell enough bonds would cause a shortage of military equipment, 49 per cent of those interviewed after the Fourth Loan said that it would. With such a conception of the nature of the economy is it not surprising that, when asked whether they thought buying bonds would help keep prices down, 54 per cent either asserted directly that bond purchases had no effect on prices or said that they could not see any relation between the two. Nor is it surprising that during the war there was a slight increase in this percentage since a number of people noted that even though bonds were being sold in large quantities prices were continuing to rise.

From this and similar evidence the conclusion seems warranted that people succeeded in maintaining an early established cognitive structure by selecting from the War Bond promotion those items which conformed to that structure and by ignoring items deviating from it.

Numerous examples of the distortion of 'messages' to make them agree with existing beliefs could be cited, but perhaps the most dramatic are those related to the conviction held by a minority of the population that the Government would not redeem the bonds. Whenever a change of procedure in the redemption of bonds was instituted, rumors cropped up among these people to the effect that the new change was a step toward 'freezing' bonds. At one point during the war a group of enthusiastic citizens (probably as a publicity stunt) conducted a bonfire in which they burned their bonds as a gesture to indicate their willingness to give money to the Government for the war. This event stimulated rumors among those distrusting the Government's intention to repay that the bonds were no good and that people were burning them because they were worthless.

To summarize the evidence presented up to this point, it is clear that changes in cognitive structure cannot be assured simply by guaranteeing wide coverage of the media of communication. By selecting the stimuli from the media which they will allow to reach their sense organs and by rejecting or distorting messages that deviate too much from existing cognitive structures, people manage to resist much of the effort made to change their thinking by techniques of mass persuasion. To the extent that changes in behavior are dependent upon changes of cognitive structure they, at the same time, resist efforts to modify their usual manner of behavior.

Creating a Particular Motivational Structure

We have now explored some of the implications of the notion that behavior is guided by a person's cognitive structure. For a satisfactory analysis of the process of social induction of behavior, however, it is necessary to examine a bit further what it is that energizes behavior. As a general statement it may be said that personal needs provide the energy for behavior and express themselves through the setting up of goals in the person's cognitive structure. That is to say, certain activities (like eating, going to the movies, running for Congress, etc.) become attractive when corresponding needs are activated, and the amount of energy that will be devoted to these activities depends upon the strength of the need (i.e., the level of need tension). It should be noted further that goals have a location in the cognitive structure so that for a given individual some activities are seen as leading to the satisfaction of certain needs and others are seen as unrelated to such satisfaction or even leading away from it. Thus, for one person 'joining a union' may be seen as a path leading to economic security, while for another 'being nice to the boss' may be seen as the path toward the same goal, with 'joining the union' being in exactly the opposite direction.

It follows from these general observations about the nature of human motivation that efforts to influence the behavior of another person must attempt either to modify needs (and goals) or to change the person's motivational structure as to which activities lead to which goals. This means that a person can be induced to do voluntarily something that he would otherwise not do only if a need can be established for which this action is a goal or if the action can be made to be seen as a path to an existing goal. Little is known at the present time about the establishment of needs, but it appears unlikely that any single campaign via the mass media can actually establish new needs. Whether or not this feat is possible, the following principle may nevertheless be stated.

3. To induce a given action by mass persuasion, this action must be seen by the person as a path to some goal that he has.

When people were asked during the war why they were buying bonds, they gave answers that could readily be interpreted in terms of the motivational principles outlined here. The most common reasons were related to the desire to win the war. People said, in essence, though they phrased it in many ways, "I want to help win the war, and buying War Bonds is one way I can help." Stated reasons of this type were the following: (percentages are given to indicate the proportion of the adult population giving them after the Seventh Loan). (a) Because the country needs the money to pay for the war (64 per cent). (b) To help the boys, to bring them back (16 per cent). (c) To get the war over sooner (6 per cent).

Another goal for which buying bonds was seen as a path may be loosely defined as 'personal economic security.' People who gave reasons of this type said in essence, "I want to provide economic security for myself and family, and buying War Bonds is one way I can achieve this goal." The most common of these reasons given after the Seventh Loan were: (a) To save for some indefinite personal use in the future (44 per cent). (b) To have reserves in case of a post-war depression (5 per cent). (c) Because bonds are a good investment (24 per cent).

A third rather common type of goal was "wanting to be a good citizen." Reasons related to this goal tended to be stated in terms of the Government's needs or objectives. To the extent that the Government's objectives were seen as also providing satisfaction of personal financial needs these reasons could also be classified under the previous heading. The more frequent of these reasons were: (a) To help prevent inflation (14 per cent). (b) Because the Government wants people to save (10 per cent). (c) To prevent a post-war depression (1 per cent).

Undoubtedly many people had other personal goals for which buying bonds was seen as a path. It appears, for example, that some people saw the buying of bonds at public rallies as a means of gaining prestige. At first glance it would seem that the number of goals that could be made to appear attainable through the purchase of bonds would be almost limitless. Further scrutiny of the facts, however, indicates that there were actually severe limitations on the kinds of connections that could be established between bond-buying and personal goals. Unless people could see something in the nature of buying bonds that made this act appear reasonably a path to a given goal, all the power of mass persuasion that could be mobilized could not get the connection accepted.

3a. A given action will be accepted as a path to a goal only if the connections 'fit' the person's larger cognitive structure.

As documentation of this principle it is necessary only to refer again to the fact that, despite efforts to explain the relation between buying bonds and inflation control, over half of the population still denied that there was such a relationship because it did not fit into their general understanding of the nature of the economy. Similarly those people who believed that the Government would not repay the bonds could not be induced to believe that buying bonds would provide them with personal economic security after the war.

3b. The more goals which are seen as attainable by a single path, the more likely it is that a person will take that path.

It is, of course, possible for a given action to be seen as leading simultaneously to more than one goal. When such a situation exists, the forces directed toward these various goals will all assume the direction of the one action which is the path common to them all. It is to be expected, then, that making a given action appear as leading to several goals will increase the likelihood that that action will be chosen. In persuading people to buy War Bonds, this meant that the more reasons they could be led to see for buying the more likely they should be to buy. Evidence from the research program consistently upported this conclusion. Consider the findings of the survey after the Seventh Loan (*Table 12-2*). It is seen that people who saw more than one type of reason for buying bonds were much more likely to buy, whether solicited or not, than were those who had only one type of reason. In order to be certain that differences in income among those giving different numbers of reasons do not produce these results, it is necessary to conduct this analysis separately within restricted income ranges. When this procedure is followed, it is found that at every income level people who gave more than one type of reason were more likely to buy than were those who mentioned only one type.

3c. If an action is seen as not leading to a desired goal or as leading to an undesired end, it will not be chosen.

3d. If an action is seen as leading to a desired goal, it will tend not to be chosen to the extent that easier, cheaper, or otherwise more desirable actions are also seen as leading to the same goal.

These two principles are simply elaborations of the general motivational scheme already outlined. They point, however, to exceedingly important practical implications for anyone desiring to influence behavior by mass persuasion. Much of the 'psychological warfare' of competing propagandists or of competing advertising programs is concerned with these principles. In such competition much effort is devoted to the objective of showing how one's own proposed course of action leads to a desired goal while the action proposed by the competitor does not lead to a desired goal or actually leads to an undesired end. The efforts of dictators to monopolize the channels of communication stem largely from the realization that competitors may offer more acceptable paths to accepted goals.

Table 12-2. The relation of the number of reasons mentioned to buying bonds in the seventh war loan

Types of Reasons Mentioned	Proportion Buying for Drive of Those	
	Personally asked to buy	Not asked to buy
	%	%
Patriotic, personal financial, and national financial	65	35
Patriotic and personal financial *or* Patriotic and national financial	57	22
Patriotic only	44	9
Number of interviews	1,232	1,104

Those people who during the war believed that the Government would not repay the bonds may be cited to illustrate *Principle 3c*. For these people, 'buying bonds' was perceived as leading to 'losing my money.' Needless to say, it was found that these people resisted efforts to get them to buy bonds and were quite ready to redeem their bonds if they were induced to purchase them. In order to make willing bond buyers out of these people it was necessary to change their motivational structure in regard to the consequences seen to be connected with the act of buying bonds. Examples of the competition of paths to the same goal may also be found in the War Bond campaigns. People who chose to invest their money in something more profitable than bonds were choosing a path to economic gain which appeared to be better than bonds. The following list of the more common reasons given for not buying bonds will be seen to illustrate the operation of both of these principles: bonds may not be redeemed; other investments are safer; bonds aren't liquid enough; bonds give less return than other investments; bonds have too long a maturity period; bonds may be no good because we might lose the war; bonds will be worthless because of inflation; bonds are not necessary for victory; bonds prolong the war; savings should be kept in several forms; and, owning bonds gives the Government a record of my savings.

The analysis presented in this and the preceding sections specifies some of the requirements for campaigns designed to influence behavior. In brief, we have seen that a campaign must reach the sense organs with 'messages,' that these 'messages' must be of such a nature as to be accepted into existing cognitive structures, and that proposed courses of action must be seen as leading to desired goals. It might appear that, if these requirements were met, a campaign would succeed in inducing desired changes of behavior. The evidence indicates, however, that a further requirement exists.

Creating a Particular Behavioral Structure

The phrase 'good intentions' suggests the nature of this further requirement. It is quite possible for a person to have a given cognitive and motivational structure for a long period of time without its ever actually gaining control of his behavior. There are certain motivational systems, like those of hunger or thirst, which gain control of a person's action periodically because of a heightened discomfort that arises and persists until action is taken. There are, however, other systems, much more commonly those with which campaigns of mass persuasion deal, which carry with them no insistent prod to action within any clear limitation of time. To the extent that a campaign attempts to induce action in regard to systems of this latter type it must be designed to deal specifically with this problem.

4. **To induce a given action, an appropriate cognitive and motivational system must gain control of the person's behavior at a particular point in time.**

Needless to say, a person's behavior is at all times under the control of some motivational system, and the problem of inducing a given action is that of getting a particular cognitive and motivational structure in control of behavior at some specific point in time. The competition among various structures for the control of behavior is often very great. When a person is asked why he has not actually done a particular thing that he seemingly had accepted as desirable, he may answer that he did not have the time, energy, or financial resources. Such a statement is equivalent to saying that other motivational systems have maintained control of his behavior to such an extent that they monopolized his time and resources.

In selling War Bonds this type of competition was most evident. Following each of the War Loan drives a sample of those not buying bonds were asked their reasons for not buying. From one-half to three-quarters of these people replied that they "could not afford to buy bonds during the drive." This answer was, of course, a socially acceptable way of excusing oneself for not having submitted to social pressure, but in most instances it also reflected the fact that other motivational systems (such as those related to the needs for food, shelter, recreation, social status, etc.), had remained in control of behavior throughout the period of the drive. Most of these people held quite favorable attitudes toward bonds, accepted the desirability of their owning bonds, and agreed that buying bonds was a patriotic act. The problem of getting them actually to buy during a campaign consisted, therefore, not so much of creating favorable cognitive and motivational structures as of getting those structures in control of behavior at some specific point in time during the drive.

4a. The more specifically defined the path of action to a goal (in an accepted motivational structure), the more likely it is that the structure will gain control of behavior.

4b. The more specifically a path of action is located in time, the more likely it is that the structure will gain control of behavior.

Examination of a number of campaigns of mass persuasion will reveal that quite commonly the course of action being encouraged is described in relatively general terms. It is rare that the proposed action is described in concrete detail or given a precise location in time. There are, of course, good reasons for couching the language of a campaign of mass persuasion in general terms: circumstances vary greatly among people in the general population, so that a specific statement may not apply realistically to all and, if a statement is made too specific, it can more easily be rejected. But despite these difficulties, the fact seems well documented that, unless a proposed action is defined quite specifically, it is probable that it will not actually be carried out in behavior, even though it has been accepted as desirable.

The experience of the Second War Loan is especially illuminating in this connection. As we have already seen, more than $12,000,000 worth of promotion was put into this campaign. Analysis of its content, however, disclosed that the major appeal to action was expressed in the phrase, "Buy War Bonds." Interviews after the campaign revealed that this statement was sufficiently broad for people to accept the desirability of the action without feeling any pressure actually to buy bonds during the time of the campaign. In the interviews many people said in effect, "I agree completely that people should buy bonds; in fact I own quite a number myself." When asked why they had not bought during the drive, many people indicated their belief that they had conformed completely with the requests of the publicity "to buy bonds," even though they had not purchased any during the campaign.

As a result of this type of analysis of the Second Loan, Treasury officials developed quite a different campaign for the Third Loan. In this campaign the major appeal to action was phrased, "Buy an *extra* bond for the Third War Loan." In addition, an individual quota of a $100 bond was given emphasis, and other devices were used to make it clear that an extra purchase was being requested during a specified period of time. From the research following the Third Drive it became abundantly clear that the revised promotion had been much more effective. It was found, for example, that the number of people asserting that they had not bought "because I am doing my share" dropped from 19 per cent after the Second Loan to 6 per cent after the Third and that the number of people buying bonds rose from 20 to 39 per cent.

There were many ways in which the act of buying bonds could be specified in publicity. The major ways employed in the War Bond publicity were by indicating the amount to be purchased, the time for buying, and the place to buy. Thus, the campaigns said in effect, "Buy an extra $100 bond during the drive from the solicitor where you work." All available evidence indicates that this type of appeal was far more effective than those couched in more general terms.

4c. A given motivational structure may be set in control of behavior by placing the person in a situation requiring a decision to take, or not to take, a step of action that is a part of the structure.

If an action, like buying bonds, has become a part of a person's motivational structure, one way to bring that structure into control over the person's behavior is to place him in a situation where he must decide whether or not he will buy a bond at that moment. The necessity of making a decision in regard to a specific action requires that motivational structures of which this action is a part be brought to bear in determining the next step in action. When such a decision is required, the action will be taken if the resultant forces in all activated motivational structures are in the direction of that particular action. This means, of course, that forcing a decision will result in the desired action only if appropriate cognitive and motivational structures have been accepted by the person. By the same token, however, it means that the desired action will result if the appropriate structures do exist.

The technique of personal solicitation in selling War Bonds made use of this principle. When a person was solicited, he was asked to make a decision to buy, or not to buy, a bond at that time. A 'solicitor' might also take the occasion to try to create favorable cognitive and motivational structures, but the essential function of solicitation lay in the fact that it required the person to make a decision. From these considerations we may conclude that personal solicitation should precipitate bond buying among people whose motivational structure was favorable to buying bonds. In other words, a campaign of personal solicitation should greatly increase the number of people buying bonds if it follows an effective campaign of publicity and education. The more effective the publicity (in creating favorable cognitive and motivational structures) the greater should be the effect of solicitation.

The great mass of data collected after each of the War Loans supports these conclusions quite strongly. In *Table 12-3* are presented only some of these findings, selected to illustrate the results under rather different conditions. It is seen that there is a close relation between the number of people solicited in a drive and the number of people actually buying bonds. Further, the percentage of people buying bonds is much greater among those solicited than among those not solicited. In all the data analyzed the same conclusion was reached: people who were personally asked to buy were always found to be more likely to buy—in every drive, in every income bracket, in every occupational group, in every section of the country.

Table 12-3.   Some relations between personal solicitation and buying

	Second Loan April, 1943	*Third Loan Sept., 1943*	*Fourth Loan Jan., 1944*	*Fifth Loan June, 1944*
	%	%	%	%
Of all income receivers				
Were personally solicited	25	50	51	58
Bought extra bonds	20	39	45	47
Of those not solicited				
Bought extra bonds	12	18	25	22
Of those solicited				
Bought extra bonds	47	59	63	66
Number of interviews	1,358	1,583	1,441	1,925

The dependence of the outcome of solicitation upon the existence of favorable motivational structures can be seen in *Table 12-3*. Solicitation among people with more favorable structures was much more likely to precipitate buying than among those with less favorable structures (among those with three reasons for buying, 65 per cent; two reasons, 57 per cent; one reason, 44 per cent).

Conclusions

The principles presented here derive from a more extensive theory of human motivation. They are concerned with the particular motivational problem of inducing behavior 'from the outside.' To the extent that they are valid, they should apply to all inductions, whether through the mass media or in a face-to-face situation. They should also apply to inductions attempted for all types of purposes, whether to sell, to train, to supervise work, to produce therapy, and so on. In all such attempts the process of induction must be concerned with the establishment of cognitive, motivational, and behavioral structures. Only when conditions are proper in respect to all three of these, will the actual induction of behavior occur.

Applied to the field of mass persuasion, these principles may serve as a yardstick for evaluating the probable success of any proposed campaign. The principles are by no means exhaustive, nor do they give detailed guides for the creative aspects of the development of campaigns. They do, however, provide a list of essential requirements for the success of any campaign of mass persuasion. It can be seen, moreover, that, because of the inherent difficulties of meeting these requirements, campaigns are not likely to make basic changes in the behavior of large numbers of people unless there is a monopolization of the channels of communication or unless the changes being encouraged are in the same direction as those being stimulated by other influences.

13

Information Theory and Mass Communication

WILBUR SCHRAMM

For most of us, information theory dates back to Claude Shannon's notable article in the *Bell System Technical Journal,* in 1948, but its roots are far older. They reach back at least as far as the statistical mechanics of Boltsmann and Gibbs, Szilard's and von Neumann's treatments of information in physics, Nyquist's and Hartley's work with communication circuits, Wiener's development of cybernetics and Shannon's own earlier work on switching and mathematical logic. But since 1948 the theory has been responsible for significant advances in the design of electronic "brains" and governors, and for deeper understanding of electronic communication generally. It has been applied to the study of biological processes (Quastler and others), human mental processes (Wiener, McCulloch and others), mental tests (Cronbach and others), psycholinguistics (Miller, Osgood, Wilson and others) and the problem of readability (Taylor). Application has, so far, stopped short of mass communication. There has been a feeling that information theory might help us understand what goes on in a newspaper or a broadcast, but we have never been able to say just how.

It is proposed in this paper to take a brief overview of information theory itself, then to examine broadly its applicability to mass communication, and finally to look in more detail at some of the areas of mass communication in which it promises to be most helpful.

The Nature of Information Theory

Let us be clear at the outset that information theory is not a theory of information in the same sense in which that term is ordinarily used

Reprinted from *Journalism Quarterly* (Spring, 1955), pp. 131-146, by permission of the author and publisher.

by social scientists. In fact, as Kellogg Wilson has cogently remarked (10), it might well be called a *theory of signal transmission*. Its highly ingenious mathematics are concerned chiefly with the entropy or uncertainty of sequences of events in a system or related systems. Therefore, let us begin by saying what information theory means by "system."

A *system* is any part of an information chain which is capable of existing in one or more states, or in which one or more events can occur. The vibrating metal diaphragm of a telephone or a microphone is a system. So is the radio frequency amplifier circuit of a radio receiver. So is a telegraph wire. So is the air which carries the pulsations of sound waves. So is the basilar membrane of the ear. So is the optic nerve. So, in a little different sense, is the semantic system of an individual. Each of these is capable of assuming different states or playing host to different events, and each can be coupled to other systems to make a communication chain.

If information is to be transferred, systems must obviously be *coupled*. We say systems are coupled when the state of one system depends to some degree on the state of the system that adjoins it. Thus when a microphone diaphragm is depressed so as to cause a coil to cut magnetic lines of force and generate a current in a wire, those systems are coupled. When light frequencies strike the eye and cause discharges in the optic nerve, those systems are coupled. A break in the coupling will obviously prevent any information from being transferred. That is what happens when a microwave link goes out during a television broadcast, or when a student's attention wanders in class.

Most human communication chains contain a large number of coupled systems, and they contain one kind of system which Dr. Shannon has not primarily dealt with: the *functional*, as opposed to the *structural*, system. A functional system is one that *learns*; its states depend on its own past operation. The air that carries sound waves or the metal diaphragm of the microphone, is a structural system. So is the sensory system of a human being. But the central nervous system, and especially the aspect of it to which we refer as the semantic system, is a functional system. It is capable of learning. It codes and decodes information on the basis of past experience. Incidentally, this is one of the pitfalls in the way of applying information theory mathematics to human communication. These are probability formulas, and if the probabilities are altered—i.e., if any learning takes place—during the experiment, the events can no longer be regarded as a stochastic process and the formula will not apply. It is therefore necessary rigidly to control the learning factor.[1]

Systems may be either *corresponding* or *non-corresponding*. Corresponding systems are capable of existing in identical states. Thus, the sound input of the microphone and the sound output of the loudspeaker are capable of

---

[1]Which may be accomplished either by keeping the periods of experimentation very short, or by using a response already over-learned.

existing in identical states—therefore corresponding. But the air and the diaphragm are not corresponding. Neither are the diaphragm and the current, or the light signal and the central nervous system.

We can now say what information theory means by *communication*. Communication occurs when two corresponding systems, coupled together through one or more non-corresponding systems, assume identical states as a result of signal transfer along the chain. Unless the sound that goes into the telephone is reproduced by the sound that comes out of the telephone at the other end of the line, we do not have communication. Unless the concept in the semantic system of Mr. A. is reproduced in the semantic system of Mr. B., communication has not taken place. Begging the question of whether a meaning as seen by one individual can ever be reproduced exactly by another individual—or whether we can test it accurately enough to be sure—we have no great difficulty in adapting this definition to our common understanding of the term communication.

But when we define *information* in terms of information theory, then we have to get used to a somewhat different approach. We can, of course, measure the "information" transmitted along a communication chain in terms of many kinds of units—letters, morphemes, phonemes, facts (if we can satisfactorily define a fact). But none of these is satisfactory for the precise needs of information theory. Information is there defined in terms of its ability to reduce the uncertainty or disorganization of a situation at the receiving end.

Let us take an example. Suppose I tell you one "fact" about a coin toss and one "fact" about typewriter keys. I tell you that tails will not come up when the coin is next tossed, and that the letter G will not be struck when the next key is depressed on the typewriter. Now it is obvious that the information about the coin is more useful to you than the information about the typewriter in predicting what will happen. You will have no remaining doubts as to which side of the coin will come up, whereas you will still be uncertain which of the remaining 41 keys of the typewriter will be struck. In terms of information theory, more information has been transferred about the coin than about the typewriter. When a transmitted signal succeeds in reducing the number of equally probable outcomes at the receiving end by one-half, one *bit* of information is said to have been transferred. (*Bit* comes from *binary digit*.) Thus, when you reduce the two equally probable outcomes of a coin toss to one, you are using one *bit* of information. You can see that the computing of this information readily lends itself to using logarithms to the base 2, rather than our common base 10. In the case of the coin toss, $\log_2 2 = 1$ bit. But it would take $\log_2 42$ or about 5.4 bits of information to predict which typewriter key would be struck at random, or $\log_2 26$ (4.7 bits) to predict which letter of the alphabet will come up, if one is chosen at random.

This brings us to the basic terms of information theory, *entropy* and *redundancy*. Entropy simply means the uncertainty or disorganization of a system; redundancy is the opposite. Entropy is, of course, a famous term derived from mathematical physics, where it has been used to talk about Newton's second law of thermodynamics. The law that "entropy always increases," said Eddington, "holds, I think, the supreme position among the laws of Nature." It is this law, he also said—the tendency of physical systems to become always more shuffled, less organized—which is the only way we could tell whether a movie of the physical world were being run backward or forward. It is not surprising that Shannon, trying to describe information in terms of the reduction of uncertainty, should use the term entropy and the traditional mathematical symbol for that term H.

Entropy is measured in terms of the information required to eliminate the uncertainty or randomness from a situation within a system or involving two systems. Entropy will obviously be at its maximum when all states of the system are equally probable—that is, when they occur completely at random, as when a coin is tossed. The formula for maximum entropy is therefore the same as the formula for information,

$$H_{max} = \log_2 n$$

where n is the number of equally probable outcomes.

Most situations with which we deal in human communication do not have equally probable outcomes. For example, the letters of a language do not occur completely at random. If they did, the language would be complete chaos. Because we know that *e* in the English language occurs oftener than any other letter, we give it the simplest symbol in the radio-telegraph code—one dit, or short. Because there are certain combinations of letters and sounds more likely than others to occur together, we find it possible to learn to spell and understand speech. Therefore, in most communication situations, we use entropy formulas which measure the *degree* of predictability and randomness.

In order not to clutter up the path at this point, the principal formulas of information theory have been put in a brief appendix to this paper. The non-mathematical reader need remember only that mathematical tools are available to measure, among other things, the amount of uncertainty in a system (observed entropy), the degree of certainty or predictability in a system (redundancy), the degree of uncertainty in a system (relative entropy), the uncertainty of occurrence of pairs of events (joint entropy), the uncertainty of occurrence of events in sequence (conditional entropy), the amount of information transmitted under various conditions, and the capacity of a channel to transmit information.

How Applicable Is the Theory

The concepts of information theory have an insightful quality, an intuitive sort of fit, when they are applied freely to mass communication situations.

For one thing, it is obvious that human communication, like any other kind of communication, is merely a chain of coupled systems—thus,

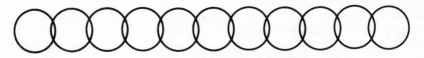

In mass communication, these chains take on certain remarkable characteristics. They are often very *long*. The account of a news event in India must
pass through very many coupled systems before it reaches a reader in Indiana.
Again, some of the systems have phenomenally high rates of output compared
to their input. Shannon would call them high-gain *amplifiers*. These are the
mass media, which have the power to produce many simultaneous and identical messages. Also, in this kind of chain, we have certain networks of systems within systems. Two of these are very important. The mass media themselves are networks of systems coupled in a complicated way so as to do the
job of decoding, interpreting, storage and encoding which we associate with
all communicators. Likewise, the individual who receives a mass media message is a part of a network of group relationships, and the workings of this
network help to determine how he responds to the message.

But each system in the mass communication chain, whatever the kind of
system, is host to a series of events which are constrained by their environments and by each other, and therefore to a certain degree predictable and subject to information theory measurements. Much of the scholarly study of mass
communication consists of an examination of the constraints on these events,
and discovering the dependency of events in one of these systems on events in
another system.

For example, a large part of what we call "effects" study is the comparison of events in one system with events in another. A readership study compares the events in a newspaper with the events in an individual's reading
behavior. A retention study compares the events in a medium with the events
in an individual's recall. And so forth. We have every reason to suspect, therefore, that a mathematical theory for studying electronic communication systems ought to have some carry-over to human communication systems.

Entropy and Redundancy

The term *entropy* is still strange to students of social communication, but *redundancy* is an old and familiar idea. The redundancy concept
of information theory gives us no great trouble. Redundancy is a measure of
certainty or predictability. In information theory, as in social communication,
the more redundant a system is, the less information it is carrying in a given
time. On the other hand, any language or any code without redundancy would
be chaos. In many cases, increasing the redundancy will make for more efficient communication.

For example, on a noisy teletype line, it helps considerably to have certain probabilities controlling what letters follow others. If a q (in English)

occurs followed by two obvious errors, the operator at the receiving end can be quite sure that the q is followed by a u and that the next letter will be another vowel. When a circuit is bad, operators arbitrarily repeat key words twice. Remember the familiar cable language—THIS IS NOT—REPEAT, NOT . . .

The amount of redundancy—using that term freely—is therefore one of the great strategy questions confronting mass communication. The most economical writing is not always the most effective writing. We could write this entire paper in the terse, economical language of mathematics, but that would not necessarily communicate most to the people who will read this paper. A newspaper reporter may choose to explain the term *photosynthesis* in twenty words, which is redundancy unnecessary to a scientist but highly necessary to a layman. There is a kind of rule of thumb, in preparing technical training materials, that two or more examples or illustrations should be given for each important rule or term. There is another rule of thumb, in broadcast commercials, that product names should be repeated three times. All these are strategy decisions, aimed at using the optimum of redundancy. And indeed, finding the optimum degree of redundancy for any given communication purpose is one of the chief problems of encoding.

Relative entropy, as we have pointed out, is merely the other side of the coin from redundancy. The lower the redundancy, the higher the relative entropy.

One of the aspects of human communication where entropy and redundancy measures have already proved their usefulness is in the study of language. Morphemes, phonemes, letters and other linguistic units obviously do not occur in a language completely at random; they are bound by certain sequential relationships, and therefore subject to measures of entropy and redundancy. We know, among other things, that the relative entropy of English is slightly less than 50%.[2] Shannon has estimated, incidentally, that if the relative entropy of the language was only 20%—if the next letter in a sequence were, on the average, 80% predictable—then it would be impossible to construct interesting crossword puzzles. But if the relative entropy were 70%—if the structure were only 30% redundant—then it would be easily possible to construct *three-dimensional* crossword puzzles (1). This information about crossword puzzles, of course, is not intended to represent the results of modern linguistic scholarship. For a more representative example, see Jacobson, Halle and Cherry on the entropy of Russian phonemes (9).

Wilson Taylor's "Cloze" procedure[3] is one of the interesting ways we have

[2]This is calculated as follows: The maximum entropy of 26 English letters is $\log_2 26$ or about 4.7 bits per letter. The sequential entropy of groups of eight letters as they occur in English usage is about 2.35 bits per letter. Therefore, the relative entropy is 2.35/4.7 or about .5. This would be lower if we figured sequential entropy for sequences longer than eight letters.

[3]See Wilson L. Taylor, "Cloze Procedure: A New Tool for Measuring Readability," JOURNALISM QUARTERLY, 30:415-33 (Fall 1953).

available for use in estimating the entropy of redundancy of prose. Taylor deletes every *n*th word in a passage, and asks readers to supply the missing words. The scatter of different words suggested for each of the missing terms provides a measure of the predictability of the passage to that particular audience. For example, if we present two paragraphs to the same group of 20 readers, and on the average this is the score they make:

Paragraph A

16 specify word A (correct)

2   B

2   C

Paragraph B

6 specify word A (correct)

4   B

4   C

3   D

1   E

1   F

1   G

—if we get this result, it is clear that the uncertainty or relative entropy of Paragraph B is considerably greater for this audience than is that of Paragraph A. Paragraph A is apparently more redundant than B. Taylor has gone into this use of information theory in his doctoral dissertation, and it is clear that the redundancy or relative entropy of a passage is closely related to its readability.

If we consider an entire mass medium as a system, then it is evident that the maximum entropy of a newpaper or a broadcasting station is immensely greater than that of a semaphor, a calling card, a personal letter or a sermon. The paper or the station has a very great freedom to do different things and produce strikingly different products. A large newspaper, like the New York *Times,* has higher maximum entropy than a smaller newspaper. If we could devise any way to make a valid comparison, I think we should find that the relative entropy of radio and television would be less than that of newspapers. If this is indeed the case, it may be that the tremendous wordage of broadcasting puts a burden on originality, and the scant feedback to a broadcasting station puts a premium on any formula which has proved popular. A successful formula is soon imitated. A popular program promptly spawns a whole family that look like it. A joke passes quickly from comedian to comedian. We might say that for comedians, joint and conditional entropy are quite low. For comic strips, relative entropy is obviously very low, and redundancy very high.

But it is also evident that no medium uses as much of the available freedom as it could. Complete freedom would mean random content. The art of being an editor or a program manager consists in no small degree of striking the right balance between predictability and uncertainty—right balance being defined as the best combination of satisfied anticipation and surprise. From time to time we have tried to quantify this amount of organization or predictability in a mass medium. One of the simpler ways to approach it is to tabulate the news sources in a paper.

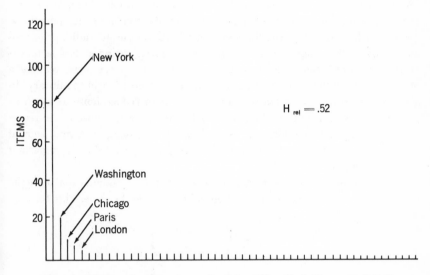

Figure 13-1.   Sources of news by cities. [New York Times, 11/8/54]

For example, Figure 13-1 is a typical distribution of news items by source in a metropolitan newspaper for one day.

The usual way we handle figures like this is by means of the statistics of central tendency—mean, standard deviation, etc. Suppose we were to handle it by information theory mathematics. If relative entropy were at a maximum, each of these news sources would be represented equally. Actually, the relative entropy of news sources in the *Times* for that day was about 52%. Throughout that week it hung around 50%, minus or plus 5. This seems quite typical of large newspapers. Four Chicago papers, two other New York papers, and the Washington *Post* and *Times Herald,* all were between 41 and 57% for the same period. The London *Times* and Paris *Figaro* were a little over 40%. During the same period, a radio news wire averaged about 45% relative entropy.

This rather remarkable order of agreement represents a pattern of constraint which, if we understood it completely, would tell us a great deal about mass media. Why do large papers, on the average, use about half the freedom open to them to represent different news sources? Availability is one reason, but the chief reason is simply that this is the editors' definition of what their clientele want, and can absorb, and *should* have, and can be given within the bounds of physical limits and custom. Information theory appears to offer us a new way to study this characteristic of the media.

The Idea of Noise

The idea of noise is another information theory concept which intuitively makes sense in the study of mass communication. Noise, as we have said, is anything in the channel other than what the communicator puts there. Noise may be competing stimuli from inside—AC hum in the radio, print visible through a thin page in a magazine, day-dreaming during a class lecture— or from outside—competing headline cues on a newspaper page, reading a book while listening to a newscast, the buzz of conversation in the library. In general, the strategy of a mass communicator is to reduce noise as much as possible in his own transmission, and to allow for expected noise in the reception. An increase in redundancy, as we have already suggested, may combat noise; a radio announcer may be well advised to repeat a highly important announcement.

The information theory formula for maximum transmission capacity in the face of noise also furnishes some guides as to what can be done. This formula is

$$W \log_2 \left(\frac{P + N}{N} \right)$$

in which W is band width, P is power of transmission, N is noise. In other words, you can approach maximum efficiency by reducing noise, increasing band width or increasing power. Two of the great problems of mass communication, of course, are to understand exactly what is meant by band width and power, for any given situation. Is the band width of a talking picture or television greater than that of a silent picture or radio?[4] Is the band width of a sight-sound medium like television greater than that of print? You can certainly increase band width by using a high fidelity phonograph, but can you also increase it by buying time on more radio stations? Similarly, what constitutes power, in this sense, within persuasive communication? Supposedly, the nature of the arguments and the source will contribute to it. Will talking louder contribute to power, so defined? Will buying bigger ads?

To basic questions like these, information theory is unlikely to contribute except by stimulating insights, but it should be pointed out that there are formu-

---

[4]Putting simultaneous and reinforcing cues in a single band of communication supposedly adds to the "power" of a message. For example, a speaker may emphasize a point by choice of words, by speaking louder, by pausing just before the key word, by gestures, by facial expression, etc. But suppose one of these cues is not congruent with the others. For example, suppose the speaker winks in the midst of all this seriousness. Or suppose his voice trails up when it should go down. This seems to be the way we use simultaneous cues in a wide band to represent satire or humor or irony.

las for calculating noise which may well prove to be useful in tests of learning and retention from mass communication, and in rumor analysis and other functions of communication chains.

Coupling

That brings us to talk of coupling, which is another point at which information theory comes very close to our usual way of thinking about human communication. We are accustomed to think of "gatekeepers." Strictly speaking, every system that couples two other systems is a gatekeeper. But there are certain especially important gatekeepers in mass communication: the reporter walking his beat, the telegraph editor deciding on what to select from the wire, the press association wire filer deciding what stories to pass on, the commentator deciding what aspect of current life to focus on, the magazine editor deciding what parts of the environment to represent, and others. All these are subject to the stability and fidelity measures of information theory: how likely are they to pass on the information that comes to them? How faithfully are they likely to reproduce it?

Even the terms used to talk about fidelity in electronic systems sound familiar to us in light of our experience with mass communication. How much of the information do the gatekeepers *filter out?* How much *fading* and *booming* do they introduce (by changing the emphasis of the message)? How much *systematic distortion* are they responsible for (through bias)? How much *random distortion* (through carelessness or ignorance)?

The newspaper itself—if we want to consider it as a system—is a gatekeeper of the greatest importance. The daily life of a city presents itself to the paper's input. Selected bits of the daily life of the rest of the world enter the input through the telegraph desk. What comes out? What is the stability of the paper for reproducing local news as compared with national news, civic news as compared with crime news, news of one presidential candidate as compared with news of another? And what about fidelity? To what extent does the paper change its input by cutting, by rewriting, by choosing a headline which affects the meaning, by giving one story better position than another?

Think of the reporter walking his beat. Everything he sees and hears is news for someone, but he must make a selection in terms of what his editors and—supposedly—his readers want. His stability is necessarily low. But how is his fidelity? Does he get the quotes from a speech right? Does he report an accident accurately?

Or think of the receiver at the end of the mass communication chain. What stories from the *Reader's Digest,* what items from the newspaper, does he pass on to his friends? And how accurately does he represent the content? Does he reproduce the part of the content which reinforces his previous attitudes? Does he get the point of an article?

Rumor analysis is a fascinating use for the coupling concepts of information theory. What kinds of rumors encourage the stability of the chain—that is, what kinds of rumors will tend to be passed on? And what factors govern how faithfully a rumor is passed on?

Content analysis codes are subject to study for stability and fidelity. How much of the information in the measured content do they respond to? How faithfully do they reproduce it? As a matter of fact, many of the concepts of information theory are stimulating to content study. For example, the heavy redundancy of Communist propaganda shows up from almost any content study, as does the relatively low entropy of the semantic systems within which the Communist propagandist works. The close coupling of units in the Communist propaganda chain is striking. And the stability and fidelity of the Communist gatekeepers, transmitting the official line, are very high. If they are not, the Party gets a new gatekeeper.

Measures of stability and fidelity are available, in information theory, and relatively easy to use. When they are applied to a long chain—such as the one, previously referred to, which carries news from "India to Indiana" and back—it becomes apparent that the stability of the main points along the chain is quite high: that is, a bureau like London is quite likely to pass along a story that comes from New Delhi. The closer one gets to the source of news, the lower the stability, because the input is large, the output capacity relatively small. Bloomington, for example, regularly publishes about 65 local stories, but can only put two or three on the wire. Delhi, likewise, can send London only a small part of the Indian news. Chicago, on the other hand, can send out more than half the stories available. The problem in measuring the fidelity of this kind of chain is to define measurable units. Using length as one criterion, it becomes apparent that the greatest loss is near the source of news. Using rewriting as a criterion, it seems that the chief rewriting is done at the first wire points and the chief national bureaus.

Channel Capacity

Channel capacity is another important concept which is common both to information theory and to mass communication. All channels, human, electronic or mechanical, have an upper limit on their ability to assume different states or carry different events. We can estimate, for example, the amount of information the eye is capable of transmitting to the optic nerve, and it is less than the information available to the eye, although apparently more than the semantic system can handle. We can estimate the capacity of a telephone line or a microphone, and have very good formulas for doing so. But when we consider the characteristics of a chain and recall that the chain is no stronger than its weakest link, then our chief interest turns to the channel capacity of man, who is the weakest link in most communication chains.

Perceptual experiments have told us a great deal about the ability of man to transmit information through some of his systems. In general, we can say that man's ability to handle information is faster than most mechanical systems (such as smoke signals and flags), but far slower than that of most electronic devices (e.g., the electronic computers). We still have a great deal to find out about man's capacity for handling language and pictorial information.

Many of the capacity problems of mass communications, of course, find man at the mercy of his works. The reporter who has only 30 minutes to write his story before deadline, the editor who is permitted to file only 200 words on the wire, the radio news bureau desk which has room for only 13 minutes of copy and must select from 300 stories, the editor who finds a big advertising day crowding out his news—all these are communicators suffering from capacity problems they have helped to make. It is also obvious that the channel capacity of *The New York Times* is greater than that of a small daily. But for the *Times* and its smaller brothers there is an even greater channel restriction: the reader. The reader of a daily can spend, on the average, about 40 minutes on his paper. And he reads rather slowly. Even so, he can read faster than he can listen, so to speak. A radio speaker usually stays under 150 words a minute, not because he cannot talk faster, but because he fears he will crowd the channel capacity of his listeners.

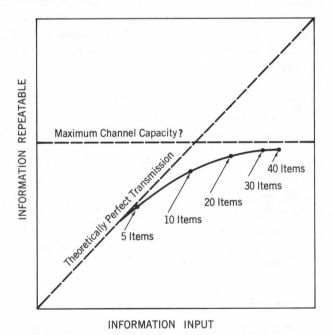

Figure 13-2. Ability to repeat information from newscasts.

Shannon has developed a theorem for a channel with noise which is both remarkable in itself and highly meaningful for persons concerned with mass communication (1). His theorem says, in effect, that for rates of transmission less than the capacity of a channel it is possible to reduce noise to any desired level by improving the coding of the information to be transmitted; but that for rates of transmission greater than channel capacity it is never possible to reduce noise below the amount by which the rate of transmission exceeds channel capacity. In other words, as Wilson notes, error can be reduced as much as desired if only the rate of transmission is kept below the total capacity of the channel; but if we overload the channel, then error increases very swiftly.

Information theory thus promises us real assistance in studying the capacity of channels. For example, in a recent publication (10) an information theory model is proposed to measure an individual's channel capacity for semantic decoding. Verbal information is to be fed the individual at increasing rates. This information consists of a group of adjectives describing an object. The receiver is asked to respond in each case by touching the corresponding object, in a group of objects, in front of him. (He has already over-learned this response, so supposedly no learning takes place during the experiment.) The time from the stimulus until the subject touches an object is taken as the total time for decoding and encoding. It is hypothesized that as the rate increases this total time will decrease until it becomes stable. As the rate increases further, the number of errors will begin to increase, until at a certain rate the time will become highly variable and the process will break down. The rate at which the total time becomes stable is taken as the optimum channel capacity, because it is there that the largest amount of accurate information is being transmitted.

This experiment has not yet been done with the accurate controls which would be required, but some striking confirmation of it comes out of experiments with retention of newscasts. Subjects were presented newscasts of increasing density but constant length—5, 10, 20, 30, 40, 50 items. The average subject's ability to recall the subject of these items leveled off vary sharply between 10 and 20. There was practically no additional learning between 20 and 30. After 20, the number of errors began to increase rather sharply. In other words, the amount of information transmitted behaved about as hypothesized above, and the resulting curve was strikingly like those typically resulting from experiments on the capacity of subjects to discriminate among stimuli—as shown in Figure 13-2 [on p. 183].

Networks

Of all the potential contributions of information theory to mass communication, perhaps the most promising is in the study of communication networks. Networks are as important in mass communication as in electronic communication. Every functional group is a communication network. The staff of a newspaper or a broadcasting station, a film production crew, the group with which a member of the mass communication audience talks over what he reads, hears and sees—all these are communication networks. The intercommunication within the network is measurable, whether it consists of conversation, print, gestures or electronic currents.

Osgood and Wilson, in a mimeographed publication,[5] have suggested a series of measures derived from information theory, for dealing with groups. In addition to the common entropy, redundancy, noise, fidelity and capacity measures, they suggest *traffic* (what members do the most talking, and how much talking is done?), *closure* (to what extent is the group a closed corporation?), and *congruence* (to what extent do members participate equally in the communication of the group, or to what extent are there members who are chiefly talkers and others who are chiefly listeners?). All these formulations can be dealt with mathematically. Measures like these suggest a quite different and stimulating way of studying small groups, and in particular they commend themselves for use in studying the important groups within mass communication.

Suppose, for example, we want to study some part of the world news network. Suppose that we take the chief newspapers of the leading cities in half a dozen countries—for example, the United States, Great Britain, France, Germany, Italy and the Soviet Union—and tabulate for one week the stories which the papers in each city carry from the other cities in the network. This has been done in a small way, with interesting results. Washington has the greatest output traffic, New York the greatest input traffic. Moscow has the greatest degree of individual closure: that is, it is most likely to talk, if at all, to itself. Within a country, there are startling differences in the amount and distribution of input. In general there appears to be a little more organization (redundancy) in the pattern of input than in the pattern of output: that is, source entropy is higher than destination entropy. And the congruence (the correlation between source and destination frequencies of points in the network) varies markedly with political conditions and cultural relationships at a particular time.

Let us take a simpler example of group communication. Here is a record of telephone calls amongst four boys (who telephoned incessantly). The calls were tabulated at periods two months apart—20 calls while the boys were organizing a school newspaper, and 20 calls two months later after the paper was well launched.

It is clear that the relative transitional entropy of this group became less

[5]"A Vocabulary for Talking about Communication," colloquium paper, Institute of Communications Research, University of Illinois.

Table 13-1. Twenty telephone calls by four boys

A. In Process of Organizing a School Newspaper

	Mike	Bud	Mike T.	John	
Mike		4	4	2	10
Bud	3		1	2	6
Mike T.	1	1		0	2
John	1	1	0		2
	5	6	5	4	

B. After School Newspaper had been Published 2 Months

	Mike	Bud	Mike T.	John	
Mike		3	1	1	5
Bud	7		1	0	8
Mike T.	5	1		0	6
John	1	0	0		1
	13	4	2	1	

in the two months—that is, it became better organized—and also that the congruence had changed so that increasingly one pattern could be predicted: i.e., the boys would call Mike. It seems that whereas Mike must have been the organizer at first, he became the leader later, and the other boys turned to him for advice or instructions.

This kind of result suggests the hypothesis that the entropy of communication within a functional group decreases as the group becomes more fully organized into work roles and better perceives the existence of leadership. By way of testing this and preparing the way for studying actual media staffs, some experiments have been done with groups of five journalism students who were given assignments that simulated the work of an actual newspaper staff, including reporting, reference, editing, copyreading and setting in type. All their intercommunications were recorded. Not enough groups have yet been put through the procedure to reveal all the variables, but the pattern so far is very clear and interesting. Some of the groups were started on their assignments entirely unstructured—that is, no roles were assigned. In others a leader was appointed. In still others, every person was assigned a job. Inasmuch as some measure of leadership almost always appeared, regardless of assignment, participants were asked at the end whether they perceived a leader or leaders, and if so, whom? This, in general, seems to be the pattern:

> (1) As the perception of leadership increases, the relative transitional entropy of communication in the group decreases—that is, it becomes easier to predict who will talk to whom.

(b) As the degree of initial organization is increased, the total amount of communication decreases and the total time required to do the job decreases.

(c) However, between the group in which a leader is appointed and the group in which all members are assigned roles, these measures change much less than between the other groups and the unstructured group. In some cases, the group in which a leader only was appointed actually finished the job more quickly than the group in which all roles were assigned. This suggests that there may be a stage in which increasing organization does not contribute to efficiency; and also, that it must make a difference who is appointed leader, even in these previously unacquainted groups.

These results are presented only to suggest that the approach is a promising one for group study, and especially for the study of the kind of functional groups that play such an important part in mass communication.

Finally

How can we sum up the import of all this for the study of mass communication?

Even such a brief overview as this must make it clear that information theory is suggestive and stimulating for students of human communication. It must be equally clear that the power of the theory and its stimulating analogic quality are greatly at variance with the puny quality of the mathematical examples I have been able to cite—that is, examples of the use so far made of information theory mathematics in studying mass communication. Why should this be?

The theory is now—1948, as I have said, for most of us. Its application is fringed with dangers. One of these has been indicated—the danger of working with stochastic processes in functional systems which may learn and thereby change the probabilities. It should also be said that we do not as yet know much about the sampling distributions of these entropy formulas, and it is therefore not always wise to use them for hypothesis testing and statistical inference. Finally, we must admit frankly the difficulty of bridging the gap between the formula's concept of information (which is concerned only with the number of binary choices necessary to specify an event in a system) and our concept of information in human communication (which is concerned with the relation of a fact to outside events—e.g., how "informative" is it?).

This is not to say that the transfer cannot be made. Certainly I have no intention of saying that the theory has only analogic value, and that the contribution of its mathematical tools is necessarily small. These tools seem to me to be extremely promising in the study of language, channel capacities, couplings, and network groups, if nowhere else. It will be to our advantage to explore these uses and others.

Appendix

The Basic Formulas

It may be helpful to explain the basic entropy formula here in order to give a better idea of what information theory has to offer mathematically.

Let us begin with an event which we call *i* within a system which we can call *I*.[6] (For example *i* may be the yellow light on a traffic light *I*.) Then let us call p(i) the probability of event i occurring within the system. This is equivalent to saying that p(i) equals 1/a, in which a is a certain number of equally probable classes. (For example, the yellow light in a traffic light occurs two times in four events, so that its probability is 1/2.) The information we need to predict the occurrence of event i is therefore $\log_2 a$. By algebraic transformation, we can say that, since p(i) equals 1/a, a equals 1/p(i). Therefore the information necessary to specify the one event i is $\log_2(1/p(i))$. Since the logarithm of x/y always equals log x — log y, we have the information necessary to specify event i equal to $\log_2 1 - \log_2 p(i)$. The log of 1 is always zero, and therefore we arrive at an equation which states the amount of information necessary to specify one event in a system (let us call this information h(i)),

$$h\ (i) = -\log_2 p(i)$$

Now what we need is an estimate of the average amount of entropy associated with all the states of a system. The average of a sample of numbers can be expressed as

$$\sum_i \frac{i\ f(i)}{n}$$

where i is the numerical value of any class of numbers, f(i) is the frequency of occurrence of that class, n is the sample size, and $\sum_i$ is the term for sum of all the i's. But f(i)/n is the same as an estimate of probability, which we called p (i), and which we can here substitute in the term for an average as follows:

$$\sum_i i\ p(i)$$

Therefore, if we want the average amount of information needed to predict the occurrence of the states of a system I, we can use this term and substitute the information symbol for the numerical value, thus,

---

[6]This explanation of the formula for observed entropy in general follows the approach of Wilson in bibliography item (10). Wilson's treatment of the subject is easy to read and still both solid and stimulating, and is recommended to beginners in this field.

$$H(I) = \sum_i h(i)\, p(i), \text{ or}$$

$$H(I) = -\sum_i p_I \log_2 p(i)$$

This last expression is the basic formula for observed entropy.

It is clear that this formula will equal zero when the probability of one event is unity and the probability of all other events is zero: in other words, when there is no uncertainty in the system. It is also clear that the formula will approach H_{max} (which, you will remember, is $\log_2 n$) as the events in the system become more nearly equally probable, so that there is maximum uncertainty in the system. In a coin toss, for example, observed entropy is the same as maximum entropy ($\log_2 2$, or 1) because the events are equally probable. However, the more events in a system, the higher the observed entropy is likely to grow. Therefore, it becomes useful to have a measure by which to compare systems which have different numbers of states. This is the formula for *relative entropy*, which is simply the observed entropy of a system divided by its maximum entropy—

$$H_{rel}(I) = \frac{H(I)}{H_{max}}$$

From the basic formula, we get the formula for *joint entropy*, which is simply the entropy for the occurrence of pairs of events (for example, q and u together in a sample of English words) and which is written,

$$H(I,J) = -\sum_{i,j} p(i,j)\log_2 p(i,j)$$

This is read exactly like the basic entropy formula except that (i,j) stands for the occurrence of events n and j together. We also get a formula for *conditional entropy*, which deals with the occurrence of two events in sequence (for example, the occurrence of *u* after *q* in a sample of English words). This is written,

$$H_I J = \sum_{i,j} p(i,j)\log_2 p_1(j)$$

in which $p_1 j$ represents the probability of the occurrence of j after i has occurred.

Among the other formulas available are those for redundancy (basically, $1 - H_{fel}$), amount of information transmitted, channel capacity, noise and maximum effective coding in the face of noise. It is not believed necessary to speak in any greater detail of these measures at this point, inasmuch as the purpose of these pages is to give a general idea of the theory rather than a complete description of it.

Computing the Commoner Measures

Maximum entropy, of course, may be computed simply by taking the log (to the base 2) of the total number of events in the system.

In computing the other entropy measures from social data, it will be necessary to estimate the probabilities of events within systems by counting frequencies of occurrence over some uniform time period. For example, if a traffic light were a new phenomenon to us, we might count the occurrence of red, yellow and green events for a certain length of time and get, say, 10 each for red and green, 20 for yellow, out of 40 events. From these we should estimate the probability of red and green as $\frac{1}{4}$ each, of yellow as $\frac{1}{2}$. To estimate the probabilities of events in two systems or of sequential events in one system, it is helpful to use a table like this one:

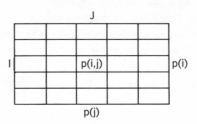

Having computed the values of $H(I)$, $H(J)$, $H(I,J)$ from this kind of table, the values of the conditional entropies may be obtained, if desired, by the following relationships:

$$H_I(J) = H(I,J) - H(I)$$
$$H_J(I) = H(I,J) - H(J)$$

It is not necessary to do all the calculation which would seem to be required to turn the probabilities into entropy scores, if one uses such a table as that of Dolansky and Dolansky (see bibliography) which is recommended to anyone making extensive use of these formulas.

A Short List of Readings on Information Theory

The Basic Theory:

1. SHANNON, C. E., and WEAVER, WARREN, *The Mathematical Theory of Communication.* Urbana, 1949. (Contains the classical article by Shannon, with comments by Weaver. For readers without a good mathematical background, Weaver is a better beginning article than Shannon.)
2. WEINER, NORBERT, *Cybernetics.* New York, 1948. (Stimulating in that it contains much of the viewpoint for Shannon's later development.)
3. FANO, R. M., *The Transmission of Information.* MIT Technical Reports 65 and 149. Cambridge, 1949-50. (Highly mathematical.)
4. GOLDMAN, STANFORD, *Information Theory.* New York, 1953. (Textbook for graduate students in electrical engineering.)

5. MILLER, G. A., "What Is Information Measurement?", *American Psychologist,* 8:3-11 (1953). (Non-technical, and a good beginning point for non-mathematicians.)

Tables for Computing Information Theory Measures:

6. DOLANSKY, L., and DOLANSKY, M. P., *Table of $log_2 1/p$, $p\ log_2 1/p$, $p\ log_2 +$ $(1—p)\ log_2\ (1—p)$.* MIT Technical Report 277. Cambridge, 1952. (The most complete tables.)
7. NEWMAN, E. B., "Computational Methods Useful in Analyzing Series of Binary Data," *American Journal of Psychology,* 64:252-62 (1951).

Examples of Applications:

8. GARNER, W. H., and HAKE, H. W., "The Amount of Information in Absolute Judgments," *Psychological Review,* 58:446-59 (1951). (Joint and conditional entropy used to measure stimulus-response relationships.)
9. JAKOBSON, R., HALLE, H., and CHERRY, E. C., "Towards the Logical Description of Languages in Their Phonemic Aspect," *Language,* 29:34-46 (1953).
10. OSGOOD, C. E., editor, SEBOCK, T. A., and others, *Psycholinguistics: A Survey of Theory and Research Problems.* Supplement to *International Journal of American Linguistics,* 20:4 (1954). (Sections on information theory are stimulating and easy to read; they are written mostly by K. Wilson.)

IV

INFLUENCE,
ADOPTION,
AND INNOVATION

MASS COMMUNICATORS HAVE LONG BEEN VAGUELY AWARE THAT their messages did not stop at the point where they initially reached the ears or eyes of listeners and readers. Instead, the messages are often passed along from person to person. Informal communications among individuals may be quite different from the original message of the mass communicator, a fact that can be disturbing and also nearly impossible to control.

Communications between individuals may or may not originate as the result of mass communication messages. The consumer who had a dissatisfying experience with a product may initiate a pattern of communications that devastates the image that the seller had intended to establish. On other occasions buyers may add reinforcement to the sellers' messages. In a sense, the impersonal mass communication becomes a personal communication that can influence still additional persons. The impact of this personal influence is exceptionally strong, and sellers generally agree that negative informal influences can cancel the effects of the best and most extensive of advertising campaigns.

A special case of informal communication effects is found in innovation and new-product studies. Investigations in rural sociology, advertising research, and new-product research show similar patterns of innovation, adoption, or trial by individuals in contact with new ideas and products. Some of these studies show clearly the importance both of favorable response from the initial users of new ideas and products and their patterns of influence.

193

14

The Communications Process and Innovation

WILLIAM LAZER
and WILLIAM E. BELL

One of the most perplexing, yet important, problems in market communications is that of ascertaining the influence of innovators. Since an innovator, by definition, is the first to adopt a product or idea, it seems logical to assume that he would serve as an important agent in the dissemination of practices and ideas—would serve as a local demonstrator, an influencer of local change, and as a direct line of communication for the remainder of the community. If this is true, extensive effort could then be directed at communicating with and selling the innovator on a new idea, product, or practice.

However, some researchers report that because innovators are "different," they are not, in fact, the influentials. In reality the next adopter group rather than the innovators are the influentials, because the former are more like the rest of the population (Beal and Bohlen, 1957; Copp, Still and Brown, 1958; Wilkening, 1956). As far as innovators are concerned, perhaps it is proper to say that they are watched but are not followed (Lionberger, 1960).

Research Literature

To date, the research literature contains insufficient evidence on which to draw valid conclusions about the actual influence of innovators. Much of the research concerning the flow of communications in marketing new products has been done by rural sociologists. They have as their major concern the dissemination of communications about new ideas and products related to farming. On the basis of over 200 research projects, tentative conclusions have been formulated about the acceptance of innovations with particular attention given to the adoption process.

Reprinted from *Journal of Advertising Research* (September, 1966), pp. 2-7, by permission of the authors and publisher. ©Advertising Research Foundation, Inc., (1966).

The adoption process means the acceptance of new ideas and products. It concerns various mental and action states of consumers from the time of awareness that a new idea or product is available until it is accepted. In consumption terms, it is congruent with the problem-solving steps taken by innovators. Five progressive phases have been delineated: 1) Awareness, 2) Interest, 3) Evaluation, 4) Trial, and 5) Adoption. (See Beal, 1958; Beal, Rogers and Bohlen, 1957; Cooperative Extension Service, 1961; Hassinger, 1959.)

Awareness

At the awareness stage, a person first learns about new ideas, products, or practices. He has only general information about them, knows little or nothing about their special qualities or potential usefulness, or how they would likely work for him.

Interest

The individual develops an interest in the new thing that he has learned about. No longer satisfied with mere knowledge of its existence, he wants more detailed information about what it is, how it will work, and what it will do. He is willing to listen, read, and learn more about it, and is inclined actively to seek the desired information.

Evaluation

After developing interest, he weighs the information and evidence accumulated in the previous stages in order to decide whether the new ideas, products, or practices are basically good—especially whether they are good for him. In a sense, he reasons through the pros and cons mentally, and applies them to his own situation. This might be referred to as the "mental trial stage." While evaluation is involved at all stages of the adoption process, it is most evident and needed at this level.

Trial

The individual is confronted with a distinctly different set of problems. He must actually put the change into practice—he must learn. Competent personal assistance may be required in deciding how, when and where, to use the innovation. The usual pattern of acceptance is to try a little at first and then, if the small-scale experiment proves successful, to make large-scale use of it.

Adoption

Adoption is the last stage in the process. Here a person decides that the new idea, product, or practice is good enough for full scale and continued use, and a complete change is made with that end in view.

This pattern has been discerned for innovation in farm products. It establishes innovators as deliberate problem solvers and careful purchasers. The universality of this process seems to be widely accepted, but is this truly the case? Are these stages applicable to purchase decisions for products other than the farm products studied? Research findings have not conclusively established this. In fact, a major study relating to innovation in non-farm products suggests that the problem-solving approach is not applicable. Among the salient points recorded in this research were:

1. Little or no family discussion precedes a durable goods purchase in 71 per cent of families surveyed.

2. Only one store was visited by 47 per cent of the people who bought a new TV set, refrigerator, washer or stove.

3. Only 21 per cent of the buyers remembered receiving information from advertisements and circulars.

4. Sixty-two per cent said that they did not receive information from any reading material, ads, billboards, or point of purchase.

5. More than half of all buyers did not choose between models in different price classes, and considered only one price.

6. The older and presumably more seasoned the consumer, the less deliberate his purchases become.

7. As active information seekers, rural consumers are almost as circumspect as those in large metropolitan markets.

Innovators were not found to be rational problem solvers. In fact through the use of a scaling technique, this research data revealed that only 20 per cent of the sample could be classified as careful purchasers. In this case, the problem-solving approach had relatively little validity, particularly in the evaluation stage.

Research has been done on the information used during each phase of

Table 14-1. Rank order of information sources by stage in the adoption process

Awareness: learns about a new idea or practice	Interest: gets more information about it	Evaluation: tries it out mentally	Trial: uses or tries a little	Adoption: accepts it for full-scale and continued use
1. Mass media— radio, TV, newspapers, magazines	1. Mass media	1. Friends and neighbors	1. Friends and neighbors	1. Friends and neighbors
2. Friends and neighbors— mostly other farmers	2. Friends and neighbors	2. Agricultural agencies	2. Agricultural agencies	2. Agricultural agencies
3. Agricultural agencies, Extension, Vo-Ag.	3. Agricultural agencies	3. Dealers and salesmen	3. Dealers and salesmen	3. Mass media
4. Dealers and salesmen	4. Dealers and salesmen	4. Mass media	4. Mass media	4. Dealers and salesmen

Personal experience is the most important factor in continued use of an idea.

the adoption process in the purchase of farm products. Information sources vary with each stage. Table 14-1 (derived from C.E.S., 1961) presents a summary of the frequency ranking of information sources as they relate to various stages of the adoption process.

Mass media are mentioned most often as information sources at the awareness and interest stages. Farm magazines and farm papers are used in greater frequency than other mass media such as newspapers, radio, and television. When a final purchase decision is to made, however, neighbors and friends become the sources consulted most often. Thus, informal groups become most influential after the formal media create awareness and interest (Beal and Bohlen, 1957; Copp, Still and Brown, 1958; Wilkening, 1956).

Empirical Investigation

Study Criteria

An immediate problem in studying innovations is the development of an operational definition of innovation and the establishment and selection of criteria for the kinds of innovations to be studied. The following criteria were adopted for the study:

1. A product is an innovation if less than 10 per cent market penetration exists in a given geographic location.

2. Any product studied should have a potential market among a broad cross-section of consumers. This excludes products which appeal to a specific social class, ethnic group, or other special market segments.

3. The products should not be necessities so that potential consumers can exercise discretion in deciding whether to accept or reject them.

4. Information identifying purchasers must be available so that they can be studied. This criterion excludes innovations which are purchased mainly as gifts.

5. The purchase should be relatively recent so that the innovator's recall of the selection process is adequate.

Products from a single industry, the household appliance industry, were chosen for investigation. The specific items and their market saturation are shown in Table 14-2.

Table 14-2. Products studied

Innovation	Per Cent of Market Saturation
Color television	0.6
Stereophonic equipment	9.3
Automatic dishwashers	5.2
Air conditioners (room & central)	6.1

The Sample

The published data which form the background for this study are part of the Sixth Quinquennial Survey of the Detroit Market, published by the Detroit News. An analysis of product ownership of this group revealed that 498 households in the Detroit area had at least one of the four innovistic products being studied. The Detroit area was then divided into five geographic strata and a quota sample was drawn up from each. A minimum of 20 households were selected from each of the five strata. One hundred and nine interviews were obtained from innovators, and they constitute the basis for this investigation of the communications process of innovators.

Selected Findings

Awareness of Innovations

Several researchers have found that mass media are the primary sources of information in making innovators aware of innovations. This study revealed some contradictory evidence. When the owners of the innovations were asked "Where did you first hear about the product(s) you own?", responses were as follows.

Only 13.8 per cent of the responses referred to the four major mass media, radio, TV, magazines, and newspapers. This contrasts with the importance of informal, personal communications, which accounted for 38.5 per cent of the responses. The category, "other," was comprised mainly of owners of dishwashers, and here, home builders made the suggestion and explained the product. It is interesting that store displays and other point-of-sale merchan-

Table 14-3. Sources of original information about innovations

Sources	Per Cent of Times Items Mentioned*
Friends	38.5
In store	11.0
TV	4.6
Newspaper	4.6
Magazines	3.7
Radio	.9
Other	45.9
Don't know	20.2

Total greater than 100 per cent owing to multiple responses.

dising techniques outranked the mass media as communications media for the appliances. The sources of original information about innovations are displayed in Table 14-3.

Media Exposure

It was hypothesized that perhaps individuals who are innovators may not get the exposure to mass media that the "average consumer" does. Perhaps their socioeconomic strata and the social life they lead preclude them from watching television and reading magazines to the same degree as other consumers. This does not seem to be the case.

The response to the question, "On the average, how many hours a week do you watch television?" is shown in Table 14-4. Almost 50 per cent of the innovators are exposed to three or more hours of television per day. Since a tendency often exists to underestimate the number of hours spent viewing television, the actual figure may even be higher.

Table 14-4. Number of hours a week spent viewing television

Number of Hours	Per Cent Responding
Less than 6	19.3
6 but less than 11	12.8
11 but less than 16	11.9
16 but less than 21	6.4
21 but less than 26	14.7
26 or more	34.9

Innovators were exposed to a larger number of magazines in their home than the national average. The 109 homes interviewed had 659 magazines, slightly over six per household. An indication of the type of magazine and the relative frequency of its appearance can be gained from Table 14-5.

Table 14-5. Magazines in the innovistic household

Type of Magazine	Per Cent Obtaining (N = 659)
Home and garden	33.3
General magazines	31.6
News and business	7.1
Sports and men's	4.7
Hobby	3.8
Fashion	3.2
Fiction	2.4
Buying guides	2.0
Literary	1.7
Other	10.2

Interest and Evaluation of Innovations

After becoming aware of a new product offering, where do innovators gain the information desired to enable them to evaluate new products? Being the first to buy, they cannot benefit from the experience of friends and neighbors. Over 75 per cent of the respondents did not seek any advice from other individuals. Even when innovators consult others, they do not consult individuals outside the family. Thus while informal sources of information are of prime importance for awareness, their influence seems to be negligible during the interest and evaluation stage.

There was an indication, however, that after awareness was created, additional information about the products was sought, and that innovators did attempt to evaluate prospective purchases. Over 53 per cent of the respondents indicated they sought additional information about new products. Mass media, of some type, were mentioned as a source of such information by over 96 per cent of the respondents. Over 74 per cent mentioned the use of publications and organizations established for providing consumer information. Examples cited were: *Consumers' Report, Consumers' Guide, Changing Times,* and the *Better Business Bureau.* Table 14-6 shows the sources utilized as a percentage of those consulting.

Table 14-6. Consulting sources of information

Source	Per Cent of Those Consulting
Mass media	96.5
Consumer publications and organizations	74.1
Friends and relatives	56.8
Salesmen and dealers	6.8
Technical	6.8
Other	13.8

Influence on Purchases

Are mass media effective in selling innovators on the new product? One possible indication of their effect may be found in the amount of shopping done by the innovators. If innovators have made up their minds about particular models, brands, and styles before visiting retail outlets, then it would seem that the information given in mass media has some effect. On the other hand, if they actively shop for innovative products, then mass media may not be very effective. It should be noted that household appliances are usually considered shopping goods since potential customers shop different stores before purchasing them.

Table 14-7 shows the number of stores visited by respondents before purchasing new products. It points out clearly that innovators are not shoppers—they have made up their minds prior to store visits. Fifty-six per cent of the responses indicate that only one retail store was contacted and the purchase

Table 14-7.   Number of stores visited

No. of Stores	Per Cent Responses*
0	20.2
1	56.0
2	10.1
3	10.4
4	15.6
5	3.7
More than 5	11.0

Total greater than 100 per cent because of multiple product ownership in some instances with a different number of visits for each product.

was then made. Eighty-six per cent of the innovators visited two or fewer stores. A surprising number of innovistic products were also purchased outside the normal retail outlet. This applied particularly to dishwashers which were frequently purchased through the home builder.

Innovators as Influentials

Do innovators play an influential role in the communication process? Researchers investigating farm products and the communication of ideas found that they do, but we are concerned exclusively with new consumer products.

To assess the role the innovator plays as an influential, two questions were asked. The first was whether anyone who might be interested in buying any of the innovistic products had asked to see the ones owned. Almost half of the respondents had shown their products to prospective buyers, but almost half did not; one per cent did not remember.

The second question was whether innovators had been asked their opinions of their purchases. While slightly less than half actually exhibited their products, a higher proportion (65.1 per cent) reported that they had been asked their opinion of the products owned.

What about the purchase reaction of inquiring potential buyers? Of those respondents who said they either demonstrated or were questioned about their products, 64 per cent asserted that inquiring people did purchase at a later date, 28 per cent reported that the potentials did not, and 8 per cent did not know. Innovators, therefore, seem to play a significant role in the informal communications process.

Since innovators by definition reflect a situation where market saturation is less than 10 per cent, they may form unique social groups where all their associates already own the products studied. Thus, the people being studied would not then be innovistic leaders among their friends and neighbors, but perhaps followers. The respondents were asked what proportion of their friends owned any of the innovistic products. The replies, summarized in Table 14-8, show that respondents were truly innovistic leaders. Over 60 per cent reported that few of their friends owned the products.

Table 14-8. Friends owning innovistic products

Number of Friends Owning Innovistic Products	Per Cent Responding*
All	5.5
Most	22.0
Half	22.9
Few	61.5
None	9.2
Don't know	6.4

Total exceeds 100 per cent owing to multiple product owners having different responses.

Additional evidence is given in Table 14-9. When asked if their friends purchased before, at the same time, or after their own purchase, it became evident that twice as many innovistic owners bought before their friends.

Table 14-9. Comparison of time of purchase: friends and innovators

Time of Purchase of Friend	Per Cent Responding*
Before the innovator	22.9
At the same time as innovator	14.7
After the innovator	45.9
Some before, some after the innovator	21.2
No friends own	9.2
Don't know	12.8

Total exceeds 100 per cent owing to multiple product owners having different responses.

Implications for Marketing

The following marketing implications are suggested by the findings of this study:

1. Mass media may not be effective channels for making innovators aware of innovation. Informal personal communications, displays, and point-of-sales techniques may be better.

2. After awareness is created, however, innovators do seek additional information about innovations from mass media. They are significantly influenced in their evaluations of innovations and in their purchase decisions by mass media. This would suggest the importance of informative advertising copy.

3. Before visiting retail stores, innovators are presold. They do not shop for innovations. Advertising, therefore, performs the major portion of the actual selling task.

4. Two conflicting inferences are suggested by the fact that innovators do not recognize mass media advertising as an important source of information post facto. First, advertising may be doing an effective job but the innovators do not consciously recognize it. Second, advertising may not be doing a good job in introducing product innovations. In the light of research finding concerning farm practices and ideas, which show that mass media are most important in the awareness stage, marketing executives should explore this dilemma.

References

BEAL, G. M. "Information Sources in the Decision-Making Process." *The Research Clinic on Decision Making.* Pullman, Wash.; State College of Washington, August 1958, pp. 36-51.

BEAL, G. M. and J. M. BOHLEN. *The Diffusion Process.* Ames, Iowa: Agricultural Extension Service Report No. 18, March 1957.

BEAL, G. M., E. M. ROGERS, and J. M. BOHLEN. "Validity of the Concept of Stages in the Adoption Process." *Rural Sociology,* Vol. 22, June 1957, pp. 166-168.

BLAKE, JAMES K. "How Much Thinking Before Buying." *Dun's Review and Modern Industry,* Vol. 66, August 1955, pp. 38-41.

CLARK, LINCOLN. (ED.) *Consumer Behavior, the Dynamics of Consumer Reaction.* New York: New York University Press, 1954, pp. 30-87 by George Katona and Eva Mueller.

COOPERATIVE EXTENSION SERVICE. *Adapters of New Farm Ideas.* East Lansing, Mich.: Cooperative Extension Service, North Central Regional Publication No. 13, 1961.

COPP, J. H., M. L. STILL, and E. J. BROWN. "The Function of Information Sources in the Farm Practice Adoption Process." *Rural Sociology,* Vol. 23, June 1958, pp. 146-157.

HASSINGER, E. "Stages in the Adoption Process." *Rural Sociology,* Vol. 24, March 1959, pp. 52-53.

LIONBERGER, HERBERT F. *The Adoption of New Ideas and Practices.* Ames, Iowa: Iowa State University Press, 1960.

WILKENING, E. A. "Role of Communicating Agents in Technological Change in Agriculture." *Social Forces,* Vol. 34, May 1956, pp. 361-367.

15

Mass Media Sources of Information and Influence

The mass media include radio, television, newspapers and magazines, farm journals, and specialized publications. College bulletins or other material issued by agency sources are not included here.

Sources of Information

Mass media are most important at the awareness stage in the adoption process. From a peak at this stage, the importance of the source declines steadily for both products studied (Figure 15-1).

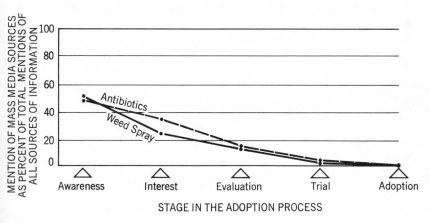

Figure 15-1. Importance of mass media sources of information at successive stages in the adoption process

Reprinted from *The Adoption of New Products: Process and Influence.* Ann Arbor, Michigan, the Foundation for Research on Human Behavior, 1959, pp. 35-39.

Again there are major differences among the adopter categories (Table 15-1). The mass media are far more important in the awareness stage for the middle categories than they are for either innovators or laggards. The innovators rely on the mass media more at the interest stage. They hear about the new products somewhere else first, but then use the mass media to secure additional information.

According to the research done both at Iowa State and at Missouri, innovators and influentials take more farm magazines and specialized publications, and are exposed to more other sources of mass media information, than are any other group. Adopter categories can be ranked according to the number of publications they receive, and the ranking is the same as the ranking by time of adoption. Innovators receive the most; laggards receive the least. Farm publications stand out as an important source of information about new farming practices, as might be expected.

Mass Media Sources of Influence

In the Missouri research, radio turned up as an important source of influence at both early and late stages in the adoption process. Its importance in "clinching decisions," as shown in this research, is contrary to most findings of other research. This importance in these two communities is probably due to the facts that radio is an information source that is well institu-

Table 15-1. Mentions of mass media sources as per cent of mentions of all information sources

2-4D Weed Spray

Adopter category	Awareness	Interest	Evaluation	Trial
Innovator	20%	40%	20%	0%
Early adopter	45%	35%	30%	0%
Early majority	64%	32%	14%	0%
Late majority	53%	23%	11%	4%
Laggard	35%	10%	10%	0%

Antibiotics

Innovator	25%	25%	25%	25%
Early adopter	46%	27%	18%	9%
Early majority	36%	36%	14%	0%
Late majority	61%	45%	21%	2%
Laggard	47%	12%	0%	0%

tionalized in both communities and that the persons who do the broadcasting are trusted for their judgment and integrity.

Farmers did not mention television as influential in their decision to try new products. However, in a second study undertaken to explore this further, 45 per cent of the farmers owning sets in Prairie and 23 per cent of those in Ozark were activated in some way by television. They had either purchased something, tried an idea, gone to the county agent, or talked with other farmers about it. A comparison of the television-activated and non-activated farmers presents some interesting differences. Activated farmers had more schooling and higher farm practice adoption scores, and they had decidedly higher gross incomes. Such people are more often mentioned as innovators and decision-influencers than are farmers who are not activated. On the basis of this, it may be assumed that television does perform an important communication role for the people who are most likely to adopt first. How it compares with other sources, such as farm magazines, is not known. Research done elsewhere suggests that television is usually a more effective source of influence than can be assumed on the basis of this study.

In another Missouri study where television was better institutionalized as a source of farm information, 92 per cent of the household heads and 88 per cent of the wives living in the open country recalled at least one of the program subjects telecast during six months of a farm and home show. Furthermore, a sizeable number did something about what they saw. Their responses appear in Table 15-2.

Table 15-2. Actions based on viewing television show

Action	Household Head	Wife
Talked to others	26%	17%
Wrote for a bulletin	8%	11%
Went to county extension agent	10%	6%
Did at least one of above	36%	37%

An NBC before-and-after television study showed that television advertising sharpened awareness of brand names, riveted brand names to the product, drove home the product trademark, sold the product slogan, enhanced the brand reputation, shifted brand preferences, and most of all, increased by substantial margins the sales of products advertised on television.

Conclusion

The mass media are important sources of information at the awareness stage of the adoption process, particularly for the middle adopter categories. Innovators find out about new products elsewhere and use mass media as a source of additional information. The innovators, early adopters, and early majority are the ones who are most exposed to the mass media. They take the most publications and are activated by what they learn. Farm magazines appear to be the most important source of information on new farm products and practices. Daily newspapers are also important. The importance of both radio and television as sources of information probably depends upon the extent to which they are institutionalized in the community. People who are motivated by television seem to be more influential than those who are not. What these people learn they probably pass on to others in the community who are less likely to be activated by television.

16

The Process of Mass Acceptance

When a large investment is required to launch a radically new idea in packaging, two big questions always confront the decision makers:

- How can consumers be persuaded to accept the new idea?
- How long will it take to put it over?

For years marketers have been searching for a foolproof formula to predict acceptance, whether the question at hand is a new design for an automobile or a pushbutton container for packaging whipped cream.

Whether a universal formula ever will be found is open to question. But in a summary of 35 research studies on how people accept new ideas, conducted in nine states over the past 20 years, there is the promise of more light on this subject than has ever been found before.

The compilation of these research studies has been made and fitted into a framework by Drs. George M. Beal and Joe M. Bohlen, sociologists at Iowa State College, Ames, Ia.[1] Recently, the professors presented some of their findings at the eighth annual United Fruit Forum in New York. Their deduction, based on work done so far, is that the process through which people accept new practices is much the same whether it's frozen foods, synthetic fabrics, mechanical equipment or wonder drugs; whether the people are urban or rural; whether they live in Midtown Manhattan, a small town in Iowa or Arizona.

If this is the case, then an examination of the basic pattern of their thesis should be helpful to all packagers—faced, as they so often are, with a decision on an entirely new packaging concept which may require breaking the barriers of entrenched consumer habits.

Analysis of the behavior pattern indicated by these studies also may provide a key as to where and how to concentrate the promotional program—to what age groups, to individuals of what economic levels, with what educational background and with what value orientation.

The data are presented in the framework of two over-all generalizations.

Reprinted from the February, 1959, issue of *Modern Packaging Magazine,* pp. 75ff.
[1]George M. Beal and Joe M. Bohlen. "The Diffusion Process," Special Report No. 18, Agricultural Extension Service, Iowa State College, Ames, Ia., 1957.

The first is that the process by which people accept new ideas is not a single-unit act, but a series of complex ones—a mental process that can be divided for analysis and action into five stages.

The second is that all people do not adopt new ideas at the same time. Some people are quick to adopt them; others wait a long time, while some never adopt them. And the time span in accepting a new idea can vary from six months to 15 years or more, according to these studies.

In this article we relate to packaging the five stages into which Drs. Beal and Bohlen divide the mental process by which the individual accepts a new idea, accompanied by our own interpretation of its significance in package planning. The five stages, as they have been outlined, are as follows:

1. *The awareness stage.* An individual becomes cognizant of a new idea, such as a cook-in-the-bag food. But the prospective consumer lacks details about it. She may not know a brand name, whether it tastes good or how to prepare it.

2. *The interest stage.* Awareness of the product piques her interest to find out more about it. She wants to know who makes it, how long it takes to prepare, whether the package contains one or more servings, whether it is really a convenience that saves work in the kitchen.

3. *The evaluation stage.* She applies the information obtained in the first two stages to her own situation, gives the cook-in-the-bag package a mental trial—perhaps asking herself: Will my family like this labor-saving food? How much will it cost? Do I have to keep it frozen in the refrigerator before use?

4. *The trial stage.* If the evaluation indicates that the packaged product has possibilities for her, she will buy it and give it a trial. She finds out for herself how easy it is to prepare, whether her family likes it, whether it can be served economically within her budget.

5. *The adoption stage.* The final stage is the adoption stage, characterized by continued use of the product and, most of all, by satisfaction with the idea. It is pointed out that this does not mean a consumer who has accepted an idea must use it constantly, but that she has accepted it as good and intends to include it in her on-going program. She no longer goes through the process of "Should I or should I not buy it?"

The research indicates that mass media—newspapers, magazines, TV and radio—play the dominant role as the source of information in providing awareness and interest. And in the case of rural population, the Government agencies, such as the Agricultural Extension Service, exert a strong influence in the diffusion of new ideas. Families are frequently influenced, also, by new ideas brought from school by the children.

When it comes to the evaluation stage, neighbors and friends appear to be the most influential. And there is evidence that the further away from the time at which an idea was created, the more people depend upon neighbors and friends as the source of information.

Table 16-1. Behavior pattern for the adoption of a new idea

Innovators 3-5% →	Early Adopters 10-15% →	Early Majority 15-20% →	Majority 40-60%	Non-adopters 5-10%
High income	Younger	Slightly above average age	Older	Older
High social status	Well educated	Medium-high social and economic status	Less education	Less education
Active in community	More formal participation in formal community activities—hold offices in church organizations, PTA, farm groups	Above-average education	Less social participation	Less social participation
Contacts outside community (travel more)	Receive more newspapers, magazines, specialized publications	Receive more newspapers, magazines, bulletins	Receive fewer newspapers, magazines and other publications	Apt to be satisfied with the status quo
Have direct sources of information beyond that available in mass media		Earlier to adopt than majority		Receive fewer publications

People react to new ideas in much the same way, no matter what product or practice is involved, Drs. Beal and Bohlen conclude after researching more than 40 products from hybrid seed corn to canned frozen fruit juices. First to accept is a small group of innovators, followed in time sequence by other groups as categorized from left to right in the table above. Time span in accepting a new idea can vary from six months to more than 15 years.

At the trial and adoption stages, the dealer or retailer and salesmen are called on for the detailed information about how to use a new product.

People apparently go through these stages of acceptance at different rates, depending upon their individual characteristics, the social situation in which they live and the type of product involved.

And it is not believed that they go through this process every time they pick up a bar of soap or a tube of toothpaste—an impulse purchase—in the same way they would in the adoption of synthetic textiles as against materials made from natural fibres—a choice that requires longer evaluation before trial and final acceptance. However, the research does show that they go through the process in the adoption of frozen foods as opposed to canned foods, or in the acceptance of new wonder drugs as against old standbys, in much the same way as they did some 40 other products researched in the studies, indicating the validity of the thesis without over-generalizing, say the authors.

The community in which people live affects their values, influencing how rapidly they adopt ideas and the kinds of ideas they adopt, Drs. Beal and Bohlen point out. In some communities there is an attitude toward acceptance of change. When a new idea comes out in that community, it will be accepted rapidly. In other communities, there is an attitude toward the status-quo and it takes hard sell to get people to accept. The communities might be right next to each other within a county, a suburb or a metropolitan area, they say. Also of importance are the groups to which they belong and the values they hold toward the product, the seller and toward change itself.

This being the case, it follows that a knowledge of such characteristics is an important consideration in selecting test markets for a new package.

The findings also indicate, as might be expected, that those practices which cost little seem to be adopted more rapidly than those which are more expensive. The marketer of a popular-priced packaged item whose future success depends on frequency of purchase has a better chance of winning rapid favor than one whose product carries an initial high price. The choice of electrical appliances or farm equipment, for example, requires a great deal of time at the evaluation stage and offers little opportunity of trial before actual adoption. Generally, packaged products are in a favorable position here. A consumer can afford to buy a flip-top box of cigarettes just to try it out, whereas his adoption of an electric refrigerator must depend almost entirely on his evaluation of the various makes and their prices before purchase.

The studies divide people exposed to new ideas into five time-of-adoption categories, with regard to acceptance:

1. *The innovators*, estimated at 3 to 5% of any group or community. They are the well-established, high-income people, financially able to take risks in being first to try something new. They are not influenced greatly by other local community members. They are active beyond the community; they travel more, secure more technical information and have information sources beyond the local community and therefore are looked up to by the rest of the community. They are change oriented.

2. *The early adopters*, about 10 to 15%. These people make up a relatively younger group in the community than those to follow, usually with more education than those who adopt more slowly. They participate actively in community organizations such as churches, parent-teacher and civic associations, often holding elected offices. They receive significantly more newspapers and magazines than the average. There is evidence that this group furnishes a disproportionate amount of formal leadership in a community. Thus, what they do is almost sure to be emulated by other formal and informal group members.

3. *The early majority*, about 15 to 20%. These individuals are the informal opinion leaders of the community, usually slightly older than the early

adopters. Their contacts are mostly in their own community and the opinions which their neighbors and friends hold of them is their main source of prestige and social status. They are less active in local organizations than those who adopt earlier. Their position of leadership is informal; they are not elected to it. They have a following only insofar as people respect their opinions. If their informal leadership fails a few times, their following looks elsewhere for leadership. But their judgment is usually sound, because they have more limited resources than early adopters and cannot afford to make poor decisions. They seem to be most influential in getting the majority to adopt new practices.

4. *The majority,* about 40 to 60%. This group is usually older, with a little less education, and less prone to change. It is composed of individuals who probably form the major part of formal organization membership, but who are less active in leadership. They probably read less, but make up the large percentage group on which the ultimate success of a product or package depends. They seem to be most influenced by what their neighbors and friends do—strive more to conform to group expectation.

5. *The non-adopters,* the remaining 5 to 10% are the oldest, with the least education. They participate least in community organizations, come in contact with less direct information, are apt to be resistant to change and, in many cases, probably have fewer consumer needs than the younger groups.

Some families or certain members of it place a high value, apparently, on being first to adopt and thus accept new products more rapidly. The professors think that probably the most influential patterns of association affecting attitudes toward change in the community are the informal groups, the people who play cards together, visit together, ride to work together, engage in sports or other recreational patterns.

In the case of new packages, these findings strongly indicate the need for a carefully planned advertising and promotional program, properly timed with the distribution of the new package. The best package in the world can be a failure if there is a time lag between the promotion and the distribution of the packaged merchandise. Consumers—especially the innovators—must be able to buy it when they become aware of it. The stages in acceptance often suggest the effectiveness of an extensive sampling program to lists of community leaders, followed by store demonstrations, to attract the innovators and early adopters. Also pointed out is the weakness of depending on a one-shot saturation program because not all of the potential adopters are reached or even made aware of the product by the one shot.

And in this day of self service, when there is so little clerk service, the process of adoption calls for packages and display materials that give complete information about the product, how to use and how to care for it. More and more today, informative packaging must take over the job of the dealer and salesman in acquainting the prospective consumer with its advantages of convenience, performance and economy.

The research report, of course, does not answer what makes a good idea in the first place. Seemingly, it presupposes that the idea—translated into a commercial product or package—has possibilities for mass acceptance, as previously determined by established market-test procedures. Nor does it cover the question of whether the timing of a new idea is right. For example, one important supplier of cartons reported recently that he went to leading tobacco companies with the idea for a reclosable cigarette carton back in the '30s, but got nowhere. It was not until 20 years later, when the Philip Morris Co. was willing to put money behind its flip-top box in an extensive promotional campaign to put over Marlboros, that the cigarette industry gave serious consideration to a revolutionary change in cigarette packaging. Nor was serious consideration given to the packaging of soft goods in transparent film packages until self-service merchandising forced it.

Perhaps packages need further study to show (a) how to sell a bright idea to top management and (b) how to put it across to distributors and retailers.

The studies discussed here, however, should be especially useful, it is believed, to point up the importance of delineating the various segments of a potential market and planning the educational and promotional campaign for a new package in relation to adoption process and time of adoption groups.

17

Communication Research and the Image of Society: Convergence of Two Traditions

ELIHU KATZ

Research on mass communications has concentrated on persuasion, that is, on the ability of the mass media to influence, usually to change, opinions, attitudes, and actions in a given direction. This emphasis has led to the study of campaigns—election campaigns, marketing campaigns, campaigns to reduce racial prejudice, and the like. Although it has been traditional to treat audience studies, content analysis, and effect studies as separate areas, there is good reason to believe that all three have been motivated primarily by a concern with the effective influencing of thought and behavior in the short run.[1]

Other fields of social research have also focused on the effectiveness of campaigns, a prominent example being the twenty-year-old tradition of research by rural sociologists on the acceptance of new farm practices. Yet, despite this shared concern, the two traditions of research for many years were hardly aware of each other's existence or of their possible relevance for each other. Indeed, even now, when there is already a certain amount of interchange between them, it is not easy to conceive of two traditions that, ostensibly, seem more unrelated. Rural sociology suggests the study of traditional values, of kinship, primary relations, *Gemeinschaft*; research on mass communications, on the other hand, is almost a symbol of urban society.

This is a revision of a paper prepared for the Fourth World Congress of Sociology, 1959, and is part of a larger inventory of research on social and psychological factors affecting the diffusion of innovation supported by the Social Science Research Committee of the University of Chicago and the Foundation for Research on Human Behavior. Thanks are due to Martin L. Levin, who has assisted with this project, and to Professors C. Arnold Anderson and Everett M. Rogers for helpful criticism. Reprinted from *The American Journal of Sociology* (March, 1960), pp. 435-440, by permission of the publisher, University of Chicago Press. ©Copyright 1960.

[1]This point is elaborated in Elihu Katz and Paul F. Lazarsfeld, *Personal Influence: The Part Played by People in the Flow of Mass Communication* (Glencoe, Ill.: Free Press, 1955).

The recognition that these two traditions of research have now begun to accord each other is, in large measure, the product of a revision of the image of society implicit in research on mass communications. Thus, although the convergence now taking place has surely proceeded from both directions, this paper attempts to present the story from one side only.[2]

Communication Research and the Image of Society

Until very recently, the image of society in the minds of most students of communication was of atomized individuals, connected with the mass media but not with one another.[3] Society—the "audience"—was conceived of as aggregates of age, sex, social class, and the like, but little thought was given to the relationships implied thereby or to more informal relationships. The point is not that the student of mass communications was unaware that members of the audience have families and friends but that he did not believe that they might affect the outcome of a campaign; informal interpersonal relations, thus, were considered irrelevant to the institutions of modern society.

What research on mass communications has learned in its three decades is that the mass media are far less potent than had been expected. A variety of studies—with the possible exception of studies of marketing campaigns—indicates that people are not easily persuaded to change their opinions and behavior.[4] The search for the sources of resistance to change, as well as for the effective sources of influence when changes *do* occur, led to the discovery of the role of interpersonal relations.[5] The shared values in groups of family, friends, and co-workers and the networks of communication which are their structure, the decision of their influential members to accept or resist a new

---

[2]It would be interesting if a rural sociologist would tell it from his point of view. In any case, this meeting of traditions is timely, in view of the pessimism expressed by C. Arnold Anderson's "Trends in Rural Sociology," in Robert K. Merton *et al.* (eds.), *Sociology Today* (New York: Basic Books, 1959), p. 361. Anderson regards research on diffusion as the most sophisticated branch of rural sociology.

[3]Cf. similar conclusions of Eliot Freidson, "Communications Research and the Concept of the Mass," in Wilbur Schramm (ed.), *The Process and Effects of Mass Communication* (Urbana: University of Illinois Press, 1954), pp. 380-88, and Joseph B. Ford. "The Primary Group in Mass Communication," *Sociology and Social Research*, XXXVIII (1954), 152-58.

[4]For a review of such studies see Joseph T. Klapper, *The Effects of the Mass Media* (New York: Bureau of Applied Social Research, 1949) ; relevant excerpts from this document appear in Schramm (ed.), *op. cit.*, pp. 289-320. G. D. Wiebe suggests reasons why marketing campaigns fare better than others, in "Merchandising Commodities and Citizenship on Television," *Public Opinion Quarterly*, XV (1951-52), 679-91. See also Paul F. Lazarsfeld and Robert K. Merton, "Mass Communication, Popular Taste and Organized Social Action," in Wilbur Schramm (ed.), *Mass Communications* (Urbana: University of Illinois Press, 1949), 459-80.

[5]This parallels the discovery of the relevance of interpersonal relations in other modern institutions, especially in mass production.

idea—all these are interpersonal processes which "intervene" between the campaign in the mass media and the individual who is the ultimate target. These recent discoveries, of course, upset the traditional image of the individuated audience upon which the discipline has been based. Moreover, there is good reason to believe that the image of society in the minds of students of popular culture needs revision in other dimensions as well.[6] But these remarks are concerned only with the discovery that the mass audience is not so atomized and disconnected as had been thought.

Interpersonal Relations and Mass Communications

Given the need to modify the image of the audience so as to take account of the role of interpersonal relations in the process of mass communications, researchers seem to have proceeded in three directions. First of all, studies were designed so as to characterize individuals not only by their individual attributes but also by their relationship to others. At the Bureau of Applied Social Research of Columbia University, where much of this work has gone on, a series of successive studies examined the ways in which influences from the mass media are intercepted by interpersonal networks of communication and made more or less effective thereby. These were studies of decisions of voters, of housewives to try a new kind of food, of doctors to adopt a new drug, and so on.[7] Elsewhere, studies have focused on the relevance of such variables as relative integration among peers or membership in one kind of group rather than another.[8] These studies are rapidly multiplying.

A second strategy is the study of small groups; indeed, a number of links have been forged between macroscopic research on the mass media and the microscopic study of interpersonal communication.[9]

But, while research on small groups can provide many clues to a better

[6]See Edward A. Shils, "Mass Society and Its Culture" (paper presented at the Daedalus-Tamiment Institute Seminar, June, 1959), for a critique of the common tendency among students of communication to conceive of mass society as disorganized and anomic.

[7]For a review of these studies see Elihu Katz, "The Two-step Flow of Communication: An Up-to-date Report on an Hypothesis," *Public Opinion Quarterly*, XXI (1957), 61-78.

[8]For a recent systematic exposition of a number of these studies see John W. Riley, Jr., and Matilda W. Riley, "Mass Communication and the Social System," in Merton *et al.* (eds.), *op. cit.*, pp. 537-78, and Joseph T. Klapper, "What We Know about the Effects of Mass Communication: The Brink of Hope," *Public Opinion Quarterly*, XXI (1957-58), 453-74.

[9]E.g., Carl I. Hovland, Irving L. Janis, and Harold H. Kelley, *Communication and Persuasion* (New Haven, Conn.: Yale University Press, 1953), chap. v, "Group Membership and Resistance to Influence," and John W. C. Johnstone and Elihu Katz, "Youth Culture and Popular Music," *American Journal of Sociology*, LXII (1957), 563-68. For a review of the implications of research on the small group for the design of research on mass communication see Katz and Lazarsfeld, *op. cit.*, Part I.

understanding of the role of interpersonal relations in the process of mass communications, it focuses almost exclusively on what goes on *within* a group. The third strategy of research, then, was to seek leads from research concerned with the introduction of change from *outside* a social system. Here the work of the rural sociologists is of major importance.[10] For the last two decades the latter have been inquiring into the effectiveness of campaigns to gain acceptance of new farm practices in rural communities while taking explicit account of the relevant channels of communication both outside and inside the community.[11] Yet, despite the obvious parallel between rural and urban campaigns, it was not until after the "discovery" of interpersonal relations that the student of mass communications had occasion to "discover" rural sociology.

Interpersonal Relations and Rural Communication

If the assumption that interpersonal relations were irrelevant was central to the research worker on mass communications, the opposite was true of the student of rural campaigns. And the reasons are quite apparent: rural sociologists never assumed, as students of mass communications had, that their respondents did not talk to each other. How could one overlook the possible relevance of farmers' contacts with one another to their response to a new and recommended farm practice? The structure of interpersonal relations, it was assumed, was no less important for channeling the flow of influence than the farm journal or the county agent.[12]

Why did relationships among members of the audience figure so much more prominently in research on new farm practices than in research on mar-

[10]Relevant also is the anthropological study of underdeveloped areas where social structure may sometimes be taken into account along with culture in explaining the acceptance of change (e.g., Benjamin D. Paul [ed.], *Health, Culture and Community: Case Studies of Public Reactions to Health Programs* [New York: Russell Sage Foundation, 1955]).

[11]For reviews of research in this field see Subcommittee on the Diffusion and Adoption of New Farm Practices of the Rural Sociological Society, *Sociological Research on the Diffusion and Adoption of New Farm Practices* (Lexington: Kentucky Agricultural Experiment Station, 1952), and Eugene A. Wilkening, "The Communication of Information on Innovations in Agriculture," in the forthcoming volume by Wilbur Schramm (ed.), *Communicating Behavioral Science Information* (Stanford, Calif.: Stanford University Press). A recent bibliography on *Social Factors in the Adoption of Farm Practices* was prepared by the North Central Rural Sociology Subcommittee on Diffusion (Ames: Iowa State College, 1959).

[12]Yet rural sociologists have justifiably berated their colleagues for not taking more *systematic* account of interpersonal structures (e.g., Herbert F. Lionberger, "The Diffusion of Farm and Home Information as an Area of Sociological Research," *Rural Sociology*, XVII [1952], 132-44).

keting campaigns, campaigns to reduce prejudice, and the like? Consider the following explanations.

It is obvious, in the first place, that rural sociologists define their arena of research, at least in part, by contrast with the allegedly impersonal, atomized, anomic life of the city. If urban relationships are "secondary," rural life must be somewhere near the other end of the continuum. Hence primary, interpersonal relations—their location, their sizes and shapes, and their consequences—are of central concern.[13]

Second, research on mass communications, linked as it is to research on opinions and attitudes, is derived more directly from individual psychology than sociology. Students of rural change, on the other hand, have a sociological heritage and a continuing tradition of tracing the relations of cliques, the boundaries of neighborhoods, the web of kinship and the like.[14] Only recently has sociological theory begun to have a cumulative impact upon research on mass communications.

Rural sociologists, moreover, who study the adoption of new farm practices are, typically, in the employ of colleges of agriculture, which, in turn, are associated with state colleges and universities. The locale of operations is somewhat more circumscribed, as a result, than it is in the case of the student of urban mass media. The student of the adoption of new farm practices is not interested in, say, a representative national sample. Sometimes, therefore, he will interview all the farmers in a given county or a very large proportion of them, and this makes it possible to collect data on the relations among individual respondents, which, obviously, is impossible in random cross-sectional sampling where respondents are selected as "far apart" from each other as possible. By the same token, the investigator of rural communication is more a part of the situation he is studying; it is more difficult for him to overlook interpersonal influence as a variable.

Finally, a fact, related in part to the previous one, is that the rural sociologist has been primarily interested in the efficacy of the local agricultural agency's program, and, while the local agent employs the mass media as well as personal visits, demonstrations, and other techniques, his influence is plainly disproportionately effective among the more educated and those enjoying prestige in the community and considerably less so among others. Research workers soon were able to suggest, however, that the county agent's effectiveness for a majority of the population may be indirect, for the people he influences may influence others. This idea of a "two-step" flow of communication

[13]See the propositions concerning the systems of social interaction in rural, as contrasted with urban, society in Pitirim Sorokin and Carle C. Zimmerman, *Prnciples of Rural-urban Sociology* (New York: Henry Holt & Co., 1929), pp. 48-58.

[14]The work of Charles P. Loomis is outstanding in this connection; on his approach to the relationship between interpersonal structures and the introduction of change see Loomis and J. Allan Beegle, *Rural Sociology: The Strategy of Change* (Englewood Cliffs, N.J.: Prentice-Hall, Inc., 1957). Sociometry has played an important role in this development.

also suggested itself as a promotional idea to magazines and other vehicles of mass communications, but it was not actually studied—perhaps because it was more difficult to define operationally—until rather recently.[15]

Some Consequences of Convergence

That research on mass communications and on the diffusion and acceptance of new farm practices have "discovered" each other is increasingly evident from the references and citations in recent papers in both fields.[16] The realization of the shared interest in the problem of campaigns—or, more accurately now, in the shared problems of diffusion—has evidently overcome academic insulation. From the point of view of students of mass communications, it took a change in the image of the audience to reveal that the two traditions were studying almost exactly the same problem.

Now that the convergence has been accomplished, however, what consequences are likely to follow? First of all, the two will be very likely to affect each other's design of research. The problem of how to take account of interpersonal relations and still preserve the representativeness of a sample is paramount in studies of mass communications, while that of rural sociologists is how to generalize from studies of neighborhoods, communities, and counties. What is more, despite their persistent concern with interpersonal relations, students of rural diffusion have never mapped the spread of a particular innovation against the sociometric structure of an entire community; paradoxically, a recent study deriving from the tradition of research on mass communications has attempted it.[17] Clearly, both fields can contribute to the refinement of research design, and their contributions, moreover, would have implications not only for each other but for a growing number of substantive

---

[15]For mention of the claims of communicators that members of their audiences are influential for others see one of the earliest pieces of research on opinion leaders: Frank A. Stewart, "A Sociometric Study of Influence in Southtown," *Sociometry*, X (1947), 11-31.

[16]E.g., Everett M. Rogers and George M. Beal, "The Importance of Personal Influence in the Adoption of Technological Changes," *Social Forces*, XXXVI (1958), 329-35, and Herbert Menzel and Elihu Katz, "Social Relations and Innovation in the Medical Profession," *Public Opinion Quarterly*, XIX (1955-56), 337-53. More important, perhaps, is the "official" recognition of the relevance of research on mass communications in the 1959 bibliography of the North Central Rural Sociology Subcommittee, *op. cit.*

[17]See James S. Coleman, Elihu Katz, and Herbert Menzel, "The Diffusion of an Innovation among Physicians," *Sociometry*, XX (1957), 253-70. See also the reports of "Project Revere," e.g., Stuart C. Dodd, "Formulas for Spreading Opinions," *Public Opinion Quarterly*, XXII (1958-59), 537-54, and Melvin L. DeFleur and Otto N. Larsen, *The Flow of Information* (New York: Harper & Bros., 1958). Extensive work on informal cliques as facilitators and barriers to interpersonal communication in rural communities has been reported by Herbert F. Lionberger and C. Milton Coughenor, *Social Structure and the Diffusion of Farm Information* (Columbia: University of Missouri Agricultural Experiment Station, 1957).

fields which are interested in tracing the spread of specific innovations through social structures. This includes the work of students of technical assistance programs, of health campaigns, of marketing behavior, of fads and fashions, and the like.

Second, the convergence has already revealed a list of parallel findings which strengthen theory in both. Several findings that seem most central are:

1. In both urban and rural settings personal influence appears to be more effective in gaining acceptance for change than are the mass media or other types of influence. A number of studies—but by no means all—have found that there is a tendency for adopters of an innovation to credit "other people" with having influenced their decisions.[18] What is of interest, however, is not the precise ranking of the various sources of influence but the undeniable fact that interpersonal communication plays a major role in social and technical change both in the city and on the farm.

2. When decision-making is broken down into phases (e.g., becoming aware of an innovation, becoming interested in it, evaluating it, deciding to try it, etc.), the mass media appear relatively more influential in the early informational phases, whereas personal influences are more effective in the later phases of deliberation and decision. The tendency in both traditions is no longer to look at the media as competitive but, rather, as complementary by virtue of their function in various phases of an individual's decision.[19]

3. The earliest to accept an innovation are more likely than those who accept later to have been influenced by agricultural agencies, mass media,

---

[18]Typically, the respondent is asked to recall the sources influencing him, arrange them chronologically, and then select the one which was "most influential." The shortcomings of this are obvious. There are many exceptions, but a sizable number of studies have reported that the influence of "other people" is more influential than other sources. See, e.g., Herbert F. Lionberger, *Information-seeking Habits and Characteristics of Farm Operators* (Missouri Agricultural Experiment Station Research Bull. 581 [Columbia, 1955]) ; E. A. Wilkening, *Adoption of Improved Farm Practices as Related to Family Factors* (Wisconsin Agricultural Experiment Station Research Bull. 183 [Madison, 1953]) ; Marvin A. Anderson, "Acceptance and Use of Fertilizer in Iowa," *Croplife*, II (1955) ; George Fisk, "Media Influence Reconsidered," *Public Opinion Quarterly*, XXIII (1959), 83-91; and Katz and Lazarsfeld, *op. cit.*, Part II. The more important question, however, is under what conditions certain sources of influence are more or less likely to be influential. Different innovations, different social structures, and different phases of the process of decision and of diffusion have been shown to be associated with variations in the role of the media. The latter two factors are treated below.

[19]Cf. James S. Coleman, Elihu Katz, and Herbert Menzel, *Doctors and New Drugs* (Glencoe, Ill.: Free Press, 1960), with such recent rural studies as Rogers and Beal, *op. cit.*; James H. Copp, Maurice L. Sill, and Emory J. Brown, "The Function of Information Sources in the Farm Practice Adoption Process," *Rural Sociology*, XXIII (1958), 146-57; and Eugene A. Wilkening, "Roles of Communicating Agents in Technological Change in Agriculture," *Social Forces*, XXXIV (1956), 361-67. Earlier formulations tended to *infer* the psychological stages of decision-making from the typical sequence of the media reported by respondents, but more recent formulations define the phases of decisions and the media employed in each phase independently. The studies cited above representing the most advanced approach to this problem are also considering the consequences of the use of media "appropriate" or "inappropriate" to a given stage of decision.

and other formal and/or impersonal sources, whereas the latter are more likely to be influenced by personal sources (presumably, by the former).[20] Furthermore, the personal sources to which early adopters respond are likely to be outside their own communities, or at a greater distance, than are the personal sources influencing later adopters.[21] The orientation of early adopters —"cosmopolitan," "secular," "urbanized," "scientific" (to choose from among the terms that have been employed)—also reveals an openness to the rational evaluation of a proposed change and a willingness for contact with the world outside their communities.[22] Many of the studies support the notion of a "two-step" flow of communication in which innovators are influenced from outside and in which they, in turn, influence others with whom they have personal contact.

This is not to claim that there are no differences between communication in urban and rural society or that the direction of the difference between the two kinds of communities may not be essentially as originally perceived by social theorists. Nor is it claimed that all research findings are mutually compatible. Instead, the purpose of this paper is to call attention to the image of society implicit in two fields of research on communication, pointing to the influence of such images on the design of research and on "interdisciplinary" contacts, and to call attention to a few remarkably similar findings in these heretofore unrelated fields, suggesting that the study of communication will surely profit from their increasing interchange.

[20]This, of course, is the "two-step" flow of communication, a conception which finds support in the studies reviewed by Katz, *op. cit.*; Rogers and Beal, *op. cit.*; Lionberger, *op. cit.*; and F. E. Emery and O. A. Oeser, *Information, Decision and Action: Psychological Determinants of Changes in Farming Techniques* (Melbourne, Australia: University of Melbourne Press, 1958).

[21]Cf. Coleman, Katz, and Menzel, *op. cit.*, with E. A. Wilkening, *Acceptance of Improved Farm Practices in Three Coastal Plain Counties* (North Carolina Agricultural Experiment Station Technical Bull. 98 [Chapel Hill, 1952]), and James Copp, *Personal and Social Factors Associated with the Adoption of Recommended Farm Practices* (Kansas State College, Agricultural Experiment Station Research Bull. [Manhattan, 1956]).

[22]See Bryce Ryan and Neal Gross, *Acceptance and Diffusion of Hybrid Seed Corn in Two Iowa Communities* (Iowa State College, Agricultural Experiment Station Bull. 372 [Ames, 1950]), and Emery and Oeser, *op. cit.* The latter, however, suggest that, under certain conditions, personal contact may be more important for early adopters even though they, in turn, are primary sources of influence for those who follow their lead.

18

Communicating with the Innovator in the Fashion Adoption Process

CHARLES W. KING

The consumer fashion adoption decision is the product of a complex procedure of information processing. To develop a contemporary theory of fashion adoption, the marketer must understand the dynamics of fashion communication on the time-of-adoption continuum. The innovator or early buyer represents a discrete market segment and a key consumer change agent in the diffusion process. The central question is, what are the communication characteristics of the fashion innovator? How can the marketer communicate with the fashion innovator or early buyer?

Communicating with the Fashion Innovator

The Role of the Fashion Innovator or Early Buyer in the Adoption Process—An Overview

In earlier research, fashion adoption has been treated as a specific type of innovative behavior within the broader context of social change. Fashion adoption has been defined as "a process of social contagion by which a new style or product is adopted by the consumer after commercial introduction by the designer or manufacturer[1]." The consumer adoption decision is made within the time dimension of a season. The buying and wearing of a particular season's new fashions by the mass consumer market involve a shift

Reprinted from *Proceedings, American Marketing Association Conference*, Peter D. Bennett, ed. (September, 1965), pp. 425-439, by permission of the publisher, the American Marketing Association.

[1]For a detailed critique of the fashion adoption process, see Charles W. King, "Fashion Adoption: A Rebuttal of the 'Trickle Down' Theory", in Stephen A. Greyser (Ed.), *Toward Scientific Marketing*, Proceedings of the Winter Conference of the American Marketing Association, 1963, Boston, Massachusetts, pp. 108-125.

from the styles appropriate the previous year to the current season's fashion offerings. Consumers across socio-economic classes adopt new styles early in the season, and the contagion spreads horizontally within social strata and to a more limited extent, vertically across strata. Consumers may select from a wide range of styles in the current season's inventory and be "in fashion."

In this adoption process, the innovator or early buyer plays a key role as a consumer change agent. The early buyer initiates the adoption cycle within the season through her early purchase and is the earliest visual communicator of the new season's styles to the mass of fashion consumers. Fashion retailers and manufacturers monitor the early buyers' selections and make major decisions regarding the season's fashion trends and inventory based on the early buyers' purchase patterns.

Among the mass fashion consumers, the early buyers give legitimacy to the season's styles through displaying the season's offerings to their social networks in various social settings. In some social networks, the early buyer may also be a fashion opinion leader and may define broad fashion standards for the group as well as display the season's inventory.

The Fashion Innovator as a Discrete Market Segment

Empirical research focusing on the early buyer in the millinery product category has suggested that the early buyer may be a discrete market segment.[2] Comparative analysis of early buyers and other consumers has indicated that the early buyers are differentiated from other consumers by consistent differences in demographic and life style characteristics rather than by isolated idiosyncracies. More specifically, the early buyers were found to be higher in social status, more psychologically compatible with fashion involvement, more gregarious and involved in social activities where fashion consciousness would be appropriate and more interested in personal grooming and hat wearing per se.

Communicating with the Fashion Innovator

The fashion innovators or early buyers represent a prime sales target for the fashion merchandiser because of their key position in the adoption process and because of their sales potential as a major market segment. The central question is, how can the fashion marketer communicate with the early buyer?

Communications variables as discriminants of innovative behavior

In previously reported multiple discriminant analysis of the early buyer

[2]Charles W. King, "The Innovator in the Fashion Adoption Process", in L. George Smith (Ed.), *Reflections on Progress in Marketing*, Proceedings of the Winter Conference of the American Marketing Association, 1964, Chicago, Illinois, pp. 324-339.

and other consumer groups to be studied in depth in this paper, ten selected communications variables were analyzed as an independent predictive battery of measures. The resulting linear discriminant function was not significant at the .05 level and accurately classified only 65 percent of the respondents.[3] While these data suggest that differences between these groups on these variables were not pronounced, there may be subtle differences between adopter groups that were not detected by the variables used or the linear analysis.

Other research on fashion communication

Other published empirical research on fashion communication has not included time of adoption as a dimension of analysis. Barber and Lobel performed a content analysis of fashion copy in leading fashion journals from 1930 to 1950 but did not consider differential communication processes within the fashion market.[4] Rich generated a body of evidence on communication behavior and information usage in fashion but did not pursue communication in the time of adoption context.[5]

Fashion journalists and media researchers have segmented the fashion market into socio-economic groups, and various fashion journals focus on particular segments. Each journal typically testifies to reaching *the* "fashion leader," but media research has focused on reader profiles rather than on the dynamics of fashion communication within the adoption process.[6]

Hypotheses from adoption research

Research on innovative behavior in other contexts, particularly by rural sociologists, indicates that early adopters tend to differ from later adopters in terms of communication behavior.[7] Early adopters tend to rely more on impersonal rather than personal sources of information concerning the innovation adopted. Early buyers use more "cosmopolite" sources (sources external to the adopters' social system). In turn, the early adopters utilize more technical sources, e.g., agricultural scientists, county agents, agricultural extension service bulletins, etc. and report more involvement with all kinds of information sources. In the area of social interactions and communications, early adopters are more gregarious and have more contacts outside their immediate social system. In turn, the early adopters appear to be more active

[3]Ibid., pp. 331-332.

[4]Bernard Barber and Lyle S. Lobel, "Fashion in Women's Clothes and the American Social System", *Social Forces*, 31 (1952) pp. 124-131.

[5]Stuart U. Rich, *Delivery Service and Telephone Ordering: Department Store Policies and Consumer Demand*, Division of Research: Harvard Graduate School of Business Administration, 1963.

[6]Based on interviews with fashion editors, journalists and researchers. For a simplified report on the marketing strategies of leading fashion journals, see "The Fashion Beat", *Time*, 86:7, August 13, 1965, p. 58.

[7]For a review of research dealing with communication behavior in the adoption process, see Everett M. Rogers, *Diffusion of Innovations*, New York: Free Press, 1962, pp. 98-105, 178-188, 217-247.

as personal communicators within their social system. Though these conclusions have been drawn from adoption contexts markedly different from
the fashion environment, do similar communication patterns characterize
the innovator in fashion adoption?

The objective of this paper is to explore the communication characteristics of the innovator or early buyer in the category of women's millinery.
More specifically, the following issues have been studied:

1) What are the communication characteristics of the early buyer
in comparison with other consumers?

2) What are the implications of these findings in terms of fashion
adoption behavior and in terms of fashion merchandising strategy?

The Research Methodology

The Data

The data analyzed in this paper were collected in an exploratory
consumer survey of the innovator or early buyer and the influential or opinion
leader within the product category of women's millinery. The research design was built around defining the time of adoption as the critical variable.
Respondents were qualified on a time of adoption continuum based on their
Fall, 1962, hat buying behavior. Time of adoption was defined as the month
of first purchase of a hat during the Fall season. The adoption decision was
not defined as the purchase of any specific style, because the consumer can
purchase a wide range of styles *within the current season's merchandise* and
be "in style" regardless of the specific style selection.

Adopter Groups Analyzed

In this paper, two adopter groups have been analyzed in depth:

1) Innovators or early buyers—late August or September buyers
representing the first 35% of the Fall, 1962, season's millinery buyers.

2) All other consumers—later buyers and consumers that did not
buy in the Fall, 1962 season.

The Dynamics of Communication Behavior in Fashion Adoption

Do the dynamics of communication behavior differ among
adopter groups on the time of adoption continuum? The communication

characteristics of the early buyer and other consumer groups have been studied on four major dimensions:

    1) exposure to mass communications;
    2) involvement in general social communications and specific social activities;

Table 18-1. Exposure to mass communications by adopter category

Mass Communications Variable	Early Buyers	Other Consumers	X^2. Test of Significance
Radio Listening:			
Low	48%[a]	51%[a]	p <.70[a]
High	52	49	
Total	100%	100%	
TV viewing:			
Low	56%	44%	p<.02
High	44	56	
Total	100%	100%	
Newspaper readership:			
Low	61%	67%	p<.20
High	39	33	
Total	100%	100%	
General interest magazine readership:			
Low	28%	42%	p<.05
Medium	41	35	
High	31	23	
Total	100%	100%	
Fashion magazine readership:			
Low	41%	48%	p<.20
High	59	52	
Total	100%	100%	
News magazine readership:			
Low	65%	71%	p<.50
High	35	29	
Total	100%	100%	
Total magazine readership:			
Low	43%	56%	p<.02
High	57	44	
Total	100%	100%	
Base Sample Size	112	395	

[a]Read: 48% of the early buyers and 51% of the other consumers reported "low" radio listening. The difference was not statistically significant at the 5% level based on X^2 analysis.

3) social communications about fashion and hats;
4) preferred fashion information sources.

Exposure to Mass Communication

Fashion theory and adoption research in other contexts suggest the early buyer group should have higher mass communication exposure than other consumers. The early buyer and other consumer groups, however, report very similar exposure to print and broadcast media based on the data presented in Table 18-1, though the direction of the differences does favor the hypothesis of higher exposure of the early buyers.

The early buyers' lower TV viewing and higher general interest and total magazine readership reflected the only statistically significant differences from the exposure patterns of the other consumers. More subtle support for the hypothesis is found, however, when the *direction of difference* is noted on each communication dimension. With the exception of TV viewing, the early buyer group reported higher exposure to each of the 6 other media suggesting a non-random distribution of the direction of the differences that is significant and supports the hypothesis.

Involvement in General Social Communications and Specific Social Activities

Involvement in general social communications and specific social activities reflects consistent and fundamental differences in the dynamics of the communication process among early buyers compared with other consumers. The data presented in Table 18-2 have been confined to those activities on which the groups reported statistically significant differences using the 5 percent significance criterion. The complete array of activities measured also included telephone conversations with women, family visiting with friends, church-synagogue attendance, pleasure driving, shopping in neighborhood centers, wedding attendance and traveling by public transportation (subway, bus, etc.).

The early buyer group is more involved in general social communications and specific social activities in which the communication of fashion cues is an integral part of the personal interaction process. The early buyers' higher frequency of social visiting with other women provides the setting for oral exchange of fashion information. In turn, the greater frequency of downtown shopping may enable the early buyer to canvass a wider inventory of current fashion merchandise.

Higher participation in more formal and fashion oriented activities such as cocktail parties, teas, club meetings, etc. gives the early buyer a role in a complex fashion information exchange network. The early buyer monitors the fashion standards and preferences of the social environment and contrib-

Table 18-2. Involvement in general social communications and specific activities by adopter category

Social Activities Variable	Early Buyers	Other Consumers	X^2 Test of Significance
Frequency of social visiting with women:			
Low	49%	66%[a]	p<.01[a]
High	51	34	
Total	100%	100%	
Shop downtown:			
Low	31%	46%	p<.01
High	69	54	
Total	100%	100%	
Eat lunch or dinner out at a restaurant:			
Low	26%	44%	p<.01
High	74	56	
Total	100%	100%	
Attend cocktail parties, and open houses:			
Low	52%	66%	p<.01
High	48	34	
Total	100%	100%	
Attend night clubs:			
Low	71%	81%	p<.05
High	29	19	
Total	100%	100%	
Attend conventions, business and professional meetings:			
Low	69%	80%	p<.02
High	31	20	
Total	100%	100%	
Attend morning or afternoon teas:			
Low	65%	79%	p<.01
High	35	21	
Total	100%	100%	
Attend PTA, fraternal and club meetings:			
Low	32%	46%	p<.01
High	68	54	
Total	100%	100%	
Attend theatrical plays, concerts, lectures:			
Low	46%	60%	p<.02
High	54	40	
Total	100%	100%	
Organization membership:			
Low	52%	67%	p<.01
High	48	33	
Total	100%	100%	
Total activities index:			
Low	20%	36%	
Medium	38	38	p<.02
High	42	26	
Total	100%	100%	
Base Sample Size	112	395	

[a]*Read: 49% of the early buyers and 66% of the other consumers reported "low" frequency of social visiting with other women. The difference was statistically significant at the 1% level based on X^2 analysis.*

utes the display of her fashion selections to the network. While oral exchange of cues may occur, visual monitoring is typically a continuous activity of all participants.

The early buyer is also more exposed to fashion cues from outside her immediate social environment as indicated by her higher attendance at conventions, professional meetings, etc. This coincides with the greater "cosmopoliteness" of early adopters noted in farm practice adoption.

In turn, the early buyer is generally more gregarious as measured by total organization membership and the total activities index. Further analysis of the direction of the differences on all 17 measures of social communications and activities indicated that the early buyers reported higher involvement on every measure except use of public transportation. As in the case of the exposure to mass media, the consistency of the direction of the differences is significant and supports the higher gregariousness of the early buyer.

Table 18-3. Social communications about fashion and hats by adopter category

	Early Buyers ("Yes" Answer)	Other Consumers ("Yes" Answer)
"Generally like to talk to someone to get ideas about fashion before going shopping . . ."	34%[a]	33%[a]
"Talked to someone recently to get ideas about fashion . . ."	24%	21%
"Know someone in particular you generally like to talk to about fashion . . ."	30%	30%
"Someone recently asked your advice about fashion . . ."	33%	27%
"Recently offered someone suggestion about fashion . . ."	23%	23%
"Talked with someone recently to get ideas about hats . . ."	7%	8%
"Know someone you generally like to talk to about hats . . ."	12%	11%
Placed "high" dependence on millinery saleswoman when buying a hat.	20%	24%
Base Sample Size	112	395

[a]*Read: 34% of the early buyers and 33% of the other consumers reported they generally like to talk with someone to get ideas about fashions before going shopping for clothes. None of the differences are statistically significant at the 5% level based on X^2 analysis.*

Social Communications About Fashion and Hats

The traditional "trickle down" theory of fashion adoption and other adoption research suggest that the early buyers would be high transmitters while the other consumers would be high receivers of person-to-person communications about fashion and hats. The data presented in Table 18-3 challenge that hypothesis. The early buyers and other consumers *have essentially identical involvement* in information receiving (talking to someone to get ideas about fashion) and information transmission (respondent's advice requested or respondent offered information).

The similarity in personal communication patterns across adopter categories is due in part to the level of interest in fashion throughout the population. Approximately 50 percent of the total sample reported "high" interest and less than 7 percent of the total population reported no interest in fashion.[8] While more early buyers (60 percent) reported high fashion

Table 18-4. Preferred fashion information sources by adopter category

	Fashion Sources Designated "Helpful"			Fashion Sources Designated "Most Helpful"		
	Early buyers	Other consumers	X^2 test of significance	Early buyers	Other consumers	X^2 test of significance
Specialized fashion sources	42%[a]	34%[a]	p<.05[b]	40%	31%	p<.10[b]
Going shopping in stores	22	26	p<.30	33	45	p<.05
General mass media	18	20	p<.50	14	12	p<.80
Personal communications	18	20	p<.50	13	12	p<.80
Total	100%	100%		100%	100%	
Base	273[c]	893[c]		112	395	

[a]*Read: 42% of the early buyers and 34% of the other consumers designated specialized fashion sources such as fashion shows, fashion magazines and newspaper fashion ads as "helpful" in keeping informed on fashion trends.*

[b]*X^2 analyses based on differences by individual information source.*

[c]*Total number of sources mentioned. Multiple answers accepted.*

[8]Somewhat similar data have been reported by Rich, *op. cit.*, p. 67 using the same measure of fashion interest.

interest compared with other consumers (46 percent), the topic has high relevance to the attitudes of both groups.

The *level of information seeking* within both groups attests to the initiative of the adopters in information gathering. The information seeking by the early buyer may make the task of communicating with this market segment easier for the fashion marketer.

Preferred Fashion Information Sources

Fashion information sources selected as "helpful" and "most helpful" in keeping informed about fashion are presented in Table 18-4. In general both adopter groups reported using a variety of types of fashion information. Technical fashion sources, such as fashion shows, fashion magazines and newspaper fashion ads and shopping in the stores, clearly rank as the most important categories.

In turn, the adopter groups differ somewhat in their information preferences. In general, early buyers tended to prefer technical sources more than did the other consumers. In turn, the other consumers reported greater usage of in-store shopping.

A Profile of the Early Buyers' Communications Characteristics

A broad profile of the early buyers' fashion communications characteristics emerges from the data analysis. Compared with other consumers, the early buyers report:

1) moderately higher exposure to the mass communications media;

2) markedly higher involvement in general social communications and specific activities where fashion communication is an integral part of the social interaction;

3) higher general gregariousness as measured by organization membership and total activities;

4) higher exposure to communications from outside the immediate social environment as measured by attendance at professional meetings, etc. and attendance at formal activities where new fashion concepts might be introduced by "visitors" to the environment:

5) preferences for different kinds of fashion sources over others. Though both the early buyer and other consumer groups assigned greater importance to technical fashion sources and shopping in stores, the early buyers placed significantly greater emphasis on the technical sources than did the other consumers and less importance on shopping in the store;

6) equally high involvement in person-to-person information seeking and information transmission about fashion and hats.

Implications for Adoption Theory and Fashion Marketing Strategy

The analysis of the dynamics of the communications process among the early buyers and the other consumers supports two major conclusions:

1) The innovator or early buyer in the fashion adoption process within the millinery context appears to differ in communication characteristics compared with other consumers.

2) The innovator or early buyer is differentiated from the other consumers by consistent though subtle differences in communication exposure and usage rather than by particular idiosyncrasies in communication behavior.

What are the implications of these findings to adoption theory and to fashion marketing strategy?

Implications for Adoption Theory

The analysis of the communication behavior of the fashion early buyer and other consumer groups has significant implications for adoption theory across product categories. The bulk of research in product adoption and diffusion has been conducted within the context of farm practices adoption. A basic question of concern to marketers is, how applicable are the generalizations derived from farm practices adoption research to consumer product adoption in the mass market?

Communication behavior across adoption contexts

The findings regarding fashion communication behavior are relevant to this question. Despite the diversity of the environments and adoption contexts, i.e., farm practices adoption among farmers in rural farming communities versus fashion adoption among women in Boston, Massachusetts, *a consistent pattern of communication behavior on the time-of-adoption continuum appears to exist across adoption contexts.*

The fashion early adopter and the farm practices early adopter both have similar communication exposure and usage patterns. The early adopters from both contexts report higher exposure to communication in general, are more gregarious and are more exposed to communication from outside their immediate social environments. In terms of communication source preferences and usage, both early adopter sets report greater preferences for impersonal sources than their later adopter counterparts. Both early adopter groups prefer technical information sources over other types of communication.

Adaptive communication behavior

Though consistent patterns of communication behavior appear to exist across adoption contexts, the fashion personal communication data indicate that *communication behavior is adaptive to the adoption context.* Rural sociologists have reported that personal influence and person-to-person information exchange are more important in the adoption decisions of later adopters. In contradiction to this conclusion, however, the fashion early buyer was as involved in person-to-person information seeking as her other consumer counterpart.

The difference in communication patterns is explained in part by the differences in the adoption environments. In the farm practices adoption context, few expert personal sources may be available to early adopters since their relatives, friends and neighbors are unlikely to have expertise regarding the innovation at the time of the early adopter's evaluation and trial decision. In the fashion adoption context, however, interest in keeping informed about fashion is high and early buyers and other consumers have substantial exposure to fashion cues via mass media, shopping and visual and oral information exchange. Therefore, at the evaluative stage in her adoption decision, the early buyer may get valuable information from personal communication within her social network.

The functions of communication sources

The fashion communication patterns suggest that *different information sources may perform different and complementary functions.* The early buyer prefers technical sources for keeping informed about fashions yet also shops in stores and actively seeks information in the social network. An analysis of the functions of the various sources might indicate that technical sources are used to maintain general awareness, while shopping in stores focuses on fashion trends within the early buyer's shopping environment and affords a basis for evaluation through trying on styles, matching colors with the existing wardrobe, etc. The social network may provide information on the fashion norms and attitudes of the network relevant to the early adopter's fashion behavior.

Implications for Fashion Marketing Strategy

As noted earlier, the early buyer and other consumer groups appear to represent discrete market segments. The different life styles of the early buyers and the other consumers suggest that the groups may have different millinery style preferences for functional and aesthetic reasons. The early buyers may have more current and high fashion wardrobes with which new mil-

linery styles must be coordinated. In turn, the early buyers and other consumers may have learned different fashion "rules" and style preferences in
their respective social environments.

To integrate the unique market segment notion into the marketing strategy
of the fashion industry, specific marketing programs involving product line,
promotion and retail selling tactics should be directed at the individual market
segments. Given the role of the early buyer as a prime sales target and as a
consumer change agent, at least one objective should be to accelerate the first
purchase by the early buyer group to initiate the season and to maximize the
time for repeat purchases by the segments during the season.

To implement these strategies, the fashion marketer must improve his
communication with the market segments. The differential communication behavior of the early buyers and other consumers reinforces the discrete market
segment notion and has basic implications for fashion industry promotion and
retail selling tactics.

Communication source selection and market segmentation

How can the early buyer of the other consumer set be reached most efficiently by fashion marketers? The research findings indicate that *no single
fashion source can be used to reach either market segment.* The optimum communication program should include a combination of technical fashion sources
such as fashion shows, fashion magazines and newspaper fashion ads and in-
store promotion display and personal selling, general mass media and personal
communications. The data indicate that *individual information sources are not
used to the exclusion of others but in conjunction with one another.*

The communication program should differ *in emphasis and in message
content* over the fashion season. The season's styles and major fashion themes
should be introduced through the technical sources with reinforcement by the
in-store retailing effort. Later in the season, emphasis should shift to more
localized communication centered around the in-store shopping experience in
conjunction with factual newspaper advertising.

The communication message

Given that an optimum combination of information sources is selected,
what kinds of fashion information do the market segments need? Though these
data have not probed content preferences per se, the demographic and life style
profiles of the early buyer and late buyer groups suggest that the segments'
information needs may differ. The more fashion conscious and informed early
buyer group may need more technical information on new styles, silhouettes,
etc. while later buyers may need more detailed fashion "rules" to guide their
fashion behavior and reduce perceived risk. The communication preferences of
the market segments suggest that the early buyers and other consumers do
seek different types of information. If the information needs do differ, promo-

tional copy and retail selling tactics should be planned accordingly over the season.

The information seeking function

The high level of information seeking and information transmission about fashion and hats should be integrated into the broad communication program. Though the complexities of message transmissibility and rumor networks are inadequately understood, the high level of information seeking suggests that the formal communication effort need not seek to reach all consumers in each segment. The introduction of instructive information relevant to the segments' particular environments will travel through social networks as a result of the purposive information seeking activity among consumers.

Summary

To develop a contemporary theory of fashion adoption, the marketer must understand the dynamics of fashion communication on the time-of-adoption continuum. The analysis of the communication characteristics of the early buyer and other consumer groups in the millinery product category has indicated that consistent though subtle differences exist in communications exposure and usage between the early buyers and the other consumers.

The differences in communication behavior for the two groups give additional support to the concept that the early buyer and the other consumer groups represent discrete market segments. The differential communication characteristics of the adopter groups have implications for generalizations regarding adoption behavior in fashion and in other product categories. To the fashion marketer, the communication patterns of the early buyers and the other consumers suggest marketing strategies that may improve the marketer's communication with the market segments on the time-of-adoption continuum.

While this analysis has been confined to the fashion category of millinery, the concept of market segmentation by time-of-adoption and the concept of differential communication behavior across market segments have applicability across fashion categories. While the characteristics of the market segments may change by fashion category, understanding the dynamics of communication behavior by market segment is essential to the fashion marketer.

19

Sources of Influence in the Acceptance of New Products for Self-medication: Preliminary Findings

JAMES F. ENGEL
DAVID A. KNAPP
and DEANNE E. KNAPP

The direct use of over-the-counter drugs by consumers is an important factor in American medicine as attested by the fact that sales of proprietary remedies reached approximately $1.3 billion in 1964. Self-medication, moreover, is growing rapidly, due to the following factors: (1) rising educational levels; (2) increased availability of information about medicine and drugs in advertising and articles; (3) the declining ratio of general practitioners to specialists and greater consumer reluctance to call a specialist for treatment of minor ailments; and (4) the low socioeconomic level of a portion of the public which leaves only the alternatives of a crowded welfare clinic or the use of home and/or patent remedies.

The pharmaceutical industry has responded to this market need with a veritable flood of new products, but wise marketing planning is severely hampered by the virtual absence of data on how consumers arrive at self-medication decisions. This information gap also has important public policy ramifications. Therefore, a long-term research project is needed to answer such questions as the following: "What information sources are most influential in an individual's decision to pursue a specific self-therapy?" "Are appropriate uses being made of self-medication drugs?" "What is the importance of price in the purchase and use of a home remedy?" This paper reports findings from

This research was supported, in part, by grants from The Ohio State University Council on Research and The Division of Community Health Services (Grant No. CH-00177-01). Reprinted from *Proceedings, American Marketing Association Conference*, Raymond M. Haas, ed. (September, 1966), pp. 776-782, by permission of the publisher, the American Marketing Association.

a pilot study and focuses on the sources of information used in the acceptance of new drug products.

Pilot Study Methodology

An exploratory study was undertaken during Summer, 1965 with the objective of identifying and delineating the motivating factors involved in the self-medication process. Six group interviews were held in the Behavioral Sciences Laboratory of the College of Commerce and Administration. In addition, 30 individual depth interviews were undertaken with Columbus, Ohio housewives. Although a random sample was not utilized, a good socioeconomic cross section was attained.

To shed further light on the sources of information which might be consulted for specific ailments, an attitude scale, referred to as the Disease Scale, was developed to measure the potency of sources of information about health. Seventeen diseases are scaled as to their perceived seriousness and subjects were asked to indicate whose advice would be accepted (i.e., a doctor, friend, and so on) for each. It was not utilized, however, in the pilot study with housewives.

The Self-medication Process

It was interesting to discover the degree of sophistication shown by most respondents in the use of drugs, although they often lacked specific knowledge. In addition, respondents were concerned about this lack as evidenced by the amount of gossip reported regarding health and the appeal of health articles. Suprisingly, the amount of misinformation exhibited in the interviews was small and, for the most part, inconsequential.

Most of those studied presented unmistakable signs that the absence of specific knowledge about a drug or treatment procedure leads to a significant degree of perceived risk that a wrong decision might be made. As a result, they are quite cautious in pursuing new self-medication strategies and show a strong propensity to search for additional information. Obviously some housewives possess a greater degree of knowledge and hence are less prone to inquire further.

The findings verified the risk-reducing role of well-known brand names. This, of course, is the most widely-cited advantage of brands to the consumer, but seldom has it been verified empirically in such convincing fashion. Many respondents commented that a reputable manufacturer would not put his name on a product which is impure or which might offer dangerous side effects. A new product from such companies, therefore, seems certain to be tried more readily, all things being equal.

For those who required additional information, the following sources were mentioned most frequently: (1) doctors; (2) advertisements; (3) friends and relatives; (4) pharmacists; and (5) articles.

Doctors

It is clear that those interviewed placed their greatest confidence in a doctor's recommendation, although most will not call their physician immediately when they have a cold. There is a prevailing fear of being labeled a hypochondriac, and there appears to be a strong reluctance to bother the doctor outside of office hours. This tendency is less evident, however, if a child is sick rather than an adult.

The doctor's impact in recommending self-medication procedures seems to be greatest at times other than when a minor ailment occurs. Many consumers, for example, reported raising questions on the reliability of branded products to their doctor during regular visits. Once verification is given from this source, product and brand loyalty can become deeply imbedded, because the doctor is legitimately regarded by most respondents as being quite authoritative.

Advertisements

As might be expected, great indignation and disapproval was expressed regarding drug advertising, especially overstated television commercials. Yet, the high incidence of brand names mentioned and the reported use of branded products attest to the tremendous impact of advertising. It seemed that those who protested the loudest were most able to give a verbatim playback of copy and also were most likely to be users of the product in question.

The primary effects of advertising were to develop an awareness of the existence of a new remedy and arouse initial interest in its use. Most respondents were reluctant, however, to act on this information alone, apparently because of some doubt regarding the authenticity of the claims. As a result, it was common for respondents to inquire further of doctors, friends and relatives, or pharmacists. Of great interest to the researchers was the amazing impact made by advertisements for a new cold remedy which extends therapeutic usefulness over a relatively long period of time. It has become a market leader at least in part because of the success its advertising had in stimulating great interest which, in turn, led to a remarkable number of inquiries aimed at other information sources.

In some cases, advertising is viewed as having a sufficient degree of authority to stimulate direct action. This was especially true when the remedies were mentioned and endorsed by leading personalities. Arthur Godfrey was mentioned in this context, for example, as were local personalities in the Columbus market.

Friends and Relatives

This communication channel was widely used to verify information about product innovations gathered from other sources. The consumer apparently values the informal channel quite highly and actively seeks reports on the practical results experienced by trusted friends and relatives in treating a specific ailment or in trying a new product. It was encouraging to note in this context that proper precautions were frequently mentioned regarding the advice of others (i.e., what works for one might not work for another).

There were some instances where friends and relatives *volunteered* information, but these were not frequent. Volunteered information was most frequently reported after friends and relatives used the new cold remedy mentioned above. The impetus, however, most frequently lay with the person *seeking* the information as opposed to those who *gave* it.

The relative incidence of use of this communication channel was such that the success or failure of a patent remedy may be dependent in large part upon the evaluation which is given by word-of-mouth.

Pharmacists

As might be expected, the druggist was frequently mentioned as a source for further information, especially once initial interest was given in response to specific questions by the consumer rather than volunteered. There is no doubt that a majority of those interviewed regard the pharmacist as an expert in his field.

A number of housewives, however, voiced concern over the changing role of the pharmacist as indicated by the rise of discount drug outlets. Many indicated that the sharply reduced opportunity for personal contact leads to an unconcern about the welfare of the customer. Many, for this reason, will pay the higher prices to shop at neighborhood pharmacies where they know the owner and trust his professional judgment. The need of this segment of drug users for a pharmacist who knows and understands their requirements and expresses personal concern should not be ignored.

It also is of interest to inquire whether or not pharmacists are willing and able to be a source of drug information. Some preliminary findings from a research project now underway raise some rather disturbing questions in this regard.

Articles

Articles in magazines and newspapers are read with varying degrees of interest and skepticism. Most respondents indicate little faith in reports of "miracle cures," but they apparently are influenced by *negative* reports about remedies. Thus, articles seem to serve as motivators to avoid a product or treatment rather than to try it.

The Disease Scale

While the group and depth interviews indicated an active search for information and the sources used, the researchers also desired to have a more precise indication of whose advice is likely to be accepted if proffered, all things being equal. Therefore, the Disease Scale mentioned earlier was developed, and it consists of 17 diseases which have been scaled as to their perceived seriousness using equal-appearing interval and paired comparison procedures (see Table 19-1). It has proven to be reliable and valid.

Table 19-1. Scale values for diseases

Scale Value	Disease	Scale Value	Disease
0.000	1. dandruff	3.420	10. stomach ulcer
0.989	2. headache	3.608	11. arthritis
1.160	3. upset stomach	3.835	12. kidney stones
1.420	4. in-grown toenail	4.013	13. pneumonia
1.565	5. common cold	5.035	14. tuberculosis
1.694	6. sunburn	5.377	15. heart disease
2.513	7. sinus trouble	5.434	16. stroke
2.661	8. flu	6.209	17. cancer
3.111	9. hemorrhoids		

The diseases were arranged along a vertical continuum of seriousness at points corresponding to their appropriate scale values (Figure 19-1), and the subjects (introductory psychology students) were asked to indicate at what point on the continuum they would no longer accept advice from a given source of health information. The sources rated included friends, pharmacists, physicians, television advertisements, articles by physicians, and articles by pharmacists.

Results are shown in Figure 19-2, and it will be noted that, on the average, a physician's advice is accepted for all diseases up to and including stroke. The advice presented by a pharmacist in person or that given in an article written by a physician would be accepted if the ailment were no more serious than

Figure 19—1   Figure 19—2

The Disease Scale   Communicator Rankings

cancer   —   cancer   —

stroke   —   stroke   —   ◄——————— Physician
heart disease   —   heart disease   —

tuberculosis   —   tuberculosis   —

pneumonia   —   pneumonia   —
kidney stones   —   kidney stones   —

arthritis   —   arthritis   —

stomach ulcer   —   stomach ulcer   —

hemorrhoids   —   hemorrhoids   —

                                                          ◄——————— Pharmacist
flu   —   flu   —   Article written
                                                          by physician
sinus trouble   —   sinus trouble   —

sunburn   —   sunburn   —   ◄——————— Article written by
                                                          a pharmacist
common cold   —   common cold   —

in-grown toenail   —   in-grown toenail   —
                                                          ◄——————— Friend
upset stomach   —   upset stomach   —   TV Advertisement

headache   —   headache   —

dandruff   —   dandruff   —

Figures 19-1, 19-2.

"flu." The written advice of a pharmacist, however, would be disregarded if the ailment were more serious than "sunburn." Finally, friends and television advertisements would be regarded favorably for such minor difficulties as "upset stomach." All differences are statistically significant at the 0.01 level.

These results verify the findings of the group and depth interviews. The perceived risk of ineffective or even dangerous treatment no doubt increases with the scale value of an ailment, and the need for authoritative information shows a corresponding rise. Many sources are used, however, for colds and related illnesses, with the degree of perceived risk and information seeking varying widely from individual to individual.

Future Research

These findings, of course, are based only on pilot studies. As a result, they should only be regarded as tentative. Even if more elaborate methodology had been used, however, the limitations of a cross sectional study would remain. No attempt is made in cross sectional research to study behavior "in the act," so to speak, with the result that the opportunity exists for memory distortions of all types. Decision-making processes can be studied with clarity *only* through the use of longitudinal analysis which focuses on individual patterns of change over time.

Assuming the availability of adequate financing, a long-term longitudinal study will begin in Summer, 1967* at The Ohio State University involving personnel from the College of Commerce and Administration and the College of Pharmacy. It will be focused on the questions discussed in this report as well as many others which are of widespread interest in many fields related to public health. Of special interest to marketing would be the opportunity to study decision-making as a process, a type of inquiry which is as yet done quite infrequently. Much can be learned about decision processes in general, as well as clarifying to an extent not previously possible the role of various types of communication sources in influencing consumer behavior in self-medication.

* [Editor's note: The research began as scheduled.]

20

A Sociometric Analysis of
Group Influences on Consumer
Brand Preferences

JAMES ELLIS STAFFORD

A major question facing marketing today is exactly how, in what way, and to what extent social factors influence consumer behavior. It has been shown, for example, that consumer brand preferences are related to economic considerations such as price. But are there other forces, both psychological and social, at work which also influence the consumer in his brand selection? The basic problem of this dissertation, therefore, was to determine experimentally if one type of social factor—informal membership groups—influenced brand preferences, and then to analyze and describe in detail the process of this influence.

The design of this experiment consisted of sociometrically selecting and analyzing ten groups of women from Austin, Texas, who were neighbors, close friends, or relatives; who enjoyed shopping together; and who were given a common experimental task to perform—the selection of a loaf of bread from four previously unknown brands twice a week for eight weeks.

Each of the ten groups were sociometrically analyzed to determine internal leadership patterns, communication networks, and degree of cohesiveness. Similarly, the actual brand choices of the women were observed, recorded and analyzed on an individual basis to determine the degree of brand loyalty, and on a group basis to determine whether group influences existed, how they functioned, and what impact they had on particular brand preferences and brand loyalty. Analysis of variance and chi square were the primary statistical techniques employed in the testing of the following general hypotheses:

    1. Small, informal social groups exert influences toward conformity on member brand preferences.

    2. The degree of influence exerted on a member toward certain

Reprinted from *Proceedings, American Marketing Association Conference*, Peter D. Bennett, ed. (September, 1965), pp. 459-460, by permission of the publisher, the American Marketing Association.

brand preferences by the group is related directly to the "cohesiveness" of that group.

3. Within a group, the "leader" is the most influential member with respect to member brand preferences.

The study led to the following tentative conclusions. First, hypothesis 1 was supported. While no significant preference was shown for any one of the four brands used in the study, there was a definite indication that the groups influenced the members toward conformity of brand preference. Second, hypothesis 2 was partially rejected. No statistical significance was found between the level of cohesiveness and member brand loyalty. Only when cohesiveness and leadership patterns were combined was any relationship with member brand loyalty uncovered. In more cohesive groups, the probability was much higher that the members would prefer the same brand as the group leader. Third, the results gave significant support to the third hypothesis. Leaders were found to influence group members in two ways. First, the higher the degree of brand loyalty exhibited by a group leader, the more likely were the other members to prefer the same brand. Second, the greater the degree of leader brand loyalty, the higher was the percentage of his group becoming brand loyal also.

With respect to the concept of brand loyalty per se, it was found, for example, that many consumers became brand loyal even where there was no discernible difference between brands. In most cases, however, this loyalty developed only after a period of search or exploratory behavior among the test brands. Once each brand had been tried, then the probability of brand loyal behavior increased appreciably beyond the level expected by chance. Similarly, each time an individual repeated a brand choice, the probability was much higher that he would select the same brand again. Finally, an individual's degree of "suggestibility" was found to be closely related to a "readiness" to become brand loyal. The more suggestible individuals became brand loyal significantly quicker than less suggestible individuals.

In conclusion, while an exploratory experiment of this nature is more often suggestive than conclusive, it appears that there is sufficient evidence to conclude that small, informal social groups do influence member brand preferences.

21

The Two-step Flow of Communication: An Up-to-date Report on an Hypothesis

ELIHU KATZ

Analysis of the process of decision-making during the course of an election campaign led the authors of *The People's Choice* to suggest that the flow of mass communications may be less direct than was commonly supposed. It may be, they proposed, that influences stemming from the mass media first reach "opinion leaders" who, in turn, pass on what they read and hear to those of their every-day associates for whom they are influential. This hypothesis was called "the two-step flow of communication."[1]

The hypothesis aroused considerable interest. The authors themselves were intrigued by its implications for democratic society. It was a healthy sign, they felt, that people were still most successfully persuaded by give-and-take with other people and that the influence of the mass media was less automatic and less potent than had been assumed. For social theory, and for the design of communications research, the hypothesis suggested that the image of modern urban society needed revision. The image of the audience as a mass of disconnected individuals hooked up to the media but not to each other could not be reconciled with the idea of a two-step flow of communication implying, as it did, networks of interconnected individuals through which mass communications are channeled.

This may be identified as Publication No. A-225 of the Bureau of Applied Social Research, Columbia University. It is an abridged version of a chapter in the author's "Interpersonal Relations and Mass Communications: Studies in the Flow of Influence," unpublished Ph.D. thesis, Columbia University, 1956. The advice and encouragement of Dr. Paul F. Lazarsfeld in the writing of this thesis are gratefully acknowledged. Reprinted from *Public Opinion Quarterly* (Spring, 1957), pp. 61-78.

[1] Paul F. Lazarsfeld, Bernard Berelson and Hazel Gaudet, *The People's Choice*, New York: Columbia University Press, 1948 (2nd edition), p. 151.

Of all the ideas in *The People's Choice,* however, the two-step flow hypothesis is probably the one that was least well documented by empirical data. And the reason for this is clear: the design of the study did not anticipate the importance which interpersonal relations would assume in the analysis of the data. Given the image of the atomized audience which characterized so much of mass media research, the surprising thing is that interpersonal influence attracted the attention of the researchers at all.[2]

In the almost seventeen years since the voting study was undertaken, several studies at the Bureau of Applied Social Research of Columbia University have attempted to examine the hypothesis and to build upon it. Four such studies will be singled out for review. These are Merton's study of interpersonal influence and communications behavior in Rovere;[3] the Decatur study of decision-making in marketing, fashions, movie-going and public affairs, reported by Katz and Lazarsfeld;[4] the Elmira study of the 1948 election campaign reported by Berelson, Lazarsfeld and McPhee;[5] and, finally, a very recent study by Coleman, Katz and Menzel on the diffusion of a new drug among doctors.[6]

These studies will serve as a framework within which an attempt will be made to report on the present state of the two-step flow hypothesis, to examine the extent to which it has found confirmation and the ways in which it has been extended, contracted and reformulated. More than that, the studies will be drawn upon to highlight the successive strategies which have been developed in attempting to take systematic account of interpersonal relations in the design of communications research, aiming ultimately at a sort of "survey sociometry." Finally, these studies, plus others which will be referred to in passing,

[2]For the discussion of the image of the atomized audience and the contravening empirical evidence, see Elihu Katz and Paul F. Lazarsfeld, *Personal Influence: The Part Played by People in the Flow of Mass Communications,* Glencoe, Illinois: The Free Press, 1955, pp. 15-42; Eliot Friedson, "Communications Research and the Concept of the Mass," *American Sociological Review,* Vol. 18, (1953), pp. 313-317; and Morris Janowitz, *The Urban Press in a Community Setting,* Glencoe, Illinois: The Free Press, 1952.

[3]Robert K. Merton, "Patterns of Influence: A Study of Interpersonal Influence and Communications Behavior in a Local Community," in Paul F. Lazarsfeld and Frank N. Stanton, eds., *Communications Research, 1948-9,* New York: Harper and Brothers, 1949, pp. 180-219.

[4]Elihu Katz and Paul F. Lazarsfeld, *op. cit.,* Part Two.

[5]Bernard R. Berelson, Paul F. Lazarsfeld and William N. McPhee, *Voting: A Study of Opinion Formation in a Presidential Campaign,* Chicago: University of Chicago Press, 1954.

[6]A report on the pilot phase of this study is to be found in Herbert Menzel and Elihu Katz, "Social Relations and Innovation in the Medical Profession," *Public Opinion Quarterly,* Vol. 19, (1955), pp. 337-52; a volume and various articles on the full study are now in preparation. [Editor's note: See Coleman, Katz, and Menzel, "The Diffusion of an Innovation among Physicians," *Sociometry,* XX (1957), 253-270, and *Doctors and New Drugs,* Glencoe, Ill., Free Press, 1960.]

will provide an unusual opportunity to reflect upon problems in the continuity of social research.[7]

Findings of *The People's Choice*

The starting point for this review must be an examination of the evidence in the 1940 voting study which led to the original formulation of the hypothesis. Essentially, three distinct sets of findings seem to have been involved. The first had to do with *the impact of personal influence*. It is reported that people who made up their minds late in the campaign, and those who changed their minds during the course of the campaign, were more likely than other people to mention personal influence as having figured in their decisions. The political pressure brought to bear by everyday groups such as family and friends is illustrated by reference to the political homogeneity which characterizes such groups. What's more, on an average day, a greater number of people reported participating in discussion of the election than hearing a campaign speech or reading a newspaper editorial. From all of this, the authors conclude that personal contacts appear to have been both more frequent and more effective than the mass media in influencing voting decisions.[8]

The second ingredient that went into the formulation of the hypothesis concerned *the flow of personal influence*. Given the apparent importance of interpersonal influence, the obvious next step was to ask whether some people were more important than others in the transmission of influence. The study sought to single out the "opinion leaders" by two questions: "Have you recently tried to convince anyone of your political ideas?", and "Has anyone recently asked you for your advice on a political question?" Comparing the opinion leaders with others, they found the opinion leaders more interested in the election. And from the almost even distribution of opinion leaders throughout

---

[7]Other authors who have drawn upon the concepts of opinion leadership and the two-step flow of communication, and developed them further, are Matilda and John Riley, "A Sociological Approach to Communications Research," *Public Opinion Quarterly*, Vol. 15 (1951), pp. 445-460; S. N. Eisenstadt, "Communications Processes Among Immigrants in Israel," *Public Opinion Quarterly*, Vol. 16 (1952), pp. 42-58 and "Communication Systems and Social Structure: An Exploratory Study," *Public Opinion Quarterly*, Vol. 19 (1955), pp. 153-167; David Riesman, *The Lonely Crowd*, New Haven: Yale University Press, 1950; Leo A. Handel, *Hollywood Looks at its Audience*, Urbana: University of Illinois Press, 1950. The program of research in international communications at the Bureau of Applied Social Research has given considerable attention to opinion leadership; see Charles Y. Glock, "The Comparative Study of Communications and Opinion Formation," *Public Opinion Quarterly*, Vol. 16 (1952-53), pp. 512-523; J. M. Stycos, "Patterns of Communication in a Rural Greek Village," *Public Opinion Quarterly*, Vol. 16 (1952), pp. 59-70; and the forthcoming book by Daniel Lerner, Paul Berkman and Lucille Pevsner, *Modernizing the Middle East*. Studies by Peter H. Rossi and by Robert D. Leigh and Martin A. Trow are also concerned with the interplay of personal and mass media influences in local communities.

[8]Lazarsfeld, Berelson and Gaudet, *op. cit.*, pp. 135-152.

every class and occupation, as well as the frequent mention by decision-makers of the influence of friends, co-workers and relatives, it was concluded that opinion leaders are to be found on every level of society and presumably, therefore, are very much like the people whom they influence.[9]

A further comparison of leaders and others with respect to mass media habits provides the third ingredient: *the opinion leaders and the mass media.* Compared with the rest of the population, opinion leaders were found to be considerably more exposed to the radio, to the newspapers and to magazines, that is, to the formal media of communication.[10]

Now the argument is clear: If word-of-mouth is so important, and if word-of-mouth specialists are widely dispersed, and if these specialists are more exposed to the media than the people whom they influence, then perhaps "ideas often flow from radio and print to opinion leaders and from these to the less active sections of the population."[11]

Design of the Voting Study

For studying the flow of influence as it impinges on the making of decisions, the study design of *The People's Choice* had several advantages. Most important was the panel method which made it possible to locate changes almost as soon as they occurred and then to correlate change with the influences reaching the decision-maker. Secondly, the unit of effect, the decision, was a tangible indicator of change which could readily be recorded. But for studying that part of the flow of influence which had to do with contacts among people, the study design fell short, since it called for a random sample of individuals abstracted from their social environments. It is this traditional element in the design of survey research which explains the leap that had to be made from the available data to the hypothesis of the two-step flow of communication.

Because every man in a random sample can speak only for himself, opinion leaders in the 1940 voting study had to be located by self-designation, that is, on the basis of their own answers to the two advice-giving questions cited above.[12] In effect, respondents were simply asked to report whether or not they were opinion leaders. Much more important than the obvious problem of validity posed by this technique is the fact that it does not permit a comparison

[9]*Ibid.*, pp. 50-51.
[10]*Ibid.*, p. 51.
[11]*Ibid.*, p. 151.
[12]Strictly speaking, of course, if a respondent reports whether or not he is a leader he is not speaking for himself but for his followers, real or imagined. Furthermore, it ought to be pointed out for the record that it is sometimes possible for a respondent to speak for others besides himself. The voting studies, for example, ask respondents to report the vote-intentions of other family members, of friends, of co-workers, though this procedure is of undetermined validity.

of leaders with their respective followers, but only of leaders and non-leaders in general. The data, in other words, consist only of two statistical groupings: people who said they were advice-givers and those who did not. Therefore, the fact that leaders were more interested in the election than non-leaders cannot be taken to mean that influence flows from more interested persons to less interested ones. To state the problem drastically, it may even be that the leaders influence only each other, while the uninterested non-leaders stand outside the influence market altogether. Nevertheless, the temptation to assume that the non-leaders are the followers of the leaders is very great, and while *The People's Choice* is quite careful about this, it cannot help but succumb.[13] Thus, from the fact that the opinion leaders were more exposed to the mass media than the non-leaders came the suggestion of the two-step flow of communication; yet, manifestly, it can be true only if the non-leaders are, in fact, followers of the leaders.

The authors themselves point out that a far better method would have been based on "asking people to whom they turn for advice on the issue at hand and then investigating the interaction between advisers and advisees. But that procedure would be extremely difficult, if not impossible, since few of the related·'leaders' and 'followers' would happen to be included in the sample."[14] As will be shown immediately, this is perhaps the most important problem which succeeding studies have attempted to solve.

Designs of Three Subsequent Studies

To this point, two aspects of the original statement of the two-step flow hypothesis have been reviewed. First of all, the hypothesis has been shown to have three distinct components, concerning respectively the impact of personal influence; the flow of personal influence; and the relationship of opinion leaders to the mass media. The evidence underlying each has been examined. Secondly, the design of the study has been recalled in order to point up the difficulty that arises from attempting to cope with the fundamentally new problem of incorporating *both* partners to an influence transaction into a cross-sectional study.

From this point forward, the major focus will turn to those studies that have succeeded *The People's Choice*. We will first report the different ways in which three of the four studies selected for review approached the problem of

[13]There is an alternatives procedure which is something of an improvement. Respondents can be asked not only whether they have given advice but whether they have taken advice. This was done in the Decatur and Elmira studies which are cited below. Thus the non-leaders can be classified in terms of whether or not they are in the influence market at all, that is, whether or not they are "followers."

[14]Lazarsfeld, Berelson and Gaudet, *op. cit.*, pp. 49-50.

designing research on interpersonal influence.[15] Thereafter, the substantive findings of the several studies will be reviewed and evaluated so as to constitute an up-to-date report on the accumulating evidence for and against the hypothesis of the two-step flow of communication.

1. *The Rovere Study.* Undertaken just as the 1940 voting study was being completed, the earliest of the three studies was conducted in a small town in New Jersey. It began by asking a sample of 86 respondents to name the people to whom they turned for information and advice regarding a variety of matters. Hundreds of names were mentioned in response, and those who were designated four times or more were considered opinion leaders. These influentials were then sought out and interviewed.[16]

Here, then, is the initial attempt, on a pilot scale, to solve the problem of research design posed by *The People's Choice*. To locate influentials, this study suggests, begin by asking somebody, "Who influences you?" and proceed from the persons influenced to those who are designated as influential.

Two important differences between this study and the 1940 voting study must be pointed out. First, there is a difference in the conception of opinion leadership. Whereas the voting study regards any advice-giver as an opinion leader if he influences even one other person (such as a husband telling his wife for whom to vote), the leaders singled out by the criterion employed in Rovere were almost certainly wielders of wider influence.

Secondly, the voting study, at least by implication, was interested in such questions as the extent of the role of interpersonal influence in decision-making and its relative effectiveness compared to the mass media. The Rovere study took for granted the importance of this kind of influence, and proceeded to try to find the people who play key roles in its transmission.

A final point to make in connection with the design of this study is that it makes use of the initial interviews almost exclusively to *locate* opinion leaders and hardly at all to explore the *relationships* between leaders and followers. Once the leaders were designated, almost exclusive attention was given to classifying them into different types, studying the communications behavior of the different types and the interaction among the leaders themselves, but very little attention was given to the interaction between the leaders and the original informants who designated them.

2. *The Decatur Study,* carried out in 1945-46, tried to go a step further.[17] Like the voting study, but unlike Rovere, it tried to account for decisions—specific instances in which the effect of various influences could be discerned and assessed. Like Rovere, but unlike the voting study, it provided for inter-

---

[15]The Elmira study will be omitted at this point because its design is essentially the same as that of the 1940 voting study except for the important fact that it obtained from each respondent considerably more information about the vote-intentions of others in his environment, the kinds of people he talks with, etc., than was done in *The People's Choice*.

[16]Merton, *op. cit.*, pp. 184-185.

[17]Katz and Lazarsfeld, *op. cit.*, Part Two.

views with the persons whom individuals in the initial sample had credited as influential in the making of recent decisions (in the realms of marketing, movie-going, and public affairs). The focus of the study this time was not on the opinion leaders alone, but (1) on the relative importance of personal influence and (2) on the person who named the leader as well as the leader—the adviser-advisee dyad.

Ideally, then, this study could ask whether opinion leaders tended to be from the same social class as their followers or whether the tendency was for influence to flow from the upper classes downwards. Were members of the dyads likely to be of the same age, the same sex, etc? Was the leader more interested in the particular sphere of influence than his advisee? Was he more likely to be exposed to the mass media?

Just as the dyad could be constructed by proceeding from an advisee to his adviser, it was also possible to begin the other way around by talking first to a person who claimed to have acted as an adviser, and then locating the person he said he had influenced. The Decatur study tried this too. Using the same kind of self-designating questions employed in the voting study, persons who designated themselves as influential were asked to indicate the names of those whom they had influenced. By "snowballing" to the people thus designated, there arose the opportunity not only to study the interaction between adviser and advisee but also to explore the extent to which people who designated themselves as influential were confirmed in their self-evaluations by those whom they allegedly had influenced. Proceeding in this way, the researchers hoped to be able to say something about the validity of the self-designating technique.[18]

The authors of *The People's Choice* had said that "asking people to whom they turn and then investigating the interaction between advisers and advisees . . . would be extremely difficult if not impossible." And, in fact, it proved to be extremely difficult. Many problems were encountered in the field work, the result of which was that not all the "snowball" interviews could be completed.[19] In many parts of the analysis of the data, therefore, it was necessary to revert to comparisons of leaders and non-leaders, imputing greater influence to groups with higher concentrations of self-designated leadership. Yet, in principle, it was demonstrated that a study design taking account of interpersonal relations was both possible and profitable to execute.

But about the time it became evident that this goal was within reach, the goal itself began to change. It began to seem desirable to take account of chains

[18]About two-thirds of the alleged influences confirmed the fact that a conversation had taken place between themselves and the self-designated influential on the subject matter in question. Of these, about 80 per cent further confirmed that they had received advice. The extent of confirmation is considerably less in the realm of public affairs than it is in marketing or fashion. *Ibid.*, pp. 149-161 and 353-362.

[19]Partly this was due to inability to locate the designated people, but partly, too, to the fact that original respondents did not always know the person who had influenced them as is obvious, for example, in the case of a woman copying another woman's hat style, etc. See *Ibid.*, pp. 362-363.

of influence longer than those involved in the dyad; and hence to view the adviser-advisee dyad as one component of a more elaborately structured social group.

These changes came about gradually and for a variety of reasons. First of all, findings from the Decatur study and from the later Elmira study revealed that the opinion leaders themselves often reported that their own decisions were influenced by still other people.[20] It began to seem desirable, therefore, to think in terms of the opinion leaders of opinion leaders.[21] Secondly, it became clear that opinion leadership could not be viewed as a "trait" which some people possess and others do not, although the voting study sometimes implied this view. Instead, it seemed quite apparent that the opinion leader is influential at certain times and with respect to certain substantive areas by virtue of the fact that he is "empowered" to be so by other members of his group. Why certain people are chosen must be accounted for not only in demographic terms (social status, sex, age, etc.) but also in terms of the structure and values of the groups of which both adviser and advisee are members. Thus, the unexpected rise of young men to opinion leadership in traditional groups, when these groups faced the new situations of urbanization and industrialization, can be understood only against the background of old and new patterns of social relations within the group and of old and new patterns of orientation to the world outside the group.[22] Reviewing the literature of small group research hastened the formulation of this conception.[23]

One other factor shaped the direction of the new program as well. Reflecting upon the Decatur study, it became clear that while one could talk about the role of various influences in the making of fashion *decisions by individuals,* the study design was not adequate for the study of fashion in the aggregate— *fashion as a process of diffusion*—as long as it did not take account of either the content of the decision or the time factor involved. The decisions of the "fashion changers" studied in Decatur might have cancelled each other out: while Mrs. X reported a change from Fashion A to Fashion B, Mrs. Y might have been reporting a change from B to A. What is true for fashion is true for any other diffusion phenomenon: to study it, one must trace the flow of some specific item over time. Combining this interest in diffusion with that of studying the role of more elaborate social networks of communication gave birth to a new study which focused on (1) a specific item, (2) diffusion over time, (3) through the social structure of an entire community.

3. *The Drug Study.* This study was conducted to determine the way in which doctors make decisions to adopt new drugs. This time, when it came to

[20]*Ibid.,* p. 318; Berelson, Lazarsfeld and McPhee, *op. cit.,* p. 110.

[21]This was actually tried at one point in the Decatur study. See Katz and Lazarsfeld, *op. cit.,* pp. 283-287.

[22]See, for example, the articles by Eisenstadt, *op. cit.,* and Glock, *op. cit.;* the Rovere study, too, takes careful account of the structure of social relations and values in which influentials are embedded, and discusses the various avenues to influentiality open to different kinds of people.

[23]Reported in Part I of Katz and Lazarsfeld, *op cit.*

designing a study which would take account of the possible role of interpersonal influence among physicians, it became clear that there were so few physicians (less than one and one-half per 1000 population) that it was feasible to interview all members of the medical profession in several cities. If all doctors (or all doctors in specialties concerned with the issue at hand) could be interviewed, then there would be no doubt that all adviser-advisee pairs would fall within the sample. All such pairs could then be located within the context of larger social groupings of doctors, which could be measured by sociometric methods.

Doctors in the relevant specialties in four midwestern cities were interviewed. In addition to questions on background, attitudes, drug-use, exposure to various sources of information and influence, and the like, each doctor was also asked to name the three colleagues he saw most often socially, the three colleagues with whom he talked most frequently about cases, and the three colleagues to whom he looked for information and advice.[24]

In addition to the opportunity of mapping the networks of interpersonal relations, the drug study also provided for the two other factors necessary for a true diffusion study: attention to a specific item in the course of gaining acceptance, and a record of this diffusion over time. This was accomplished by means of an audit of prescriptions on file in the local pharmacies of the cities studied, which made it possible to date each doctor's earliest use of a particular new drug—a drug which had gained widespread acceptance a few months before the study had begun. Each doctor could thus be classified in terms of the promptness of his decision to respond to the innovation, and in terms of other information provided by the prescription audit.

Altogether, compared with the earlier studies, the drug study imposes a more objective framework—both psychological and sociological—on the decision. First of all, the decision-maker himself is not the only source of information concerning his decision. Objective data from the prescription record are used as well. Secondly, the role of different influences is assessed not only on the basis of the decision-maker's own reconstruction of the event, but also on the basis of objective correlations from which inferences concerning the flow of influence can be drawn. For example, doctors who adopted the new drug early were more likely to be participants in out-of-town medical specialty meetings than those who adopted it later.

Similarly, it is possible to infer the role of social relations in doctor's decision-making not only from the doctor's own testimony concerning the role of social influences but also from the doctor's "location" in the interpersonal networks mapped by the sociometric questions. Thus, on the basis of sociometric data, it is possible to classify doctors according to their integration into the medical community, or the degree of their influence, as measured by *the number of times* they are named by their colleagues as friends, discussion-partners, and consultants. They can also be classified according to their mem-

[24]See footnote 6.

bership in one or another network or clique, as indicated by *who* names them. Using the first measure makes it possible to investigate whether or not the more influential doctors adopt a drug earlier than those who are less influential. From the second kind of analysis one can learn, for example, whether or not those doctors who belong to the same sub-groups have similar drug-use patterns. In this way, it becomes possible to weave back and forth between the doctor's own testimony about his decisions and the influences involved, on the one hand, and the more objective record of his decisions and of the influences to which he has been exposed, on the other hand.

Note that the networks of social relations in this study are mapped "prior" to the introduction of the new drug being studied, in the sense that friendship, consultation, and so on, are recorded independently of any particular decision the doctor has made. The study is concerned with the potential relevance of various parts of these sociometric structures to the transmission of influence. For example, it is possible to point to the parts of the structure which are "activated" upon the introduction of a new drug, and to describe the sequence of diffusion of the drug as it gains acceptance by individuals and groups in the community. While the Decatur study could hope to examine only the particular face-to-face relationship which had been influential in a given decision, the drug study can locate this relationship against the background of the entire web of *potentially* relevant relationships within which the doctor is embedded.

The Findings of Studies Subsequent to *The People's Choice*

Having examined the *designs* of these studies, the next step is to explore their *findings* insofar as these are relevant to the hypothesis about the two-step flow of communication. It will be useful to return to the three categories already singled out in discussing *The People's Choice*: (1) the impact of personal influence; (2) the flow of personal influence; and (3) opinion leaders and the mass media. Evidence from the three studies just reported, as well as from the 1948 Elmira study[25] and from others, will be brought together here; but in every case the characteristics of each study's design must be borne in mind in evaluating the evidence presented.

A. The Impact of Personal Influence

1. *Personal and the mass media influence*

The 1940 study indicated that personal influence affected voting decisions

[25]Berelson, Lazarsfeld, and McPhee, *op. cit.*

more than the mass media did, particularly in the case of those who changed their minds during the course of the campaign. The Decatur study went on to explore the relative impact of personal influences and the mass media in three other realms: marketing, fashions and movie-going. Basing its conclusions on the testimony of the decision-makers themselves, and using an instrument for evaluating the relative effectiveness of the various media which entered into the decisions, the Decatur study again found that personal influence figured both more frequently and more effectively than any of the mass media.[26]

In the analysis to date, the drug study has not approached the problem of the relative effectiveness of the various media from the point of view of the doctor's own reconstruction of what went into the making of his decision. Comparing mere frequency of mention of different media, it is clear that colleagues are by no means the most frequently mentioned source. Nevertheless, exploration of the factors related to whether the doctor's decision to adopt the drug came early or late indicates that the factor most strongly associated with the time of adoption of the new drug is the extent of the doctor's integration in the medical community. That is, the more frequently a doctor is named by his colleagues as a friend or a discussion partner, the more likely he is to be an innovator with respect to the new drug. Extent of integration proves to be a more important factor than any background factor (such as age, medical school, or income of patients), or any other source of influence (such as readership of medical journals) that was examined.

Investigation of why integration is related to innovation suggests two central factors: (1) interpersonal communication—doctors who are integrated are more in touch and more up-to-date; and (2) social support—doctors who are integrated feel more secure when facing the risks of innovation in medicine.[27] Thus the drug study, too, provides evidence of the strong impact of personal relations—even in the making of scientific decisions.

2. Homogeneity of opinion in primary groups

The effectiveness of inter-personal influence, as it is revealed in the studies under review, is reflected in the homogeneity of opinions and actions in primary groups. The medium of primary group communication is, by definition, person-to-person. Both the voting studies indicate the high degree of homogeneity of political opinion among members of the same families, and among co-workers and friends. The effectiveness of such primary groups in pulling potential deviates back into line is demonstrated by the fact that those who changed their vote intentions were largely people who, early in the campaign, had reported that they intended to vote differently from their family or friends.[28]

[26]Katz and Lazarsfeld, op. cit., pp. 169-186.

[27]On the relationship between social integration and self-confidence in a work situation, see Peter M. Blau, The Dynamics of Bureaucracy, Chicago: University of Chicago Press, 1955, pp. 126-129.

[28]Lazarsfeld, Berelson and Gaudet, op. cit., pp. 137-145; Berelson, Lazarsfeld and McPhee, op. cit., pp. 94-101, 120-122.

The drug study, too, was able to examine the extent of homogeneity in the behavior of sociometrically related doctors, and was able to demonstrate that there were situations where similar behavior could be deserved. For example, it was found that, when called upon to treat the more puzzling diseases, doctors were likely to prescribe the same drug as their sociometric colleagues. The study also showed that, very early in the history of a new drug, innovating doctors who were sociometrically connected tended to adopt the new drug at virtually the same time. This phenomenon of homogeneity of opinion or behavior among interacting individuals confronting an unclear or uncertain situation which calls for action has often been studied by sociologists and social psychologists.[29]

3. The various roles of the media

The 1940 voting study explored some of the reasons why personal influence might be expected to be more influential in changing opinions than the mass media: It is often non-purposive; it is flexible; it is trustworthy. It was suggested that the mass media more often play a reinforcing role in the strengthening of predispositions and of decisions already taken. Nevertheless, it was assumed that the various media and personal influence are essentially competitive, in the sense that a given decision is influenced by one *or* the other. The Decatur study tended toward this assumption too, but at one point the study does attempt to show that different media play different parts in the decision-making process and take patterned positions in a sequence of several influences. The drug study elaborates on the roles of the media even further, distinguishing between media that "inform" and media that "legitimate" decisions. Thus in doctors' decisions, professional media (including colleagues) seem to play a legitimating role, while commercial media play an informing role.

B. The Flow of Personal Influence

The 1940 voting study found that opinion leaders were not concentrated in the upper brackets of the population but were located in almost equal proportions in every social group and stratum. This finding led to efforts in subsequent studies to establish the extent to which this was true in areas other than election campaigns and also to ascertain what it is that *does* distinguish opinion leaders from those whom they influence.

The first thing that is clear from the series of studies under review is that the subject matter concerning which influence is transmitted has a lot to do with determining who will lead and who follow. Thus, the Rovere study suggests that within the broad sphere of public affairs one set of influentials is

[29]That men, faced with an unstructured situation, look to each other to establish a "social reality" in terms of which they act, is a central theme in the work of Durkheim, Kurt Lewin and his disciples, H. S. Sullivan ("consensual validation"), and in the studies of Sherif, Asch and others.

occupied with "local" affairs and another with "cosmopolitan" affairs.[30] The Decatur study suggests that in marketing, for example, there is a concentration of opinion leadership among older women with larger families, while in fashions and movie-going it is the young, unmarried girl who has a disproportionate chance of being turned to for advice. There is very little overlap of leadership: a leader in one sphere is not likely to be influential in another unrelated sphere as well.[31]

Yet, even when leadership in one or another sphere is heavily concentrated among the members of a particular group—as was the case with marketing leadership in Decatur—the evidence suggests that people still talk, most of all, to others like themselves. Thus, while the marketing leaders among the older "large-family wives" also influenced other kinds of women, most of their influence was directed to women of their own age with equally large families. In marketing, fashions, and movie-going, furthermore, there was no appreciable concentration of influentials in any of the three socio-economic levels. Only in public affairs was there a concentration of leadership in the highest status, and there was some slight evidence that influence flows from this group to individuals of lower status. The Elmira study also found opinion-leaders in similar proportions on every socio-economic and occupational level and found that conversations concerning the campaign went on, typically, between people of similar age, occupation, and political opinion.

What makes for the concentration of certain kinds of opinion leadership within certain groups? And when influential and influencee are outwardly alike —as they so often seem to be—what, if anything, distinguishes one from the other? Broadly, it appears that influence is related (1) to the *personification of certain values* (who one is); (2) to *competence* (what one knows); and (3) to *strategic social location* (whom one knows). Social location, in turn, divides into whom one knows within a group; and "outside."

Influence is often successfully transmitted because the influencee wants to be as much like the influential as possible.[32] That the young, unmarried girls are fashion leaders can be understood easily in a culture where youth and youthfulness are supreme values. This is an example where "who one is" counts very heavily.

But "what one knows" is no less important.[33] The fact is that older women, by virtue of their greater experience, are looked to as marketing advisors and that specialists in internal medicine—the most "scientific" of the

[30]Merton, *op. cit.*, pp. 187-188.

[31]For a summary of the Decatur findings on the flow of interpersonal influence, see Katz and Lazarsfeld, *op. cit.*, pp. 327-334.

[32]That leaders are, in a certain sense, the most conformist members of their groups— upholding whatever norms and values are central to the group—is a proposition which further illustrates this point. For an empirical illustration from a highly relevant study, see C. Paul Marsh and A. Lee Coleman, "Farmers' Practice-adoption Rates in Relation to Adoption Rates of Leaders," *Rural Sociology*, Vol. 19 (1954), pp. 180-183.

[33]The distinction between "what" and "whom" one knows is used by Merton, *op. cit.*, p. 197.

practicing physicians—are the most frequently mentioned opinion leaders among the doctors. The influence of young people in the realm of movie-going can also be understood best in terms of their familiarity with the motion picture world. The Elmira study found slightly greater concentrations of opinion leadership among the more educated people on each socio-economic level, again implying the importance of competence. Finally, the influence of the "cosmopolitans" in Rovere rested on the presumption that they had large amounts of information.

It is, however, not enough to be a person whom others want to emulate, or to be competent. One must also be accessible. Thus, the Decatur study finds gregariousness—"whom one knows"—related to every kind of leadership. The Rovere study reports that the leadership of the "local" influentials is based on their central location in the web of interpersonal contacts. Similarly, studies of rumor transmission have singled out those who are "socially active" as agents of rumor.[34]

Of course, the importance of whom one knows is not simply a matter of the number of people with whom an opinion leader is in contact. It is also a question of whether the people with whom he is in touch happen to be interested in the area in which his leadership is likely to be sought. For this reason, it is quite clear that the greater interest of opinion leaders in the subjects over which they exert influence is not a sufficient explanation of their influence. While the voting studies as well as the Decatur study show leaders to be more interested, the Decatur study goes on to show that interest alone is not the determining factor.[35] In fashion, for example, a young unmarried girl is considerably more likely to be influential than a matron with an equally great interest in clothes. The reason, it is suggested, is that a girl who is interested in fashion is much more likely than a matron with an equally high interest to know other people who share her preoccupation, and thus is more likely than the matron to have followers who are interested enough to ask for her advice. In other words, it takes two to be a leader—a leader and a follower.

Finally, there is the second aspect of "whom one knows." An individual may be influential not only because people within his group look to him for advice but also because of whom he knows outside his group.[36] Both the Elmira and Decatur studies found that men are more likely than women to be opinion leaders in the realm of public affairs and this, it is suggested, is because they have more of a chance to get outside the home to meet people and talk politics. Similarly, the Elmira study indicated that opinion leaders belonged to more organizations, more often knew workers for the political

[34]Gordon W. Allport and Leo J. Postman, *The Psychology of Rumor*, New York: Henry Holt, 1943, p. 183.
[35]Katz and Lazarsfeld, *op. cit.*, pp. 249-252.
[36]It is interesting that a number of studies have found that the most integrated persons within a group are also likely to have more contacts outside the group than others. One might have expected the more marginal members to have more contacts outside. For example, see Blau, *op. cit.*, p. 128.

parties, and so on, than did others. The drug study found that influential doctors could be characterized in terms of such things as their more frequent attendance at out-of-town meetings and the diversity of places with which they maintained contact, particularly far-away places. It is interesting that a study of the farmer-innovators responsible for the diffusion of hybrid seed-corn in Iowa concluded that these leaders also could be characterized in terms of the relative frequency of their trips out of town.[37]

C. The Opinion Leaders and the Mass Media

The third aspect of the hypothesis of the two-step flow of communication states that opinion leaders are more exposed to the mass media than are those whom they influence. In *The People's Choice* this is supported by reference to the media behavior of leaders and non-leaders.

The Decatur study corroborated this finding, and went on to explore two additional aspects of the same idea.[38] First of all, it was shown that leaders in a given sphere (fashions, public affairs, etc.) were particularly likely to be exposed to the media appropriate to that sphere. This is essentially a corroboration of the Rovere finding that those who proved influential with regard to "cosmopolitan" matters were more likely to be readers of national news magazines, but that this was not at all the case for those influential with regard to "local" matters. Secondly, the Decatur study shows that at least in the realm of fashions, the leaders are not only more exposed to the mass media, but are also more affected by them in their own decisions. This did not appear to be the case in other realms, where opinion leaders, though more exposed to the media than non-leaders, nevertheless reported personal influence as the major factor in their decisions. This suggests that in some spheres considerably longer chains of person-to-person influence than the dyad may have to be traced back before one encounters any decisive influence by the mass media, even though their contributory influence may be perceived at many points. This was suggested by the Elmira study too. It found that the leaders, though more exposed to the media, also more often reported that they sought information and advice from other persons.[39]

Similarly, the drug study showed that the influential doctors were more likely to be readers of a large number of professional journals and valued them more highly than did doctors of lesser influence. But at the same time,

---

[37]Bryce Ryan and Neal Gross, *Acceptance and Diffusion of Hybrid Seed Corn in Two Iowa Communities*, Ames, Iowa: Iowa State College of Agriculture and Mechanic Arts, Research Bulletin 372, pp. 706-707. For a general summary, see Ryan and Gross, "The Diffusion of Hybrid Seed Corn in Two Iowa Communities," *Rural Sociology*, Vol. 8 (1943), pp. 15-24. An article, now in preparation, will point out some of the parallels in research design and in findings between this study and the drug study. [Editor's note: See *Studies of Innovation and of Communication to the Public* (Stanford, Calif.: Institute For Communication Research, Stanford University, 1962), pp. 5-35.]

[38]Katz and Lazarsfeld, *op. cit.*, pp. 309-320.

[39]Berelson, Lazarsfeld and McPhee, *op. cit.*, p. 110.

they were as likely as other doctors to say that local colleagues were an important source of information and advice in their reaching particular decisions.

Finally, the drug study demonstrated that the more influential doctors could be characterized by their greater attention not only to medical journals, but to out-of-town meetings and contacts as well. This finding has already been discussed in the previous section treating the *strategic location* of the opinion leader with respect to "the world outside" his group. Considering it again under the present heading suggests that the greater exposure of the opinion leader to the mass media may only be a special case of the more general proposition that opinion leaders serve to relate their groups to relevant parts of the environment through whatever media happen to be appropriate. This more general statement makes clear the similar functions of big city newspapers for the Decatur fashion leader; of national news magazines for the "cosmopolitan" influentials of Rovere; of out-of-town medical meetings for the influential doctor; and of contact with the city for the farmer-innovator in Iowa[40] as well as for the newly-risen, young opinion leaders in underdeveloped areas throughout the world.[41]

Conclusions

Despite the diversity of subject matter with which they are concerned, the studies reviewed here constitute an example of continuity and cumulation both in research design and theoretical commitment. Piecing together the findings of the latter-day studies in the light of the original statement of the two-step flow hypothesis suggests the following picture.

Opinion leaders and the people whom they influence are very much alike and typically belong to the same primary groups of family, friends and co-workers. While the opinion leader may be more interested in the particular sphere in which he is influential, it is highly unlikely that the persons influenced will be very far behind the leader in their level of interest. Influentials and influencees may exchange roles in different spheres of influence. Most spheres focus the group's attention on some related part of the world outside the group, and it is the opinion leader's function to bring the group into touch with this revelant part of its environment through whatever media are appropriate. In every case, influentials have been found to be more exposed to these points of contact with the outside world. Nevertheless, it is also true that, despite their greater exposure to the media, most opinion leaders are primarily affected not by the communication media but by still other people.

[40]Ryan and Gross, *op. cit.*, choose to explain "trips to the city" as another index of the non-traditional orientation of which innovation itself is also an index. In the case of the drug out-of-town meetings, trips to out-of-town centers of learning, etc., but the latter were also mentioned as key sources of advice by doctors who were innovators and influentials [Sic].

[41]See Lerner, *et al.* cited above.

The main emphasis of the two-step flow hypothesis appears to be on only one aspect of interpersonal relations—interpersonal relations as channels of communication. But from the several studies reviewed, it is clear that these very same interpersonal relations influence the making of decisions in at least two additional ways. In addition to serving at networks of communication, interpersonal relations are also sources of pressure to conform to the group's way of thinking and acting, as well as sources of social support. The workings of group pressure are clearly evident in the homogeneity of opinion and action observed among voters and among doctors in situations of unclarity or uncertainty. The social support that comes from being integrated in the medical community may give a doctor the confidence required to carry out a resolution to adopt a new drug. Thus, interpersonal relations are (1) channels of information, (2) sources of social pressure, and (3) sources of social support, and each relates interpersonal relations to decision-making in a somewhat different way.[42]

The central methodological problem in each of the studies reviewed has been how to take account of interpersonal relations and still preserve the economy and representativeness which the random, cross-sectional sample affords. Answers to this problem range from asking individuals in the sample to describe the others with whom they interacted (Elmira), to conducting "snowball" interviews with influential-influencee dyads (Decatur), to interviewing an entire community (drug study). Future studies will probably find themselves somewhere in between. For most studies, however, the guiding principle would seem to be to build larger or smaller social molecules around each individual atom in the sample.[43]

[42]These different dimensions of interpersonal relations can be further illustrated by reference to studies which represent the "pure type" of each dimension. Studies of rumor flow illustrate the "channels" dimension; see, for example, Jacob L. Moreno, *Who Shall Survive*, Beacon, N. Y.: Beacon House, 1953, pp. 440-450. The study by Leon Festinger, Stanley Schachter and Kurt Back, *Social Pressures in Informal Groups*, New York: Harper and Bros., 1950, illustrates the second dimension. Blau, *op. cit.*, pp. 126-129, illustrates the "social support" dimension.

[43]Various ways of accomplishing this have been discussed for the past two years in a staff seminar on "relational analysis" at the Bureau of Applied Social Research. The recent study by Seymour M. Lipset, Martin A. Trow and James S. Coleman, *Union Democracy*, Glencoe, Ill.: The Free Press, 1956, illustrates one approach in its study of printers within the varying social contexts of the shops in which they are employed. The study by Riley and Riley, *op. cit.*, is another good example.

22

A Revision of the Two-step Flow of Communications Hypothesis[*]

A. W. VAN DEN BAN

Summary

Some unpredicted findings have been discovered in a study on voting habits made twenty years ago by a group of research workers of Columbia University who formulated their discovery thus: 'Ideas often flow *from* radio and print *to* the opinion leaders and *from* them to the less active sections of the population.' This statement, known as the two-step flow of communications hypothesis, has attracted wide attention in communication literature. At present, however, most research workers agree that the situation in real life is more complicated than this hypothesis suggests. Research on the diffusion of new ideas, techniques, etc., and especially a recent study on the diffusion of new farming methods in the Netherlands, shows that both opinion leaders and their followers are influenced by mass media as well as by personal influence. Farmers usually hear for the first time of the existence of a new method through the mass media, but the decision to adopt an innovation is mainly influenced by personal contacts. However, the kinds of mass media influencing opinion leaders and the kinds of personal contacts influencing them differ from those which influence their followers.

The conclusions drawn from various studies of communication processes differ with regard to the question whether people are mainly influenced by persons of a higher social status or by persons of the class they themselves belong to. The Dutch study suggests that this depends upon the need people feel for new information. If they are badly in need of information, they will

Quoted with permission from *Gazette*, International Journal for Mass Communication Studies, Vol. X, no. 3 (1964), 237-249.

*I am indebted to Dr. H. H. Felstehausen, of the University of Wisconsin, and to Prof. F. F. H. Kolbé, of the University of Pretoria, for their valuable criticism of an earlier draft of this article.

turn to well informed persons who often belong to a higher social status, but they are likely to receive most information on new ideas they do not very badly want to know about through casual conversations with people of their own status group.

Review of Literature

Few findings in communications research have aroused so much interest as the 'two-step flow of communications hypothesis'. This hypothesis originated from an analysis of the 1940 presidential election campaign in the United States which unexpectedly revealed that the majority of the voters were not only influenced by mass media, but that they were even more influenced by other people. These findings led to the hypothesis: 'Ideas often flow *from* radio and print *to* the opinion leaders and *from* them to the less active sections of the population.'[1] Later research showed that communication processes are often more complicated than this hypothesis indicates. In an up-to-date test of this hypothesis published in 1957,[2] Katz found that 'despite their greater exposure to the (mass) media, most opinion leaders are primarily affected not by the communication media but by still other people.' Katz mainly used the studies of the Bureau of Applied Social Research of Columbia University for his 'up-to-date test', but he did not give much attention to the analyses made by rural sociologists of the adoption of new farming methods.

In the tradition of this rural sociological research, Ryan and Gross published their famous study on the adoption of hybrid seed corn already twenty years ago.[3] Subsequent research confirmed their findings that the adoption of new farming methods is usually a rather lengthy process during which people become aware of new ideas mainly through mass media, but where the decision to adopt the new idea is predominantly made as a result of personal influence.[4] It was also found that, as a rule, opinion leaders are better informed than their followers.[5] In the study which forms the subject of this article, we tried to combine these findings by analysing which sources of information were used by opinion leaders and which by their followers during the various stages of the adoption process.

A student of journalism, Mason, had made an attempt to study the same problem. He is rather critical of rural sociological research in this field, but in my opinion his study is only of limited value because of some weaknesses

[1]P. F. Lazarsfeld, B. Berelson and H. Gaudet, *The People's Choice*, 2nd ed. New York, Columbia University Press, 1948, p. 151.

[2]*Public Opinion Quarterly*, 21, pp. 61-78.

[3]B. Ryan and N. Gross, "The Diffusion of Hybrid Seed Corn in Two Iowa Communities," *Rural Sociology*, 8 (1943) pp. 15-24.

[4]This research is summarized in: E. M. Rogers, *The Diffusion of Innovations*, Free Press, New York, 1962, ch. IV.

[5]Summarized in Rogers, *op. cit.*, ch. VIII.

in his methodology.[6] Rural sociologists had asked farmers, subsequent to their having adopted a new idea, about their sources of information while they went through the various stages of the adoption process. Mason, however, asked the farmers at different stages of the adoption process questions such as: 'How much have you talked to someone at the State College about a community drainage project? A lot, quite a bit, a little, or not at all?' This method has two weaknesses. In the first place, in the case of those who had already adopted the new method, the replies related not merely to the sources of information which influenced them during the period which led to their final decision to adopt the new method, but also to the sources from which they got their initial information about this project. In the second place, the differences in the use of the sources of information found in the different stages of the adoption process are partly due to the well known fact that innovators use different sources of information than people do who lag behind in adopting anything new. In addition, it seems doubtful to me whether all those who said that they had used a certain source of information quite a bit, had actually made use of this source to the same extent.[7]

In a study of an election campaign in the United States, Deutschmann and Pinner found that over 80% of the informed people got their initial information on two major campaign events from mass media. Personal conversations usually take place subsequent to people having been informed by these media. Such conversations usually exert a greater influence on the intention how to vote than mass media do. However, a large number of people who were only influenced by mass media also changed their intention how to vote to some extent.[8] These findings confirm the two-step flow hypothesis. This is also true of the studies on the diffusion of the news of the death of Senator Taft[9] and on that of the assassination of President Kennedy.[10] In the case of the shooting of President Kennedy, it was found that over half the population had got their information from personal sources, but that they had usually turned to the mass media for confirmation and additional information. In the less sensational case of Senator Taft, far fewer people were found to have got their initial information from personal sources, but here too, many had

[6]R. Mason, *Information Source Use in the Adoption Process*, Ph. D. dissertation, Dept. of Communication, Stanford University, Stanford, Cal. R. Mason, "The Use of Information Sources by Influentials in the Adoption Process," *Public Opinion Quarterly*, 27 (Fall 1963), pp. 455-466, and R. Mason, "The Use of Information Sources in the Adoption Process," *Rural Sociology*, 29 (March 1964), pp. 40-52.

[7]Perhaps this is an indication of the rather weak interviewing techniques Mason has used throughout his study. Among other things he reports that out of 97 farmers who had not tested their soils, 38 incorrectly claimed that they had done so (Ph.D. dissertation, table 7, p. 59).

[8]J. Deutschmann and F. A. Pinner, *A Field Investigation of the Two-stage Flow of Communication*, paper read for the Association for Education in Journalism, mimeograph, Communication Research Center Michigan State University, East Lansing, 1960.

[9]O. N. Larsen and R. J. Hill, "Mass Media and Interpersonal Communication in the Diffusion of a News Event," *American Sociological Review*, 19 (1954), pp. 426-433.

[10]B. S. Greenberg, *Diffusion of News of the Kennedy Assassination*, mimeograph, Institute of Communications Research Stanford University, 1964.

turned to the mass media for additional information, although over half of the total sample were found not to have consulted any other medium for additional information.

These studies give one the impression that people usually get their news first from the mass media, except in cases of very important and unexpected events which cause a lot of excitement and comment. If they are interested in the event, they may consult mass media for additional factual information, but they are perhaps more inclined to listen to personal sources for interpretation and evaluation of these events. The correctness of the hypothesis that one group of people is informed through mass media, and another group through personal contacts, is, therefore, very doubtful.

Research Methods

In the case of our study in the Netherlands, interviews were conducted with all of the approximately one hundred farmers in each of three communities with widely different cultural patterns.[11] In order to establish opinion leadership, three sociometric questions were asked:

    1) Which two farmers do you ask for advice when you are not sure of the merits of new farming methods?
    2) Which two farmers do you consider to be good farmers?
    3) Which two farmers do you talk to most frequently?

This method enabled us to count how often each farmer was mentioned in the replies to each of these questions. In addition, in each community, six or seven 'judges', mostly influential farmers, were asked to give each farmer a rating, ranging from a low zero to a high ten, according to the farmer's influence during discussions on farm management. These ratings were then averaged. A factor analysis showed that each of these four 'measures' mainly gave an indication of the same dimension: social status.

In order to measure the information sources used, each farmer was given a card with seven different sources: mass media; meetings and lectures; excursions, demonstrations and experimental plots; the local agricultural advisory officer (in the U.S.: county agent of the extension service); other farmers; salesmen; personal experience.[12] They were then asked which of these sources was usually the most important to them with regard to learning for the first time about a new farming method. The next question was: 'Many farmers await the effect of a new method before deciding whether to apply it themselves. If you make such a decision, which of the information sources on this card is usually the most important to you?' The replies showed that some farmers chose one of the mass media and said that to them the radio or their

[11]Except 2% refusals and not-at-homes.
[12]T.V. has not been included, because television is not (yet) used by the agricultural advisory service in the Netherlands. Dutch television programmes only give an agricultural programme for people living in towns; half an hour a month. There are no commercials on the Dutch T.V.

farming paper was the most important. These replies were also coded. The main reason why these questions were not asked with regard to specific methods was that it would then have been difficult to get any idea about the information sources influencing the late-comers who usually follow in the wake of the opinion leaders.

In addition to the questions on the importance farmers attached to the different information media, questions were also asked about the extent to which farmers used the major information sources.[13]

Information Sources Used by Leaders and Followers

According to the two-step flow hypothesis one would expect lead-

Table 22-1. The average 'judge's' rating of the influence of farmers using information media to various extents—scale: 0–10

Information Media Used	Average Influence Rating		
	Noord-Beveland[1]	Milheeze[2]	Dwingeloo[3]
Number of farming papers			
None		[4]	6.0
1	5.5		6.3
2	6.0		7.6
3 or more	7.0		7.6
Listening to radio farming programmes			
Never	5.8	5.8	6.5
Sometimes	5.9	5.9	6.8
Nearly always	6.4	5.7	6.3
Number of agricultural meetings attended			
None	5.1	4.9	6.1
1–5	5.8	5.1	6.7
6 or more	6.8	6.6	7.2
Number of farm visits by agricultural advisory officer last year			
None	5.3	5.0	5.4
1–3	6.1	6.0	6.6
4 or more	6.5	7.1	6.8
Demonstrations attended			
None	5.6	5.3	6.5
Some	6.3	6.2	6.6

[1] A community with modern farm management and many contacts with urban culture.
[2] A community with modern farm management and few contacts with urban culture.
[3] A community with traditional farm management and few contacts with urban culture.
[4] All farmers in this community receive a farming paper, but only 7% more than one.

[13] A more complete discussion of these research methods and of the research findings is given in A. W. van den Ban, *Boer en Landbouwvoorlichting; De Communicatie van Nieuwe landbouwmethoden* (The Communication of New Farm Practices in the Netherlands, English summary), Assen. Netherlands, Van Gorcum, 1963.

ers to make more use of mass media than their followers. Table 22-1 shows that this is true with regard to the number of farming papers received by the farmers, but not with regard to listening to farming programmes on the radio, with the exception—to some extent—in the Noord Beveland community. The other information media too, including personal contacts with the local advisory officer, were used more frequently by the opinion leaders than by their followers.

Stages in the Adoption Process

A second reason to revise the two-step flow of communications hypothesis is based on the results of Table 22-2, showing the sources of information used during the different stages of the adoption process.

For initial information about new methods 75% of the farmers men-

Table 22-2. The percentage of farmers considering various sources of information to be the most important

Source of Information	To Learn[1]	To Decide[2]
Farming papers	16	1
Radio	13	0
Mass Media in general	41	3
Mass Media plus some other source	5	3[3]
Demonstrations, meetings, etc.	6	12
Advisory officer	3	20
Other farmers	11	43
Other farmers plus some other source	3[3]	8
Salesmen	3	4
Personal experience	0	3
Other combination of sources	2	3
No answer	0	4

[1] Initial information about new farming methods.
[2] On the adoption of those methods.
[3] Coded as other combination.

tioned mass media as their most important source of information, but these media have hardly any importance when it comes to decide to adopt the new method. During the decision stage of the adoption process, personal contacts with other farmers, advisory officers and salesmen were mentioned as the major information sources by 75% of the respondents. Under these conditions it is hardly possible for opinion leaders to have been exclusively influenced by mass media, or for their followers to have been influenced only by personal contacts.

In accordance with the two-step flow hypothesis we found that those farmers who usually first hear from other farmers about new methods, exert very little influence themselves. However, there are so few of these farmers—only 33 out of 303 respondents—that this can hardly be considered sufficient evidence for the correctness of the hypothesis. Furthermore, the eleven farmers who mentioned mass media as their major source of information in the decision stage of the adoption process were not exceptionally influential.

We may therefore conclude that opinion leaders as well as their followers are influenced both by mass media and by other people, but during different stages of the adoption process.

Who Influences Whom?

According to the original two-step flow hypothesis there is one group of opinion leaders who influence all others. Later research has shown, however, that there may actually be a hierarchy of leaders. How this process works is not quite clear from previous research. Some authors say that 'opinion leaders and the people whom they influence are very much alike and typically belong to the same primary groups.'[14] But other studies showed that 'farmers were generally inclined to look up the status scale for advice on matters related to farming.'[15]

The replies to our three sociometric questions enable us to analyze how this process worked within one community. We do not possess any information on the farmers outside this community who may influence farmers within, or vice versa.[16] In order to analyze who influences whom within a community, the farmers were first divided into four groups ('quartiles') according to the scores showing their contacts with the advisory service.[17] It was then possible to calculate how many choices had been made for farmers in the same quartile according to their contact with 1, 2 or 3 quartiles more or less contact and, also, how many choices would have been made if each farmer had chosen two other farmers at random. By dividing these two sets of figures we obtained Table 22-3.

The last line of this table shows that not all farmers made the two choices they were requested to make; if they had done so, all the figures on this line would have been 100. More interesting are the columns showing that there is a tendency to choose as friends, farmers with a little more contact

14Katz, op. cit.
15H. F. Lionberger, *Adoption of New Ideas and Practices*, Iowa State University Press, 1960, p. 86.
16Rogers found that the innovators, that is the first 2.5% to adopt new methods, have many contacts with colleagues outside their community. E. M. Rogers, "Characteristics of Innovators and Other Adopter Categories," *Ohio Agr. Exp. Station, Research Bull.* 882. Columbus, 1961.
17These scores included not only the personal contacts with the local advisory officer, but also the readership of farming papers and publications of the advisory service, visits to farm demonstrations and meetings, etc.

Table 22-3. The number of sociometric choices made according to the differ-ence in scores for contact with the advisory service between the chooser and the farmers chosen, in percentages of the number of choices which would have been made if every farmer had made two choices at random

Number of Quartile Differences	Adviser			Good Farmer			Friend		
	N. Bev.[1]	*Mlh.*[2]	*Dw.*[3]	*N. Bev.*	*Mlh.*	*Dw.*	*N. Bev.*	*Mlh.*	*Dw.*
− 3 Farmer chosen, far less contact	0	17	0	0	9	9	9	43	17
− 2	8	21	26	31	13	37	42	73	59
− 1	41	27	42	62	27	35	77	60	66
0 as much contact	61	84	47	90	100	69	74	98	79
+ 1	94	87	75	108	108	97	113	90	87
+ 2	111	111	66	138	158	117	126	94	80
+ 3 Farmer chosen, much more contact	112	69	43	197	248	103	84	69	52
Total	62	64	49	87	88	69	82	80	71

[1] = *Noord-Beveland*   [2] = *Milheeze*   [3] = *Dwingeloo*

with the advisory service than the respondents maintain themselves; but to choose as 'good farmers', farmers who maintain much more contact, whereas the choice for the advisor lies between the two others. The reason for this difference between the people chosen in reply to the three sociometric questions probably is, that the contact with the advisory service is correlated with social status, especially in the communities with modern farm management. It is a well known fact that people tend to spend their leisure with people belonging more or less to the same social status, but that people prefer to work together with group members of higher social status.[18] If this is the case here too, we should find this tendency more clearly expressed by dividing the farmers, not according to their contact with the advisory service, but according to their social status. For this reason a table, similar to Table 22-3, was made for the "judges" rating of the farmers' influence.[19]

For the communities with modern farm management—Noord-Beveland and Milheeze—this table shows a strong tendency to select as 'good farmers', farmers with much more influence than the respondents exerted themselves.

[18]G. C. Homans, *Social Behaviour; Its Elementary Forms*, New York, Burlingame, Harcourt, Brace and World, 1961, Ch. 15.

[19]The ratings 2, 3 and 4 and the ratings 8 and 9 have been combined, because few farmers received such an extreme rating. Otherwise, some percentages in Table 22-4 would have been calculated on the basis of very small numbers of observations.

In the community with traditional farm management this was shown to be true to a lesser extent. Moreover, the tendency to select as friends, farmers of about the same social status, is more pronounced in Table 22-4 than in Table 22-3.[20]

These findings show, in accordance with the opinion of Katz, that opinion leaders sometimes belong to the same primary groups as their followers, but that at other times people prefer to ask advice from others with a higher social status, and probably belonging to quite different primary groups, in accordance with Lionberger's findings. Katz is correct with regard to information gathered in casual conversation, probably on subjects like films one wants

Table 22-4. Number of sociometric choices made according to the difference in the 'judge's' rating of the influence exerted by the chooser and the farmers chosen, expressed in percentages of the number of choices which would have been made if every farmer had made two choices at random

Points Difference in 'Judge' Rating	N. Bev.	Mlh.	Dw.	N. Bev.	Mlh.	Dw.	N. Bev.	Mlh.	Dw.
− 4 Farmer chosen had far less influence	0	0	19	0	0	0	0	0	58
− 3	0	0	0	0	0	7	0	32	14
− 2	0	0	8	23	0	15	8	31	30
− 1	18	37	39	26	3	18	49	96	83
0 Farmer chosen had about as much influence	54	85	73	77	83	101	112	110	101
+ 1	120	93	49	109	120	72	148	102	60
+ 2	107	114	49	145	184	110	107	83	76
+ 3	157	150	107	278	221	165	100	79	79
+ 4 Farmer chosen had much more influence	98	0	96	343	407	154	74	41	115
Total	62	64	49	87	88	69	82	80	71

to see, or about the qualities of the different candidates in an election. Few people feel an urgent need for information on such subjects. On the other hand, for information on new farming methods—the problem studied by Lionberger—many farmers badly need this information because they know that this may have a considerable influence on their income. In the latter case, therefore, they will turn for advice to farmers they consider more competent than themselves, in spite of the fact that crossing such a social barrier may

[20]The exceptions in Dwingeloo, for farmers with 4 points more or less influence, are probably caused by chance because of the small number of observations in these cells.

further diminish the social status of the farmer asking for advice, as has been shown by Homans.[21]

This indicates that the question as to whether or not the diffusion of new ideas is a two-step process, does depend on the need for information people feel. When they urgently need information about a new idea, a two-step process within the community will occur most frequently. Certainly our data show that in these Dutch farming communities most farmers know which farmers are best informed about new methods. However, as long as people believe that they can get along quite well without specific information, as is often the case, new ideas have to pass along a rather long chain of people before they have moved from the top to the bottom of the social status scale.

Characteristics of Opinion Leaders Depend upon the Progressiveness of Their Community

The analysis of three communities, differing in their willingness to adopt new ideas, enabled us to study the influence on opinion leadership of the community norms. In this study, community norms have not merely been inferred by means of the average adoption and contact-with-advisory-service scores, but also with the aid of the interview question: 'What is the general opinion in this village about farmers who are always among the first to try new methods?' Table 22-5 shows that the community norms are much less

Table 22-5. The general opinion in the village about farmers who are always among the first to try new methods, expressed in percentages of interviewees per community

Opinion	Noord-Beveland	Milheeze	Dwingeloo
Favourable	31	45	10
Favourable with qualifications	12	5	12
No general opinion	29	30	20
Unfavourable	26	14	49
No answer	3	5	8

favourable in the Dwingeloo area than in Noord-Beveland, and most favourable in the Milheeze area. The figures relating to the contact with the advisory officer and the adoption scores show about the same tendency.

While trying to formulate a general theory on opinion leadership, Homans presented the hypothesis that a person becomes an opinion leader by 'providing rare but valuable services to others.'[22] In progressive communities like Milheeze and Noord-Beveland, farmers are apt to put a much higher value on

[21]Op. cit., p. 324.
[22]Op. cit., p. 314.

information about new methods than farmers in traditional communities like Dwingeloo. We would, therefore, expect opinion leaders at Dwingeloo to be less well informed about new methods than in the other two communities. Tables 22-1 and 22-3 have already shown some indications that this is indeed the case. Table 22-1 shows that the difference in influence between the farmers who do and those who do not use various sources of information, often is smaller in the Dwingeloo area than in the other, more progressive communities. Similarly, Table 22-3 shows that Dwingeloo farmers are least inclined to select as good farmers or advisers, farmers who maintain a closer contact with the advisory service than they do themselves. These indications become clearer when we correlate the contact-with-advisory-service scores of Table 22-6 with the four different measures of opinion leadership.

Table 22-6. Correlation coefficient of contact with advisory service scores and four measures of opinion leadership

Measure of Opinion Leadership	Noord-Beveland	Milheeze	Dwingeloo
Number of times chosen as:			
adviser	0.480	0.506	0.371
good farmer	0.336	0.528	0.253
friend	0.394	0.355	0.218
Judges' rating of influence	0.482	0.707	0.280

This table shows indeed that the correlation coefficients between opinion leadership and contact with extension are higher in the Noord-Beveland and Milheeze communities, where more farmers are interested in information about new methods than in a traditional community like Dwingeloo.

Similar conclusions have been drawn from investigations on opinion leadership among farmers in Kentucky[23] and in another part of the Netherlands.[24]

Conclusions

On the basis of the research reported in this article, it seems necessary to replace the two-step flow of communications hypothesis by a more complicated set of hypotheses:

1. The adoption of a new idea usually takes quite a long time, cer-

[23]C. P. Marsh and A. L. Coleman, "Farmers' Practice-adoption Rates in Relation to the Adoption Rates of 'Leaders'," *Rural Sociology*, 19 (1954) pp. 180-181.

[24]A. W. van den Ban, *op. cit.*, p. 168.

tainly in the case of methods which imply many changes in related spheres.

2. Mass media are major agents in arousing the interest in new methods early in the adoption process, but during a later stage personal contacts are especially influential in the decision to adopt a new method. Basically, this process is the same for opinion leaders and for their followers.

3. The first persons to adopt a new idea make intensive use of all sources which can provide reliable information about the idea including mass media as well as personal contacts with qualified informants.

4. Often these innovators and early adopters are also the opinion leaders of their group, but the relationship between pioneering and opinion leadership is much closer in progressive than in traditional groups.

5. Problems, about which more information is badly needed, will often make people turn for advice to the best informed people in the community. These are usually people of a high social status.

6. On most new ideas, however, people will not feel an urgent need for information. In this case, people will get their information personally through casual conversations, mainly with people of about the same social status.

Considerable evidence for these hypotheses is found in a study on the diffusion of new farming methods in the Netherlands whereas the study of other innovations also offers some evidence, especially the study on new farming methods in the United States. There is no certainty, however, that these hypotheses will also be found to be true for different cultures and different new ideas. Further research will be needed to test the validity of these hypotheses, for instance with regard to ideas about political candidates in Latin America.

V

COMMUNICATION
IN ADVERTISING

THE ADVERTISING PROCESS AND THE INSTITUTIONS OF ADVERTISING make a fascinating study from many points of view. The core of all that is written about Madison Avenue, mass manipulators, advertising copy, advertising media, creative advertising geniuses, and similar topics is communications. The social critic, the advertising client, the advertsing agency, and the economist measure the effects of communications from different perspectives and with reference to different goals. Each may emphasize a different aspect of the advertising industry such as size, creative talent, economic impact, sales-generating potential, aesthetic features, ethical standards, or institutional arrangements; yet, if it is not taken into account that advertising is a complex institutionalized form of buyer-seller communications, each aspect will become rather pointless.

From the communications point of view, it is difficult to identify common elements of advertising much beyond the most elementary description. However, students of advertising must someday identify these elements if we expect to understand why one ad sells and another fails.

The readings in this part not only relate advertising practice to elements of communication theory, but they also explore a few other related problems. Knowledge of the changing nature of the message-carrying media is critical in the evaluation of the impact of advertising. The patterns of word-of-mouth advertising, which may or may not arise directly from paid advertising, are one of the frontiers of advertising research efforts. Surely, no reader can escape the frustration that his inquiry into advertising leads to more problems and avenues of further research than he had previously assumed.

23

What Advertising Does

M. ARGUNOV

People with initiative, energy, and attentiveness work in the No. 12 Textile store in Novosibirsk. The store's director Maria Ivanovna Khodzinskaya is a good, staunch friend and adviser to her customers. She tries to do everything to help them to buy the goods they want with the maximum of convenience and the least expenditure of time.

Some time ago, Maria Ivanovna began to notice that more and more linen cloth and items made from linen were accumulating in the store even though Russian linen and items made from it are fine products. What was the matter? True, some people bought, but sales came to only 250-300 rubles per day (277.50-$333 at the official rate of exchange).

The store director talked with her women customers—with one, then another. She found that they knew little about linen cloth, its qualities, and its characteristics. She began to ponder how she could do a better job of telling about these things. As a result, there developed an interesting plan for an advertising campaign. It was carried out, and the results surpassed all expectations. Here is what happened.

With the help of a decorator, the shop windows and interior of the store were rearranged to emphasize linen cloth. Sections of two rooms were set up in the sales area. The walls of the improvised rooms were made of light wooden frames three by four meters in size covered with linen cloth. The windows in each room were show windows which were hung with linen curtain cloth. On the table there were tablecloths and napkins made of linen. And there was also a female mannequin draped with linen cloth. Every day during the advertising period the cloth and the items in these rooms were changed.

To make a more eye-catching display of suit and dress cloth, 15 dresses were made in new styles and from different kinds of linen cloth. The dresses

Translation of an article in "Sovetskaya Torgovlya" (Russian Trade), No. 2, February 1966, published monthly in Moscow by the U.S.S.R.'s Ministry of Trade. Reprinted from *Journal of Advertising Research*, (December, 1966), pp. 2-3, by permission of the publisher, ©Advertising Research Foundation, Inc. (1966).

were put on display mannequins in the store's sales area. In addition, live models demonstrated the dresses.

The decorator placed linen piece goods on stands and counters. Posters which described linen cloth and its qualities were hung at the store's entrance and in the sales area. Customers were given advertising leaflets.

Television was also used in the campaign. During the advertising period (15 days), two televised reports were made directly from the store. These reports did a good job of showing the assortment of linen cloth and linen goods. They showed the arrangement of the improvised rooms with the curtains, tablecloths, napkins, and other things made of linen, as well as the dress designs on the display and "live" mannequins. At the same time, television viewers were told that linen cloth and items made of Russian linen are strong, durable, attractive, and hygienic. It was pointed out that things made of linen last twice as long as items made of cotton.

Advertising messages saying almost the same thing about linen cloth and also telling where it could be bought were broadcast by the city's radio station and published in the local newspaper.

On the day following the start of the coordinated advertising campaign, sales of linen cloth and linen items increased more than 30-fold. On this one day, linen sales came to 9,200 rubles ($10,212). Sales for the following two weeks were:

Sales of Linen

	(rubles)
Second day	8,800
Third	6,000
Fourth	5,570
Fifth	6,400
Sixth	4,300
Seventh	3,000
Eighth	2,300
Ninth	1,700
Tenth	2,500
Eleventh	1,300
Twelfth	700
Thirteenth	560
Fourteenth	570
Fifteenth	485

During the 15 days, total sales of linen cloth and linen items came to 50,000 rubles, or 45,500 rubles more than were ordinarily sold in the same period of time before the advertising campaign; all the linen cloth in the store was sold.

Expenses for the advertising campaign came to 1,112 rubles. This total included outlays for promotional rearrangement of the store, setting up the

sections of the two model rooms, the telecast, the radio and newspaper advertising, and making the dresses that were put on display. (Incidentally, these
dresses were sold to customers who asked to buy them.) The benefit obtained
from the advertising campaign is indisputable. There was economic profit, and
the campaign was undoubtedly useful to the customers as well.

Of course, this success did not come by itself. The advertising campaign
was carefully prepared. In particular, store personnel selected additional linen
items at the local distribution base of the Textile Trade Administration in
order to broaden the assortment. No less important a role was played by the
well thought-out advertising texts for television, radio, the local newspaper and
posters, and for the show-windows.

Store No. 12 is now conducting such advertising campaigns regularly.
Recently, for example, woolen cloth was widely advertised. All this helped the
store systematically to overfulfill its assigned sales volume plan. At the same
time, expenditures for advertising have totaled only 0.1-0.15% of sales volume.

As we see, the store did a great deal to advertise its goods. But, unfortunately, it did far from everything it might have done in such circumstances.
The colored promotional movie "Russian Linen" was not shown during the
campaign. It seems that the store managers did not know of its existence.

I would like to recommend that all directors of trade establishments really
publicize their goods, help customers select the things they want, find new ways
and means of showing goods to the best advantage, and undertake coordinated
advertising campaigns.

All this will not only help to fulfill the plan for selling goods and increase
the quality of merchandising, but will also have an effect on correct formulation
of consumer demand.

We should spare no effort in the organization of good advertising. Neither
should we economize on advertising, because expenditures for it are repaid a
hundredfold.

24

Clues for Advertising Strategists

DONALD F. COX

Basically there are two ways of viewing the audience—what I call the "egotistical" and the "realistic" views. Of these two, the most satisfying to the mass communicator is the first, which enables him to think of the audience as a relatively inert and undifferentiated mass that he can often persuade or influence. It is "egotistical" because it attributes great powers to the communicator and regards the audience as a swayable mass. Proponents of this view would probably hold that if you "hit them hard enough" (or "loud enough, long enough, and often enough"), sooner or later they will buy your product.

Perhaps the "realistic" view is more valid. With it, the audience is regarded as a body of individuals who may respond to a communication or commercial in a variety of ways, depending on their individual predispositions. This view also holds that while the communicator, the communication, and the medium play important roles in the communications process, in the final analysis it is the audience which decides whether (and to what extent) it will be influenced. Further, this view acknowledges the importance of the audience in its own right, through the process of social and personal influence.

Let us examine some evidence which should demonstrate that the "realistic" view *is* realistic, and the "egotistical" view *is* egotistical.

In order for an audience to be influenced in the desired manner by a communication, several conditions must be met:

- The audience must, somehow, be *exposed* to the communication.

- Members of the audience must interpret or *perceive* correctly what action or attitude is desired of them by the communicator.

- The audience must remember or *retain* the gist of the message that the communicator is trying to get across.

Reprinted from *Harvard Business Review* (November-December, 1961), pp. 160-182, by permission of the publisher, Harvard Graduate School of Business Administration, Boston.

•Members of the audience must *decide* whether or not they will be influenced by the communication.

We might consider these four conditions—exposure, perception, retention, and decision—as the gateways to effective communication and persuasion.

Communications research has established beyond much doubt that the processes of exposure, perception, retention, and decision do not often occur in a random fashion among the population. To varying degrees, people are predisposed to expose themselves to certain kinds of communications and media and not to others. Different people tend to get different meanings from the same communication and to remember or forget different aspects of a communication. Finally, different people make different decisions as to whether or not they will be influenced.

Since each of these processes involves a selection or choice by individual members of the audience, we may refer to them as *selective exposure, selective perception, selective retention,* and *selective decision.* Let us first examine some studies which illustrate the operation of the selective processes, and later discuss the implications of these studies in the area of advertising strategy.

Selective Exposure

The conditions under which people engage in selective exposure and the extent to which this process is operative have not been fully specified or documented by communications research. However, the general conclusion seems to be that most people tend to expose themselves to communications in which they are interested or which they find congenial to their existing attitudes and to avoid communications that might be irritating, or uninteresting, or incompatible with their own opinions. The following studies are illustrative:

•Danuta Ehrlich, Isaiah Guttman, Peter Schönbach, and Judson Mills found that new car owners were much more likely to read advertisements for the car they had just purchased than were owners of the same make but an earlier model.[1] The new car owners were also much more likely to read ads about their own car than they were to read about other makes. The hypothesis is that the new car owners were seeking reassurance by exposing themselves to what were, no doubt, very "congenial" communications.

•Charles F. Cannell and James C. MacDonald found that only 32% of a sample of male smokers were consistent readers of articles on health (including articles dealing with the relationship between smoking and lung cancer), whereas 60% of non-smoking males read such articles.[2]

[1]"Postdecision Exposure to Relevant Information," *Journal of Abnormal and Social Psychology*, Volume 54, 1957, pp. 98-102.
[2]"The Impact of Health News on Attitudes and Behavior," *Journalism Quarterly*, Volume 33, 1956, pp. 315-323.

Selective Perception

Even when people are accidentally or involuntarily exposed to a communication, they sometimes misinterpret or distort the intended meaning of the communication. For example, Patricia L. Kendall and Katherine M. Wolf report a study in which cartoons which were intended to ridicule prejudice were misinterpreted in some way by 64% of the people who saw them.[3] Misinterpretation was most frequent among prejudiced respondents who either saw no satire in the cartoons or interpreted them as supporting their own attitudes. One respondent felt that the purpose of a cartoon intended to ridicule anti-Semitism was "to show that there are some people against the Jews and to let other people feel freer to say they're against 'em too, I guess."

Carl I. Hovland, O. J. Harvey, and Muzafer Sherif presented communications arguing the desirability of prohibition to three types of people—"Drys," "Wets," and those "Moderately Wet."[4] They found that the greater the difference between the attitude of the recipient and the position advocated by the communication, the more likely the recipient was to regard the communication as propagandistic and unfair, and even to perceive the stand advocated by the communication as further removed from his own position than it actually was. Conversely, when the distance was small between the recipient's own stand and the position advocated by the communication, the recipient was likely to view the communication as being fair and factual and to perceive it as being even closer to his own stand than it actually was.

Habits also can cause distortion of a communication because people often see or hear that which, on the basis of past experience, they expect to see or hear. Gordon Allport and Leo Postman report that a picture in which a Red Cross truck was shown loaded with explosives was ordinarily perceived by subjects as a Red Cross truck carrying medical supplies (because that is the way it "ought" to be).[5]

In summary, the research cited indicates that under certain conditions people misinterpret or distort a communication so that it will be more compatible with their own attitudes, habits, or opinions.

[3]"The Analysis of Deviant Cases in Communications Research," in *Communications Research*, edited by Paul F. Lazarsfeld and Frank N. Stanton (New York, Harper & Brothers, 1949), pp. 152-179.

[4]"Assimilation and Contrast Effects in Reactions and Attitude Change," *Journal of Abnormal and Social Psychology*, Volume 55, 1957, pp. 244-252.

[5]"The Basic Psychology of Rumor," *Transactions of the New York Academy of Sciences*, Series II, Volume 8, 1945, pp. 61-68. Reprinted in *Readings in Social Psychology*, edited by E. E. Maccoby, T. M. Newcombe, and E. L. Hartley (New York, Henry Holt & Company, Inc., 1958), pp. 54-64.

Selective Retention

There is another way a person can reduce the dissonance or lack of internal harmony resulting when there is a discrepancy between his attitudes and those expressed by a communication with which he is faced. He can simply forget rather quickly the content of the communication! If this process is operative, we should also expect that a person would learn more quickly, and remember for a longer period, communications which *are* compatible with his own attitudes.

A study by Jerome M. Levine and Gardner Murphy supports these contentions.[6] Here it was found that procommunist material was better learned and better remembered by procommunists than by anticommunists; and the reverse was true for anticommunist material. Another example of selective retention occurred in an experiment by Claire Zimmerman and Raymond A. Bauer.[7] Given some material which was to be used in preparing a speech, subjects remembered fewer of the arguments which might have been received unfavorably by the audience they were slated to address.

Selective Decision

Even when a person has been exposed to a message, correctly perceives its intent, and remembers the main content, he still must decide whether or not to be influenced in the manner intended by the communicator. Because of individual predispositions, different people make different decisions as to whether or not (and to what extent) they will be influenced.

For example, in not one of the studies which I have reported has there been an instance in which every member of the audience made the same decision. In every case, some people decided to be persuaded; others did not. We can only assume that just as certain people are predisposed to expose themselves selectively to certain kinds of communications and to avoid others, they are also predisposed (i.e., more susceptible) to being influenced by some types of communications and appeals and not by others. In the Hovland, Harvey, and Sherif experiment, those whose attitudes strongly favored prohibition

[6]"The Learning and Forgetting of Controversial Material," *Journal of Abnormal and Social Psychology*, Volume 38, 1943, pp. 507-517.

[7]"The Influence of an Audience on What is Remembered," *Public Opinion Quarterly*, Volume 20, 1956, pp. 238-248.

were predisposed *not* to be influenced by arguments against prohibition, and vice versa. Persuasion occurred most often when the individuals' attitudes toward prohibition were only slightly different from those advocated by the communication.

The evidence which I have thus far introduced seems to indicate quite clearly that people are very capable of resisting attempts to *change* their attitudes and behavior. If a persuasive communication seems incompatible with their own attitudes, they may avoid it, distort its meaning, forget it, or otherwise decide not to be influenced.

If these conclusions are valid (as they seem to be), what are the implications for advertising? Although I am unable to offer much in the way of direct evidence, I can put forth two suggestions:

● A great deal of advertising must function either to *reinforce* existing attitudes and behavior (e.g., maintenance of brand loyalty), or to *stimulate* or activate people who are already predisposed to act in the desired manner (e.g., people who enjoy reading murder mysteries are most likely to be on the lookout for, and to be influenced by, advertising of murder mysteries).

● A related implication is that advertising is not, in itself, a cause of audience effects, but rather works with and through various mediating factors such as audience predispositions and personal influence (e.g., word-of-mouth advertising).[8]

It would be a mistake to contend that predispositions are so highly developed and so rigid that attitudes and behavior patterns never change. They do. However, I would argue that *changing* a person's attitudes or behavior (as opposed to *reinforcing* present attitudes or *activating* those already predisposed) is beyond the scope of most advertising, *except* where:

> (1) The attitude or behavior involved is of little importance to the individual. People to whom it makes little difference which brand of toothpaste they use are more likely to be influenced to switch brands by toothpaste advertising. Even here, however, some activation of predispositions is involved; people with false teeth are less likely to use any toothpaste.
>
> (2) The mediating factors (predispositions and personal influence) are inoperative. People may be influenced directly by the advertising for a new product because they have not been able to form attitudes which would predispose them against the product.
>
> (3) The mediating factors, which normally favor reinforcement, themselves favor change. If for some reason our friends begin buying color television sets, we are more likely to be influenced by advertising for color TV sets.[9]

If these contentions are realistic, it would then appear that a major function of effective advertising is to "select" people who are already predisposed

---

[8]See Joseph T. Klapper, "What We Know About the Effects of Mass Communications: The Brink of Hope," *Public Opinion Quarterly*, Volume 21, 1957-1958, pp. 453-474.
[9]Points (2) and (3) are taken from Klapper, op. cit.

to buy a product and present them with appeals (appropriate to the types of potential customers) which would hopefully trigger the desired response. *In those instances where change of important attitudes or behavior is the advertising objective, failure is more likely than success unless the advertiser can somehow work with or through the mediating factors.*

Now let me offer two generalizations that may shed more light on the predisposition factor:

•Some people or groups are more predisposed than others to be influenced by advertising for a particular product or brand.

•Within that group which is more predisposed toward a particular product, some individuals or subgroups will be more predisposed to be influenced by certain kinds of appeals, while others will be predisposed by different kinds of appeals.

In order to indicate the bases of these predispositions, I will discuss the three groups of factors which interact to make an individual more (or less) predisposed to be influenced by any particular communication: (1) the physical and economic reality which an individual experiences, (2) his personality, and (3) the social environment in which he lives.

Physical and Economic Reality as a Basis of Predisposition

This is the most obvious of the predisposing factors. It is well recognized that a person's income, age, sex, and so on, will predispose him or her to buy certain products and to refrain from buying others. Similarly, products he has owned or now owns may be partial determinants of his future susceptibility to advertising. For some products it is relatively easy to predict, on the basis of physical and economic predispositions, which large group within the populaton will be most likely to buy.

Within this large group, however, it is sometimes possible to distinguish several subgroups, each of which—though predisposed to buy the product—could best be reached by different communications or different appeals. Taking new owners and old owners of automobiles, for instance, and assuming that both groups were predisposed to buy the same make of auto within the following two or three years, I wonder if an auto manufacturer's advertising would not be more effective if different appeals were made to each group.

Maybe present advertising could be retained to reach both groups and be as effective as could be expected for old owners, but in addition specific appeals could be directed to new owners (by direct mail). This might be effective in giving them greater reassurance at a time when they most need it and thus increase the probability that their next car will be of the same make.

Personality as a Basis of Predisposition

Various studies (such as that by Irving L. Janis et al.[10]) have attempted to show that some personality types are more susceptible to influence than others are. There may be some truth in this supposition, but it is rather difficult to prove that *in general* one person is more persuasible than another. More likely, people are predisposed (on the basis of their habits, attitudes, and motives) to be more susceptible to persuasion on certain issues or by certain kinds of appeals. For example, the study by Irving L. Janis and Seymour Feshbach of fear-arousing appeals aimed at changing dental hygiene practices (discussed in Part I, pp. 164-166) * found that people who were high in anxiety were least likely to be influenced by strong fear appeals.[11] Other examples of personality as a basis of predisposition can be found in the preceding discussion of selective exposure, perception, retention, and decision. One further example is the finding of Elihu Katz and Paul F. Lazarsfeld that women who are low in "gregariousness," or who report that they "worry more than others," or who are "sometimes blue and depressed" are more likely to have higher exposure to "popular fiction" (such as movie and "true story" type magazines and daytime serials).[12]

These findings can hardly be considered exhaustive, but they represent an interesting beginning. As the study of personality advances, we should expect to see a great many more relationships revealed between personality variables and predispositions to being influenced by certain specific kinds of appeals. The real difficulty at the present time seems to be the lack of reliable and useful tests for measuring individual personality differences. However, just because the effect of personality is not well documented in the research on communications does not mean that it is not important. It may turn out to be *the* most important determinant of predispositions.

The Social Environment as a Basis of Predisposition

In this age of the "organization man" and the "other-directed" man it is well known, and even accepted, that to varying degrees our behavior is influenced by other people and groups. What is not so well known is the

---

[10]See *Personality and Persuasibility* (New Haven, Yale University Press, 1959).

*[Editor's note: see *Harvard Business Review* (September-October, 1961).]

[11]"Effects of Fear-Arousing Communications," *Journal of Abnormal and Social Psychology*, Volume, 48, 1953, pp. 78-92.

[12]*Personal Influence* (Glencoe, Illinois, The Free Press, 1955), p. 378.

extent to which our social environment shapes our behavior and attitudes in subtle ways we may not even be aware of. When I speak of the social environment as a basis of predisposition, I do not refer to direct, overt attempts by one person to influence another (which is called personal influence); instead I refer to indirect, often barely noticeable social influences.

A classic experiment by Solomon A. Asch offers a striking example of the effect of unmentioned group "norms" on individual behavior.[13] Subjects in groups of eight were asked to match the length of a given line with one of three unequal lines. The correct answer was quite obvious, but seven of the eight subjects had been previously instructed to give the same *wrong* answers. In one third of the cases the person who was not let in on the experiment agreed with the unanimous (though visibly incorrect) majority—even though he "knew" what the correct answer was, and even though no overt attempt at influence was made.

Another example of social influence is reported by Francis S. Bourne.[14] He found that women who made negative statements about a food product, but who said the product was popular with their friends, used more of the product than did women who made positive statements about the product, but who said it was unpopular with their friends. In other words, if you know your friends favor a particular brand or product you may be more predisposed to use it yourself.

Bourne offers some evidence which suggests that social influence of this sort is operative chiefly among products which are conspicuous (i.e., both visible and unique). This remains to be seen, but it is fairly clear that in some situations group norms or sentiments play a considerable part in predisposing us to act in certain ways—probably much more so than most of us realize. Since different people belong to different reference groups which may hold varying attitudes toward a particular brand or product, it follows that some groups will be more, or less, predisposed to be influenced by advertising for a product than will others.

And within these groups some people may be more susceptible to advertising (or certain appeals) than others. For example, Harold H. Kelley and Edmund H. Volkart found that individuals who least valued their membership in a group were not so likely to resist attempts at influence which were counter to the values of the group.[15]

The effect of group norms and other social pressures raises many interesting question and problems for advertising strategy—questions which I can-

---

[13]"Effects of Group Pressure upon the Modification and Distortion of Judgements," in *Readings in Social Psychology*, see footnote 5.

[14]"Group Influence in Marketing Decisions," in *Some Applications of Behavioural Research*, edited by Rensis Likert and Samuel P. Hayes, Jr. (Paris, UNESCO, 1957).

[15]"The Resistance to Change of Group-anchored Attitudes," *American Sociological Review*, Volume 17, 1952, pp. 453-465. The findings are summarized by Carl I. Hovland, Irving L. Janis, and Harold H. Kelley, *Communication and Persuasion* (New Haven, Yale University Press, 1953), Chapter 5.

not now explore. Let me try, however, to offer two generalizations for advertisers to consider:

(1) The fact that the economic and physical reality, the personality, and the social environment act to predispose certain groups to be more, or less, susceptible to influence than others is well recognized by marketing and advertising strategists. Most successful marketing programs begin with an appraisal of "Who buys (or is most likely to buy) the product?" or "To whom will (or does) the product appeal?" In addition, we see a good deal of the practice of selective marketing or market segmentation; that is, producing and marketing products which have a particular appeal for a limited and specific segment of the market.

(2) But only rarely do we notice an advertiser making use of *selective advertising*; that is, the use of different appeals to sell the *same* product to different segments of the market. The research to date clearly suggests that the possibility of making greater use of selective advertising is, for many companies, well worth investigating (and I shall discuss it in more detail later).

Earlier I excluded personal influence from our discussion of predisposing factors. But personal influence, of course, cannot be long excluded. Not only are members of the audience themselves influenced by mass communications; they also are stimulated at times through personal communication.

Many of the studies of personal influence were stimulated by an earlier study of voting behavior which had suggested a hypothesis called the "two-step flow of communication." According to this theory, ideas "flow from radio and print to opinion leaders and from them to less active sections of the population."[16]

Two pioneering studies which are of particular significance in studying the process of personal influence have been conducted. One is by Elihu Katz and Paul F. Lazarsfeld on the flow of influence among housewives in Decatur in the areas of marketing (food and household products primarily), fashions, public affairs, and movie-going.[17] The other is by Herbert Menzel and Elihu Katz on the spread of a new drug among doctors.[18]

Based on respondents' own assessments (the accuracy of which may be questioned), the Decatur study concluded that in marketing, personal influence has greater impact than has advertising because respondents reported "more exposure to personal advice than to advertisements; and second, among those exposed to each source, 'most important influence' is more often attributed to people than to formal advertisements." The drug study did not attempt to evaluate relative impact, but did conclude that interpersonal communication and social support are important factors in encouraging doctors to face the risks of medical innovation.

The two studies suggest that influence is related "to the personification of

---

[16]Paul F. Lazarsfeld, Bernard Berelson, and Hazel Gaudet, *The People's Choice* (New York, Duell, Sloan & Pearce, 1944), p. 151.

[17]Katz and Lazarsfeld, op. cit.

[18]"Social Relations and Innovation in the Medical Profession," *Public Opinion Quarterly*, Volume 19, 1955-1956, pp. 337-352.

certain values (who one is) ; . . . to competence (what one knows) ; and . . . to strategic social location (whom one knows) ."[19]

For example, the Decatur study suggests that:

•There is little overlap in opinion leadership—a person tends to specialize in one sphere—e.g., marketing *or* fashion *or* movies.

•In marketing, there is a concentration of opinion leadership among "large family wives" (older women with two or more children).

•Influence flows among people of the same social status and usually among the same age group.

•Women who are "gregarious" are more likely to be opinion leaders.

The Decatur study also shows that opinion leaders are more likely to be exposed to the mass media than are the people whom they influence, and also that they are particularly likely to be exposed to the media appropriate to their own sphere of influence. In the case of fashion, it even appears that the opinion leaders are "not only more exposed to the mass media but are also more affected by them in their own decisions."[20] The drug study also showed that "influential doctors were more likely to be readers of a large number of professional journals and valued them more highly than did doctors of lesser influence."[21]

The obvious implication is to advertise to opinion leaders and let them carry the ball from there. Opinion leaders are very interested in a specific sphere, are more exposed to media, and hence are probably more likely to notice and read advertisements appropriate to their sphere of influence. However, just because they are exposed to the advertising does not necessarily mean that they will be influenced by it. (In the Decatur study, only the fashion leaders were.)

Actually, a good case can be made for the proposition that as far as *change* is concerned, opinion leaders are more likely to show high resistance than are their followers in many cases. This point was not brought out in the Decatur study, but the drug study noted that it was not the influential doctors who *first* began using the new drugs, but rather doctors who were relatively isolated from the rest of the medical community. If these innovators were isolated because they were not too highly regarded by the influential doctors, it is not likely that they had a great deal of direct personal influence over the influential doctors.

In studying the process of personal influence (rather than looking at "opinion leaders" as such) we would probably be more realistic if we distinguished between two kinds of leaders—the *innovators* and the *"influentials."* Influentials may have considerable personal influence over others in the group,

---

[19]Elihu Katz, "The Two-step Flow of Communication," *Public Opinion Quarterly,* Volume 21, 1957, p. 73.

[20]Ibid., p. 75.

[21]Ibid., p. 76.

but they may enjoy this influence because they recognizably hold the norms and values of the group.

If, as is often the case, the norms of the group favor the status quo, the influentials have an investment in this status quo, hence are more likely to be resistant to change. Unless the norms of the group favor innovation (as in fashion or in some areas of the medical profession), the innovators are very likely to be the deviant or isolated members of the group, none too popular with the rest of the group, and with little direct personal influence over anyone in the group. However, the innovators may affect the behavior of others (including the influentials) through a process of "social influence by example." For example, in a study of the adoption of hybrid seed corn, Bryce Ryan and Neal Gross discovered that the influential farmers took their cue from innovating farmers after seeing the good results they had obtained.[22] Adoption by most of the others in the community followed adoption by the influentials.

In sum, unless the norms of the group favor innovation, innovating and influencing are two separate processes which are carried out by two different types of people. It is therefore necessary to redefine the simpler notion of opinion leadership in order to take into account two types of opinion leaders—the innovators and the influentials.

The implications of these findings for advertising strategy are not clear. The process of personal influence is undoubtedly of major importance in the marketing of goods and services; yet, at the present time only a handful of relevant studies on this important topic are available. It is fairly clear, though, that it is beneficial to have the right people talking about your product, provided they are saying the right things. What should be done in order to encourage this is not self-evident. As a start, though, I would suggest that word-of-mouth activity be used as one measure of advertising effectiveness. In this way, a campaign could be judged partly on the basis of the amount of word-of-mouth activity it stimulated. It may well be that having one person talk about your product to his friends is worth more than having the friends exposed to a commercial or advertisement for the product.

What implications does research on mass communications have for testing advertising effectiveness? This is a problem which has always been of concern to advertisers. The research supports two propositions (which, incidentally, confirm what most advertising researchers already know—that measuring advertising effects is a delicate and difficult operation). However, the following propositions, and the research and theory underlying them, do more than confirm the obvious; they may help establish a useful basis for measuring ad effectiveness.

In general, the essence of the two propositions is that the connection between a person's factual knowledge and his attitudes or opinions and between

---

[22]"The Diffusion of Hybrid Seed Corn in Iowa Communities," *Rural Sociology*, Volume 8, 1943, pp. 15-24.

the latter and his behavior is not necessarily a direct, one-to-one relationship. More specifically:

(1) *It is possible for a person to change his factual knowledge without changing his attitudes or his behavior.*

One illustration of this proposition is found in the Janis and Feshbach study of the effect of fear-arousing appeals on changing attitudes and behavior regarding dental hygiene practices.[23] Similarly, a study by Carl I. Hovland, Arthur A. Lumsdaine, and Fred D. Sheffield found that the film *The Battle of Britain* was considerably more effective in changing factual information than it was in changing opinions—based on tests before and five days after the film showing.[24]

Does this mean that measures of advertising effectiveness such as the Starch Readership Service and the Gallup-Robinson IMPACT technique are of dubious value? Both services measure name association and recall (i.e., factual information), and research has shown it is possible to effect changes in information without eliciting corresponding changes in attitudes or behavior—or, in other words, without achieving the goals of most advertising. Let us reserve judgment on these measures until we consider the next proposition. At that time they may appear potentially more useful than they do here.

(2) *It is possible for a person to change his behavior without first changing his attitudes (i.e., attitude change may follow behavior change).*

It is often impractical to attempt to relate advertising effects to sales. The closest substitute would seem to be a measure of changes in attitudes produced by an advertisement. The assumption would be that advertising works by first causing changes in attitude that in turn produce changes in behavior. Therefore, since we cannot measure the behavior, the next best thing is to measure that which immediately precedes the behavior—attitudes.

This procedure sounds logical, but, unfortunately, it so happens that attitude changes may *follow* rather than precede behavior changes. For example, it is possible that a person will see an advertisement, buy the product, and then change his attitude toward the product in the direction advocated by the ad. Raymond A. and Alice H. Bauer suspect "that one of the major ways in which mass media influence public attitudes is via the second-order effect of having first elicited behavior based on other existing attitudes."[25] If this contention is realistic, measurement of changes in attitudes may not be a valid criterion for evaluating the effectiveness of an ad. For example:

•Let us imagine that a number of consumers bought a particular brand of shoe polish after having seen some advertising for that brand, but without

    [23]Janis and Feshbach, op. cit. See also the discussion of the study in *Harvard Business Review*, September-October 1961, pp. 164-166.

    [24]*Experiments on Mass Communications* (Princeton, Princeton University Press, 1949).

    [25]"America, Mass Society and Mass Media," *Journal of Social Issues*, Volume 16, No. 3, 1961, pp. 3-66 (published in 1961).

exhibiting any measurable change in their attitudes toward the brand. Assume that the advertising was influential, not because it changed their basic attitudes, but because it reminded them, at the point of purchase, that the brand existed, and they therefore decided to try it.

Suppose the manufacturer was trying to evaluate the effectiveness of his campaign so that he could better focus his advertising efforts. If he had measured the consumers' attitudes before and after advertising (but before they had bought the product), he would have found no change in their attitude toward his brand. He probably would have concluded that the advertising had no effect whatever.

But advertising had, in fact, triggered the purchase by reminding consumers of the brand's existence. The manufacturer would have thus erred in evaluating the effects of his advertising. On the other hand, if he had measured consumers' attitudes before advertising, and again after they had made the purchases (and had changed their attitudes), he would have concluded that advertising had caused consumers to change their attitudes and thus buy his product.

This, too, would have been a mistake and might have led him to the wrong conclusions about how he should advertise his product. If, as we have assumed, the real reason why his advertising was effective was because it reminded people to buy the product, a campaign of "reminder" advertising would be indicated. The manufacturer, however, after studying the results of either type of attitude survey, would probably have concluded that (a) the advertising *was not* effective, or (b) the advertising *was* effective because it changed consumers' attitudes. This might have led him to the erroneous conclusion that (a) he did not have to advertise, or (b) that he should launch a campaign which would change people's attitudes.

Unfortunately, it is difficult to find direct evidence in support of the proposition that behavior change can take place without being preceded by attitude change. When Jack W. Brehm asked young women first to rate the desirability of eight products (mostly appliances), then offered them their choice between two of these products, and again asked them to rate the products, he found that after making their choice, the subjects showed a marked increase in preference for the product chosen.[26] They also showed a marked *decrease* in their preference for the product *not* chosen. The extent of this decrease in post-decision preference was considerably greater if the subject had initially given both products about the same rating. In other words, the more difficult the choice she had to make, the more likely she was (after the decision) to prefer the chosen product more and the rejected product less.

Similarly, Judson Mills tested students' attitudes toward cheating, then

[26]"Post-decision Changes in the Desirability of Alternatives," *Journal of Abnormal and Social Psychology*, Volume 52, 1956, pp. 384-389.

created a situation where some of them were able to cheat during a test.[27] He remeasured their attitudes, and found that those who had cheated became more lenient in their attitudes toward cheating, while those who had not cheated became more severe.

The theory which predicts these kinds of behavior is called the *theory of cognitive dissonance*. This theory was developed by Leon Festinger,[28] and holds that when a person chooses between two or more alternatives, discomfort or dissonance will almost inevitably arise because of the person's knowledge that while the decision he has made has certain advantages, it also has some disadvantages. The girl who chose a toaster in the Brehm experiment did so because she liked it, but she would have liked the iron, too. Also, the cheaters knew there was an advantage to cheating, but they recognized that it was not the right thing to do, hence a disadvantage.

The theory holds that dissonance arises after almost every decision, and further that the individual will invariably take steps to reduce this dissonance. There are several ways in which this can be done, but the most likely way is to create as many advantages as you can in favor of the alternative you have chosen and to think of as many disadvantages as possible relating to the other alternatives. Thus the girl who chose the toaster decided that she really liked it much more than the iron, and so on. The same explanation accounts for the new car owners reading more ads about their cars than old car owners.

It is important to remind you: I am not suggesting that attitude changes may not also precede changes in behavior. Undoubtedly they do. However, while the evidence I have offered is only suggestive, there are some grounds for believing that behavior change can take place without being preceded by attitude change. This, combined with the fact that some attitude change almost always follows any important decision or behavior change, makes any attempt at using attitude change to measure advertising effects a delicate and potentially misleading operation.

Having built up a little background on dissonance theory, we can now return to the other possible indirect measures of advertising effectiveness—recognition and recall. The theory of cognitive dissonance would hold that when a person faces the chance of being exposed (or is exposed) to knowledge or opinions (i.e., cognitions) which are related to, but in conflict with, some of his own cognitions, dissonance arises. For example, if I own a Ford but suddenly hear an announcer extolling the wonders of a Chevrolet, the cognition that I own a Ford will be dissonant with the cognition that the Chevrolet is a wonderful car. As we know, the theory suggests that I will take steps to reduce his dissonance. But how? I have several alternatives:

[27]"Changes in Moral Attitudes Following Temptation," *Journal of Personality,* Volume 26, 1959, pp. 517-531.

[28]*A Theory of Cognitive Dissonance* (Evanston, Illinois, Row, Peterson and Company, 1957).

•To buy or consider buying a Chevrolet *(selective decision)*.

•To turn off the set or otherwise ignore the commercial *(selective exposure)*.

•To distort the communication—"Sure, Chevrolet is good, but that model is probably very expensive to operate compared with my Ford" *(selective perception)*.

•To forget the entire communication very quickly or forget parts of the communication that produce the most dissonance *(selective retention)*.

If I am somewhat predisposed to buy a Chevrolet, and if the commercial has been effective in acting on my predisposition, I may take the first alternative—even if it is only so far as to say I will certainly consider a Chevrolet next time. In this case, the advertising has been effective and I am less likely to engage in the alternative defenses. If, however, I am not so predisposed and the commercial has not been effective, then I will certainly try to reduce the dissonance by avoiding the commercial, distorting it, and/or forgetting some or all of it rather quickly.

If I am somewhat predisposed to the information, is it not possible that measures of exposure and recall can be very useful in evaluating the effectiveness of an advertisement? As I have argued earlier, advertising seems to work by selecting and acting on those people who are already predisposed to buy the product. Therefore, a good measure of exposure and recall should offer valid testimony to the ad's ability to select and act on those so predisposed. The ones who are not predisposed, or who were not acted on, will already have taken steps either to avoid exposing themselves, or to distort or not recall properly all or part of the message.

What criteria then should be met by a good indirect measure of advertising effectiveness? In addition to meeting acceptable standards of research methodology, an indirect measure should:

•*Measure exposure under natural conditions (or allow for the effects of forced exposure).* Any artificial medium must be suspect because it reduces the opportunity for selective exposure.

•*Measure respondents some time (at least a week—preferably two weeks) after they have been exposed to the communication.* This is to allow the process of selective retention to operate.

•*Measure a verbatim playback of the message.* That is, respondents' unaided recollections of the contents of an ad should be recorded *in toto*. It is important to know not only *how much* has been remembered, but also what portions of the message have been forgotten or remembered—what portions are dissonant or consonant, and *with whom*. Respondents can also be identified on the basis of relevant characteristics in order to determine how different types of people react to the advertisement.

•*Measure distortion of the message.* It is important to know what parts of the message are distorted and the nature of these distortions. This would be partially handled by the verbatim playback, but might also require one or two probing questions.

Unhappily, neither the Starch system nor the Gallup-Robinson IMPACT technique meets *all* of these criteria. But the IMPACT technique does come very close, and with a few slight modifications would meet the suggested criteria. The needed modifications would include delaying the measure of recall for several weeks where practicable, measuring distortion more systematically, and classifying responses by types of respondents.

For those who want high readership or viewership scores we should note that by measuring recall immediately after exposure, under forced exposure conditions, by probing deeply, and so on, it is possible to achieve inflated results. However, all the evidence indicates that people tend to set up barriers against communications which are incompatible with their own attitudes or which do not interest them. I feel, therefore, that an indirect measure of advertising effectiveness which determines whether or not, and to what extent, a consumer has engaged in the processes of selective exposure, perception and retention will be more realistic and hence more valuable to a company in evaluating its advertising efforts.

I would like to close by putting forward an advertising strategy which seems to be supported by much of the research evidence which has been presented—*the strategy of selective advertising*. This strategy is based on two key assumptions:

●Advertising works primarily by reinforcing or otherwise acting upon people already predisposed to act.

●The closer the match between the appeals used and the individual's predispositions, the more likely he is to expose himself to the advertisement, and to act as desired.

Ideally, since we consider people to be different from one another, every individual should be approached with slightly different appeals in order to come closest to matching his predispositions. Obviously, this is quite impractical. What has happened instead is that most advertisers operate at the other end of the continuum; that is, they assume that for practical purposes everyone is more or less alike, and that an appeal which is good for one is good for all.

This approach also may be quite impractical—if we think in terms of opportunity cost. It seems that an ideal strategy would involve a compromise somewhere between these two extremes. The advertiser cannot advertise selectively to everyone, but neither should he think that "for all practical purposes" everyone is alike. People are not all alike. However, some segments of the population do have many common characteristics. We would expect much more similarity among people in the same social class than we would among people of different classes. We would also expect more similarity among young people than between people of two age groups, and so on. There are many ways in which the population might be segmented into groups reasonably homogeneous in their predispositions toward any particular product.

If this is the case, then the task of selective advertising is to select those groups and subgroups which are relevant to the particular product and to match appeals with group predispositions. In other words, a selective advertising campaign would not usually rely on only one appeal or one type of media but would run as many different appeals in as many different media as were necessary to match particular groups which make up the potential market for a product—up to the point where this increased number of appeals maximized the return on advertising investment. Just where the optimum point is located is rather beyond the scope of this article. It seems likely, however, that in most cases the optimum strategy would be to use more than one appeal.

There is still another argument for the use of a variety of appeals. Not only do people differ from one another, but any one individual has many needs which might be satisfied by a product. Dorwin Cartwright suggests that the "more goals which are seen as attainable by a single path, the more likely it is that a person will take that path."[29] In other words, the product is the path by which the person may attain certain goals. Use of a variety of appeals increases the number of goals or needs which the product might be seen as satisfying, and hence increases the probability of triggering off one or more predisposing factors.

In addition, the use of a variety of relevant appeals allows the advertiser to repeat his product story several times in several ways without arousing the wrath of the listener who might be irritated by constant repetition of the same appeal.

Robert K. Merton's analysis of Kate Smith's marathon effort in selling war bonds offers testimony to the power of selective advertising.[30] Merton identified some sixty different appeals used and found that "each new entreaty sought out a new vulnerability in some listeners." As I have suggested, Miss Smith's use of a variety of appeals was effective in two ways: (1) it offered one person more reasons to buy, and (2) it touched some predisposition in a wide variety of people. An appeal which was not relevant to the predispositions of some would likely trigger off responses in others, and so on.

To conclude, the strategy of selective advertising would strongly reject the notions that there is but *one* market for a product and that this market can best be reached by *one* appeal which has universal selling power. The strategy of selective advertising would hold that such contentions are myths which have little basis in reality.

Perhaps the day will come when advertisers will abandon their belief in the undifferentiated market and the universal appeal. This day should mark a considerable step forward in the art of advertising strategy.

[29]"Some Principles of Mass Persuasion," *Human Relations*, Volume 2, 1949, pp. 253-267.
[30]*Mass Persuasion* (New York, Harper & Brothers, 1946).

25

How Word-of-mouth Advertising Works

ERNEST DICHTER

Each year members of our organization* talk to over 10,000 consumers in various parts of the world. "What made you buy this brand or particular product?" is one question which usually is part of our motivational study. No matter how our depth interviews approach the question, the answer invariably reveals that there he is again—the mysterious friend, expert, or relative who "told me about it." At times, the figures show this influence of "recommenders" to run as high as 80%. Why in a time of increasing advertising volume does Word-of-mouth recommendation loom so high?

Apparently, there are several ways of influencing people that coexist with, or go beyond, radio, TV, magazines, and newspapers as media for recommending goods and services. These unconventional forms of "advertising," or influence, include *Consumer Reports* and similar publications; refrigerator, freezer, and pantry shelves ("Every time I look at my shelves, I am sold or unsold on products which I bought"); seals of approval; and, most important of all, the advice of a friend.

We decided, therefore, in order to develop a better understanding of the mechanism involved in these informal channels of communication, to initiate a research study of our own (see the box on page 298). Then, as we proceeded, listening to consumers recalling their experiences, a number of key research questions emerged. The most significant of these included:

- What are the reasons for the growing importance of Word-of-mouth recommendation? In what psychological needs is it rooted?

- What motivates people to talk about their experiences?

- What motivates them to listen to recommendations? To act or not to act on them?

Reprinted from *Harvard Business Review* (November-December, 1966), pp. 147-166, by permission of the publisher, Harvard Graduate School of Business Administration, Boston.
*[Editor's note: Institute For Motivational Research, Inc.]

The Research Approach

This article is based on research findings of the Institute for Motivational Research, Inc.:

●Depth interviews were conducted with 255 consumers in 24 localities in the United States, with emphasis on the New York metropolitan area. Respondents were encouraged to recall freely (and in full detail) conversations in which products, services, and advertising had been discussed, including recommendations made as well as received.

●Conditions and circumstances under which recommendations were accepted or rejected were carefully probed. Altogether, 352 individual instances of what we call "active Word-of-mouth" recommendations and 488 instances of recommendations received and acted on (purchases) were reported. (There were some instances of negative Word-of-mouth, which are beyond the scope of this article.)

●Verbal tests regarding the most "talked about" advertising were conducted with 103 adult persons in the New York metropolitan area— to get some indications about the nature and structure of sales messages which, in themselves, invited Word-of-mouth.

Also included is research material developed by the Ziff-Davis Publishing Company, under the direction of its marketing vice president, Stanley R. Greenfield, which the company has kindly put at our disposal.

●How does Word-of-mouth recommendation affect advertising, and how does advertising affect Word-of-mouth?

●How does this whole process influence the purchasing behavior of the contemporary American consumer?

Answers to these questions have now enabled us to develop recommendations as to how the processes involved in Word-of-mouth can be successfully adapted and used by advertising and public relations practitioners.

Effective Advertising

We all have the desire to re-create the situation where the shoemaker, the tailor, or the grocer gave information and friendly advice based on personal knowledge of the consumer, his or her family, and their needs and means. Such intimate relationships created a feeling of trust and security and reduced the confusions of cold "commercialism."

When the consumer believes that an advertisement is more of a sales tool than information and guidance, he feels threatened. He rejects the advertising claim. He turns for a solution of his buying problem to Word-of-mouth. When the consumer feels that the advertiser speaks to him as a friend or as an unbiased authority, creating the atmosphere of Word-of-mouth, the consumer will relax and tend to accept the recommendation.

There are two kinds of Word-of-mouth: pre-decision and post-decision. They do not have the same object, and they probably do not take place in the same way. The most effective Word-of-mouth for the advertiser is the post-decision speaker who is bent on eliminating all dissonance in his post-decision situation. He is the man to sell to because he will be an active propagandist. For this same reason, advertising should perhaps be oriented much more toward present than potential customers and use them to spread the good word.

Effective advertising and effective Word-of-mouth are *not* worlds apart. On the contrary, it is the sense of our findings that *the most effective advertising is that which follows the same psychological channels of communication and satisfies the same motivations on which the whole importance and success of Word-of-mouth rest.*

This article is organized into two parts. Part I—the psychological findings about Word-of-mouth—deals with the discovery and charting of the channels of communication. Then, in Part II, the findings obtained are applied to the practical problems of advertising.

Part I. Psychological Findings

I shall first focus attention on the two specific problems of the psychology of Word-of-mouth recommendation:

    1. What motivates a person to *talk* about a product or service?

    2. What motivates a person to *listen* to a recommendation and to act on it?

Speaker Motivation

The power and the significance of everyday Word-of-mouth lie mainly in the *speaker's* lack of *material* interest. This does not imply, however, that he has no investment in the process of recommendation. Our investigation confirms that—generally—nobody will speak about products or services unless the talking itself, or the expected action of the *listener*, promises *satisfaction* of some kind—popularly speaking, unless he "gets something out of it."

We found further that the speaker is likely to choose such products, such listeners, and such "words" as are most apt to serve his underlying needs and ends (of which he is only rarely or partially aware).

Involvement categories

Motivations to talk about products or services were found to fall into four main categories, frequently overlapping or combined. I shall identify these categories briefly, and then discuss each in turn:

1. *Product-involvement.* Experience with the product (or service) produces a tension which is not eased by the use of the product alone, but must be channeled by way of talk, recommendation, and enthusiasm to restore the balance (provide relief).

2. *Self-involvement.* In other cases the accent is more on the self of the person than on the product, with the latter serving as a means through which the speaker can gratify certain emotional needs. As we shall see, there exists potentially a whole host of them, but they can all be subsumed under the over-all category of "self-confirmation."

3. *Other-involvement.* Here the product chiefly fills the need to "give" something to the other person, to "share" one's pleasure with him or her, or to express care, love, or friendship. In these instances the recommendation takes the place of a "gift," just as a thoughtful gift often expresses a tacit "recommendation." ("Because I have had pleasure in this, I want you, too, to have it—here it is.")

4. *Message-involvement.* This refers to talk which is mainly stimulated by the way the product is presented through advertisements, commercials, or public relations, but is not necessarily based on the speaker's experience with the product proper.

Naturally, products and services will vary, according to their potential role in the consumer's life, in their capacity for producing excitement, expressing care or love, and so on. And, certainly, the kind and degree of emotional involvement aroused by a car and a detergent, a dish and a dress, or a cigarette lighter and a perfume will differ a great deal. (This study presents the average reactions in a number of incidents covering a wide variety of products. It could be refined by future investigations aimed at product categories.)

Product involvement

Of the 352 talking episodes reported by our respondents, 33% belong in this category.

Distinctly pleasurable (but also certain unpleasurable) experiences have a tendency to call for mental repetition in the form of speech whenever a fitting occasion offers itself. This category includes incidents of strongly felt, gratifying experiences with a product or a service which make the speaker "flow over." Talk in this case may also serve to relive the pleasure the speaker had obtained, such as on a boat trip to Europe, or from a dish served in a restaurant, the pickup and power of a car, and so forth; it also helps to dispose of the excitement aroused by the use of the product, or by the fact of having obtained it. In many instances it is talk about the product which confirms for the speaker his ownership and joy in the product, or his discovery of it. For example:

> She asked if I'd ever used Guardsman. She said, 'You ought to get some—it's terrific!' Well, I said I'd try it, and I did. I mentioned to this friend later that I had used it, and she seemed pleased that I had bought it and anxious to know if I'd liked it. I told her it seemed to be pretty good, but she was hardly satisfied with that comment, and began to rave about it all over again. I don't rave much as a rule anyway. She seemed convinced she'd done me a huge favor by recommending it, and if I wouldn't get all excited after using it, she had to get excited for me. You'd think there was something in it for me.

The question, "What's in it for me?" is brought up by another respondent, a New York housewife. But one can easily see from her response that her "reward" is in the "verbal consumption" of those precious cookies:

> You'd think there was something in it for me the way I talk it up for Sandies. I think they're the best cookies ever, and that's why I like to have other people try them. That's the way I got to know about them. I was spending a weekend with an old girl friend of mine at her house on Long Island. She served these cookies in a dish, and they tasted so delicious and had such a real homemade flavor and look that I congratulated her on making such wonderful cookies. I really thought they were homemade. They don't look all even and perfectly rounded like the usual package cookies. And besides there was something about their taste that I can't describe but that usually seems to go with homemade cakes and cookies. I was amazed when she told me what they were. I had never heard of them.

Self-involvement

The depth interviews revealed, in 24% of all talking instances, that self-confirmation plays the major part in motivating talk.

Here the experience with the product is immediately put to use in the service of self-confirmation of the speaker and of his need to reassure himself in front of others. The product is employed in many, often clever, ways as a vehicle to carry him safely, even victoriously, through his self-doubts and insecurity. Most of us use such techniques occasionally and involuntarily, without being aware of it. The most frequent goals of self-confirmation through talk about products and services are:

Gaining attention—the products and services which, in their totality, represent what could be called the "machinery of living" take the place of topics centered around people or ideas. (Introducing a product into a conversation can be a way of "having something to say.")

Showing connoisseurship—talking about certain products can serve as proof of being "in the know," or having refined judgment, and so on.

Feeling like a pioneer—newness and "difference" of products provide the speaker with an opportunity to identify with them and their makers.

Having inside information—some products or services permit the speaker to feel clever—that is, to know "more" about them and their production than the listener is expected to know.

Suggesting status—talking about products with "social status" provides an "elevator" for the talker by which he can reach the level of the product and its users.

Spreading the gospel—"converting" the listener to using a product can provide the speaker with occasion to enlist the listener in a "good cause"—that is, to "preach the gospel."

Seeking confirmation of own judgment—the more people there are who follow the speaker's advice, the more justified will he feel in his own judgment; he needs followers to feel reassured about his own decisions.

Asserting superiority—recommendation of products can be used as a tool for assuming leadership and exercising power over the listener, and may even serve as a sort of test to determine whether the listener really respects the speaker ("Will he or won't he heed my advice?").

Here is but one example from many reported in which self-involvement is channeled through product recommendation:

> I recommended it to my sister-in-law Ruby and to Rosie Gibson, my friend up on the hill, and I don't know how many more. And I feel rather good that something I recommended was so well liked because it makes me feel that my judgment is good, and I know that people respect my judgment. Yes, there's been many a time when one friend or another would ask me how I felt about a certain thing, and I'd tell them. Many times that was all they needed and went along on my advice. I'd say that if you establish a feeling of confidence about yourself, and there's a feeling of dependability about you, people sort of take your word because they know that you have had some experience with the thing they are talking about, and that you will tell all you know about it and if you don't, you won't.

Usually, the follower is reassured by the power and strength of his leader. However, in Word-of-mouth we often found the reverse to be true: followers are sought by the leader (speaker) so that he feels less lonely and more secure in his own product choice. Knowing that others will conform to his choice makes him feel good. Consider: "I want to feel there are others. . . . I use this as a test. . . . If he comments favorably, he's your kind of guy. . . . You know you share not only the product but your approach to the world."

The "bandwagon effect" is reversed in cases in which consumers are proud to use what they consider an "underdog" product. They feel gratified in defying the majority by publicly using an unpopular brand; but the real self-confirmation lies in converting others to their own "peculiar" choice:

> People think I'm an odd duck for smoking Raleighs. Although Raleigh is one of the popular brands, in the sense that one sees them everywhere, they're hardly popular from the standpoint of the number of people who smoke them that I see. It's as if buying them makes you stand out like a jerk or poverty-struck, a guy who can only afford to smoke Raleighs if additional merchandise is added. So I say, 'Look at me!' by recommending them. . . . Also smoking an unpopular brand makes me feel I'm bucking the headwind. I'm handicapping myself in

advance, saying to people, 'You're going to like me in spite of my peculiarities, maybe even because of them.' If I can get them to smoke Raleighs, that really clinches it. Maybe that's why I recommend them.

The degree to which the need for self-confirmation motivates Word-of-mouth recommendation is reflected in the speaker's reaction to a rejection of his advice. In cases of nonacceptance, the self-involved speaker feels hurt, rejected, or abandoned as a person:

> I think when people reject a suggestion violently, they are aware that in a sense they are rejecting the person. And, on the other side of the coin, I do feel rejected when somebody won't take a suggestion I've made. I feel real bad when they refuse out of hand to consider the idea. I'm likely to sing its praises even louder—and that's not really because I think I've not been convincing, but because either my ideas are worthwhile and acceptable, or in some small sense I'm not.

Rejection is particularly resented when another person's advice has prevailed:

> Well, I don't mind telling you I felt pretty angry about it, but I didn't say much. I felt like I had been kicked in the face. Here I tell her about something I think tastes good; then someone else tells her it's no good, and she takes this other person's opinion just like that—just as if I didn't know the difference between a good taste and a bad taste. It's really not anything to get excited about, but sometimes things like that get under a person's skin.

Frequently, the hurt and resentment about nonacceptance turn into hostility against the unwilling follower. In a rapid process of depreciation, the erstwhile friend or neighbor, or relative, is now accused of "double-crossing" the speaker; he is called stubborn, set in his ways, lazy, foolish; and the aggrieved speaker's sentiments range from false pity to malice: "Now he is having mechanical difficulties with it [the car purchased against the speaker's recommendation]. He made his bed, and now he has to lie in it. He has to live with his decision. That's all there is to it."

Generally, the self-involved speaker feels that the listener has a moral duty not only to try the recommended product, but also to share his—the speaker's —feelings about it, to report back to him, to be grateful, and thus to confirm the speaker's judgment. It is one of the characteristics of the next category that these symptoms of intolerance on the part of the speaker are missing.

Other-involvement

This motivation appeared to prevail in 20% of all talking events.

Here the prevailing attitude is the need and intent to help, to share with the other person enthusiasm in, and benefits of, things enjoyed. Products serve mainly as instruments which help to express sentiments of neighborliness, care, friendship, and love.

This case example was chosen to illustrate the way in which an "other-

involved" person accepts and respects the reasons for the rejection of her recommendation, however strongly she may feel about the product as such:

> I was telling my mother about Ivory Liquid and how much I liked
> it. She said she would try it, but just couldn't because she has an allergy
> condition with her hands and finds it impossible to use any kind of
> detergent. I felt that it was so good I wanted her to know about it—
> especially for her dishes. I was at my mother's house and just happened
> to mention it in the course of conversation . . . about the sample and
> how I had tried it and all that. I was pretty enthusiastic about it, and
> wanted to share that enthusiasm with her—especially because it was my
> mother. I did try hard to convince her—even advised her to use rubber
> gloves in order that she could use it and see how wonderful it was—but
> Mother said she can't do a thing with gloves on, and we dropped the
> whole subject. Well, there just wasn't anything that I could do about it.
> Knowing the condition of her hands and knowing that it is important,
> I didn't renew my efforts for her to try the detergent any more.

Message-involvement

That the current "age of advertising consciousness" leads to a particularly
strong position of Word-of-mouth has been previously mentioned. However,
this very orientation of sophisticated skepticism toward modern sales messages
is accompanied by three other consumer attitudes which, strangely enough,
give Word-of-mouth a good chance to operate by using them as the topics of
talk and thus, in many instances, making them "sell" in an indirect way. The
three phenomena that ushered in the age of advertising consciousness—similarity of claims, conspicuousness of the advertising profession, and intrusion
of advertising into most aspects of living—have also produced several widespread audience attitudes:

'The Show Is the Thing.' Since it is difficult for consumers to avoid exposure to advertising, many people have turned to accepting it for its independent attraction and entertainment value. They are inclined to lean back and let
the advertisers compete with the "shows." Thus entertainment value and originality of ads have become topics of talk.

Shop Talk. Knowing that hundreds of highly paid brains are competing
for their favor, readers and listeners have become judges and experts of advertising effectiveness. They assume the critical attitude of an advertising manager
and tell each other about "clever" ads.

Verbal Play. Whether or not the product is desired or the content
of the sales message is of interest, readers and listeners like to quote playfully
and apply verbally ad lines and slogans. Even where the original mood is one
of mockery or irony at the ad, the advertiser, or the product, it is usually super-
seded by the pleasure gained in the act of the perhaps often-repeated and varied
application. A certain gratefulness is the price one pays for the opportunity
offered by the ad to "play" with it.

Listener Motivation

Whereas in the preceding discussion I explored the motivations of the speaker (the one who recommends), in this section I shall explore the motivations of the listener in those instances in which he or she *acted* as a result of the recommendation—that is, purchased the product in question.

What—on the basis of our investigation—are the factors that decide whether a recommendation is to be rejected, or accepted and acted on? The answer is that to make a recommendation "carry," the three points of the tri-angle—speaker, listener, and product—have to "fit" each other in certain ways. (To some degree the quality of the message also is involved.) We found to be of particular importance the *speaker-listener* relationship, as seen by the listener, and the *speaker-product* relationship, again as the listener perceives it.

Naturally, we do not intend to minimize the importance of the listener's "need" for the product. The degree of need-urgency, the propinquity of points of sale, and all other factors which make up the "logistics" of the situation contribute considerably to every buying decision. However, we have accepted the fact that need is not necessarily a "given" entity; it can within certain limits be produced or stimulated. Where this is not the case, it has to be added to those variables which cannot be controlled anyway and therefore do not belong within the scope of this study.

Key conditions

In analyzing the 488 instances of purchases ensuing from Word-of-mouth, we found that in weighing the value and validity of a recommendation, the listener is primarily concerned about two key conditions: a. that the person who recommends is interested in him and his well-being, and b. that the speaker's experience with and knowledge about the product are convincing. More or less consciously, the listener asks himself a number of tacit questions: "Is it the speaker's intention to sell me the product for any material reasons, or to help me with his true experience? What is his relation to me? May I fully trust him as a friend? What is the speaker's relation to the product? How authentic is it? How much does he know about the product, apart from his experience with it? Does he know more about it than I do?"

'Influential' groups

The factors that make a recommendation "click" are not always clear-cut and definite. In many instances several determinants combine in bringing about the decision. But it was our goal to trace through careful probing the main motivational emphasis in each case to the most decisive single condition. Therefore, it became important to define as closely as possible the main sources of potentially successful recommendations and the respective psychological forces behind their effectiveness.

Analysis of our sample yielded seven divisions among the recommending groups:

1. *Commercial Authorities.* Under this heading are listed those persons who, on the basis of their training and/or work, appear to be closer to the product and more knowing about it than the average consumer.

Recommending groups within this commercial authority division include *professional experts* and *sales persons.* To the former group belong, for example, mechanics (in the case of car recommendations), pharmacists, beauticians, and so on. Recommendation by experts was responsible for the buying decision in 3% of the cases. On the other hand, advice from sales personnel was instrumental in 6½% of all the buying events we analyzed. (I shall later discuss incidents of salesmen's influence in which factors other than the mere "authority" of the salesmen were involved.)

2. *Celebrities.* Included are movie, theater, TV, and radio personalities whose "authority" is attributed to prominence in show business, also persons prominent in any other fields not directly connected with the product. Although these speakers are in the strict sense part of advertising, we include them here because they have actually entered our living rooms and represent industry's closest approach to a synthetic Word-of-mouth production. In 7½% of our incidents, a celebrity's recommendation was directly responsible for the purchase.

3. *Connoisseurs.* Into this group fall those cases in which the listener was chiefly influenced by the speaker's close and authentic, but nonprofessional, contact with the product. The connoisseur may know as much or more about the product and its background than the expert, but he does not make his living in connection with it; he merely enjoys it and his know-how about it. But he is still a consumer, and as such is perceived by the listener as someone like himself but with more special product knowledge. This kind of product relation provided the main motivating force in 10% of the purchasing events.

Such a group of connoisseurs are, for example, the readers of *Car & Driver* magazine. Research on members of this group demonstrated conclusively that they do play a major role in influencing the automotive brand decision making of millions of Americans. One study indicated that 50% of *Car & Driver's* subscribers were asked for their opinions or advice on cars more than 50 times in one year, and another 20% reported that they were asked at least 12 to 18 times a year. In other words, since the magazine has over 300,000 subscribers, this 70% gave advice or opinions to literally millions in the consumer audience. Or to put it in another way, several million decisions on automobile purchases were to one degree or another influenced by this group of opinion leaders.

It is also of extreme importance to note that opinion leaders rap as well as boost. In fact, the tabulation of brands mentioned as having been discussed in the last interaction reported in the study showed that there were 80% as many raps by brand as there were boosts by brand.

4. *Sharers of Interests.* The influence of speakers in this group rests on the fact (or impression) that they have something special in common with the listener, be it a definite life situation (they are both young mothers, or they are junior executives living under similar circumstances) or a similarity of interest or taste. This sort of influence prevailed in 18% of all buying decisions.

5. *Intimates.* What is meant here is the influence of mother, father, big brother or sister, husband, wife, boyfriend or girlfriend which expresses itself not necessarily by means of verbal communication, but by the speaker's action. Thus, for example, keeping in the house a certain brand of soap, cigarette, toothpaste, and so on, may replace verbal advice or recommendation. Life in a family, marriage, or in any close relationship includes to some degree the taking-over of prevailing patterns of product-use and buying, "empathic" adaptation to the leader's habits and taste. The kind of "authority" which operates in these cases is, of course, one based on personal closeness and not, as in the commercial group, on relation to the product. (The effect on the listener may, in accordance with the emotional trend of the relationship, not always be acceptance of, but sometimes rebellion against, the speaker's choice of product or brand.) Our depth interviews revealed that 14% of the buying instances analyzed fall into this category.

6. *People of Goodwill.* In these instances, the listener sees the speaker as a person who is genuinely interested in his well-being. The speaker is trusted as a genuine friend, or as a friendly neighbor, and shows the sincerity of his intention and interest in the listener frequently through his knowledge and understanding of the listener's special and individual needs. Such feeling on the part of the listener was responsible for 24½% of the buying decisions.

7. *Bearers of Tangible Evidence.* Where the speaker has at his disposal perceivable proof of a product's efficacy, this fact may override all other factors of personal and product relations and easily tip the scales. Demonstrable effects ("before" and "after") of cosmetics and home remedies, observable or somehow memorable performances of household machines, cars, and gadgets, belong in this group. Combinations of this motivation with categories of personal relationship are frequent. However, we have tried to isolate in this group only those instances where tangible evidence prevailed (16½% of the purchase decisions).

Role of 'intention'

An analysis of the foregoing frequencies reveals the predominant position of "intention" in the listener's motivational system. The "hierarchy" of factors which were instrumental in bringing about the buying decisions is:

As the tabulation shows, closer knowledge of the psychological forces at play leads to the reduction of the seven influential groups into three main cate-

Table 25-1.

People of goodwill	24½% ⎫	"Disinterested"	
Intimates	14 ⎬	friendliness	38½%
Sharers of interests	18 ⎫	Community of	
Connoisseurs	10 ⎬	consumership	28%
Salesmen	6½ ⎫		
Celebrities	7½ ⎬	Commercial	
Professional experts	3 ⎭	authority	17%
Bearers of tangible evidence	16½		
	100%		

gories of motivating factors. (The "bearers of tangible evidence" may belong to any of the three categories.) Let us examine them:

'Disinterested' Friendliness. The first two groups, i.e., "people of goodwill" and "intimates," were formed into a unit because their main motivating power rests on the listener's feeling that the speaker (or, in the case of "silent" Word-of-mouth, the "model") is motivated to contribute to the listener's well-being or, a least, that his intention is divorced from material interests.

Community of Consumership. The next two groups which were combined are "sharers of interest" and "connoisseurs," since in both of these the common interest in the product is the bond that united the speaker and the listener.

Commercial Authority. The Word-of-mouth influences by sales personnel, professional experts, and celebrities were combined because in these instances a certain "authority" is assigned to the speaker on the basis of his *position*, without his necessarily having the backing of a strong inner conviction about the product or a personal relationship to the listener.

'Aha' experience

Our research at the Institute has shown that only a dialogue—that is, a two-way communication—is truly effective. This applies to formal communication in mass media, but even more to the informal influence of Word-of-mouth interaction.

Many advertising copy tests are based on the erroneous assumption that the recipient of a message "gets the word" passively. Thus Ad A, if it makes a deeper groove in his brain, is assumed to be more effective than Ad B.

In reality we are dealing with what we call a motivated reaction. It is a dialogue between the sender and the receiver of a message. Three different people, a hunter, a forester, and an artist, going into the same forest see three different forests. Their interests differ, and a varied communication dialogue takes place.

The same thing applies to commercial communication. When the reader or viewer can say, "Yes, that's true," or nod in agreement, we talk about an "aha" experience. But it is this "aha" experience which mass media often fail to produce.

Appraisal of advertising effectiveness often does not match what actually happens between a commercial message and a consumer. Criteria such as attention, recognition, and recall were not the key factors which differentiated successful commercial campaigns from unsuccessful campaigns.

The reason for this is that most advertising effectiveness testing, as it has been practiced up to now, seems to have proceeded on the premise that commercial messages represent a stimulus; the consumer is exposed to this stimulus, and something registers in his mind. This registration has been researched in terms of the attention aroused, the recognition created, and the recall brought about. At first glance, these approaches sound reasonable.

However, our practical experience and modern psychological understanding challenge the whole basis on which these research approaches have been built; they violate everything we know about how perceptive processes really take place.

The "recommender" is often much more capable of establishing this "aha" experience, this dialogue of conviction. In doing so, four factors help him a great deal:

'*Expressive Movements.*' Psychologists have established the fact that "truth" in terms of a person's inner experience is expressed by the conveyance of emotions in the form of "expressive movements" which can be perceived by the other person. Indeed, it is considered one of the functions of emotions to inform the other person about the speaker's inner experience. Thus the real meaning of a product and of its effect to the user is revealed not only through the choice of the speaker's words, but also through the discharge of emotions in inflection, face and body expressions, and gestures.

A Philadelphia housewife, for example, expresses her desire to be swayed by the speaker's enthusiasm for the recommended product: "I'm not really an explorer; I'm a creature of habit. I don't try new things. Someone has to try them and rant and rave, ooh and ah . . . and then I'll try them."

Understanding of Needs. That the speaker is genuinely concerned with the listener's well-being or has his advantage at heart becomes eminently believable in cases in which the recommendation is geared to, and takes into account, the individual needs or special circumstances of the listener. This serves, as it were, as a "passport" for the message to the listener's heart. Consider this listener's response:

> Well, I have very fine hair and not everyone knows how to set that type of hair. If done wrong, it's a great waste of money and time for everyone concerned—the beauty operator and the one getting her hair done. But, you see, in the first place, the person who recommended the beauty shop knew about my soft hair and didn't send me to just anyone. She was thoughtful enough to know just what I wanted in a beauty operator. Oh, she was a new neighbor—a very lovely person.

Tangible Evidence. In our tabulation we have treated "tangible evidence" as a separate group. However, it frequently serves to strengthen the impact of an ad or of a recommendation in cases in which personal intention or product relationship are not sufficiently convincing in themselves.

In instances of home appliances, food, or garden equipment, the results are often at the listener's disposal right in the speaker's home, yard, or garden. In the case which follows, the combined strength of an attractive product name, advertising, and the "commercial" authority of a salesgirl did not suffice to motivate the purchase; it was the "tangible" proof of the speaker's beautiful skin that clinched the sale:

> I think an ad that stands out in my mind was a product put out by Revlon called Moondrops. It is a skin lotion, and I saw the ad on TV and in the magazines and newspapers. The ad stressed it was good for the skin and made one look younger. The name also attracted me— it sounded so cool and pretty. Some girl who worked in a cosmetic department in a department store here also told me about it. I was not very friendly with the girl, but she had such beautiful skin. It may not have anything to do with the lotion, but after seeing the lotion so nicely advertised and then the recommendation from her and her lovely skin —well, I just thought I would invest in it.

Secrecy or Hesitation. Expressed in the form of a paradox, the best proof of the speaker's disinterestedness is his reluctance to divulge the source or brand name of a product which is wanted by a "listener." This refers to the well-known psychological phenomenon that the harder it is to get a desired object, the more desirable it becomes.

In Summary

In talking to other people about products and services, "speakers" expect and/or receive certain gratifications; they will not recommend things "for nothing." However, in typical Word-of-mouth incidents, these rewards are always purely psychological, and never material. This very assumption—that no material interest is involved in the recommendation—is the most basic motivation for the "listener" in accepting and acting on the recommendation. He desires to learn the "truth" about the product and expects to obtain it most safely under two conditions: a. that the one who recommends is interested in him and his well-being, and b. that this recommender's experience with and knowledge about the product are convincing.

If we transfer these conditions to the relationship between advertiser and reader and consider the former the "speaker" and the latter the "listener," it becomes obvious that the advertiser faces a fundamental difficulty in filling this psychological role. Is it not the avowed purpose of advertising to sell and to make money? And is not the product to him a means to this end rather than an object of personal experience and interest? And yet the ad-conscious attitude of modern audiences compels the advertiser to attack the problem of closing this gap and to try to absolve himself of his "original sin."

Part II. The Applications

In the preceding section it was reported how, in the light of our investigation, everyday Word-of-mouth processes come about in the area of product and service recommendations. However, in order to utilize some of the selling power of Word-of-mouth in advertising, it will be necessary to apply our findings to the practical realities of advertising. Specifically, the two main problems are:

1. How to *simulate* Word-of-mouth.
2. How to *stimulate* Word-of-mouth.

Simulation Requirements

If we see in the advertiser the recommending "speaker," he has to be as effective as possible in making his "listener" accept his word and act on it. No commercial ad can help having the ultimate intention of selling for monetary profit. On the other hand, the foremost source of selling power in Word-of-mouth lies in the belief that this very intention is missing. In order to escape this contradiction, the advertiser has to attempt to approximate, at least, the position of the disinterested and noncommercial speaker, and to absolve himself to some degree of his original sin.

According to the study findings, there are two approaches which can lead the advertiser closer to the position of the reader's friend and fellow consumer: (1) proving his "intention," (2) improving his authentic relationship to the product. Practical applications of these findings open up a number of ways to which other-than-profit motives can be expressed.

Proof of 'friendship'

Most consumers have a strong secret desire to be "loved" by their suppliers for their own sake. Thus every time an advertiser "speaks," he has to *separate himself*, as it were, from the commercial camp and become an intermediary between the producer and the consumer—but one who can be believed to be a "friend" of the consumer. He must give proof through understanding, attitude, and action that he is one of them, or at least that he has their well-being at heart. This may, according to the size and scope of operations, extend to community, country, or even to mankind.

There are a number of methods by which you, as the advertiser, can prove your intention and ally yourself with your readers (listeners):

Anticipate Consumer's Attitude. Meet the consumer's ad-consciousness by showing that you are ad-conscious yourself! Once you anticipate the increasingly ad-conscious attitude of your audiences, your ads will avoid a sense of grim urgency and gain a more pleasurable attitude toward themselves and their audience. Invite readers and listeners to join you in the fun of advertising, even to some extent at your expense!

By taking the audience into your confidence and placing it on your own level, you will prove your friendship for it and absolve yourself, within limits, of the original sin.

'Gift Package' Sales Message. Go beyond the selling purpose of your ad by giving it some independent value which the reader-listener can enjoy. In expressing your sales message by means of something genuinely beautiful, exciting, entertaining, insightful, or humorous, you reveal your care for your listener, who is free to benefit from your thoughtful efforts—whether he follows your recommendation or not.

Understating the actual sales message may in such ads even enhance the selling effect. For example: "We must be doing something right"—the Rheingold ad.

Establish Audience Kinship. Match yourself and your product's appeals with the customer you are aiming at. Prove to him that you and he understand each other, that you have something in common with him, and that in some way you and he are kindred souls. (This, remember, is the feeling which in everyday Word-of-mouth makes a listener so much more susceptible to a speaker's message.) Refer to some of his most probable group or individual characteristics, leanings, tastes, and needs; make him feel that the man behind the ad is his kind of person.

Make the style of your ad your password to your consumer. The choice of medium and style of artwork and copy is in itself an important step in the establishment of a community of taste and interest between advertiser and audience. The style reassures the consumer: "See, you and I have a similar taste, style of life, and so on; this is why I feel that this product which I am recommending is just right for *you.*"

Initiate 'Exclusive' Group. Join your prospective customers, through your ad, in an act of initiation: suggest that the product is not meant for everybody, and only those who belong to the circle of the initiated (which includes the advertiser) may know about and take advantage of it. Again, some proof should be in the ad that the advertiser understands the prospective members of the "exclusive" group and shares with them that of which they are proud.

Be a Friend of Man. There is nothing new about institutional advertising and the use of public relations for the creation of goodwill in the interest of large companies. Ford Motor Company, Humble Oil & Refining Company, Container Corporation of America, and many others, have—through their foundations, donations, general research, and rewards—demonstrated that they are interested in the community at large. But one does not have to represent a giant corporation in order to prove that the company has nonprofit interests and is a friend of man. The yearly pleasure trip on which a Florida businessman takes his 47 employees every Christmas may make a more personal and moving impression than the millions spent by those who everybody knows have millions to spend. Small but thoughtful and original acts of friendship may do a lot to prove a company's intention.

Convey Personal Experience. We have seen that the Word-of-mouth recommendation draws a great deal of its power from the fact that the speaker is in a position to convey his personal experience with the product, and to express it in the authentic language of his experience or enthusiasm. The advertiser, however, has not always really "experienced" his product, and often does not know enough of its effects on others to talk about it in an authentic, spontaneous way.

Ads that express and reveal genuine interest in and love for the advertised product, and understanding of its role in the consumer's life, will go far in proving the advertiser's intention above and beyond his monetary motivation.

Relation to product

The second role to be played by the advertiser is his authentic relation to the product. The following suggestions can serve as guideposts toward the application of this principle:

Become a Consumer. From our findings, we remember that the greatest chance for the salesman to sell is in leaving his role as a salesman and momentarily slipping into the role of a consumer who has had (or witnessed) a genuine experience with the product in question. Accordingly, give yourself a chance to "live with your own product" as a consumer. Thus you can step out of the (suspect) role of advertiser and tell your audience of your real experience.

Personalize the Producer. Demonstrate an immediate relationship between producer and product which should show some of the love and care the old craftsman used to feel for the things he made. If this is not feasible, personalize the people who are closer to the product: the brewmaster, the engine designer, and the like.

Trace 'Company Myth.' Find out about the circumstances under which the company was organized, and how its product or products were created or adopted. In many cases someone will be found who was once creatively involved in, or "obsessed" with, the product. On other occasions, interesting material about the product may come to light. Such material can help the advertiser to show his or the company's product involvement, and thus help to "absolve" him.

Instances of this sort which have proved effective in advertising and public relations are: the cooperative founding of Nationwide Insurance by 26 farmers who needed inexpensive insurance for themselves; Sell's Liver Paté, which owes its existence to a gourmet-turned-producer; Mrs. Pepperidge's bread which, we are told, she first baked herself for her sick son, and later for the many thousands of "sons" and "daughters" who became her customers; and Mrs. Gerber, as the developer of baby food for her children.

Describe Organization Climate. Find an aspect of the product or its production which calls for special care or is unique or exciting. Fit this into the company climate and describe it as one of general care, appreciation, respect, and love for the product.

Reflect an Adventure. Whenever possible avoid the polished anonymity of the conventional copywriter and turn your ad into a personal statement about some kind of adventure with the product. Try to embed the product into your private life—that is, let your friends and family make contact with it, and turn your ad into a "documentary."

Consumer testimonials

In cases in which the advertiser's own voice is not convincing enough, he may call in a third person as an intermediary between him and the listener (testimonial). What happens in testimonials comes particularly close to the Word-of-mouth process; here a "user" or alleged user of the product is called on by the advertiser to convey to the nonuser or prospective user his experience with, or opinion about, the product. Consequently, everything that applies to everyday Word-of-mouth can be applied to testimonials, and gains particular significance in this advertising technique. The principle of "fittingness" among the three factors—speaker, listener, product—prevails.

The success of the message, therefore, will rest to a large degree on the reader's (listener's) belief that the auxiliary consumer (speaker) is talking to him spontaneously and disinterestedly, that he has *not* been called in as a "hired hand," and that he has no monetary interest whatsoever in the matter. Being a paid agent is the endorser's "original sin." But the reader's belief in the endorser's message will also depend on the believability of the latter's relationship to the product and the authenticity of his language.

For example, sometimes it is better to state, "I really don't drink Lipton tea, but I have been told it is very good."

Stimulation Appeals

Another of the advertiser's tasks is to provoke, stimulate, and produce Word-of-mouth about his product, company, or message. He must supply his messages with motivations and ammunition to this end, and turn them into topics of talk.

We have seen from everyday Word-of-mouth incidents that "a person does not talk for nothing"; if one wishes to motivate him to talk, the message has to offer him a promise of emotional gain or some sort of mental gratification. This, as we have seen, may be the chance to channel the excitement aroused by an experience with a product, to obtain some kind of self-confirmation and enhance his ego, or to get the satisfaction that he has shown interest in or care for others. Finally, the emotional gain may consist of those gratifications which derive from an involvement in the message rather than in the product, leading to talking about or quoting from an ad or commercial.

Topics of talk

Numerous applications for the advertiser suggest themselves to stimulate Word-of-mouth:

Use the "shock of difference"—but with an orientation. Try to stop reader-listeners in their tracks by presenting your cause from an unusual angle, show-ing a not-so-obvious facet of your product, setting it off sharply from or against what others are doing in the same area. But don't be "different" at all costs and without an orientation! Successful applications of this technique are the Schweppes bearded Commander, who lends his product the desired touch of upper class distinction; Hathaway's black eyepatch, which endows its shirts with an atmosphere of adventurous and romantic virility; Maidenform's dream-walk in the seminude, which associates the bra with "wishful dreams" of passion; the glamorous hand from nowhere, which offers an attractive prom-ise to the simple man; and so on.

Accordingly, let the incongruency, extremity, or unusualness of your ad express the "climate" in which you expect your product to thrive or the direc-tion in which you want it to "move" psychologically. The shock of difference is likely to produce in the reader-listener a "tension" which in turn may use talk as an outlet. People also like to show their alertness in spotting the "differ-ence."

Employ the effect of "heightened reality" (stagecraft). All talked-about ads, commercials, and so forth have one thing in common: they use the artistic effects of heightened reality; they "stage," as it were, their content by trans-forming the features of reality into a selective, condensed, symbolic, and styl-ized presentation—whether visual, audible, or both. If you want your adver-tising itself to stimulate talk, don't be satisfied with presenting "reality as is." Do make use of the expressive power of the art forms—the suspense of drama, the lifts and moods of poetry, the relief of comedy, the irony of anecdote, the bluff of paradox, and the startling truth of a documentary close-up.

Invite "listeners" to join you in poking fun at yourself. We have previously discussed this friendship-promoting aspect of self-mockery in advertising. The same feature that makes the consumer feel the advertiser takes him into his confidence also loosens his tongue. Where you intend to use humor or comedy, include humorous ad-consciousness in your advertising performance; it will encourage and stimulate the reader-listener to join you in this vein and to pro-long and vary the fun through his own Word-of-mouth.

Equip your message with "wings." Verbal play is not a child's prerogative; people will quote widely, and often with compulsive repetitiveness, what is made easy and pleasurable for them to quote. See to it that your message contains some good *coinage*—a sequence of words (and sounds) which provokes verbal play through its rhythm, alliteration, and pointedness. It should be applicable to a wide variety of life situations and should offer a plug for symbolic, figurative, ironic, aggressive, or suggestive use.

Leave room for your reader's wit or ingenuity. In coining your slogans or jingles, give your reader-listener a chance to fill in left-out words or to exploit ambiguous meanings for his own purposes! In this way you provoke him to make your message really his own.

(Whether such verbal play will tend to preserve the original sales message, or will bypass and eventually obliterate the product-association, is another problem which cannot be elaborated on in this study.)

Do not leave your customer alone with your product. Advertising in order to win customers is not enough. If you wish them to become your product's advertisers, if you want to stimulate them to talk about your product, you cannot afford to leave them alone with it! You must try and steel their experience with your product along the lines which you expect will make them talk.

For instance, if you advertise a cleanser, ask your customers whether they notice that in using this product they no longer have to bend down in order to get the dirt rings out of the bath tub. Ask them for a report about their experience, and they surely will be talking about it. If you advertise a car, tell those who own it how to turn the key, open rear doors in station wagons, and make them aware of pleasurable driving experiences peculiar to your make. (Ford is doing an excellent job with its approach: "Ford has a better idea.")

Most products have an aspect which answers some specific need or emotional desire on the part of the public. Often that desire is not quite obvious and the customer is only vaguely aware of it. The advertiser should have his ear to the ground to find out about this desire and to make his customers aware that his product does answer it.

Link your products with needs and trends of the time. Certain topics are "in the air" in certain periods of time. It is the job of the advertiser to hit on that aspect of his product which can be most readily and productively linked with these topics and trends, and thus to secure the product a place in the "talk of the time."

Satisfy the urge for "newness." Present your product from time to time from a new angle. The best product is usually taken for granted and ceases to be discussed once it has become part of the accepted pattern of use and of living. From time to time it has to be revived, rejuvenated, and brought in line with changes which have already occurred. Moreover, it has to be presented in ways which *anticipate* such changes and, through new facets of the product, make the public aware of them. The reward will be not only sales, but also talk, and thus more sales.

Give your reader a chance to gain attention. Supply him with "unusual"

and interesting material which might be anything from impressive or sensational to anecdotic. See to it that the product or company forms an indispensable background for the "story" or is meaningfully linked with it. Give him
cultural, scientific, or technical ammunition, but always make it pointed and
highlighted so as to be "ready for use." Again, don't allow the product or
company to get lost in the process. In a general way, *The New York Times*
began appeal to this desire with its slogan: "It's more interesting—and you
will be, too!"

Provide him with "inside information." Take the reader behind the scenes
of your product or company and give him the feeling of being in-the-know.
The information may refer to the making of the product, to company personalities, or to product history. The interest-value of the piece of knowledge will
promote and facilitate talk about the product.

Give him the feeling of secrecy or exclusivity. Analysis earlier pointed to
the fact that, in all probability, the spreading of a message will be facilitated
when a certain degree of secrecy or exclusivity is connected with it. What
motivates the one who "gives it away" is the desire to show that he himself is
initiated, and that he is gracious enough to initiate the listener into a chance
that is restricted or rare.

Supply users of your product with material to show them that in using
the product they have, as it were, joined a "club" of people who really "know"
—have more taste, understanding, or connoisseurship than most others—and
you will have propelled them psychologically in the direction of "talk."

If your product shows some new angle, or represents an attempt at a new
solution, do not try only to sell or to convince your reader, but "hire" him in
the role of a pioneer. Your ad should leave him with the feeling that in understanding and accepting the novelty and "differentness" of the product, he can
share some of the credit that will go to it, and that it is his job to pave the way
for it in talking to others. Let your ad mobilize his ambitions and supply him
with the "weapons" for assuming his leadership and exerting his power in the
interest of the product.

Make your reader feel that recommendation is a gift. We pointed out
earlier how close the recommendation of a cherished product comes to being
a gift, and that, conversely, a thoughtful gift always represents a recommendation. Make your readers aware of what your product can do for those for
whom they "care," and that a recommendation can take the place of a gift:
without the reader acting as an intermediary between the product and the
cared-for person, a wish may remain frustrated and a gratification missed.
Thus talking about the product can do a lot for the reader in his relation to
those he cares for; it will give him a chance to do a favor, earn praise, make
friends, or simply express his attention, care, or love.

Offer a bridge of friendship. Make it easy for consumers who like or
cherish your product to send a free, gift-packed sample of it to their relatives
or friends. It can be accompanied by a brief, personal-looking note which

explains that "this is one of the things that has made life more enjoyable (or easier) for me, and I don't want you to miss it." All the giver has to do is to send you his personal signature and the names of his friends. Keep the company in the background; make the "gift" serve as an invisible bridge.

Conclusion

I consider the establishment of a close link between successful, everyday Word-of-mouth recommendations and effective advertising to be one of the implicit findings of the present study. It emphasizes the new role of the advertiser as that of a friend who recommends a tried and trusted product, as against that of a salesman who tries to get rid of merchandise.

Tracing the reasons for effective advertising in step-by-step fashion back to its person-to-person roots will, we hope, help the advertiser in reviewing his mass media approaches and in carrying through his new role. It is evident that in addition there are other avenues that *complement* mass media advertising. There is a symbiotic relationship between the impersonal and the personal, or the formal and the informal, avenues of communication.

I have tried to demonstrate in this presentation that mass media advertising does indeed make people aware of a product and may stimulate sufficient interest in the product to make it desirable. Mass media advertising may even be sufficient to sell the product. But for the latter statement to be true, generally speaking, the risk factor has to be extremely low. Consider the difference, for example, in the choice between detergents and in the choice between two automobiles. In the first case there is little economic or psychic risk; in the second case the economic risk is great, and important psychological and sociological considerations are involved.

I have also tried to demonstrate, particularly with products whose risk value is high, that Word-of-mouth recommendation is a strong, if not the strongest, ally a product can have. Recent anthropological, sociological, and psychological studies have shown that mass media can raise questions or define issues; they can be informative and entertaining; and, to some degree, they can influence public opinion, but in the final analysis they cannot shape or mold it. People mold opinion. The glossy, brightly colored magazine page or the 21-inch TV screen can never replace the influence and the value of a personal recommendation. Were that the case, the consumer public would have to be very passive—simply sitting back and receiving information, and enough of it to permit proper evaluation.

However, our recent studies have shown quite the opposite: the consumer public is in fact active. Consequently, in a buying situation a dynamic interpersonal relationship—where ideas are discussed, opinions are exchanged, questions are asked, and answers are given—will frequently exist. Moreover, such an exchange will almost always outweigh the passivity of a one-sided and purely formal advertiser-audience relationship. Advertising cannot sell against personal influence.

We have further endeavored to point out that there is a ready-made market of "influences," "experts," and "aficionados," who can be reached and, in turn, influenced by advertising in existing specialized publications or by the appropriate creative approach.

The advertiser with a good product to sell will do his best to stimulate information-seeking by prospective buyers, and he will make every effort to have as much favorable information as possible in the hands and heads of these various influentials. The "aficionado" is the person who can take the buyer into his confidence and make him a "member of the club." The bond created by this relationship of people dedicated to the same hobbies can often replace, and often produce, real friendships. To the extent that the advertiser joins this club, he too offers friendship, trust, and confidence.

26

The Informative Role of
Advertising

LOUIS P. BUCKLIN

The central market place facilitates the meeting of buyers and sellers interested in the exchange of certain products. Without such a common ground, both buyers and sellers must make extensive searches for suitable trading partners. The central market place helps minimize the cost of these activities.

Advertising serves a similar purpose by providing information about the nature, availability, and location of products. Informative advertising may complement or even substitute for the central market. Advertising may limit the need for person-to-person search, or may actually supplant the negotiation process of the market place, for example, mail order advertising.

The potential value of this role is ever increasing. The demand for convenience by dispersed suburban consumers has weakened the vast markets of the major metropolitan cities. In addition, manufacturers' product lines have become increasingly diverse. Together these factors mean that there is scant likelihood for individual buyers and sellers to be exposed to even a major fraction of the possible trading opportunities. Advertising can help close this gap.

Similar conceptions of this information role of advertising may be found in most advertising treatises (e.g., Britt, 1960, pp. 159-167). Support for such views comes from examination of advertisements with respect to their fact-carrying qualities (e.g., Sandage and Fryburger, 1958, Chap. 5). Unfortunately, however, this only indicates that certain advertisements *could* play this role. Little evidence exists as to whether consumers indeed use them in this way, leaving one to wonder whether this concept is a valid argument for advertising or merely product puffing.

This article presents evidence as to whether consumers actually use advertising the way this informative role implies. Data were collected in a survey of consumer shopping patterns among a group of randomly selected female

Reprinted from *Journal of Advertising Research* (September, 1965), pp. 11-15, by permission of the author and publisher. © Advertising Research Foundation, Inc., (1965).

household heads residing in the communities which approximate the trading area of Oakland, California. To be included in the sample, the person sampled had to have made one shopping trip in the past month for some item (excluding foods, homes, and automobiles) costing over five dollars. If she had not, she was replaced from a substitute home in the same block.

The 506 women finally included in the sample were quizzed extensively about their shopping activities on this trip. They also were asked whether they had shopped for these products by checking advertisements before the trip.

Use of Advertising

Respondents reported checking advertisements for 210, or 24 per cent, of the 891 products, worth five dollars or more, reported upon. There were no replies in four products. This rate of recall, of course, does not purport to measure total exposure to advertising. What it does show is that respondents could not recall using advertising as a shopping aid more than one-quarter of the time for five-dollar-or-better products. One might thus conclude that advertising's role as an active guide to shopping is quite restricted.

But before accepting that conclusion, let's examine the use of advertising with respect to the type of product, the last time such a product was purchased, and the item's value. Table 26-1 gives a breakdown of the answers on the checking of advertising by products. Rate of recall varies significantly, from nine per cent for shoes to 52 per cent for furniture. These differences appear to reflect the degree of consumer familiarity with the type of product. Where

Table 26-1. The checking of advertisements by various product categories

	Ads Checked	No Ads Checked	Total	Base
Shoes	9%	91%	100%	(166)
Personal accessories	12	88	100	(34)
Apparel	23	77	100	(420)
Other	23	77	100	(56)
Home furnishings	26	74	100	(81)
Large appliances	42	58	100	(31)
Small appliances	43	57	100	(21)
Toys	46	54	100	(28)
Auto accessories	50	50	100	(8)
Furniture	52	48	100	(42)
Total	24	76	100	(887)

$\chi^2 = 48.1, p < .001$

the consumer likely is most informed, such as in personal accessories, apparel, and shoes, she relies least upon advertising. Where she is not apt to know product quality, as in appliances and furniture, the effort spent checking advertising is substantially increased.

As Table 26-2 shows, consumers checked advertising in 18 per cent of the product cases when the last purchase had been within three months. This rose to 30 per cent when the most recent purchase had been 18 months ago or more, or the item had never been bought before.

Table 26-2. The checking of advertisements by date of last purchase

Date of Purchase	Ads Checked	No Ads Checked	Total	Base
Last purchased less than 3 months ago	18%	82%	100%	(236)
4 to 18 months	23	77	100	(311)
More than 18 months, or never	30	70	100	(274)
Total	24	76	100	(821)

$\chi^2 = 10.0, p < .01$

Table 26-3 breaks down the data according to the product's value. Advertising is used much more extensively in the search for high-priced products. Advertising was checked only 14 per cent of the time for products in the five to nine dollar bracket. This rose to 46 per cent in the 50 dollar and over price range, a substantial and highly significant difference.

Table 26-3. The checking of advertisements by product price level

	Ads Checked	No Ads Checked	Total	Base
$5–$9	14%	86%	100%	(370)
$10–$19	22	78	100	(198)
$20–$49	31	69	100	(176)
$50 or more	46	54	100	(123)
Total	24	76	100	(867)

$\chi^2 = 58.2, p < .001$

So the conclusion that advertising plays a limited role in perfecting the market place must be tempered in light of these results. The data led to the hypothesis that the consumer uses advertising to the extent that she feels a need for information. If she is unfamiliar with the product, if she has not shopped for the item for some time, if it is expensive, then she will be more likely to use advertising. According to Howard (1963, p. 58), ". . . the further along the learning curve the buyer is, the less inclined he is to seek information." The survey data, and the hypothesis generated therefrom, closely support this position.

Effect of Advertising

This noting of advertisements might not broaden the consumer's knowledge of the alternative products available. Instead, it might sell her on a single brand and actually reduce the scope of her information-gathering activities. To investigate this possibility, respondents were asked whether they had decided upon the brand before undertaking the trip in question. Answers were cross tabulated with the checking of advertisements, and are shown in Table 26-4.

Table 26-4. Relationship between checking of ad and brand preference

	One Brand Preferred	No Brand Preferred	Total	Base
Ads checked	24%	76%	100%	(209)
No ads checked	22	78	100	(673)
Total	22	78	100	(882)

$\chi^2 = .59, p < .50$

These data show little difference in the extent of brand preference between the two categories: 24 per cent of those who checked advertisements expressed a brand preference, compared with 22 per cent where advertising had not been checked. This difference is not significant and the notion that advertising served only to pre-sell is not substantiated.

Indeed, another computation shows that noting advertising seems to enlarge the consumer's knowledge of desirable product characteristics (Table 26-5).

Respondents were asked as to whether they knew all, some, few, or none of the product features before they started the trip. Table 26-5 shows that of those who checked advertisements, 51 per cent knew all the features wanted, 30 per cent knew some, and only 19 per cent were aware of few or none. On

Table 26-5. Relationship between checking advertisements and knowledge of product features wanted

| | Features Known | | | | |
	All	Some	Few or none	Total	Base
Ads checked	51%	30%	19%	100%	(207)
No ads checked	38	29	33	100	(672)
Total	41	29	30	100	(879)

$\chi^2 = 17.1$, p < .001

products for which the respondents had not checked advertisements, just 38 per cent knew all features, 29 per cent knew some, and 33 per cent were aware of just a few. These differences clearly suggest that advertisements aided the respondent in selecting the product characteristics that she most desired, without prejudicing her as to brand.

Store Preferences

Respondents who noted advertising also seemed much less wedded to particular stores. Respondents were asked whether they had a favorite store for purchasing each of the five-dollar-or-more products. Cross tabulation of replies with the checking of advertisements reveals, in Table 26-6, a negative association: 28 per cent of those who checked advertisements stated they had a preferred store for the product, as compared with 47 per cent among those who did not check ads.

Table 26-6. The relationship between checking advertisements and store preferences for the product

	Preferred Store	No Preferred Store	Total	Base
Ads checked	28%	72%	100%	(210)
No ads checked	47	53	100	(676)
Total	42	58	100	(886)

$\chi^2 = 22.8$, p < .001

This relationship receives further support from evidence that respondents who checked advertising were more concerned with price. Respondents were asked for each product mentioned, what factors they considered in selecting a store. Price was mentioned as a factor for 319 of the products. Table 26-7 shows the cross tabulation of this question with the checking of advertisements. Price was stated as a factor for 46 per cent of the products for which advertising was noted, 34 per cent for those where advertising was not noted.

Table 26-7. The relationship between checking advertisements and price as a product choice factor

	Price Mentioned	Price Not Mentioned	Total	Base
Ads checked	46%	54%	100%	(209)
No ads checked	34	66	100	(669)
Total	36	64	100	(878)

$\chi^2 = 9.85$, p < .001

Shopping Efforts

Studying the extent of shopping effort by the respondents provided another view of the role of advertising. This was accomplished in two ways. First, to measure the number of shopping stops, or interstore comparisons, made for a given product, respondents were asked, with respect to the shopping trip that qualified them for the sample, to name the stores visited and the products shopped for in each. Table 26-8 shows the number of interstore comparisons, calculated from this information, cross tabulated with the checking of advertisements. Where advertising was not checked, 14 per cent of the products were shopped for in more than one store, compared with 25 per cent when advertising was checked.

Table 26-8. The relationship between checking advertisements and number of interstore comparisons made upon shopping trip

	Only One Store	One or More	Total	Base
Ads checked	75%	25%	100%	(210)
No ads checked	86	14	100	(677)
Total	84	16	100	(887)

$\chi^2 = 14.2$, p < .001

Second, respondents were asked, on each product, whether they had shopped for it in a store prior to the qualifying shopping trip. A particularly strong association exists between this characteristic and the checking of advertising, as shown in Table 26-9. Where advertising was not checked, only 21 per cent of the products had been shopped for previously; the corresponding figure where advertising had been checked was 53 per cent.

Table 26-9. The relationship between checking advertisements and previous shopping trips for the product

	Previous Shopping	No Previous Shopping	Total	Base
Ads checked	53%	47%	100%	(210)
No ads checked	21	79	100	(677)
Total	29	71	100	(887)

$\chi^2 = 78.1$, p < .001

Since checking of advertisements is associated with concern for price, it is fair to ask whether the relationships just cited merely reflect the price variable. To evaluate this, the two shopping activity variables were further analyzed by holding price constant within the four brackets shown on Table 26-3. For both interstore comparisons and extent of previous shopping, each of the four subtables revealed more extensive search activity for products for which advertising had been checked. Additive chi-squares were significant as well (p < .001). As a result, the relationship between shopping assiduity and the checking of advertisements, as shown in Tables 26-7 and 26-8, is well supported.

Conclusions

The survey data build a strong case that shoppers use advertising intelligently and effectively for at least an important minority of products purchased. Advertising is used more in shopping for less familiar items, items that they have not bought recently, and high-priced items. Further, such use of advertising does not appear to lead to brand preference. On the contrary, it was associated with better product information, lower store preference, greater concern about price, and increased search.

Advertising cannot properly be termed the causative factor in all of this. Rather, advertising is part of a rather clearly definable, rational shopping syndrome. Advertising is simply one of several check points upon which consumers rely to improve their purchasing abilities. In many cases where advertising was not checked, this seemed to be the result of a lack of consumer interest in investigating alternative purchases. Many such consumers perhaps felt that because of their past relationship with stores and/or brands, that making any extra effort in shopping would not be worth the time spent. Thus it may be concluded that where consumers feel a need for market information, advertising will be used as an aid to purchasing activities. In this sense, advertising may be regarded as a positive influence in the perfection of markets.

A corollary to this conclusion is ironic in the light of increasing advertising expenditures. Despite continuous exposure to advertisements, many consumers seem to have difficulty in actively checking advertisements, as indicated by their failure to do so. For the products studied in this survey, few consumers seem to be exposed to the advertising precisely when they are ready to buy. This may be because the location and whereabouts of advertisements for a wide variety of alternative products are hard to find. There is no source index with which to zero in on advertisements. Purchasing newspapers and magazines indiscriminately is too expensive. In short, the dissemination of advertisements for more expensive products, from the standpoint of aiding the consumer when she desires this help, is very inefficiently organized. Some kind of medium is needed which the consumer can activate to produce quickly the information that she needs.

The survey by no means shows that all advertising operates in an informational role. The survey provided no means to reconstruct the effect of all advertisements that the consumer might have absorbed. In other circumstances the persuasive effect of advertising might be found to inhibit the consumer from learning about alternative products. Still, the data nevertheless demonstrate that, at least under some circumstances, advertising plays an important and informational role. They also hint that if consumers could more easily find advertisements when needed, this role of advertising might well be increased.

References

BRITT, STEUART H. *The Spenders*, New York: McGraw-Hill, 1960.

SANDAGE, C. H., AND VERNON FRYBURGER. *Advertising Theory and Practice*. 5th ed. Homewood, Ill.: Irwin, 1958.

HOWARD, JOHN A. *Marketing Management*. Rev. ed. Homewood, Ill.: Irwin, 1963.

27

Is Advertising Believability Really Important?

JOHN C. MALONEY

The use of presently available advertising testing methods has encouraged an oversimplified view of the ways in which advertising works.

Many of these methods suggest that X% of an advertising audience noted an advertisement while Y% did not; that X% understood it while Y% did not; or that X% "believed" it while Y% did not. Thus, a single advertisement's performance is often seen as a series of "jumps" over a number of successive hurdles, with belief of the advertisement being the last of these.

Although such assumptions may be true in general, they may be dangerously misleading in their particulars. Research in recent years has clearly demonstrated that noting, understanding, and believing are *not* either-or, or go or no-go occurrences.

More importantly, it is now apparent that *no advertisement is likely to be completely "believable" when its purpose is to change people's minds. Moreover, an advertisement need not be believed completely to be effective.*

These views are based on three years of background research; a continuing program of communication research conducted by the Leo Burnett Company, and from a survey of hundreds of books and articles concerning all phases of persuasive communication.[1]

Competition Between Persuasive Messages and Old Beliefs

Advertising believability *does* represent the net effect of adver-

Reprinted from *Journal of Marketing* (October, 1963), pp. 1-8, by permission of the publisher, the American Marketing Association.

[1]For a description of one of the author's own studies in this area see John C. Maloney, "Curiosity vs. Disbelief in Advertising," *Journal of Advertising Research*, Vol. 2 (June, 1962), pp. 2-8.

tising upon the mind of the reader, listener, or viewer. Few advertisers, advertising researchers, or psychologists would disagree with the statement that an
advertisement is "believed" when it leaves the consumer with that attitude,
belief, or intention toward the product which the advertiser intended that he or
she should have after exposure to the advertisement.

However, *believability is not an inherent property of the advertisement
itself.* It is not a mystic something that some advertisements have and others
do not have. Believability depends upon the *interaction* of each advertisement
with the consumer's attitudes and memories accumulated from prior experience.

Each person's predispositions to note, understand, and accept or reject
certain messages is *learned.* Different people have different expectations about
the trustworthiness of various kinds of advertising; they have developed different kinds of knowledge and different types of feelings about the products
or brands being advertised. This means that an advertisement completely believable to one person may not be at all believable to another.

In other words, we must specify *believable to whom* when we consider the
"believability" of an advertisement.

We must also take the advertiser's intentions into account in a very explicit
way. What was it that was to be believed? What *specific* attitudes or beliefs
should be left in the consumer's mind if the advertisement is believed? It is
important to know which understandings or feelings toward the product amount
to belief, and which amount to disbelief after exposure to the advertisement.

Decoding, Apperception, and "Seeing in the Light of Past Experience"

A great deal has been learned in recent years about how people
"make sense out of new information by viewing it in the light of past experience." Communications researchers often refer to this very general process
as message *decoding;* psychologists may use the general term *apperception.*
Either term refers to the process by which advertising messages interact with
people's pre-existing memories, attitudes, and beliefs.

One thing is certainly apparent: "Reminder messages" can be believed
very easily. If a message is aimed at the reinforcement of already existing beliefs, it will be easily accepted. To use the psychologist's terms, such a message
easily finds a place in the "cognitive structure" of what people think they know,
and in the "affective structure" of how they feel about a product or service.

However, when the message is not intended as a "reminder" message, but
rather as a *persuasive* message aimed at *changing* people's minds about something, we have a different story. The persuasive message is sure to run into a
conflict or competition with the pre-existing beliefs which the message seeks to
change. Since these pre-existing beliefs make up part of the past-experience
mechanism used to decode the persuasive message, these old beliefs have a
clearcut advantage over the newer beliefs called for by the message.

Decoding, apperception, and the competition between new information and old beliefs have been studied intensively from many different points of view. The clinical psychologist has studied these phenomena as part of the *ego-defense* mechanisms involved in personality formation and change. The same phenomena are crucial to the *trial-and-check* phases of most of the newer learning theories and perception theories (whereby new information "inputs" are compared with old information "memories"). These same processes are also central to a whole range of new *homeostatic* or *balance* theories of attitude change.[2]

In whatever context the conflict between new information and old beliefs is studied, the implications are the same. All such research leads to this conclusion: *By its very nature persuasion calls for the communication of messages that will NOT be believed easily.*

This conclusion is supported by hundreds of actual studies of mass communication effects. Thus, one reviewer of dozens of communication research studies concludes that mass media are much more likely to maintain, rather than to change, people's states of mind.[3] This basic fact is attributed to three aspects of apperception, commonly referred to as factors of "perceptual defense:"[4]

1. Selective attention
2. Selective perception
3. Selective recall

Selective Attention and Belief of Advertisements

Selective attention is a general term which has this implication for advertisers: *People tend to select out for attention those advertisements which are quickly recognizable as being in accord with interests or beliefs which they already hold; and they are much less likely to pay attention to other advertisements.*

[2]The newer balance theories of attitude change are particularly relevant to the basic processes described here; see Robert B. Zajonc, "The Concepts of Balance, Congruity, and Dissonance," *Public Opinion Quarterly*, Vol. 24 (Summer, 1960), pp. 280-296. For a review of the literature on trial-and-check phases of perception and learning theory, see Charles M. Solley and Gardner Murphy, *Development of the Perceptual World* (New York: Basic Books, Inc., 1960), pp. 220-237.

[3]Joseph T. Klapper, *The Effects of Mass Communication* (Glencoe, Illinois: The Free Press, 1960), p. 8.

[4]For a discussion of these perceptual defense factors in a broader context of mass media audience expectations, see Raymond A. Bauer, "The Initiative of the Audience," *Journal of Advertising Research*, Vol. 3 (June, 1963), pp. 2-7.

Other elements of attention relate to the intensity of the advertisement's sight or sound stimuli, and the intrigue or "affective value" of the advertisement itself.[5]

The selective attention phenomenon accounts for the fact that users of an advertised product are more likely than nonusers to note an advertisement for the product in question. The same phenomenon probably accounts for the fact that readership "noting scores" are typically much higher for advertising for high-interest products than for advertising which features products of low interest.

Since the advertiser finds it easiest to arrest the consumer's attention by using illustrations or sounds of considerable general interest, he is sometimes tempted to resort to featuring interesting but irrelevant material in an advert sement. If the product itself is not relevant to an active consumer interest, this tactic will solve the problems imposed by selective attention; but mere noting is not believing, and such action may easily impair ultimate belief in the advertisement.

Selective Perception and Belief of Advertisements

If an advertisement arrests the consumer's attention, it will have some effect upon the beliefs of the consumer, if only to confirm or strengthen already existing beliefs. However, there is no assurance that beliefs concerning the advertised product will be affected in the intended way.

Thus, people may fail to believe the persuasive message because of the way in which they *selectively perceive* the meaning of the message in accordance with old beliefs. More specifically, selective perception can lead to the misunderstanding of a message because of *misindexing* or *message distortion*.

The Problem of Misindexing

Any particular communication may seem relevant to many different kinds of beliefs; it might be "viewed in the light of" many different past experiences. The question of *which* attitudes will be influenced by a given advertisement depends upon the way in which the reader, listener, or viewer classifies or categorizes the tentative meaning of the advertising message as he or she begins to decode it.

This kind of classification of messages has been variously referred to by

[5]Daniel E. Berlyne, *Conflict Arousal and Curiosity* (New York: McGraw-Hill Book Company, Inc., 1960), pp. 73 ff.

communications researchers and psychologists as "cognitive tuning" or "message indexing."[6]

Belief in advertising messages is commonly impaired by three kinds of misindexing. The reader, listener, or viewer may "get hung up on the advertisement itself" and never get around to thinking about the advertised product or service. The mind may be led astray by some "borrowed attention" device in the advertisement. The advertisement may stir up thoughts about competing products or more general issues than the advertiser had in mind.

The first of these kinds of misindexing is graphically described by Alfred Politz: "Imagine a room with a large window that looks out on a beautiful countryside. On the wall opposite the window are three mirrors. The first mirror is uneven, spotted, and dirty looking. The second mirror is clean and neat, and in addition is framed by a beautiful ornamental engraving. The third mirror has no frames or ornament, and is nothing but a plain, but perfectly flawless mirror. Now, an observer (critic or client) is taken into the room and his guide points to the first mirror and says, 'What do you see?' The observer says, 'I see a bad mirror.' His guide points to the second mirror and asks again, 'What do you see?' The observer says, 'I see a beautiful mirror.' Finally, his guide points to the third mirror and says, 'What do you see?' The observer says, 'I see a beautiful scene out of an open window.' "[7]

Just as many supposedly fine mirrors are much too gaudy and distract attention from that which they are supposed to reflect, many advertisements have a comparable defect. The "addy" advertisement may attract attention, but it often distracts from the message about the product or service. People tend to react to such advertisements as *ads*. They may think them very bad, very good, very pretty, or very novel; but they never quite get around to reacting to what it is the ad is "saying" about the product.

The second common type of misindexing of advertising relates to the hazards of using attention-getting devices not appropriate to consumers' attitudes toward the product being advertised. In such instances the reader, listener, or viewer is not likely to respond to the advertisement as a message about the product or service being advertised. The advertisement is more likely to stimulate thoughts about the subject from which attention was "borrowed."

Some advertisers argue that the main illustration in a print advertisement need not be appropriate to the reader's way of looking at the product in question. "After all," they contend, "the picture is just to 'stop' the reader. Once I pull him into the ad, he will get my message from the copy."

However, people are *not obliged* to understand the intended advertising message once they are "pulled into the ad." The reader can "get into the ad,"

[6]Percy H. Tannenbaum, "The Indexing Process in Communication," *Public Opinion Quarterly*, Vol. 3 (Summer, 1955), pp. 292-302.

[7]Alfred Politz, "The Dilemma of Creative Advertising," *Journal of Marketing*, Vol. 25 (October, 1960), pp. 1-6, at pp. 4-5.

reflect upon the personal meaning of the borrowed-attention device, and "get out of the ad" without ever having any compunction about reading the body copy or understanding the intended meaning of the advertisement.

Attention-getting devices should start the reader's stream of consciousness toward, not away from, the intended meaning of the message.

The third manner in which advertisements are commonly misindexed is by "me-tooism." Some advertisers apparently cannot resist the temptation to emulate claims made by their more successful competitors, or to imitate the advertising styles of such competitors, even though these claims or styles may have become fixed in people's minds as the "hallmarks" for competing brands.

Television commercials have an advantage over printed advertisements in this regard. The most noticeable features of a printed advertisement must quickly stir the reader's recollections or expectations about the product if the message is to be properly indexed. But the television commercial can have greater influence on the viewer's "stream of consciousness" than that.

The commercial can begin with a human interest drama and lead gradually into the advertising message, so long as the "tie-in" is accomplished in a way that is remindful of the viewer's own experiences with the product. Repeated tests have shown that failure to relate the "story line" to typical ways in which the consumer sees the product often lead to strong recall of the commercial, but without any "stirring up" of attitudes toward the product itself.

Aids to Proper Indexing

Evidence accumulated from the Leo Burnett Company's studies of over 50 television commercials reflects upon the extreme importance of the advertiser's ability to *empathize* with consumers' memories of or expectations about the advertised product. Commercials which show the product in unusual positions or unfamiliar settings are not conducive to proper indexing.

But the liberal use of "product experience cues" does clearly seem to enhance the chances of proper indexing. A "product experience cue" is a sight or sound stimulus exactly like those experienced by the consumer when he or she buys, serves, eats, rides in, or otherwise experiences the product himself or herself.

At the same time "across-message cues"—elements that are common to consumers' exposures to printed advertisements *and* commercials *and* package designs *and* other representations of the product—can also go a long way toward "pulling together all of the consumers' impressions of a product. Unique and consistently used trademarks, slogans, and type faces are examples of such "across-message cues."

Without the use of such common-to-all-messages aids to proper indexing, the cumulative effects of a product's advertising are impaired; and each commercial, each advertisement, and each display piece is likely to "trigger" separate and unrelated associations in the consumer's mind.[8]

The Problem of Distortion

Suppose that an advertisement has arrested attention of the intended audience and has been properly indexed. Is the advertiser now *assured* that his message will be believed? Of course not. The old beliefs already lodged in people's minds still have ample opportunity to resist the change called for by the advertising message.

People see meanings which they *expect* to see. If the message meaning does not "fall into place" with old beliefs, an uncomfortable "imbalance" is created, and feelings of curiosity or doubt are likely to ensue. Such imbalance —often referred to as *cognitive dissonance*—can be resolved in one of two ways: *by changing old beliefs to conform to the message; or through distortion of the meaning of the message so that the message more easily fits in with old beliefs.*[9]

The advertising message may be distorted by being *leveled* or *sharpened*.

An advertising message is *leveled* when people distort the meaning, by overlooking something in the advertising message which is out of phase with pre-existing beliefs:

A message is most likely to be leveled when it presents information which is *generally* in accord with what the reader, listener, or viewer would expect, but when at the same time it contains information just a little out of the ordinary. Under these circumstances the person quickly characterizes the advertisement as something quite familiar ("something I already know all about") and overlooks the new details in the message.

The advertiser who wishes to avoid the risk of nonbelief due to leveling should ask himself what it is in his message that deviates from what the consumer feels that he already knows about the product or service. He should make this portion of his message stand out *sharply,* and not bury it in the midst of many other familiar-to-the-consumer ideas about his product or service.

The advertising message is *sharpened* when people "read into the message" additional or unintended meanings in order to make the message conform to pre-existing beliefs.

The message is quite likely to be sharpened if it represents a departure from long-standing advertising themes for the product. Thus, out of any 100 respondents to an advertisement for a product of the Campbell Soup Company,

[8]For a selective review of the literature on empathy see Kenneth Gompertz, "The Relation of Empathy to Effective Communication," *Journalism Quarterly*, Vol. 37 (1960), pp. 533-546.

[9]Leo Festinger, *A Theory of Cognitive Dissonance* (Evanston, Illinois: Row, Peterson and Company, 1957). Also see Jack W. Brehm and Arthur R. Cohen, *Explorations in Cognitive Dissonance* (New York: John Wiley & Sons, Inc., 1962).

a few respondents may be expected to report that the advertisement contained pictures of the Campbell Kids, whether or not the Campbell Kids actually were pictured. Because of many repeated past experiences, many people have come to expect Campbell advertisements to picture the Campbell Kids.

Strangely enough, while the believability of advertising often is adversely affected by people's tendencies to think the advertising says something different from what it actually does say, *sharpening can and often does work to the advertiser's advantage.*

Virtually all "reminder advertising" depends on people's tendencies to sharpen messages. If the advertiser knows that the attitudes which people already have for his product are quite favorable, and if his main intention is to reinforce such attitudes—rather than to create new attitudes or change old ones—he needs only to provide the consumer with a pleasant reminder of the product.

If the advertiser can count on the favorability of the consumer's attitudes to lead to a favorable kind of "filling in," it may be well to create an implicit advertising message, leaving room for the consumer to decide for himself why the product or service is to be preferred.

On the other hand, *if the advertiser wants to change people's attitudes or create new attitudes, he should be very explicit,* with a detailed explanation of the product or service benefits and the reasons underlying these benefits.[10]

Selective Recall and Belief of Advertisements

Belief of an advertising message shortly after the consumer is exposed to the advertisement is often misleading. With the passage of time, belief may either increase or fade away. Both an increase of belief with passage of time (often referred to as positive *sleeper effect*) and a decrease in belief are forms of *selective recall.*

Positive Sleeper Effect

Positive sleeper effect is most likely to occur when an advertising message is initially discredited as having come from an insincere advertiser or advertising spokesman but later becomes "the best information I have to go on" in making a buying decision.

There is good reason to believe that much "at-home disbelief" of advertising changes to "in-the-store belief" when an actual buying decision must be made. However, the evidence on this point is not conclusive; and it may be that

[10]Herbert I. Abelson, *Persuasion* (New York: Springer Publishing Company, 1959), pp. 10-13.

the repetitive nature of advertising precludes any chance for a sleeper effect to operate.[11]

The fading of belief with the passage of time might be viewed in very general terms as mere forgetting of the advertising message, but this is an oversimplification. Actually the fading of belief can be attributed to *"overcrowding the active file space"* in the reader, listener, or viewer's mind (known technically as *retroactive inhibition*), or to *failure to reinforce tentative beliefs*.

"Overcrowding the Active File Space"

The consumer is usually much less interested in a product or service than the advertiser. People can ordinarily retain only a limited amount of information about a product, service, or brand in their "active file memories." In trying to fill his advertisements with more and more information about his product or service, the advertiser can easily diminish his chances of leaving a clear, unitary impression of his product or service in the consumer's mind.

However, the problem of "active file space" is complicated somewhat in the case of infrequently purchased items which involve greater than average purchase risk. Automobile purchases are an example. The minority of consumers who are in-the-market automobile buyers at any one time act somewhat like businessmen who set up a special, temporary "mental file" for information related to a special project. Typically they will notice and remember many more advertising messages about automobiles than less interested persons would ever notice or remember.

In this regard, advertisers for major-purchase items face a dilemma. They can create advertising which provides a little bit of information to a lot of potentially interested people, or they can provide a lot of information to a few very actively interested people.

If they elect the former alternative, advertisements will be simple and uncluttered—with every element in the advertisement making a single idea easy to believe. If they elect the latter alternative, advertisements are likely to have a very "busy" look—with seven, eight, or nine separate selling points for the product. Either type of advertisement might be very "believable"; but the two types are likely to be believable in different ways to different audiences.

Thus, competitors' selling messages, the advertiser's own irrelevant claims, or many other factors may crowd out basic attitudes toward a product from the consumer's conscious memory. But this is only one cause for the fade of belief over time.

[11]Martin Weinberger, "Does the 'Sleeper Effect' Apply to Advertising?" *Journal of Marketing*, Vol. 25 (October, 1961), pp. 65-67.

Failure to Reinforce Tentative Belief

Many advertising messages are believed on a pending-further-evidence ("I'll believe it when I see it") basis.

Tentative beliefs of this sort may be crystallized by first-hand experience with the product itself; or such beliefs may be "shored up" by comments or examples offered by a consumer's friends or associates. However, such tentative belief or attitude imbalance represents an unsatisfactory state of affairs for the consumer; and such beliefs will give way to older modes of thinking if not reinforced.

The advertiser can cope with these problems in a variety of ways:

•By frequent exposure to the consumer of the same or similar advertising messages.

•By use of advertising messages with highly compatible messages in point-of-purchase materials, package designs, direct mail, etc.

• By use of advertising messages which can easily be confirmed by those who have already used the product—that is, those to whom the consumer might turn for advice or example once he or she becomes tentatively convinced of the product's merits.

Special Role of Advertising in Gradual Formation of Beliefs

In the past 25 years social scientists, particularly sociologists, have conducted numerous "diffusion research" studies to determine the way in which new ideas, opinions, and preferences "catch on" and spread throughout groups of people. A good deal has been learned from such studies about the ways in which "brand loyalty" develops for everything from political issues and candidates to consumer products.

One of the major findings, often confirmed and reconfirmed by such research, is that people's beliefs in new ideas develop gradually. The obvious implication is that new products usually are not accepted or adopted by people suddenly. People gradually *become aware* of new products . . . *become interested* in them or curious about them . . . *mentally evaluate* them in terms of their own needs or interests . . . and finally *try* them and *adopt* or reject them.

These or similar stages of belief formation have been variously described as the "product adoption process," the "marketing communications spectrum," the "staircase of persuasion," and by other terms.[12]

Advertising and the Adoption Process

The influence of advertising is found at each step in the adoption process—from making people *aware* of the product initially, to making them more willing to buy it again after they have already bought it and used it. *However, advertising usually has its greatest effects prior to use of the product.* Advertising may make someone buy a "bad" product once, but not more than once.[13]

The implications seem clear. *No single advertisement is likely to produce absolute "belief" in a product. Rather, each advertisement is likely to make its most significant contribution by "nudging" the consumer onto and along the path of the adoption process.*

This is especially true for infrequently purchased products with high purchase risk. It should be noted that the duration of the gradual product adoption process may vary from a matter of seconds for an inexpensive product (such as a potato peeler) to many months for products which involve considerable purchase risk. For many products, it may be better to work gradually toward belief of favorable attitudes toward a product or service one step at a time.

Automobile advertisers have used this approach effectively. "Teasers" may be used prior to new model introductions each year. No pictures of the cars are shown, and no specific facts are presented; and the sole purpose of such advertising is to intrigue consumers. Teaser advertisements may be followed by more detailed illustrations of the car, after new-model introductions, to stimulate further interest. These advertisements may be followed, later in the model year, with detailed facts about the car for aware, interested, fact-seeking buyers. In turn, these advertisements are backed up by dealers' local advertising to provide the try-it-here, buy-it-now impetus to actual trial or purchase.

"Opinion Leaders" and the "Two-step Flow"

As indicated above, many tentative beliefs of advertising crystallize *only* after the advertising message is given support from the example or advice of consumers' friends or acquaintances. However, many studies have shown that certain people are more likely to be "opinion leaders," acting with

[12]H. F. Lionberger, *Adoption of New Ideas and Practices* (Ames, Iowa: Iowa State University Press, 1960).

[13]Steuart Henderson Britt, *The Spenders* (New York: McGraw-Hill Book Co., Inc., 1960), at p. 106.

a minimum need for support or word-of-mouth confirmation from others, while others are more likely to be "opinion followers."[14]

The "opinion leaders" within any consumer group have been found to be more likely to expose themselves directly to advertising and to other mass media information sources than other people. Thus, they may by advice or example pass along the influence of advertising to less interested or less well-informed segments of the population.

This process has been described as the "two-step flow" of advertising influence—from advertising to the "opinion leaders," and from the "opinion leaders" to others.[15] The consumer goods manufacturer who advertises to the "retail trade" which sells his goods provides an example of trying to capitalize on this "two-step flow."

The "opinion leadership" and "two-step flow" concepts have been widely popularized, but not always accurately. While it is true that advertising believability *can* be enhanced a good deal by word-of-mouth support of "opinion leaders," it should be noted that:

Opinion leadership is typically very informal in its operation. The two-step flow of information is most likely to occur via subtle comment or example, without opinion leader or opinion follower being especially conscious of what is happening.

Opinion leadership is not a matter of social leadership. Opinions about most products or brands do not flow from upper class to lower class. Opinion leaders are found at all social strata, as people "take their cues" about new products or brands from neighbors, friends, fellow workers, or others with whom they have social contacts.

There are different opinion leaders for each product class. Although the opinion leader has been characterized in many general ways (for example, in terms of his or her gregariousness, social and geographic mobility, and so on) the main characteristic of an opinion leader is greater-than-average interest in or heavier-than-average use of the type of product or service in question.

The very first people to adopt a new product will not necessarily be the opinion leaders for that product. Such "innovators" are often an extremely interested minority, with specialized and largely unshared interests in the product class. Widespread belief of an advertising message or adoption of the product will likely require that the message or product "catch on" with a larger minority who have many contacts with the slow-to-believe or slow-to-adopt majority.

The advertiser may gain very little advantage from any attempt to cater

[14]Elihu Katz and Paul F. Lazarsfeld, *Personal Influence: The Part Played by People in the Flow of Mass Communications* (Glencoe, Illinois: The Free Press, 1955).
[15]Elihu Katz, "The Two-step Flow of Communication: An Up-to-date Report on an Hypothesis," *Public Opinion Quarterly*, Vol. 21 (Spring, 1957), pp. 61-78.

to the opinion leader or to reinforce the two-step flow of beliefs. If his product can be accepted with a minimum of financial or social risk—if people typically make up their own minds about such products—the advertiser should ignore the opinion leader and short-circuit the "two-step flow."

Curiosity Versus Disbelief

In the light of the foregoing discussion, one thing is very clear. *Advertising is most likely to be believed when its purpose is to reinforce already existing attitudes toward the product.*

While such "reminder" advertising is usually very believable, "it is *minding* them in the first place" (creating a new attitude or changing an old one) that causes problems.

When the advertiser's task involves *persuasion*—that is, a change, rather than a mere reinforcement of attitudes—belief is likely to come slowly. A single advertisement will rarely account for a change from complete nonbelief or disbelief to complete belief in the merits of a product or service.

Therefore, it may be more important for advertisers to forget about the "believability" of single advertisements and to turn attention to the individual advertisement's potential for contributing to a cumulative influence upon consumers' beliefs. *There is an important difference between the expectation that a single advertisement should be believed in an absolute sense and the expectation that it should contribute to a gradual, eventual belief.*

If asked about his reaction to a given advertisement, a consumer may say, "I don't believe it." Such responses can be very misleading. The consumer may be reflecting *actual disbelief* of the message, or he may be reflecting a *curious nonbelief* of the sort that implies, "It sounds too good to be true."

The author's own research has shown that the latter sort of response, although it may seem negative in a superficial sense, is actually conducive to "nudging" the consumer along the path of the product adoption process.[16]

Ten Conclusions

Here are ten important conclusions to be drawn:

1. Different consumers bring different beliefs, interests, and attitudes to an advertisement; and an advertisement which is believable to some people will not be believable to others. To evaluate the belief of advertising, one must

[16]Same reference as in footnote 1, at p. 3.

know *who* should believe and *what* should be believed in terms of the advertiser's intentions.

2. Consumers' already existing beliefs or attitudes relate to many separate stages of believing advertisements. As a preliminary to belief, the consumer must focus attention upon the advertisement once he is exposed to it. In doing this, he makes a very general "what-this-is-all-about" judgment of the advertisement. At this early stage, the advertisement loses any chances of being believed unless it somehow relates to previously developed beliefs, interests, or attitudes.

3. Once the consumer focuses attention on an advertisement, the advertising message must find its way to the consumer's already existing attitudes *toward the product* without being side-tracked. Too often the advertising message is "misindexed" at this stage because: (a) it is too "addy" and simply reminds the consumer of advertising rather than the product; (b) it is too remindful of competitors' products or services; or (c) it starts a chain of thoughts about irrelevant attention-getting devices in the advertising.

4. Once the advertisement is seen as being germane to the consumer's way of looking at the product or service, the main impediment to belief is unconscious distortion of the intended meaning of the advertising message. In order to make the meaning of the message fit in with his old attitudes, the consumer may "level" the message, overlooking parts of the message with which he disagrees; or he may "sharpen" the message, adding certain meanings to the advertisement which the advertiser had not really intended. In either case, the distortion of the message meaning precludes any chance of belief. ("Sharpening" *sometimes* works to the advertiser's advantage *if* the consumer's attitudes toward the product are already favorable.)

5. If the consumer focuses attention on the advertisement, indexes it properly, and does not distort its meaning, he may believe the advertising message only temporarily. There are two main reasons that much apparent belief of advertising fails to hold up over time. One is the simple fact that consumers cannot or will not remember all the things about a product that advertisers might like them to remember. Second, much belief of advertising is tentative belief, not sufficiently well supported by the consumer's earlier experiences or previously developed attitudes. Such tentative belief will fade unless there is early support from future experiences with the product, repeated exposure to similar advertising, or word-of-mouth advertising.

6. No single advertisement is likely to be believed completely if belief requires the consumer to change his mind about the product. Unless the consumer is already "sold" on a product, complete belief in new products, involving "adoption" of them, may take months or even years.

7. Advertising is especially effective for making people aware of, interested in, *or curious about* new or improved products; and thus advertising is a very effective aid to developing *tentative belief* in a product. While advertising

also helps to induce trial of the product, complete belief in the product's merits usually requires that the selling messages be supported by sales personnel, and the comments or example of family members or acquaintances.

8. Within the groups of people to whom consumers look for example and guidance in making product or brand choices, there is a minority of people who are especially interested in the product class. These "opinion leaders" often relay advertising messages to others or reinforce the "believability" of these messages for others—by example or by word of mouth. Thus, there often tends to be a "two-step flow" of advertising influence—from the advertising to "opinion leaders," and from "opinion leaders" to "opinion followers."

It is sometimes to the advertiser's advantage to cater to the "opinion leaders" and to capitalize upon the "two-step flow" of advertising influence. Sometimes, however, the advertiser is better off to ignore the potential "opinion leaders" and to shortcircuit the "two-step flow" of advertising. The latter course of action is no doubt best when the consumer feels little risk in believing in the product or service, that is, when he can make a brand choice without feeling any need to depend upon the guidance of others.

9. The advertiser must always be concerned about having his message noticed; and consumers should be able to recognize easily that the message relates to the advertised product in a way that is relevant to their own needs or interests. However, the advertiser need not be too concerned about advertising messages which "sound too good to be true" *if* the consumer has a real opportunity to find out that they *are* true.

10. Finally, the advertiser must remember that the most persuasive advertising messages are those which are most congruent with the consumer's experiences, both past and future. And it is not just the consumer's experience of seeing, hearing, or reading advertisements that matters.

One-at-a-time advertising exposures do not account for belief by themselves. ALL BELIEVABLE ADVERTISING IS, TO SOME DEGREE, "REMINDER ADVERTISING."

28

From Mass Media to
Class Media

THEODORE PETERSON

Last October *Coronet* magazine died, a month short of its 25th anniversary. At that time it had more than two million subscribers (most of them attracted by bargain offers) and single-copy sales of about 750,000 a month. It had made considerable gains in advertising linage and revenue in 1960. Even so, it had been running at a loss—$600,000 a year, according to trade reports. In short, its situation was similar to that of many other magazines.

Coronet's fall, however, was a mere thud compared with the loud crash that Crowell-Collier Publishing Co. sent reverberating through the industry in 1956 when it killed off *Collier's, Woman's Home Companion* and *American,* with a combined circulation of well over 11 million. But it made enough noise to remind publishers of the essential mortality of their offspring.

It was a reminder they scarcely needed. Twelve of the 47 magazines that had circulations of at least one million a decade ago are gone today. In recent months, to strengthen their hold on readers and advertisers, both *Life* and *Saturday Evening Post** have come up with drastic design changes. Even before December, when Curtis Publishing Co. told stockholders that its operating loss for the previous nine months had been more than $11 million, insiders knew that the publisher of *Ladies' Home Journal, Saturday Evening Post* and other magazines were having a hard time. Probably every publisher has worried to some degree about the economic health of the industry.

Just what is the condition of magazine publishing today? How has it fared in the past dozen or so years since television emerged as a major competitor for advertising and audiences? What is the outlook for the future?

In some ways, the industry seems in remarkably robust health. Advertising revenues in 1960 were $941 million, an all-time high. And indications are that the 1961 revenues are only slightly behind this record. Forecasters expect

Reprinted from *Challenge*, The Magazine of Economic Affairs, a publication of Challenge Communications, Inc., 475 Fifth Ave., New York, N. Y. 10017. (March, 1962), pp. 6-9.
*[Editor's note: *Saturday Evening Post* folded in February, 1969.]

present advertising income to double by 1975. Individual magazines continue to pull in advertising grosses that would have made publishers of an earlier day envious. *Life* alone in 1960 had advertising receipts substantially larger than the combined total for the 30 magazines that led in advertising revenues in 1925. Just one issue last November, the pre-Christmas peak, brought in $5,202,000, a sum that many a major publisher of the 1920s or 1930s would have considered a good showing for the entire year.

Circulations, too, are at an all-time peak, and there is little evidence that they have approached the saturation point. Even the Television Bureau of Advertising, scarcely an agency to give comfort to a competitor, has acknowledged that increases in magazine circulation have kept a pace or two ahead of increases in the population.

Despite those encouraging signs, however, publishers have good cause for gloomy day and fretful nights. Two out of every five consumer magazines are running at a loss, according to the industry's own estimates, and profits for the remainder have slid alarmingly downward in the past decade. In 1950, 35 of the largest publishers had average profits, after taxes, of 4.3 per cent. By 1960 that figure had fallen to 1.7 per cent, and in 1961 it was almost certainly lower.

Most of the troubles afflicting magazines, some commentators say, stem from the spectacular growth of television as a competing medium in the past 15 years. TV now penetrates 90 per cent of American homes, and today the typical youngster leaving high school has spent more time before his family's set than in the classroom. Advertising billings of networks and local stations climbed from virtually nothing in 1947 to about $1.8 billion in 1961.

Actually, however, researchers have found little proof that television has seriously diminished the amount of reading done by the public. What it apparently does curtail is certain *kinds* of reading. TV evidently cuts into reading time once given to fantasy and escape, but it does not seem to affect reading for information. That is the assumption of magazine editors who have drastically reduced their fiction offerings while expanding the space devoted to nonfiction. And it is the conclusion reached by Dr. Edwin Parker of the Institute of Communications Research at the University of Illinois in several of his investigations.

Parker found that TV has made inroads into the time that children spend on such escapist fare as comic books, movies and radio; it does not seem to have cut into their use of such informational media as books, newspapers and magazines. The same general pattern seems to hold for book reading among adults, according to a still-unpublished study Parker has made of the effects of television on library circulations in Illinois. On the average, TV reduced circulations by just slightly more than one book per capita per year—and that drop was in fiction. Parker found no change in the circulation of nonfiction attributable to TV, although it has increased as a result of other factors.

Nor is there any really convincing proof that television has deprived magazines of advertising revenues. The $941 million that advertisers spent in magazines in 1960 was about 52 per cent more than they spent in 1947, when TV began its meteoric rise. No one can say, of course, how much more money they would be spending in magazines today if television had never come along.

But, by some standards, the advertising income of magazines seems to have grown at about the same rate since the advent of television as in the past. Except for dips in 1949 and 1958, revenues have grown at a steady pace since the 1930s. From 1935 through 1950 the number of dollars that magazines took in from advertising closely paralleled consumer expenditures on goods. That ratio has not fallen in the age of television. If anything, it has slightly increased.

The real banes—and boons—of magazine publishing go back to the 1890s, when a few publishers saw that mass production was beginning to stimulate a boom in advertising. To take advantage of it, they produced magazines, not for the educated well-to-do, as most publishers had in the past, but for the growing middle class. This approach revolutionized the publishing business.

The principle on which these publishers operated, and which they have bequeathed to their successors, is really quite simple. The publisher typically sells his product at less than production cost. By holding down the price to readers, he hopes to build a large circulation; that circulation can bring him enough advertising money to cover his costs and to provide him a profit as well.

In practice, however, the system rarely works that simply. Things over which the publisher has little or no control can quickly convert the black ink in his ledgers to red. If advertisers curtail their budgets, his large circulation is a liability instead of an asset. Seldom can he cut his costs far enough or fast enough to keep income and outgo in balance. His costs, in fact, are quite rigid since he cannot drastically alter his product if he expects to hold his readers and reattract advertisers.

Since the publisher must have a following among advertisers as well as among readers, even editorial success carries its dangers. He may have millions of readers, as *Coronet* did, but not enough advertising to make a profit. And if circulation jumps ahead rapidly, advertising rates may lag behind. The classic case is that of *Life* in its early days, when circulation bounded so far ahead of advertising rates that the magazine lost $5 million in a year and a half.

The whole system makes the publisher especially vulnerable in a period of rising costs. And publishers will tell you glumly how much their basic costs have gone up since 1950—paper by 31 per cent, printing by 44 per cent, postage by 89 per cent, salaries by 41 per cent.

Today fierce competition has intensified these inherent problems. Although publishers have been scrabbling for large circulations since the 1890s, television has made some of them more concerned than ever about reaching mass audiences. Television can deliver a mammoth audience to the advertiser at a comparatively small cost per viewer. Some publishers, fighting TV on its own ground, have gone after mammoth audiences of their own. The A. C. Nielsen Co., a professional audience-counting firm, reports that *Reader's Digest* now reaches 27 per cent of all adults in the U.S., *Life* more than 25 per cent, *Look* 21 per cent and *Saturday Evening Post* approximately 18 per cent.

Fifty magazines now have circulations of one million or more, and for 26 of them the million is simply a floor. Ten have sales of between two million and four million; four between four million and six million; and six between six million and eight million. One, the *Reader's Digest*, which increased its circulation guarantee by one million during 1961, has sales of more than 13 million.

But it is not just television that magazines are battling in their fight for numbers. The leaders are struggling among themselves for supremacy, even for survival. The most dramatic internecine warfare in recent years has been among the women's magazines. A decade ago, *Ladies' Home Journal*, the queen, sat primly on her throne, and advertisers paid her tribute to the tune of about $22 million a year. At her feet were *Woman's Home Companion* and *McCall's*. In 1956 the *Companion* vanished, its advertising far too lean for its circulation. Two years later *McCall's*, under its aggressive new editor, Herbert Mayes, set out to depose the *Journal*.

Mayes gave *McCall's* a new dress, crammed its fat issues with works by well-known authors and loudly proclaimed its changes among advertising agencies. Speaking confidently of sales of 11 million by 1965, he has already pushed *McCall's* ahead of the *Journal* in advertising and circulation. Ad income is almost three times what it was a decade ago. Some issues are hitting sales of eight million to give advertisers a bonus circulation of a million over the base at which rates are pegged. The *Journal* has retaliated by promising advertisers that it will deliver them readers at the same cost per thousand. Throughout the tussle, the magazines have screeched at one another in most unregal fashion.

Magazines have waged their circulation war at heavy cost. Publishers now can build large circulations only at considerable expense, by luring readers with bargain offers. Most major magazines offer new subscriptions at reduced rates, usually at about half the regular price. And such bargain subscriptions make up a large share of the circulations of many magazines. More than 99 per cent of the new subscriptions and renewals for *Reader's Digest* in the first half of 1961 were at reduced rates. For *Life* the figure was 75 per cent, for *McCall's* 59 per cent.

Some magazines have picked up readers by taking over the subscription lists of publications going out of business. *Look* took over the unexpired *Collier's* subscriptions in hopes of adding a million to its circulation; *Reader's Digest, Saturday Evening Post, Ladies' Home Journal* and *Holiday* have divided up *Coronet's* subscription list.

One reason for all this is that single-copy sales have fallen considerably in recent years. During World War II newsstand sales accounted for about 55 per cent of the circulations of *Life* and *Look;* today they account for less than 10 per cent. For magazines generally, single-copy sales are at about their 1950 levels, although total circulation has risen by about 21 per cent.

The mad race for circulation, some publishers think, is inherently unhealthy. "The lesson for other magazines is to stop chasing numbers," said the editor of *Coronet* upon the demise of that magazine. "If the numbers game continues, it will destroy many more magazines."

Advertisers, too, are concerned about the practice of capturing new readers at any cost. Increasingly, they have complained that they are being called on to bear too large a share of the publisher's cost, the reader too little.

Since circulation costs money unless it pulls in a corresponding volume of advertising, some magazines have had to dip into their reserves or tap other sources of income to stay in business. Several leading publishers have branched out into other areas as profits in their industry have slumped.

Time Inc., which has owned TV stations since 1952, has expanded its broadcasting operations at home and abroad in the past year. It has also aggressively entered the book publishing field. *Reader's Digest* last year added a record club to its book club. Meredith Publishing Co. has long had broacasting stations and a book department besides its *Better Homes and Gardens* and *Successful Farming.* In the past two years it has bought up several trade, text and technical book publishing firms and has begun selling teaching machines and related materials. Macfadden Publications last year acquired new interests in radio stations, pay television and paperback books.

In their preoccupation with sheer numbers, some observers think, magazines have renounced one of their traditional strengths—the ability to attract a highly selected audience for the advertiser. Last December, Fairfax Cone, advertising agency head, said that the huge circulations magazines boast about are not really very impressive. He pointed out that the advantage of numbers lies clearly with TV, and that the unassailable advantage of magazines is their selective market.

America no doubt will continue to have its super magazines of multi-million circulation. But the big successes in the years ahead quite probably will be among magazines that pinpoint their appeal to some clearly defined audience with special taste, needs or interests.

The plight of the circulation leaders with their high costs, high risks and low profits should discourage anyone but the most venturesome from starting a new publication of broad appeal. A mass-oriented publication needs millions of readers before it can even begin to divert the attention of advertisers from television. It needs an almost prohibitively hefty bankroll to get it started and to keep it going until it attracts advertiser and reader followings—if it ever does.

In contrast, a publisher can experiment with a specialized magazine at much lower cost. If his experiment fails, as it well might, he may be able to count his losses in the thousands or hundreds of thousands instead of in the millions. But if the publication finds a receptive audience that advertisers want to reach, the backers may get a good return on their investment.

The case of *Playboy* offers a striking example. Its publisher, Hugh Hefner, recently remarked: "In our own case, we happily decided to try reaching and entertaining the young urban male market, and in eight years *Playboy* has blown our personal investment of $600, plus a borrowed additional $7,000, into a complex of corporations, the present value of which must be somewhere in the neighborhood of $20 million, with most of the expansion still ahead."

Strange as it may seem, television has helped to give publications with sharply limited audiences a new reason for existence. TV and the mass magazines are aiming at a substantial proportion of the total population, and they are bound by the tastes, interests and beliefs of the great majority. They cannot afford to explore at great length and depth subjects of concern to just a minority, even a sizable minority. They have left a big place for specialized magazines that can give the hi-fi fan or the boating enthusiast or the sports car buff the specialized information that he wants and in the desired detail.

Vernon C. Myers, publisher of *Look*, has neatly summed up the case for the specialized magazine: "As education, income and leisure time have continued to rise, the interests of the American people have ranged more broadly and more deeply into more subjects than ever before. Hence, it's not surprising that many new magazines are appearing to cater to specific needs and interests."

And appear they have. In the past year publishers have hopefully launched or planned dozens of new magazines aimed at modest followings among persons interested in campus life, antique airplanes, the effects of environment on human life, high fashion, FM listening, the problems of growing old, European travel and a good range of other subjects, some bordering on the esoteric. The very titles of some of the new magazines reflect their limited appeal—*Asia, Back Stage, Candlepin Bowler, Country Club Woman, Pool Life, Private Pilot, Show, Ski Life, Tape, Underwater.*

Odds are strong, of course, that a high proportion of the magazines started in the past year or two will fail. Some already have. Some of those projected were abandoned before their first issue. Some were begun with more faith than finance, and still others seem to have woefully overestimated their potential.

Yet publishers of sharply focused magazines can take a good deal of encouragement from what has been happening to their kind of publishing in the era of the picture tube. Specialized magazines, especially the chiefly informational ones, have made some of the greatest gains in circulation and in pages of advertising. Magazines beamed at high-brow audiences have soared ahead while those attuned to less educated segments of the public have definitely lost ground.

Take, for example, *Scientific American*. It was a feeble publication, long past its prime, when two young journalists bought it for $40,000 in 1947.

Their aim was to bridge a gap between the educated layman and scientists working at the outposts of discovery. Their contributors have included 25 Nobel Prize winners and scientists such as Albert Einstein, Jonas Salk, Linus Pauling and James Van Allen. In 14 years, circulation increased sevenfold to 300,000 and advertising income 63 times to some $4,667,000.

Their story is more dramatic than most, but what happened to *Scientific American* has been happening on a lesser scale to other magazines. Consider a few figures. Between 1950 and 1960, total magazine circulations increased by 21 per cent, the number of pages of advertising by 10 per cent. In that same period, the combined circulations of the major newsweeklies—*Newsweek, Time, U.S. News & World Report*—climbed by 89 per cent, their advertising pages by 27 per cent. Two monthly magazines usually identified with the intellectual elite—*Atlantic* and *Harper's*—raised their combined circulations by 50 per cent, their advertising pages by 85 per cent. *Saturday Review's* sales were up by 145 per cent, its advertising pages by 63 per cent.

On the other hand, the three leading mass circulation weeklies and bi-weeklies—*Life, Look* and *Saturday Evening Post*—carried 30 per cent fewer advertising pages in 1960 than in 1950, although their revenues had grown as a result of rate increases.

As existing magazines of special purpose have been pushing ahead, they have been joined by a flock of newcomers. *The Reporter* was launched in 1949 to interpret national and international affairs. More recently *Current* has come along to combine excerpts from speeches, documents and other sources into coherent discussions of current issues and *Atlas* provides an interesting sampling of the world's press. *American Heritage, Horizon* and *Wisdom* have been started for cultured and affluent readers. *Sports Illustrated* in 1954 began reporting the "wonderful world of sport" for fans who do not have to sit in the bleachers.

Meanwhile magazines that drew their readers from the lower educational levels have been dropping behind. The combined circulations of five leading "confession" magazines last year were only 90 per cent of what they were in 1950. Those of four top movie fan magazines were 53 per cent.

Publishing for closely knit interest groups neither guarantees big profits nor provides immunity from the ills that have killed scores of magazines in recent years. Yet, for more than three decades, the *New Yorker* has shown that a magazine can earn a comfortable living by worrying less about the number of its readers than about the kind.

The *New Yorker* has never pretended to be a magazine for everyone; its pitch is to the sophisticated, urban reader with money. Although it gently reminds readers when their subscriptions are about to expire, the *New Yorker* has little use for circulation campaigns and bargain offers. It counts on people who want it to seek it out. Yet its circulation has grown steadily, and its renewal rate is one of the highest in the industry.

The *New Yorker* likes advertisers, but it does not fawn over them. It has been turning down some $250,000 worth of advertising a year because the products would not appeal to its readers, or because the copy and layout were below its standards, or because space was unavailable. Late in 1959 it announced that it would hold advertising to 5,000 pages in 1960 because it could not obtain high-quality editorial matter to balance more than that. Grumbled one advertising executive: "Their salesmen do not see you, they grant you an audience; their advertising departments do not sell advertising, they accept it."

The *New Yorker* has made money every year except for the first faltering three. Its 1960 profits after taxes were 10 per cent of its revenues of $18,606,488. That is a record many a publisher would envy.

Some magazines are growing lustily; others show signs of decay; still others are only memories. There is little likelihood that new mass circulation magazines will appear. But, by and large, the prospects for specialty magazines seem bright.

29

The Impact of Television Advertising: Learning Without Involvement

HERBERT E. KRUGMAN

Among the wonders of the twentieth century has been the ability of the mass media repeatedly to expose audiences numbered in millions to campaigns of coordinated messages. In the post-World War I years it was assumed that exposure equaled persuasion and that media content therefore was the all-important object of study or censure. Now we believe that the powers of the mass media are limited. No one has done more to bring about a counterbalancing perspective than ex-AAPOR president Joseph Klapper, with his well-known book *The Effects of Mass Media*,[1] and the new AAPOR president Raymond Bauer, with such articles as "The Limits of Persuasion."[2]

It has been acknowledged, however, that this more carefully delimited view of mass media influence is based upon analysis of largely noncommercial cases and data. We have all wondered how many of these limitations apply also to the world of commerce, specifically advertising. These limitations will be discussed here as they apply to television advertising only, since the other media include stimuli and responses of a different psychological nature, which play a perhaps different role in the steps leading to a purchasing decision.

The tendency is to say that the accepted limitations of mass media do apply, that advertising's use of the television medium has limited impact. We tend to feel this way, I think, because (1) we rarely feel converted or greatly persuaded by a particular TV campaign, and (2) so much of TV advertising content is trivial and sometimes even silly. Nevertheless, trivia have their own special qualities, and some of these may be important to our understanding of the commercial or the noncommercial use and impact of mass media.

To begin, let us go back to Neil Borden's classic Harvard Business School

Reprinted from *Public Opinion Quarterly* (Fall, 1965), pp. 349-356.
[1]Joseph Klapper, *The Effects of Mass Media*, Glencoe, Ill., Free Press, 1960.
[2]Raymond Bauer, "The Limits of Persuasion," *Harvard Business Review*, September-October, 1958, pp. 105-110.

351

evaluation of the economic effects of advertising.[3] Published in 1942, it concluded that advertising (1) accelerates growing demand or retards falling demand, i.e. it quickens the pulse of the market, and (2) encourages price rigidity but increases quality and choice of products. The study warned, however, that companies had been led to overlook price strategies and the elasticity of consumer demand. This was borne out after World War II by the rise of the discounters!

The end of World War II also brought mass television and an increased barrage of advertising messages. How much could the public take? Not only were early TV commercials often irritating, but one wondered whether all the competition would not end in a great big buzzing confusion. Apparently not! Trend studies of advertising penetration have shown that the public is able to "hold in memory," as we would say of a computer, a very large number of TV campaign themes correctly related to brands. The fact that huge sums and energies were expended to achieve retention of these many little bits of information should not deter us from acknowledging the success of the overall effort.

It is true that in some categories of products the sharpness of brand differentiation is slipping, as advertising themes and appeals grow more similar. Here the data look, as one colleague put it, "mushy." In such categories the product is well on its way toward becoming a commodity; even while brand advertising continues, the real competition is more and more one of price and distribution. But prices, too, are advertised, although in different media, and recalled.

What is lacking in the required "evaluation" of TV advertising is any significant body of research specifically relating advertising to attitudes, and these in turn to purchasing behavior or sales. That is, we have had in mind a model of the correct and effective influence process which has not yet been verified. This is the bugaboo that has been the hope and the despair of research people within the industry. Always there looms that famous pie in the sky: If the client will put up enough money, if he will be understanding enough to cooperate in blacking out certain cities or areas to permit a controlled experiment, if the cities or areas under study will be correctly matched, if the panels of consumers to be studied will not melt away in later not-at-homes, refusals, or changes of residence, if the sales data will be "clean" enough to serve as adequate criteria—*then surely* one can truly assess the impact of a particular ad campaign! Some advertisers, too, are learning to ask about this type of evaluation, while the advertising agencies are ambivalent and unsure of their strength.

This seems to be where we are today. The economic impact of TV advertising is substantial and documented. Its messages have been learned by the public. Only the lack of specific case histories relating advertising to attitudes

---

[3]Neil Borden, *The Economic Effects of Advertising*, Chicago, Irwin, 1942.

to sales keeps researchers from concluding that the commercial use of the medium is a success. We are faced then with the odd situation of knowing that advertising works but being unable to say much about why.

Perhaps our model of the influence process is wrong. Perhaps it is incompletely understood. Back in 1959 Herbert Zielske, in "The Remembering and Forgetting of Advertising," demonstrated that advertising will be quickly forgotten if not continuously exposed.[4] Why such need for constant reinforcement? Why so easy-in and easy-out of short-term memory? One answer is that much of advertising content is learned as meaningless nonsense material. Therefore, let us ask about the nature of such learning.

An important distinction between the learning of sense and nonsense was laid down by Ebbinghaus in 1902 when he identified the greater effects of order of presentation of stimuli on the learning of nonsense material. He demonstrated a U curve of recall, with first and last items in a series best remembered, thus giving rise also to the principles of primacy and recency.[5]

In 1957, many years later, Carl Hovland reported that in studying persuasion he found the effects of primacy and recency greater when dealing with material of lesser ego-involvement. He wrote, "Order of presentation is a more significant factor in influencing opinions for subjects with relatively weak desires for understanding, than for those with high 'cognitive needs'."[6] It seems, therefore, that the nonsensical à la Ebbinghaus and the unimportant à la Hovland work alike.

At the 1962 AAPOR meetings I had the pleasure of reading a paper on some applications of learning theory to copy testing. Here it was reported that the spontaneous recall of TV commercials presented four in a row formed a distinct U curve. In the same paper a re-analysis of increment scores of fifty-seven commercials tested in a three-position series by the Schwerin television testing method also showed a distinct U curve, despite the earlier contentions of the Schwerin organization. That real advertising materials presented in so short a series could produce distinct U curves seemed to confirm that the learning of advertising was similar to the learning of the nonsensical or the unimportant.[7]

What is common to the learning of the nonsensical and the unimportant is lack of involvement. We seem to be saying, then, that much of the impact of television advertising is in the form of learning without involvement, or what Hartley calls "un-anchored learning."[8] If this is so, is it a source of weakness

---

[4]H. A. Zielske, "The Remembering and Forgetting of Advertising," *Journal of Marketing*, January 1959, pp. 239-243.

[5]H. Ebbinghaus, *Grundzuge der Psychologie*, Leipzig, Germany, Veit, 1902.

[6]C. T. Hovland *et al.*, *The Order of Presentation in Persuasion*, New Haven, Yale University Press, 1957, p. 136.

[7]H. E. Krugman, "An Application of Learning Theory to TV Copy Testing," *Public Opinion Quarterly*, Vol. 26, 1962, pp. 626-634.

[8]This is the title of a working manuscript distributed privately by E. L. Hartley in 1964, which concerns his experimentation with new methods of health education in the Philippine Islands.

or of strength to the advertising industry? Is it good or bad for our society? What are the implications for research on advertising effectiveness?

Let us consider some qualities of sensory perception with and without involvement. Last October I participated along with Ray Bauer, Elihu Katz, and Nat Maccoby in a Gould House seminar sponsored by the Foundation for Research on Human Behavior. Nat reported some studies conducted with Leon Festinger in which fraternity members learned a TV message better when hearing the audio and watching unrelated video than when they watched the speaker giving them the message directly, i.e. video *and* audio together.[9] Apparently, the distraction of watching something unrelated to the audio message lowered whatever resistance there might have been to the message.

As Nat put it, "Comprehension equals persuasion": Any disagreement ("Oh no! That can't be true!") with any message must come after some real interval, however minute. Ray asked Nat if he would accept a statement of this point as "Perception precedes perceptual defense," and Nat agreed. The initial development of this view goes back before World War II to the psychologist W. E. Guthrie.[10] It receives more recent support from British research on perception and communication, specifically that of D. E. Broadbent, who has noted the usefulness of defining perception as "immediate memory."[11]

The historical importance of the Maccoby view, however, is that it takes us almost all the way back to our older view of the potent propaganda content of World War I, that exposure to mass media content is persuasive per se! What is implied here is that in cases of involvement with mass media content perceptual defense is very briefly postponed, while in cases of noninvolvement perceptual defense may be absent.

Does this suggest that if television bombards us with enough trivia about a product we may be persuaded to believe it? On the contrary, it suggests that persuasion as such, i.e. overcoming a resistant attitude, is not involved at all and that it is a mistake to look for it in our personal lives as a test of television's advertising impact. Instead, as trivia are repeatedly learned and repeatedly forgotten and then repeatedly learned a little more, it is probable that two things will happen: (1) more simply, that so-called "overlearning" will move some information out of short-term and into long-term memory systems, and (2) more complexly, that we will permit significant alterations in the *structure* of our perception of a brand or product, but in ways which may fall short of persuasion or of attitude change. One way we may do this is by shifting the relative salience of attributes suggested to us by advertising as we organize our perception of brands and products.

Thanks to Sherif we have long used the term "frame of reference," and

[9]L. Festinger and N. Maccoby, "On Resistance to Persuasive Communications," *Journal of Abnormal and Social Psychology,* Vol. 68, No. 4, 1964, pp. 359-366.

[10]E. R. Guthrie, *The Psychology of Learning,* New York, Harper, 1935, p. 26.

[11]D. E. Broadbent, *Perception and Communication,* London, Pergamon Press, 1958, Chap. 9.

Osgood in particular has impressed us with the fact that the meaning of an object may be perceived along many separate dimensions. Let us say that a number of frames of reference are available as the primary anchor for the percept in question. We may then alter the psychological salience of these frames or dimensions and shift a product seen primarily as "reliable" to one seen primarily as "modern."[12] The product is still seen as reliable and perhaps no *less* reliable than before, but this quality no longer provides the primary perceptual emphasis. Similarly, the product was perhaps previously seen as modern, and perhaps no *more* modern now—yet exposure to new or repeated messages may give modernity the primary role in the organization of the percept.

There is no reason to believe that such shifts are completely limited to trivia. In fact, when Hartley first introduced the concept of psychological salience does not tell the whole story, it seems to be one of the dynamics operat- anti-Semitic attitudes in Germany as bring already existing anti-Semitic attitudes into more prominent use for defining the everyday world.[13] This, of course, increased the probability of anti-Semitic behavior. While the shift in salience does not tell the whole story, it seems to be one of the dynamics operating in response to massive repetition. Although a rather simple dynamic, it may be a major one when there is no cause for resistance, or when uninvolved consumers do not provide their own perceptual emphases or anchors.

It may be painful to reject as incomplete a model of the influence process of television advertising that requires changes in attitude *prior to* changes in behavior. It may be difficult to see how the viewer of television can go from perceptual impact directly to behavioral impact, unless *the full perceptual impact is delayed.* This would not mean going into unexplored areas. Sociologists have met "sleeper effects" before, and some psychologists have long asserted that the effects of "latent" learning are only or most noticeable at the point of reward. In this case, it would be at the behavioral level involved in product purchases rather than at some intervening point along the way. That is, the purchase situation is the catalyst that reassembles or brings out all the potentials for shifts in salience that have accumulated up to that point. The product or package is then suddenly seen in a new, "somehow different" light although nothing verbalizable may have changed *up to that point.* What we ordinarily call "change of attitude" may then occur after some real interval, however minute. Such change of attitude after product purchase is *not*, as has sometimes been said, in "rationalization" of the purchase but is an emergent response aspect of the previously changed perception. We would perhaps see it more often if products always lived up to expectations and did not sometimes create negative interference with the emerging response.

I have tried to say that the public lets down its guard to the repetitive

---

[12]Psychological salience was first discussed in this manner by E. L. Hartley, *Problems in Prejudice*, New York, Kings Crown Press, 1946, pp. 107-115.

[13]*Ibid.*, p. 97.

commercial use of the television medium and that it easily changes its ways of perceiving products and brands and its purchasing behavior without thinking very much about it at the time of TV exposure or at any time prior to purchase, and without up to then changing verbalized attitudes. This adds up, I think, to an understandable success story for advertising's use of the television medium. Furthermore, this success seems to be based on a left-handed kind of public trust that sees no great importance in the matter.

But now I wonder about those so-called "limits of effectiveness" of the noncommercial use of the mass media. I wonder if we were not overusing attitudes and attitude changes as our primary criterion of effectiveness? In looking for behavioral changes, did we sometimes despair too soon simply because we did not find earlier attitude changes? I wonder if we projected our own attitudes and values too much onto the audiences studied and assumed that they, too, would treat information about such matters as the United Nations as serious and involving? I wonder also how many of those public-spirited campaigns ever asked their audiences to *do* something, i.e. asked for the kind of concrete behavior that at some point triggers whatever real potentials may have developed for an attitude change to begin or perhaps to complete its work.

I would like to suggest, therefore, that the distinction between the commercial and the noncommercial use of the mass media, as well as the distinction between "commercial" and "academic" research, has blinded us to the existence of two entirely different ways of experiencing and being influenced by mass media. One way is characterized by lack of personal involvement, which, while perhaps more common in response to commercial subject matter, is by no means limited to it. The second is characterized by a high degree of personal involvement. By this we do *not* mean attention, interest, or excitement but the number of conscious "bridging experiences," connections, or personal references per minute that the viewer makes between his own life and the stimulus. This may vary from none to many.

The significance of conditions of low or high involvement is not that one is better than the other, but that the processes of communication impact are different. That is, there is a difference in the change processes that are at work. Thus, with low involvement one might look for gradual shifts in perceptual structure, aided by repetition, activated by behavioral-choice situations, and *followed* at some time by attitude change. With high involvement one would look for the classic, more dramatic, and more familiar conflict of ideas at the level of conscious opinion and attitude that precedes changes in overt behavior.

I think now we can appreciate again why Madison Avenue may be of little use in the Cold War or even in a medium-hot presidential campaign. The more common skills of Madison Avenue concern the change processes associated with low involvement, while the very different skills required for high-involvement campaigns are usually found elsewhere. However, although Madison Avenue generally seems to know its limitations, the advertising researchers tend to be less clear about theirs. For example, from New York to Los Angeles researchers in television advertising are daily exacting "attitude change" or "persuasion" scores from captive audiences, these scores based on question- naires and methods which, though plausible, have not demonstrated predictive validity. The plausibility of these methods rests on the presence of a more or less explicit model of communication effectiveness. Unfortunately, the model in use is the familiar one that assumes high involvement. Perhaps it is the ques- tionnaires and the research procedures themselves that are responsible for creating what high involvement is present, which would not otherwise exist. The wiser or more cautious researchers meanwhile retreat to the possibilities of impersonal exactness in controlled field experiments and behavioral criteria. What has been left out, unfortunately, is the development of a low-involvement model, and the pre-test measures based on such a model. The further develop- ment of this model is an important next step, not only for the perhaps trivial world of television advertising but for the better understanding of all those areas of public opinion and education which, socially important as they may be, may simply not be very involving to significant segments of the audience.

In time we may come to understand the effectiveness of mass media pri- marily in terms of the *consistency* with which a given campaign, commercial or noncommercial, employs talent and research sensitively attuned to the real level of audience involvement. In time, also, we may come to understand that behavior, that is, verbal behavior and overt behavior, is always consistent pro- vided we do not impose premature and narrowly conceived rules as to which must precede, or where, when, and how it must be measured.[14]

[14]The consistency of verbal and overt behavior has also been reasserted by Hovland, who attributes pseudo–differences to those *research designs* which carelessly compare results of laboratory experiments with results of field surveys (C. I. Hovland, "Reconciling Con- flicting Results Derived from Experimental and Survey Studies of Attitude Change," *American Psychologist*, Vol. 14, 1959, pp. 8-17) ; by Campbell, who attributes pseudo- differences to the fact that verbal and overt behaviors have different situational thresholds (D. T. Campbell, "Social Attitudes and Other Acquired Behavioral Dispositions," in S. Koch, ed., *Psychology: A Study of a Science*, Vol. 6, McGraw-Hill, 1963, pp. 94-172) ; and by Rokeach, who attributes pseudo-differences to the fact that overt behavior is the result of interaction between *two* sets of attitudes, one toward the object and one toward the situation, and that most research leaves one of the two attitudes unstudied (M. Rokeach, "Attitude Change and Behavior Change," paper presented at the annual conference of the World Association for Public Opinion Research, Dublin, Ireland, Sept. 9, 1965).

30

Mass Media and Community
Identity in an Interurban Setting

LEO BOGART
and FRANK E. ORENSTEIN

The polar concepts of "community" and "society" have fascinated sociologists for nearly a century of mankind's movement into an epoch
of mass production, mass contact, mass media, and mass mobility. The warm
personal relationships which characterize community ties are often contrasted
with the tenuous, impersonal, secular relationships which we associate with
the Great Society.[1]

If the concept of community involves those human relationships based on
spatial propinquity which are personal, intimate and based on the primary
group, so the concept of the market reflects, in it origins, at least, those relationships based on spatial propinquity which are economic and, therefore, as impersonal as they can be.

To be sure, the relation between seller and buyer, between merchant and
customer, can be as intimate and intense as any that human beings can have.
Anyone who has struck a bargain in an Oriental bazaar knows that the prevailing code of negotiation places more stress on the game, on the contest of
wills and wits, than on the actual economics of the transaction.

But in its historical origins, the emergence of the market suggests the
evolution of an impersonal social order. In the classic folk society where neighbors are bound together by kinship and friendship ties that pervade all areas
and aspects of life, economic activity is indistinguishable from other cooperative effort that expresses the feelings of solidarity and cohesion.

A market must be on neutral ground. It must provide a physical location

Reprinted from *Journalism Quarterly* (Spring, 1965), pp. 179-188, by permission of
the authors and publisher.

[1]*cf.* Ferdinand Toennies, *Community and Society* (East Lansing: Michigan State
University Press, 1957). Also Robert Redfield, *The Little Community: Viewpoints for the
Study of a Human Whole,* the Gottesman Lectures, Uppsala University, 1935 (Almquist &
Wiksells Boktrycker, AB Uppsala, 1955). See also Henry Maine, *Village Communities East
and West* (New York: Henry Holt & Company, 1889).

which is symbolically separate from personal ties. The bazaar, at the cross-roads or at the ford on the river, admirably fills this function. It is a place to which people from different villages may come to exchange their specialized goods and services. In the market one encounters friends in the midst of strangers. Since earliest history, the exchange of gossip and news has been intermingled with the exchange of goods and services. The market is the point at which the horizons of the individual's daily world are extended to encompass the surrounding environment. In the context of the market the division of labor becomes most meaningful in human terms, as common interests or occupational roles provide a better basis for rapport than mere residential contiguity.

The weekly bazaar settles down and becomes permanent as tradesmen and vendors establish their habitations where they trade and as still others come to provide them with services. The market as an event in time is replaced by the market as a place where people live as well as visit and (later) as inseparable from the community itself.

In time the notion of a market as identical with a town broadened into the concept of the trading area from which people are drawn to do their business. The American rural sociologists of the 1920s were fascinated with the radius of influence that a town casts upon its hinterland.[2] They observed that people were subject to the competing influence of different markets, and that they would be drawn to one or the other depending on distance, the expense and importance of the purchase, and the size of the market.

In the late nineteenth century, the invention of the street car permitted the expansion of cities by extending the feasible range of commuting to work or shopping.[3] But the invention of the automobile has even more drastically changed the relationship between markets and their hinterlands. Throughout the Western world, but most notably in the United States, the explosion of population has created vast built-up areas in which the civic boundaries laid out a hundred years earlier on a surveyor's map no longer set realistic limits on the daily flow of population, the movement of goods, the relationship of residence to work, schooling or friendship associations.

In his book, *Megalopolis*,[4] the French geographer, Jean Gottmann, has vividly portrayed the development of a vast urbanized population belt in the American Northeast. A densely populated connective tissue along highways and railroads leads from town to town in a continuous sprawl with occasional focal or nodal points. The inhabitants of this urbanized zone share the common culture and values of the metropolitan society. The traditional definitions of community, city, market are made obsolete. The Census Bureau, in defining

[2] As an illustration *cf.* Augustus Washington Hayes, *Rural Sociology* (New York: Longmans Green & Company, 1929), pp. 284-98.
[3] Samuel B. Warner, Jr., *Street Car Suburbs* (Cambridge: Harvard University Press, 1962).
[4] Jean Gottmann, *Megalopolis, the Urbanized Northeastern Seaboard of the United States* (New York: The Twentieth Century Fund, 1961).

its Standard Metropolitan Statistical Areas, is constantly faced with the problem of reconciling the diverse interests of different civic groups.

The Yale University Institute of Urban Studies and the J. Walter Thompson Company have used the term "Interurbia" to describe the growing tendency of major metropolitan areas to link up with each other.[5]

The development of interurban sprawl is unthinkable except as the product of a population growth which has taken place far more rapidly in suburban areas than in central cities. Between 1940 and 1960, the suburban population of the United States grew by 102%, while that of the central metropolitan cities grew by 27% and of non-metropolitan areas by 12%. This concentrated growth has been one of the features of a mobile society in which one out of five persons moves every year and in which three out of four families live today in a residence different from the one they occupied ten years ago.

The world of Interurbia is not one which fits the descriptions of suburbia given by George Lundberg and others a generation ago.[6] In the classical suburbia of the commuter trains (Bronxville, Winnetka, Newton or Chevy Chase) life has a simple two-way flow from suburb to city and back. Every resident has a certain primary loyalty to his community. This is where he sends his children to school, goes to church, has friends, plays, and does his shopping for the main necessities of life. The central city is the place of employment, the place where he goes for major shopping and entertainment, where special private interests can be pursued. Membership in the local community and membership in the metropolitan area community are compatible and clearly differentiated as to function.

By contrast, the very nature of residence in the interurban society involves multi-lateral pressures. The outside attraction is not all from one direction. It may come from a number of different places. There is a choice of focal points for work, for voluntary association, for friendship contacts, for the pursuit of avocational interests and for shopping. Men living next door to each other on the same street in an identical row of houses may leave for work in the morning with entirely different destinations. On the weekend, they may head for still different places to go shopping or to a show.

To be sure, they retain residual loyalties to those institutions which are rooted in their community of residence, to the common schools and churches. They share common interests in the local institutions which minister to the physical space—the police, fire and sanitation departments, and the like. But these functions may assume relatively less significance in a community which lacks the consensus which arises in suburbia where everyone is oriented toward the same metropolitan center.

The changing pattern of human activity within a geographical area has

[5]*Interurbia, the Changing Face of America* (J. Walter Thompson Company).

[6]George Lundberg, *Leisure: A Suburban Study* (New York: Columbia University Press, 1934), Ch. II. Also, Harlan Douglass, *The Suburban Trend* (New York: Century, 1925), pp. 3-37.

weakened the traditional definition of the market as a place where people live and buy. Thus it has become common to use the term "market" differently than in the past, to define a sector of society distinguished by a common state of mind, a common set of interests or a common position in the life cycle.

It is common to speak of the teenage market, the market of junior executives, the market of fashion-minded upper income matrons, or the market of young mothers. This way of thinking has its roots in the very realistic observation that people's social relationships and social identities no longer always center on the places where they live. Similarity of occupational or social roles may be much more important in providing them with a common realm of discourse or interest.

This has been reinforced by the emergence of media, particularly magazines, which cater to special interests and which give them a sense of identity, both to the members of the particular group to whose interests they are directed and also to advertisers.

Mass media only came into existence when the web of interpersonal contact and gossip grew too complex to serve the needs of a society increasingly segmented in its interests and spread over space. Historically, the mass media have been a force of social cohesion insofar as they provide commonly known symbols and heroes and a sense of vicarious participation in events of common interest.

If the mass media give people a sense of identity with others who share common interests, we may wonder how they serve this function in an interurban setting. There the individual may have some loyalty to his local neighborhood, but his contacts may range over a number of surrounding cities and towns. Many of his marketing needs are filled by the shopping centers that have sprung up, without community roots, on the interurban plain. Here nationally branded merchandise is displayed in a setting which is uniform from Maine to California and is supported by advertising directed through the national media to reach consumers at large without regard to the local context.

Among the mass media, magazines and television are generally perceived as having a national orientation and newspapers as local in character. Although newspapers use a great volume of syndicated and wire service material which is the same across the board, they also provide detailed information on local happenings which radio or television cannot match.

The Intercity Study

The present study starts from the hypothesis that even in Interurbia there is a middle range of identification and involvement between the local community of residence and the greater American society which all the mass media reflect and report. Our assumption is that people in an interurban zone have patterns of strong attraction to nearby cities. Among residents of the same interurban community, there should be a wide variety of orientations that arise from different personal mobility patterns; the choice of mass media should reflect the same type of selectivity that is reflected in living, visiting, travelling, shopping and working behavior.

The town of about 25,000 which we shall call Intercity was selected precisely because it lay under cross-pressure from a number of different surrounding towns. Intercity has a relatively long history, an established core or center, and a surrounding suburban sprawl of new development. It lies within easy access of a number of communities ranging in size from several thousand to several hundreds of thousands. Apart from a weekly newspaper it has no mass media of its own, but it is served by mass media emanating from five big cities no more than 40 miles away. (See Table 30-1.) There are a number of other smaller towns and villages within a 25-by-40-mile area around Intercity. Interviews were conducted with 501 household heads on a probability sampling basis by the research firm of Iber Zeisel in October 1962.

Table 30-1. Frequently visited places 20 miles or less from intercity

	Number of Daily Papers	Number of TV Stations
Metropolitan area		
Central City	2	2
Naborcity	1	1
Elm City	2	–
Plant City	2	1
River City	2	1
Non-metropolitan		
Metal Town	1	
Mill Town	1	
Factory Town	0	
North Village	0	
South Village	0	
Middle Village	0	

Intercity comes close to being an average kind of town. The 1960 Census gives the median family income as just short of $7,000, with 17% of the families having incomes between $10,000 and $25,000, and 7% reporting less than $3,000 a year. Over half the wage earners are employed in manufacturing mostly in metals, machinery or machine parts, and the most common jobs are held by skilled workers or operatives. The median number of years of schooling completed by those 25 or over is almost 11. Half the respondents in the survey had completed high school or gone beyond; 28% had had at least some high school; 21% had not gone beyond grade school. Only 7% were college graduates; 12% had some college education. Like any interurban area, Intercity is characterized by a high degree of personal mobility: 18% of the respondents had lived there for less than two years; less than half had been in the town for over ten years. Most of those who had been born elsewhere came from one of the other towns in the area, but no one city accounted for any preponderant number. In fact, no one city accounted for any more than 17% of the moves within the last 15 years. (Contrast this with the classic move from central city to suburbs.)

Intercity, in spite of its interurban location, is an independent community rather than an appendage or suburb of any big town nearby. This is shown by the high proportion of its principal wage earners who work in Intercity itself—37%—and also by the fact that the remainder are spread among a great many of the surrounding communities. (See Table 30-2.)

Table 30-2.   Place of work of main breadwinner (N = 503)

Intercity	37%
Elm City	7
Naborcity	11
Plant City	5
Central City	12
Central City metropolitan area	4
Mill Town	1
Metal Town	4
North Village	6
South Village	2
River City	4
All other places	6
Works in no one place	1

The automobile makes mobility a daily commonplace in Intercity, and it is by no means confined to the principal wage earners who commute to out-of-town jobs. Nearly everyone interviewed (97%) had been out of Intercity for some purpose within the previous four weeks, and 89% had been outside the previous week. Almost everyone left town by car; only a handful had used the bus or train.

Those who did not travel outside Intercity at all in the last week include disproportionately more women, more people at the lower income and educational levels, more old people.

Like work patterns, travel outside Intercity covers a broad array of communities. There is no single "main line" of travel. Within the past week, Elm City and Naborcity had each drawn over a third of the Intercitizens, three other towns had each drawn about a fourth, and eight other communities had been visited by between 2% and 14% each. (Table 30-3.)

Table 30-3.   Places visited in last seven days and in last four
weeks (N=503)

	In Last Four Weeks	In Last Seven Days
Towns in immediate area		
Elm City	58%	37%
Naborcity	51	35
Plant City	27	14
Metal Town	43	29
North Village	31	24
South Village	9	6
Towns in general area		
Central City	44	28
Rest of Central City metropolitan area	15	10
River City	21	11
Mill Town	3	2
Middle Village	6	4
Factory Town	5	3
More distant points		
Far City	6	3
Megalopolis	7	2

People travel out of Intercity for a considerable variety of reasons, and
there are remarkably small differences between men and women. During the
past half year, over a third have gone out of town for medical or dental treatment.

Table 30-4.   Extent of participation in selected out-of-town
activities

	In Last Four Weeks		In Last Seven Days	
	Men (N = 241)	Women (N = 262)	Men (N = 241)	Women (N = 262)
Shopping	67%	79%	50%	53%
Visiting friends or relatives	64	69	47	45
Snack or drink	42	48	26	28
Entertainment	23	23	11	10
Group or club meeting	21	14	13	11

In the past seven days over half have gone shopping in other towns; nearly half of those interviewed have visited out-of-town friends or relatives; over
a fourth have gone elsewhere for a snack, drink or meal; one in ten has gone
to a movie or show; one in ten to a religious service; one in eight has gone to
a meeting of some out-of-town group or club. (Table 30-4.) In addition 31% of

men and 39% of women had sought medical treatment out of town in the last six months.

Sports teams or clubs represent the principal voluntary association activity outside of Intercity. However, most of the athletic teams which people report that they follow with interest are teams from one of the major national centers rather than from one of the nearby cities.

Each of the surrounding towns has a variety of attractions for Intercitizens and yet each town balances these attractions in a way which is uniquely its own. Respondents were asked what the main reason was for their last trip to each city during the past four weeks. Half of those who had gone to Elm City had gone there to shop. In the case of Plant City, the proportion was one in six. Work and social visiting were the two main reasons for visiting Plant City; entertainment was an important reason for a visit to the Central City area; social visiting was the most frequent reason for visiting River City.

Mass Media in Intercity

Most people in Intercity are exposed every day to both daily newspapers and television. "Yesterday," 89% read one or more papers, an average of 1.8 per reader, mostly home-delivered. All but 17% of these people also watched TV, and an additional 9% watched TV "yesterday," though they did not read a newspaper.

Table 30-5. Daily newspapers read "yesterday" (N=503)

Elm City—either paper		35%
Paper 1	11%	
Paper 2	28	
Naborcity		18
Plant City—either paper		6
Paper 1	4	
Paper 2	4	
Central City—either paper		54
Paper 1	47	
Paper 2	14	
Mill Town		*
Metal Town		1
River City—either paper		14
Paper 1	14	
Paper 2	1	
Megalopolis—any paper		12
Paper 1	10	
Paper 2	1	
Others	3	
All other papers		1

*Less than 0.5%.

Intercity is one of those towns where a visitor can drive down a typical street of identical houses and find the different colored mailboxes of papers which originate in different nearby cities. (See Table 30-5.)

In general, those people who read *only* a paper published in one of the larger, more distant cities of the group show a more cosmopolitan outlook than do those who read a paper from one of the smaller, more nearby cities (*regardless* of whether they also read a paper from the more distant metropolis).

Protestants and Catholics, and to a lesser degree Republicans and Democrats, show some interesting but on the whole minor variations in preference for individual daily newspapers.

Table 30-6.   Newspaper choice and place of employment

	Read "Yesterday" Newspaper Published in Each Town		
	All (503) respondents	Respondents in household where someone works in town of publication	
	%	%	n
Elm City	35	61	(59)
Naborcity	18	62	(69)
Plant City	6	44	(27)
Central City	54	67	(92)
Metal Town	1	15	(69)
River City	14	33	(24)
Mill Town	*	33	(3)

*Less than 0.5%.

Intercitizens report themselves to be more interested in national and international news than in local news. However, individual dailies show substantial variation in the extent of their appeal to people who have a national or a local news orientation. One of the Central City papers appeals strongly to readers with a cosmopolitan orientation and one does not. Conversely, one of the Elm City papers appeals strongly to readers with a parochial orientation and one does not. In short, the character of the individual newspaper seems to shape its audience regardless of where that newspaper originates.

Looking at the reasons why people no longer read newspapers that they read in the past, only one out of five refers to the editorial character of the paper as a reason for dropping his subscription. In most cases, situational or geographic reasons are given to explain why a paper is no longer read: a change in job, residence, delivery routes or in family circumstances.

The Daily Newspaper and Personal Mobility

Why do some readers choose to read a daily newspaper that is published in one city while their neighbors pick a paper from another? A number of factors turn out to be highly predictive. Persons who formerly have lived in a nearby town, or who say they might move to another community in the next five years, are present readers of that town's newspaper in seven cases out of ten.

If someone in the family works in a town outside Intercity, this increases the likelihood that members of his family will read a paper published in that town. To take just two illustrations, 6% of the Intercitizens read the Plant City paper "yesterday" but in families where a breadwinner commutes to Plant City, the proportion is 44%. In families with a commuter to Naborcity, 62% read the Naborcity daily; the overall readership is 18%. (Table 30-6.)

Those who go to a particular town are more likely to read that town's newspapers than those who do not. Moreover, the more frequently they visit, the greater likelihood they will read the local paper. (Table 30-7.)

The relationship between visiting and newspaper reading remains the

Table 30-7.   Proportion of visitors and non-visitors to a town who read its newspapers

	Readership among People Who						
	Did not visit in last four weeks[b]		Visited in last four weeks[b]		Visited in last week		Visited five or more times in last week	
		N		N		N		N
Elm City	18%	(212)	47%	(291)	53%	(188)	74%	(27)
Naborcity	4	(249)	32	(254	37	(175)	79	(43)
Plant City	2	(365)	19	(138)	28	(72)	(10)[a]	(16)
Central City	43	(283)	67	(220)	70	(140)	83	(35)
River City	11	(398)	28	(105)	35	(54)	(3)[a]	(12)
Metal Town	–	(288)	3	(215)	3	(144)	(2)[a]	(11)
Mill Town	*	(490)	–	(13)	–	(9)	–	(1)
Far City	–	(472)	–	(31)	–	(17)	–	(1)
Megalopolis	11	(466)	19	(37)	(2)[a]	(12)	–	–

*Less than 0.5%.

[a]Number of visitors too small to permit percentaging of readers.

[b]Chi^2 values were computed for readership among visitors and non-visitors in the last four weeks for each of the first five towns in the table, plus Megalopolis. All observed comparisons were significant beyond the .05 level, except for Megalopolis, an urban complex whose papers enter Intercity in force, but which is too far for easy commutation.

same regardless of the reasons that bring people to visit a town. Whether people went to a nearby community to visit friends, see the doctor, go to a show, restaurant or club meeting, between 40% and 50% had read that town's newspaper "yesterday."

Altogether 41% of the Intercitizens had gone shopping in the past week in a town where a daily newspaper is published. Others, of course, had shopped only in Intercity (which has a complete variety of stores in its business district) or in nearby hamlets, villages or shopping centers where there is no daily newspaper. Of those who had shopped in a newspaper town, 60% had read that town's newspaper "yesterday."

The matter of shopping was narrowed down to a number of specific items in the interview. Between a third and half the respondents reported that they had gone to a newspaper town outside Intercity for their last purchase of a television set, an easy chair or couch, sheets, towels or other linens, a man's suit or better dress, or an automobile.[7] Between half and two-thirds of these people, depending on the item, read "yesterday" a newspaper published in the town where the item was bought.

We found a similar pattern when we asked people where they would go to make their *next* purchase of a suit, better dress or television set.

The presence and substantial (70%) readership of the local weekly newspaper did not appear to have any bearing on the daily newspaper's capacity to select its readers from the ranks of those who were oriented in the direction of its home town. The local weekly's detailed listings of real estate transactions and neighborhood social events appear to supplement rather than conflict with the daily local spot news coverage by those daily papers which maintain bureaus or correspondents in Intercity. This conforms to the findings of Morris Janowitz in his study of "The Community Press in an Urban Setting,"[8] in which he found that neighborhood urban weeklies and metropolitan dailies served complementary functions. (Table 30-8.)

Table 30-8.   Proportions reading intercity weekly paper
among readers and non-readers of daily papers

		n
Total Sample	70%	(503)
Readers of a daily paper "yesterday"	72	(447)
Non-readers of a daily paper	46	(56)

The relationships already discussed have been based on the number of visitors to a town for one purpose or another who read that town's newspapers. Looking at the data from another point of view, the proportion of readers of a paper who visit the town of publication, the same sort of relationship is re-

[7]This last item was covered in a special second interview with 297 respondents.
[8]Morris Janowitz, *The Community Press in an Urban Setting* (Glencoe, Ill.: The Free Press, 1952).

vealed: the readers of a town's papers are much more likely to visit that town than are other people. For instance, in the course of the last week, 57% of the readers of an Elm City paper went to Elm City, while the same is true of only 11% of those who were not among this reader group.

Table 30-9. Watching TV stations located in nearby cities "yesterday" by total sample and visitors

	Total sample	Visitors			
		In last four weeks	n	In last seven days	n
Naborcity	30%	30%	(254)	28%	(175)
Plant City	1	—	(138)	—	(72)
Central City	50	48	(220)	45	(140)
River City	37	42	(105)	41	(54)

Television Viewing and Personal Mobility

Since there is such a strong relation between shopping and visiting a nearby town and reading its daily newspaper, it is reasonable to ask whether television viewing shows the same relationship. Intercity is within viewing range of channels originating in four nearby cities, one of which yielded only 1% of "yesterday" viewers. But between 30% and 50% had watched a channel from one of the other three cities "yesterday." Unlike the daily newspaper data, there is no significant difference between the viewers and non-viewers in the proportion who have in the past week or month visited each of the towns whose TV station they watched yesterday. (Table 30-9.)

Since people are likely to watch more than one channel on a given day, we also asked what channel they watch most often. Here again, there is no difference in visiting between those who watch a town's station most and those who watch channels originating in other communities. (Table 30-10.)

The same pattern applies to shopping—the most frequent reason for visit-

Table 30-10. Channel most frequently watched by visitors

Town of Origin of Most Frequently Watched TV Station	Visitors in Last Four Weeks			
	Naborcity (n = 254)	Plant City (n = 138)	Central City (n = 220)	River City (n = 105)
Naborcity	13%	13%	15%	12%
Plant City	*	—	—	—
Central City	32	36	35	31
River City	17	16	11	15

*Less than 0.5%.

ing another town. Whether we consider those who describe a channel as the one they watch most often or the larger group that watched that channel yesterday, the percentage of those who shop in that TV town is no different than among the non-viewers. (Table 30-11.)

Table 30-11.   TV viewing by shoppers and non-shoppers

	% Naming Channel of TV City (four-city average)	
	"Watched yesterday"	*Watched most often*
During last week		
Shopped in TV cities	31%	19%
Did not shop in TV cities	30	16
During last four weeks		
Shopped in TV cities	32	21
Did not shop in TV cities	30	17

The percentage who have been in each town for any reason within the last seven days shows no particular difference between yesterday viewers and non-viewers. As an example, 33% of those who watched a Naborcity channel yesterday have been in Naborcity within the past seven days. So have 35% of all the other people. But of those who yesterday read the Naborcity newspaper, 72% have gone to that town in the last week, compared to 27% of the non-readers. The results are similar for the other markets.

Of those in Intercity who went shopping within the past week in a television town, 31% watched that town's TV channel yesterday. Of those who have gone shopping within the past week in a newspaper town 60% read one of that town's newspapers yesterday. In a period of growing urban complexity, each daily newspaper sorts out its readers from the surrounding population. Its audience selectively concentrates on those who look to that community as the place to visit and shop.

Additional Conclusions

●The reader's choice of an individual newspaper may reflect his politics, his cosmopolitanism or his ethnicity. But in an area where people have a range of choices, the cities of origin of the newspapers they read reflect their patterns of mobility and orientation.

●In an era of interurban sprawl, people seem to be able to think of different towns accessible to them as having differentiated functions, much as a resident of a metropolis may look to specialized districts or neighborhoods for different services or facilities. There may be a town to work in, a town to play in, a town to shop in, a town where friends or relatives may be found. Each place may evoke a different set of associations with movements that take place at a different time of the day or week.

•Media do seem to define a market, not only in the national sense, as specialized magazines do when they single out people who share an occupational or social interest, but also locally, spatially in the traditional sense. The relation between the newspaper and its market appears to be a two-way affair. People go from Intercity to Plant City, River City or Central City because they see the ads in the papers describing the specials of the day. But they are drawn to read those papers because they are the voice of the very towns where they are accustomed to shop. And the day-after-day, month-after-month exposure to the news minutiae of a particular nearby town inevitably creates a sense of identity with its people and institutions.

•This study adds to the body of literature which shows that media serve complementary rather than competing functions for the public. The weekly paper of the local community is not in competition with the surrounding dailies. It provides a different kind of coverage and focus of interest than the dailies do. Television, with its aura of show-business glamour and the national hook-up, represents a different kind of experience to the consumer than the daily newspapers which reflect primarily informational needs that reflect the individual's local orientation.

•Increased personal mobility in America's growing interurban regions may make meaningless the classical designations of community and society as terms defined in space which determine social allegiances and social ties. In Intercity, there is a crisscrossing of mobility patterns, orientations and allegiances from one community to the next. The areas dominated by each central city interpenetrate with those dominated by others. Each of the surrounding larger centers reaches into Intercity for part of its human traffic and loyalties, and in turn Intercitizens borrow from each.

This study offers a modest demonstration of how people may experience identifications at many different levels. Their actions as consumers in the marketplace are inseparable from their other social roles.

VI

COMMUNICATION
IN PERSONAL
SELLING

MUCH ADVICE ON HOW TO HELP BOOST SALES HAS BEEN OFFERED
to salesman and sales manager alike. The advice has varied considerably in
nature because different formulas work in different situations. Few writers on
salesmanship, particularly ex-salesmen, can be convinced that their method is
not universally applicable. All of these observations demonstrate that personal
selling, like advertising, is a complex applied field for communications science
to tackle. Universal principles for effective personal selling are, alas, unlikely
to be simple statements for salesmen to apply in every situation.

The salesman is an expensive medium for marketing communications, but
experience shows that his flexibility and personal touch, among other potential
qualities, gain the favor of buyers in consumer and industrial marketing situations. In fact, costs notwithstanding, the salesman just cannot be replaced in
many firms' marketing programs.

Numerous false principles of salesmanship have become accepted because
of a lack of scientific testing. The selections in this part explore some of the
unwarranted assumptions made about personal selling. In addition, the reader
will find positive attempts to set forth what is known about personal selling.

31

Research in Personal Selling
JAMES G. HAUK

Personal selling today is regarded largely as a process of personalized persuasion, communication, and service. From the firm's viewpoint it is carried out by individuals who are given titles such as company representative, sales engineer, communications consultant, account executive, detail man, and other titles which partly describe the nature of the job. Because persuasion, communication, and service pervade nearly all selling positions, however, each is elaborated on below. They represent alternative points of view which can be emphasized in developing theory in personal selling and in conducting empirical research on it.

Psychology of Persuasion

One of the major purposes of the salesman is to persuade present and prospective customers to buy. In order to persuade effectively he must communicate and serve the customer so that needs are satisfied. Some would argue that emphasis should be placed on discovering the motives responsible for purchase, measuring their relative importance, and manipulating the most important motives. Salesmanship books have presented various theories oriented in this general direction. Professor Bursk has offered an additional hypothesis.

> I claim that persuasion is more a matter of strategy than of manipulation; that it is a process of arraying logical forces so that people themselves decide to do what you want them to do, rather than actually changing people's minds; and that any effort to get action by tampering with people's emotions not only runs up against the psychological limi-

Reprinted from *Science in Marketing*, George Schwartz, ed., New York, John Wiley & Sons, Inc., 1965, pp. 219-228.

tations of resistance, but also can be prohibitively time consuming and expensive.[1]

His hypothesis also emphasizes the importance of discovering the self-approved motives which will give the customer a rationalization for buying. Appeals to these motives are often more effective than appeals to the real motives for purchase.

Many practicing salesmen emphasize the significance of the individual situation. They maintain that no single approach holds the key unless the approach is to adjust to each customer situation according to the circumstances. One of the frequently stated advantages of personal selling over advertising is flexibility in adapting messages to individual customer motives and needs.

In placing selling theory on a sound foundation there is need for utilizing the basic research conducted in psychology and sociology. For example, Festinger's theory of cognitive dissonance could provide a basis either for formulating theory in selling or for empirical testing as applied to the selling process. Dissonance often exists before the purchase decision is made as well as subsequent to it. It has been maintained that the buyer may go into a state of "virtual panic" as he reaches the point of decision in buying an automobile for example. He may rush into the purchase as an escape from the problem or he may simply put off the purchase because of the difficulty of deciding on the car which is best for him. The salesman's role at this point in the purchase cycle would differ from that during the early stages of the consumer's search process.

Salesmanship could also be approached with the hypothesis suggested in an early paper that the relationship between the salesman's characteristics and the customer's characteristics is pertinent in explaining the salesman's persuasive power. This appears to be the one used in a study of life insurance agents. The attempt is to determine the characteristics of both the salesman and his prospects, half of whom purchased from him and half of whom did not purchase from him. The research covers the salesman's opinion of the prospects, the prospect's opinion of the salesman, personality, social and sociometric characteristics of both salesman and prospect, as well as a number of other phenomena.[2]

Ethics of Persuasion

Some would argue that the study of ethics has no place in the development of science in marketing, but for a number of reasons, which I will

[1]Edward C. Bursk, "Opportunities for Persuasion," *Harvard Business Review*, Vol. XXXVI, No. 5 (September-October 1958), p. 111.
[2]Franklin B. Evans, "A Sociological Analysis of the Selling Situation: Some Preliminary Findings," *Emerging Concepts in Marketing*, William S. Decker (ed.), AMA, Chicago, 1963, pp. 476-482.

not discuss here, my opinion differs. Certainly if the empirical and philosophical study of ethics in selling is excluded we will never attain completely the kind of knowledge about marketing which is desirable and necessary in a free society.

It has been noted that the significant ethical problem is not *whether* persuasion should be exercised but *how* it should be exercised. There may be a number of unanswered questions in both areas, however. They are particularly pertinent in a highly specialized economy where the salesman usually knows more about the product at the time of negotiation than does the buyer. Many of the problems are ignored or, in some cases, examined in a biased way.

First, I am referring to the question of whether or not it is acceptable for a knowledgeable person to persuade a less knowledgeable one to buy his product when the competitor's product would do a better job. Certainly there is often uncertainty as to which product would work in the customer's best interests. In addition, one might argue that if all competing salesmen persuade on behalf of their own products the outcome of the rivalry will be desirable for the customer. In this sense the competitive persuading is analogous to the court of law where prosecutor and defense each present a one-sided case.

It may be that the question of relative knowledge between the seller and the buyer is not significant. However, if the knowledge and maturity discrepancy is taken to the extreme, cases arise which cause one to wonder. Advertising frequently is directed at children, but is it acceptable for a mature salesman to persuade children to buy products?

No attempt will be made to evaluate such issues. Instead, the point is that there are many questions which could be dealt with more intensively. In addition to those already cited, the following continue to be relevant to the selling field: Does the salesman have any obligation to present the "truth" about his product or service to the customer? Should he withhold facts from the customer which will damage his chances for securing the sale, even though the customer requests them? How far can selling justifiably go in invading the privacy of the individual? Is subliminal selling acceptable?

A study of 129 executives attending the 1963 Graduate School of Sales Management and Marketing at Syracuse University yielded an interesting result. The executives were independently asked whether or not they thought sales management had an ethical responsibility to the customer beyond the requirements of the law. Nearly all the executives felt that such responsibilities did exist, and the vast majority were very strong in their feelings. While one can interpret such findings in a number of ways, they are symptomatic of some basic issues.

Studying the ethical question from a historical point of view is also revealing: ". . . and there shall be no praising goods, or oath taken about them. If a person disobey this command, any citizen who is present, not being less than thirty years of age, may with impunity chastize and beat the swearer."[3]

---

[3] William T. Kelley, "Development of Early Thought in Marketing and Promotion," *Journal of Marketing*, Vol. XXI, No. 1 (January, 1957), pp. 62-63.

Of course, as Kelley points out, there were merchants in ancient Athens (who undoubtedly praised their goods), and they were probably not beaten. Plato's laws were proposals for an "ideal" state.

The later views of Thomas Aquinas suggest a tolerance for persuasion but insistence on high standards, particularly with regard to the sale of defective goods. Such a philosophy is markedly different from that implied in the Law Merchant during the Middle Ages: Every bargain, once consummated was to remain closed, "and if the purchaser repents of his purchase, and wished to recede from the contract, let him lose what he has given."[4]

Selling as a Communications Process

Personal selling can also be researched from the communications point of view. Some would argue that all communication has persuasion as its intent or result. Others simply define selling as a communication process with emphasis on the outflow of information from the salesman to the buyer. It is designed to cause the buyer to perceive the product as an aid in achieving his goals. It can be accurate or untruthful, and while persuasion may be the purpose, it accomplished this purpose by the provision of information. A variation of this view is to regard personal selling as *two-way* communication, while advertising is one-way communication. Salesmanship cannot only individualize and personalize outflow messages, it can also facilitate the informational feedback which is necessary to the development of a system.

In integrating personal selling with communications theory, it should be recognized that the communications process is basically a medium of social interaction. With selling, it is a medium between the salesman and the customer. Consequently, any integration attempt should recognize basic knowledge about human interaction as well as about communications. With respect to the latter, the major elements are the source, encoding, the message, the channel, decoding, and the receiver. Selling could be studied with these elements as the general structure. This requires an understanding of the psychology and sociology of each element, if the study is to be effective.

The informational role of the salesman justifies a communications emphasis. Not only must specialized firms be coordinated, but, in an economy where the rate of product innovation is high, sound buying depends on sound information. For example, buyers need information on the existence of the innovation, on whether to try it out, and on how to put it into effect, including instructions on use and perhaps repair. Where and how does the salesman fit in the process of providing the needed information?

[4]W. Mitchell, *An Essay on the Early History of the Law Merchant*, University Press, Cambridge, 1904, p. 3.

One early study of the introduction and acceptance of hybrid seed corn among farmers indicated that salesmen were the most important source of information regarding the *existence* of the product.[5] His importance declined, however, as the product was diffused through the market. Several years subsequent to product introduction the new purchaser was most likely to hear about it from neighbors.

The sources of information most influential in actually inducing the farmer to buy also varied over time: salesmen were most influential during early years and neighbors most influential in later years. A more recent study indicates that mass media, agricultural agencies, and other farmers were the most important sources of first knowledge, while commercial sources ranked high in providing information on how much material to use, where to use it, and other problems of application.[6] As the studies suggest, the salesman's communication function relative to that of other information sources will vary over time and between products.

In introducing new technical products to the market, the salesman may be crucial, for potential users may have to be located and the benefits of the product explained. And in marketing established products, new users enter the market, often as ignorant of the facts pertinent to selection as the consumer who purchased the product during the innovation stage of the product cycle. Personal communication is particularly significant in marketing high priced products where careful deliberation characterizes customer buying behavior.

Such questions as the following should be answered: What proportion of the total communication task should be allocated to the salesman? What kinds of informational outflow should be assigned to them? What kinds of information are best collected by the salesman? In what industry situations is the sales representative primarily a disseminator of information and in what situations is he primarily a collector of information? These are only a few of the questions on the communication role of the salesman which deserve attention.

Service for Need Satisfaction

Another view to take is to regard selling as a process of providing individualized service to satisfy the customer's needs. The sales representative may go far in surveying the customer's operations as a basis for designing the product or for recommending the product best able to solve his problems. He may also help in installing it, in demonstrating it, in training the customer's employees to use it, and in repairing it subsequent to sale. In this respect the

[5]Bryce Ryan and Neal C. Gross, "The Diffusion of Hybrid Seed Corn in Two Iowa Communities," *Rural Sociology*, Vol. VIII, No. 1 (May 1943), p. 19.

[6]Eugene A. Wilkening, "Roles of Communicating Agents in Technological Change in Agriculture," *Social Forces* (May 1956), pp. 361-367.

selling function may be one of supplying individualized service to the customer rather than attempting to deal with his emotions.

One sales manager in the industrial paint industry argues that technical service is the essence of selling in his company. Another sales manager in handling orthopedic products does not employ salesmen. Service to the customer is so important in selling his product that he employs only "service representatives." Others find that selling is a highly complex job which may call for a group approach where several company specialists combine their specialized skills to solve customer problems. In some cases technical representatives from competing concerns cooperate in designing and installing a system which requires the use of the products produced by each of the competing firms.

In this general area the lack of knowledge is embarrassing. Not much is known, for example, about the condition under which selling and technical service should be assigned to the same company representatives and, conversely, the conditions under which it should be specialized. In part, the lack of attention springs from the fact that until recently service itself had been largely ignored in marketing literature. This has helped to hide the very existence of specialization possibilities. A thorough examination could be made of business practice to identify the factors conducive to specializing the two.

There is also the question of how far the salesman should go in specifying the product needed by the customer and in specifying the need itself. One manager in the roller bearing industry maintains that product specifications is the prerogative of the salesman, at least in his own company. Here several thousand varieties of roller bearings are available for customer purchase, and the salesman knows far more about their correct application than does the customer. In view of the problems created by incorrect application, refusal to sell is in order unless the company retains the specification task.

In other industries it is precarious for the salesman to assume much responsibility in this respect. Where needs are emotional, for example, the customer is usually most qualified to determine whether the product will satisfy him. In other cases product specification is not the crucial issue. Services which help the customer manage or operate his business are more useful as a sales tool. But the product specification question is not only basic to marketing in general but is also basic to sound personal selling in most industries. For both reasons additional analysis in this area can contribute to marketing thought in a fundamental way.

Section 15 (1) of the Uniform Sales Act indicates the minimum amount of specification advisable and the circumstances under which it should be performed:

> Where the buyer expressly or by implication makes known to the seller the particular purposes for which the goods are required, and it appears that the buyer relies on the seller's skill and judgment (whether

he be the grower or the manufacturer or not) there is an implied war-
ranty that the goods shall be fit for such purposes.[7]

This provision may necessitate the supply of survey work, installation, and
demonstration as a way of seeing to it that the product is adapted to buyer
needs and that it satisfies the particular purpose designated by him.

The revised Uniform Commercial Code, which has gone into effect in a
few states, appears to shift some additional responsibility to the seller.[8] It
recognizes, implicitly at least, that the salesman may designate the purpose or
function to be fulfilled by the product rather than rely on the buyer for this
task. The buyer may indicate only that he has problems in inventory control
for example (or leave it up to the salesman to point out the problem). The
salesman may define the problem, recommend a system or process which will
alleviate it, and specify the kind of products necessary to enable the system to
function correctly.

Strategy of Need Satisfaction

Cash and Crisy have elaborated on the need satisfaction theory
of selling, where the ratio between the time the salesman talks during the
interview and the time the customer talks is supposed to change over the interview. However, when technical service is involved in selling the talking time
may be minor compared with the time devoted to surveying the customer's
business, demonstrating the product, and other services prior to securing the
order. The question here is how far the salesman should go in assisting the
prospective customer when there is no guarantee that he will purchase the
product. If the service is charged for separately, the problem is minimized, but
separate pricing is the exception when the primary purposes of the business is
to sell tangible products.

One salesman representing an office equipment firm draws up sketches
showing how the customer might best arrange the office operation. The purpose
is to sell their own office equipment, but prospective customers sometimes use
the proposals as a basis for buying the products of discount firms. The same
thing happens in other firms and industries, and at the retail level.

In another case, a plumbing and heating contractor refuses to run surveys
or to submit proposals in selling to industrial concerns unless the prospective
customer assures him beforehand that he will buy. In selling to home owners,
however, no commitment is required, for residential surveys are more stand-

[7] U.S.A. Section 15 (1).
[8] Lawrence Vold, *Cases and Materials on the Law of Sales*, 2nd ed., West Publishing
Company, St. Paul, 1949, p. 805.

ardized, less complex, and less expensive. There is some justification for both policies although one might question the wisdom of the first one. An inexpensive preliminary study can be conducted to estimate the expense of a more elaborate survey and to keep the negotiations alive. During the process the salesman can also estimate the probability of securing an order from the customer and can use the preliminary survey, along with the promise of a more elaborate one, to promote sales.

More formalized methods are being developed for handling such uncertainties. In some cases where negotiated bidding is used, the salesman may have to take into account the competitor's service expenditures as well as his price strategy, for the probability of securing an order will depend on what the competitor does in both areas. Suppose an analysis of the competitor's past behavior, customer motivation, and the relative characteristics of the products offered by the two firms leads to some judgment on the probability of securing the order with various combinations of service and price. The probabilities are estimated and placed in matrix form as in Table 31-1. Assume also that other incremental expenses associated with the order amount to 20 per cent of sales.

With this information, an expected contribution to profit can be computed for each combination of price and service by applying the equation: $Cij = (pij)$ $(Pi - Sj - .20Pi)$, where Cij is the expected contribution to profit associated with the ith price and the jth service expenditure, pij is the probability of securing the order with a price of i and a service expenditure of j, Pi is the i selling price, and Sj is the j service expenditure.

Table 31-1. Probability of securing the customer's order with varying combinations of price and sales-service expenditures

		Price (i)		
Sales-service		P_1	P_2	P_3
Expenditure (j)		$10,000	$12,000	$15,000
S_1	$1000	0.50	0.40	0.30
S_2	3000	0.70	0.55	0.45
S_3	5000	0.90	0.65	0.50

Given the probability coefficients presented in Table 31-1, a contribution to profit matrix can be constructed (Table 31-2). The price-service combination which maximizes expected profit contribution is $S_2 - P_2$, or a price of $12,000 and a sales service expenditure of $3,000. Here expected contribution to profit is $4,180.

This analysis for decision making obviously assumes that probabilities can be estimated with some accuracy. It is also clear that if the salesman does secure the order at a price of $12,000 and a service expenditure of $3,000, he

Table 31-2. Expected contribution to profit of varying combinations of price and sales-service expenditure

	Price (i)		
	P_1	P_2	P_3
Sales-service Expenditure (j)	$10,000	$12,000	$15,000
S_1 $1000	$ 3500	$ 3840	$ 3300
S_2 3000	3500	4180	4050
S_3 5000	2700	3640	3500

will not actually contribute $4,180 to profits. Instead, faced with a very large number of sales situations, identical to the one under consideration, he will contribute an *average* amount of $4,180 over the long run if he follows the $P_2 — S_2$ strategy on every occasion. He will lose the order 45 per cent of the time using this strategy, which means that he will contribute nothing to profits on these occasions.

If he follows strategy $P_1 — S_3$ in contrast, he will lose the order only 10 per cent of the time. Stated differently, he is almost certain of making a sale if he quotes a $1,000 price and supplies $5,000 worth of service. For this reason, and because identical sales situations are rarely encountered over time, one might reason that the $P_1 — S_3$ strategy is preferable. That is, expected profits are maximized by simply selecting the strategy which has the highest probability of resulting in an order, assuming that incremental revenues exceed incremental costs. The effect on future profits should also be considered.

32

Communications and Industrial Selling

THEODORE LEVITT

●Does corporate or institutional advertising by industrial-product companies pay?

●Do the salesmen of well-known industrial products companies have an automatic edge over the salesmen of little-known or unknown companies?

●Is it better for an industrial product company to spend its limited funds on aggressive advertising of its general competence or on more careful selection and training of its salesmen?

●Are the decisions of prospective buyers of new industrial products affected by the amount of personal risk these decisions expose them to?

●Are the buying decisions of practicing purchasing agents affected more by the reputation of a vendor-company than are the decisions of practicing engineers and scientists?

●Does the effect of a company's reputation on a customer's buying decision hold up over time, or does it erode as time passes?

These are some of the questions that have been investigated in a study recently completed at the Harvard Graduate School of Business Administration. Specifically, the questions focused on the extent to which an industrial-product company's generalized reputation affects its ability to launch new products. The accelerating flood of new and often complex industrial products, coupled with the continuing shortage of capable salesmen and the rising costs of advertising make the above questions particularly timely.

'Source Effect'

This timeliness is further enhanced by studies by Harvard Busi-

Reprinted from *Journal of Marketing* (April, 1967), pp. 15-21, by permission of the publisher, the American Marketing Association.

ness School Professor Raymond A. Bauer, which have suggested that business communicators have been inadequately aware of the extent to which their audiences influence the communicators, rather than the usual one-way preoccupation with how the communicators (or advertisers) influence their audiences.[1] To illustrate:

Research shows that a newspaper editorial identified to one group of Americans as emanating, say, from *The New York Times* and to a similar group of Americans as emanating, say, from *Pravda* would lead one to expect that a change in audience opinion in the direction advocated by the editorial would be greater for those who believed it was a *New York Times* editorial than those who believed it to be a *Pravda* editorial. In other words, the audience's feelings about the credibility of the message source help determine the persuasive effectiveness of the message itself. The greater the prestige or the more believable the message source, the more likely that it will influence the audience in the direction advocated by the message. The less prestigeful or believable the source, the less likely that it will influence the audience in the direction advocated by the message.

This phenomenon is now generally referred to as "source effect." Obviously what source effect amounts to is some sort of independent judgment by the audience such that it is either more or less affected by the message. The audience takes a form of initiative, independent of the message, which affects its susceptibility to the message.[2]

If in their private lives people such as businessmen and scientists exhibit source effect and audience initiative in response to political communications and propaganda, there is the question of whether they do this same thing in their business lives in response to advertising and direct sales presentations. McGraw-Hill expresses its belief that source effect works powerfully in industrial selling in its famous advertisement of a stern-looking purchasing agent facing the reader (salesman) from behind his desk and saying:

> I don't know who you are.
> I don't know your company.
> I don't know your company's product.
> I don't know what your company stands for.
> I don't know your company's customers.
> I don't know your company's record.
> I don't know your company's reputation.
> Now—what was it you wanted to sell me?
> MORAL: Sales start before your salesman calls—with business publication advertising.

[1]Bauer, "The Obstinate Audience," *American Psychologist*, Vol. 19 (May 1964), pp. 319-328, and "Communication as a Transaction," *Public Opinion Quarterly*, Vol. 27 (Spring 1963), pp. 83-86.

[2]For the seminal research in this area, see Carl I. Hovland and Walter Weiss, "The Influence of Source Credibility on Communication Effectiveness," *Public Opinion Quarterly*, Vol. 15 (Winter 1951-1952), pp. 635-650, and Carl I. Hovland, A. A. Lumsdaine, and Fred D. Sheffield, *Experiments in Mass Communication* (Princeton: Princeton University Press, 1949).

To test this and a variety of related hypotheses, an elaborate communications simulation was devised and administered. Participants included 113 practicing purchasing agents from a wide variety of companies, 130 engineers and scientists, and 131 business school graduate students. (For simplifying purposes, the engineers and scientists are in this article referred to as "chemists.") This article is a report on the results of this simulation. But while it is a "report," it is not a simple document. As will be seen, it is full of moderating qualifications and carefully-phrased conclusions. It cannot be read with easy speed or casual comfort. The more complex a subject, the more involuted its rhetoric. In the present case, the reader must be prepared to go slow along an agonizing path.

Methodology

Basically what was done in the research was to divide each audience group (purchasing agents, chemists, and students) into six separate subgroups and then to expose each subgroup to a ten-minute filmed sales presentation for a new, but fictitious, technical product for use as an ingredient in making paint. Each audience member was put into the position of assuming he was listening to the presentation as it would be given by a salesman sitting across his desk. Some groups were asked to assume they were purchasing agents for a paint firm and some were asked to assume they were chemists. The film presentation technique and audience setup were created to make conditions as realistic as possible, with great care taken to prevent communications between subgroups and to create realistic and thoughtful responses by the subjects. All saw what was basically the same ten-minute film with the same actors. However, some subgroups saw a relatively good presentation and some a relatively poor one; for some the selling company was identified in the film as a relatively high-credibility company (the Monsanto Company), for other subgroups it was identified as a relatively lower credibility and less well-known company (the Denver Chemical Company), and for still others the company identity was kept anonymous. Immediately after the film was run, and then again in five weeks, each respondent filled out a detailed questionnaire.[3]

Results

Let us now take up each of the question areas posed at the outset of this article, and see how our findings respond to them.

[3]The details of the research mechanism are spelled out in Theodore Levitt, *Industrial Purchasing Behavior: A Study in Communications Effects* (Boston, Massachusetts: Division of Research, Harvard Business School, 1965).

1. Does Corporate or Institutional Advertising by Industrial-product Companies Pay?

For complex industrial products or materials, a company's generalized reputation does indeed have an important bearing on how its sales prospects make buying decisions. While the research did not specifically investigate the influence of corporate or institutional advertising, the results show that to the extent that such advertising helps in building a company's reputation it clearly helps in making sales. Whether such advertising specifically helps build a reputation is, however, a separate question. But the presumption is that mere visibility of a company is in some way helpful and reassuring, provided that the impressions that are created are not negative.

Generally speaking, the better a company's reputation, the better are its chances (1) of getting a favorable *first hearing* for a new product among customer prospects, and (2) of getting early *adoption* of that product. Vendor reputation influences buyers, decision makers, and the decision-making process. But since industrial products, and particularly new products, generally require direct calls by salesmen, does the value of company reputation automatically give an edge to the salesman from a well-known company over the salesman from a less well-known or anonymous one?

2. Do Well-known Company Salesmen Have an Edge over the Salesmen of Other Companies?

The answer is "yes," but it is a more complex answer than one might offhand suspect. Just because his company is favorably well known and to this extent puts the customer in a more favorable frame of mind toward that company, does not give the salesman a simple and automatic leg up over the salesman of a less-known company. The fact seems to be that customers *expect* more, or at least a better sales-presentation job, from well-known company salesmen. Hence they judge their performance somewhat differently from the way they judge the performance of other salesmen. Indeed there is some indication that some types of customers (or "audiences" of sales presentations) almost unconsciously "help" the salesmen of lesser-known companies by lowering their expectations in order to encourage competition between vendors. Thus, when they eventually make buying decisions, while these customers tend clearly to favor the better known companies, they seem to give disproportionate encouragement to the salesmen of the less well-known companies.

Still, everyone knows from experience that a good sales presentation is always better than a poor one, regardless of company reputation. A vital question that therefore arises is whether it is generally better for an industrial products company to spend its limited funds on more aggressive or effective

advertising of its general competence, or on more careful selection and training of its salesmen.

3. Is It Better to Advertise More or to
Select and Train Salesmen Better?

As would be expected, the research found that the quality of a
salesman's presentation in support of a technically-complex new product is an
important variable in obtaining a favorable customer reaction. In other words,
there is a "presentation effect" in favor of the product supported by a well-done
sales presentation.

When the influences of source effect and presentation effect are combined,
the research suggests that when a relatively unknown or anonymous company
makes a good direct sales presentation, it may be just as effective in getting a
favorable first hearing for a complex new industrial material as a well-known
company making a poor presentation. Thus a well-known company loses the
advantage of its reputation if its direct sales presentation is clearly inferior to
that of an unknown or little-known company. Against a good sales presentation
by a little-known company, a well-known one must also have a good presentation if the customer-getting value of its reputation is to be realized. Conversely,
a little-known company, by concentrating strongly on training its salesmen to
make good presentations, may be able to make considerable progress toward
overcoming the liability of its relative anonymity.

Combining this with the finding that certain buyers apparently want to
favor less well-known companies and expect more of better-known companies,
even though they are strongly attracted to the latter, the conclusion seems to be
that the lesser-known company—particularly when its resources are limited—
can do an unexpectedly effective job for itself through more careful salesman
selection and training.

On the other hand, everyone knows that every buying decision for a new
product, and some for an established product, involves a certain amount of risk
for the buyer. Moreover, the buyer's personal risk (as opposed to the risk for
his company) varies as between whether he has sole personal responsibility
for the buying (or, indeed, the "rejection") decision or whether it is a shared
or committee decision. To what extent does the degree of the decision-maker's
personal risk affect the importance of vendor reputation and quality of a sales
presentation in the buyer's decision process?

4. The Role of Personal Risk in Buying Decisions

The amount of personal risk to which the individual decision-
maker is exposed in a buying or rejection decision proves to be a vital factor
in his decisions. And it is vital in the extent to which source effect is influential.
Company reputation clearly results in a higher proportion of high-risk deci-

sions in favor of the well-known company. Presentation quality tends substantially to strengthen the position of the less well-known company in high-risk buying situations, but not as much in low-risk buying situations. While careful attention to salesman selection and training can be said to help equalize greatly the competitive position of lesser known firms, these help it more to get a foot in the door than help it get an immediate adoption for its product. When it comes to the most important and most risky of customer actions—actually deciding to buy or reject a new product—assuming the various suppliers' products to be equal in all respects, source credibility exerts a dominant influence over other considerations.

But this still leaves unanswered the question of whether and to what extent all of these influences are equal among customers with varying degrees of technical competencies. Do they apply equally, for example, to purchasing agents and technically-trained personnel such as chemists?

5. The Influence of Customer 'Competence'

The research found that the power of source effect (company reputation for credibility) varies by the character and "competence" of the recipient of a sales message. Thus, there is some indication that, in the case of complex industrial materials, purchasing agents, who are usually highly competent as professional buyers, may be less influenced by a company's generalized reputation than are technical personnel, who are presumably less competent as buyers but more competent as judges of a complex product's merits. In first appraising complex new materials on the basis of sales presentations made directly to them, technically-sophisticated personnel seem to be influenced by the seller's reputation to a point that is unexpectedly higher than the influence of that reputation on such technically less sophisticated personnel as purchasing agents. In short, technical personnel are probably influenced far more by company reputation than has been widely assumed, and certainly more than such technically less sophisticated people as purchasing agents.

While all audiences seem to be influenced by the quality of the sales presentation, important differences apparently exist between purchasing agents and technical personnel. In the lower-risk decision situation of whether to give a newly presented complex new product a further hearing, technical personnel are more powerfully influenced by the quality of a direct sales presentation than are purchasing agents. Put differently, on low-risk purchasing decisions, the technically less sophisticated purchasing agents seem to rely less heavily on the quality of the sales presentation than do the technically more sophisticated personnel in making their decisions. But on high-risk decisions (whether actually to buy the product) the reverse is true: that is, the greater the risk, the more favorably purchasing agents are influenced by good sales presentations, and the less favorably technical personnel are influenced by such presentations. The greater the risk, the more likely technical personnel are to rely on their technical judgments about a new product's virtues rather than on the quality of the sales presentation in favor of that product. But purchasing agents, being technically less sophisticated, seem forced, in high-risk situations, to rely more heavily on the seller's presentation.

6. The Durability of Vendor Reputation on Buying Decisions

Philip Wrigley, of the chewing gum empire, is alleged to have answered a query about why his company continues to spend so much on advertising now that it is successful with this observation: "Once you get a plane up in the air you don't turn off the engines." For industrial-product companies, a related question concerns the durability of buying inclinations (and even of buying decisions) that sales prospects exhibit immediately after hearing a sales presentation. Since few new industrial products are immediately purchased on the making of a sales presentation to a customer—since, for many reasons, there is generally a time lag before a decision is made, the question is: Does source effect hold up over time? For example, with the passage of time does the prospect forget the source of a new product presentation, remembering only the facts and the claimed product performance, such that when the actual buying decision is made at some later time the vendor's reputation plays little or no role? Similarly, does the importance of quality of the sales presentation hold up over time?

The present research indicates that there is in industrial purchasing a phenomenon which communications researchers call the "sleeper effect." The favorable influence of a company's generalized good reputation (source effect) does indeed erode with the passage of time. But the conditions under which this happens appear to be quite special. Based on what the present research was able to test, what can be said is that this erosion occurs specifically when there is no intervening reinforcement or reinstatement of the identity of the source. Put differently, in the absence of repeated sales callbacks or advertisements to reinstate the identity of the source, the seller tends, over time, to lose the favorable impact of his good reputation on the attitudes and actions of his sales prospects.

But the declining power of source effect over time on audience decision-making works *in opposite directions* for the well-known company than for the lesser-known company. Sleeper effect, in a manner of speaking, hurts the well-known company but helps the lesser-known company. In the case of the former, as the sales prospect forgets the well-known source his originally favorable attitude toward the product declines; and in the case of the latter, as he forgets the lesser-known source his originally less-favorable attitude toward the product also declines. That is, the likelihood of his buying from the high credibility company declines while the likelihood of his buying from the low-credibility company rises—even though the high-credibility company is still likely to get more customers in absolute terms.

Implications and Reservations

The implications of the present research for industrial products companies are numerous, but so also are the reservations and qualifications which must be attached to the research findings. While the research sought to simulate reality as carefully as possible, it still remains only a simulation. Moreover, individual competitive situations, product characteristics, and a vast variety of other conditions can greatly affect the value of these findings in specific cases. But in the absence of better information and research, the present findings may be viewed as at least a beginning toward unravelling some age-old mysteries.

Reputation and Presentation

From the point of view of a producer of industrial materials or components, it seems safe to conclude that the cultivation of a good reputation among potential customers will have some payoff in the sense that it will help his salesmen to get "a foot in the door" of a prospect. But the value of cultivating a good reputation seems to be considerably less when it comes to its effect on the likelihood of the prospect's *actually buying* a new product on being first exposed to it. A good reputation always helps, but it helps less as the riskiness of the customer's decision rises and as he has something else to rely or draw on.

Hence it seems safe also to suggest that a producer of technically-advanced products which are used as components or as ingredients by other manufacturers would be wise systematically to cultivate for himself a strongly favorable generalized reputation among technical personnel of prospective manufacturing customers. In other words, in trying to sell such products to technically-trained personnel it may not be wise to rely so extensively, as many such companies do, on the product's inherent virtues and on making strong technical product presentations. Technical personnel are not human computers whose purchasing and product-specification decisions are based on cold calculations and devoid of less rigorously rational influences. They do indeed seem to be influenced by the seller's general reputation.

However, as might have been expected, the quality of a salesman's presentation in support of a product is an important variable in obtaining favorable buyer reactions, regardless of the technical or purchasing competence of the audience. A good direct sales presentation is generally more effective than a poor one. There is a "presentation effect" in favor of the product supported by a well-done sales presentation. But, as in the case of source effect, the research indicates that a good sales presentation is generally more useful in getting a favorable first hearing for a new product (that is, in what is, for the prospect, a low-risk decision) than it is in getting a favorable buying decision (that is, a high-risk decision). A good sales presentation is definitely better than a poor one in getting product adoption, but it has even more leverage than a poor one in getting a favorable first hearing for a product.

All this indicates that both the reputation of a vendor company and the quality of its direct sales presentations are important elements in sales success, but that the way the importance of these elements varies as between audiences and between types of audience decision-situations greatly affects how a vendor might wish to shape his marketing tactics.

"Sleeper Effect"

The findings on "sleeper effect" are particularly interesting in that, contrary to the other findings, they suggest that some policies appropriate for the well-known company may not be appropriate for the lesser-known company. Thus, repeat advertising and sales callbacks reinstate the well-known company's indentity and therefore influence the prospect in its favor. But since the sales prospect tends to forget the source over time and therefore makes a more "objective" decision, reinstating the identity of the lesser-known company could actually tend to hurt that company. All other things being equal, the lesser-known company may find it better to leave well enough alone. But whether "all other things" are equal is highly doubtful, and in any case varies by the situation. The most that can be said here is that there can conceivably be circumstances in which sleeper effect can work to the advantage of the lesser-known company.

However, the research also found that the passage of time has different consequences for source effect than for presentation effect. A good sales presentation is more effective over time than a good reputation. Moreover, the better the original sales presentation, the greater the durability of its influence over the audience with the passage of time. That is, regardless of the presence of sleeper effect (the declining influences of source credibility with the passage of time), if the original sales presentation was relatively good, the prospects tend more strongly to favor the product in question at a later date than if that presentation had been poor. The originally favorable influence of the highly credible source declined less, and the originally unfavorable influence of the less credible source hurt less, as the original sales presentation was better. A good sales presentation has greater durability than a good company reputation. Company reputation, in order to work for that company, has to be more regularly reinforced (possibly through advertising repetition) than does the effect of a good sales presentation.

A related finding on the dynamics of sleeper effect involves the strength of a sales prospect's reaction to a sales presentation. Thus, there is some evidence that the more self-confidently a prospect refuses at the outset to permit a new product to be viewed and reviewed by others in his firm, the greater the likelihood later that he will change his mind and give such permission. That is, a strong outright refusal for a further hearing at the time of the first sales call may suggest greater probability of getting permission later than does a weak and vacillating original refusal. Hence the very vigor with which a new product is at first rejected by a prospect may, instead of signaling that it is a lost cause, actually signal that a later repeat call is likely to get a good hearing.

High Risk Situations

But this refers only to relatively low-risk decisions—decisions in which the prospect is asked merely to give the product serious consideration, not actually to buy it at that time. In high-risk decision situations the findings were different. The research confirms the common-sense expectation that the greater the personal risk to the responding sales prospect, the more persuasion it takes to get him to switch from a product he is currently using. Moreover, once a prospect has made a decision in a high-risk situation, the seller will generally have considerable difficulty both in getting the negative respondent subsequently to change his mind and in keeping the affirmative respondent from changing his mind. This means that, especially in high-risk situations, it pays to try to get a favorable customer decision at the outset. Once he has rejected a product, it appears to be extremely difficult to get the prospect to be willing to reopen the discussions. Similiarly, once he has accepted a new product under high-risk conditions, the customer appears to suffer from considerable self-doubt about whether he has made the right decision. He is probably very susceptible to being "unsold" by a competitor. This suggests the need for continuous followup by the original seller to reassure the customer and thus keep him sold.

Salesman or Company?

It has already been pointed out that, generally speaking, the more credible the source the more likely it is that its message will get a favorable reception. But the question arises as to who "the" source is: Is it the salesman who makes the sales call, or is it the company he represents? Do customers perceive this "source" as being one and the same or different? The present research indicates that they think of them as being two different sources. The salesman is not automatically thought of as being the company. When asked to rank the trustworthiness of the salesman on the one hand and then the trustworthiness of the company he represented, respondents consistently scored the salesman lower than his company.

While this might reflect the relatively low esteem with which salesmen are generally held, paradoxically, in our highly sales-dependent society, a closer look at the results suggests a great deal more. It was found, for example, that respondents are more likely to favor the products of salesmen whom they rank low in trustworthiness when these salesmen represent well-known companies than they are to favor the products of salesmen whom they rank relatively high in trustworthiness but who represent unknown companies. A similar result occurred in connection with respondents' feelings about how well informed and competent the salesmen from high-vs.-low credibility companies are. Thus, offhand it would seem that favorably well-known companies opperate at the distinct advantage of being able to afford to have less "trustworthy" and less "competent" salesmen, at least in the short run, than little-known or anonymous companies. But close examination suggests something else. It suggests that source effect is such a uniquely powerful force that for respondents to favor well-known companies, their need to trust the salesmen of these companies and to think highly of their competence is much less urgent than it is in order for them to favor less-well-known and anonymous companies. In other words, the favorably well-known company does indeed have an advantage over its less well-known competitor in that its salesmen need to *seem* less trustworthy and competent in order to be effective. Well-known companies need not be as scrupulous in their hiring and training of salesmen. Source effect seems almost to conquer everything.

But not entirely everything. As noted above, presentation quality and quality of the message can overcome some of the disadvantages of being relatively anonymous. So can, of course, trust in the salesman. What is it then that makes for an appearance of salesman trustworthiness? First of all, the results of the present research suggest that trustworthiness of the communicator (such as, for example, a salesman, television announcer, etc.) is not as clearly related to the audience's feeling about his knowledge or understanding of the product he is selling as might be expected. While there is some relationship, trust is much more closely related to the overall quality or character of the salesman's sales presentation. Poor presentations in particular reduce trust in the message transmitter (salesman). They also reduce trust in the message source (the salesman's company). The better the presentation the more trustworthy both the company and the salesman are perceived to be. To say this, and what has been said before, is equivalent to saying that there is obvious merit in making sure that salesmen have quality sales presentations, and this holds true particularly for less well-known companies.

It is interesting to note from the research that there was only a very modest, certainly not a clear, connection between audience ratings of a salesman's trustworthiness and their judgments regarding the extent of his product competence. An audience's willingness either to recommend or adopt a product was not clearly related to its judgment about a salesman's product knowledge. Nor was it related, in the short run, to how much of the information which the salesman gave out was actually retained by the audience.

All this suggests that in making his adoption decisions the customer is influenced by more than what the salesman specifically says about the product or even how effectively he communicates product facts. It seems very probable that the communicator's personality and what he says about things other than the product in question play a vital role in influencing his audience. The effective transmission of product facts seems to be more important in the long run than in the short run. With the passage of time since the date of the original sales presentation, persons who retained more product information right after that presentation were more likely to make and hold decisions favorable to the source. Hence the importance of the effective transmission of product facts during the original presentation seems to increase as the product-adoption decision is delayed. But it is not clear that detailed recall of product facts ever becomes a paramount ingredient in obtaining favorable buying decisions.

Summary

It seems clear that company reputation is a powerful factor in the industrial purchasing process, but its importance varies with the technical competence and sophistication of the customer. The quality of a sales message and the way it is presented are capable of moderating the influence of this source effect, but again it varies by audience. Generally speaking, it pays for a company to be favorably well known, and perhaps especially among customers having some degree of technical sophistication, such as engineers and scientists. But superior sales messages and well-trained salesmen can help less well-known companies to overcome some of the disadvantages of their relative anonymity. A well-planned and well-executed direct sales presentation can be an especially strong competitive weapon for the less well-known company. Moreover, the greater the riskiness of the purchasing decision the customer is asked to make, the more likely it is that a good sales presentation will produce a customer decision in favor of the direction advocated by the source.

33

The Salesman's Role in Household Decision-making

LAUREN EDGAR CRANE

This discussion is concerned with the role of the salesman in household decision-making. An attempt will be made to relate the discussion to that concerning family decision-making presented last year by Granbois.[1] It is hoped that by concentrating on *problem* rather than on *project*, I can stimulate a mutual exchange of ideas which may encourage work in this area. Our experience at Notre Dame this last year has convinced me that we need a research program, rather than a research project—a program which can attack this problem from many viewpoints with a wide diversity of methods.

Our own viewpoint and our methods stem more from a communications rather than a marketing orientation. First of all, we are less interested in the actual decisions which households make as a result of an encounter with a salesman than with the process by which those decisions are reached. Second, we are as much interested in ways of improving customers' skill in such encounters as we are with finding ways by which salesmen can perform more successfully. Third, we define communications rather broadly as the use of symbols to influence another person's behavior, and thus, to some extent, we part company with men like Cox,[2] who regard consumer decision-making as a search for and evaluation of information, or those like Hughes[3] who describe the sales encounter as a "dual learning" situation. And fourth, we are concerned with communications as a process, involving sources and messages,

Reprinted from *Proceedings, American Marketing Association Conference*, George L. Smith, Ed. (December, 1964), pp. 184-196, by permission of the publisher, the American Marketing Association.

[1] Donald H. Granbois, "The Role of Communication in the Family Decision-Making Process," *Toward Scientific Marketing*, Stephen A. Greyser, Ed. (Chicago: American Marketing Association, 1963).

[2] Donald F. Cox, "The Audience as Communicators," *Toward Scientific Marketing*, Stephen A. Greyser, Ed. (Chicago: American Marketing Association, 1963), pp. 58-72.

[3] G. David Hughes, "A New Tool for Sales Managers," *Journal of Marketing Research*, May 1964, pp. 32-38.

channels and receivers. That is, we are *not* interested solely in messages; we are equally interested in the selection of audiences and of channels and in the effect of audiences upon sources.

Choice of Problem Area

What were the effects of this commitment to a communications point of view? To begin with, it had a good deal to do with our original choice of the problem area itself.

There are, of course, good marketing reasons for studying personal selling. As all of us know, in comparison to the amount of money spent on preparing and transmitting messages, less money is spent on publishable research in marketing communications than in any other type of communications. Moreover, what little research of this kind is done in the area concentrates on advertising rather than personal selling, although data cited by Hughes[4] indicates that selling costs are nearly triple those of advertising.

The communications reasons for studying personal selling are somewhat different: we are interested because the salesman uses face-to-face channels for his messages; and face-to-face channels, we believe, represent the most effective channels by which human behavior can be influenced.

The reasons for our belief are obvious and familiar. First, face-to-face audiences tend to be smaller, so that messages can be aimed more precisely at receivers' interests, needs, and abilities. Second, feedback is instantaneous, so that a message can be modified while it is being delivered. Third, the communicator can employ a wide variety of symbol systems. Beginning with the great denotative and connotative resources of the human voice, he can add, if he wishes, the symbol systems of print and picture, words and numbers. Fourth, a face-to-face communicator can reward his listeners by interaction which is pleasurable in itself, aside from any other functions, such as the provision of information, which it may perform. Fifth, a face-to-face communicator has the advantage of calling forth the special attitudes and behaviors by which we react to human beings in contrast to our behavior toward inanimate objects.

From both a marketing and a communications standpoint, the reasons for studying personal selling seem compelling. And yet, as became very clear to me when I started to look for experimental data on personal selling in the course of writing a text in marketing communications these reasons have *not* compelled us.

One reason for the failure to study marketing communications in general is the failure of the business community to finance basic, publishable research.

[4]*Ibid.*

As a result, studies of bomber crews and the diffusion of farm practices have contributed far more to communications theory than have studies of marketing.

But why the special neglect of personal selling? Here, in a sense, I believe we have ourselves to blame. Most of us most of the time first decide on a favorite method of gathering and analyzing data so that our methods perforce limit *what* we can study. Face-to-face communications is a tangled jungle full of unknown terrors to a researcher who has deadlines to meet, whether those deadlines are set by a commercial sponsor, a foundation grant, a Ph.D. committee, or a dean's demand for a list of publications for his annual report. Thus, even the small group researchers, who have been as inventive of method as they have been productive of theory, almost as a matter of course drain the juice out of the face-to-face situation by erecting screens to prevent participants from seeing one another and by forcing their subjects to communicate via written messages and push-buttons.

Choice of Method

Despite the difficulty involved in studying the salesman's role in household decision-making as an example of face-to-face communications, our commitment to the communications point of view urged us to venture into the jungle. In addition, our communications commitment also influenced our choice of methods.

Had we been interested primarily in marketing, we might have asked participants to report the relative influence which each perceived himself as having on a given purchase. This is what Blood and Wolfe[5] did: 68% of the housewives they questioned said that their husbands had most influence on car purchase, 42% said he had most influence on home purchase. (Husband and wife had equal influence, reported 25% of respondents for cars, 41% for life insurance and 58% for housing.) Or we might have gone a step further, and questioned both husband and wife. As one would expect, and as a study by Wolgast[6] indicates, spouses' perceptions differ: although 23% of Wolgast wives said car purchase was a joint decision, 31% of husbands made this claim.

Even from a marketing viewpoint, however, such studies have their shortcomings. By treating purchase as a single, unitary event, for example, they gloss over the many separate decisions which must be made in buying a car, a house or an insurance policy. By depending on self-reports, researchers may discover, merely, that respondents are aware of social norms and of the roles which society says are appropriate to each sex. From a communica-

[5]Robert O. Blood, Jr., and Donald M. Wolfe, *Husbands & Wives* (Glencoe, Ill.: The Free Press, 1960).

[6]Elizabeth H. Wolgast, "Do Husbands or Wives Make the Purchasing Decisions?" *Journal of Marketing*, October, 1958, pp. 151-158.

tions viewpoint, one concerned less with the decision that is made than with the process by which the decision is reached, such methods miss the main point. We chose to intervene in the decision-making process at the point when husband and wife invite the salesman into their living room. Having chosen to locate our study in time and space at this point in the decision-making process, the most appropriate method seemed to us an adaptation of the "revealed differences" technique of Strodtbeck.[7]

Strodtbeck starts with a paper-and-pencil checklist of questions concerning such family policies as a teenager's use of the car or school-night curfew. The researcher quickly scans the completed checklists and selects issues in which husband or wife or teen-ager successively play the role of one isolated and facing a coalition of other two. He then asks the family to discuss each issue in turn and try to reach a joint decision. The discussion is tape-recorded and analyzed subsequently by applying Bales' categories of interaction analysis or by having judges rate family members either on a series of semantic differential scales or such qualities as "warmth." Similar discussions in marketing have been coded into Bales' categories by Kenkel[8] who asked college students and their wives to spend a half-hour discussing how they would spend a gift of $300. Such studies have exposed a number of the factors which affect the amount of influence husbands and wives exert over household decisions. *Culture* is one; Strodtbeck[9] reports that among the matriarchal Navaho, women won 58% of contested decisions, as compared with only 41% among the patriarchal Mormons. *Amount* of communications activity is another; Strodtbeck notes that the one who talks most wins. *Nature* of communications is also important; Kenkel[10] finds that men predominate in task-centered comments and women in supportive, group maintenance remarks.

From our standpoint, Kenkel's design has one advantage and two drawbacks: it permits us to observe interaction between husband and wife, but the occasion of the interaction is itself somewhat artificial and the salesman appears to have no necessary part in the design.

The Blood-Wolfe and Wolgast design, in contrast, involves real prospects exposed to real salesmen and an actual exchange of money and product, but it does not permit us to observe the interaction among them, only to reconstruct it on the basis of verbal reports by the participants.

To avoid the limitations of either method, we decided to begin our exploratory work by tape-recording actual sales interviews of real salesmen trying to sell real products to real people.

This decision, of course, places limits of it own on our study. Effectively, it limits us to sales capable of being consummated in a single encounter of

[7]Fred L. Strodtbeck, "Husband-wife Interaction Over Revealed Differences," *American Sociological Review*, Vol. 16, pp. 468-473.

[8]William F. Kenkel, "Husband-wife Interaction in Decision Making and Decision Choices," *Journal of Social Psychology*, Vol. 54, pp. 255-262.

[9]Strodtbeck, *loc. cit.*

[10]Kenkel, *loc. cit.*

some two hours, scheduled in advance and taking place in a home where a tape recorder could be placed.

Limits on Prospects and Products

Our goal and our method, taken together, introduce additional constraints, limiting both the type of products and the type of prospects we can study. These limits can be analyzed in terms of the three classes of independent variables listed by Granbois[11] as appropriate to studies of household decision-making.

Granbois' first class is *situation:* High uncertainty, he says, is necessary for information-seeking and deliberate decision-making to occur. Such uncertainty appears when a product is being purchased for the first time or when its relatively high unit-cost displaces many alternative expenditures. Granbois' second class of variables consists of *product type.* In our case this means we cannot study products which, although sold in the home, do not involve a joint decision by husband and wife. This excludes all those products such as Fuller brushes, Avon's cosmetics, Tupperware, and vanilla extract, whose purchase is delegated to the wife. Since our interest in the interaction limits us to joint decisions, we also face constraints as regards Granbois' third class of variables—decision-makers' characteristics. It restricts us to respondents in early stages of the family life cycle, since the longer a household exists, the more decisions tend to be delegated and the less interaction tends to precede them. It restricts us to middle socio-economic strata, since wives tend to dominate at the bottom of the ladder and husbands at the top.

In addition to these limits suggested by Granbois, we placed two additional restraints on the situation.

First, we wanted to limit ourselves, by our choice of product, to households whose entry into the market as prospects could be dated by some observable event, such as the birth of a first baby and the resultant entry of its parents into the market for pablum, safety pins, and bath powder. We had two reasons for this. One was that we wanted to be able to specify and manipulate the length of time between prospects' entry into the market and their encounter with a salesman. Since part of the selling job is performed by advertising and by word-of-month communications with friends and neighbors and since the behavior of both household and salesman would be affected by the amount of prospects' exposure to such influences, we wished to know the length of time during which such exposure could take place. The second reason was that we wanted to compare the incidence of purchase and non-purchase, exposure to a salesman and non-exposure among prospects who had been in the market equal lengths of time.

[11]Granbois, *loc. cit.*

Second, we wanted to avoid situations in which the sales encounter becomes a dialogue between husband and salesman, with the wife as a silent spectator. There were reasons to suspect that this might occur—the "publicity" of a visible tape-recorder and the presence of a stranger, the salesman, would tend to push both husband and wife toward behavior perceived as appropriate to their sex roles. To counter this tendency, we used all three of Granbois' variables. By recording interviews in a home rather than a laboratory setting, we hoped to reduce the public nature of the encounter. Since Blood and Wolfe[12] report that influence varies with relative contribution to the household, we planned to increase wives' influence by including working wives in our study. Finally, we looked for products on which wives were, in some sense, experts, hoping thus to increase wives' participation. Three products, we felt, met these criteria.

Children's Encyclopedias

This is a big-ticket item, usually purchased just once by a family. Since parents typically become live prospects for the product when their oldest child reaches a class in school where themes are required, we could date their entry into the market. This would also mean studying prospects fairly early in the life cycle. Salesmen, for their own reasons, typically insist on talking to both husband and wife. The situation was one of high uncertainty, since neither decision-maker actually uses the product. The wife's role in the decision is strengthened to the extent she regards social mobility achieved through education as important, and supervises the children's homework.

Insurance

Here we limited ourselves to first-policy purchases. Again the product represents a major commitment of funds and involves high uncertainty. By limiting ourselves to the married college student who first experiences a need for the product either at the time of his marriage or, even more intensely, on the arrival of his first child, we made it possible to date prospects' entry into the market, and at the same time focus on prospects at an early stage in the life cycle.

Band Instruments

This was a late addition to our design. Again we limited ourselves to the first purchase which means that prospects' entry into the market can be dated by the time their oldest child becomes eligible for the band, usually about the fifth grade. Uncertainty is high, since purchasers do not ac-

12Blood, *loc. cit.*

tually use the product themselves and because they lack experience with a relatively high-unit-cost product. As with encyclopedias, the wife's sensitivity to cultural values and mobility implications of the product and the likelihood that she will supervise children's use of the product, strengthen her hand in decision-making. The one artificial aspect of this situation is introduction of a salesman into the home. Sales efforts in real life tend to occur at a mass meeting of parents at the school or in response to written announcements from the school. In a sense, the school child himself, the prospective user, becomes a surrogate salesman, whose efforts are likely to extend over a period of time rather than be concentrated in a single evening.

Independent and Dependent Variables

Having narrowed the scope of our study by this selection of products and prospects, what independent variables do we have left? At least three appear to us to be of potential importance. First, we can vary the number of persons involved in the interaction. We begin with a triad—husband, wife, and salesman. Since the triad is basically unstable, tending to break up into a two-person coalition and one isolated, we might expect the salesman to spend considerable effort to prevent a coalition being formed against him, or to himself become frozen into a coalition which leaves either husband or wife as hostile isolated participant. We can change this triad into a tetrad by adding another prospect, as we have done in having parents explore purchase of an insurance policy for a teen-age son. Or we can transform the triad into a tetrad by adding another representative of the seller. Interestingly enough, as Tucker[13] points out, by using an offstage associate as a "villain," an automobile salesman often wins good will by appearing to battle against his associate on behalf of the prospect. The automobile salesman frequently casts the used-car appraiser or the sales manager in such a villain's role; a tract builder's engineer or architect may give similar air to the builder's salesman.

Second, we can compare the interaction that occurs when the sales encounter is initiated by the salesman with that which occurs when the prospects themselves request a salesman to call. Third, we can strengthen one side or the other in the sales interview. We can do this by comparing experienced and inexperienced salesmen or by observing any changes in the bargaining strategy a couple employs as it moves from the first to the second and third salesman for a given product. (Although in "real life" prospects often see only one salesman, our study schedules three salesmen for each household, varying their order from family to family.) We can also manipulate this variable by giving

13W. T. Tucker, *The Social Context of Economic Behavior* (New York: Holt, Rinehart and Winston, Inc., 1964).

prospects product information or training in bargaining strategy and compare experimental and control couples or make before-and-after studies of a given couple. In similar fashion, we can compare the communications behavior of high-producing and low-producing salesmen. We can, as suggested earlier, increase a wife's influence *vis-a-vis* her husband's by including working wives who, by reason of their greater contribution to the family, exercise more influence over household decisions.

Our principal dependent variables are the amount and nature of the messages emitted by each member of the triad or tetrad. We are interested in such questions as these: What percent of the total messages does the salesman emit? Whom does he send most messages to and receive most messages from? What changes occur as the interview moves out of the initial stage of setting the social scene to the salesman's feeling-out of prospects' attitudes, to his provision of information, to his answering of objections and his attempt of a close? Following Bales' schema, how do participants differ in the proportion of task-centered messages, either questions or answers, and in the proportion of positive and negative emotional reactions incidental to group maintenance?

Information or Influence?

These, then, were the constraints and the variables with which we embarked upon our study. This was, in rough outline, the design in mind as we made our first tapes of encounters between encyclopedia or insurance salesmen, husbands and wives.

It was at this point that we realized we must part company with those who regard household decision-making as essentially a process of gathering and evaluating information. This may be true, so long as the decision-makers depend upon printed sources of information, upon word-of-mouth contacts with their friends, or even on visits to retail outlets. So long as they gather information by these methods, they retain effective control of the process.

When they invite a salesman into their home, however, a change takes place. Husband and wife give up much of their control over subsequent events. They greatly reduce their power to end the interview. For example, this power passes to the salesman, who takes on the role of a quasi-guest when he steps into the living room. They give up their freedom to bargain by pretending to lose interest in purchase of the product. By putting the salesman to the inconvenience and expense of coming to them, they have expressed a fairly high degree of interest in the product if not actually of commitment to purchase it. At the same time, they make brand comparison—another bargaining device— inconvenient, even inappropriate; brand-comparison belongs to an earlier state of decision-making. Moreover, it is widely recognized that the role of the salesman is not one of merely providing information; attempts to influence others' behavior is a legitimate, expected part of the salesman's role. Although the information he provides may be expert, it is obviously chosen for the purpose of influencing purchase.

In short, as was anticipated in our definition of communications as the use of symbols to influence human behavior, when the salesman steps into the prospects' living room, the information-seeking model must give way to a "games strategy" model involving the interplay of influence attempts made and resisted.

This means that our analysis of the sales encounter must isolate the bargaining devices which prospects use. Do they try to counter the salesman's influence attempts with questions of price, or comments on alternative brands, or doubts about the desirability of the product itself? But the shift to an "influence" model also raised a fundamental question about our original choice of time and place at which to intervene in the decision-making process.

If, as we have suggested, the salesman's presence converts an information-handling process into a contest of influence attempts, why do prospects permit this change to occur by consenting to see a salesman? As we have pointed out, the very invitation drastically limits the prospects' bargaining ability. Moreover, it must be obvious to any prospect that he is ill-matched, in terms of product knowledge, experience in bargaining, and motivation to "win," in any such game played with a salesman. Perhaps the prospect puts himself at a disadvantage only because he finds himself in Lewin's Type IV conflict, double approach-avoidance, in which all action tends to be blocked[14] and only introduction of the salesman can resolve the dilemma.

In any case, it seemed clear to us that the most important decision which the household makes may well be the invitation to the salesman or the acceptance of his request for a visit. If so, then a study which focuses on events occurring *after* this decision enters the picture too late. If the sales encounter is an influence rather than an information process, we need to know a lot more about how each participant defines the situation when he enters into it.

How many salesmen, for example, and how many prospects look upon the encounter as a zero-sum game? How many of them look upon it as a battle of wits, enjoyable in itself, regardless of the outcome? What motives does each attribute to the other? What range of negotiation does each perceive for himself and the others? What tactics does each regard (a) as permissible and (b) as likely to be employed by each participant? How do these different definitions of the situation affect communications in it? How often and why and how do these definitions change during the encounter?

We have tried to answer some of these questions by giving each participant a series of semantic differential scales. Before an interview, insurance salesmen rate life insurance, life insurance salesmen, life insurance customers,

[14]C. I. Hovland and R. R. Sears, "Experiments on Motor Conflict. I. Types of Conflict and Their Modes of Resolution," *Journal of Experimental Psychology*, Vol. 23, pp. 477-493.

and themselves. After the interview they rate each prospect and also indicate how they think each prospect rates them. Insurance prospects, similarly, rate life insurance, life insurance salesmen, and themselves before an interview. Afterwards they rate life insurance and the specific agent seen and indicate how they think the agent rates them.

These ratings, we hope, will give us an index of each participant's sensitivity to the others. Thus we expect to find that the salesman or prospect who correctly perceives how the other is rating him will be more effective because of his greater sensitivity to interpersonal cues. At the same time, of course, the scales give us a somewhat more sensitive measure of a salesman's success in influencing prospects than mere success or failure in the sale of a policy. A salesman may produce a significant change in attitudes toward insurance, toward salesmen or toward both, even if no sale develops. Finally, we are interested in comparing self-ratings and role stereotypes for both salesmen and customers.

Homogeneity of Prospects

In addition to these two reasons for believing that our study must begin prior to the sales encounter itself, a cursory comparison of the first encyclopedia and insurance tapes provided a third reason.

We had expected to find a minimum of real interaction in the encyclopedia tapes; folk lore is full of stories of encyclopedia salesmen who, when interrupted, have to start back at the beginning of a canned pitch. We were surprised, however, to see the extent to which insurance salesmen dominated the interviews, presenting a standardized presentation that avoided any extensive interaction with their prospects—and deprived salesmen of the advantage of feedback in the face-to-face situation.

A possible explanation for this has come to light during the interviews which we conduct with salesmen following taping of the sales encounter itself. Salesmen tell us that their most successful colleagues are those who discover the type of prospects with whom they are most successful and concentrate on them.

To the extent that this occurs, to the extent that there is high similarity among the prospects whom any given salesman contacts, we would expect salesmen to sell a highly-standardized product and to use highly-standardized messages about the product.

There are two plausible explanations as to why this should be true. One is the principle of least effort. If a salesman can concentrate on a homogeneous clientele, he can save the effort involved in having dozens of policy options at his fingertips and in being able to shift smoothly from one type of message to another. His communications activity, both sending and receiving, is sim-

plified. The other is that he is likely to have a high ratio of sales made compared with sales attempted. An encyclopedia publisher might find it profitable
to make a relatively low proportion of sales—but the salesman is likely, no
matter what he is paid, to find frequent failure highly punishing from a psychological viewpoint. The same, we suspect, is true of the insurance agent.

Corroboration for this viewpoint comes from Evans,[15] who has also told
us in a personal interview that successful insurance salesmen tend to focus on
a homogeneous clientele of persons much like themselves despite pressure by
their employers who insist that a "good salesman" can and should be able to
sell to anyone.

We are now attempting to follow up on this lead. A leading life insurance
firm has tentatively agreed to review the policies written by some 250 of their
agents to determine how much product standardization exists within the
policies written by individual agents. We have suggested that the sample of
agents be stratified in terms of their ability to resist management pressure as
indexed by years of experience, value of policies written, and if possible, support from their peers.

In short, our interest is shifting from an analysis of the messages which
salesmen and prospects exchange in the sales encounter to a study of the
process by which a salesman discovers the audience and market with which he
is most successful and the methods by which he gains access to such prospects.

Shift in Product

Just as our feeling that starting our study with the salesman's
interview may mean entering the scene after the most significant communications events have already occurred affects our method of study, so a shift in
method of study affects the products being studied.

Two of the biggest decisions, in terms of cost, which a household makes
are those involving the purchase of a house and an automobile. However, the
decision-making involved in these purchases tends to involve a whole series of
lesser decisions made over a long period of time and occurring in many different places. We had excluded them from our study since they were not amenable to the tape-recording of a single sales encounter. Since it now appears that
this method may miss the crucial decision-making events even for insurance
policies and encyclopedias, autos and houses come back into the picture.

These two products meet many of our criteria. The uncertainty associated
with high unit cost attaches to both. It is particularly high if one concentrates
on the first home which a family purchases, as we plan to. Although prospects
may have considerable product experience as renters, they do not have previ-

[15]Franklin B. Evans, *Dyadic Interaction in Selling*, multilithed by author, University
of Chicago, 1964.

ous experience in the process of bargaining and decision-making that goes into purchase, thus heightening uncertainty. On the other hand, the purchase of a house involves a great number of decisions, many of which may be delegated to one spouse rather than made jointly; this is particularly true because of the episodic nature of house and car purchase and the several times and places in which these decisions are made. To this extent a study of home purchase departs from the criteria set down earlier. The relative influence of each spouse may be reflected less in his communications behavior in an encounter with a salesman than in the number and relative importance of each of these preliminary decisions which each makes.

On the other hand, the definition of the situation which each participant carries into the encounter remains important, and we can manipulate the relative strength of each participant at the bargaining table. Although we cannot date entry of a prospect into the housing market by reference to some intra-family event with any exactitude, we can compare families who have been engaged in the process of search-and-comparison for various periods of time and who have varying distances from the actual purchase itself.

Our plan is to pick up subjects on their first contact with local builders or their first visit to a model home. In a focused interview we will then have them retrace for us their information-seeking efforts up to the present, and we will ask them to keep a diary, from this point on, of the information-seeking activity they engage in and of the influences they are exposed to. It is our hope that across our families we will have both recall and diary data for similar phases in the decision-making process, so that we can compare the results of these two different methods. (If necessary, we can pick up some families at a later contact with the builder.)

We plan to add an experimental phase to the survey phase just described by asking each spouse on our first contact with them, in a variant of the Kenkel technique, to indicate which "extras" from a list of some $15,000 housing choices they would choose, given a budget of some $3,000.

In a control group of subjects, husbands and wives will be asked to reconcile their differences and reach a joint decision; we will tape their discussion at the time we pick up their diaries. The remaining subjects will be assigned to experimental groups in a study of the effects of peer group influence and a comparison of two methods of increasing prospects' relative influence in the sales encounter. Here is how it will work. In return for keeping diaries, randomly-selected subjects will be given free tuition to a "workshop on home buying." Couples assigned to the "peer group influence" condition will be split up; husbands and wives will meet separately to discuss the list of "extras" and come to a joint decision. After this, each individual will again indicate how he, personally, would spend the $3,000 budget. Then spouses will be reunited and asked to come to a joint household decision on the choice of extras. Other couples, representing a control group, will go directly to the joint-decision session.

Half of each of these groups, peer group and control group, will then be assigned to a "product information" session and half to a "bargaining strategy" session. The first of these will be given product information by architects, lending agencies and other "impartial" experts. The other group will be provided with information about builders' margins and practice in bargaining strategy. It is our hope that, by tape-recording the final conference between builder and buyer at which terms of the purchase are agree upon and the contract signed and by analyzing the actual contract terms themselves, we will be able to compare the effects of these two ways of increasing the influence which prospects can exert in the sales encounter.

This, then, is the road we have traveled. It has taken us from concentration on the sales encounter itself to a feeling that perhaps the most important decisions of all, from a communications point of view, have occurred prior to the encounter itself. Let me end, therefore, with a plea for the serendipity of research without deadlines. Let me urge more false starts, more changing of horses in midstream, and let me hope for a host of friends and colleagues who will find in the pieces we have strewn along the way some part they can fit into a grander design.

VII

SOCIAL IMPACT OF COMMUNICATIONS

Much controversy about several forms of communication is found in books, articles, press releases, and private conversation. Members of advertising trade groups, for instance, devote considerable needed attention to dealing with criticisms and correcting abuses in the industry. Selling communications make an ideal subject for controversy because they are by nature trying to attract attention and interest from nearly all members of American society above the age of one—and even this age exception might be argued.

The readings in this part suggest that the impact of the advertising form of communication may be more deeply involved in the fabric of society and the individual's daily life than a careless glance would detect. The complications that result can be viewed as insignificant, minor, or major—and, similarly, as either correctable or hopeless. Some solutions to the problems implied in these short essays on life with advertising would have profound impact on the economy and certainly on the mass communications media. Solutions, however, await the definition and measurement of the problems. These well-written, critical selections show some different dimensions of the problems.

34

The Day the Ads Stopped

GEORGE G. KIRSTEIN

The day the advertising stopped began just like any other day—
the sun came up, the milk was delivered and people started for work. I noticed
the first difference when I went out on the porch to pick up *The New York
Times*. The newsdealer had advised me that the paper would now cost 50c a
day so I was prepared for the new price beneath the weather forecast, but the
paper was thinner than a Saturday edition in summer. I hefted it thoughtfully,
and reflected that there really was no alternative to taking the *Times*. The *News*
had suspended publication the day before the advertising stopped with a final
gallant editorial blast at the Supreme Court which had declared the advertising prohibition constitutional. The *Herald Tribune* was continuing to publish,
also at 50c, but almost no one was taking both papers and I preferred the *Times*.

As I glanced past the big headlines chronicling the foreign news, my eye
was caught by a smaller bank:

> 1 KILLED, 1 INJURED IN
> ELEVATOR ACCIDENT AT MACY'S.

The story was rather routine; a child had somehow gotten into the elevator pit
and his mother had tried to rescue him. The elevator had descended, killing
the woman, but fortunately had stopped before crushing the child. It was not
so much the story as its locale that drew my attention. I realized that this was
the first time in a full, rich life that I had ever read a newspaper account of an
accident in a department store. I had suspected that these misfortunes befell
stores, as they do all business institutions, but this was my first confirmation.

There were other noticeable changes in the *Times*. Accounts of traffic accidents now actually gave the manufacturers' names of the vehicles involved as,
"A Cadillac driven by Harvey Gilmore demolished a Volkswagen operated
by . . ." The feature column on "Advertising" which used to tell what agencies
had lost what accounts and what assistant vice president had been elevated was
missing. As a matter of fact, the whole newspaper, but particularly the Financial Section, exhibited a dearth of "news" stories which could not possibly

Reprinted from *The Nation* (June 1, 1964), pp. 555-557, by permission of the publisher.

interest anyone but the persons mentioned. Apparently, without major expenditures for advertising, the promotion of Gimbels' stocking buyer to assistant merchandising manager was not quite as "newsworthy" as it had been only yesterday. Movies and plays were listed in their familiar spot, as were descriptions of available apartments in what used to be the classified section. The women's page was largely a catalogue of special offerings in department and food stores, but no comparative prices were given and all adjectives were omitted. One could no longer discover from reading the *Times,* or any other paper, who had been named Miss National Car Care Queen or who had won the Miss Rheingold contest.

Driving to work, I observed workmen removing the billboards. The grass and trees behind the wall of signs were beginning to reappear. The ragged posters were being ripped from their familiar locations on the walls of warehouses and stores, and the natural ugliness of these structures was once more apparent without the augmenting tawdriness of last year's political posters or last week's neighborhood movie schedules.

I turned on the car radio to the subscription FM station to which I had sent my $10 dues. The music came over the air without interruption, and after awhile a news announcer gave an uninterrupted version of current events and the weather outlook. No one yet knew which radio stations would be able to continue broadcasting. It depended on the loyalty with which their listeners continued to send in their subscription dues. However, their prospects were better than fair, for everyone realized that, since all merchandise which had previously been advertised would cost considerably less on the store counter, people would have funds available to pay for the news they read or the music or other programs they listened to. The absence of the familiar commercials, the jingles, the songs and the endless repetition of the nonsense which had routinely offended our ears led me to consider some of these savings. My wife's lipsticks would now cost half as much as previously; the famous brand soaps were selling at 25 per cent below yesterday's prices; razor blades were 10 per cent cheaper; and other appliances and merchandise which had previously been nationally advertised were reduced by an average of 5 per cent. The hallowed myth that retail prices did not reflect the additional cost of huge advertising campaigns was exploded once and for all. Certainly these savings should add up to enough for me to pay for what I listened to on my favorite radio station or read in the newspaper of my choice.

After parking my car, I passed the familiar newsstand between the garage and the office. *"Life* $1," the printed sign said. *"Time* and *Newsweek,* 75c." Next to these announcements was a crayon-scrawled message! *"Consumer Reports* sold out. Bigger shipment next week." I stopped to chat with the newsie. "The mags like *Consumer Reports* that tell the truth about products are selling like crazy," he told me. *"Reader's Digest* is running a merchandise analysis section next month." I asked about the weekly journals of opinion. He said, "Well now they are half the price of the news magazines—*The Nation* and *The*

New Republic prices have not gone up, you know, but I don't think that will help them much. After all, a lot of magazines are going to begin printing that exposé-type stuff. Besides, people are buying books now. "Look!" He pointed across the street to the paperback bookstore where a crowd was milling around as though a fire sale were in progress.

I walked over to the bookstore and found no special event going on. But books represented much better value than magazines or newspapers, now that the latter were no longer subsidized by advertisements, and the public was snapping up the volumes.

Sitting in my office, I reviewed the events and the extraordinary political coalition that had been responsible for passing the advertising prohibition law through Congress by a close margin. The women, of course, had been the spearhead of the drive. Not since the Anti-Saloon-League days and the militant woman-suffrage movement at the beginning of the century had women organized so militantly or expended energy more tirelessly in pursuit of their objective. Their slogans were geared to two main themes which reflected their major grievances. The first slogan, "Stop making our kids killers," was geared mainly to the anti-television campaign. The sadism, killing and assorted violence which filled the TV screens over all channels from early morning to late at night had finally so outraged mothers' groups, PTAs and other organizations concerned with the country's youth that a massive parents' movement was mobilized.

The thrust of the women's drive was embodied in their effective two-word motto, "Stop lying." Women's organizations all over the country established committees to study all advertisements. For the first time in history, these common messages were analyzed in detail. The results were published in anti-advertising advertisements, by chain letter and by mouth. The results were devastating. No dog-food manufacturer could claim that pets loved his product without having the women demand, "How in the name of truth do you know? Did you interview the dogs?" No shampoo or cosmetic preparation could use the customary blandishments without having the women produce some witch who had used the particular product and who had lost her hair, developed acne or had her fingernails curl back.

Women led the attack, but the intellectuals soon joined them, and the clergy followed a little later. The intellectuals based their campaign largely on the argument that the English language was losing its usefulness, that word meanings were being so corrupted that it was almost impossible to teach youth to read to any purpose. One example commonly cited was the debasement of the superlative "greatest." The word had come to mean anything that didn't break down; viz., "the greatest lawn mower ever," interpreted realistically, was an instrument that, with luck, would cut grass for one summer. The clergy's campaign was geared simply to the proposition that it was impossible to teach people the virtues of truth when half-truths and lies were the commonly accepted fare of readers and viewers alike.

Opposition to the anti-advertising law was impressive, and at the beginning it looked as if all the big guns were arrayed against the women. Spokesmen for big business contended throughout the campaign that elimination of advertising meant elimination of jobs. The fallacy of this argument was soon exposed when all realized that it was not men's jobs but simply machine running time that was involved. By this decade of the century, the cybernetic revolution had developed to a point where very few men were involved in any of the production or distribution processes. No one could feel much sympathy for the poor machines and their companion computers because they would be running only four hours daily instead of six.

Some merchants tried to blunt the "stop lying" slogan by telling the absolute truth. One San Francisco store advertised: *2,000 overcoats—only $12. Let's face it—our buyer goofed! These coats are dogs or you couldn't possibly buy them at this price. We're losing our shirt on this sale and the buyer has been fired. But, at least, many of these coats will keep you warm.*

The trouble with this technique was that it backfired in favor of the women. The few true ads, by contrast, drew attention to the vast volume of exaggeration, misrepresentation and outright lies that were printed as usual. The advertising industry published thirteen different editions of its "Advertisers Code" in the years preceding the law's passage, but few could detect any difference from the days when no code at all existed.

The press, of course, was the strongest opponent and loudest voice against the advertising prohibition. Its argument was largely legalistic, based on the First Amendment to the Constitution, for the publishers had decided at the outset of their defense not to emphasize the fact that if advertising stopped, readers would actually have to pay for what they read, rather than have America's largest corporations pay for the education and edification of the public. However, the words "Free Press" came to have a double meaning—both an unhampered press and a press that charged only a nominal fee for the publications.

The constitutional argument was really resolved in that final speech on the floor of the Senate before a gallery-packed audience, by Senator Thorndike of Idaho. His memorable ovation, certainly among the greatest in the Senate's distinguished history, concluded:

> *And so, Mr. President, the opponents of this measure* [the advertising prohibition] *claim that the founders of this republic, our glorious forefathers, in their august wisdom, forbade the Congress to interfere with the freedom of the press to conduct itself in any way it found profitable. But I say to you, that the framers of our Constitution intended to protect the public by permitting the press, without fear or favor, to examine all of the institutions of our democracy. Our forefathers planned a press free to criticize, free to analyze, free to dissent. They did not plan a subsidized press, a conformist press, a prostitute press.*

The applause was thunderous and the bill squeaked through the Senate by four votes. Three years later, the Supreme Court upheld Senator Thorndike's interpretation. That was two days ago, and today the advertising stopped.

All morning I worked in the office, and just before noon I went uptown for lunch. The subway cars were as drab as ever and seemed a little less bright because of the absence of the familiar posters. However, in one car the Camera Club of the Technical Trades High School had "hung" a show of New York City photographs chosen from student submissions. In another car, the posters on one side carried Session I of a course in Spanish for English-speaking riders, while the opposite side featured the same course in English for those speaking Spanish. This program was sponsored by the Board of Education which had subcontracted the administration of it to the Berlitz School. A poster in both languages in the middle of the car explained that the lessons would proceed on a weekly basis and that by sending $1 to the Board of Education, review sheets and periodic tests would be available upon request.

On Madison Avenue, the shopping crowds were milling around as usual, but there was a noticeable absence of preoccupied and hatless young men hurrying along the street. The retirement plan that the advertising industry had worked out through the insurance companies was fairly generous, and the majority of key personnel that had been laid off when the agencies closed were relieved not to have to make the long trek from Westport or the nearer suburbs each day. Some of the copywriters who had been talking about it since their youth were now really going to write that novel.

Others had set up shop as public relations counselors, but the outlook for their craft was not bright. Without the club of advertising, city editors looked over mimeographed press releases with a new distaste, and it is even rumored that on some newspapers the orders had come down to throw out all such "handouts" without exception. On the magazines, the old struggle between the editorial staff and the advertising sales staff for dominance had finally been resolved by the elimination of the latter. There were even some skeptics who believed that public relations counseling would become a lost art, like hand basket weaving. So most former advertising copywriters planned to potter about in their gardens, cure their ulcers and give up drinking. They were not so many. It was a surprise to most people to learn that the advertising industry, which had had such a profound effect on the country's habits and moral attitudes, directly employed fewer than 100,000 people.

Outside 383 Madison Avenue, moving vans were unloading scientific equipment and laboratory accessories into the space vacated by Batten, Barton, Durstine & Osborn. The ethical drug industry had evolved a plan, in the three-year interim between the passage of the advertising prohibition and the Supreme Court's validation of it, to test all new drugs at a central impartial laboratory. Computers and other of the latest information-gathering machinery were massed in the space vacated by this large advertising agency to correlate the results of drug tests which were being conducted in hospitals, clinics, laboratories and doctors' offices throughout the world.

The Ford Foundation had given one of its richest grants, nearly three-quarters of a billion dollars, to the establishment of this Central Testing Bureau. The American Medical Association had finally agreed, under considerable public pressure, to take primary responsibility for its administration. It was pointed out to the doctors that when the drug companies could no longer make their individual claims through advertisements in the AMA bulletin or the medical society publications, a new and more reliable method of disseminating information would be required. At the outset, the AMA had joined the drug companies in fighting bitterly against the prohibition, but the doctors now took considerable pride in their centralized research and correlation facilities. The AMA bulletin, once swollen to the bulk of a small city's telephone directory, was now only as thick as a summer issue of *Newsweek*. Doctors no longer would find their mail boxes stuffed with throw-away material and sample pills; but they would receive the weekly scientific report from Central Testing Bureau as to the efficacy of an experience with all new preparations.

Late in the afternoon, I began to hear the first complaints about the way the new law worked. One of the men came in and picked up a folder of paper matches lying on my desk. "I'm swiping these; they're not giving them out any more, you know." Someone else who had been watching TV said that the two channels assigned to the government under a setup like that of the B.B.C., were boring. One channel showed the ball game, but the other had been limited to a short session of the Senate debating the farm bill, and a one-hour view of the UN Security Council taking up the latest African crisis. My informant told me the Yanks had won 8 to 0, and the Senate and the UN weren't worth watching. I reminded him that when the channel that was to be supervised by the American Academy of Arts and Sciences got on the air, as well as the one to be managed by a committee of the local universities, things might improve. "Cheer up," I told him, "At least it's better than the Westerns and the hair rinses."

Oh, there were some complaints, all right, and I suppose there were some unhappy people. But personally I thought the day the advertising stopped was the best day America had had since the last war ended.

35

A Sad Heart at the Supermarket
RANDALL JARRELL

The emperor Augustus would sometimes say to his Senate: "Words fail me, my Lord; nothing I can say could possibly indicate the depth of my feelings in this matter." But I am speaking about this matter of mass culture, the mass media, not as an Emperor but as a fool, as a suffering, complaining, helplessly nonconforming poet-or-artist-of-a-sort, far off at the obsolescent rear of things: what I say will indicate the depth of my feelings and the shallowness and one-sidedness of my thoughts. If those English lyric poets who went mad during the eighteenth century had told you why the Age of Enlightenment was driving them crazy, it would have had a kind of documentary interest: what I say may have a kind of documentary interest.

The toad beneath the harrow knows
Exactly where each tooth-point goes;

if you tell me that the field is being harrowed to grow grain for bread, and to create a world in which there will be no more famines, or toads either, I will say, "I know"—but let me tell you where the tooth-points go, and what the harrow looks like from below.

Advertising men, businessmen, speak continually of "media" or "the media" or "the mass media"—one of their trade journals is named, simply, *Media*. It is an impressive word: one imagines Mephistopheles offering Faust media that no man has ever known; one feels, while the word is in one's ear, that abstract, overmastering powers, of a scale and intensity unimagined yesterday, are being offered one by the technicians who discovered and control them— offered, and at a price. The word, like others, has the clear fatal ring of that new world whose space we occupy so luxuriously and precariously; the world that produces mink stoles, rockabilly records, and tactical nuclear weapons by the million; the world that Attila, Galileo, Hansel and Gretel never knew.

Reprinted from *Culture for the Millions*, Norman Jacobs, editor. Princeton, N. J., D. Van Nostrand Company, Inc., 1961, pp. 97-110. Permission granted by *Daedalus*, Journal of the American Academy of Arts and Sciences.

And yet, it's only the plural of "medium." "Medium," says the dictionary, "that which lies in the middle; hence, middle condition or degree. . . . A substance through which a force acts or an effect is transmitted. . . . That through or by which anything is accomplished; as, an advertising *medium*. . . . *Biol.* A nutritive mixture or substance, as broth, gelatin, agar, for cultivating bacteria, fungi, etc." Let us name *our* trade journal *The Medium*. For all these media (television, radio, movies, popular magazines, and the rest) are a single medium, in whose depths we are all being cultivated. This medium is of middle condition or degree, mediocre; it lies in the middle of everything, between a man and his neighbor, his wife, his child, his self; it, more than anything else, is the substance through which the forces of our society act upon us, make us into what our society needs.

And what does it need? For us to need . . . Oh, it needs for us to do or be many things—to be workers, technicians, executives, soldiers, housewives. But first of all, last of all, it needs for us to be buyers; consumers; beings who want much and will want more—who want consistently and insatiably. Find some spell to make us no longer want the stoles, the records, and the weapons, and our world will change into something to us unimaginable. Find some spell to make us realize that the product or service which seemed yesterday an unthinkable luxury is today an inexorable necessity, and our world will go on. It is the Medium which casts this spell—which is this spell. As we look at the television set, listen to the radio, read the magazines, the frontier of necessity is always being pushed forward. The Medium shows us what our new needs are—how often, without it, we should not have known!—and it shows us how they can be satisfied: they can be satisfied by buying something. The act of buying something is at the root of our world: if anyone wishes to paint the beginning of things in our society, he will paint a picture of God holding out to Adam a checkbook or credit card or Charge-A-Plate.

But how quickly our poor naked Adam is turned into a consumer, is linked to others by the great chain of buying!

> No outcast he, bewildered and depressed:
> Along his infant veins are interfused
> The gravitation and the filial bond
> Of nature that connect him with the world.

Children of three or four can ask for a brand of cereal, sing some soap's commercial; by the time that they are twelve they are not children but teen-age consumers, interviewed, graphed, analyzed. They are on their way to becoming that ideal figure of our culture, the knowledgeable consumer. I'll define him: the knowledgeable consumer is someone who, when he goes to Weimar, knows how to buy a Weimaraner. He has learned to understand life as a series of choices among the things and services of this world; because of being an executive, or executive's wife, or performer, or celebrity, or someone who has inherited money, he is able to afford the choices that he makes, with knowing familiarity, among restaurants, resorts, clothes, cars, liners, hits or best-sellers of every kind. We may still go to Methodist or Baptist or Presbyterian churches on Sunday, but the Protestant ethic of frugal industry, of production for its own sake, is gone. Production has come to seem to our society not much more than a condition prior to consumption: "The challenge of today," writes a great advertising agency, "is to make the consumer raise his level of demand." This challenge has been met: the Medium has found it easy to make its people feel the continually increasing lacks, the many specialized dissatisfactions (merging into one great dissatisfaction, temporarily assuaged by new purchases) that it needs for them to feel. When, in some magazine, we see the Medium at its most nearly perfect, we hardly know which half is entertaining and distracting us, which half making us buy: some advertisement may be more ingeniously entertaining than the text beside it, but it is the text which has made us long for a product more passionately. When one finishes *Holiday* or *Harper's Bazaar* or *House and Garden* or *The New Yorker* or *High Fidelity* or *Road and Track* or—but make your own list—buying something, going somewhere seems a necessary completion to the act of reading the magazine. Reader, isn't buying or fantasy-buying an important part of your and my emotional life? (If you reply, *No*, I'll think of you with bitter envy as more than merely human; as deeply un-American.) It is a standard joke of our culture that when a woman is bored or sad she buys something to make herself feel better; but in this respect we are all women together, and can hear complacently the reminder of how feminine this consumer-world of ours is. One imagines as a characteristic dialogue of our time an interview in which someone is asking of a vague gracious figure, a kind of Mrs. America: "But while you waited for the Intercontinental Ballistic Missiles what did you *do?*" She answers: "I bought things."

She reminds one of the sentinel at Pompeii—a space among ashes, now, but at his post: she too did what she was supposed to do. . . . Our society has delivered us—most of us—from the bonds of necessity, so that we no longer need worry about having food enough to keep from starving, clothing and shelter enough to keep from freezing; yet if the ends for which we work, of which we dream, are restaurants and clothes and houses, consumption, possessions, how have we escaped? We have merely exchanged man's old bondage for a new voluntary one. But *voluntary* is wrong: the consumer is trained for his job of consuming as the factory worker is trained for his job of producing; and the first is a longer, more complicated training, since it is easier to teach a man to handle a tool, to read a dial, than it is to teach him to ask, always, for a name-brand aspirin—to want, someday, a stand-by generator. What is that? You don't know? I used not to know, but the readers of *House Beautiful* all know, and now I know: it is the electrical generator that stands in the basement of the suburban houseowner, shining, silent, until at last one night the lights go out, the freezer's food begins to—

Ah, but it's frozen for good, the lights are on forever; the owner has switched on the stand-by generator.

But you don't see that he really needs the generator, you'd rather have seen him buy a second car? He has two. A second bathroom? He has four. He long ago doubled everything, when the People of the Medium doubled everything; and now that he's gone twice round he will have to wait three years, or four, till both are obsolescent—but while he waits there are so many new needs that he can satisfy, so many things a man can buy.

> Man wants but little here below
> Nor wants that little long,

said the poet; what a lie! Man wants almost unlimited quantities of almost everything, and he wants it till the day he dies.

We sometimes see in *Life* or *Look* a double-page photograph of some family standing on the lawn among its possessions: station wagon, swimming pool, power cruiser, sports car, tape recorder, television sets, radios, cameras, power lawn mower, garden tractor, lathe, barbecue set, sporting equipment, domestic appliances—all the gleaming, grotesquely imaginative paraphernalia of its existence. It was hard to get them on two pages, soon they will need four. It is like a dream, a child's dream before Christmas; yet if the members of the family doubt that they are awake, they have only to reach out and pinch something. The family seems pale and small, a negligible appendage, beside its possessions; only a human being would need to ask, "Which owns which?" We are fond of saying that something-or-other is not just something-or-other but "a way of life"; this too is a way of life—our way, the way.

Emerson, in his spare stony New England, a few miles from Walden, could write:

> Things are in the saddle
> And ride mankind.

He could say more now: that they are in the theater and studio, and entertain mankind; are in the pulpit and preach to mankind. The values of business, in an overwhelmingly successful business society like our own, are reflected in every sphere: values which agree with them are reinforced, values which disagree are cancelled out or have lip-service paid to them. In business what sells is good, and that's the end of it—that is what *good* means; if the world doesn't beat a path to your door, your mousetrap wasn't better. The values of the Medium (which is both a popular business itself and the cause of popularity in other businesses) are business values: money, success, celebrity. If we are representative members of our society, the Medium's values are ours; even when we are unrepresentative, non-conforming, our hands are (too often) subdued to the element they work in, and our unconscious expectations are all that we consciously reject. (Darwin said that he always immediately wrote down evidence against a theory because otherwise, he'd noticed, he would forget it; in the same way we keep forgetting the existence of those poor and unknown failures whom we might rebelliously love and admire.) *If you're so smart why aren't you rich?* is the ground-base of our society, a grumbling and quite unanswerable criticism, since the society's nonmonetary values *are* directly convertible into money. (Celebrity turns into testimonials, lectures, directorships, presidencies, the capital gains of an autobiography *Told To* some professional ghost who photographs the man's life as Bachrach photographs his body.) When Liberace said that his critics' unfavorable reviews hurt him so much that he cried all the way to the bank, one had to admire the correctness and penetration of his press-agent's wit: in another age, what mightn't such a man have become!

Our culture is essentially periodical: we believe that all that is deserves to perish and to have something else put in its place. We speak of "planned obsolescence," but it is more than planned, it is felt—is an assumption about the nature of the world. The present is better and more interesting, more real, than the past; the future will be better and more interesting, more real, than the present. (But, consciously, we do not hold against the present its prospective obsolescence.) Our standards have become, to an astonishing degree, those of what is called "the world of fashion," where mere timeliness—being orange in orange's year, violet in violet's—is the value to which all other values are reducible. In our society "old-fashioned" is so final a condemnation that a man like Norman Vincent Peale can say about atheism or agnosticism simply that it is old-fashioned; the homely recommendation of "Give me that good old-time religion" has become after a few decades the conclusive rejection of "old-fashioned" atheism.

All this is, at bottom, the opposite of the world of the arts, where commercial and scientific progress do not exist; where the bone of Homer and Mozart and Donatello is there, always, under the mere blush of fashion; where the past—the remote past, even—is responsible for the way that we understand, value, and act in, the present. (When one reads an abstract expressionist's remark that Washington studios are "eighteen months behind" those of his colleagues in New York, one realizes something of the terrible power of business and fashion over those most overtly hostile to them.) An artist's work and life presuppose continuing standards, values stretched out over centuries or millennia, a future that is the continuation and modification of the past, not its contradiction or irrelevant replacement. He is working for the time that wants the best that he can do: the present, he hopes—but if not that, the future. If he sees that fewer and fewer people are any real audience for the serious artists of the past, he will feel that still fewer are going to be an audience for the serious artists of the present, for those who, willingly or unwillingly, sacrifice extrinsic values to intrinsic ones, immediate effectiveness to that steady attraction which, the artist hopes, true excellence will always exert. The past's relation to the artist or man of culture is almost the opposite of its relation to the rest of our society. To him the present is no more than the last ring on the trunk, understandable and valuable only in terms of all the earlier rings.

The rest of our society sees only that great last ring, the enveloping surface of the trunk; what's underneath is a disregarded, almost hypothetical foundation. When Northrop Frye writes that "the preoccupation of the humanities with the past is sometimes made a reproach against them by those who forget that we face the past: it may be shadowy, but it is all that is there," he is saying what for the artist or man of culture is self-evidently true; yet for the Medium and the People of the Medium it is as self-evidently false—for them the present (or a past so recent, so quick-changing, so soon-disappearing, that it might be called the specious present) is all that is there.

In the past our culture's frame of reference, its body of common knowledge (its possibility of comprehensible allusion) changed slowly and superficially; the amount added to it or taken away from it in any ten years was a small proportion of the whole. Now in any ten years a surprisingly large proportion of the whole is replaced. Most of the information people have in common is something that four or five years from now they will not even remember having known. A newspaper story remarks in astonishment that television quiz programs have "proved that ordinary citizens can be conversant with such esoterica as jazz, opera, the Bible, Shakespeare, poetry and fisticuffs." You may exclaim, "Esoterica! If the Bible and Shakespeare are esoterica, what is there that's common knowledge?" The answer, I suppose, is that Elfrida von Nardoff and Teddy Nadler (the ordinary citizens on the quiz programs) are common knowledge; though not for long. Songs disappear in two or three months, celebrities in two or three years; most of the Medium is lightly felt and soon forgotten. What is as dead as day-before-yesterday's newspaper, the next-to-the-last number on the roulette wheel? and most of the knowledge we have in common is knowledge of such newspapers, such numbers. But the novelist or poet or dramatist, when he moves a great audience, depends upon the deep feelings, the live unforgotten knowledge, that the people of his culture share; if these have become contingent, superficial, ephemeral, it is disastrous for him.

New products and fashions replace the old, and the fact that they replace them is proof enough of their superiority. Similarly, the Medium does not need to show that the subjects that fill it are timely or interesting or important—the fact that they are its subjects makes them so. If *Time, Life,* and the television shows are full of Tom Fool this month, he's no fool. And when he has been gone from them a while, we do not think him a fool—we do not think of him at all. He no longer exists, in the fullest sense of the word "exist": to be is to be perceived, to be a part of the Medium of our perception. Our celebrities are not kings, romantic in exile, but Representatives who, defeated, are forgotten; they had always only the qualities that we delegated to them.

After driving for four or five minutes along the road outside my door, I come to a long row of one-room shacks about the size of kitchens, made out of used boards, metal signs, old tin roofs. To the people who live in them an electric dishwasher of one's own is as much a fantasy as an ocean liner of one's own. But since the Medium (and those whose thought is molded by it) does not perceive them, these people are themselves a fantasy: no matter how many millions of such exceptions to the general rule there are, they do not really exist, but have a kind of anomalous, statistical subsistence; our moral and imaginative view of the world is no more affected by them than by the occupants of some home for the mentally deficient a little farther along the road. If, some night, one of these outmoded, economically deficient ghosts should scratch at my window, I could say only, "Come back twenty years ago." And if I, as an old-fashioned, one-room poet, a friend of "quiet culture," a "meek lover of the good," should go out some night to scratch at another window, shouldn't I hear someone's indifferent or regretful, "Come back a century or two ago"?

When those whose existence the Medium recognizes ring the chimes of the writer's doorbell, fall through his letter slot, float out onto his television screen, what is he to say to them? A man's unsuccessful struggle to get his family food is material for a work of art—for tragedy, almost; his unsuccessful struggle to get his family a stand-by generator is material for what? Comedy? Farce? Comedy on such a scale, at such a level, that our society and its standards seem, almost, farce? And yet it is the People of the Medium, those who long for and get, or long for and don't get, the generator, whom our culture finds representative, who are there to be treated first of all. And the Medium itself— one of the ends of life, something essential to people's understanding and valuing of their existence, something many of their waking hours are spent listening to or looking at—how is *it* to be treated as subject matter for art? The writer cannot just reproduce it; should he satirize or parody it? But often parody or satire is impossible, since it is already its own parody; and by the time the writer's work is published, the part of the Medium which is satirized will already have been forgotten. Yet isn't the Medium by now an essential part of its watchers? Those whom Mohammedans speak of as the People of the Book are inexplicable, surely, in any terms that omit it; we are people of the magazine, the television set, the radio, and are inexplicable in any terms that omit them.

Oscar Wilde's wittily paradoxical statement about Nature's imitation of Art is literally true when the Nature is human nature and the Art that of television, radio, motion pictures, popular magazines. Life is so, people are so, the Medium shows its audience, and most of the audience believe it, expect people to be so, try to be so themselves. For them the People of the Medium are reality, what human beings normally, primarily are: and mere local or personal variations are not real in the same sense. The Medium mediates between us and raw reality, and the mediation more and more replaces reality for us. In many homes either the television set or the radio is turned on most of the time the family is awake. (Many radio stations have a news broadcast every half hour, and many people like and need to hear it.) It is as if the people longed to be established in reality, to be reminded continually of the "real," the "objective" world—the created world of the Medium—rather than be left at the mercy of actuality, of the helpless contingency of the world in which the radio receiver or television set is sitting. (And surely we can sympathize: which of us hasn't found a similar refuge in the "real," created world of Cézanne or Goethe or Verdi? Yet Dostoievsky's world is too different from Wordsworth's, Piero della Francesca's from Goya's, Bach's from Hugo Wolf's, for us to be able to substitute one homogeneous mediated reality for everyday reality in the belief that it *is* everyday reality.) The world of events and celebrities and performers, the Great World, has become for many listeners, lookers, readers, the world of primary reality: how many times they have sighed at the colorless unreality of their own lives and families, sighed for the bright reality of, say, Lucille Ball's —of some shadow dyed, gowned, directed, produced, and agented into a being as equivocal as that of the square root of minus one. The watchers call the celebrities by their first names, approve or disapprove of "who they're dating," handle them with a mixture of love, identification, envy, and contempt—for the Medium has given its people so terrible a familiarity with everyone that it takes great magnanimity of spirit not to be affected by it. These celebrities are not heroes to us, their valets.

Better to have these real ones play themselves, and not sacrifice too much of their reality to art; better to have the watcher play himself, and not lose too much of himself in art. Usually the watcher is halfway between two worlds, paying full attention to neither: half distracted from, half distracted by, this distraction—and able for the moment not to be affected too greatly, have too great demands made upon him, by either world. For in the Medium, which we escape to from work, nothing is ever *work*, nothing ever makes intellectual or emotional or imaginative demands which we might find it difficult to satisfy. Here in the half-world everything is homogeneous—is, as much as possible, the same as everything else: each familiar novelty, novel familiarity, has the same texture on top and the same attitude and conclusion at bottom; only the middle, the particular subject of the particular program or article, is different. (If it *is* different: everyone is given the same automatic "human interest" treatment, so that it is hard for us to remember, unnecessary for us to remember, which particular celebrity we're reading about this time—often it's the same one, we've just moved to a different magazine.) Heine said that the English have a hundred religions and one sauce; so do we; and we are so accustomed to this sauce or dye or style, the aesthetic equivalent of Standard Brands, that a very simple thing can seem perverse, obscure, without it. And, too, we find it hard to have to shift from one art form to another, to vary our attitudes and expectations, to use our unexercised imaginations. Poetry disappeared long ago, even for most intellectuals; each year fiction is a little less important. Our age is an age of nonfiction; of gossip columns, interviews, photographic essays, documentaries; of articles, condensed or book length, spoken or written; of real facts about real people. Art lies to us to tell us the (sometimes disquieting) truth; the Medium tells us truths, facts, in order to make us believe some reassuring or entertaining lie or half truth. These actually existing celebrities, of universally admitted importance, about whom we are told directly authoritative facts—how can fictional characters compete with them? These *are* our fictional characters, our Lears and Clytemnestras. (This is ironically appropriate, since many of their doings and sayings are fictional, made up by public relations officers, columnists, agents, or other affable familiar ghosts.) And the Medium gives us such facts, such photographs, such tape recordings, such clinical reports not only about the great, but also about (representative samples of) the small; when we have been shown so much about so many—*can* be shown, we feel, anything about anybody—does fiction seem so essential as it once seemed? Shakespeare or Tolstoy can show us all about someone, but so can *Life;* and when *Life* does, it's someone real.

The Medium is half life and half art, and competes with both life and art. It spoils its audience for both; spoils both for its audience. For the People of the Medium life isn't sufficiently a matter of success and glamor and celebrity, isn't entertaining enough, distracting enough, *mediated* enough; and art is too difficult or individual or novel, too restrained or indirect, too much a matter of tradition and the past, of special attitudes and aptitudes: its mediation sometimes is queer or excessive, and sometimes is not even recognizable as mediation. The Medium's mixture of rhetoric and reality, which gives people what we know they want in the form we know they like, is something more efficient and irresistible, more habit-forming, than any art. If a man all his life has been fed a sort of combination of marzipan and ethyl alcohol—if eating, to him, is a matter of being knocked unconscious by an ice cream soda—can he, by taking thought, come to prefer a diet of bread and wine, apples and well-water? Will a man who has spent his life watching gladiatorial games come to prefer listening to chamber music? And those who produce the bread and wine and quartets for him—won't they be tempted either to give up producing them, or else to produce a bread that's half sugar, half alcohol, a quartet that ends with the cellist at the violist's bleeding throat?

The Medium represents to the artist all that he has learned not to do: its sure-fire stereotypes seem to him what any true art, true spirit, has had to struggle past on its way to the truth. The artist sees the values and textures of this art substitute replacing those of his art with most society, conditioning the expectations of what audience he has kept. Any outsider who has worked for the Medium will have noticed that the one thing which seems to its managers most unnatural is for someone to do something naturally, to speak or write as an individual speaking or writing to other individuals, and not as a subcontractor supplying a standardized product to the Medium. It is as if producers, editors, supervisors were particles forming a screen between maker and public, one that will let through only particles of their own size and weight (or, as they say, the public's) ; as you look into their bland faces, their big horn-rimmed eyes, you despair of Creation itself, which seems for the instant made in their own owl-eyed image. There are so many extrinsic considerations about everything in the work, the maker finds, that by the time it is finished all intrinsic considerations have come to seem secondary. It is no wonder that the professional who writes the ordinary commercial success, the ordinary script, scenario, or article, resembles imaginative writers less than he resembles advertising agents, columnists, editors, and producers. He is a technician who can supply a standard product, a rhetorician who can furnish a regular stimulus for a regular response, what has always made the dog salivate in this situation. He is the opposite of the imaginative artist: instead of stubbornly or helplessly sticking to what he sees and feels, to what seems right for him, true to reality, regardless of what the others think and want, he gives the others what they think and want, regardless of what he himself sees and feels.

Mass culture either corrupts or isolates the writer. His old feeling of one-ness, of speaking naturally to an audience with essentially similar standards, is gone; and writers do not any longer have much of the consolatory feeling that took its place, the feeling of writing for the happy few, the kindred spirits whose standards are those of the future. (Today they feel: the future, should there be one, will be worse.) True works of art are more and more produced away from, in opposition to, society. And yet the artist needs society as much as society needs him: as our cultural enclaves get smaller and drier, more hys-terical or academic, one mourns for the artists inside them and the public out-side. An incomparable historian of mass culture, Ernest van den Haag, has expressed this with laconic force: "The artist who, by refusing to work for the mass market, becomes marginal, cannot create what he might have created had there been no mass market. One may prefer a monologue to addressing a mass meeting. But it is still not a conversation."

Even if the rebellious artist's rebellion is whole-hearted, it can never be whole-stomached, whole-Unconscious'd. Part of him wants to be like his kind, is like his kind; longs to be loved and admired and successful. Our society (and the artist, in so far as he is truly a part of it) has no place set aside for the dif-ferent and poor and obscure, the fools for Christ's sake: they all go willy-nilly into Limbo. The artist is tempted, consciously, to give his society what it wants, or if he won't or can't, to give it nothing at all; is tempted, unconsciously, to give it superficially independent or contradictory works which are at heart works of the Medium. (Tennessee Williams' *Sweet Bird of Youth* is far less like Chekhov than it is like Mickey Spillane.) It is hard to go on serving both God and Mammon when God is so really ill-, Mammon so really well-organized. Shakespeare wrote for the Medium of his day; if Shakespeare were alive now he'd be writing *My Fair Lady*; isn't *My Fair Lady*, then, our *Hamlet?* shouldn't you be writing *Hamlet* instead of sitting there worrying about your superego? I need my *Hamlet!* So society speaks to the artist; but after he has written it its *Hamlet*, it tries to make sure that he will never do it again. There are more urgent needs that it wants him to satisfy: to lecture to it; to make public ap-pearances, to be interviewed; to be on television shows; to give testimonials; to make trips abroad for the State Department; to judge books for contests or Book Clubs; to read for publishers, judge for publishers, be a publisher for publishers; to be an editor; to teach writing at colleges or writers' conferences; to write scenarios or scripts or articles, articles about his home town for *Holi-*

day, about cats or clothes or Christmas for *Vogue*, about "How I Wrote *Hamlet*" for anything; to . . .

But why go on? I once heard a composer, lecturing, say to a poet, lecturing: "They'll pay us to do *anything*, so long as it isn't writing music or writing poems." I knew the reply that, as a member of my society, I should have made: "So long as they pay you, what do you care?" But I didn't make it—it was plain that they cared. . . . But how many more learn not to care, love what they once endured! It is a whole so comprehensive that any alternative seems impossible, any opposition irrelevant; in the end a man says in a small voice, "I accept the Medium." The Enemy of the People winds up as the People—but where there is no Enemy, the people perish.

The climate of our culture is changing. Under these new rains, new suns, small things grow great, and what was great grows small; whole species disappear and are replaced. The American present is very different from the American past: so different that our awareness of the extent of the changes has been repressed, and we regard as ordinary what is extraordinary (ominous perhaps) both for us and the rest of the world. For the American present is many other peoples' future: our cultural and economic example is, to much of the world, mesmeric, and it is only its weakness and poverty that prevent it from hurrying with us into the Roman future. Yet at this moment of our greatest power and success, our thought and art are full of troubled gloom, of the conviction of our own decline. When the President of Yale University writes that "the ideal of the good life has faded from the educational process, leaving only miscellaneous prospects of jobs and joyless hedonism," are we likely to find it unfaded among our entertainers and executives? Is the influence of what I have called the Medium likely to make us lead any good life? to make us love and try to attain any real excellence, beauty, magnanimity? or to make us understand these as obligatory but transparent rationalizations, behind which the realities of money and power are waiting?

Matthew Arnold once spoke about our green culture in terms that have an altered relevance (but are not yet irrelevant) to our ripe one. He said: "What really dissatisfies in American civilization is the want of the *interesting*, a want due chiefly to the want of those two great elements of the interesting, which are elevation and beauty." This use of *interesting* (and, perhaps, this tone of a curator pointing out what is plain and culpable) shows how far along in the decline of the West Arnold came; it is only in the latter days that we ask to be interested. He had found the word in Carlyle. Carlyle is writing to a friend to persuade him not to emigrate to the United States; he asks, "Could you banish yourself from all that is interesting to your mind, forget the history, the glorious institutions, the noble principles of old Scotland—that you might eat a better dinner, perhaps?" We smile, and feel like reminding Carlyle of the history, the glorious institutions, the noble principles of new America, that New World which is, after all, the heir of the Old. And yet . . . Can we smile as comfortably, today, as we could have smiled yesterday? listen as unconcernedly, if on taking leave of us some tourist should say, with the penetration and obtuseness of his kind:

I remember reading somewhere: that which you inherit from your fathers you must earn in order to possess. I have been so much impressed with your power and possessions that I have neglected, perhaps, your principles. The elevation or beauty of your spirit did not equal, always, that of your mountains and skyscrapers: it seems to me that your society provides you with "all that is interesting to your mind" only exceptionally, at odd hours, in little reservations like those of your Indians. But as for your dinners, I've never seen anything like them: your daily bread comes *flambé*. And yet—wouldn't you say?—the more dinners a man eats, the more comfort he possesses, the hungrier and more uncomfortable some part of him becomes: inside every fat man there is a man who is starving. Part of you is being starved to death, and the rest of you is being stuffed to death. . . . But this will change: no one goes on being stuffed to death or starved to death forever.

This is a gloomy, an equivocal conclusion? Oh yes, I come from an older culture, where things are accustomed to coming to such conclusions; where there is no last-paragraph fairy to bring one, always, a happy ending—or that happiest of all endings, no ending at all. And have I no advice to give you, as I go? None. You are too successful to need advice, or to be able to take it if it were offered; but if ever you should fail, it is there waiting for you, the advice or consolation of all the other failures.

VIII

NEW DIRECTIONS
FOR
COMMUNICATIONS

THE BRIEF INTRODUCTION TO SOME OF THE BASIC RELATIONSHIPS
between communications and other fields provided in earlier parts hopefully
raised more questions and heightened some creative anxiety about the progress
of the practice of communications in modern society. While not masters of
most of the fundamental issues, writers are already looking ahead to new problems and new research methods in communications.

The selections in this part cover a potpourri of subjects that give a glimpse
of the additional opportunities for communications studies. Whether a true
science of communications will some day develop is a provocative question;
but even more important is the complete and confident knowledge that our
present knowledge is neither complete nor worthy of great confidence. This
alone will transform the first reading of these selections into an earnest search
by the reader for more answers.

36

The Marketing Strategy of
Planned Visual Communications

GERALD STAHL

Marketing executives today are authorizing—unwittingly—the expenditure of millions of dollars to *contradict* the specific corporate, product, and brand messages they are spending other millions of dollars to promote.

Incongruous company and brand identifications are often visual contradictions of messages projected in advertising. Packaging is hindered by complicated or outmoded symbols and trademarks which weaken consumers' recognition and acceptance of products. Visually unrelated advertisements and packaging fail to establish company identification emphatically enough to sustain favorable recognition with consumer, customer, stockholder, dealer, distributor.

Because of this lack of *planned* identification—which is consistent, appropriate to the company, and distinctive—each element of visual communications is allowed to function separately. Each thereby fails to support or profit from the company's total investment in *all* forms of visual communications.

Many marketing specialists do appreciate that distinctive visual identification helps gain favorable recognition for their companies and products. But these same executives often miss the fact that their companies' identifications appear constantly in marketing media *other than* paid advertising, packaging, and signs.

Indeed, *all* visual media are instrumental: company signature and trademark, business forms, calling cards, checks, invoices, labels and tags, transportation vehicles, product identifications, catalogs, sales brochures, promotion and collateral materials, exhibits and displays, as well as packaging and advertising.

Each of these agents is constantly exhibiting information about the company, its products, its divisions, its standards, its character. When various media expose dissimilar identifications of the same company, the total corporate impression is confusing and frequently negative.

Reprinted from *Journal of Marketing* (January, 1964), pp. 7-11, by permission of the publisher, the American Marketing Association.

Planned Visual Communications Defined

Planned Visual Communications is *the visibly distinctive and consistent projection of related company, division, and product identity into its markets.*

This is achieved successfully through the organization and control of *all* visual media at a corporation's disposal. In this way a company gains maximum return from the considerable exposure it realizes through the millions of impressions its visual media may make.

With each medium visibly supporting every other, consistency of communications is achieved. This is a major key to attaining positive recognition and recall. Favorable recall motivates publics to buy from, invest in, and deal

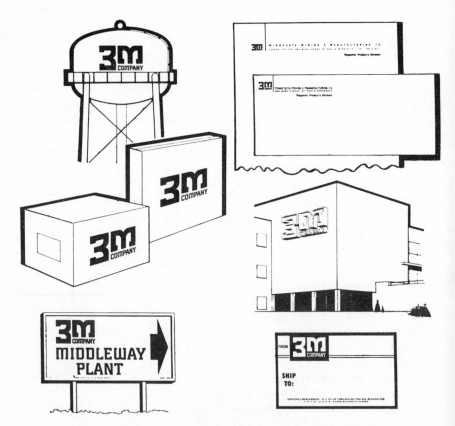

Figure 36-1. Some visual communications of 3M company

with the company. *Visible consistency that is unique, contemporary, and pertinent becomes a direct instrument of profits and future company growth.*

While business managements are alert to replace obsolete equipment and revamp outmoded purchasing systems, many still do not act with similar marketing intelligence in improving obtuse visual communications. As such, profitable business is actually deterred. The point is that corporate and product identification *can* be controlled as carefully as other areas of business management.

Planned Visual Communications in Action

An effective Visual Communications system functions in many ways. Advertising projects the same corporate and brand identification carried on packaging and sales literature. Discernible visual reminders transport the recognition value of advertising to the time and place of the buying decision. Obvious evidence of corporate character and planned direction stimulates interest and respect within the business and financial community. The franchise of familiarity and confidence, built by all the company's products and activities, is established for the introduction of new products and the penetration of new markets.

Organized visual communications makes advertisements and packages work as more than transient message carriers which promote only one brand at a time. *In the same paid space and at the same time packages and advertisements help to build sustained recognition for the total company—for all its products and all its divisions.*

A pertinent example is the 3M Company's coordinated program of corporate, division, and product identification. See Figure 36-1.

3M's philosophy is worth noting: when anyone sees *any* 3M package, product, advertisement, sign, brochure, label, catalog or tag, he probably will recognize it immediately and favorably as part of the 3M Company.

Management believes this helps to strengthen total company recognition as well as to boost the given product or division through clear *visible* association with the parent company. A logical technique, it still is not being used by the majority of America's corporations.

Rebuilding Brand Loyalties

Brand loyalties have been weakened by three main factors:

(1) streams of new products launched with separate names and identities that bear no relation to other products of the same company or to the company itself;

(2) look-alike packaging of national, regional, and private-label brands, and

(3) competitive price-incentive deals and discount operations.

Strong company identification that is clearly shown in packaging and advertising helps to counteract these profit deterrents.

Creating Merchandising Confidence

General Foods, for one, has rechanneled its corporate identification to accomplish two major objectives:

(1) provide the "elbow room" to endorse any new product of any kind the company may elect to market in coming years, and

(2) help strengthen brand loyalties of existing products.

Its methods: emphatic visual emphasis on the General Foods name, character, and identity. Brand and product identities, once merchandised separately, are now visibly linked with the total corporate identity. Advertisements focus major visual attention on the General Foods corporate design, to demonstrate that all of its vast assortments of products are part of the reputable GF family.

Marketing New Products

Effective Visual Communications helps to gain space and recognition for new products in the average supermarket, where 6,000 to 12,000 separate categories of items are displayed, sometimes a dozen or so brands within a category.

Most of these stores have become buy-everything outlets, where foods and cosmetics must compete with garden tools and record albums. In this situation, dynamic company and brand identifications are vital to achieve product distinction. Immediately visible identity also helps to penetrate consumers' "immunization" against "new, new, new" appeals.

Planned company identification helps to reduce the payout periods for new products by cutting needs for saturation advertising, couponing, and sampling. The reason is clear: with strong recognition, a company is freer to tackle new product introductions. It uses its established identification to push successfully for a greater share of the market with maximum return on investment.

Informing Business and Financial Audiences

Helping to keep business and financial audiences correctly apprised of corporate progress is another function of Visual Communications.

Inaccurate representation of its diversified operations was the major problem faced by the company known for many years as the American Machine and Metals Corporation. Its limiting name, outmoded trademark, and unrelated corporate and division signatures did not convey the fact that the company was involved in a score of profitable activities which had nothing to do with machinery, and which too few influential publics knew about.

In order to counteract the erroneous impression created by its name and disorganized visual identification, management changed the corporate name to AMETEK, Inc. A carefully related visual-identity plan was developed to project its true operations and character. See Figure 36-2.

The elements of the identity plan were a precision trademark designed to express technical skill, a related and consistent system of corporate and division signatures, and a distinctive graphic format.

These identity elements united to form a unique, visual character that was consistently carried out in all visual media. The new Ametek name and visual identity was first introduced in a series of corporate advertisements and then gradually incorporated in all visual media. Substantially increased interest by the financial community in the company and its operations is one of the results.

Development of Successful
Visual Communications

The Audit

The first step is for a qualified designer to analyze existing visual communications materials and messages.

Much like a financial audit, the communications analysis "pinpoints" specific areas of weakness (the debits) and areas of strength (the assets). The simplest method is to assemble examples of all items being used to identify, label, tag, package, promote, or advertise products, services, divisions, and the company. This includes even technical manuals, direct-mail literature, merchandising promotions, point-of-purchase displays, nameplates, signs, business forms, catalogs, and stationery.

Areas of weakness to look for are these:

(1) company or brand identity in advertising that is weak or ordinary;

(2) packages which have little visual relationship with advertisements;

(3) vastly varying ways of imprinting, applying, and using company or brand trademarks and logotypes;

(4) shipping containers which carry slight, if any, identifying marks;

(5) packaging that obscures or misuses product identification;

(6) collateral material and printed literature that is visually inconsistent;

(7) packaging and labeling that is illegible or confusing;

(8) identification practices of divisions or product lines that are contradictory to those of the company as a whole.

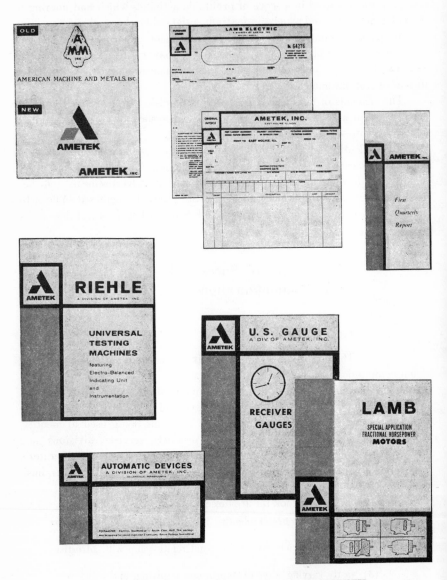

Figure 36-2.   Some visual communications of AMETEK

Assets to look for are those identity elements which have value and can be salvaged from the "scramble," and represented with force and clarity.

After the audit is completed and analyzed, an outline of specific aims and objectives is prepared. The next job is to determine what overall corporate message is being transmitted, and should appropriately be transmitted. A look at competitors' programs is also in order to review their successes and weaknesses, and to avoid even slight imitations.

Implementation

The actual Visual Communications program is then planned and designed.

After the system of identification is approved by management, it is implemented in all visual marketing media. Execution of the new communications plan follows, with built-in control to make sure that all new elements of visual communications which come along continue to convey the same distinctive message.

Usually a small committee or the advertising department of the company is charged with the responsibility of guiding the new programs. With the designer acting as adviser to the committee, all new material is cleared through the committee to assure continuity and adherence to the objectives.

Most companies publish a manual that sets standards, rules, and procedures to be followed. The manual acts as a guide and set of specifications that assures control and continuity.

Design Attributes

Any message is most effective when it requires the least effort to understand and remember. This is especially true of corporate design. *Simplicity* is a prime necessity of Visual Communications design. Good examples are IBM and the J & L design for Jones & Laughlin Steel.

Relevancy is a second attribute. Design and graphics must be pertinent to the nature of the company, its products, services, and markets. For example, a design which appears frivolous or feminine would not be appropriate for a manufacturer of industrial chemicals.

Functionalism is vital. It must be adaptable to all subsidiaries, divisions and products. U. S. Industries, for example, has solved this with a basic trademark, signature, and design scheme flexible enough to show both USI and division identities and still promote individual products.

Distinctiveness and *individualism* set the corporate's Visual Communications system apart from competition. Imitation detracts from the impression of leadership, integrity, and character.

Impact and *memorability* are additional requirements. Impact gains immediate attention. When design is also memorable, the initial impact is more readily sustained. The successful Visual Communications program must also project special corporate characteristics tailored specifically for the company. Qualities of strength, vitality, dynamism and progress, for example, must be interpreted and expressed visually.

In Conclusion

A distinctive Visual Communications program is one of the most prominent and most marketable corporate assets. Without it, even the superlative product may be hampered.

Mere repetition of attractive design, however, is not enough. The successful plan requires skilful *inter-media* implementation of a unique, contemporary identity which indicates vigorous management, company organization, and product distinction.

37

The Silent Language in
Overseas Business

EDWARD T. HALL

With few exceptions, Americans are relative newcomers on the international business scene. Today, as in Mark Twain's time, we are all too often "innocents abroad," in an era when naiveté and blundering in foreign business dealings may have serious political repercussions.

When the American executive travels abroad to do business, he is frequently shocked to discover to what extent the many variables of foreign behavior and custom complicate his efforts. Although the American has recognized, certainly, that even the man next door has many minor traits which make him somewhat peculiar, for some reason he has failed to appreciate how different foreign businessmen and their practices will seem to him.

He should understand that the various peoples around the world have worked out and integrated into their subconscious literally thousands of behavior patterns that they take for granted in each other.[1] Then, when the stranger enters, and behaves differently from the local norm, he often quite unintentionally insults, annoys, or amuses the native with whom he is attempting to do business. For example:

•In the United States, a corporation executive knows what is meant when a client lets a month go by before replying to a business proposal. On the other hand, he senses an eagerness to do business if he is immediately ushered into the client's office. In both instances, he is reacting to subtle cues in the timing of interaction, cues which he depends on to chart his course of action.

Abroad, however, all this changes. The American executive learns that the Latin Americans are casual about time and that if he waits an hour in the outer office before seeing the Deputy Minister of Finance, it does not neces-

Reprinted from *Harvard Business Review* (May-June, 1960), pp. 87-96, by permission of the publisher, Harvard Graduate School of Business Administration, Boston.
[1]For details, see my book, *The Silent Language* (New York, Doubleday & Company, Inc., 1959).

sarily mean he is not getting anywhere. There people are so important that nobody can bear to tear himself away; because of the resultant interruptions and conversational detours, everybody is constantly getting behind. What the American does not know is the point at which the waiting becomes significant.

•In another instance, after traveling 7,000 miles an American walks into the office of a highly recommended Arab businessman on whom he will have to depend completely. What he sees does not breed confidence. The office is reached by walking through a suspicious-looking coffeehouse in an old, dilapidated building situated in a crowded non-European section of town. The elevator, rising from dark, smelly corridors, is rickety and equally foul. When he gets to the office itself, he is shocked to find it small, crowded, and confused. Papers are stacked all over the desk and table tops—even scattered on the floor in irregular piles.

The Arab merchant he has come to see had met him at the airport the night before and sent his driver to the hotel this morning to pick him up. But now, after the American's rush, the Arab is tied up with something else. Even when they finally start talking business, there are constant interruptions. If the American is at all sensitive to his environment, everything around him signals, "What am I getting into?"

Before leaving home he was told that things would be different, but how different? The hotel is modern enough. The shops in the new part of town have many more American and European trade goods than he had anticipated. His first impression was that doing business in the Middle East would not present any new problems. Now he is beginning to have doubts. One minute everything looks familiar and he is on firm ground; the next, familiar landmarks are gone. His greatest problem is that so much assails his senses all at once that he does not know where to start looking for something that will tell him where he stands. He needs a frame of reference—a way of sorting out what is significant and relevant.

That is why it is so important for American businessmen to have a real understanding of the various social, cultural, and economic differences they will face when they attempt to do business in foreign countries. To help give some frame of reference, this article will map out a few areas of human activity that have largely been unstudied.

The topics I will discuss are certainly not presented as the last word on the subject, but they have proved to be highly reliable points at which to begin to gain an understanding of foreign cultures. While additional research will undoubtedly turn up other items just as relevant, at present I think the businessman can do well to begin by appreciating cultural differences in matters concerning the language of time, of space, of material possessions, of friendship patterns, and of agreements.

Language of Time

Everywhere in the world people use time to communicate with each other. There are different languages of time just as there are different spoken languages. The unspoken languages are informal; yet the rules governing their interpretation are surprisingly *ironbound*.

In the United States, a delay in answering a communication can result from a large volume of business causing the request to be postponed until the backlog is cleared away, from poor organization, or possibly from technical complexity requiring deep analysis. But if the person awaiting the answer or decision rules out these reasons, then the delay means to him that the matter has low priority on the part of the other person—lack of interest. On the other hand, a similar delay in a foreign country may mean something altogether different. Thus:

• In Ethiopia, the time required for a decision is directly proportional to its importance. This is so much the case that low-level bureaucrats there have a way of trying to elevate the prestige of their work by taking a long time to make up their minds. (Americans in that part of the world are innocently prone to downgrade their work in the local people's eyes by trying to speed things up.)

• In the Arab East, time does not generally include schedules as Americans know and use them. The time required to get something accomplished depends on the relationship. More important people get fast service from less important people, and conversely. Close relatives take absolute priority; nonrelatives are kept waiting.

In the United States, giving a person a deadline is a way of indicating the degree of urgency or relative importance of the work. But in the Middle East, the American runs into a cultural trap the minute he opens his mouth. "Mr. Aziz will have to make up his mind in a hurry because my board meets next week and I have to have an answer by then," is taken as indicating the American is overly demanding and is exerting undue pressure. "I am going to Damascus tomorrow morning and will have to have my car tonight," is a sure way to get the mechanic to stop work, because to give another person a deadline in this part of the world is to be rude, pushy, and demanding.

An Arab's evasiveness as to when something is going to happen does not mean he does not want to do business; it only means he is avoiding unpleasantness and is side-stepping possible commitments which he takes more seriously than we do. For example:

•The Arabs themselves at times find it impossible to communicate even to each other that some processes cannot be hurried, and are controlled by built-in schedules. This is obvious enough to the Westerner but not to the Arab. A highly placed public official in Baghdad precipitated a bitter family dispute because his nephew, a biochemist, could not speed up the complete analysis of the uncle's blood. He accused the nephew of putting other less important people before him and of not caring. Nothing could sway the uncle, who could not grasp the fact that there is such a thing as an *inherent* schedule.

With us the more important an event is, the further ahead we schedule it, which is why we find it insulting to be asked to a party at the last minute. In planning future events with Arabs, it pays to hold the lead time to a week or less because other factors may intervene or take precedence.

Again, time spent waiting in an American's outer office is a sure indicator of what one person thinks of another or how important he feels the other's business to be. This is so much the case that most Americans cannot help getting angry after waiting 30 minutes; one may even feel such a delay is an insult, and will walk out. In Latin America, on the other hand, one learns that it does not mean anything to wait in an outer office. An American businessman with years of experience in Mexico once told me, "You know, I have spent two hours cooling my heels in an executive's outer office. It took me a long time to learn to keep my blood pressure down. Even now, I find it hard to convince myself they are still interested when they keep me waiting."

The Japanese handle time in ways which are almost inexplicable to the Western European and particularly the American. A delay of years with them does not mean that they have lost interest. It only means that they are building up to something. They have learned that Americans are vulnerable to long waits. One of them expressed it, "You Americans have one terrible weakness. If we make you wait long enough, you will agree to anything."

Indians of South Asia have an elastic view of time as compared to our own. Delays do not, therefore, have the same meaning to them. Nor does indefiniteness in pinpointing appointments mean that they are evasive. Two Americans meeting will say, "We should get together sometime," thereby setting a low priority on the meeting. The Indian who says, "Come over and see me, see me anytime," means just that.

Americans make a place at the table which may or may not mean a place made in the heart. But when the Indian makes a place in his time, it is yours to fill in every sense of the word if you realize that by so doing you have crossed a boundary and are now friends with him. The point of all this is that time communicates just as surely as do words and that the vocabulary of time is different around the world. The principle to be remembered is that time has different meanings in each country.

Language of Space

Like time, the language of space is different wherever one goes. The American businessman, familiar with the pattern of American corporate life, has no difficulty in appraising the relative importance of someone else, simply by noting the size of his office in relation to other offices around him:

• Our pattern calls for the president or the chairman of the board to have the biggest office. The executive vice president will have the next largest, and so on down the line until you end up in the "bull pen." More important offices are usually located at the corners of buildings and on the upper floors. Executive suites will be on the top floor. The relative rank of vice presidents will be reflected in where they are placed along "Executive Row."

• The French, on the other hand, are much more likely to lay out space as a network of connecting points of influence, activity, or interest. The French supervisor will ordinarily be found in the middle of his subordinates where he can control them.

Americans who are crowded will often feel that their status in the organization is suffering. As one would expect in the Arab world, the location of an office and its size constitute a poor index of the importance of the man who occupies it. What we experience as crowded, the Arab will often regard as spacious. The same is true in Spanish cultures. A Latin American official illustrated the Spanish view of this point while showing me around a plant. Opening the door to an 18-by-20-foot office in which seventeen clerks and their desks were placed, he said, "See, we have nice spacious offices. Lots of space for everyone."

The American will look at a Japanese room and remark how bare it is. Similarly, the Japanese look at our rooms and comment, "How bare!" Furniture in the American home tends to be placed along the walls (around the edge). Japanese have their charcoal pit where the family gathers in the *middle* of the room. The top floor of Japanese department stores is not reserved for the chief executive—it is the bargain roof!

In the Middle East and Latin America, the businessman is likely to feel left out in time and overcrowded in space. People get too close to him, lay their hands on him, and generally crowd his physical being. In Scandinavia and Germany, he feels more at home, but at the same time the people are a little cold and distant. It is space itself that conveys this feeling.

In the United States, because of our tendency to zone activities, nearness carries rights of familiarity so that the neighbor can borrow material possessions and invade time. This is not true in England. Propinquity entitles you to nothing. American Air Force personnel stationed there complain because they have to make an appointment for their children to play with the neighbor's child next door.

Conversation distance between two people is learned early in life by copying elders. Its controlling patterns operate almost totally unconsciously. In the United States, in contrast to many foreign countries, men avoid excessive touching. Regular business is conducted at distances such as 5 feet to 8 feet; highly personal business, 18 inches to 3 feet—not 2 or 3 inches.

In the United States, it is perfectly possible for an experienced executive to schedule the steps of negotiation in time and space so that most people feel comfortable about what is happening. Business transactions progress in stages from across the desk to beside the desk, to the coffee table, then on to the conference table, the luncheon table, or the golf course, or even into the home—all according to a complex set of hidden rules which we obey instinctively.

Even in the United States, however, an executive may slip when he moves into new and unfamiliar realms, when dealing with a new group, doing business with a new company, or moving to a new place in the industrial hierarchy. In a new country the danger is magnified. For example, in India it is considered improper to discuss business in the home on social occasions. One never invites a business acquaintance to the home for the purpose of furthering business aims. That would be a violation of sacred hospitality rules.

Language of Things

Americans are often contrasted with the rest of the world in terms of material possessions. We are accused of being materialistic, gadget-crazy. And, as a matter of fact, we have developed material things for some very interesting reasons. Lacking a fixed class system and having an extremely mobile population, Americans have become highly sensitive to how others make use of material possessions. We use everything from clothes to houses as a highly evolved and complex means of ascertaining each other's status. Ours is a rapidly shifting system in which both styles and people move up or down. For example:

•The Cadillac ad men feel that not only is it natural but quite insightful of them to show a picture of a Cadillac and a well-turned out gentleman in his early fifties opening the door. The caption underneath reads, "You already know a great deal about this man."

•Following this same pattern, the head of a big union spends an excess of $100,000 furnishing his office so that the president of United States Steel cannot look down on him. Good materials, large space, and the proper surroundings signify that the people who occupy the premises are solid citizens, that they are dependable and successful.

The French, the English, and the Germans have entirely different ways of using their material possessions. What stands for the height of dependability and respectability with the English would be old-fashioned and backward to us. The Japanese take pride in often inexpensive but tasteful arrangements that are used to produce the proper emotional setting.

Middle East businessmen look for something else—family, connections, friendship. They do not use the furnishings of their office as part of their status system; nor do they expect to impress a client by these means or to fool a banker into lending more money than he should. They like good things, too, but feel that they, as persons, should be known and not judged solely by what the public sees.

One of the most common criticisms of American relations abroad, both commercial and governmental, is that we usually think in terms of material things. "Money talks," says the American, who goes on talking the language of money abroad, in the belief that money talks the *same* language all over the world. A common practice in the United States is to try to buy loyalty with high salaries. In foreign countries, this maneuver almost never works, for money and material possessions stand for something different there than they do in America.

Language of Friendship

The American finds his friends next door and among those with whom he works. It has been noted that we take people up quickly and drop them just as quickly. Occasionally a friendship formed during schooldays will persist, but this is rare. For us there are few well-defined rules governing the obligations of friendship. It is difficult to say at which point our friendship gives way to business opportunism or pressure from above. In this we differ from many other people in the world. As a general rule in foreign countries friendships are not formed as quickly as in the United States but go much deeper, last longer, and involve real obligations. For example:

•It is important to stress that in the Middle East and Latin America your "friends" will not let you down. The fact that they personally are feeling the pinch is never an excuse for failing their friends. They are supposed to look out for your interests.

Friends and family around the world represent a sort of social insurance that would be difficult to find in the United States. We do not use our friends to help us out in disaster as much as we do as a means of getting ahead—or, at least, of getting the job done. The United States systems work by means of a series of closely tabulated favors and obligations carefully doled out where they will do the most good. And the least that we expect in exchange for a favor is gratitude.

The opposite is the case in India, where the friend's role is to "sense" a person's need and do something about it. The idea of reciprocity as we know it is unheard of. An American in India will have difficulty if he attempts to follow American friendship patterns. He gains nothing by extending himself in behalf of others, least of all gratitude, because the Indian assumes that what he does for others he does for the good of his own psyche. He will find it impossible to make friends quickly and is unlikely to allow sufficient time for friendships to ripen. He will also note that as he gets to know people better, they may become more critical of him, a fact that he finds hard to take. What he does not know is that one sign of friendship in India is speaking one's mind.

Language of Agreements

While it is important for American businessmen abroad to understand the symbolic meanings of friendship rules, time, space, and material possessions, it is just as important for executives to know the rules for negotiating agreements in various countries. Even if they cannot be expected to know the details of each nation's commercial legal practices, just the awareness of and the expectation of the existence of differences will eliminate much complication.

Actually, no society can exist on a high commercial level without a highly developed working base on which agreements can rest. This base may be one or a combination of three types:

1. Rules that are spelled out technically as law or regulation.
2. Moral practices mutually agreed on and taught to the young as a set of principles.
3. Informal customs to which everyone conforms without being able to state the exact rules.

Some societies favor one, some another. Ours, particularly in the business world, lays heavy emphasis on the first variety. Few Americans will conduct any business nowadays without some written agreement or contract.

Varying from culture to culture will be the circumstances under which such rules apply. Americans consider that negotiations have more or less ceased when the contract is signed. With the Greeks, on the other hand, the contract is seen as a sort of way station on the route to negotiation that will cease only when the work is completed. The contract is nothing more than a charter for serious negotiations. In the Arab world, once a man's word is given in a particular kind of way, it is just as binding, if not more so, than most of our written contracts. The written contract, therefore, violates the Moslem's sensitivities and reflects on his honor. Unfortunately, the situation is now so hopelessly confused that neither system can be counted on to prevail consistently.

Informal patterns and unstated agreements often lead to untold difficulty in the cross-cultural situation. Take the case of the before-and-after patterns where there is a wide discrepancy between the American's expectations and those of the Arab:

•In the United States, when you engage a specialist such as a lawyer or a doctor, require any standard service, or even take a taxi, you make several assumptions: (a) the charge will be fair; (b) it will be in proportion to the services rendered; and (c) it will bear a close relationship to the "going rate."

You wait until after the services are performed before asking what the tab will be. If the charge is too high in the light of the above assumptions, you feel you have been cheated. You can complain, or can say nothing, pay up, and take your business elsewhere the next time.

•As one would expect in the Middle East, basic differences emerge which lead to difficulty if not understood. For instance, when taking a cab in Beirut it is well to know the going rate as a point around which to bargain and for settling the charge, which must be fixed before engaging the cab.

If you have not fixed the rate *in advance*, there is a complete change and an entirely different set of rules will apply. According to these rules, the going rate plays no part whatsoever. The whole relationship is altered. The sky is the limit, and the customer has no kick coming. I have seen taxi drivers shouting at the top of their lungs, waving their arms, following a redfaced American with his head pulled down between his shoulders, demanding for a two-pound ride ten Lebanese pounds which the American eventually had to pay.

It is difficult for the American to accommodate his frame of reference to the fact that what constitutes one thing to him, namely, a taxi ride, is to the Arab two very different operations involving two different sets of relationships and two sets of rules. The crucial factor is whether the bargaining is done at the beginning or the end of the ride! As a matter of fact, you cannot bargain at the end. What the driver asks for he is entitled to!

One of the greatest difficulties Americans have abroad stems from the fact that we often think we have a commitment when we do not. The second complication on this same topic is the other side of the coin, i.e., when others think we have agreed to things that we have not. Our own failure to recognize binding obligations, plus our custom of setting organizational goals ahead of everything else, has put us in hot water far too often.

People sometimes do not keep agreements with us because we do not keep agreements with them. As a general rule, the American treats the agreement as something he may eventually have to break. Here are two examples:

•Once while I was visiting an American post in Latin America, the Ambassador sent the Spanish version of a trade treaty down to his language officer with instructions to write in some "weasel words." To his dismay, he was told, "There are no weasel words in Spanish."

•A personnel officer of a large corporation in Iran made an agreement with local employees that American employees would not receive preferential treatment. When the first American employee arrived, it was learned quickly that in the United States he had been covered by a variety of health plans that were not available to Iranians. And this led to immediate protests from the Iranians which were never satisfied. The personnel officer never really grasped the fact that he had violated an ironbound contract.

Certainly, this is the most important generalization to be drawn by American businessmen from this discussion of agreements: there are many times when we are vulnerable *even when judged by our own standards*. Many instances of actual sharp practices by American companies are well known abroad and are giving American business a bad name. The cure for such questionable behavior is simple. The companies concerned usually have it within their power to discharge offenders and to foster within their organization an atmosphere in which only honesty and fairness can thrive.

But the cure for ignorance of the social and legal rules which underlie business agreements is not so easy. This is because:

●The subject is complex.

●Little research has been conducted to determine the culturally different concepts of what is an agreement.

●The people of each country think that their own code is the only one, and that everything else is dishonest.

●Each code is different from our own; and the farther away one is traveling from Western Europe, the greater the difference is.

But the little that has already been learned about this subject indicates that as a problem it is not insoluble and will yield to research. Since it is probably one of the more relevant and immediately applicable areas of interest to modern business, it would certainly be advisable for companies with large foreign operations to sponsor some serious research in this vital field.

A Case in Point

Thus far, I have been concerned with developing the five check points around which a real understanding of foreign cultures can begin. But the problems that arise from a faulty understanding of the silent language of foreign custom are human problems and perhaps can best be dramatized by an actual case.

A Latin American republic had decided to modernize one of its communication networks to the tune of several million dollars. Because of its reputation for quality and price, the inside track was quickly taken by American company "Y."

The company, having been sounded out informally, considered the size of the order and decided to bypass its regular Latin American representative and send instead its sales manager. The following describes what took place.

The sales manager arrived and checked in at the leading hotel. He immediately had some difficulty pinning down just who it was he had to see about his business. After several days without results, he called at the American Embassy where he found that the commercial attaché had the up-to-the-minute information he needed. The commercial attaché listened to his story. Realizing that the sales manager had already made a number of mistakes, but figuring that the Latins were used to American blundering, the attaché reasoned that all was not lost. He informed the sales manager that the Minister of Communications was the key man and that whoever got the nod from him would get the contract. He also briefed the sales manager on methods of conducting business in Latin America and offered some pointers about dealing with the minister.

The attaché's advice ran somewhat as follows:

1. "You don't do business here the way you do in the States; it is necessary to spend much more time. You have to get to know your man and vice versa.

2. "You must meet with him *several times* before you talk business. I will tell you at what point you can bring up the subject. Take your cues from me. [Our American sales manager at this point made a few observations to himself about "cookie pushers" and wondered how many payrolls had been met by the commercial attaché.]

3. "Take that price list and put it in your pocket. Don't get it out until I tell you to. Down here price is only one of the many things taken into account before closing a deal. In the United States, your past experience will prompt you to act according to a certain set of principles, but many of these principles will *not* work here. Every time you feel the urge to act or to say something, look at me. Suppress the urge and take your cues from me. This is very important.

4. "Down here people like to do business with men who *are* somebody. In order to be somebody, it is well to have written a book, to have lectured at a university, or to have developed your intellect in some way. The man you are going to see is a poet. He has published several volumes of poetry. Like many Latin Americans, he prizes poetry highly. You will find that he will spend a good deal of business time quoting his poetry to you, and he will take great pleasure in this.

5. "You will also note that the people here are very proud of their past and of their Spanish blood, but they are also exceedingly proud of their liberation from Spain and their independence. The fact that they are a democracy, that they are free, and also that they are no longer a colony is very, very important to them. They are warm and friendly and enthusiastic if they like you. If they don't, they are cold and withdrawn.

6. "And another thing, time down here means something different. It works in a different way. You know how it is back in the States when a certain type

blurts out whatever is on his mind without waiting to see if the situation is right. He is considered an impatient bore and somewhat egocentric. Well, down here, you have to wait much, much longer, and I really mean *much, much* longer, before you can begin to talk about the reason for your visit.

7. "There is another point I want to caution you about. At home, the man who sells takes the initiative. Here, *they* tell you when they are ready to do business. But, most of all, don't discuss price until you are asked and don't rush things."

The Pitch

The next day the commercial attaché introduced the sales manager to the Minister of Communications. First, there was a long wait in the outer office while people kept coming in and out. The sales manager looked at his watch, fidgeted, and finally asked whether the minister was really expecting him. The reply he received was scarcely reassuring, "Oh yes, he is expecting you but several things have come up that require his attention. Besides, one gets used to waiting down here." The sales manager irritably replied, "But doesn't he know I flew all the way down here from the United States to see him, and I have spent over a week already of my valuable time trying to find him?" "Yes, I know," was the answer, "but things just move much more slowly here."

At the end of about 30 minutes, the minister emerged from the office, greeted the commercial attaché with a *doble abrazo*, throwing his arms around him and patting him on the back as though they were long-lost brothers. Now, turning and smiling, the minister extended his hand to the sales manager, who, by this time, was feeling rather miffed because he had been kept in the outer office so long.

After what seemed to be an all too short chat, the minister rose, suggesting a well-known café where they might meet for dinner the next evening. The sales manager expected, of course, that, considering the nature of their business and the size of the order, he might be taken to the minister's home, not realizing that the Latin home is reserved for family and very close friends.

Until now, nothing at all had been said about the reason for the sales manager's visit, a fact which bothered him somewhat. The whole setup seemed wrong; neither did he like the idea of wasting another day in town. He told the home office before he left that he would be gone for a week or ten days at most, and made a mental note that he would clean this order up in three days and enjoy a few days in Acapulco or Mexico City. Now the week had already gone and he would be lucky if he made it home in ten days.

Voicing his misgivings to the commercial attaché, he wanted to know if the minister really meant business, and, if he did, why could they not get together and talk about it? The commercial attaché by now was beginning to show the strain of constantly having to reassure the sales manager. Nevertheless, he tried again:

What you don't realize is that part of the time we were waiting, the minister was rearranging a very tight schedule so that he could spend tomorrow night with you. You see, down here they don't delegate responsibility the way we do in the States. They exercise much tighter control than we do. As a consequence, this man spends up to 15 hours a day at his desk. It may not look like it to you, but I assure you he really means business. He wants to give your company the order; if you play your cards right, you will get it.

The next evening provided more of the same. Much conversation about food and music, about many people the sales manager had never heard of. They went to a night club, where the sales manager brightened up and began to think that perhaps he and the minister might have something in common after all. It bothered him, however, that the principal reason for his visit was not even alluded to tangentially. But every time he started to talk about electronics, the commercial attaché would nudge him and proceed to change the subject.

The next meeting was for morning coffee at a café. By now the sales manager was having difficulty hiding his impatience. To make matters worse, the minister had a mannerism which he did not like. When they talked, he was likely to put his hand on him; he would take hold of his arm and get so close that he almost "spat" in his face. As a consequence, the sales manager was kept busy trying to dodge and back up.

Following coffee, there was a walk in a nearby park. The minister expounded on the shrubs, the birds, and the beauties of nature, and at one spot he stopped to point at a statue and said: "There is a statue of the world's greatest hero, the liberator of mankind!" At this point, the worst happened, for the sales manager asked who the statue was of and, being given the name of a famous Latin American patriot, said, "I never heard of him," and walked on.

The Failure

It is quite clear from this that the sales manager did not get the order, which went to a Swedish concern. The American, moreover, was never able to see the minister again. Why did the minister feel the way he did? His reasoning went somewhat as follows:

I like the American's equipment and it makes sense to deal with North Americans who are near us and whose price is right. But I could never be friends with this man. He is not my kind of human being and we have nothing in common. He is not *simpatico*. If I can't be friends and he is not *simpatico*, I can't depend on him to treat me right. I tried everything, every conceivable situation, and only once did we seem to understand each other. If we could be friends, he would feel obligated to me and this obligation would give me some control. Without control, how do I know he will deliver what he says he will at the price he quotes?

Of course, what the minister did not know was that the price was quite firm, and that quality control was a matter of company policy. He did not realize that the sales manager was a member of an organization, and that the man is always subordinate to the organization in the United States. Next year maybe the sales manager would not even be representing the company, but would be replaced. Further, if he wanted someone to depend on, his best bet would be to hire a good American lawyer to represent him and write a binding contract.

In this instance, both sides suffered. The American felt he was being slighted and put off, and did not see how there could possibly be any connection between poetry and doing business or why it should all take so long. He interpreted the delay as a form of polite brushoff. Even if things had gone differently and there had been a contract, it is doubtful that the minister would have trusted the contract as much as he would a man whom he considered his friend. Throughout Latin America, the law is made livable and contracts workable by having friends and relatives operating from the inside. Lacking a friend, someone who would look out for his interests, the minister did not want to take a chance. He stated this simply and directly.

Conclusion

The case just described has of necessity been oversimplified. The danger is that the reader will say, "Oh, I see. All you really have to do is be friends." At which point the expert will step in and reply: "Yes, of course, but what you don't realize is that in Latin America being a friend involves much more than it does in the United States and is an entirely different proposition. A friendship implies obligations. You go about it differently. It involves much more than being nice, visiting, and playing golf. You would not want to enter into friendship lightly."

The point is simply this. It takes years and years to develop a sound foundation for doing business in a given country. Much that is done seems silly or strange to the home office. Indeed, the most common error made by home offices, once they have found representatives who can get results, is failure to take their advice and allow sufficient time for representatives to develop the proper contacts.

The second most common error, if that is what it can be called, is ignorance of the secret and hidden language of foreign cultures. In this article I have tried to show how five key topics—time, space, material possessions, friendship patterns, and business agreements—offer a starting point from which companies can begin to acquire the understanding necessary to do business in foreign countries.

Our present knowledge is meager, and much more research is needed before the businessman of the future can go abroad fully equipped for his work. Not only will he need to be well versed in the economics, law, and politics of the area, but he will have to understand, if not speak, the silent languages of other cultures.

38

Toward a Theory of
Nonverbal Communication

JURGEN RUESCH
and WELDON KEES

In broad terms, nonverbal forms of codification fall into three distinct categories:

•*Sign language* includes all those forms of codification in which words, numbers, and punctuation signs have been supplanted by gestures; these vary from the "monosyllabic" gesture of the hitchhiker to such complete systems as the language of the deaf.

•*Action language* embraces all movements that are not used exclusively as signals. Such acts as walking and drinking, for example, have a dual function: on one hand they serve personal needs, and on the other they constitute statements to those who may perceive them.

•*Object language* comprises all intentional and nonintentional display of material things, such as implements, machines, art objects, architectural structures, and—last but not least—the human body and whatever clothes or covers it. The embodiment of letters as they occur in books and on signs has a material substance, and this aspect of words also has to be considered as object language.

Analogic, nonverbal forms of codification stand in a somewhat conplementary relationship to digital or verbal forms of denotation, particularly in *spatial and temporal characteristics*. Sign, action, and object languages usually require a certain space that ordinarily cannot be modified. This is not true of spoken and written languages, whose spatial requirements are minimal. For example, print can be modified in size, and microfilming makes it possible to reduce an entire library to a fraction of the space occupied by the original material. The distinctions in terms of the temporal characteristics are even more impressive. In order to be understood, words must be read or heard one after another. In written communication, the amount of time that elapses between the act of writing and the act of reading may be considerable, since a piece of writing may be

Reprinted from *Nonverbal Communication*. Berkeley, University of California Press, 1956, pp. 189-193, by permission of the publisher.

composed over a long period of time and may not be read or come to light until years afterward. In contrast, the appreciation of objects and gestures is based less upon impressions that follow each other in serial order but more upon multiple sensory impressions that may impinge simultaneously.

Verbal and nonverbal languages do not appeal to the same *sensory modalities*. Silently executed sign language is perceived exclusively by the eye, much in the way that spoken language is perceived by the ear. Action language may be perceived by the eye and the ear and—to a lesser degree—through the senses of touch, temperature, pain, and vibration. Object language appeals to both distance and closeness receivers, including the senses of smell and taste. This fact has notable effects upon the mutual position of the participants in a communication network. In practice, sign and action languages depend upon immediacy, requiring the participants to be within the range of each other's vision. Object language requires various kinds of perception, usually at a much closer range, but transmitter and perceiver need not be within reach. As a matter of fact, the transmitter may be dead when the receiver obtains the object and the message that is coded therein. In this respect, object language closely resembles written language, except that it is more universally understood.

The *selection* of a particular type *of codification* depends upon the communicative versatility of an individual and his ability to vary statements in keeping with the nature of a situation. The use of object language is indicated, for example, because of its succinct and immediate nature, in situations where a person needs to make statements to himself—he may tie a knot in his handkerchief to remind himself of something important. Action language is indicated when people wish to convey the exact nature of a situation to others; for example, certain concepts are involved in the performance of music and in the servicing of machinery—in brief, the transmission of skills—that can be conveyed only nonverbally. Verbal language is most adapted to dissecting aspects of events and to codifying such knowledge in spoken or written terms, and to carrying on meaningful discourse.

Nonverbal languages take on prime importance in situations *where words fail completely*. Words are particularly inadequate when the quality of space has to be symbolized. Photographs, paintings, drawings, material samples, or small-scale, three-dimensional models are indispensable to an appreciation of the distinctions between a Gothic cathedral and its baroque counterpart. Analogic forms of representation are equally necessary in the reporting of extreme situations, when emotional experiences are difficult to convey to those who did not personally participate in them. In an effort to suggest the quality of such events, a speaker or a writer attempts to use verbal signals that are designed to evoke emotions similar to those he or others experienced. If the listener or reader has never been exposed to or is not familiar, either through reading or other experience, with situations similar to or evocative of those described, the account will fail altogether. However, with the aid of objects and pictures, or through reënactment, even the least imaginative can be given some sense of what happened. Such verbally oriented specialists as lawyers are aware of the necessity of supplementing their verbal arguments with courtroom reënactments and of documenting them with material and pictorial evidence.

The characteristic functions of each of the various types of nonverbal language are not necessarily interchangeable. *Object language,* because of its time-enduring qualities, plays an enormous role in archaeology, anthropology, and history. Until the discovery of the first written documents to come down to us, the only enduring traces we had of the remote past were those that survived in the forms of objects and buildings. Tools and weapons were known as early as the Stone Age, and the fact that material articles almost always carry either implicit or explicit instructions with them makes it possible to reconstruct events of prehistoric times, even though we lack knowledge of the verbal language of a particular period. When we observe a tool or an implement, we consciously or unconsciously connect such objects with human activities. Somehow, when an object is assessed, the missing craftsman, inventor, or operator—either the projected self or another person—is present at the rim of consciousness, vaguely outlined though not insistent, but nonetheless felt. The interpretation is made easier because of the fact that objects either refine and increase the scope of our sensory end organs or serve to extend or replace our muscles. The modern version of sensory extension is the scientific recording instrument; that of motor extension is the labor-saving machine. In very recent years, a third kind of extension has been developed: giant calculators, computing machines, and other devices vastly extend the scope of our thinking, predicting, and decision making.

Objects may be intentionally shaped *as symbols,* or they may come to be looked upon as symbols. When they are not used for sharpening perception, facilitating evaluation, or simplifying action, they may consequently stand for something else and assume functions similar to those of words, standing for individuals, animals, activities, or other objects. The decorative aspects of materials and objects are closely related to their language functions. Whereas the referential properties of objects bear upon events that, if expressed in words, would be referred to as the subject, decoration is an expression of activities that, if expressed in words, would be called the predicate.

Nonverbal language is frequently used to effect *social control.* In interpersonal situations, many ideas, concepts, and things must be stated in ways that will not be considered obtrusive or offensive. Among such considerations is the definition of boundaries. Marks of ownership, expressed by means of objects, may be found near entrances, at gateways and doors, identifying owners or residents of a certain property and indicating how they may be reached. Such marks are particularly suitable for denoting statements to whom it may concern. Objects that stand permanently in one place and can be seen at any time impose prohibitions through their impact. Some objects are addressed to particular people; appealing interpersonally, they may invite, seduce, or repel, or demand to be looked at, touched, or tried out. We all consciously look for nonverbal clues in buildings, landscapes, and interiors, for we know that these clues have something to say about the status, prestige, taste, and other values of those who own them. Such an awareness is used by architects, decorators, and owners to set the scene for social encounters.

Object language may also be called into play when persons who make unethical, immoral, slanderous, or *profane statements* wish to hide their identity. Object language is ideal for such purposes, since it is less rigidly governed by rules than are actions or words; frequently, too, such messages are difficult to track down to their source. Thus, where words might be considered to be in bad taste or in violation of the law, many of the subtleties touching on social discrimination, emotional expression, and selective appeal are entrusted either completely or in part to nonverbal codifications.

Although verbal language often necessitates uneconomical denotation, object language allows concise and *economic phrasing*. Abbreviated statements are frequently expressed through a mixture of verbal and nonverbal language that in turn necessitates a particular kind of grammar. For example, the subject may be denoted by a three-dimensional object, whereas the predicate may be expressed in words. Here, the object identifies, the words qualify. Other statements may be repeated in nonverbal terms to avoid repetitions that might be considered boring. Human tolerance for redundancy in analogic language is far greater than its tolerance for redundancy in verbal language.

In contrast to object language, *action language* is transitory, although at the same time it represents the most universal kind of language. Among animals, auditory and visual perception of movements tend to set in motion other actions on the part of the perceiving animal. These actions may in turn influence the animal who gave the first signal. This is true of human behavior as well. Since action language exerts a kinesthetic effect, often initiating abortive movements in the perceiver, the deaf, for example, depend upon this phenomenon in the interpretation of lip reading. Indeed, almost everyone attempts to "get into the act" when watching certain physical or social actions, as can be observed from the behavior of people watching parades or from the lack of reserve on the part of sports enthusiasts. This fact is apparent in any activity that depends upon the reciprocal responses of the participants. The members of a team of acrobats in action cannot signal to each other through words or objects, but instead must rely upon split-second comprehension of each other's timing. Similarly, a spectator must experience the impact of such action himself, either visually or by actual participation, to understand fully the scope and extent of the communicative aspects of such movements.

Action language is the principal way in which *emotions* are expressed. When, in the course of a deadlocked argument, a person slams his fist upon the table, this action, along with other signs of tension, is universally understood. Other participants, almost by necessity, react with avoidant, protective, or fighting reactions. By making a switch from words to action, the referential properties of language are abruptly shifted from conflict to a context in which agreement may be possible. By means of such expression, the discussants are capable of reëstablishing contact, and may either resume their verbal discussion or separate altogether. In any event, a deadlock is broken.

Closely related to action language are *sign language and gesture.* Over the course of centuries, every social group has developed systems of communication in which particular words, signs, and gestures have been assigned communicative significance. There is a kind of gesture that assumes the auxiliary role of an emphasizing, timing, and directional device—for example, a pointed finger. Another kind of gesture takes the place of verbal signs themselves, as in Indian sign language. Because such denotation systems are not bound to phonetics, they enable persons who speak different languages to communicate with each other in ways analogous to the pictographic symbolizations that cut across verbal language barriers.

The *relationship between verbal and nonverbal codifications* can be conceptualized best through the notion of metacommunication. Any message may be regarded as having two aspects: the statement proper, and the explanations pertaining to its interpretation. The nature of interpersonal communication necessitates that these coincide in time, and this can be achieved only through the use of another channel. Thus, when a statement is phrased verbally, instructions tend to be given nonverbally. The effect is similar to an arrangement of a musical composition for two instruments, where the voices in one sense move independently and in another change and supplement each other but nonetheless are integrated into an organic and functional unity.

Combinations of the verbal and the nonverbal may be employed not only to enlighten but also *to obscure the issues* involved. In politics, business, advertising—indeed in every walk of life—words may be used to conceal forthcoming actions, and contradictory expressions are consciously used to create confusion, since human communication almost always involves object, action, and word. If all the symbolic expressions of an individual refer to the same event, then the referential aspects of the statement are clear. But when action codifications contradict verbal codifications, then confusion is almost certain to result. For example, when a mother repeatedly exclaims, "Darling, you're so sweet," simultaneously pinching her child to the extent of producing black and blue marks, the child has to learn to disregard either the action or the verbal statement in order to avoid confusion.

Finally, *verbal language* is based upon entirely different principles than the nonverbal languages. In its denotative capacity a single word can refer to a general or universal aspect of a thing or event only. In order to particularize and specify, words must be combined with other words in serial order. Words enable us to express abstractions, to communicate interpolations and extrapolations, and they make possible the telescoping of far-flung aspects of events and diversified ideas into comprehensible terms. Unlike nonverbal codifications, which are analogic and continuous, verbal codifications are essentially emergent, discontinuous, and arbitrary. The versatility of words—and this includes numbers—may, however, have dangerous consequences. Words and—to a lesser degree—gestures are commonly thought to be the principal means through which messages are conveyed. Even though such a view is not substantiated by fact, it is convenient—especially for purposes of public administration and law —to assume that we live in an almost exclusively verbal world. This emphasis upon the verbal is a by-product of modern civilization, with its accelerated centralization of control, in which increasingly more people do clerical work and fewer people are engaged in productive work. One of the consequences has been the creation of a staggering variety of middlemen who traffic solely in information. Not only salesmen but even many executives seem to have become credulous of their own propaganda, a situation that is further aggravated by the fact that most of these men have rather limited contact with many of the processes they symbolically deal with or control. The danger of this remoteness from reality lies in the tendency to regard abstract principles as concrete entities, attributing body and substance to numbers and letters and confusing verbal symbols with actual events. Such a way of thinking is an almost inescapable occupational hazard of those who use words for purposes of control.

When verbal and digital symbols are not repeatedly checked against the things they purport to stand for, *distortions of signification* may develop that *nonverbal languages seldom bring about.* Since in everyday communication these shortcomings of verbal language are difficult to avoid, people often intuitively resort to the use of nonverbal, analogic language, which is more closely tied to actual events. But this is not enough. If human beings are to protect themselves against the onslaughts of modern communications machinery and the distortions of propaganda, they must ultimately learn once again to use words scrupulously and with a sense of integrity. Only by a renewal of emphasis on the individual, with all his personal and unique characteristics—and this involves to a great extent the nonverbal—can a sense of proportion and dignity be restored to human relations.

39

Mass Communications and the Consumer Movement

LEE RICHARDSON

Only rarely does a social scientist have the good fortune to observe important nonrecurring phenomena of direct relevance to his field of study. This is particularly true of conflict situations that have a tendency to occur unexpectedly. Only a few insightful and detailed studies of conflict and unusual social events are available that could not have been written even a few months after the events occurred.[1]

In the autumn of 1966, multiplied thousands of normally placid American housewives in countless cities, suburbs, and towns in the United States staged a series of meetings, protest demonstrations, and outright boycotts of supermarkets.[2] In one city[3] with a population of 100,000 to 500,000, this observer was granted permission to view the activities of the housewives' organization from inside the unofficial headquarters of the group.

While the underlying conditions that led to the furious activities of the housewives may be explained in terms of a conflict between the housewives' pocketbooks and the economics of the food industry,[4] the boycotts and protests themselves cannot. The explanation of the nature and duration of the protest movement lies with the mass media. The mathematical odds against several hundred protest movements springing up randomly within a period of two weeks and then disappearing, for the most part, within a month are infinitesimal. No evidence exists of similar movements occurring in preceding or immediately subsequent periods. No informal communication pattern between cities can be

[1]A classic attempt to reconstruct an unexpected social event is *Invasion from Mars* by H. Cantril, H. Gaudey, and H. Herzog (Princeton: Princeton University Press, 1940).

[2]See news summaries in "Housewives Skewer High Food Prices," *Business Week*, October 22, 1966, pp. 42-43; "Food," *Time*, November 4, 1966, p. 89; and "Housewives Revolt in Grocery Stores," *U.S. News & World Report*, October 31, 1966, pp. 59-61.

[3]The fictitious name of Pine City is used. The city is reasonably representative of other cities in the nation as evidenced by its frequent use as a test market for new products and by various socio-economic comparisons.

[4]See *U.S. News & World Report, op. cit.*, p. 59.

cited as a cause,[5] nor were food prices attacked by the protestors suddenly different in this one-month period.[6]

Table 39-1. Housewives' actions and newspaper publicity

	Newspaper Lines[1]		Pine City Housewives' Activity Turning Points in Group Action[4]
Date	Local events[2]	National events[3]	
Oct. 16		31*	
Oct. 17		197*	
Oct. 18		112*	Plan activity[5]
Oct. 19	281*	127*	Increase activity[6]
Oct. 20	230*	206*	
Oct. 21	221*	293*	
Oct. 22	267*	392*	
Oct. 23	46*	216	Increase activity[7]
Oct. 24	115*	0	
Oct. 25	230*	230	
Oct. 26	108*	133*	
Oct. 27	211*	235*	
Oct. 28	103	564*	
Oct. 29	83*	476*	
Oct. 30	82	126	
Oct. 31	43	188	
Nov. 1	62	292*	
Nov. 2	170	141	Decrease activity[8]
Nov. 3	72	55	
Nov. 4	26	0	
Nov. 5	60	0	
Nov. 6	0	0	
Nov. 7	67	0	Decrease activity[9]
Nov. 8	49	0	
Nov. 9	0	0	

*Includes at least one front-page article.
[1]Morning and afternoon news and editorial commentaries, combined linage. Pictures were omitted.
[2]Pine City metropolitan area events relative to housewives' actions.
[3]All events except Pine City area.
[4]All actions were taken by the group being observed.
[5]A decision to announce that a group was being organized was made by a small group of friends. The decision was based on actions in other cities as reported by the newspaper.
[6]Large numbers of "volunteers" responding to the news of the organization's birth gave strength to the original group who decided to confront the local supermarket managements and to circulate petitions.
[7]Failure to achieve any noticeable impact upon the supermarkets and continued "volunteer" response prompted decision to picket supermarkets. With much fanfare, the picketing continued strong until November 2.
[8]Failure to achieve anything and unseasonably cold weather prompted sharp cutback in picketing and resumption of more planning meetings.
[9]Defeat admitted privately and pickets virtually eliminated. Further activity locally became disorganized.

[5]Some telephone calls were made by the Pine City group to persons in other states identified as leaders of similar groups in their respective communities.
[6]Federal Reserve Bulletin, August, 1967, p. 1424.

The day-to-day activities of the movement in Pine City can be explained basically in terms of the impact of the Pine City newspaper. It was observed that the participants in the movement relied upon the newspaper rather than upon radio or television for all types of information. After comparison of the several basic turning points in the movement's activities with the volume of newspaper coverage in Table 39-1, the reader should ponder the following plausible hypotheses that can be developed from the information:

1. Business-customer relations are affected heavily by the involvement of the mass media.

2. The consumer movement[7] in the United States can be largely effective or ineffective because of mass media's decisions to publicize or not publicize events pertaining to it.

3. The housewives' boycotts of autumn, 1966, were strongly influenced by the mass media.

4. The Pine City housewives' organization made its important decisions primarily because of local and national consumer movement publicity in the Pine City newspaper.

Further testing of these statements awaits the analysis of similar events and communications patterns in other communities. Final answers to the many questions raised in Table 39-1 should not be expected, even if sophisticated research techniques could be readied for the next similar occurrence. However, business and consumer organizations can draw one firm lesson in mass communications from the episode: mass communications media can influence the length and nature of conflicts of public importance.

[7]Helen Sorenson, *The Consumer Movement* (New York: Harper & Brothers, 1941).

40

Is Communications Research
Really Worthwhile?

ALLAN GREENBERG

Knowledge about communications in advertising and other phases of marketing emanates largely from what are called "principles" of communication.

Journals in marketing, communications, psychology, and the other behavioral sciences contain many detailed articles about communications and human behavior—many of the studies conceived with ingenuity and analyzed with mathematical tools. But usually the conclusions drawn are tentative in nature only, awaiting further studies among other populations or replications of the studies under different conditions; or else they are presented as evidence furthering the acceptance or rejection of various concepts and deductions.

Some of the conclusions are even presented as "principles." Then with passage of time, many of these "principles" come to be accepted as if they have been "proved," turning up in textbooks, speeches, and articles as if they were irrefutable "laws." Some of them become almost ritualistic dogma.

Examples of Communications Principles

Various books represent excellent compendiums of findings and conclusions that form the basis of many of the principles or laws in advertising and communications.[1] And some of the principles of mass communications and advertising that have come to be widely accepted are the following:[2]

Reprinted from *Journal of Marketing* (January, 1967), pp. 48-50, by permission of the publisher, the American Marketing Association.

[1]Bernard Berelson and Gary A. Steiner, *Human Behavior, An Inventory of Scientific Findings* (New York: Harcourt, Brace & World, 1965) ; Joseph T. Klapper, *The Effects of Mass Communication* (Glencoe, Illinois: Free Press, 1960) ; Herbert I. Abelson, *Persuasion* (New York: Springer Publication Company, 1959).

[2]Berelson and Steiner, same reference as footnote 1, at pp. 529, 544, 548, 550, and 552.

People tend to see and hear communications that are favorable or congenial to their predispositions; they are more likely to see and hear congenial communications than neutral or hostile ones. And the more interested they are in the subject, the more likely is such selective attention.

The higher a person's level of intelligence, the more likely it is that he acquires information from communications.

The communication of facts is typically ineffective in changing opinions in desired directions against the force of audience predispositions. The stronger the predispositions, the less effective the communication of facts.

Anticipating a subsequent use increases retention even of uncongenial material.

Strong appeals to fear, by arousing too much tension in the audience, are less effective in persuasion than minimal appeals.

Another example is this: "There will probably be more opinion change in the direction you want if you explicitly state your conclusions than if you let the audience draw their own."[3]

One review of empirical studies on the optimum size of newspaper advertisements emphasized the principle that as the size of advertisement increases, there is less than a proportionate increase in number of "noters."[4]

But how useful are these findings? Very few researchers or practitioners would consider findings such as the above as "proved" in the same sense as a law of physics or chemistry.

Limited Usefulness of Communications Principles

These principles or laws or conclusions or findings, whatever one calls them, are at best statistical statements, with varying but unknown probabilities of occurring. Dogmatic use of such principles is not too meaningful; and the circumstances under which the law or principle is meant to hold rarely are specified.

Actually the level of generality is not known to any degree of precision. As Berelson and Steiner say: "In the behavioral sciences, if not in human behavior, it is always 'more complicated than that.' The qualifications may derive from size of sample, composition of sample, level of proof, techniques of measurement, factors left uninvestigated, or other conditions, but they are usually there. . . . For nothing is true in the behavioral sciences (or in life) except 'under certain circumstances.' "[5]

Even when one accepts a principle in advertising and communications as largely true, in a particular set of circumstances a problem arises. Advertising

[3]Abelson, same reference as footnote 1, at p. 10.
[4]"What's Best Size for a Newspaper Ad." *Media/scope*, Vol. 9 (July, 1965), pp. 48-51.
[5]Berelson and Steiner, same reference as footnote 1, at p. 7.

deals with unique instances—a given campaign at a given point in time for a particular brand.

Because every instance in human affairs is unique, the question is—does the principle apply in *this* case? And the "this" case is not an abstraction but is made up of content—a specific advertisement, a specific media decision for a specific campaign, a brand with a particular share of market, and so on. The true answer to the question is not really known.

The problem is somewhat similar to that of statistical and clinical prediction, substituting for a person the specific case as one out of a universe of such cases. Statistically, the principle may hold over a large enough number of cases, even under unknown or unspecified sets of circumstances; but the problems faced by marketing executives practically always call for a clinical prediction. In such circumstances the value of a principle or law is a moot point.

At best, laws or principles of communication might be used as a guide in the absence of empirical data. A law or principle in communications is only *one additional guidepost* that might be used.

Scientifically proved laws in communications could stifle innovation in marketing. The very nature of an innovation in marketing tends to disregard some principles or laws. However, this does not negate the need for attempts to study communications and human behavior, to theorize, to propound principles or laws, and to attempt to catalog the circumstances under which the principles or laws seem to hold.

The Experimental or Observational Study

The gathering of empirical data for a "clinical" judgment implies an experimental or observational study, and a subsequent prediction based on the results of the study.

But in the experimental or observational study, predictions can be made only by making a host of assumptions or allowances, in order to equate the conditions under which the study is conducted to actual conditions that would be likely to exist at the time involved in the prediction.

Seeing a new package held by an interviewer is not quite the same as seeing it on the shelf in a store. Similarly, an advertisement seen outside a magazine is not the same as when seen inside a magazine. An idea presented to a respondent in a face-to-face interview is not the same as when the respondent meets it in an actual situation. Answers to hypothetical questions asked about future actions are not the exact equivalent of the actions themselves taken later.

Time and time again advertising researchers have been prodded to become increasingly scientific in their research methodology. A tacit assumption underlying such urgings is that the tools and the techniques used in some of the physical sciences should be adapted, so as to achieve predictive accuracy.

However, differences between the kinds of experiments in research in the physical sciences and in marketing are so fundamental as to make the attainment of the same predictive accuracy impossible in marketing.

Careful sampling, painstaking questionnaire construction, reliability checks, and measures of validity tend to make sample survey predictions of estimated universe parameters more accurate than otherwise. However, actual evidence of the effectiveness of these and other techniques in increasing the accuracy of predictions about communications is not easy to obtain.

In predicting in chemical research, for instance, the assumptions that have to be made are few in number, and to a great extent the assumptions will hold or the conditions can be controlled so as to make them hold. Thus, water of a certain composition will always boil at 212°F., given certain barometric pressure. But between this type of prediction and the ones usually expected of marketing researchers there are worlds of differences.

The differences are fundamental and not functions of the present state of the art. The physical sciences aim to determine numerical laws and constants of nature. Marketing research has a somewhat less ambitious aim: to develop general principles and concepts and direct empirical knowledge.

Marketing research deals with human beings who act and react on the basis of value judgments. Where personal interviews are used, there is the problem of the interactions between respondents and interviewers. There are problems of human perception, memory, moods, feelings, motivations, and expectations.

Also, *time* is an all-important factor in marketing research. Between the point in time that the study is made and the period covered by the prediction, uncontrolled time has played a significant role. The prediction made from a research study could be perfectly valid at one point in time, but the degree of validity at a second point in time may not be known.

Finally, the conditions under which the results of marketing research will hold true cannot be duplicated exactly in real life.

It is true that predictive accuracy of population parameters as a result of a well-conducted survey can be very high. One need only check major media study projections on age, sex, family composition, and so on of the total population against complete census figures to note the high degree of accuracy of well-done studies. However, such consistent accuracy is difficult to find in the case of experimental studies dealing with prediction of attitudes and behavior.

An Acceptable Set of "Principles"

On the other hand, the fact that limitations exist need not inhibit researchers from utilizing communications principles and conducting empirical research with specific content.

For instance, informative material has been forthcoming on decision theory, and on the use of the Bayesian approach to making choices under uncertainty. Questions of whether subjective probability has anything in common with mathematical probability or "obeys" psychological rules of its own continue to await further research.[6]

And now, in spite of having questioned the validity of various "principles," here is a set of conclusions for the field of marketing.

1. Communications findings stemming from research in fields other than marketing cannot be generalized readily to the field of marketing, and thus can not be used as guidelines without major qualifications.

2. Even when applicable, a marketing communications principle should not be construed as "absolute truth."

3. The focus for decision always revolves around the specific content of the problem.

4. The results of a marketing study have an unknown degree of precision when used for prediction at a later period in time.

5. The greater the risks that an incorrect decision might involve, the more is additional information required.

[6]John Cohen, "Subjective Probability," *Scientific American*, Vol. 205 (November 1957), pp. 128-134.

41

Experimental Method in Communication Research

PERCY H. TANNENBAUM

As a procedure of scientific inquiry, experimentation has not enjoyed particularly widespread use or success in journalism and communication research. The research literature in this field contains only a handful of reports of experimental undertakings. Nor can it be said that the focus and caliber of such undertakings have been such as to lead to striking theoretical developments or practical innovations.

But if communication is to achieve any status at all as a science—and this, presumably, is its *raison d'être* as an academic discipline—it must largely be founded upon, though not necessarily limited to, the experimental method. Speculation and conjecture, intuition and insight, classification and correlation —all these have their place in any scientific system; they are the raw materials from which theory is built. But scientifically considered, any theory, however elegant and ingenious it may be, is sterile unless it eventually lends itself to demonstration and verification. Within the scientific method of inquiry, experimentation is one of the principal procedures for determining such verification —a specialized procedure that attempts to reduce the degree of external contamination and internal ambiguity of the results of the inquiry.

This is not to suggest that verification is the only criterion for the acceptance of a theory. Nor does this imply that experimentation is the only method of scientific verification. It is *a* scientific procedure, but not *the* scientific procedure. Also, it is a means and not an end; it is part of the warp and woof of science but should not be confused with science itself. If it possesses certain properties which are customarily labeled as "scientific," there are other procedures which, although they do not share these same properties, also are legitimately within the scientific domain. In short, experimentation might be a condition necessary for the development of a science, but it is not the sufficient condition.

Reprinted from *Introduction to Mass Communications Research*, Ralph H. Nafziger, ed., Baton Rouge, La., Louisiana State University Press, 1963, pp. 51-76, by permission of the publisher.

In this chapter, we shall attempt to explore some of the bases for that particular system of inquiry we call experimentation, to consider its chief ingredients, and to consider, too, some of its shortcomings. A particular focus throughout will be the role of experimentation in the fledgling field of communication research. This will not be, however, a how-to-do-it exposition, largely for the reason that no one experimental procedure exists for all given problems. But there are certain characteristics that any experimental undertaking should possess, the *modus operandi* of experimentation, so to speak, and these will be considered.

The Setting for Experimentation

The Motivation of Research

In this age of technological advancement it has become fashionable to think of science as being all clearness and light. To be sure, there is a real and important sense in which science does stand for law and certainty. But enter the portals of an experimental scientist's laboratory—be it a nuclear physicist's, a biologist's, a laboratory psychologist's, or even a communication researcher's—and the impression you get is more likely to be one of confusion than of the order he allegedly yearns for. This impression applies not only to the disarray of his gear and gadgetry but to his thinking and tinkering as well. He usually bears as little resemblance to the deep-eyed, furrow-browed Searcher for Truth as he does to the caricature of the mad scientist frenetically engaged in mystical alchemy. If he does exhibit some zeal and anxiety, it is as likely to be a function of his preoccupation with apparent trivia as of his being on the threshold of great discovery: scurrying around in quest of subjects for his experiments; trying to get some piece of apparatus to work; trying to measure something more exactly, and the like.

Only in moments of retrospective thought is he consciously aware of engaging in genuine science. As B. F. Skinner,[1] among others, has indicated, he need not enter the scientific arena to do battle with the Great Unknown, armed with a Hypothesis and with an Experimental Design. Nor is it necessary for him to tote along a Model, mathematical or otherwise, of the phenomenon he is studying. His Basic Assumptions are many but are rarely derived from a Deductive Theory. If he proceeds by Logic, as he must, it is often less relentless and rigorous than he might hope for. To be a good researcher he need not be consciously aware of all of these elements of scientific procedure—at least not in the sense that the capitalization of these terms implies.

If there is any one thing that characterizes experimental research, it is a type of trial-and-error probing; one might almost say groping. This is not to

[1]B. F. Skinner, "A Case History in Scientific Method," *American Psychologist*, 11 (1956), 221-33.

say that the researcher operates in a vacuum. On the contrary, there is often a body of knowledge that precedes his particular investigations, along with a more or less defined methodology for conducting them. But it is largely a chance proposition, and he is never quite certain what the outcome will be.

Paradoxically, it is this very uncertainty that accounts for the motivation of research as well as for its disenchantments. For experimental research is almost always a by-product of that curious mixture of doubt and certainty, of curiosity and faith, that separates the empiricist from the strictly rational pure theorist. A singular characteristic of scientific inquiry, then, is that it encourages doubt instead of suppressing it. From such a faith in doubt, as it were, is generated the motivation for conducting a particular piece of research.

Being a "doubting Thomas," the researcher is never fully sure nor satisfied. The exhilaration he may experience on completing an individual experiment is almost always blunted by the very uncertainty which initiates it. So he investigates and reinvestigates, checks and rechecks, always searching for something new.

Why all this relentless activity? It has, of course, a reason and an end purpose. This ultimate goal is difficult to pin down, but if one were pressed to do so, the issue might well resolve itself into the principle of *parsimony*: to describe accurately and predict a maximum number of events from a minimum number of postulates. So that while he may be largely motivated by an everpresent doubt, the experimentalist also has an unvarying faith—faith in the existence of an underlying *order*, if not in a basic lawfulness. His activity is almost always predicated on the belief that a basic set of principles does in fact exist to explain a particular phenomenon. And this search for parsimony is not merely a matter of elegance or economy. It is a matter of uncovering order and of understanding that order. From such understanding comes prediction and possibly control.

The experimentalist, of course, is usually a more modest and unassuming soul than such a lofty goal would imply. In a real sense, his motivation is not unlike that of the mountain climber who, when asked why he attempted to scale the world's highest peak, replied simply and honestly: "Because it is there." So, too, with the research scientist. Ask him why he pursues a particular line of inquiry, and he is liable to reply, "It interests me," or words to that effect. But underlying both his activity and that of the mountain climber—or the butterfly collector, for that matter—is an intense curiosity and a particular, even peculiar, faith. Like all faiths, science has its rituals and its procedures.

Establishing Functional Relationships

The procedures of science are outlined elsewhere in this book. These characterize the body of knowledge and experience that comprises the so-called scientific method—the way in which science progresses from doubt to certainty.

The scientific method aims at precision and exactness. This is why it relies so heavily on the use of rigorous logic and equally rigorous procedures for verification. By use of logic, it seeks to establish relationships that assume the form of *functions*. Although such relationships do not have to be expressed in mathematical terminology, they should, ideally, have the characteristics of mathematical functions.

There are three such characteristics to consider in defining any function: There must be a *domain* of one variable, a *range* of the second variable, and a *rule* or function that associates every element in the domain with some element in the range. It is then possible to chart any value of the domain into a value of the range via the prescribed rule.

In science we usually seek to establish such functions between two sets of variables—moreover, functions which imply *causal* relationships. The factors of causation that belong to the domain are called the *independent variables;* the factors of effect that belong to the range are called the *dependent variables.* We usually can specify the dependent variables quite readily; i.e., we know what effects we are interested in studying. But we are often in the dark regarding the crucial independent variables: we are not certain which factors cause these effects. On the basis of theory or hunch, or both, we can often surmise such causal relationships, but science also demands that we prove these suspicions. One role of experimentation, then, is at this more or less exploratory stage to test whether or not the presence of a particular independent variable does have a significant effect on some dependent variable.

But this is not enough. To have a well-defined function we must be able to go beyond just indicating that two variables are related. To say that variable A "leads to" variable B, or that B "is a function of" A, or that A and B "are correlated," indicates only the *what* of the relationship and not the *how*—i. e., we also must be able to specify the rule if the information is to be scientifically useful. Again, theory may provide some clues, but usually we have to plod along in tedious fashion to determine this rule: We induce different levels of independent variable A and get different measures of dependent variable B, and try to deduce the rule from these two sets of data. And this is a second role of experimentation.

In the last analysis science calls for the demonstration of such functional relationships beyond their logical development; it demands *verification*. A central criterion of a science, then, lies in its method of verification. Experimentation is an integral feature of the scientific method in that it provides for such verification under exact and exacting conditions. In a sense it is the acid test for any scientific hunch, hence for any scientific theory.

The Focus for Experimentation in Communication

How and where does experimentation specifically fit into the field of communication? To examine this question we must first take a brief look at the communication process itself.

For our purposes here the communication process may be considered simply as one in which a source transmits some information or meaning to a receiver. To elaborate somewhat, the *source* (which may be an individual person or a complex social institution such as a newspaper, etc.) is motivated to convey some intentions, which it translates into some convenient set of symbols (e. g., written or spoken language, pictures, combinations of musical notes, etc.). We refer to this process of translation of intentions into symbols as *encoding*, and the resulting set of symbols is called the *message*.

The communications process does not stop here. The message, in turn, provides a distinctive source of stimulation for whoever is exposed to it, the *receiver*. But for communication, as such, to take place, it is not sufficient that mere exposure take place. The message also must have some meaning for the receiver: i. e., he must be able to retranslate, or *decode*, the symbols into significances of his own, which may or may not agree with the intentions of the source. This decoding activity is at once the awareness of the significance of the message and a necessary prior condition if the decoder is to do anything as a result of the message.

It is obvious from this too brief representation of the communication process (cf. Wilbur Schramm[2] for a more thorough presentation) that the critical activities are the encoding and decoding behaviors of the source and receiver respectively. The other elements of the process are either necessary products for initiating such behaviors (there must be a source if encoding is to occur, and a message for decoding to occur) or specific products resulting from such behaviors. But both encoding and decoding are learned and implicit processes. They reside within the individual organism and are not directly observable. As a result, we are forced to make *inferences* of these implied processes from their observable consequences. The consequence of encoding is the set of symbols we call the message, and that of decoding is the set of instrumental acts we call the response. These two sets of observable data indicate the two main approaches to communication research and provide the subject matter for that research.

The first or "content-oriented" approach to communication research is best illustrated by studies of content analysis. Here the units for investigation are the characteristics of content and/or structure of the message as such. The analysis of such data allows for inferences of the intentions of the source and of his resulting encoding behavior, and sometimes for inferences of the effects it may produce. Experimentation has been used very little, if at all, in this area of research. Its most significant contribution would be more in bolstering the methodology of content-oriented research than in the formal testing of hypotheses. For example, in the study of daily newspaper performance in the 1956 presidential election proposed by the Association for Education in Journalism's Council on Communication Research,[3] experimental research would have been

---

[2]W. Schramm, "How Communication Works," in W. Schramm (ed.), *The Process and Effects of Mass Communication* (Urbana: University of Illinois Press, 1954).

[3]R. B. Nixon *et al.*, "A Proposal for the Study of the Role and Performance of the American Daily Newspaper in the 1956 Presidential Election Campaign," Sigma Delta Chi Committee on Ethics and News Objectivity (1955, *mimeo.*).

used in establishing more meaningful categories for content analysis. The proposal was that different suspected message characteristics (e. g., size of story, location of story, headline treatment) would be tested to determine whether they constituted biased news treatment.

The second or "effects-oriented" approach is concerned more directly with communication effects per se. Here the inquiry is directed at establishing and demonstrating functional relationships of the kinds indicated above, and this type of research provides the main focus for experimentation in communication.

The causal or independent variables in this research are usually of two kinds: factors of the message (e. g., the studies on the "indexing process" reported by Percy Tannenbaum)[4] and the factors of the receivers (e. g., the studies of the effect of various social and personality characteristics on susceptibility to persuasion through communication reported by C. I. Hovland, I. L. Janis, and H. H. Kelley).[5] This is why content analysis and audience research are so important for the development of a theory of communication behavior; among other things, they help specify the critical variables that may be operative in determining the why and wherefore of communication effects. The dependent variables in this research are the changes in the kind of decoding activity elicited in the receivers and in the resulting overt behavior. Here we typically focus on the more apparent changes: acquisition of new information and skills; attitude change; etc. Often, however, we are concerned with more remote consequences: e. g., sales fluctuations in studies of advertising effects; voting behavior; and the like.

Where do the specific problems—i. e., the specific cause-effect relationships to be investigated—come from for experimental research in communication? One source has already been hinted at—the results of other inquiry, e. g., from previous content analysis or audience research, and so on. To cite but one possible case: If a content analysis shows a high proportion of violence in television content, and if an audience survey shows a larger number of juvenile viewers of such content, experimentation may be used to test the notion (we can, if we wish, dignify it by calling it an *hypothesis*) that the amount of juvenile delinquency is positively related to the amount of TV violence. Similarly, a review of the research literature such as Schramm's[6] often produces research problems; it both summarizes the findings of earlier research and provides many tantalizing hypotheses for new research.

Another source of problems is established theory. A comprehensive theory will not only be based on the findings of research but should itself lead to detailed predictions of effects. If these predictions stand up under rigorous experimental scrutiny, then the theory becomes accepted. If experimental research

---

[4]P. H. Tannenbaum, "The Indexing Process in Communication," *Public Opinion Quarterly*, 19 (1955), 292-302.

[5]C. I. Hovland, I. L. Janis, and H. H. Kelley, *Communication and Persuasion* (New Haven: Yale University Press, 1953).

[6]W. Schramm, "The Effects of Mass Communications: A Review," *Journalism Quarterly*, 26 (1949), 397-409.

fails to substantiate such predictions, then the theory is suspect and must either be revised or rejected. In the field of communication no such established theory exists at the present. But we do have a whole host of hunches, guesses, rules of thumb, and the like, and from such speculation and conjecture stem many of the hypotheses and problems for experimental research.

The Fundamentals of Experimentation

What is meant by "experimentation"? We have used the term rather extensively but have yet to define it. This is not a simple matter, largely because there is no single experimental procedure, and, like so many other concepts, it may have different implications in different contexts. One could attempt a direct frontal approach by encompassing the characteristics that are common to all experiments in a single definition; but, like most attempts at finding a common denominator, this would probably be too trite and sterile for our purposes. Or one could try a back-door approach by blueprinting a model experiment. This, too, would probably be too pristine and unrealistic to be of much use. Perhaps the best procedure would be a rather oblique approach—to start with the most obvious and fundamental characteristics of experiments and proceed from there.

Experimentation is a type of activity we call inquiry, and it deals with observations. This is not to say, of course, that all inquiry and observation are experiments. But the converse is true: all experiments are inquiries and rest on observation. One way to understand more clearly what we mean by experimentation, then, is to establish a dichotomy between experimental and nonexperimental inquiry and to differentiate between them. R. L. Ackoff,[7] following historical precedence, has suggested two dimensions for such differentiation: the problems that are investigated (i. e., the subject matter) ; and how these problems are investigated (i. e., the methodology).

The Subject Matter of Experiments

All inquiry and research, experimental or otherwise, has a particular problem as its point of initiation. As John Dewey[8] has suggested, people are confronted with a perplexity and from this they isolate a specific problem. As far as the researcher is concerned, it should be noted that such states of perplexity can be aroused while he is considering the work of other people or while he is observing nature first hand. Similarly, the manifestation of the perplexity— i. e., the actual problem he focuses on—can stem from a variety of sources. In any event the researcher must have the mental acuity and alertness to recognize a genuine problem.

[7] R. L. Ackoff, *The Design of Social Research* (Chicago: University of Chicago Press, 1953).

[8] J. Dewey, *How We Think* (New York: Heath, 1933).

But what constitutes a genuine problem? A common criticism of experimentation is that it deals with less pressing and less utilitarian problems than are warranted by the required effort. On the other hand, nonexperimental inquiry is often said to deal with problems of more immediate and practical significance. The history of science, however, contains abundant evidence for the utility of the long-range view and demonstrates that what are seemingly trivial problems may, in the long run, prove to be important ones. From the small acorns of plodding research on atomic structures have grown the big oaks of atomic and hydrogen bombs; from countless, relatively minute experiments there emerged a polio vaccine.

Likewise, not all nonexperimental inquiry deals with problems of the moment. Historical research, for example, is replete with instances of painstaking examination dealing with generalized, long-range problems—e. g., A. J. Toynbee's[9] exhaustive work on the uniformity of historical development, or within the communication field itself, F. S. Siebert's[10] effort to trace the development of press freedom in relation to changing political and social conditions. The distinguishing characteristic between experimental and nonexperimental inquiry does not lie in their respective subject matters.

Before proceeding with this comparison, one might well consider in further detail this charge of triviality of experimentation within the communication area. It is in the behavioral sciences, in general, and communication, in particular, that this criticism appears to be more widespread and, at least at first glance, more valid. Few, if any, examples of the type cited above from the natural sciences exist in the social sciences to support the notion that experimentation will ultimately pay off, and the communication researcher is often berated for investigating trifling issues or "just trying to prove the obvious."

Much of this criticism is obviously warranted. Many of the critical problems in communication have been side-stepped in research to date, and much of the research has been redundant. There are reasons for this, of course. For one thing, there is a pronounced lack of appropriate measuring devices for many of the presumably critical variables, and without an adequate way of indexing something, it is impossible to study it properly. For another thing, the lack of a systematic theory has forced communications research—which, like most other forms of inquiry, follows a first-things-first procedure—to focus on the multitude of hunches and rules of thumb for problems. The field of communication abounds in such conjecture and speculation, largely because it developed as an academic discipline *after* a considerable period of applied practice. As a consequence, practices and procedures have been adopted without the prior benefit of research and theory. In time they became so established that they are now accepted as fact. When research techniques and measuring instruments are finally developed, it will behoove the researcher to put some of these hunches to test.

---

[9]A. J. Toynbee, *A Study of History* (New York: Oxford University Press, 1947).

[10]F. S. Siebert, *Freedom of the Press in England 1476-1776* (Urbana: University of Illinois Press, 1952).

This is not to belittle the role that intuition and conjecture play in scientific theory-building. Indeed, every science, even the highly advanced ones, starts from a series of brilliant hunches and usually is dependent on keen intuition and insight for its advancement. But in the final analysis every hunch and every product of inductive or deductive logic must be tested and demonstrated if it is to belong to the body of scientific fact. It follows that the more a particular field relies on such speculation at a given time, the greater is the need for eventual rigorous research; and the area of communication is no exception.

The Methodology of Experimentation

We turn now to the second criterion for distinguishing between experimental and nonexperimental inquiry: how the problem, once it is isolated, is investigated. The difference here is largely a matter of the *degree of control* of the inquiry. In his quest for precision in the solution of a problem the experimentalist exercises a freedom of choice in directing his inquiry so that he relies progressively less on common sense and progressively more on objective control. There are three main characteristics of experimental inquiry that account for this difference: (1) The observations are more objective in experimental inquiry. (2) Possible contamination of the inquiry by outside variables is controlled. (3) There usually is involved a systematic manipulation of the specific variables under observation. Let us examine each of these characteristics in more detail.

Objective observation

In much but not all nonexperimental inquiry, the observations made are subjective ones—i.e., they are dependent on the personal judgments of the individual investigator and are thus subject to his biases and predispositions. This is most apparent perhaps in historical research where the conclusions reached are based on a person's own interpretation of available data. It is apparent, too, in studies of content analysis. For example, two investigators may use somewhat different sets of categories to analyze the same message and hence yield different findings, or two investigators may even use the same categories and yet come out with somewhat different relative frequencies of certain content types.

While scientific research generally aims at reducing such subjectivity, experimental research demands such reduction. This does not mean that experimental research must deal only with cold, hard, impersonal data. If this were true it would have only a limited application in communication research, where many of the problems involve attributes and judgments of human beings. Rather, objective observation means that the data generated must be unadulterated by the personal influence of the investigator; he must maintain a certain aloofness from his data and not allow his own biases to enter in the data-gathering and treatment. Many otherwise well-designed experiments suffer from this lack of objectivity, and hence their findings are suspect. It is equally true, however, that many of the crucial variables in communications are not amenable to objective observation, at least not today, and thus cannot be studied except by subjective judgment.

Another criterion of objectivity often cited is that the observations should yield *quantitative* data. This is actually more a matter of convenience and precision than of objectivity as such. It is true that quantitative data do lend themselves to various statistical treatments that often allow for an objective evaluation of the results of the inquiry, but quantitative data are not objective data in and of themselves. For example, the data from a content analysis may be expressed in quantitative terms but may still be derived from highly subjective judgment.

Controlled conditions

The keystone of the experimental method is the element of control—more specifically, as we shall use the term here, control of all variables other than those under investigation. Many of the dependent variables which a communication researcher is apt to study are susceptible to influence by a wide variety of independent variables. In an experiment we focus our attention on one or more of these independent variables and attempt to control the influence of all the others. The effects of uncontrolled variables may obscure the true nature of the relationships under investigation, or they may lead to fallacious interpretation of the results of the investigation. It is often impossible, particularly in communication, to exercise such control over all possible sources of influence. This is why replication of an experiment is such a desired procedure and not merely a matter of research redundancy. If the results of experimental investigations under a variety of conditions are consistent, then and only then can the demonstrated functional relationship be accepted as fact. If reproducibility of results is not apparent, then the relationship still cannot be regarded as tenable.

As a simple illustration of the pitfalls that are possible under inadequately controlled conditions, consider the following example: An experiment is conducted to measure the difference in learning material presented to two groups, one via television, the other in a standard classroom situation. Analysis of the data shows that the TV group makes a superior score. But unless the two groups were matched for intelligence, initial (pre-exposure) knowledge of the subject matter, and so on, we could not say that TV was the superior form of instruction. In this instance, matching the groups with respect to previous knowledge, IQ, etc., is equivalent to controlling for the influence of these variables.

Or consider another example, this one a little less obvious: There have been literally dozens of studies demonstrating attitude change as a function of an intervening communication. While most of these studies showed significant change, there were several where no significant change occurred, or where the changes were in a direction opposite to that implied in the message. However, when the data from some of these latter studies were reanalyzed, it was found that the pre-exposure attitudes were already very intense and hence not readily amenable to change. When this "external" variable of intensity of original attitude was controlled, we had one explanation for this seeming impasse.

Generally speaking, there are three ways of providing for control:

1. Isolation of effect. If, for one reason or another, a particular variable is considered to be relevant to the behavior in question, one obvious way of controlling its effects is to treat it as an experimental variable itself—i.e., subject it to experimental manipulation and observe its effects. As we shall see later, the current availability of more powerful statistical techniques permits the simultaneous experimental treatment of several independent variables. Under such conditions, it becomes possible to isolate as it were, the respective (and, incidentally, interactive) effects of the various variables under treatment. However, for reasons of economy and elegance of design, it is usually undesirable if not impossible to treat all such potential variables at the same time. The experimentalist then directs his attention to what, on a priori grounds, he figures to be the few most critical variables and attempts to control the remaining variables in some other way.

2. Constancy of effect. In experimental research we usually have several groups of subjects exposed to somewhat different treatments—e.g., we may have an experimental group which receives a communication and a control group which does not receive it, and then we compare the two groups with respect to some dependent variable. One way of controlling the influence of variables other than the experimental one (the absence or presence of the communication message, in this case) is to keep such other variables at a constant level in both groups. Whatever effect is exercised by the experimental variables is then a real one beyond the contaminating influence of the external factors.

There are, in turn, two ways generally available for providing for such constancy of effect: We can *remove* a contaminating variable from the experimental situation and thereby give that variable a constancy level of zero, or we can *induce the same level* of that variable in all our treatment groups. Removal of a variable is probably the more exact procedure, but it is usually the more difficult to accomplish. This is particularly true in communication research where the variables often are properties of the individual that cannot be turned on or off at will. Under some conditions, however, it is possible to remove the variable. For example, if one were studying the information and attitude change resulting from a bona fide magazine article, it is conceivable that knowledge of the magazine from which the article was taken might be a contaminating factor. By hiding the source of the article from all subjects, this variable could be controlled. There are times when we must go to somewhat greater lengths to insure such control. In studies of attitude change it is believed that subjects may react differentially and not give honest responses if they know the purpose of the study. For this reason we often attempt to disguise the purpose of the study in such a manner that the subjects are unaware that their change in attitude is being measured. Tannenbaum[11] even introduced an entirely extraneous test into the experiment to provide for such control.

Inducing a common level of the contaminating variable is usually a much easier and more commonly used procedure. For example, in almost all communication-effects experiments it is assumed that the effect will vary with the degree of attention to the message; we thus try to insure—via instructions and the like—equal exposure and motivation to attend in all subjects. In Tannenbaum's[12] study of the effect of headlines on news story interpretation, the potential contaminating factors of content and size of the story were controlled by having all subjects read the identical stories with only the headline being varied. Similarly, in C. E. Swanson's[13] investigation of readership as a function of readability, two versions of the same content were used as the test material. And there are numerous other examples.

3. Randomization of effect. The above procedures may be used to control those variables which we suspect may contaminate the experimental findings. We specify and isolate such variables and go to some pains to keep their effects constant or at least known. But what about those variables which we do not suspect or which, though we may be suspicious of their influence, we cannot keep constant for one reason or another?

In communication research we deal with many different sources of variation, several of which reside within the individual. Theory has simply not progressed to the stage where many of these variables can be specified—e.g., we suspect that there are factors within the personality of an individual which can influence communication effects, but we cannot identify these factors specifically. The few that can be specified are often not amenable to control either because they cannot—on ethical grounds, if for no other reason—be manipulated at will, or they cannot be indexed adequately with available techniques. As an example of the former we suspect that attitudes derived from family and friends are factors in the development of communication behavior in children, but we cannot legitimately raise a group of children in complete isolation to use as a true control group. As an example of the latter, susceptibility to external influence is regarded as a vital personality factor in any communication effects study, but there is no generally accepted way of measuring this variable.

To accommodate for the influence of such vague and generalized factors, we usually make a tacit assumption. We accept the principle of homogeneous distribution of such variables and assume that they are randomly distributed in our various treatment groups. This assumption is not made blindly, of course.

[11]P. H. Tannenbaum, "Initial Attitudes Toward Source and Concept as Factors in Attitude Change Through Communication," *Public Opinion Quarterly*, 20 (1956), 413-25.

[12]P. H. Tannenbaum, "The Effect of Headlines on the Interpretation of News Stories," *Journalism Quarterly*, 30 (1953), 189-97.

[13]C. E. Swanson, "Readability and Readership: A Controlled Experiment," *Journalism Quarterly*, 25 (1948), 339-43.

We try to select our groups and control our experimental conditions in such a manner that this becomes at least a tenable assumption for that particular experiment. This is why we select our experimental and control groups so that they are not too divergent in basic attributes—intelligence, motivation, etc.—prior to the experimental treatment. For example, if we are forced to use college undergraduates as our subjects, as we often are, we usually select two or more sections from the same course to serve as our treatment group. Or if we are focusing on the general population, we try to use adequate sampling procedures so that many of these factors will be controlled through random distribution.

Another manifestation of this assumption of homogeneous distribution is the use of larger sized samples than might otherwise be necessary. By increasing the number of his observations the researcher has a more reasonable basis for his assumption of randomization, and the larger the sample size the more stable and more representative are his data. Such procedures may not guarantee complete control, but they are steps in approaching it.

Manipulation of experimental variable

The prototype of an ideal experiment is one in which all causal factors but one are kept constant, and that one (the experimental variable) is allowed to vary in a systematic manner while observations of concommitant or successive changes in the dependent variable are made. We have used the term "control" to refer to keeping the nonexperimental variables constant. The term "manipulation" is used to refer to the controlling of the experimental variable by systematic manipulation.

Many times, particularly in so-called "laboratory" experiments, the manipulation is deliberate and intentional. Under such conditions the investigator intervenes to influence the events to be observed and exercises almost complete control over the experimental variables. For example, when Jean Kerrick[14] was interested in investigating the effects of captions on the interpretation of ambiguous pictures, she kept the pictures constant and inserted her own, deliberately manufactured captions. Similarly, C. Hovland and W. Weiss[15] purposely assigned specific sources to the same stories in their study of the effect of source credibility.

But not all experiments must have this element of forced manipulation. The astronomer cannot manipulate the stars and planets of the solar system, yet he can effectively conduct controlled inquiries into their movements and relationships. The social scientist likewise cannot vary the groups of people he studies, but this does not stop him from conducting experiments with groups.

In the field of journalism and communication there are times when con-

[14]Jean S. Kerrick, "The Influence of Captions on Picture Interpretation," *Journalism Quarterly*, 32 (1955), 177-82.

[15]C. I. Hovland and W. Weiss, "The Influence of Source Credibility on Communication Effectiveness," *Public Opinion Quarterly*, 15 (1951), 635-50.

ditions are such that deliberate manipulation is not necessary to conduct efficient experiments. When former President Truman spoke in Minneapolis some years ago, C. E. Swanson, J. Jenkins, and R. L. Jones[16] were able to capitalize on the situation and conduct a controlled study. Similarly, Tannenbaum[17] used a live situation in studying the effects of a TV coverage of a congressional subcommittee hearing. More dramatic perhaps was the good fortune of I. L. Janis, A. A. Lumsdaine, and A. I. Gladstone.[18] In June, 1949, they had started a study in which opinion measures were obtained before and after exposure to an "optimistic" message that claimed Russia could not produce atomic bombs for some time to come. Less than three months later the unexpected announcement was made that the Soviets had exploded such a bomb, and the investigators were able to use this situation to study the effect of preparatory communication on reactions to the news event.

The identification of deliberate manipulation with control has a historical basis in terms of the ideal experiment indicated before. Here, one independent variable is allowed to vary while all others are controlled or held constant, and its effect on the dependent variable is measured. But today the dependence of the dependent variable on any number of independent ones can be determined by modern statistical analysis. Consequently deliberate manipulation is no longer necessary to the same degree as before. It also permits the experimentalist greater freedom; he is no longer confined to the laboratory but can study many relevant problems where they actually occur.

We can now return to our original question: What do we mean by experimentation? A definition may go something like this: Experimental research is research in which one or more independent variables that are assumed to be relevant are systematically manipulated, and their effects, both independent and interactive, on some dependent variables are observed under objective conditions with the possible contaminating effect of other independent variables held constant. This is admittedly a rather lengthy definition, but as we have seen, each element is important.

The Design and Procedure of Experiments

Experimentation is but one form of research activity, and, as such, shares many of the characteristics of design and procedure that any re-

---

16C. E. Swanson, J. Jenkins, and R. L. Jones, "President Truman Speaks: A Study of Ideas vs. Media," *Journalism Quarterly*, 27 (1950), 251-62.

17P. H. Tannenbaum, "What Effects When TV Covers a Congressional Hearing?" *Journalism Quarterly*, 32 (1955), 434-40.

18I. L. Janis, A. A. Lumsdaine, and A. I. Gladstone, "Effects of Preparatory Communications on Reactions to a Subsequent News Event," *Public Opinion Quarterly*, 15 (1951), 487-518.

search undertaking assumes. Most of these will be indicated in some detail. However, at the risk of redundancy many of these points may profitably be repeated within the context of experimental research. Instead of amplifying these points by resorting to generalized statements of experimental procedure, the author has selected the case-history approach, a step-by-step presentation of one of his own studies. This is not the most representative study in communication nor is it the most significant, but what it lacks in importance is offset to a degree by the accessibility and intimacy of detail.

A Typical Communication Experiment

The experiment to be reported was conducted some years ago at the University of Illinois with a minimum of expense (estimated cost: $200) and was reported in the literature.[19] For this reason many of the smaller details (e.g., the exact nature of the test material, the specific findings, etc.) may be omitted here. We shall attempt merely a survey of what motivated the study and how it was designed and conducted, with reference to the usual steps through which most experiments proceed.

Isolation of the problem

The particular problem for this study stemmed from the author's experience on the news desk of a metropolitan daily newspaper. In the course of his duties he became aware that often radically different headlines decked the same wire-service news story in different papers. He wondered if these different headlines really had different effects on persons exposed to them. This suggested to him an interesting intellectual exercise, but it was not until he arrived at Illinois as a graduate student that the opportunity to test this experimentally was available.

Review of the literature

The first step was to see if anyone else had been titillated by the same problem, and a survey of the available literature was undertaken. He uncovered a number of studies that had investigated the problem to a degree, but none of them had attacked it directly, and the decision was made to proceed with an experimental study.

Formulation of hypotheses

This may not be an essential step in all experimental undertakings, but (especially for the novice) it is more than mere elegance. Experiments are rarely conducted to "explore" a problem. They usually test a possible solution to the problem. We call such possible solutions hypotheses, and if we can state

[19]Note 12 supra.

them in concise and precise nomenclature, they often help focus the entire investigation and reduce extraneous detail.

So it was in this case. I had rather vague ideas of what it was I wanted to measure, but under prodding from my mentors, I narrowed the problem down to two hypotheses: (1) Different headlines presented with the same material give rise to different impressions of the content. (2) This effect of the headline is in inverse proportion to the extent to which the story was read. We now had isolated the variables: For the first hypothesis the independent variable was "The headline," and the dependent variable the "impression of the total story"; for the second hypothesis the independent variable was the "extent of reading," and the dependent variable the "effect of the headline."

Operational indices

The next step was defining, in terms of the actual measurement operations to be employed, just what was meant by the concepts indicated in quotation marks above. This is an important step that is often by-passed in research, as it first was in the present study. It was not until after a good deal of time and effort had been put into the planning of the study that these important questions were raised: What do these things mean? How are you going to measure them?

Many of the variables in communication research can be measured with available techniques. Far more cannot be measured—in the sense of using scales with properties of the number system—at present. Yet, if we are to study a variable, we must be able to index it in some way.

Identifying the headline was not too difficult. It was finally decided that here the interest should be in the gross content of the headline as it reflects a particular point of view on a controversial issue. Thus, given a story about a trial, three headlines—one indicating guilt of the defendant, one indicating innocence, and one being noncommittal—would allow for testing the effect of this independent variable. Identifying the dependent variables—impression of the total story—was another matter. After some consideration it was decided to index this variable by a simple opinion question regarding belief in the guilt or innocence of the defendant. Similarly, for the second hypothesis "the extent to which the story is read" was indexed by a simple—and probably inadequate —question asking the respondents to indicate in one of the four categories their own extent of reading the particular story. As an index of the dependent variable a simple dichotomy of replies on the first question into those in line with the headline and those discordant with the headline's intention was employed. These were probably not the most sensitive measures, and if we were to repeat the study today, we might employ somewhat more sophisticated ones.

Experimental design

Having an experimental design is usually desirable but not always possible. This refers to setting down a schematic representation of the treatment groups, which offers the advantage of pointing to a proper design for analysis of the data—i.e., which statistical procedure to use. In the present instance this was relatively straightforward. (In other instances the researcher often has to gather his data and then see how he can best handle and analyze it.) At any rate, for the first hypothesis the experimental design looked something like the chart below; and a similar one was available for the second hypothesis. After the appropriate numbers were placed in each cell of the grid, a Chi-square analysis was rendered (since the data would be expressed in frequencies) to see if there was any significant difference between the three groups in their distribution of replies. Of course, this was easier said than done. We first had to administer the material, get the replies, etc., before we could fill in those magic numbers.

| | Number of Replies | | |
Treatment Group	Guilty	Innocent	No opinion
Guilty-headline Group			
Innocent-headline Group			
Neutral-headline Group			

Test material

We had decided at the very outset that we would try to make this study as realistic as possible. Countless different procedures to insure reality presented themselves and were quickly discarded because they were impractical in view of the money and time available. (Most experimental procedures were usually results of such compromise between the ideal and the practical.) For the test material we decided to use news stories written in regular newspaper style and presented on a regular front page. Fate was not too kind, however, and no such realistic situations presented themselves. It was decided to make one up. We selected a plausible though hypothetical topic—an account of a murder trial. The story was written in standard Associated Press style, and three adequate and plausible headlines were prepared. Then, a back copy of the student paper at the University of Iowa was borrowed, and one story that seemed to fit was deleted. In its place the planted story was set up in the same type as used by the *Daily Iowan*. The three altered front pages—one for each headline—were then duplicated by offset printing.

We also had done the same for another story, one dealing with alternate forms of accelerated college programs. This required at least three additional front pages to be run off. For one reason or another it was surmised that there might be some interaction between the two stories, so we arranged for nine front pages to be run off, representing all possible combinations of the two stories and their respective headlines. This was probably unnecessary and more than doubled the printing costs.

Subjects

It was decided, for reasons of economy and availability, to use college undergraduates as subjects in the experiment. But we wanted to have all groups (remember, we had nine by now) matched. For this reason, nine different quiz sections of a Psychology 100 course were selected as subjects (and we would hate to relate the hours spent writing memoranda and holding conferences until this hurdle was cleared).

Questionnaire and instructions

Running off the questionnaire was a fairly simple matter. We knew by now which key questions we wanted to ask, but in order to disguise the aim of the experiment somewhat, these questions were embedded among a larger number. Subjects were told that this was a study of "newspaper reading behavior of a college population" and that they should read the page as they would read it ordinarily. Their attention was also called to the two test stories, along with several others, as typical stories that might interest the average college student.

Was everything under control?

We were all set to go at this stage. The test material was ready, so was the questionnaire, and arrangements had been made for subjects. This perhaps is the most crucial moment in any experimental undertaking. One must pause at this point and check every detail to see that none has been overlooked.

Everything looked ship-shape. The test material was such that all groups had the same material except for the particular headlines, the main independent variable. The groups seemed as matched as we could make them. The experimental situation was still of the laboratory type, but it was the closest we could get to a realistic situation under the circumstances.

Collection and analysis of data

The data collection went fairly smoothly. The subjects seemed to co-operate quite readily and appeared reasonably motivated with the task. They read the pages, filled in the questionnaire, and we had our data. Not every study proceeds quite as smoothly, of course. Often, subjects do not co-operate, or something else goes wrong, and the experimenter has to repeat the entire procedure.

For this study the data treatment was also quite simple. We merely counted the number of replies in each category for the different groups, plugged these frequencies into the analysis designs, and ran the Chi-squares. Again, not all analysis proceeds as simply as this. Most studies require many hours of poring over data and often the use of electric computers.

The study was now completed. In writing it up, we merely reported what was done and tried to interpret the findings, which were generally quite clear cut, within a meaningful framework.

This was one of the first experiments we conducted, which partially explains its simplicity. Since then we have been exposed to other, more advanced procedures, and if we were to repeat the study today it would probably be a little more complicated. For one thing, we would attempt to obtain more sensitive measures of "impression" and "extent of reading." For another, we would probably use an analysis of variance design and make one of the independent variables the content of the story. In this way one could pull out the effect of the interaction between headline and story content, which is probably the critical factor involved in this type of behavior. And we might try to get different types of subjects.

Did this study prove anything? As an isolated investigation it probably does not add up to very much. But it did set the stage for a number of other studies all focused on the central theme of an indexing process in communication effects.[20] Considered together, these studies do tell us a little more about how a message achieves its effects. And this is the way science develops: one study leads to another; methodology becomes sharpened; and before too long, a body of knowledge develops.

Other communication experiments differ from this illustrative one in various ways. But almost every one has to go through similar if not identical steps. A problem and a hypothesis must be formulated; a design of some kind must be set up; appropriate test material must be lined up if it is not already available, and so on. All along, the experimenter must pay careful attention to each little detail, because experience has shown him that often the little things turn out to be the big things. Even when the decks are finally cleared and he does embark on a systematic investigation, all well planned and laid out, the pitfalls are many. Apparatuses break down; side issues crop up unexpectedly; his findings may turn out to be unrelated to what he was looking for. But one of the charms of experimental research is that such pitfalls often have their rewards. From broken down apparatuses, newer and better ones are constructed; from an initially distracting side problem may emerge a major issue; he may not find what he set out to find, but what he does find may be more rewarding in the long run.

Experimentation in Communication—
Past and Future

The scientific study of journalism and communication is still in its infancy, but there are signs of a growing maturity. Not the least of these omens has been a marked increase in the number and caliber of research under-

[20]Note 4 *supra*.

takings, including experimental research. When C. L. Allen[21] wrote his summary of experimentation in communication less than a decade ago, there was only a handful of such studies to be cited. Today there are only several handfuls, but the rate of such undertakings is definitely on the upsurge. More important, the quality of the research has also improved.

One of the principal reasons for the paucity of research in the past has been the inherent difficulty in conducting experiments. With its demands for exactness, it is often too exacting. Or, as one wag put it: "If you insist too much on experimental rigor, you get rigor mortis in your findings." This is still true to an extent, and there are many authorities who believe that the hallowed role that experimentation has in the physical and natural sciences should not be carried over, lock, stock, and severity of method, to the behavioral sciences. The phenomena are different, they argue, and so should the methods be different. This is neither the time nor the place to speculate on this matter, which only time and experience will decide. In the meantime, it is probably just as well to proceed with what we have available.

But do we have enough available? We can borrow the method of experimentation, but can we apply it to meaningful situations within the field of communication? This points to another source of reasons for the relative lack of experimentation to date: We cannot measure what we would like to measure; we cannot manipulate what we would like to manipulate, and so on. Actually, this has been more true in the past than it is today and will probably be less true in the very near future. In the years since the end of World War II there has been a tremendous upsurge in social science research, and many of the resulting developments appear to be readily applicable to communication.

Foremost among these developments has been the emergence of valid measurement instruments. For example, we now have available a number of scientifically developed scales for the assessment of attitude. Even more promising has been the development of an instrument to measure certain aspects of meaning,[22] another most crucial variable in communication. This instrument, which has been dubbed the "semantic differential," provides a multidimensional measure—i. e., it measures across several different and mutually independent dimensions at once. There are other such instruments being developed at this writing. Together they hold great promise for communication research, because more and more we have been finding that the effects a communication message may have do not vary only in single ways but involve several different attributes at once. Indeed, many of the most striking applications of the semantic differential technique have been directly in the communication area, not only in

    [21]C. L. Allen, "The Experimental Method and Communications," in R. O. Nafziger and M. M. Wilkerson (eds.), *An Introduction to Journalism Research* (Baton Rouge: Louisiana State University Press, 1949).
    [22]C. E. Osgood, G. J. Suci, and P. H. Tannenbaum, *The Measurement of Meaning* (Urbana: University of Illinois Press, 1957).

straight effects studies,[23] but also in such critical yet unexplored areas as aesthetics and psycholinguistics.[24]

Along with this development of measuring instruments, there has been a corresponding—and in many ways, even more encouraging—evolution of new statistical designs and techniques. Most striking among these has been the improvement in sampling techniques, which cut down a good deal of the guesswork involved in drawing a sample and making inferences from that sample to the larger population. Similarly, the analysis of variance technique seems to be tailor-made for communication research. Not only does it allow for the assessment of the effects of a number of independent variables at once, but it also makes possible the identification and indexing of the effects of the interaction between these variables. We have paid considerable lip-service to this concept of interaction in communication, but we rarely have tried to demonstrate it experimentally or to measure its significance in particular situations.

The powerful statistical technique of factor analysis also bodes well for the future of communication research. While it is more an exploratory rather than a hypothesis-testing technique, and hence not directly involved in experimental research, it still can provide the impetus for experimentation. It provides a means for determining the basic dimensionality of large arrays of data and hence may be valuable in specifying the kinds of variables—independent and dependent—that experimentation should focus on. A prime example is M. S. MacLean's and W. R. Hazard's[25] study on news picture preferences. Another is the use of factor analysis in the development of categories for analysis of mental health content in the mass media and in the subsequent application of such findings in experimental situations.[26]

Given such new tools and techniques, it is only natural to expect that more and better experiments will be conducted in communication, along with a focusing on more immediate and practical problems. Lacking the resources to study some of these pressing problems, the communication researcher has had to occupy himself with less significant issues. Now, given the tools, he is in a better position to do the job.

There is still one risk, albeit a calculated one, that experimentation always faces. This is the matter of the derivation of general principles from the findings of single experiments. It is one thing to conduct a neatly designed and well-executed experiment, but it is another to interpret and convert the results of such experimentation into principle and law.

[23]See, e. g., note 17 *supra*.

[24]Note 11 *supra*.

[25]M. S. MacLean and W. R. Hazard, "Women's Interest in Pictures: the Badger Village Study," *Journalism Quarterly*, 30 (1953), 139-62.

[26]C. E. Osgood, J. C. Nunnally *et al.*, *Communication of Mental Health Information; Phase I Report* (Urbana: Institute of Communication Research, University of Illinois, 1955, mimeo.).

This involves two steps. The first is making logical inferences from the data of observation. Even if our observations are obtained under the most carefully controlled conditions, even greater caution must be exercised in their interpretation. The most common failing here is in assuming that because our data do not disprove the hypothesis, they necessarily demonstrate it to be true. Rigorous application of the principles of formal logic is what is required to prevent our going astray, and this point cannot be overemphasized. The man who conducted a large-scale survey and found that more people died in bed than anywhere else made a very accurate observation. But when he concludes from such data that beds are more dangerous than, say, foxholes, he fails to follow the principles of logical inference. In much the same manner attributing cause-and-effect relationships from correlation data has also led to fallacious and misleading interpretation.

Similarly, there is no substitute for formal logic in the next step of science; organizing these inferences into a generalization or law. In the field of communication we are still a long way from approaching this stage, but when the time comes, we must be sure to be on the alert. There seems to be an almost irresistible urge in the behavioral sciences to generalize the inferences drawn from a series of separate experiments into some short-hand formula or law. This is not necessarily bad, except that all too often it has been premature and has attempted to incorporate too much of behavior under one heading. The rule here is that the law must not attempt to go beyond the data presented and should not include classes of data which have not themselves been subjected to careful observation. This necessitates a lot of work and effort, but such are the ways of science. In the long run, cautious scientific statements may lead to final answers more readily than jumping to quick conclusions. To draw general conclusions from experimental findings is an obvious criterion for their acceptance, but we need not be carried away with it. Not every experiment has to be the key to our knowledge of the communication process. By the same token, the reporting of negative experimental findings—i. e., results which do not confirm the original hypotheses—is also vital in building a theory. There is no need to be apologetic about such findings; they should be presented in much the same manner as positive, tangible results. This will both serve to avoid unnecessary replication of experiments and also point the way to more crucial problems.